POLIN
STUDIES IN POLISH JEWRY

VOLUME EIGHT
Jews in Independent Poland
1918–1939

Edited by
ANTONY POLONSKY
EZRA MENDELSOHN and JERZY TOMASZEWSKI

Published for
The Institute for Polish–Jewish Studies

The Littman Library of Jewish Civilization
in association with Liverpool University Press

*The Littman Library of Jewish Civilization
in association with Liverpool University Press
4 Cambridge Street, Liverpool* L69 7ZU, UK

www.liverpooluniversitypress.co.uk/littman

Managing Editor: Connie Webber

*Distributed in North America by
Oxford University Press Inc., 198 Madison Avenue,
New York,* NY 10016, USA

*First published in hardback 1994
First published in paperback 2004*

© *Institute for Polish–Jewish Studies 1994*

*All rights reserved.
No part of this publication may be reproduced,
stored in a retrieval system, or transmitted, in any form or by
any means, without the prior permission in writing of
The Littman Library of Jewish Civilization*

*The paperback edition of this book is sold subject to the condition
that it shall not, by way of trade or otherwise, be lent, re-sold,
hired out or otherwise circulated without the publisher's prior consent
in any form of binding or cover other than that in which it is published
and without a similar condition including this condition
being imposed on the subsequent purchaser*

*Catalogue records for this book are available from the
British Library and the Library of Congress*

*ISSN 0268 1056
ISBN 978-1-904113-22-5*

*Publishing coordinator: Janet Moth
Copy-editing: John Waś
Proof-reading: Anna Zaranko
Index: Meg Davis
Design: Pete Russell, Faringdon, Oxon.
Typesetting: Datix International Limited, Bungay.*

THE INSTITUTE FOR POLISH–JEWISH STUDIES

The Institute for Polish–Jewish Studies in Oxford and its sister organization, the American Association for Polish–Jewish Studies, which publish *Polin*, are learned societies that were established in 1984, following the International Conference on Polish–Jewish Studies, held in Oxford. The Institute is an associate institute of the Oxford Centre for Hebrew and Jewish Studies, and the American Association is linked with the Department of Near Eastern and Judaic Studies at Brandeis University.

Both the Institute and the American Association aim to promote understanding of the Polish Jewish past. They have no building or library of their own and no paid staff; they achieve their aims by encouraging scholarly research and facilitating its publication, and by creating forums for people with a scholarly interest in Polish Jewish topics, both past and present.

To this end the Institute and the American Association help organize lectures and international conferences. Venues for these activities have included Brandeis University in Waltham, Massachusetts, the Hebrew University in Jerusalem, the Institute for the Study of Human Sciences in Vienna, King's College in London, the Jagiellonian University in Kraków, the Oxford Centre for Hebrew and Jewish Studies, the University of Łódź, University College London, and the Polish Cultural Institute and the Polish embassy in London. They have encouraged academic exchanges between Israel, Poland, the United States, and western Europe. In particular they seek to help train a new generation of scholars, in Poland and elsewhere, to study the culture and history of the Jews in Poland.

Each year since 1986 the Institute has published a volume of scholarly papers in the series *Polin: Studies in Polish Jewry* under the general editorship of Professor Antony Polonsky of Brandeis University. Since 1994 the series has been published on its behalf by the Littman Library of Jewish Civilization, and since 1998 the publication has been linked with the American Association as well. In March 2000 the entire series was honoured with a National Jewish Book Award from the Jewish Book Council in the United States. More than twenty other works on Polish Jewish topics have also been published with the Institute's assistance.

Further information on the Institute for Polish–Jewish Studies can be found on its website, <www.polishjewishstudies.co.uk>. For the website of the American Association for Polish–Jewish Studies, see <www.aapjstudies.org>.

---

*This publication has been supported by
a donation in memory of*
DR GEORGE WEBBER
(1899–1982)
scholar, Hebraist, jurist

THE LITTMAN LIBRARY OF
JEWISH CIVILIZATION

Dedicated to the memory of
LOUIS THOMAS SIDNEY LITTMAN
*who founded the Littman Library for the love of God
and as an act of charity in memory of his father*
JOSEPH AARON LITTMAN
and to the memory of
ROBERT JOSEPH LITTMAN
who continued what his father Louis had begun
יהא זכרם ברוך

'*Get wisdom, get understanding:
Forsake her not and she shall preserve thee*'

PROV. 4: 5

*The Littman Library of Jewish Civilization is a registered UK charity
Registered charity no. 1000784*

This volume is dedicated to
MIRIAM FRUSZTAJER
(née Vitenson)
who perished in Siberian exile, and
MOSHE FRUSZTAJER
who survived the war and settled in Israel in 1949

Editors and Advisers

EDITORS
Monika Adamczyk-Garbowska, *Lublin*
Israel Bartal, *Jerusalem*
Antony Polonsky (Chair), *Waltham, Mass.*
Michael Steinlauf, *Philadelphia*
Jerzy Tomaszewski, *Warsaw*

REVIEW EDITORS
Władysław T. Bartoszewski, *Warsaw*
ChaeRan Freeze, *Waltham, Mass.*
Joshua Zimmerman, *New York*

EDITORIAL BOARD

Chimen Abramski, *London*
David Assaf, *Tel Aviv*
Władysław T. Bartoszewski, *Warsaw*
David Engel, *New York*
David Fishman, *New York*
Józef Gierowski, *Kraków*
Jacob Goldberg, *Jerusalem*
Yisrael Gutman, *Jerusalem*
Jerzy Kłoczowski, *Lublin*
Ezra Mendelsohn, *Jerusalem*

Elchanan Reiner, *Tel Aviv*
Jehuda Reinharz, *Waltham, Mass.*
Moshe Rosman, *Tel Aviv*
Henryk Samsonowicz, *Warsaw*
Robert Shapiro, *New York*
Adam Teller, *Haifa*
Daniel Tollet, *Paris*
Piotr S. Wandycz, *New Haven, Conn*
Jonathan Webber, *Birmingham, UK*
Steven Zipperstein, *Stanford, Calif.*

ADVISORY BOARD

Władysław Bartoszewski, *Warsaw*
Jan Błoński, *Kraków*
Abraham Brumberg, *Washington*
Andrzej Chojnowski, *Warsaw*
Tadeusz Chrzanowski, *Kraków*
Andrzej Ciechanowiecki, *London*
Norman Davies, *London*
Victor Erlich, *New Haven, Conn.*
Frank Golczewski, *Hamburg*
Olga Goldberg, *Jerusalem*
Feliks Gross, *New York*
Czesław Hernas, *Wrocław*
Maurycy Horn, *Warsaw*
Jerzy Jedlicki, *Warsaw*
Andrzej Kamiński, *London*
Hillel Levine, *Boston*

Lucjan Lewitter, *Cambridge, Mass.*
Stanisław Litak, *Lublin*
Heinz-Dietrich Löwe, *Heidelberg*
Emanuel Meltzer, *Tel Aviv*
Czesław Miłosz (Hon. Chair), *Berkeley*
Shlomo Netzer, *Tel Aviv*
David Patterson, *Oxford*
Zbigniew Pełczyński, *Oxford*
Szymon Rudnicki, *Warsaw*
Alexander Schenker, *New Haven, Conn*
David Sorkin, *Madison, Wisc.*
Edward Stankiewicz, *New Haven, Conn*
Norman Stone, *Ankara*
Shmuel Werses, *Jerusalem*
Jacek Woźniakowski, *Lublin*
Piotr Wróbel, *Toronto*

Preface

THIS volume of *Polin* is the first to appear under the imprint of the Littman Library of Jewish Civilization. Major changes have been made in the editorial structure: it will now be run by a committee chaired by Antony Polonsky, Brandeis University, and whose members are Israel Bartal, Hebrew University, Jerusalem; Gershon Hundert, McGill University, Montreal; Magdalena Opalski, Carleton University, Ottawa; and Jerzy Tomaszewski, University of Warsaw. This editorial committee has also been significantly enlarged to reflect both our relocation and our interest in the whole of the area covered by the Polish–Lithuanian Commonwealth, including Ukraine, Belarus, and Lithuania.

This issue, which is edited by Antony Polonsky and two guest editors, Ezra Mendelsohn, Professor in the Institute for the Study of Contemporary Jewry at the Hebrew University, and Jerzy Tomaszewski, Professor of History at the University of Warsaw and Director of the Mordecai Anielewicz Center for the Study of the History and Culture of Polish Jews at Warsaw University, is devoted to the history of the Jewish community in interwar Poland. A number of the articles which appear in it were first delivered as papers at the international conference on the history of the Jews in Poland held in Jerusalem in 1988, and we are happy that some of the proceedings of that memorable occasion will be given a permanent character.

For Volume 9, we have chosen as our theme 'Poles, Jews, Socialists: The Failure of an Ideal'. The aim will be to investigate why the socialist ideal, whether in its social democratic or in its revolutionary variant, was unable to transcend national divisions on the Polish lands. Volume 10 will contain a core of articles on the history of the Jews in the Polish–Lithuanian Commonwealth down to the partitions at the end of the eighteenth century. Volume 11 will be devoted to investigating the perspectives which sociology can provide on Polish–Jewish relations and the history of the Jews in Poland.

In addition, each volume will contain a section in which new views about key issues in the history of the Jews in Poland can be discussed (considerations of space have meant that this section has had to be omitted from this volume), together with review essays, a full review section, and a record of new publications in the field of Polish Jewish history.

Polin is sponsored by the Institute for Polish–Jewish Studies, an associate centre of the Oxford Centre for Hebrew and Jewish Studies, and by the American Association for Polish–Jewish Studies, which is linked with the Department of Near Eastern and Judaic Studies, Brandeis University, Waltham, Massachusetts. We should like here to express our gratitude to the former President of the Oxford Centre, Dr David Patterson, the current President, Professor Philip Alexander, and especially the chairman of the Publications Committee, Dr Jonathan Webber. We should also like to acknowledge the invaluable support of Professor Jehuda Reinharz, Provost and Senior Vice-President for Academic Affairs, Brandeis University; Professor Jonathan Sarna, Chair, Department of Near Eastern and Judaic Studies, Brandeis University; and Mrs Irene Pipes, President, American Association for Polish–Jewish Studies. The volume would never have appeared without the assistance and supervision of Connie Webber, managing editor of the Littman Library, Janet Moth, publishing co-ordinator, and the tireless copy-editing of John Waś.

A.P.

Contents

Note on Transliteration, Names, and Place Names	xii
Abbreviations	xiii
Introduction ANTONY POLONSKY	xv

PART I
JEWS IN INDEPENDENT POLAND, 1918–1939

Jewish Historiography on Polish Jewry in the Interwar Period EZRA MENDELSOHN	3
Britain, a British Jew, and Jewish Relations with the New Poland: The Making of the Polish Minorities Treaty of 1919 MARK LEVENE	14
The Social Consciousness of Young Jews in Interwar Poland ALINA CAŁA	42
Polish–Jewish Relations as Reflected in Memoirs of the Interwar Period SZYJA BRONSZTEJN	66
Shtetl Communities: Another Image ANNAMARIA ORLA-BUKOWSKA	89
The Civil Rights of Jews in Poland 1918–1939 JERZY TOMASZEWSKI	115
The Jewish Question in Polish Religious Periodicals in the Second Republic: The Case of the *Przegląd katolicki* FRANCISZEK ADAMSKI	129
The Image of the Jew in the Catholic Press during the Second Republic ANNA LANDAU-CZAJKA	146
The Jewish Press in the Political Life of the Second Republic ANDRZEJ PACZKOWSKI	176
Polish Political Parties and Antisemitism JERZY HOLZER	194

The Polish *Kehillah* Elections of 1936: A Revolution Re-examined 206
ROBERT MOSES SHAPIRO

Jewish Artisans 227
ZBIGNIEW LANDAU

Some Aspects of the Life of the Jewish Proletariat in Poland during the Interwar Period 238
B. GARNCARSKA-KADARY

The Expulsion of Polish Jews from the Third Reich in 1938 255
KAROL JONCA

The Jewish Boycott Campaign against Nazi Germany and its Culmination in the Halbersztadt Trial 282
ALFRED WIŚLICKI

What Shall We Tell Miriam? A Tale for the Present 290
RAFAEL F. SCHARF

Poyln: Land of Sages and *Tsadikim* 299
YEHIEL YESHAIA TRUNK

PART II
REVIEWS

REVIEW ESSAYS

Why Did Assimilation Fail in the Kingdom of Poland between 1864 and 1897? 325
STANISLAUS A. BLEJWAS

In the Shadow of the Facts 330
DARIUSZ STOLA

Readings and Misreadings: A Reply to Dariusz Stola 345
DAVID ENGEL

BOOK REVIEWS

Gershon David Hundert, *The Jews in a Polish Private Town* 382
MAGDALENA M. OPALSKI

Walentyna Najdus, *Ignacy Daszyński, 1866–1936* 384
ADAM A. HETNAL

Stephen D. Corrsin, *Warsaw before the First World War* 388
STEFAN KIENIEWICZ

Józef Wróbel, *Tematy żydowskie w prozie polskiej 1939–1987* LAURA QUERCIOLI	392
Jan T. Gross, *Revolution from Abroad* DAVID ENGEL	396
Wolfgang Wippermann, *Der konsequente Wahn* MICHAEL BURLEIGH	398
Yury Boshyk (ed.), *Ukraine during World War II* SHIMON REDLICH	401
Halina Nelken, *Images of a Lost World* RICHARD L. COHEN	404
Vivian B. Mann (ed.), *Gardens and Ghettos* TADEUSZ CHRZANOWSKI	407
Polska Sztuka Ludowa, special issue (1989) TADEUSZ CHRZANOWSKI	410
Jerzy Malinowski, *Grupa 'Jung Idysz' i żydowskie środowisko 'Nowej Sztuki' w Polsce* SERGIUSZ MICHALSKI	413
Janet Hadda, *Passionate Women, Passive Men* LAURA QUERCIOLI	415

OBITUARIES

Stefan Kieniewicz (1907–1992)	421
Artur Eisenbach (1906–1992)	423
'A Small Memorial Candle' for Adolf Rudnicki (1912–1990)	427

Editor's Notes
   The Jan Karski and Pola Nirenska Award
   Bibliography of Polish Jewish Studies
	430

Notes on Contributors and Translators	431
Glossary	436
Index	443

Note on Transliteration, Names, and Place Names

IT has not been possible to achieve total consistency in the transliteration of Yiddish and Hebrew in this book, nor in the spelling of people's names. In the case of Hebrew, this is because both modern and traditional Ashkenazic styles of pronunciation were used in pre-war Poland, the latter moreover in a variety of regional and other dialectical forms; it was considered inappropriate and unhistorical to impose standardization. For Hebrew bibliographic references, however, a system of transcription has been used that aims at representing the pronunciation prescribed today for modern Hebrew to an English-speaking reader. For Yiddish, the transcription adopted follows the YIVO system—except for people's names, where the spellings they themselves used (which normally followed the Polish orthographic system) have been retained. Place names, in contrast, are spelled in the correct Polish way, even though Jews often used Yiddish names; this has been done so as to enable readers to find the places on maps and correlate information with Polish sources.

Abbreviations

AAN MSZ	Archiwum Akt Nowych, Ministerstwo Spraw Zagranicznych (Archive of Modern Documents, Ministry of Foreign Affairs)
AJS Review	*Association of Jewish Studies Review*, Cambridge, Mass.
AK	Armia Krajowa (Home Army), the principal underground resistance movement in Poland during the Second World War
BBWR	Bezpartyjny Blok Współpracy z Rządem: (Non-Party Bloc for Co-operation with the Government), an organization set up to support the Piłsudski regime, after the *coup* of May 1926
ChNSP	Chrześcijańsko-Narodowe Stronnictwo Polski (Christian National Party of Poland)
CISZO	Tsentral shul organisatsie (in the abbreviation, a Polish method of transliterating Yiddish is used). Central School Organization, the body which controlled the private schools established by the Jewish Labour Bund
Encyclopedia Judaica	*Encyclopedia Judaica*, chief editor Geoffrey Wigoder, Keter Publishing Company, Jerusalem, 1972
KPD	Kommunistische Partei Deutschlands (Communist Party of Germany)
KPP	Komunistyczna Partia Polski (Communist Party of Poland)
NKVD or NKWD	Narodni Komitet Vnutriennykh Diel (National Committee for Internal Affairs; the Soviet Secret Police)
NPR	Narodowa Partia Robotnicza (National Workers' Party)
NSDAP	Nationalsozialistische Deutsche Arbeiterpartei (National Socialist German Workers' Party)
ONR	Obóz Narodowo-Radykalny (National Radical Camp)
OZON	Obóz Zjednoczenia Narodowego (Camp of National Unity)
PPR	Polska Partia Robotnicza (Polish Workers' Party)

PPS	Polska Partia Socjalistyczna (Polish Socialist Party)
PPS-lewica	Polska Partia Socjalistyczna–lewica (Polish Socialist Party–left wing), a small radical secession group from the PPS
PPSD	Polska Partia Socjalno-Demokratyczna (Polish Social Democratic Party), the main socialist party in Galicia (Austrian Poland)
PSChD	Polskie Stronnictwo Chrześcijańsko-Demokratyczne (Polish Christian Democratic Party)
PSL	Polskie Stronnictwo Ludowe (Polish Peasant Party)
RZP	Reprezentacja Żydostwa Polskiego (the Representative Body for Polish Jewry), an organization established in Palestine during the Second World War to protect the interests of Polish Jewry
SA	Sturmabteilung (Storm Division), the radical Nazi paramilitary organization
SDKPiL	Social-Demokracja Królestwo Polskiego i Litwy (the Social Democracy of the Congress Kingdom and Lithuania)
SL	Stronnictwo Ludowe (Peasant Party)
SN	Stronnictwo Narodowe (National Movement)
SPD	Sozialdemokratische Partei Deutschlands (Social Democratic Party of Germany)
SS	Schutzsaffel: literally 'guard detachment', élite Nazi paramilitary organization
TOZ	Towarzystwo Ochrony Zdrowia (Society for the Protection of Health), a Jewish organization which aimed to improve public health standards within the Jewish community of Poland between the two world wars
YIVO	Yidisher Vissentshaftlikhe Institut (Jewish Scientific Organization)
ZLN	Związek Ludowo-Narodowy (Popular National Union)
ZMN	Związek Młodych Narodowców (Union of Young Nationalists)

Introduction

ANTONY POLONSKY

I am a poor assimilated soul. I am a Jew and a Pole, or rather I was a Jew, but gradually, under the influence of my environment, under the influence of the place where I lived, and under the influence of the language, the culture, and the literature, I have also become a Pole. I love Poland. Its language, its culture, and most of all the fact of its liberation and the heroism of its independence struggle, all pluck at my heartstrings and fire my feelings and enthusiasm. But I do not love that Poland which, for no apparent reason hates me, that Poland which tears at my heart and soul, which drives me into a state of apathy, melancholy, and dark depression. Poland has taken away my happiness, it has turned me into a dog who, not having any ambitions of his own, asks only not to be abandoned in the wasteland of culture but to be drawn along the road of Polish cultural life. Poland has brought me up as a Pole, but brands me a Jew who has to be driven out. I want to be a Pole, you have not let me; I want to be a Jew, but I don't know how, I have become alienated from Jewishness. (I do not like myself as a Jew.)
I am already lost.

THIS tragic quotation from the memoirs of the young Warsaw Jew, Abraham Rotfarb, quoted in Alina Cała's article, 'The Social Consciousness of Young Jews in Interwar Poland', encapsulates the main themes of this volume of *Polin*, devoted to the history of the Jewish community of Poland in the years between the two world wars. In a provocative essay entitled 'Interwar Poland: Good for the Jews or Bad for the Jews?'[1] Ezra Mendelsohn argued that in the historiography of interwar Polish Jewry two basic camps, one 'optimistic' the other 'pessimistic', can be observed. According to him:

The attitude of most Jewish scholars has been, and continues to be, that interwar Poland was an extremely anti-semitic country, perhaps even uniquely anti-semitic. They claim that Polish Jewry during the 1920s and 1930s was in a state of constant and alarming decline, and that by the 1930s both the Polish regime and Polish society were waging a bitter and increasingly successful war against the Jewish population.

This view is shared by surviving pre-war Polish Jewish scholars including

[1] In C. Abramsky, M. Jachimczyk, and A. Polonsky (eds.), *The Jews in Poland* (Oxford, 1986).

Raphael Mahler, Jacob Lestchinsky, and Isaiah Trunk.[2] Their standpoint has been echoed by the post-war Polish–Jewish historian, Paweł Korzec, and by a number of Israeli historians, including Moshe Landau, Shlomo Netzer, and Emanuel Meltzer.[3] The point of view is most clearly expressed by Celia Heller in her book *On the Edge of Destruction*,[4] whose thesis is clearly summarized by the title. In her view, the period between the two world wars was a rehearsal for the Holocaust. Polish actions had by 1939 pushed the Jews to the 'edge of destruction' and it only remained for the Nazis to complete what they had begun.

This 'pessimistic' view of the situation of Jews in interwar Poland has not gone unchallenged, both by Jewish and non-Jewish (mostly Polish) historians. The most eloquent of the Jewish 'optimists' is Joseph Marcus. Marcus, who is a supporter of the Orthodox party Agudas Yisroel, reserves his greatest condemnation for what he refers to as the 'reformers' of Jewish life in Poland. Blinded by their Zionist and socialist obsessions, they had a great deal to do with the economic decline of Polish Jewry. According to Marcus, Jews in Poland were able to hold their own economically and were, in fact, better off than the majority of the population. They were more than capable of withstanding the assaults to which they were subjected in the 1930s. The real problem in Marcus's view was Polish poverty and Jewish over-population: 'The Jews in Poland were poor because they lived in a poor, undeveloped country. Discrimination added only marginally to their poverty.'[5]

These views have been echoed by many Polish scholars. Their position has been best articulated by the British historian, Norman Davies. In his challenging and stimulating history of Poland, he claims that 'the condition of Polish Jewry in the interwar period is often described out of context'. This, he claims, is the responsibility of the Zionists, who needed to paint the situation in Poland in the blackest colours in order to justify their own political position. Like Marcus, he argues that the intractable nature of the

---

[2] For Mahler's views see *Yehudei polin bein shtey milkhamot olam* (Tel Aviv, 1968); for Lestchinsky's, see 'The Anti-Jewish Program: Tsarist Russia, the Third Reich, and Independent Poland', *Jewish Social Studies*, 3: 2 (Apr. 1941), 141–58; for Trunk's, see 'Der ekonomisher antisemitizm in Poyln', in Joshua A. Fishman (ed.), *Studies on Polish Jewry 1919–1939* (New York, 1974), 3–98.

[3] Paweł Korzec, *Juifs en Pologne: La Question juive pendant l'entre-deux-guerres* (Paris, 1980), and 'Antisemitism in Poland as an Intellectual, Social and Political Movement', *Studies on Polish Jewry*, 12–104; Moshe Landau, *Miyut leumi lohem: Ma'avak yehudei polin 1918–1928* (Jerusalem, 1986); Shlomo Netzer, *Ma'avak yehudei polin al zekhuyoteihem ha'ezrahiyot vehale'umiyot (1918–1922)* (Tel Aviv, 1982); Emanuel Meltzer, *Ma'avak medini bemalkodet: Yehudei polin 1935–1939* (Tel Aviv, 1982).

[4] New York, 1977.

[5] Joseph Marcus, *Social and Political History of the Jews in Poland, 1919–1939* (Berlin, New York, Amsterdam, 1983), p. 231.

Jewish question was the result of the poverty of the reborn Polish state and 'an unprecedented demographic explosion' which 'countermanded all attempts to alleviate social conditions'. The Jews were only one of many ethnic groups in conflict in Poland and they were not singled out for special treatment by Polish chauvinists, who were equally hostile to Germans and Ukrainians. They also had important allies in the Polish political scene. Davies also argues that the scale of anti-Jewish violence in Poland has been exaggerated, referring to the 'so-called pogroms' of 1918 and 1919. He cites the cultural creativity of the Polish Jewish community as evidence that its situation was not as desperate as has sometimes been claimed: 'Anyone who has seen the remarkable records which these people left behind them, and which have been collected in YIVO's post-war headquarters in New York, cannot fail to note the essential dynamism of Polish Jewry at this juncture. All was not well: but neither was it unrelieved gloom.' He explicitly rejects Heller's claim that the oppression which the Jews experienced in the last years before the outbreak of the war paved the way for the successful implementation by the Nazis of their policies of mass murder, asserting that 'the destruction of Polish Jewry during the Second World War was . . . in no way connected to their earlier tribulations'.[6]

It is easy to understand why the history of Jews in Poland between the two world wars should have aroused such passion. At this time, as Ezra Mendelsohn points out in his article in the present volume, Poland's Jewish community was second in size only to that of the United States and its fate was seen as a touchstone for how the Jews would fare in the newly independent states of east-central Europe. Poland was seen as a laboratory in which the various autonomist Jewish ideologies—Zionism, Bundism, Folkism—could be tested. It was also the place where much of the Nazi policy of mass murder was implemented and this has inevitably raised the question of how far the earlier experience of the Jews there, above all the deterioration of their situation in the 1930s, aided the Nazis in carrying out their genocidal plans. On the Polish side equally strong passions were in play. The re-establishment of Polish independence after the First World War came after 130 years of struggle against foreign rule, and the interwar period was seen by most Poles as a period of national revival and creativity, in contrast to the depressing and grey reality of Communist rule. To call into question the behaviour of the governments and population in those years seemed to undermine the legitimacy of the renewed Polish struggle for national independence and freedom from Communism.

This discussion has, however, been marked by a very high degree of

---

[6] Norman Davies, *God's Playground. A History of Poland in Two Volumes*, ii: *1795 to the Present* (Oxford, 1981), 240–66.

generalization, and the various participants have not always seemed clear what they were disagreeing about. They have also tended to argue past rather than with each other, confirming the truth of the adage that the difference between a monologue and a dialogue is that, in the former, one person speaks to himself and, in the latter, two people speak to themselves. Some attempts have been made in recent years to clarify the issues involved. The collection *The Jews of Poland Between Two World Wars* provided a much more sophisticated approach to the problem,[7] while Ezra Mendelsohn, in his *The Jews of East Central Europe Between the World Wars*,[8] has furnished a valuable and nuanced introduction to the history of the Jews in Poland in these years.

Our aim in this volume has been to carry this discussion further. Rather than attempting to provide a comprehensive account of the period, our contributors have examined specific topics which can shed light on the nature of the Jewish experience in Poland in the interwar years. Ezra Mendelsohn surveys critically the Jewish historiography on interwar Poland. His conclusions, which establish the framework of the volume, go considerably beyond those he expressed in his article in 1986. On that occasion, he concluded:

Interwar Poland was, therefore, bad for the Jews, in the sense that it excluded them from first-class citizenship in the state. This led, by the late 1930s, to a widespread feeling among Polish Jews, and especially among the youth, that they had no future in Poland and that they were trapped. Interwar Poland was good for the Jews because, among other things, it provided an environment in which forces were unleashed in the Jewish world which many Jews regarded then, and today, as extremely positive.[9]

Now, he writes:

All of us would do well to keep in mind something that the Polish historians have emphasized, correctly in my opinion—namely, that the Jewish problem in interwar Poland really was a *problem* for the new Polish state and for Polish society. The question of how to deal with this large, economically powerful but poverty-stricken, unacculturated but polonizing Jewish community that spoke with many voices and made contradictory demands—this constituted a real dilemma. Historians have a duty to present the 'problem', to analyse the various options available for dealing with it, and to explain why, in various periods, various policies were or were not put forward. (p. 13).

He also stresses the importance of using the comparative method in studying the Jews of Poland and reminds us that we 'should . . . take into account the

---

[7] Yisrael Gutman, Ezra Mendelsohn, Jehuda Reinharz, and Chone Shmeruk (eds.), *The Jews of Poland between Two World Wars* (Hanover and London, 1990).
[8] Bloomington, Ind., 1983.   [9] Mendelsohn, 'Interwar Poland', 139.

knowledge we have gained since 1939 of the extreme complexity of ethnic, racial, and national relations within the framework of the modern or modernizing state'.

All the articles in this volume attempt to analyse the complex problems of Jews in interwar Poland in the light of these observations. Mark Levene shows how the effects of the war had greatly exacerbated Polish–Jewish relations. It was in conditions in which the Jews had suffered greatly from Tsarist accusations of disloyalty and from Polish resentment at their unwillingness to support all Polish territorial claims that the community found itself again in an independent Polish state. In these conditions, the bold attempt of the Anglo-Jewish statesman, Lucien Wolf, to reconcile Jewish aspirations for national autonomy with Polish concern for their sovereignty was probably doomed to failure. The contrast between the legal framework, which established the individual and national rights of the Jews, and the actual situation is also brought out by Jerzy Tomaszewski. How the position of the Jews in Poland and Polish–Jewish relations were perceived at the time and subsequently in memoirs, diaries, and in the memory of individuals is analysed in the three articles by Alina Cała, Szyja Bronsztejn, and Annamaria Orla-Bukowska. Jerzy Holzer examines the way the different Polish political parties, from those who were openly hostile to the Jews to those who regarded antisemitism as a reactionary aberration, saw the Jewish issue. One specific feature of antisemitism in Poland, the role of Catholic belief and the influence of the Catholic Church itself, is investigated by Franciszek Adamski and Anna Landau-Czajka. Discussions of antisemitism have tended to distinguish the ideology in its modern form, which is linked with the development of the 'scientific' study of racial differences and the impact of modernization on traditional societies, from the anti-Judaism which was espoused by the Christian churches, above all the Catholic Church. The relationship of this Christian anti-Judaism to the political antisemitism which emerged in the second half of the nineteenth century is complex. What is clear, however, from these articles is that in societies like Poland's in which the traditional value system was still strong, the old anti-Judaism should not be seen as merely the soil out of which the new ideology grew. Rather, the old and new beliefs merged in a manner which makes it impossible to separate them. Thus, as Landau-Czajka shows, in October 1932, the Warsaw Catholic paper *Pro Christo* could write:

'Today the chosen people no longer exist, but there exists a people cast out—the seed of the God-killers. And today, it seems that the only justification for the existence of Jews is that they are an instrument by which the rebellious angel carries out his designs—to oppose God and His Church.' (p. 156)

Two articles deal with aspects of Jewish politics in the period. Andrzej Paczkowski examines the extensive Jewish press in Yiddish, Polish, and Hebrew, while Robert Shapiro examines the elections to the Jewish communal bodies, the *kehiles*, in 1936 and examines how far these saw the breakdown of the three-part political division of Polish Jewry into Zionist, Orthodox, and Socialist camps. The poverty and economic hardship which the community suffered and which was exacerbated by the Great Depression emerges clearly from the articles on Jewish artisans and workers by Zbigniew Landau and Bina Garncarska-Kadary. One of the factors which contributed to the worsening of the position of the Jews in the 1930s was the way in which the success of the Nazis in disenfranchizing and expropriating the property of one of the best integrated and wealthiest Jewish communities in Europe encouraged local antisemites everywhere in east-central Europe. Two aspects of the impact of Nazi policies on Poland are examined by Karol Jonca and Alfred Wiślicki. Since the articles in this volume concentrate on political and economic issues, they tend to give a rather gloomy picture of Jewish life at this time. The two memoirs by the London-based Krakovian Rafael Scharf and the Yiddish writer Yehiel Yeshaia Trunk reveal another side, the inner essence of this lost world so brutally destroyed by the Nazis. As Scharf points out:[10]

The community was fragmented and torn by internal strife, but there was also a sense of sharing a common fate that transcended social and political differences. There was a marked spirituality even among the non-religious, a response to what was felt to be the Jewish ethos, a deeply ingrained universal conviction that beyond the daily sweat and strife, men had to aspire to higher things. (p. 297)

The uniqueness of this world is even more strongly expressed by Trunk and it is perhaps appropriate that the last word should be given to him. In the 'Epilogue' to his *Poyln*, he writes:

The multi-faceted Jewish life in Poland was tied together by the style of oneness, in the style of many-sided unity of the godhead, for what is style if not unity in diversity? And, in addition, the old idealistic, prophetic, and future-orientated spirit continued to burn in the souls of Polish Jews. It went hand in hand with a cultural this-life orientation, and the spirit bridged the different and opposite forms of the consciousness of Polish Jews.

Internal Jewish conflicts were sharp and bitterly fought. The old generations warred over trifles. A butcher somewhere in a *shtetl* was an excuse for a prolonged fight. Modern times brought new needs, which literature headed by Peretz and socialism with the Bund at its helm carried to the masses, there to unearth new sources of creativity. The conflicts and battles between the old and the new raged like storm-winds inside an old and fragrant wood. The national spirit of the Jewish

---

[10] Scharf's essay was first published in Andrzej Paluch (ed.), *The Jews in Poland* (Kraków, 1992), i. 377-86.

people flamed up like a prophetic fire in people whose feet were already in the abyss of final destruction. And it seemed—rather than coming to their last days, they were just beginning the Jewish road in the world.

In the last summer before the Second World War, under the black terrible skies, the hearts of Polish Jews were heavy with premonitions of doom. And still, they knew how to turn these forebodings into a feeling of confidence. They learnt through severe trials how to cope with hot and cold without ever giving up hope. Despair which turns into confidence is perhaps part of the process of the drama of the oneness of the world, a play performed with so much feeling in the depths of the Jewish soul (p. 322).

PART I

Jews in Independent Poland
1918–1939

Jewish Historiography on Polish Jewry in the Interwar Period

EZRA MENDELSOHN

THE question of the role, status, and fate of the Jews in interwar Poland arouses unusually high passions. It is a historical subject in which many people, including historians, have a considerable vested interest; a subject involving very high stakes. This is true for both Jews and (non-Jewish) Poles. For the latter group the subject is at least potentially threatening, since claims that the Polish state of the 1920s and 1930s discriminated against Jews may be seen as a deliberate effort to blacken the good name of the much-oppressed Polish nation at the very time when, through its great heroism, it had regained its rightful place among the free nations of Europe (obviously, accusations of Polish antisemitism during the period before 1918 carry less weight, since there was then no independent Polish state). It is a subject that tends to put some Polish scholars and publicists on the defensive.

For Jews there may be even more at stake. The 'Jewish experience' in interwar Poland is often regarded as having represented a crucial, indeed fateful, test for the major political and cultural positions that had developed in the Jewish world during the nineteenth century. Poland in this sense is regarded as a kind of battleground on which the various Jewish proposals to 'solve the Jewish question' waged war, the framework in which, for example, the question as to whether the Jews could prosper 'here', in the east European diaspora, or whether they should do everything in their power to remove themselves and to resettle 'there', in Palestine, was posed in its sharpest form. The reasons why Poland was singled out for this 'honour' by Jewish historians, publicists, and ideologues are fairly obvious: there were more Jews there than anywhere else in Europe, they were free to organize

---

This paper was originally delivered at the international conference on the historiography of Polish Jewry held at the Jagiellonian University in Kraków, Sept. 1990. It does not take into account scholarly work produced since that year. A Hebrew-language version has been published: 'Ha-historiografiyah hayehudit al yehudei polin bein shtei, milḥamot haolam', *Mada'ei hayahadut*, 31 (1991), 23–32.

(as they were not in the Soviet Union), and they were not undergoing a rapid process of integration into state and society, as were the Jews of the United States. It was on Polish soil that Orthodoxy and secularism, socialism and anti-socialism, nationalism and 'assimilationism', Hebraism and Yiddishism, Zionism and diaspora nationalism, sought to impose their way of life and their 'solutions' on the Jewish population.

There is, of course, yet another reason for the passions aroused by assessments of the interwar period, namely the question of the relationship between the periods 1918–39 and 1939–45. It is extremely difficult even for the most objective scholar to write about the Jews in interwar Poland without considering what happened in that country during the Nazi occupation. I shall not discuss the historiographic debates on relations between Poles and Jews during that terrible time, but we must certainly keep in mind that for many Jewish scholars (though emphatically not for many Poles) there is some sort of connection between Jewish–Polish relations during the period of Polish independence and the mass murder of Jews on Polish soil during the war. This attitude naturally colours Jewish historians' treatment of the interwar period.

I shall begin this brief historiographical survey by discussing the main characteristics of what I would call the traditional view of the Jewish situation in interwar Poland as proposed by Jewish historians and publicists—a view based on studies during the interwar period itself and developed, mainly by Israeli scholars, during the last three decades. This view, still very much alive in the Jewish world, is enshrined in a number of key Jewish publications: it is, in a way, the 'official', Establishment Jewish attitude towards the subject, and results, I believe, from a particular worldview shared by most of the Jewish scholars and publicists engaged in the study of modern Polish Jewish history. Many of them were Polish-born, secular Jewish nationalists (of both the Zionist and autonomist persuasions, but much more often Zionists), and most were left-wingers of one kind or another. We must keep in mind the impact of this background when we consider the work of such scholars as Rafael Mahler, Isaiah Trunk, Yakov Leshchinsky, and Aryeh Tartakover, the important publicist work of the celebrated Zionist leader Yitzhak Grünbaum and of the much less famous Bundist historian Y. Sh. Hertz, and the publications of such important contemporary scholars as Yisrael Oppenheim, Shlomo Netzer, Yisrael Gutman, and Lucy Dawidowicz.

I think it is fair to say that nearly all these writers possess a similar approach to the two great questions that interest them, the two main 'fronts', so to speak, in their historiographical campaign. As far as the first 'front' is concerned, namely relations between Jews and non-Jews, they all agree that Poland was an extremely, perhaps even uniquely, antisemitic country. This is proved by the marshalling of statistics on Jewish economic decline, seen as the result of government policy, and on the decline in the percentage of Jewish students at Polish universities, by descriptions of pogroms and 'excesses', and by quotations from anti-Jewish remarks made by Polish politicians and intellectuals. Polish antisemitism is therefore demonstrated, but not usually subjected to very serious analysis: deep analysis is not really needed if one thinks of Polish antisemitism as a perfectly normal phenomenon. In this context the ideological 'baggage' of our scholars is important. Since they are all Jewish nationalists, and almost all Zionists, and since they all think in national categories, they may well assume that antisemitism is virtually inevitable. The Polish nation, seeking first to establish and then to consolidate a Polish nation-state, would obviously discriminate against the Jewish nation (and other non-Polish nations) residing within the Polish frontiers. However, the inevitability of antisemitism does not free those responsible for its perpetration from opprobrium. The anti-socialist Zev Jabotinsky, who had dealings with the right-wing leaders of eastern Europe in the 1930s, may have been willing to show understanding, but most of our scholars are full of moral indignation when they consider Polish behaviour: here, I think, the influence of the 1939–45 period comes into play, and perhaps also the high moral tone which so often informs the writings of men and women of the left. But, as I have indicated, moral indignation does not often lead to a serious historical study of the context in which Polish anti-Jewish attitudes were formed and anti-Jewish policies implemented; for our historians and publicists it is sometimes enough to enumerate. While all of them admit that there were important differences on the Jewish question between, say, the Endecja and the Polish left, they do not spend too much time analysing twentieth-century Polish politics and Polish social thought. In the great Polish Jewish film *The Dybbuk* there are no non-Jews: they are not necessary. In traditional Jewish historiography of the interwar period non-Jews are certainly necessary, but it is not always deemed necessary to study their activities too closely.

One other aspect of the conventional Jewish treatment of Polish-Jewish relations should be mentioned. Our scholars like to emphasize that even if other non-Polish citizens of interwar Poland suffered from Polish chauvinism, the Jews suffered more than anyone else. Indeed, they tend to believe that such comparisons are invidious. Jewish suffering is considered to be 'unique', not really comparable to the suffering of Ukrainians, Belorussians, Germans, or other minorities. Nor can it be profitably compared to the misery endured by the traditional underdogs of Polish society, the workers and peasants.

The second 'front' for Jewish scholars is the internal Jewish one. Generally speaking, our authors delight in emphasizing the remarkable 'flourishing' of Jewish culture and Jewish political life, achieved against great odds. They also emphasize the 'heroic struggle' of Polish Jews against the non-Jewish oppressor: the word 'struggle' (and sometimes even 'war') is present in the titles of a number of important books on the subject.[1] Not all Polish Jews, however, participated in equal measure in the cultural 'flourishing' and in the heroic struggle: the role of the so-called 'assimilationists' and of the Orthodox is often ignored, regarded as marginal, or even condemned. (These two Jewish 'camps', be it noted, produced very few historians.) The received view is of a community led by highly creative national Jews who struggled heroically against all-pervasive, morally reprehensible, but perfectly understandable Polish antisemitism and dedicated themselves to the task of building a better Jewish future, either in Poland itself or in Palestine.

This historiographical model is enshrined, as I have said, in a number of key works on Jewish history and on the history of Polish Jews. In 1969 Shmuel Ettinger of the Hebrew University published his volume on modern Jewish history in the multi-volume History of the Jewish People series edited by leading Israeli scholars. Popularly known by students as the 'red book' (after the colour of its cover), it is probably the most widely read textbook on modern Jewish history in Israel; it is also available in English and widely read in the United States. Ettinger, a scholar of great erudition and influence, does not pay much attention to interwar Poland (he was both a Jewish nationalist and a left-winger, but not Polish-born), but in what he does say he conforms perfectly to the historiographical model described above: 'the Jews of Central and Eastern Europe', he writes, summing up his remarks on the Jews of Poland and her neighbouring countries, 'lived in a state of constant terror during the last few years before the Second World War, fearing for their lives and security and afraid to voice their apprehensions in public'.[2] With regard to politics, Ettinger applauds the Jewish nationalists in Poland who fought the good fight for Jewish rights, and attacks those Jewish organizations that sided with the government in the elections of 1938. As a result of their behaviour, he tells us, 'the independence and political influence of Polish Jewry were severely affected'.[3] As far

---

[1] Thus, for example, the books by Shlomo Netzer: *Ma'avak Yehudei polin al zehuyoteihem ha'ezrahiyot 1918–1922* (Tel Aviv, 1982); Emanuel Meltzer, *Ma'avak medini bemalkodet: Yehudei polin 1935–1939* (Tel Aviv, 1982); Moshe Landau, *Miut leumi lohem: Ma'avak Yehudei polin 1918–1928* (Jerusalem, 1986); and of course Yitzhak Grünbaum, *Milhamot Yehudei polania* (Jerusalem, 1941). For details see my remarks in Yisrael Gutman, Ezra Mendelsohn, Jehuda Reinharz, and Chone Shmeruk (eds.), *The Jews of Poland between Two World Wars* (Hanover and London, 1990), 4.

[2] Shmuel Ettinger, 'The Modern Period', in H. H. Ben-Sasson (ed.), *A History of the Jewish People* (Cambridge, Mass., 1976), 959.

[3] Ibid. 960. The main culprit was the Orthodox party Agudas Yisroel, which joined the government list, the Bezpartyjny Blok Współpracy z Rządem [BBWR: Non-Party Bloc for Co-operation with the Government].

as the cultural activities of Polish Jewry are concerned, of forty-five lines devoted to this subject only six deal with Orthodox Jewish culture. Finally, Ettinger believes that at the end of the 1920s and the beginning of the 1930s '*Hehaluts* [the Zionist Pioneer movement which trained Jewish youths for their future life in Palestine] . . . became the central mass movement among socialist youth in Poland.'[4] This singling out of the Pioneer movement is highly characteristic. In fact, of all Jewish movements in interwar Poland the Haluts—activist, nationalist, socialist—is by far the most exhaustively studied. Professor Yisrael Oppenheim has devoted two massive volumes to its history, Leib Shpeizman three, and Levi Aryeh Sarid one (but it is very long) and there is yet another, more modest book on the same subject by Yisrael Otiker.[5] One might gain the impression from all of this that the Pioneer was a movement of truly epic dimensions, which in fact it never was.

If Ettinger's book is probably the single most influential work on modern Jewish history, the most influential treatment of the Holocaust period is by Lucy Dawidowicz. In *The War against the Jews* she appends a brief section on the interwar period, in which she writes that in Poland of the 1930s 'A torrent of anti-semitic legislation, brutal pogroms, and an official government policy of "evacuating" the Jews from Poland overwhelmed them.' Nevertheless, she adds, Jewish culture flourished there.[6] More relevant for our purposes is the volume on interwar Polish Jewry published by the Yidisher Vissenshaftlikher Institut (YIVO: Jewish Scientific Institute) in 1974, entitled *Shtudies vegn yidn in poylin/Studies on Polish Jewry*. This important compilation includes two long articles on Polish antisemitism, by Isaiah Trunk and Paweł Korzec, chronicling the antisemitic activities of the Polish government and Polish society. Korzec describes the Polish government as 'a regime of terror and oppression against its national minorities, especially against the defenseless Jewish population'. As for the internal Jewish front, he notes that 'A major part of the Jewish community had doubts regarding the political line of the assimilationists and the Orthodox, and believed that they were betraying Jewish interests.'[7] These are truly classic formulations. The volume also contains a long bibliography of the Jewish press, demonstrating the remarkable creativity of Polish Jewry, an article on Jewish self-defence, demonstrating the existence of the heroic struggle against the violent antisemites, and a long piece on *hakhsharah* (Zionist vocational

---

[4] Ibid. 961.

[5] Yisrael Oppenheim, *Toledot hehaluts bepolin* (Jerusalem, 1982) (this volume deals with the years 1917–29; a second volume, soon to be published, completes the story); Leib Shpeizman, *Halutsim in poylin* (3 vols.; New York, 1959–62); Levi Aryeh Sarid, *Hehaluts utenuot hanoar bepolin* (Tel Aviv, 1979); Yisrael Otiker, *Tenuat hehaluts bepolin* (Beit Lohamei Hagetaot, 1972).

[6] Lucy S. Dawidowicz, *The War against the Jews 1933–1945* (New York, 1975), 396.

[7] Joshua Fishman, (ed.), *Studies on Polish Jewry 1919–1939* (New York, 1974), 12, 46 (English section).

training, sponsored by the Pioneer movement). In all these ways it is a perfect example of Establishment Jewish historiography on interwar Polish Jewry.

Another important publication that reflects this approach is the continuing series entitled *Pinkas hakehilot* published by Yad Vashem (the Israeli institution established to commemorate and study the Holocaust). These encyclopaedic volumes chronicle Jewish life in the cities and towns of Poland and other countries. The descriptions invariably include lists of antisemitic activities. Here is a paraphrase of the relevant section on the town of Drohobycz in eastern Galicia:

Antisemitic outbursts of varying proportions were the lot of the Jews of Drohobycz during the years 1918–39. At the end of the 1920s Ukrainians attacked Jews, especially in the market. In 1930 the Endeks circulated antisemitic pamphlets. In 1936 several Jews were wounded by Ukrainian attacks. In the same year seven Jewish homes were attacked. In 1938 the Endeks broke the windows in the synagogue . . . The Polish authorities did nothing to calm things down.[8]

Finally, I will quote from Israel's most important historian of the east European Holocaust, Yisrael Gutman, and from Y. Sh. Hertz, official historian of the Jewish socialist Bund. In Hertz's work on the history of the Polish Bund we read: 'Despite the fact that a third of the population [in Poland] was comprised of national minorities, [the Poles] established a national Polish state that strongly discriminated against the minorities and especially against Jews.'[9] Gutman, in his influential book on the Warsaw ghetto, makes the same point: Poland 'stood out' in eastern Europe for its 'aggressive and intolerant nationalism. These trends, together with the traditional laws that discriminated against the national minorities in Poland, primarily affected the Jews.'[10]

In order to demonstrate that this view is still very much with us today, consider the recent book by Ettinger's student Shmuel Almog, entitled *Nationalism and Anti-semitism in Modern Europe, 1815–1945*. In his remarks on interwar Poland Almog states that

Polish anti-semitism . . . became part of the national ethos and acquired a semi-official status following independence. The partisans of the nation-state looked askance at the existence of a large and highly distinctive Jewish minority consisting of a broad stratum of traditional Jews and smaller groups of a modern Jewish identity . . . Anti-semitism in Poland, then, tended to be nearly total, and it intensified with the deterioration of the political and economic situation in the inter-war period.[11]

[8] *Polin: Pinkas hakehilot, vol. Mizraḥ galitsiyah* (Jerusalem, 1980), 167–8.
[9] Y. Sh. Hertz *et al.* (eds.), *Di geshikhte fun bund*, iv (New York, 1972), 12.
[10] Yisrael Gutman, *The Jews of Warsaw* (Bloomington, Ind., 1982), p. xvi.
[11] Shmuel Almog, *Nationalism and Anti-semitism in Modern Europe, 1815–1945* (Oxford, 1990), 107. This book was first published in Hebrew in 1988.

It may be worthwhile mentioning too that a rather extreme version of this view of Jewish–Polish relations is to be found in the writings of the most celebrated cultural figure of modern Polish Jewry, Isaac Bashevis Singer (he is not, however, an advocate of the traditional national left-wing approach to Jewish politics and Jewish culture). Thus his narrator in the novel *Shosha* sums up the situation as follows: 'The Jews in Poland are trapped. The Poles want to get rid of us. They consider us a nation within a nation, a strange and malignant body. They lack the courage to finish us off themselves, but they wouldn't shed tears if Hitler did it for them.'[12]

The 'Establishment' Jewish approach to interwar Polish Jewish history has not, until recently, been seriously challenged by non-Jewish historians. In general it seems that historians of Polish origin have tended to shy away from the 'Jewish question', for obvious reasons. Thus the old standard history of Poland by Oscar Halecki mentions it only in passing. The large number of Jews in interwar Poland and their disproportionate role in the economy are remarked on, and in such circumstances Halecki thinks that antisemitism was 'almost inevitable'. None the less, he claims, 'on the part of the Polish government it was steadily suppressed'.[13] More recently, however, non-Jewish historians have begun a sophisticated and sometimes impressive assault on the standard Jewish version.[14] The leading figure here outside of Poland is, of course, Norman Davies (his equivalent for the Holocaust period is Richard Lukas). Important Polish scholars, led by Jerzy Tomaszewski, have also entered the fray.

These revisionists, if we may so call them, are particularly interested in exposing Jewish 'myths' with regard to the question of Polish–Jewish relations, although, as we shall see, they are not entirely uninterested in the internal Jewish arena. They ask some important questions: What is really meant by 'antisemitism'? What exactly is a pogrom? The events in Lwów in November 1918, a great pogrom so far as Jewish scholars are concerned, are described by Davies as a 'so-called' pogrom.[15] They do not deny the existence of antisemitism, but they do deny its gigantic, demonic dimensions, just as Ukrainian historians have been labouring to reduce the number of Jewish victims of the Chmielnicki uprising.[16]

---

[12] Isaac Bashevis Singer, *Shosha* (New York, 1978), 138.
[13] Oscar Halecki, *A History of Poland* (New York, 1961), 297.
[14] I have discussed this in 'Inter-war Poland: Good for the Jews or Bad for the Jews?', in Ch. Abramsky *et al.* (eds.), *The Jews in Poland* (London, 1986), 130–9.
[15] Norman Davies, *God's Playground*, ii (New York, 1982), 262.
[16] See e.g the articles by Jarosław Pelenski and Frank Sysyn in Peter J. Potochnyj and Howard Aster (eds.), *Ukrainian–Jewish Relations in Historical Perspective* (Edmonton, Alta., 1988).

Beyond this they are eager to place Polish–Jewish relations in the proper perspective, and to make distinctions that are not always made—distinctions between different periods in modern Polish history, distinctions between different sorts of Polish nationalists, different kinds of Polish churchmen, and so on. Perhaps the bottom line of these efforts is the desire to demonstrate that the question of Polish–Jewish relations in the interwar period is really much more complicated than the Ettingers, Dawidowiczs, and Mendelsohns, in their simplicity, think. In order to do this they make occasional forays into internal Jewish developments. If things were so terrible, says Davies, then how can we explain the 'flourishing' of Jewish cultural and political life that Jewish scholars never fail to mention?[17] Some appear to suggest that the question of Polish–Jewish relations should really be understood not as a relationship between a majority with a monopoly of power and a defenceless minority, but as a relationship between more or less equal 'camps', neither of which held a monopoly of either good or evil.[18] If there were Polish chauvinists (the Endecja and the formations to its right), there were also Jewish chauvinists (the Revisionists). Indeed, it is striking how fascinated these historians are with Jabotinsky's movement, a kind of *deus ex machina* which allows them to claim that the Poles were not the sole advocates of what right-thinking people regard as unpleasant, intolerant integral nationalism.[19]

These non-Jewish, mostly Polish historians are not alone in their desire to look at the history of the Jews in interwar Poland in new ways. There is also a new, mostly Jewish historiography that has been emerging during the 1980s which is far more sophisticated and analytical than that of the older traditional school. Two examples are the studies of antisemitism by Frank Golczewski and Emanuel Melzer.[20] But if there is a revisionist Jewish historiography, it is selectively revisionist: the new, more sophisticated Jewish writing has not really challenged the traditional Jewish approach to

---

[17] *God's Playground*, ii. 409. See also Jerzy Tomaszewski's review of my book *The Jews of East Central Europe Between the Two World Wars* in *Polin*, i, (1986), 379–82, and his article 'Some Methodological Problems of the Study of Jewish History in Poland between the Two World Wars', ibid. 163–75.

[18] See e.g. Jacek Majchrowski, 'Some Observations on the Situation of the Jewish Minority in Poland during the Years 1918–1939', *Polin*, iii (1988), 302–9.

[19] See Jerzy Tomaszewski, 'Vladimir Jabotinsky's Talks with Representatives of the Polish Government', *Polin*, iii (1988) 276–93. Richard Lukas writes that 'There was a curious convergence between the Zionist Revisionists and the right-wing National Radical Camp': *The Forgotten Holocaust* (Lexington, Ky., 1986), 138.

[20] Frank Golczewski, *Polnisch-judische Beziehungen 1881–1922* (Wiesbaden, 1981); Melzer, *Ma'avak medini bemalkodet*. Nor should we forget the important work by Edward Wynot, e.g. his *Polish Politics in Transition* (Athens, Ga., 1974).

the question of Polish–Jewish relations, namely that interwar Poland was an extremely anti-Jewish country. Indeed, Melzer reinforces it, as does Joseph Marcus in his important book.[21] Even David Engel, a most sophisticated and careful historian of the Jewish school—so careful that he tries to avoid using the word 'antisemitism' altogether—has presented, in the introductory chapter of his impressive study on the Polish government-in-exile and the Jewish question, a more or less conventional, 'Jewish' picture of Polish–Jewish relations in the interwar period.[22] In Israel, and in the Jewish diaspora, there has not been (and I do not wish to suggest that there necessarily should be) an agonizing reappraisal of this issue, although here and there one detects that the new Polish historiography has had a certain impact.[23]

The revisionism among the Jewish historians is concerned above all with the 'second front', i.e. internal Jewish problems. New winds are blowing in the Jewish world, especially in Israel, and inevitably historians are influenced by them. The Jewish left has been in disarray, while Jewish Orthodoxy and the Jewish right have been gaining in strength. Among some members of the left-leaning intelligentsia one may detect a certain disgust with nationalism in general, including the Zionist variety, or at least a growing awareness of the complexity of ethnic relations (the Palestinian problem is relevant here). In this context we can understand the appearance of new studies on the Orthodox Jewish political party Agudas Yisroel,[24] on Hasidism in Poland,[25] and on revisionism.[26] Polish Zionism, the darling of the old school, has been cut down to size in several new studies.[27] Joseph Marcus (in his *Social and Political History*) wants to convince us that the Zionist-led Jewish political line in interwar Poland was absurd and suicidal. Even

---

[21] Joseph Marcus, *Social and Political History of the Jews in Poland 1919–1939* (Berlin, etc., 1983).

[22] David Engel, *In the Shadow of Auschwitz* (Chapel Hill, NC, and London, 1987), 12–45. He is criticized for so doing by Tomaszewski in *Studies in Contemporary Jewry*, 7 (1991), 418.

[23] See e.g. my 'Inter-war Poland' (above, n. 15), also the article on Poland by Yisrael Gutman in the new *Encyclopedia of the Holocaust*, iii (New York and London, 1990), 1153–5.

[24] See Gershon Bacon, 'Agudath Israel in Poland, 1916–1939: An Orthodox Response to the Challenge of Modernity' (diss. Columbia, 1979), and his article 'The Politics of Tradition: Agudat Israel in Polish Politics, 1916–1939', *Studies in Contemporary Jewry*, 2 (1986), 144–63.

[25] Mendel Piekarz, *Haḥassidut befolin ben shetei milḥamot uvegezarot tash–tashaḥ hashoah* (Jerusalem, 1990).

[26] Yaakov Shavit, *Jabotinsky and the Revisionist Movement* (London, 1988).

[27] Ezra Mendelsohn, 'Zionist Successes and Zionist Failures in Eastern Europe', in Ruth Kozodoy *et al.* (eds.), *Vision Confronts Reality: Historical Perspectives on the Contemporary Jewish Agenda* (Herzl Yearbook, New York, 1989), 190–209; id., 'Ha'omnam haytah yadah shel hatsionut befolin al ha'eliyonah?' in *Tsionut umitnagede'hah ba'am hayehudi* (Jerusalem, 1990), 241–6.

'assimilationism' is being looked at afresh, as is the Bund and the role of Jewish Communists.[28]

One senses, these days, the existence of a certain debunking spirit in modern Jewish historiography. A well-known debunker is Professor Chone Shmeruk, who has made clear his doubts about the 'flourishing' of Jewish culture and demonstrated the importance of the inroads of Polish acculturation and the difficulties encountered by secular Yiddish-language culture in the interwar period.[29] Moreover, both Jewish and non-Jewish scholars are now looking at new, hitherto neglected problems—relations between the sexes,[30] the Jewish stereotypes in Polish culture,[31] the 'image' of the Jew in Polish literature and of the Pole in Jewish literature.[32] There are new studies of the *shtetl*[33] and of particular Jewish communities.[34] In all this we may detect a healthy reaction against the old primacy of politics in Jewish historiography, a development partly influenced by new trends in general European and American historiography. Thanks to these new works, we are obtaining a much richer and more profound understanding of the Jewish experience in Poland.

Let me conclude with a short list of desiderata. Of course it is always good to know more, and there are projects being carried out today on the attitude of various Polish political parties to the Jewish question, on Polish legislation

---

[28] Miriam Freilich is currently writing a doctoral dissertation at the Hebrew University on the Polish Jewish circles that favoured integration and/or assimilation; on the Bund see Abraham Brumberg, 'The Bund and the Polish Socialist Party in the Late 1930s', in Gutman *et al.*, *The Jews of Poland between the Two World Wars*, 75–96; and Antony Polonsky, 'The Bund in Polish Political Life, 1935–1939', in Ada Rapoport-Albert and Steven J. Zipperstein (eds.), *Jewish History: Essays in Honour of Chimen Abramsky* (London, 1988), 547–80. Daniel Blatman has completed a doctoral dissertation at the Hebrew University on the Bund during the Holocaust period. On Jewish Communism see Moshe Mishkinsky, 'The Communist Party of Poland and the Jews', in *The Jews of Poland between the Two World Wars*, 56–74.

[29] See his article 'Hebrew–Yiddish–Polish: A Trilingual Jewish Culture', in Gutman *et al.*, *The Jews of Poland between the Two World Wars*, 285–311.

[30] Shaul Stampfer, 'Marital Patterns in Inter-war Poland', in Gutman *et al.*, *The Jews of Poland between the Two World Wars*, 173–97.

[31] Alina Cała, *The Image of the Jew in Polish Folk Culture*, to be published in the monograph series of the Center for Research on the History and Culture of Polish Jews at the Hebrew University; Władysław Bartoszewski, 'Ethnocentrism: Beliefs and Stereotypes. A Study of Polish–Jewish Relations in the Early Twentieth Century' (diss. Cambridge, 1984); Olga Goldberg, 'Postać Żyda w polskiej rzeźbie ludowej', *Polska sztuka ludowa*, 34 (1980), 219–25.

[32] Israel Bartal, 'Non-Jews and Gentile Society in East European Hebrew and Yiddish Literature 1856–1914', *Polin*, iv (1989), 53–69; Magdalena Opalski, 'Trends in the Literary Perception of Jews in Modern Polish Fiction', ibid. 70–86.

[33] Samuel D. Kassow, 'Community and Identity in the Inter-war Shtetl', in Gutman *et al.*, *The Jews of Poland between the Two World Wars*, 198–222.

[34] See e.g. Robert Moses Shapiro, 'Jewish Self-government in Poland: Łódź, 1914–1939' (diss. Columbia, 1987).

vis-à-vis the Jews, and on a host of other problems. As for the general question of how to approach the subject, I want to make one central point. All of us would do well to keep in mind something that the Polish historians have emphasized, correctly in my opinion—namely, that the Jewish problem in interwar Poland really was a *problem* for the new Polish state and for Polish society. The question of how to deal with this large, economically powerful but poverty-stricken, unacculturated but Polonizing Jewish community that spoke with many voices and made contradictory demands—this constituted a real dilemma. Historians have a duty to present the 'problem', to analyse the various options available for dealing with it, and to explain why, in various periods, various policies were or were not put forward.

Secondly, I would recommend the use of the comparative method in studying the Jews of Poland. This subject has been studied too much in isolation, as Davies has correctly pointed out, and should certainly be seen in the general context of the nationalities problem.[35] The subject of the Jews in Poland should also be studied in the context of interwar eastern Europe. Comparisons between the Polish and Russian cases are bound to be revealing,[36] as would be comparisons with such countries as Hungary, Romania, and Czechoslovakia. Such studies should give us some idea of the range of options available to the ruling powers in their dealing with the Jews, and should explain how certain historical conditions and historical traditions influence policy towards minorities in general, and Jews in particular. They should also illuminate the question as to whether Jewish behaviour was to any significant extent a factor in the crystallization of policies and attitudes towards the Jews.

Total historical objectivity is an illusion, and historians are always influenced by the events and passions of the times in which they live. But writing on the history of the Jews in Poland during the period of the Second Republic, while inevitably affected by the impact of the horrors of the Second World War, the ravages of European antisemitism, and the imposition of Communism, should also take into account the knowledge we have gained, since 1939, of the extreme complexity of ethnic, racial, and national relations within the framework of the modern or modernizing state. If it does that, we may come closer to the elusive truth.

---

[35] See Davies's article 'Ethnic Diversity in Twentieth-century Poland', *Polin*, iv (1989), 143–58.

[36] See e.g. Ezra Mendelsohn and Mordecai Altshuler, 'Yahadut berit hamo'atsot ufolin ben shetei milḥamot ha'olam: Nituaḥ hasheva'ati', in Geoffrey Wigoder (ed.), *Iyunim beyahadut zemanenu* (Jerusalem, 1984), 53–64; Mendelsohn, 'German and Jewish Minorities in the European Successor States between the World Wars: Some Comparative Remarks', in Chone Shmeruk and Ezra Mendelsohn (eds.), *Studies on Polish Jewry* (Jerusalem, 1987), pp. li-lxv.

Britain, a British Jew, and Jewish Relations with the New Poland: The Making of the Polish Minorities Treaty of 1919

MARK LEVENE

THE QUESTION OF MINORITIES IN AN INTERNATIONAL CONTEXT

ON 28 June 1919, in the great Hall of Mirrors in Versailles, the new Polish state received its international warranty. Poland had been duly recognized as a full and integral element in a 'new Europe' created through the Great War victory of the Western Allies. But there were, as the term 'warranty' implies, strings attached. Ignacy Paderewski and Roman Dmowski were on this momentous occasion being required to put their signatures to more than a treaty which would govern the future relationship between states. The peace, as determined by the Allies, also demanded specific obligations from Poland with regard to its non-Polish inhabitants. These obligations, governing Poland's *domestic* relations, were to be committed to international protocol in the form of a special and separate Minorities Treaty. Citizenship for all those living in Poland was to be guaranteed, their nationality firmly fixed as Polish. This was consistent with the agendas of previous international conferences where new states had been created or fully recognized. But the Minorities Treaty departed radically from these precedents in that it recognized not simply the existence of linguistic or cultural groups who did not belong to the dominant Polish majority but also their entitlement to rights as such within the framework of a sovereign Poland.[1]

---

[1] For more on the treaty see C. A. Macartney, *National States and National Minorities* (London, 1934); Jacob Robinson, *Were the Minorities and Treaties a Failure?* (New York, 1943); Oscar Janowsky, *The Jews and Minority Rights 1898–1919* (New York, 1933); Max Kohler, 'The Origin of the Minority Provision of the Paris Treaty of 1919', in Luigi Luzzatti (ed.), *God in Freedom* (New York, 1930), 751–94. For the full text of the Polish Minorities Treaty see Mark

The arrangements for minorities had been developed and drafted at the Paris peace conference with a view to their general applicability to all the new states created in eastern Europe, and indeed beyond. The concept of minority rights, or, in modern parlance, group rights, had for the first time, however tentatively, been addressed and endorsed at the highest international level. The creation of a League of Nations moreover provided, in theory at least, a body which would ensure that these obligations remained binding and a mechanism, through the International Court of Justice, for redressing violations or infractions. These had implications far beyond Poland. Nevertheless, the Minorities Treaty not only put Poland in the international spotlight at Paris but in a critical sense was peculiarly addressed to her. More particularly still, they concerned Poland's relationship with *one* of her minority populations, the Jews.

The new Poland had a number of non-Polish minorities who together constituted a good third of the total population. Of these the Jews, comprising not quite 10 per cent of the interwar total, were neither as significant as the Ukrainians (14.3 per cent) in demographic terms, nor as potentially problematic as the German element (3.9 per cent),[2] the majority of whom had been severed, by the territorial terms of the peace, from their traditional east Prussian homeland. If the Polish Minorities Treaty was in some sense about them, as well as significant Lithuanian and Belarussian minorities, it was above all designed to ensure the survival, security, and well-being of Poland's Jewry. In the final version of the treaty this was in fact explicit, since in two articles Jews were mentioned by name, an extraordinary departure from traditional international convention, which generally embraced their civil and political rights, as well as freedom to worship, within a general formula.

This end product begs a number of important questions. Why specifically Poland as model, or, as most Poles saw it, guinea-pig, for these new terms of international reference? Why, moreover, were the Allies demanding minority guarantees from Poland when they had no intention of extending these to their own minorities? And why such emphasis on the Jews? Polish political leaders had strenuously resisted from the moment the treaty was mooted, arguing in general terms that it was a derogation of the principle of sovereignty—a position adamantly upheld right up to the moment of

---

Levene, *War, Jews and the New Europe: The Diplomacy of Lucien Wolf 1914–1919* (Oxford, 1992), 312–15, or James Parkes, *Emergence of the Jewish Problem 1878–1939* (London, 1946), 119–23.

[2] On the basis of the 1921 census the Polish national composition by percentage was: 69.2% Poles; 14.3% Ukrainians; 7.8% Jews; 3.9% Germans and Belarussians; 0.9% others (mostly Lithuanians). See Joseph Marcus, *Social and Political History of the Jews in Poland 1919–1939* (Berlin, 1983), 16–17. The figure of 7.8% refers to those giving their 'nationality' as Jewish; in fact just under 10% gave their 'religion' as Jewish.

signing—while maintaining that in terms of Polish–Jewish relations it was the surest, quickest way to wreck them. In such circumstances, was the treaty a mistake? Could there have been an alternative arrangement or simply a better treaty? If it was not, as the Poles insisted, either in Polish or Polish–Jewish interests, then ultimately in whose interests, if anybody's, was it?

The purpose of this essay is to examine these problems not primarily in terms of the treaty's legal construction, but in terms of the contingencies, personalities, and changing viewpoints which informed its evolution. Our key witnesses will be two significant British delegates at Paris, both of whom, helpfully for historians, have left in diary form significant if self-conscious records of their actions at the conference.[3] The first, Lucien Wolf, represented the Joint Foreign Committee of British Jews (JFC), the communally sanctioned body of Anglo-Jewry with authority to speak on Jewish issues abroad. Wolf's paramount intellectual and actual position on this committee was formally acknowledged in his title of 'foreign secretary'. His imprint on the Polish Minorities Treaty is writ large. So too is that of our second key witness, Sir James Headlam-Morley, a member of the official British delegation at Paris and prime British mover in the treaty's drafting. The increasing interaction between these two players is itself revealing and, as will be argued, contributed significantly to the ultimate shape and form of the treaty arrangements.

THE POLISH JEWS AS A NATIONAL MINORITY

But what of the problem of minority rights itself and more particularly the case of the Jews of Poland? A useful and interesting place to start might be an exchange of letters, almost a year before the Paris peace conference had commenced, between Wolf and David Mowschowitch, his Russian-born adviser on east European Jewish affairs. Few English Jews at the time, including members of Wolf's own committee, understood, let alone sympathized with, the concept of minority rights, and Wolf confided to Mowschowitch his doubts on how to proceed further:

The difficulty is to obtain some authentic expression of the wishes of the Polish Jews as a whole. If they wish us to stand out for national autonomy we will do so but if there are serious differences of opinion among them on this question, I am afraid we shall have to leave them to fight it out among themselves and limit ourselves to a demand for equal rights.[4]

[3] Mocatta Library, University College, London, Lucien Wolf, Diary of the Peace Conference, Paris [hereafter Wolf, Paris Diary], and Agnes Headlam-Morley *et al.* (eds.), *Sir James Headlam-Morley: A Memoir of the Paris Peace Conference* (London, 1972).

[4] YIVO, New York, Mowschowitch Collection [hereafter MWS] 10467–8, Wolf to Mowschowitch (25 Feb. 1918).

Mowschowitch responded as follows:

> The duty of the Conjoint Committee [sic] as I understand it, is to be neutral in the international struggle between the Jewish parties but not in the struggle between the Jewish minority and the Polish majority. If the gentlemen of your committee are unable to grasp the thing for which the whole of Eastern Europe agonises, let them at least support the demand that in the Polish Constitution should be inserted a stipulation according to which a general congress ... of Polish Jews organises culturally and religiously the Jewry and represents it through its organs before the government as a whole.[5]

The exchange is revealing on a number of scores. First and foremost there is a serious doubt, at least in Wolf's mind, about whether Polish Jewry had a single, coherent, and unified position on the question. Mowschowitch had since the February revolution of 1917 been haranguing him on the degree to which the concept of national autonomy for the Jews had become common currency throughout the spectrum of Jewish political bodies and formations in the *Russian* empire.[6] Wolf himself, moreover, had become a convinced adherent, writing an important article in the *Edinburgh Review* as early as April 1917, in which he endorsed the idea for the whole of eastern Jewry, with full weight given to a conceptual framework as outlined some years earlier by the Austro-Marxist theoretician Karl Renner.[7]

This was truly a remarkable departure for an official spokesman of established Anglo-Jewry. Its historic agenda, as with comparable Western Jewish organizations, had always been geared towards the achievement of civil and political rights for Jews everywhere on a par with those of their fellow citizens. That the Jews might in some states constitute a specific national entity, with collective cultural or linguistic attributes which demanded an autonomous status *vis-à-vis* that state, seemed to contradict the very notion that what they were demanding was to be like everybody else.

Wolf had circumvented this problem in his article by drawing a distinction between Western and Eastern Jewry. The former lived in nation-states of which they were full citizens. Their nationality was therefore the same as that of everybody else. The latter, however, mostly lived in the Russian and Austro-Hungarian empires, which were multinational in their composition. If other nationality groups within these empires on the one hand automatically were, or were likely to become, full citizens of states, yet on the

---

[5] MWS 10471–5, Mowschowitch to Wolf (21 Mar. 1918).

[6] See esp. MWS 161775–81, reports on the Polish Question, n.d. [1917], MWS 6103–13, 'Some Remarks on Baron Guenzburg's Letter on Jewish Affairs in Russia', n.d. [June or July 1917], referring to a general reorganization and democratization of the former oligarchic community structure.

[7] Lucien Wolf, 'The Jewish National Movement', *Edinburgh Review* (Apr. 1917), 303–18; Karl Renner, *Der Kampf der österreichischen Nationen um den Staat* (Leipzig, 1902).

other demanded an autonomous national status within them, then, thought Wolf, it was not unjustified for Jews, should they so wish, to do the same. Renner's formula for making national status personal rather than territorial, moreover, got round the one really serious difficulty in regard to implementation, namely that the Jews, unlike most other nationalities (at least in part), had no compact territorial base but were distributed unevenly throughout great chunks of eastern Europe, inextricably mixed up with the other nationalities.

This was all well and good in theory. The problem in 1918 was that it was based on the assumption that the empires would transform themselves *from within* into fully democratic national federations and took no account of other political realities which might undermine this basic premiss. If, for instance, eastern Europe was instead to break up into a series of small or medium-sized nation-states, the idea of national autonomy for all groups was unlikely to be acceptable to the nationally dominant one. Moreover, while objectively speaking it made a very great deal of sense for the Jews if the unity of the empires were maintained, the alternative nation-state scenario might very well put them at the mercy of the dominant national group, possibly with a view to forcing them to conform or, worse, leave. In this scenario the issue of national autonomy gave way to the much more basic one of safeguarding Jewish equality before the law—in other words, back to the traditional Western Jewish stance.

Wolf's vacillation and indecision in early 1918 with regard to Poland thus had very little to do with his principled position, but was rather the pragmatic consequence of a highly fluid situation with regard to its domestic political arrangements, at that point under Austro-German occupation, and the future ramifications for these arrangements dependent on which side would ultimately win the war. Paradoxically, at that point, with the tilt towards the possibility of a peace dictated by the Central Powers, in the wake of the treaty of Brest-Litovsk, the overall chances for Jewish national autonomy both within Poland and beyond *were* enhanced.

A future Polish nation-state had been recognized by all parties to the conflict in the early stages of the war. Austro-German interests, however, were best achieved through a territorially small and essentially weak Poland which otherwise would be linked to their own satellite system. Brest-Litovsk, concluded with Bolshevik Russia in March, confirmed this intention by awarding the largely Polish-populated province of Chelm to the Ukrainians while enlarging Lithuania, again at Polish expense.[8] Such a settlement created large Polish minorities in neighbouring satellite units, a situation which would force Poland to seek safeguards for them while also, by

[8] See Fritz Fischer, *Germany's Aims in the First World War* (London, 1967) 450–72, 485–7; *The Cambridge History of Poland*, ii. *1697–1935* (Cambridge, 1951), 473.

political necessity, demanding that it pay closer attention to the position of non-Polish minorities within its boundaries.

Thus, in the absence of a Poland linked in some way to a Russian federation—a possibility only available while post-Tsarist Russia remained in the war on the side of the Allies—a *pax Germanica* represented the best, possibly only, option for preserving Polish Jewry's all-important cultural and economic links with fellow Jews in the neighbouring Ukraine, Belarus, and Lithuania. Moreover, under Austro-German rule since 1915, Polish Jewish political parties with national programmes had made major strides forward. True, the enactment of communal autonomy by the 1916 *Verordnung* had had severe limitations. It was expressly defined in religious terms and, with appointments to its governing council overseen by the German governor-general, largely valueless to the secular Bundist, Zionist, and Folkist parties most committed to goals of autonomy.[9] Nor was German or Austrian rule consistently benevolent towards the Jews. Nevertheless, the evidence suggests that Jewish national awareness did embark on a major flowering under their rule, confirmed by the take-off in the fortunes of the nationally orientated Jewish parties. With assistance from the newly created, government-backed, German Jewish organization VJOD,[10] itself committed to a clear endorsement of minority rights for Eastern Jewry, Polish Jewish aspirations for national autonomy within a future Polish state, in the spring of 1918, probably stood at their apex.

Regardless of the advantages associated with this positive scenario, however, two major obstacles, explicit in the Wolf–Mowschowitch exchange, remained. One was the Polish Jews. The other was the Poles.

THE NEW POLAND

While, as we have seen, Wolf was in general terms sympathetic to the idea of autonomy for the east, he still had nagging doubts about the particular case of Poland. In part this was a residual hangover from a pre-war view, shared by most Western Jewish observers, that as Poland would one day be reconstituted as an independent nation-state, its Jews should, in linguistic and cultural terms, assimilate to it as they had done on receiving

---

[9] Egmont Zechlin, *Die deutsche Politik und die Juden im Ersten Weltkreig* (Göttingen, 1969), 221–3; Ezra Mendelsohn, *Zionism in Poland: The Formative Years 1915–1926* (New Haven, 1981), 39–45, for these developments.

[10] Vereinigung Jüdischer Organisationen Deutschlands zur Wahrung der Rechte der Juden des Osten. For details of its formation and structure see Zechlin, *Deutsche Politik*, 221–3; Isaiah Friedman, *Germany, Turkey and Zionism 1897–1918* (London, 1977), 394–5; also MWS 21045–8, text of 10 July 1918 declaration by von Falkenhausen (Imperial Commissioner Ober-Ost), to a VJOD delegation favouring Jewish minority rights in Lithuania.

emancipation elsewhere.[11] Wolf's pre-war contacts with Polish Jewry had largely been with a small but influential metropolitan-based group, led by Professor Dickstein and members of the Natanson family, who advocated this course and who in early 1918 were still insisting that they could carry through an internal settlement by negotiation with Polish political leaders. This, moreover, they maintained could be achieved without co-operation or assistance from outside.[12] An internal settlement was in fact Wolf's preferred conclusion, while the Koło Patriotów Polsko-Żydowskich (Circle of Polish Jewish Patriots) did have the obvious advantage that their position was so in line with Polish aspirations that they undoubtedly could have reached a *modus vivendi* with the Polish political élite. Wolf, of course, knew the Circle to be totally unrepresentative of Polish Jewry and made no efforts in his following dealings at the peace conference to realign his position to theirs.[13] Nevertheless, their very existence at one end of a complicated spectrum of Polish Jewish formations did highlight Wolf's conundrum in seeking 'authentic expression of the wishes of Polish Jewry as a whole'. Efforts, primarily by Zionists, to create an elected all-Polish Jewish conference to achieve that authentic voice had so far come to naught and were to fail again at their second attempt, in October 1918, not least because the important Orthodox League boycotted the proceedings.[14] Such an eventuality had in fact already been foreseen in an important article read and carefully considered by Wolf, in the May 1918 edition of *Prawda*, the centre-left Polish-language journal published in London.[15] In this, Adam Sutherland, an expert on Poland, put a different spanner in the works of an internal settlement involving all Jewish parties by adumbrating the reasons why some of them would be unacceptable as negotiating partners to the Polish government. The Bundists, culturally nationalist in orientation, he argued, would be excluded by dint of their association with and enthusiasm for Revolutionary Russia. Zionists and Folkists, in demanding more far-reaching political national autonomy, would also be rebuffed, a view borne out in reality by Paderewski's complete refusal to countenance the concept at all when he met some Jewish leaders in February 1919.[16] That left, in

[11] *Darkest Russia* (26 Feb. 1913), Wolf leader, 'The Boycott in Poland'.

[12] MWS (118) 16203-6, report from *Die Zeit* (3 Feb. 1918). See also ibid. 16207-11, *L'Echo polonais* report (28 Apr. 1918) on the Society for Social Work among Jews in Poland, a newly created wing of the Dickstein people. Its manifesto's self-proclaimed aim was 'to facilitate and accelerate the permeation among the Jews of the fundamental ideas of Poland'.

[13] See Wolf, Paris Diary, fo. 400 (27 June 1919).

[14] Mendelsohn, *Zionism in Poland*, 91-2.

[15] Board of Deputies, London, JFC files, C11/3/1/3, encl. Sutherland, *Prawda* article (18 May 1918).

[16] Paweł Korzec, *Juifs en Pologne: La Question juive pendant l'entre-deux-guerres* (Paris, 1980), 89-90.

Sutherland's view, the great mass of Orthodoxy, who, traditionally non-political, could be brought, through organizations like Agudas Yisroel, to an arrangement on the basis of religious toleration and full civil and political rights.

This mirrored closely the public position of the Polish political Establishment, both left and right, as to what Jews and other minorities could expect in a fully sovereign Poland: namely, equality before the law. In principle, as we have already suggested, this is exactly what Western Jewish spokesmen had been seeking for decades. Sutherland's suggestion, therefore, for an internal solution based on tacit support from a sizeable section of the Jewish population while also avoiding the involvement in particular of the Zionists, Wolf's primary opponents in the international Jewish arena, should have been music to his ears.

Surprisingly, however, as the war drew to a close, now with the Western Allies as likely victors, Wolf changed tack to come out officially in favour of a line much closer to that advocated by Mowschowitch. Part of his reasoning was set out in a closely argued memorandum to the Foreign Office, in October, on the interpretation of the term 'equality before the law'.[17] In this Wolf noted that the 1862 Act of Polish Emancipation under the Russians had also offered this formula, but with the stipulation that Polish Jewry renounce the use of Yiddish in speech, writing, contracts, and court procedure. These linguistic provisions were not at that time implemented. Nor, however, were they repealed: a loophole which provided Warsaw City Council in 1916 with the opportunity to invoke them in order to defeat the setting up of a separate Jewish school system. If now, pursued Wolf, a general law were to make Polish the only legal language, 'the Jewish disability would be maintained without any technical derogation from the principle of equal rights'. This would be an injustice, he concluded, which, despite the internal differences within Polish Jewry, the Western Jewish communities would feel bound to resist, even if their interference were to risk 'a possible impropriety'. Wolf set out his committee's resolution of the issue: recognition of Jews as Polish citizens, the repeal of the 1862 linguistic provisions, guarantees for the Jewish right to Saturday rest and Sunday trade, and the autonomous management of their religious, educational, charitable, and other cultural institutions.

This was in fact a remarkable turn-about for Wolf, not least because it contradicted previous advice to Warsaw Jewish voters in the 1912 elections to the Russian Parliament, the Duma, to vote for the Polish 'national'

---

[17] Public Record Office [hereafter PRO], Kew, FO 371/3280/5373, Wolf memorandum on the 'Polish Jewish Question' (3 Oct. 1918). See also MWS 60/8108-23, Marshall to Wilson (7 Nov. 1918), where Marshall makes the same points about the issue of equality before the law to the American President.

candidate, Jan Kucharzewski[18]—in other words, to integrate to the dominant culture—not least too because the memorandum contained a quite passionate defence of the right of the majority of Polish Jews to speak and continue speaking Yiddish. This was perhaps all the more remarkable because Wolf knew he would on this score receive no support from any Polish political quarter. August Zaleski, representing the liberal, and to Wolf's mind sympathetic, Piłsudski camp in London, had warned him in 1917 that its official use 'would not find favour with any section of the Polish people'.[19] Even the Polish left would want full linguistic assimilation. Closely argued discussions on the language of instruction in Polish Jewish schools between the JFC and the Polish National Committee (PNC), eighteen months later, revealed similar right-wing opposition.[20]

At the end of 1918 it was not clear who would be leading the new Poland. The Piłsudski group, in *de facto* control at the end of the war, certainly represented, in theory at least, a framework for the continued existence of non-Polish minorities within the state. But Western recognition of Polish political leadership for the last year had not been conferred on this group—under a cloud for their collaboration with the Central Powers—but on the PNC, an amalgam of the most reactionary elements in Polish political life and headed by the openly and vociferously antisemitic, as well as ultra-nationalist, leader Roman Dmowski.[21]

The aim of Dmowski and his acolytes was not so much to deprive the Jews of their linguistic rights, or even to refuse them citizenship, but rather to rid Poland of them altogether. Their paper, *Tygodnik Polski*, carried articles which were unequivocal in their demand for mass Jewish emigration,[22] while in their control of certificates registering Poles in Britain as friendly aliens they actively sought to exclude Jews on a racial basis.[23] Paradoxically, the PNC argument on this score converged with that pro-

---

[18] See MWS 2859–60, Wolf to Meyerson (19 Feb. 1913).

[19] PRO FO 371/3280/5373, Wolf memo of interview with Zaleski (6 July 1917), encl. with Wolf to FO (3 Oct. 1918). Later Wolf referred to Zaleski as 'the most liberal Pole I know': see Wolf, Paris Diary, fo. 211 (23 Apr. 1919). The view was almost identically corroborated by the English Zionist Israel Cohen: see Norman Davies, 'The Poles in Great Britain 1914–1919', *Slavonic and East European Review*, 50 (1972), 68.

[20] PRO FO 371/3280/5373, for details of JFC–PNC meeting (23 July 1918), encl. in Wolf to FO (3 Oct. 1918); Wolf, Paris Diary, fos. 105–12 (5 Mar. 1919); also Eugene Black, 'Lucien Wolf and the Making of Poland, 1919', *Polin*, ii (1987), 5–36.

[21] On Dmowski and his antisemitism see R. M. Fountain II, *Roman Dmowski: Politics, Tactics, Ideology 1895–1907* (Columbia, Mo. 1980); also PRO FO 800/205 (Balfour files) for the record of Lord Robert Cecil's conversations with him (3 Oct. 1917).

[22] See MWS (118) 16230–6, Leon Brunn article, 'Insincerity on the Jewish Question', *Tygodnik Polski* (14 July 1918).

[23] PRO HO 45/10889/352661/4, Home Office–PNC meeting to discuss administration of certificates (8 Jan. 1918).

pounded by Zionists in Britain such as Weizmann. Early in 1919 one Home Office official defending the PNC noted: 'I have reason to believe that the best Jewish opinion is not in favour of any move towards treatment on the grounds of religion rather than nationality.'[24] Moreover, the fact that Dmowski and his supporters sought to use the idea of Jewish nationality in order to ethnically cleanse Poland of Jews was given a sharp edge by the possibility that General Haller's Polish army in France, now under the command of the PNC, might be shipped back to Poland, where it could act as its willing instrument.

If installation of a Dmowski-led administration, backed and supported by the Allies, represented a worst-case scenario, a rising tide of reported pogroms[25] in the months following the armistice raised the spectre that any Polish government, regardless of whether Dmowski or Piłsudski was in charge, would be detrimental to the Jewish interest. Even if there existed real differences in their visions of the new Poland, they had agreed, for the purposes of the Paris peace conference, a common diplomatic position, with formerly PNC wartime spokesmen Paderewski and Dmowski as representatives. Wolf's decision to challenge the Poles in the international arena, therefore, and to press a case for an albeit limited form of autonomy was to a marked degree occasioned by the failure of Poles and Polish Jews to arrive at an internal settlement, combined with an urgent awareness that without some internationally accepted guidelines the situation of east European Jewry as a whole would be put in jeopardy.

THE VIEW FROM THE BRITISH FOREIGN OFFICE

In this sense the Jewish question at Paris represented a rather critical subtext to the peace. Victory for the Allies demanded that any settlement would have to be designed to keep Germany in check as well as ensuring an effective *cordon sanitaire* against the westward extrusion of an increasingly threatening Bolshevik Russia. The territorial extents and military and political potentialities of the new east European states thus became important assets in the West's postwar power-game. Their requirement for a strong, large Poland correspondingly implied limited external interference in or control of her domestic affairs. Wolf's hopes for strong guarantees on minority rights thus implicitly clashed with what were the Allies' essentially minimalist goals.

[24] Ibid., file 58, Pedder minute (4 Feb. 1919).
[25] The extent, or cause, of the pogroms in Poland remains a subject of heated controversy. See Norman Davies, 'Great Britain and the Polish Jews, 1918–1920', *Journal of Contemporary History*, 8 (1973), 119–42.

Even before the conference had commenced, the British Foreign Office had outlined what these were:

> as regards the claim that the Jews where they form a considerable element in the population of a state should have special rights as a nationality, particularly rights of cultural or educational autonomy, it is clear that no British interests are at stake in this and that if any support or guarantee were given for such a claim it would be extremely difficult to enforce. His Majesty's Government should therefore not commit themselves to the recognition of any claim either in principle or in particular cases.[26]

Moreover:

> In all countries with Jewish inhabitants but especially in East and South East Europe where the Jews form a large and more separate element in the population than elsewhere, the spokesmen of this Jewish element, if they put forward demands for cultural autonomy as well as individual citizen rights, should be recommended in the first instance to discuss the question with the government or other representative parties of their respective countries. They should be discouraged from referring this question to outside Powers of the Peace Conference before they have done their utmost to arrive at a settlement with peoples among whom they respectively live.[27]

All the Jewish lobbies in Paris were aware of the international precedents in regard to 'individual citizen rights'. And Wolf, who knew his diplomatic history inside out and arrived in Paris forearmed with two centuries of chapter-and-verse documentation,[28] was not likely to be fobbed off on this score. But convincing the Foreign Office of the need to change their minds on the subject of autonomy, an area entirely absent from previous protocol, was likely to be much more problematic. Neither Poland nor Romania should have to 'surrender any of their sovereign rights in the case of the Jews, even as far as education is concerned', thought Sir Esmé Howard, Peace Conference delegate and their senior adviser on Polish affairs.[29] Assistant Under-Secretary of State Sir Eyre Crowe agreed: 'All that we should demand is that Jews not be penalised *qua* Jews in the eyes of the law and for purposes of citizenship.'[30]

Behind these views were in fact some rather deep-seated and intractable prejudices. Not only were Jews *per se* disliked by nearly all of the top

---

[26] PRO FO 371/3414/181911, 'Conference on the Jewish Question' (19 Nov. 1918). See Alan Sharp, 'Britain and the Protection of Minorities at the Paris Peace Conference, 1919', in A. C. Hepburn (ed.), *Minorities in History* (London, 1978), 171–88, for the FO's subsequent and changing views on the subject.
[27] Ibid.
[28] See Lucien Wolf, *Notes on the Diplomatic History of the Jewish Question* (London, 1919).
[29] PRO FO 371/3419/199696, Howard memo (9 Dec. 1918).
[30] Ibid., Crowe minute (11 Dec. 1918).

echelons of the service, they were also held collectively responsible for putting a spanner in the works of Britain's wartime efforts by actively aiding and abetting the German cause. For instance: 'The large and influential Jewish element in Poland is to a great extent actively pro-German and its members are often employed as German agents in collecting foodstuffs for export to Germany.'[31] This missive, from the British ambassador in Washington to the State Department, refusing to countenance the shipment of condensed milk to Poland by American Jewish charities, would not be extraordinary except for the fact that it was sent on the same day, 2 November 1917, as Balfour's letter to Lord Rothschild promising British support for a Jewish national home in Palestine. A tacit Foreign Office alliance with the London Zionists did not change this animus to any perceptible extent—Weizmann and Sokolow failing significantly in their attempts to promote a maximalist version of national autonomy to them[32] in marked contrast with the aristocratic *bonhomie* enjoyed particularly by Catholic Foreign Office officials with members of the PNC, such as Count Sobanski, who was described by one official as 'one of the best types an ancient social order in Eastern Europe can produce'.[33]

If, then, many officials in 1919 really believed that Jewish wartime malevolence towards the Allies would translate itself into peacetime sabotage—as one official minuted, 'the Jews are determined to do everything in their power to prevent the foundation of a great and independent Poland'[34]—it would hardly surprise to discover that this had led to an essentially negative British reading of Jewish desiderata. Certainly, Esmé Howard seems to have been of the view that even permitting schools in Jewish areas to be administered by Jews, and in Yiddish, was to provide them with an invitation to develop revolutionary or anti-state propaganda,[35] while even the more cautious, but in treaty terms more significant, Headlam-Morley could intone that 'if these schools are placed under Jewish management, the more extreme national elements ... may ... foster the use of the Yiddish language in such a way as to increase the separation ... between Jews and other citizens of Poland'.[36] British misgivings on these scores certainly

---

[31] *Foreign Relations of the United States* [hereafter *FRUS*], *1918*, suppl. 2 (Washington, 1932), 518.
[32] See PRO FO 371/3445/157260 for FO officials' bemused reactions to the Zionist Organization (Copenhagen) bureau's proposals (25 Oct. 1918) for 'national autonomy, cultural, social and political'. Sokolow led the Zionist caucus which formed the Comité des Délégations Juives [hereafter CDJ] in Paris, but seems to have had minimal contact with the British delegation, except in relation to Palestine affairs. Weizmann, according to Wolf, also failed to have any impact. See Wolf, Paris Diary, fo. 140 (25 Mar. 1919).
[33] Quoted in Davies, 'Poles', 82.
[34] PRO FO 371/3419/198168, Kidston minute (5 Dec. 1918).
[35] PRO FO/608/151/493/1/1, Howard memo (9 Dec. 1918).
[36] Headlam-Morley, *Memoir*, 158–9, Headlam-Morley to Hankey (23 June 1919).

found their way into the critical meetings of the Council of Four, which gave final decisions on the wording of the treaty. Both Lloyd George and his foreign secretary, Balfour, were adamant that the treaty's guarantee on the use of Yiddish would be limited to primary schools, while the latter's fears about 'a great central Jewish committee in Warsaw' ensured that at the end of the day educational committees were to be of a local nature only.[37]

The official British post-mortem on their position in Paris, in fact written by none other than Headlam-Morley, thus reads:

the recognition of national rights of the Jews of Poland would have been completely inconsistent with the territorial sovereignty of the state, which is the basis of our whole political system. The view taken by the British delegation throughout and supported by the Plenipotentiaries was that if there was to be a Jewish nationality it could only be by giving the Jews a local habitat and enabling them to found in Palestine a Jewish state. Any Jew who was, however, a national of the Jewish state would *ipso facto* cease to be a Polish citizen.[38]

THE AMERICAN ROLE

But if this is a clear statement of British objections to even the minimum programme of autonomy as suggested by its British Jewish advocate, Lucien Wolf, does not this suggest that this whole exposition is a red herring? Are we indeed, if we are seeking an explanation for international backing of group rights at Paris, simply looking for it in relation to the wrong people, in the wrong place?

Wolf was, of course, not the only spokesman arguing the Jewish case at Paris. An older and more august body than his British committee was the French Alliance Israélite Universelle. On home ground and with traditionally close links with the Quai d'Orsay, it might have been expected to emerge as a key intermediary in the defence of Polish Jewry. All the evidence, however, suggests that not only was it lukewarm concerning the very notion of minority rights,[39] but it also refused to cross the French foreign ministry's own belligerently pro-Polish agenda. As Eugène Sée, one of its leaders, publicly stated in one of the conference's early and fractious

---

[37] See *FRUS* v. *Paris Peace Conference, 1919* (Washington, 1946), 529–30, 624–8, Council of Four meetings (17 and 23 June 1919).

[38] H. W. V. Temperley, *A History of the Paris Peace Conference*, v (London, 1921), 137, from the chapter 'Treaties for the Protection of Minorities', written by Headlam-Morley.

[39] See Alliance Israélite Universelle, *La Question juive devant la conférence de la paix* (Paris, 1919), 38, for the official AIU statement (6 June 1919) opposing national minority rights as creating dividing-walls between Jews and their fellow citizens.

inter-Jewish meetings, 'the business of the conference is to create a sovereign state for Poland, not for the Jews'.[40]

If fear of discord between Jewish supplicant and state patron eliminates the Alliance as a possible contender, then superficially the evidence with regard to the chief American Jewish spokesmen and the American negotiating team at Paris would seem to point in a contrary and much more promising direction. If Clemenceau for France, and Lloyd George for Britain, represented the essentially pragmatic and, one might conclude, cynical interests of the two leading European players in the making of the peace, President Wilson on behalf of the Americans seemed to be promoting an entirely new and radical agenda. Constructed on the idea of an international framework which would link peace with justice, his particular emphasis on self-determination for all the peoples of Europe—if not elsewhere—could surely be interpreted as essentially benevolent to the cause of Jewish minority rights. More pertinently, perhaps, the American Jewish delegation could claim two distinct advantages over Wolf. Firstly, unlike Wolf, who could not get within striking distance of Lloyd George and who was rather out of favour, lower down the rungs, with the British Foreign Office, the American Jewish leaders, Louis Marshall and Judge Julian Mack, had not only already spoken to the President before his voyage to Europe, but had received the appropriate blessings which they believed would advance their cause.[41] Secondly, in contrast to the British Jew's almost single-handed efforts, backed by a small and highly élitist committee, Mack and Marshall could claim the backing of a strong, democratically elected American Jewish Congress which had voted unequivocally for 'national' autonomy.[42] Grouping themselves in Paris with the Zionist-dominated CDJ,[43] which claimed to speak on behalf of east European (including Polish) Jewry, and again providing credentials and legitimacy for their efforts, which Wolf seemed wholly to lack following his pointed refusal to work with the Comité,[44] the American Jewish delegation seems in every respect to have been both better placed and more capable of delivering minority rights.

[40] American Jewish Committee, New York [hereafter AJC], Adler Papers, Adler MS, 'Abstract of Report of Meetings of Representative Jewish Organisations' (31 Mar. 1919), fo. 84.

[41] See MWS 8099, Marshall to Wolf (16 Nov. 1918), encl. Marshall to Wilson (7, 14, 16 Nov. 1918) and Wilson to Marshall (16 Nov. 1918). On Wilson and his championship of self-determination see N. Gordon Levin, *Woodrow Wilson and World Politics* (Oxford, 1968); Arno J. Mayer, *Political Origins of the New Diplomacy 1917–1918* (New Haven, 1959).

[42] See Jonathan Fraenkel, *Prophecy and Politics: Socialism, Nationalism and the Russian Jews 1862–1917* (Cambridge, 1981), 541–6. See also Janowsky, *Jews and Minority Rights*, 283, for American Jewish Congress contacts with President Wilson through Rabbi Stephen Wise.

[43] Janowsky, *Jews and Minority Rights*, 283–308, for a full discussion of the American Jewish relationship to the CDJ.

[44] Wolf, Paris Diary, fos. 130–7 (24 Mar. 1919), fo. 195 (16 Apr. 1919).

Not surprisingly, the conventional wisdom endorses this assumption, generally attributing to Marshall, and to a lesser extent Mack, a key role in the making of the treaty.[45] The aim here is not to dispute that they were critical players. Their behind-the-scenes lobbying of Wilson's aide, Colonel House, decisively cut through the red tape which had delayed action in the early part of the conference and facilitated the decision of the Council of Four, in late April, to set up a special body of experts, the New States Committee (NSC), working directly and secretly under its aegis, to draft clauses for its consideration.[46] The fact that Mack and Marshall were immediately able to present their own draft formula to David Hunter Miller, its American representative, at the outset of its proceedings, and then to continue to advise both him and his successor, Manley Hudson,[47] suggests not only the conspicuous success of the American Jewish lobby in penetrating the inner coulisses of power but also an overwhelming influence in determining the shape and content of the resultant treaty.

There are, however, weaknesses in pursuing this analysis to its logical conclusion. Firstly, there is the question of the degree to which Wilson was really benevolently disposed towards minority rights. Favouring national self-determination does not necessarily equate with favouring group autonomy within nation-states. Wilson's own preferences, in fact, consistently inclined towards a strong Polish state and to the dismissal of complications which would attenuate this goal.[48] It was not just the British and French who repudiated the possibility of a full programme of Jewish autonomous management.

Secondly, Wilson's inclinations placed the American Jews' ability to deliver in some doubt. Having submitted their key minority proposal (to Hunter Miller), that Polish Jewry be recognized as 'a distinct public corporation',[49] Mack and Marshall were rudely awakened within days to his reply that the committee and its masters had rejected this as completely unacceptable.[50] This was ironic, as Marshall, a self-consciously patrician member of the old American Jewish Committee (AJC), who had been co-

---

[45] This is certainly the view of Janowsky, *Jews and Minority Rights*. See also Kohler, 'Origin of the Minority Provision', 751–94, who lays special emphasis on Marshall's role in the formulation of its provisions, and Charles Reznikoff (ed.), *Louis Marshall, Champion of Liberty* (Philadephia, 1957), 506.

[46] See Kohler, 'Origin of the Minority Provision', 755, 775–80.

[47] David Hunter Miller, *My Diary at the Conference of Paris* (London, 1924), ix. 182–5, docs. 886–7 and for subsequent minutes of the NSC. See *FRUS* v. 393–4 for Maurice Hankey's procès-verbaux of the Supreme Council meeting, of 1 May 1919 setting up the NSC, and for subsequent meetings responding to its recommendations.

[48] Seth Tillman, *Anglo-American Relations at the Paris Peace Conference* (Princeton, 1961), 203–4; F. R. Bryant, 'Britain and the Polish Settlement of 1919' (diss. Oxford, 1968), 520.

[49] Miller, *Diary*, i. 259, 262, 264.

[50] Ibid. 289–90.

opted on to Mack's Paris delegation solely because of his experience and diplomatic *savoir-faire*,[51] was not personally inclined in the direction of minority rights anyway. His decision to pursue his mandate faithfully to the bitter end[52] served only to emphasize the degree to which the American Jewish delegation was both out of favour and out of touch with the peacemakers' ultimate intention.

This was, not least, a matter of reaching a settlement which would be seen not to be humiliating Poland or infringing her sovereignty. The peacemakers' solution was a two-tier settlement combining public protocol with private arrangement. Marshall and Mack could not participate in the latter, however, as they had broken off negotiations with the Poles the previous year. As for the actual treaty, despite Marshall's success, in late May, in obtaining an interview with Wilson, the latter's opinions on the one really critical clause needed to make it function effectively—namely, the right of direct minority appeal to the League of Nations in cases of violation or infraction proved to be calamitous. Wilson's preferred course of action was for the Western Jewish organizations to act as watchmen, bringing violations of the treaty to the notice of the Great Powers, as and when appropriate.[53] While this in theory reinforced American Jewry's standing, it was in fact a return to the outmoded and totally ineffectual 1878 Treaty of Berlin model, whereby they and the other Western Jewish organizations had done exactly that in relation to Romania's contemptuous evasion of her emancipatory obligations, and in return achieved precisely nothing.

Marshall's willingness to fall into line behind the President on this occasion[54] does not in itself prove that it was the British rather than the Americans who were the genuine champions of minority rights. Nevertheless, it does seem that of those most intimately bound up with the making of the minorities settlement, it was Wolf working with the British delegate to the NSC, Headlam-Morley, rather than Marshall and his American counterpart, Hunter Miller, who most profoundly shaped it. A mid-May entry from Hunter Miller's Peace Conference diary is revealing on this score:

---

[51] See Fraenkel, *Prophecy and Politics*, 541–6, for the delegation's composition and ideological orientation.

[52] See AJC, Marshall papers, Peace Conference, Corr. Box 1, Marshall to Zuckerman (6 June 1923): 'I fought for them [minority rights] long after everybody else in the delegation recognized the fact that it would be impossible to secure them.'

[53] *FRUS* v. 680 (17 May 1919); AJC, Adler Papers, Adler Diary, fo. 257, Marshall and Adler interview with President Wilson (26 May 1919).

[54] See Wolf, Paris Diary, fos. 309–24 (29 May and 1 June 1919), for the Wolf–Marshall correspondence on this score. Wolf acerbically noted: 'unfortunately Marshall always thinks in the end as the President thinks' (ibid., fo. 337, 3 June 1919).

The attitude of the British representative, Mr Headlam-Morley, has shown an extraordinary change from the time of my first discussions with him. He was then anti-Jewish and pro-Polish but changed to the extent of being willing to go further in favour of the Jews than I thought reasonable. In the meantime I learned that Sir Herbert Samuel had lunch here with Mr Lloyd George and it was immediately after that the change in Mr Headlam-Morley appeared.[55]

In the person of Headlam-Morley, the American seems to be suggesting a change in the British stance. We have already outlined the primary motivations behind British lukewarmness to Jewish minority rights, and its preference for an out-of-court settlement. But was it really the intervention of the British Jew and politician, Herbert Samuel, which changed the goalposts, or were other factors at work?

THE IDEA OF JEWISH POWER

In fact, the overall British position had been undergoing an evolution over some period, involving high politics as well as the impact of specific personalities. The role of individuals like Herbert Samuel was certainly a contributory factor, but perhaps more in the way their presence in Paris enabled lobbyists like Wolf—and Marshall—to have much greater access to the real power-brokers than they might in the normal course of events have obtained. In part this was because Samuel, emblematically, represented an idea that was very potent at the time: Jewish power.

Samuel, as well as being in his own right a former government minister of note, also came from an important banking family which was well known for handling credits for the British government.[56] His brother, Sir Stuart Samuel, was a partner in the firm as well as being a Member of Parliament, President of the Anglo-Jewish Board of Deputies, and joint chairman of Wolf's committee. In 1919 he led one of the two official missions to Poland, the other being led by the American Jewish career diplomat Henry Morgenthau, to investigate reports of pogroms.[57] The view that such (often related) individuals constituted a collective and extremely powerful Jewish 'interest' was not only extraordinarily prevalent but seemed to be endorsed

---

[55] Miller, *Diary*, i. 306 (13 May 1919).

[56] On Herbert Samuel see Bernard Wasserstein, *Herbert Samuel: A Political Life* (Oxford, 1992). See Henry D'Avigdor-Goldsmid, 'The Little Marconi Case', *History Today*, 14 (1964), 283–6, for how Samuel's family connections in 1912 led on two occasions to charges of government insider rigging. See also Chaim Bermant, *The Cousinhood* (London, 1971), 334–8.

[57] PRO FO 3712/3905/197853 for the 'Samuel report' on his mission to Poland, Apr. 1920. On the Morgenthau mission see Cyrus Adler and Aaron A. Margalith, *With Firmness in the Right: American Diplomatic Action Affecting Jews, 1840–1945* (New York, 1946), 150–61.

by the actions of governments. Balfour's public declaration, on 14 November 1918, that 'disorders' in the east would foreclose Western assistance to the new states[58]—a half-veiled warning that anti-Jewish pogroms would rule out finance for their development and modernization—could not but confirm in their views those already convinced of its veracity. Even Dmowski, who was still persisting with his campaign for a boycott of Jewish trade and business in Poland, had the effrontery in October 1918 to talk to Marshall, on the assumption that he could thereby release American Jewish capital for the country's reconstruction.[59] Nor was it simply a question of opening purse-strings. The Polish Deputy Foreign Affairs Minister, Count Skryzński, in talks with Wolf early in 1919, ventured to suggest that an arrangement with his committee was possible if they would back Polish claims to Teschen, Danzig, and Lwów. Not surprisingly, the suggested linkage was promptly rebutted.[60]

Nevertheless, the idea of Jewish power did continue to act as an insistent, and insidious, motif throughout the conference proceedings. Thus, the stories of pogroms, according to the Polish diplomatic team, were not simply overstated but were rather part of a carefully orchestrated Jewish campaign to whip up anti-Polish sentiment in the press.[61] Moreover, in the year in which the notion of an international Jewish conspiracy really 'took off' in popular currency, to become firmly associated not just with an alleged control of capital but also with the 'Red scare' brought on by Bolshevik successes in Russia and elsewhere,[62] it is not implausible to see essentially hostile British foreign officials acting according to the same thought-patterns as a Dmowski: on the one hand wishing to hold 'collective' Jewry in check, on the other seeking ways and means by which to placate or co-opt it. Weizmann had played on these perceptions repeatedly in the critical months prior to the Bolshevik take-over in Russia, ultimately gaining thereby the Balfour Declaration. In Paris he reiterated the formula, allegedly warning that 'if the hopes of the Zionists were not realised all the Jews in

[58] See *Jewish Chronicle* (27 Nov. 1918) for the text of Balfour's speech.

[59] See MWS 8132–33, Marshall to Wilson, enclosing details of interview with Dmowski (6 Oct. 1918).

[60] Wolf, Paris Diary, fos. 197–200 (17 Apr. 1919).

[61] See e.g. PRO FO 371/3281/101651, Count Sobanski to Lord Swaythling (copy) (30 Nov. 1918), where the PNC representative in London implies that an 'entente' with the Jews can be reached if the press campaign is called off. Similarly, see PRO FO 608/67/12781, Paderewski to Balfour (30 June 1919), where the Polish prime minister argues that 'the Polish nation had never played the contemptible part of the oppressor', again implying that the pogrom reports were a fabrication.

[62] See especially on this score Norman Cohn, *Warrant for Genocide* (London, 1967); Leon Poliakov, *The History of Anti-Semitism*, iv. *Suicidal Europe, 1870–1933* (Oxford, 1985); and Sharman Kadish, *Bolsheviks and British Jews: The Anglo-Jewish Community, Britain and the Russian Revolution* (London, 1992).

Poland would go over to Bolshevism and the result would be that the policy of the Allies in Eastern Europe would crumble to pieces'.[63]

As far as Poland and the rest of eastern Europe was concerned, the Zionist demand for full national-political recognition was clearly out of court and totally unacceptable to the peacemakers. The bogy of Jewish Bolshevism could not change that. On the other hand, if the Jewish potentiality for disruptiveness was going to outdistance even that of the German minorities in the 'New Europe', it made some sense to find a mechanism whereby it could be brought within the framework of a settlement. The British were not alone in this view. Wilson at the Council of Four in June thought that 'it was perfectly clear that one of the most dangerous elements of ferment arose from the treatment of the Jews in Eastern Europe. The fact that the Bolshevist movement had been largely led by Jews was partly due to the fact that they had been treated largely as outlaws.'[64] Wilson's own rather limited solution was to ensure that the Jews were granted rights on a par with everybody else. While the British concurred with this view, they had their own pressing reasons for upping the ante if it could be shown to assist in creating a settlement which would stick. A repetition in eastern Europe of the sort of turbulence in the Balkans which, it was widely believed, had enmeshed Britain—in both human and financial terms—in the drawn-out haemorrhage of a continental war had to be avoided at all costs.

FOREIGN OFFICE REPOSITIONING

Eschewing their own strictures about non-interference, the Foreign Office began making their own discreet enquiries about the state of Polish Jewry early on in the conference, instructions to this effect going to Esmé Howard, then in Poland as part of the Inter-Allied Commission to that country.[65] His compilation of Jewish opinions led him quickly to the conclusion that if Orthodox interests in the form of confessional schools could be developed within the framework of state control, a basis for a *modus vivendi* might be found.[66] The Poles, he agreed, would be strongly opposed to separate curricula or the use of Yiddish, but this could be obviated by granting its use in primary schools only and by assimilating the confessional schools' curricula to those outside. This line closely mirrored that increasingly taken by Headlam-Morley, the mainstay of the NSC.

---

[63] Wolf, Paris Diary, fo. 140 (25 Mar. 1919), reporting an alleged conversation between Weizmann and the AIU leader, Wormser. See also Mark Levene, 'The Balfour Declaration: A Case of Mistaken Identity', *English Historical Review*, 107 (1992), 54–77, for Weizmann's success in playing on these misconceptions.

[64] *FRUS* v. 680 (6 June 1919).

[65] PRO FO 371/3903/529, Esmé Howard report on the Polish–Jewish question (2 Apr. 1919). [66] Ibid.

Headlam-Morley was from the Political Intelligence Department, the new wing of the Foreign Office created in 1917 as a kind of think-tank providing hard information and analysis, particularly on east European affairs—a subject on which its senior officials were otherwise woefully ignorant. Other recruits included Arnold Toynbee, the Leeper brothers, and of course Lewis Namier, who, from a Polish Jewish background—albeit a highly Polonized one,—had much to say to Headlam-Morley in favour of national autonomy.[67]

But Namier, who was known for his anti-Polish views and a bitter feud with Dmowski,[68] was kept out of Paris. It was therefore to Wolf that Headlam-Morley really turned for advice and more seriously for support in the creation of a settlement. The convergence was a fortuitous one. The former inspector of schools and the ex-diplomatic journalist and long-time Jewish foreign-affairs lobbyist shared common commitments to liberalism and tolerance, which provided a meeting of minds impossible to conceive of if Wolf had had to deal with hardened antisemites of the Crowe variety. The latter indeed lamented that Headlam-Morley had swallowed Wolf's bait 'hook, line and sinker'.[69]

More significantly, both were pragmatists. The failure of the peacemakers, in February 1919, to include a clause in the Covenant of the League of Nations protecting the rights of racial and national minorities in all states was a signal, Headlam-Morley warned Wolf, that its capacity to act as an instrument of minority protection would be severely limited.[70] Both men were committed advocates of the League. But if, as Headlam prophesied, it would in the main seek to look after the relations between states themselves while abstaining from interference in the relations between states and their own subjects, Wolf's focus had to be on gaining from the conference specific treaty clauses. That implied, above all, aiming for a workable settlement, the key aim of which, in Wolf's mind, would be to fix the Jews 'firmly and explicitly in the nationality of the lands of their birth'.[71] If that meant toning down the autonomy theme, particularly if in diluted form it

---

[67] For the fullest discussion on the role of the PID see Erik Goldstein, *Winning the Peace: British Diplomatic Strategy, Peace Planning and the Paris Peace Conference, 1916–1920* (New York, 1991); also Headlam-Morley, *Memoir*, pp. xx–xxiii and xxviii–xxx, specifically for Namier. V. H. Rothwell, *British War Aims and Peace Diplomacy 1914–1918* (Oxford, 1971), 17, cites on the ignorance score Namier's shock that Lord Robert Cecil assumed pre-1918 Galicia to be Hungarian as opposed to Austrian territory.

[68] See Paul Latawski, 'The Dmowski–Namier Feud 1915–1918', *Polin*, ii (1987), 37–49.

[69] PRO FO 608/51/114/1/20, Crowe minute (30 May 1919). See Sharp, 'Britain and the Protection of Minorities', 173–6, for confirmation of Headlam-Morley's commitment to the minorities cause and the League.

[70] Wolf, Paris Diary, fo. 97 (1 Mar. 1919).

[71] MWS 1603–4, Wolf to George Wolf (9 Apr. 1920).

could be made acceptable to the Poles, if that also meant playing on 'the extreme demands of the Zionists'[72] as a method for encouraging the success of his own more moderate programme, that was a price, thought Wolf, well worth paying.

The treaty in practice, and the attending private settlements, thus represented, in the main, the priorities of the British and British Jewish camp. A full programme of civil and political rights was to be guaranteed by the League of Nations. National political autonomy—in other words the CDJ desiderata, as backed by the American Jews, for a legally recognized Polish Jewish corporate entity—was to be explicitly excluded in favour of clauses which gave all the Polish minorities linguistic rights, particularly in the field of education. All such minorities were to be entitled to state funding for such purposes, while Jews in addition were to be specifically entitled to form local education committees to manage and organize their schools. Polish fears on this score were to be met by establishing an overall system of state control, with reference to the English model (which embraced Catholic, Nonconformist, and Jewish confessional schools).[73] Instruction in minority languages was specifically to be limited to the primary level, combined with the stipulation that the Polish government could, if it so wished, insist on Polish also being taught in these schools. In cases of infraction of the treaty a right of appeal would be available before the Permanent Court of International Justice which was to operate under the auspices of the League.

What could not be achieved through international protocol was to be resolved through a 'gentlemen's' agreement along the lines of the Foreign Office's memorandum of November 1918. Only now, reversing their objections to involvement, were they directly (if discreetly) involved, in the person of Headlam-Morley, acting as intermediary and broker to an agreement which took the form of an exchange of letters between Wolf and Paderewski.[74] Wolf had made a point of negotiating with the Polish delegates and continuing to do so—in contrast to the American Jews—even when privately he was despairing of their good intentions. There could be no connection with Dmowski, of course, but Wolf was convinced that cultivating Paderewski would bear fruit, as indeed it now did when he received written assurances from the Polish prime minister in reply to his demand that the Jews should have a 'rightful share in the political work of

---

[72] Wolf, Paris Diary, fos. 121–2, interview with H. J. Paton (19 Mar. 1919).

[73] This had been the subject of much discussion between Polish representatives at Paris, Wolf, and other JFC members. See Wolf, Paris Diary, fos. 105–12 (5 Mar. 1919), and JFC C11/2/4, Henriques memo., 'Jews and Education in England', n.d., [Mar. 1919].

[74] Wolf, Paris Diary, fo. 189 (14 Apr. 1919), fos. 211–13 (23 Apr. 1919); MWS 16403–4, Wolf, 'Note Verbale' on interview with Paderewski (23 Apr. 1919).

the country'.⁷⁵ Wolf's agenda for its fulfilment included a conspiracy act to outlaw the economic boycott begun in 1912 on Dmowski's initiative, and a framework of electoral and municipal laws to prevent gerrymandering and give the Jews, as near as possible, proportional representation.

In July, a month after the successful completion of the Polish Treaty, Wolf retrospectively restated his negotiating position thus:

the JFC realised from the beginning the importance of avoiding proposals which by their exacting tendencies might be calculated to abridge sovereign rights as understood by the public law of Europe and thus to stir up controversies and antagonisms which would have seriously jeopardised the end they had in view. Accordingly, they limited themselves to recommending only such amendments and amplifications of the similar formula inserted under similar conditions in the great European treaties from 1815 to 1878 as experience has shown to be absolutely necessary.⁷⁶

Wolf's chapter-and-verse references to previous protocol had in fact already been incorporated in Clemenceau's reply on behalf of the Council of Four to Paderewski's attempted repudiation, in mid-June, of the draft treaty. Far from being an unwarranted limitation on Polish sovereignty, as Paderewski had argued, the treaty, Clemenceau rejoined, represented 'an irreducible minimum' of guarantees to Jews and other minorities in the new Poland.⁷⁷

WEAKNESSES IN THE TREATY

Whether this made the Minorities Treaty a great victory for the Jewish cause, as all the Jewish parties in Paris proclaimed it to be, is, however, another matter. The CDJ was clearly engaged in wilful self-deception when it hailed it as a great charter of national rights.⁷⁸ But Wolf and Marshall, both of whom believed they deserved laurels for this achievement,⁷⁹ may

---

⁷⁵ Wolf, Paris Dairy, fos. 211–13 (23 Apr. 1919).

⁷⁶ MWS 8345–59, Wolf, 'Interim Report of the British Jewish delegation' (20 July 1919).

⁷⁷ *The Peace Conference, Paris: Report of the Delegation of Jews of the British Empire on the Peace Conference* (London, 1919) [hereafter *RDJBE*], 86, for the text of Clemenceau to Paderewski (24 June 1919). For references to Wolf's involvement in the drafting of the letter see Wolf, Paris Diary, fo. 383 (19 June 1919), fos. 389–90 (20 June 1919), fo. 404 (25 June 1919), in which he writes: 'The letter is peculiarly gratifying to me because the line of argument it adopts is that embodied in my book on the Diplomatic History of the Jewish Question.'

⁷⁸ See AJC, Adler Papers, Marshall to Motzkin (23 June 1919), where Marshall objects to the unauthorized inclusion of his name in the CDJ's appraisal of the treaty as a victory for national rights. The text of Clemenceau to Paderewski (24 June 1919) in *RDJBE* 86 clearly states that the treaty was not intended to foster Jewish national separation from the Polish state.

⁷⁹ See MWS 1603–4, Wolf to George Wolf (9 Apr. 1920); Cyrus Adler, *I have Considered the Days* (Philadelphia, 1941), 310.

also have had private doubts. Part of the treaty's weakness related to the circumstances pertaining to its creation. Arno Mayer has noted how the actual sinews of the peace settlement were laid out by committees of experts 'shielded from the political and ideological pressures that swirled around the Big Four and their first echelon advisers'.[80] This does not, however, mean that as a whole, or in terms of its constituent parts, it was a politically neutral or objective accomplishment. The Minorities Treaty was in fact a good example of one such part seriously marred by disputes between the key Jewish protagonists, Wolf and Marshall and their respective British and American sponsors. Underlying these tensions, however, were more deep-seated Anglo-American differences which ultimately showed through in the treaty itself.

Thus, though two clauses made specific reference to Jews, one of these, Article 10, was no part of Wolf's desiderata but was rather a residual concession to Marshall's persistent—yet irrelevant—efforts on behalf of national autonomy.[81] The very fact that so much time and energy was expended on the autonomy issue in the NSC, in spite of its superfluity, may indeed have been to the detriment of other elements which might ultimately have made the treaty stronger and more enforceable.

This certainly was of relevance to the subsequent Article 11. In general, Wolf was antipathetic, in the true liberal tradition, to the inclusion of clauses which seemed to single out the Jews rather than integrating them into a wider norm. Article 10 with its specific reference to Jewish educational rights fell within this negative category. On the other hand, Wolf had fought long and hard for a guarantee that liberty to rest on the Jewish Sabbath would not lead to the deprivation of the rights of the Jewish *luftmensh* to trade on the Christian Sunday. This had nothing to do with minority rights *per se*, but was rather a straightforward matter of ensuring Polish Jewish survival. Hunter Miller obstinately insisted, however, that the draft Article 11, as it stood, undermined Polish rights,[82] a position which led to the omission of the critical Sunday-trading reference and thereby deprived it of any value whatsoever.

Personal idiosyncrasy, predilection, prejudice, or what Wolf referred to as *amour propre* were certainly not Hunter Miller's monopoly. All the treaty

[80] Arno J. Mayer, *Politics and Diplomacy of Peacemaking: Containment and Counterrevolution at Versailles 1918–1919* (London, 1968), p. vii.

[81] See Wolf, Paris Diary, fos. 309–24, Marshall to Wolf and vice versa (29 May and 1 June 1919), for the difference in approach between the two men. Marshall at core put his trust in the political muscle of the Great Powers as guardian of Polish Jewish rights. Wolf, by contrast, was much more willing to conciliate the Poles if it could be shown that this would produce a durable settlement.

[82] Miller, *Diary*, i. 300; Headlam-Morley, *Memoir*, 117.

protagonists—the Jewish interlocutors,[83] the NSC drafters, the Council of Four peacemakers and their top advisers—were guilty on one or more counts, and in the case of a Clemenceau, Wilson, or Lloyd George often with devastating effect. On top of the hurried drafting of the Polish treaty, begun in early May and completed by mid-June, the Council of Four often intervened to change or delete things at will.[84] Headlam-Morley blamed both the American and American Jewish delegation for thinking more about 'the vote of New York Jews than the real advantages to be won for the Jews in Poland',[85] while hardly being himself free from blame—as a result of his objections to Yiddish as a 'real' language[86] for the clause which limited guaranteed minority-language schooling to the primary level.

Headlam-Morley's anti-American sentiments may, however, have been keen when it came to the one clause that really mattered: the final one governing the mechanism and procedure for appeal against treaty violations. Wolf had wanted this to be framed in such a way that minorities would have a direct right of appeal to the International Court of Justice, thereby circumventing both political considerations which might intervene, if it went rather to the Council of the League, and the acute dependency which had characterized Jewish supplications in the international arena since 1878.[87] Wolf made some headway in his attempts to win over Lord Robert Cecil and Philip Noel-Baker, both members of the British delegation as well as League enthusiasts who had been enlisted by the NSC specifically to draft the appeal clause.[88] His plan in part fell foul of the League covenant itself. As it was a compact between states, Headlam-Morley warned him that only the states themselves could have access to its court or council. Noel-Baker, in response, attempted a two-stage method of approach, whereby Polish minorities would go through the courts first and if that

---

[83] Wolf included. His significant failing as a result of his tensions with Marshall and the American Jewish delegation was to ignore the section in its 'Bill of Rights' which proposed provisions enabling Polish Jews who had been expelled or who had fled to return to Poland and claim their citizenship rights. No such stipulation appeared in either Wolf's JFC formula or in the final text of the treaty. In consequence, thousands of Jewish stateless refugees in postwar eastern Europe were quite unprotected by the minorities settlement. On the issue of *Staatenlosigkeit* see Mark Wischnitzer, *To Dwell in Safety: The Story of Jewish Migration since 1800* (Philadelphia, 1948), 150–3.

[84] See *FRUS* v. 529–30, 624–8 (17 and 23 June 1919), for Wilson's interventions against the right of appeal and Lloyd George's against 'separate' Jewish schools.

[85] Headlam-Morley, *Memoir*, 176; Headlam-Morley to Namier (30 June 1919).

[86] See PRO FO 608/151/493/1/1, Headlam-Morley memorandum on the definition of cultural autonomy (11 Mar. 1919): 'According to my information Yiddish is merely a bastard form of German. I should not have thought that there was any strong claim to official recognition of it; it seems to have no necessary connection with the Jewish religion.'

[87] See Wolf, Paris Diary, fo. 233 (8 May 1919). Without the right of appeal, Wolf told Headlam-Morley, the Polish Minorities Treaty would be 'mere waste paper'.

[88] Ibid., fo. 273 (23 May 1919).

failed seek international adjudication.[89] The real body-blow, however, came from Wilson in his insistence, conveyed to Wolf by Marshall, that violations could all be dealt with by the Great Powers with the assistance of the Western Jewish lobbies.

Without an effective procedure of appeal, the treaty *qua* treaty was at best likely to be of dubious applicability, at worst a dead letter. The issue led to a major blow-up between Wolf and Marshall, a vitriolic exchange of letters and the termination, so far as it had existed up to that point, of their joint work at the conference.[90] Paradoxically, it also led to the continuance of a major role for Wolf, on behalf of Polish and east European Jewry throughout the 1920s. As they were themselves denied any direct approach, and lacked an alternative American or east European secretariat to undertake the task effectively,[91] Wolf found himself elevated into the dual role of defender of the minorities settlement and international spokesman for Jewish minority rights before the League Council in Geneva.

SUMMARY

Even leaving aside the issue of group rights, the cards were already heavily stacked against a significant Jewish success at the outset of the conference at Paris. The new international situation in 1918–19, and the geo-strategic needs of the Western Allies to create strong east European states, including—and perhaps particularly—a strong Poland, militated forcefully against a diaspora Jewish interest. Even when the principle of minority protection had been conceded and the Council of Four were overseeing the work of the NSC, or endorsing its recommendations in treaty form, it should not be forgotten that they were simultaneously encouraging Polish military offensives into Lithuania and eastern Galicia[92] which in themselves threatened

---

[89] See Wolf, Paris Diary, fos. 274–9.

[90] Ibid., fos. 309–24, Marshall to Wolf and vice versa (29 May and 1 June 1919). See also Adler, *I Have Considered*, 326, and Headlam-Morley, *Memoir*, 176, Headlam-Morley to Namier (30 June 1919): 'the whole thing has ended with a definite difference between Marshall and the American Jews on the one hand and Lucien Wolf and his Committee on the other.'

[91] Marshall returned home to the USA at the end of June and played no further significant role in defending Jewish minority rights. The CDJ maintained Motzkin, but there is little evidence of their credibility in this role. See AJC, Marshall Papers, Adler to Marshall (20 June 1923), and Marshall to Adler (22 June 1923), where Marshall's own verdict on their abilities at Paris is scathing, noting that they became so bogged down in academic discussion that they did not submit their desiderata to the Peace Conference until 10 June, long after the essential details of the Polish Minorities Treaty had been formulated and concluded. The memorial was then backdated one month to 10 May, in Marshall's words 'in order to make the petitioners less ridiculous in the eyes of the world than they in fact were'. This viewpoint is confirmed in Wolf, Paris Diary, fo. 251 (12 May 1919).

[92] See John Bradley, *Allied Intervention in Russia* (London, 1968), 193.

to place Eastern Jewish life in the severest jeopardy. Meanwhile, disputes amongst the peacemakers, particularly over the role the League would play in policing the new postwar settlement, attenuated the likelihood that it would be given a powerful remit to interfere in internal disputes between states and their minority communities. This again did not favour any exposition of Jewish rights at Paris.

Bearing these factors in mind, the achievement of the Polish Minorities Treaty is all the more remarkable. Particular credit for key protagonists, notably Wolf and Headlam-Morley, *is* deserved. Through their efforts the British and other Allied leaders came to accept that east European states could not be allowed international recognition without close scrutiny of the relationship between those states and their minorities, and that this should entail the provision of substantial guarantees relating to the latter groups' cultural as well as physical protection. This particularly applied to Poland, a passionately born-again nation-state, one third of whose population underscored the inherent contradiction in the term. Poland had not prior to the Peace Conference reached an internal *modus vivendi* with her Jewish or other minority citizens, a position confirmed by Paderewski's rebuttal, in February 1919, of Zionist and Folkist proposals for an autonomous and independent *kehillah*. Moreover, no Polish party had been prepared to accept the official use of Yiddish, which was derided as a jargon yet, at the same time, an instrument of German penetration. If Polish intransigence on the language question, especially in its critical educational arena, represented one sound reason why international guarantees were necessary, the threat of a literal expunging of the Jews through pogroms, or worse, provided further grounds for international monitoring and control.

But could Polish Jewish identity—as well as physical survival—really be safeguarded and sustained by international protocol? And by focusing so closely on Jews, when there were also other larger or equally substantial Ukrainian, Belarussian, German, and Lithuanian minorities, was the effect not to single out Jews unnecessarily and dangerously? Certainly, the Jewish situation in Poland was uniquely different from that of the other groups, but it was also highly complex. It was not just at Paris, among the various Jewish delegations, that the tension between cultural and political national rights remained unresolved. The politicized Polish Jewish community—Bundists, Folkists, Zionists—had also failed to reach a consensus or a basis for a common programme. True, at Paris there was a supra-national caucus, the Comité des Délégations Juives, to which Polish Zionist delegates attached themselves, and this did clearly and unequivocally stand for full national political autonomy. But Wolf's concerns that this might not represent the views of all Polish Jews were borne out when midway through its proceedings a further, democratically elected, delegation of Polish Orthodoxy appeared, presenting their own non-national petition to Wolf.⁹³ With a Polish Jewish 'patriotic' delegation lobbying for the assimilationist position, yet with other significant groupings, notably the Bundists, unrepresented at Paris, Wolf's earlier reservations, expressed to Mowschowitch in 1918, about the lack of unanimity among Polish Jewry, could only be confirmed.

The problem, then, of who exactly represented Polish Jewry, or indeed whether one could talk about a definable entity as such, in part explains the ultimate paradox associated with the creation of the minorities settlement, namely that it was foreign Jews, notably Lucien Wolf, who had to act on their behalf—or, more correctly perhaps, act as a sort of referee between their diverse aspirations and the political realities of 1919. Wolf himself may have wanted to bow out from the scene with a parting Peace Conference gift whereby the apparatus for direct appeal to the League would be entrusted to the Polish Jews themselves. In fact, not only did Wolf have to spend the next ten years lobbying the League for this very thing,⁹⁴ but his appearance in Poland itself in 1925 as mediator between the Polish government and party political representatives of the Jewish community⁹⁵ underscored its continued lack of at least nominal unity.

We might speculate that had the Peace Conference provided a genuine mechanism whereby minorities would have been able to appeal in cases of infraction of the treaty, Polish Jewry would have been forced by circumstances and out of sheer pragmatic necessity to unite. Of course, if the peacemakers had conceded this critical point it would in practice have overturned its very stricture of not providing any basis for minority-group separateness. The Polish Jews were thus caught in a cleft stick between being internationally recognized as a community with special minority rights, yet without the power or proper authority to act as such. The result was as Wolf had feared, worse than the old Treaty of Berlin set-up.⁹⁶ The task of safeguarding the settlement thus fell entirely on those who had created it—in the absence of further American participation, the British. But they had abdicated responsibility by passing it on to the Peace Conference's other toothless creation, the League of Nations, a body with no genuine power and certainly no clear procedure for bringing violators of the settlement to book. At the bottom line, the Polish Minorities Treaty was thus based on little more than a hope that Poland would be good and agree

---

⁹³ Wolf, Paris Diary, fos. 241–2 (11 May 1919), for Szlome Emoune Israel [sic] delegation.

⁹⁴ See Joint Foreign Committee, *The League of Nations, Geneva: Report of the Secretary and Special Delegate of the Joint Foreign Committee on Jewish Questions Dealt with by the League, 1920–29* (London, 1929). See also Joint Foreign Committee, *The Procedure for Giving Effect to the League of Nations Guarantee of the Minorities Treaties and the Proposals Thereon Submitted to the 54th Session of the Council of the League* (London, 1929).

⁹⁵ Korzec, *Juifs en Pologne*, 154–5.

⁹⁶ Wolf, Paris Diary, fo. 97 (1 Mar. 1919).

to behave like something less than a nation-state. There was, of course, a genuine, potentially workable alternative, at least from a Jewish standpoint: not a Polish nation-state but a Polish state of nationalities. But this, paradoxically, could only have been realized through the perpetuation—singly or in any combination—of German, Austrian, or Russian hegemony. With the passing of these options in 1918 there passed too the best hopes for developing a just, modern, and long-lasting Polish–Jewish relationship.

The Social Consciousness of Young Jews in Interwar Poland

ALINA CAŁA

SOURCES

THIS paper attempts to analyse the Polish-language section of a collection of autobiographies of Jewish young people from the archives of YIVO[1] in New York. This collection derives from competitions organized by YIVO in Vilna in 1932, 1934, and 1939; the institute also collected and copied some older diaries. In this way it managed to collect about 900 autobiographies, of which 300 have survived in the YIVO archive in New York. A large proportion of the surviving pieces were written in Yiddish, 71 in Polish, nearly sixty in Hebrew, and a few in other languages such as German and Spanish. The oldest one was written between 1916 and 1924, but some were sent in as late as July 1939. The diaries belonged to people aged between 15 and 24.

Who were these young people who took up their pens to respond to the YIVO appeal in Polish? Contrary to what might be expected, not many of our group came from assimilated families, and not one declared affiliation to the Assimilationist movement. Half, i.e. thirty-five persons, belonged to various Zionist organizations or a least sympathized with them. Three declared their Socialist views, without, however, belonging to any party; five were Communists. Five considered themselves to be Orthodox, and two of this group combined their religious position with Zionist sympathies. The rest did not state any specific political convictions. Only six came from assimilated families, and six others described their parents as 'progressive' or 'moderately religious', by which, as appears judging from the context, they really meant that their parents maintained a tolerant stance while continuing to preserve a traditional lifestyle. The majority came from large Orthodox families, either poor or destitute. Fifteen writers, among them all

[1] Yidisher Vissenshaftlikher Institut (Institute for Jewish Research), founded in Berlin in 1925 with Vilna as the main centre. Its archives were carried away to Germany during the war, but were recovered and transferred to New York.

those who had been brought up in Polonized families, described their homes as prosperous or rich.

Only one participant had had no formal education: this is the oldest diary of 1916–24, belonging to Jula Wald. Fifteen had had only four to seven years of primary education, eighteen had completed secondary school, in either a grammar or a technical school, and seven were enrolled in higher education.

THE LANGUAGE

This collection of memoirs written by young Jewish people contains some interesting material for linguists. Thirty-seven of them wrote in correct Polish, some even with literary flair; this is noteworthy, as Polish was a second language for most of them. Only four individuals, from assimilated families, admitted to not knowing Yiddish, and three from Orthodox families to being illiterate in that language. Only six memoirs could be said to be in bad Polish, full of grammatical mistakes and Yiddish turns of phrase. In the case of four Orthodox contributors, probably the only reason they had for choosing Polish was an erroneous understanding of YIVO's requirements: they thought that one had to write in Polish to an institution such as this. In the remaining two cases the awkward style is probably attributable to the personal idiosyncrasies of the writers.

For the most part, the memoirs were written in living Polish, which includes some individual traits, small mistakes characteristic of the authors' age-group, some dialect expressions, and sometimes Russian and Ukrainian idioms and slang words. From this point of view, the most interesting of all is the oldest diary, written by Jula Wald in a self-consciously literary style and including dialect words. The author was one of those who did not know how to write Yiddish, even though it was her first spoken language. For her, Polish symbolized social advancement: this Orthodox girl mentions 'speaking in sophisticated Polish' as being the chief virtue of one of the young men seeking her hand in marriage.

'Heniek's' autobiography[2] contains numerous vulgarisms and is influenced by Warsaw's lumpenproletariat dialect.

Like most Zionists, Chaja Muszyn,[3] who belonged to the Zionist youth movement Gordonia, used a Polish–Hebrew jargon, which has a certain charm (Hebrew terms are given in italic):

Yesterday our *mnaejl* [director] had in his *liszka* [office] an *asejfa* [meeting] with the whole *kwuca* [group] of *Anoga* [short for Heb. Agudat Noár Gordonia—the youth branch of this organization], where I had the first *inion* [business, say].

[2] Józef Grzywacz. No. 115. The names of diarists in the text do not always correspond with those in the notes, since sometimes the Journal name is employed, sometimes the familiar form.
[3] No. 178.

The writer of another diary refers to pretty girls, not necessarily Jewish ones, as *yehta*s.

The autobiography of Dawid Moses Schleifer,[4] a young Orthodox Jew and an activist in the Tse'irei Agudas Yisroel (the youth branch of the organization of Orthodox Jews) in Kalusz, deserves special attention. Its final part resembles an essay, entitled 'The Talmud as a Source of Comfort'. This is an interesting piece of evidence, not only because the treatise was written in Polish, but also because it reflects the intrusion of modernity and secularism into the Orthodox tradition.

THE ESTABLISHMENT OF SELF-AWARENESS

Most of these young authors travelled the road from traditional culture via cultural Polonization to Jewish national consciousness. These changes occurred as a result of many interactions with both Jews and Poles. Their journeys were marked by many doubts, disappointments, defeats, and conflicts, but, on the other hand, were conditioned by the genesis of national consciousness which was developing under the pressure of growing antisemitism and totalitarianism.

The genesis of national consciousness was a process which followed its course under the influence of Polish culture on the one hand, and on the other under the pressure of antisemitism. Attitudes to Polishness were intricate and full of complexity. They sometimes developed on the basis of acculturation, while rejecting the concept of assimilation. This is a phenomenon commonly found in east central Europe. It constituted a contradiction which further entangled these young people in problems of identity.

Let us start with autobiographies written by Orthodox Jews. One way of gauging the nature and extent of Jewish self-awareness among these writers is to examine their attitudes towards non-Jews. It is impossible to reconstruct an image of a *goy* from them: *goyim* simply did not exist as far as traditional Jews were concerned. The latter were mainly involved in their own problems, and any contacts they had with non-Jews held so little importance for them that they did not even think them worthy of mention. The one exception is Jula Wald,[5] but her haphazard references give an unclear picture. Even though she placed high value on her suitor's 'sophisticated Polish speech', she nevertheless looked for a husband among the young Hasidim. This did not, in any way, stop her from flirting with Catholics or having Polish girlfriends and developing a friendship with the maid Stefa, but, as the years passed, one notices between the lines of her diary the

---

[4] 'Damaszek', No. 139.   [5] No. 331, dated 1916–24.

growing distance and the sharpening of her opinions about the clients she met in her father's inn. Her hesitations did not influence her firm decision to remain a faithful daughter of the tradition of Israel:

I got up very early in spite of the rain, and it being Saturday and her day off, to wish Stefa a happy Name-day ... Hanka, Maria, and I left the house to go to the market square to look at Miss Walczak's wedding ... I don't know why I had a feeling of sadness or something like to it, while I stood and watched them go off to the wedding ... Could it be jealousy that it was not my wedding which was being observed, or was I feeling bad because I could not go and have a good time there? Or was it because I remembered or rather realized that a huge gulf divided me from Mister St[aszek] Walczak? Or what was it? . . .

Well, after all it was nothing, it is just that something came into my head to make me sad.[6]

Abraham Rotfarb, who was not Orthodox, did attempt to recreate the stereotype of a *goy* which had taken shape in the Jewish district of Warsaw where he had spent his childhood:

There are more Jews than *goyim*. Because the janitor, the housemaid, the workman, and other people performing 'menial tasks' were *goyim*, I ranked them very low. What do they know, these *goyim*? A *goy* knows nothing, a *goy* does not think, the only thing he knows how to do is beat up Jews. And despite the fact that I considered Christian peasants to be soulless savages, I was still mortally afraid of them. My world was divided into Jews and *goyim*.[7]

This writer has hit the nail on the head. For Orthodox Jews, a *goy* was not so much a Pole or Christian, but a representative of the 'lower' social classes. The Polish gentry were not subjected to such harsh judgement. This stereotype was more sociological, perhaps class-orientated, than purely ethnic. Jula Wald, who was so eager to go and watch the wedding of one of her rich Catholic friends, also turned down another invitation and wrote about it contemptuously:

Today Frania is getting married. I am fed up with this wedding; they would not leave me in peace, neither she nor her fiancé nor her mother; they kept on urging me to come. For some reason Frania made up her mind that I had to come to her wedding, so I promised to come, but in the afternoon I shall send Bronka to say that mother is ill and that I can't come, because what could I do there, the only Jewess among a bunch of Catholics and such oafs as well?

In his memoirs Lipman Bosak contemplated the essence of the relationship between Jews and peasants in the following manner:

---

[6] No. 331. 'Hanka' (Hannah) and 'Maria' (Miriam) were the sisters of Julia. 'Mr St(aszek) Walczak' was the brother of 'Miss Walczak' – the Polish boy who flirted with Julia's sister Hanka.
[7] 'A. Harefuler', No. 254/581, dated 1939.

Frequently, when the market crowds abated, I watched the Jews at their stands, large and like birds' nests, and the peasants walking up and down, and I wondered what these two nations had in common to make them live side by side in near harmony. I reached the conclusion that from the point of view of the peasants the Jews were created solely so that the peasants could sell grain to them and so that they, in turn, could sell it to big dealers, and also so that they could make undercoats and boots, supply them with some of the basic food products, and runs the inns so that the peasants could get drunk on Sundays and market-days. And as far as the Jews were concerned, the peasants were created for the sole purpose of selling grain to them, buying the undercoats, boots, and other products, and spending money in the inns. Harmony is not difficult to achieve in such circumstances.[8]

The social distance which separated the Polish upper classes from the peasants, and which verged on contempt, was more pronounced in the eastern borderlands and took on ethnic overtones in these areas. The borderland peasants were called 'Russkis', i.e. Ukrainians or Belarussians; the Poles were 'the lords and masters'. These memoirs sympathize with the latter, but it is quite possible that in this instance the sample is not representative; a different picture might emerge from the portion of the collection written in Yiddish.

Most contacts between different groups occurred in school. But relationships with contemporaries of different faiths rarely followed a smooth course. The tendency on both sides was to assume an isolationist stance, as can be seen from this passage:

We lived in harmony with our Catholic peers, despite their lack of 'solidarity' with us ... My relationship with my Catholic contemporaries was strange. As a rule, I would converse with them, I sometimes helped them out just as I did other friends, I played ball with them, etc. But at the same time I made an effort to keep them at a distance, and in order to achieve this I did not always employ the best means. For in some ways I differentiated between them and Jews. For example, if one of 'us' got to me in some way or insulted me, I would always try to get it out of my system and to clear the air, and it always turned out to be all right in the end. But I remember that once when a Catholic started to make a nuisance of himself, and in the end contemptuously called me a 'scab',[9] I slapped his face. Even though he did not slap me back, we continued for a long time not speaking to each other. It was only much later that he apologized and said that he had been wrong. Because I was successful in that instance, I became more aggressive

---

[8] 'Eliezer Achimeir' No. 111, dated 1934. As I discovered recently, this fragment is not original: it was copied by the author from a book by H. and J. Tharaud, *Królestwo Bozè: Sceny życia na Ukrainie* (Zamość, 1922), 20.

[9] A contemptuous term for Jews.

towards contemporaries I did not like, and at times I was guilty of provoking them.[10]

Various authors remark on the gradual growth of hostile attitudes among Catholic colleagues, justly linking them with the antisemitic mood dominating the whole country. This development was also noted by Ludwik Stöckel:

I got through the sixth form without any problems. It was only then that the relationship with our Catholic peers began to deteriorate. These were echoes of certain incidents at the Universities...[11]

Our Catholic colleagues have now taken on board the ideology of the Lwów University thugs who were rampaging at that time pretty well openly. However, our treatment of each other remained cordial on both sides. The explosion finally came during a discussion following a lecture... We had been discussing the Jewish question... During the course of this discussion, one of the 'Greens', the name we used to refer to the National Democrats, openly stated that there was only one method to deal with us, namely the truncheon. This resulted in a number of protests from our side and also from the only Ukrainian in the class... From that day onward our personal relationships with our Polish classmates cooled down even further and became even more politely formal than before. But there still remained a few good chaps, these being usually 'free-thinkers' or Socialists, with whom we continued to have normal relations.[12]

Primary schools did not fare much better, except that ethnically based animosities were less well rationalized in younger children and tended to be on the subconscious level, manifesting themselves through physical aggression. An author writing under the pseudonym 'Kallos' described the circumstances in one of the primary schools in Kraków as follows:

I started primary school at the age of six. There were forty pupils in our class, among them four Jews. At that time antisemitism did exist, but not to the extent it does now. We Jews were up against it at every turn. The Christian pupils used to beat us up during every break, so that finally we never went out during breaks but stayed behind in the classroom. If we complained to the teachers, they only laughed at us, and later, during break, we would be in even worse trouble for having complained.[13]

Sometimes the schools themselves contributed to the consolidation of the anti-Jewish prejudices. Regina Glaser from Kołomyja remarks in her diary:

Immediately after religious instruction or before Catholic holidays, tales of ritual murder and Judas would be revived. I had good relations with my Catholic girlfriends. Every time I brought them a present, for example before the feast of

[10] Ludwik Stöckel from Tłuste, No. 95, dated 1934.   [11] Ibid.
[12] Ibid.   [13] No. 3643, dated 1939.

Purim or Easter (Pesach), they would gladly accept everything, despite the fact that the *matsot* allegedly contained Christian blood. There was no point in discussing anything with them, for whenever they had no arguments left, they would say: 'But it must be so, for this is what we have been told.' Sometimes this resulted in total disorder in the classroom, after which one could hear shouts of 'Jews go to Palestine.'[14]

Regina managed to put her finger on the essential attributes of popular culture, where group opinion is the only and sufficient criterion of truth.

It has emerged that the level of aggression depended on the attitudes of the teaching staff. Some teachers did not take conflicts among the pupils seriously. Others exhibited an open aversion to proponents of the Judaic faith and even sanctioned acts of violence against them. But there are cases of teachers with a genuinely fair-minded attitude. Markus Lieber from Krasne recalled a priest, a teacher of religion, who kept the pupils' antisemitic outbursts under control by speaking up against them in a decisive way.[15] 'Leib' Zarwanizer from Stanisławów retained a measure of genuine gratitude for the headmaster of the school where he started his education:

The headmaster, a tall, elderly gentleman with a clean-shaven stern face, taught us himself. He was very friendly toward the pupils and sometimes spoke Yiddish to the Jews. It was very easy to learn the alphabet under his direction.[16]

Hinda Fink from Sanok became such good friends with her teacher that he became her confidant:

I kept taking my poems to Dr Zalewski, who was my gym teacher in form 7. He would correct them for me and gave me various pieces of advice, also promising that he would use his influence to make it possible for me to continue my studies in the Lwów Institute. And, strangely enough, despite the fact that he was a *goy* and very, very old, I never felt embarrassed in his presence and would tell him everything, even things I would never have told my parents and definitely not a girlfriend, no matter how intimate.[17]

Friendships among pupils occurred, so frequently that one might venture to quote the well-known saying that 'every Jew had his Pole' (perhaps excluding some Orthodox Jews). Hersz Wolf Sztolcman from Sochaczew wrote in his diary:

My best friend was a Catholic, Józef Karpiński, whom I knew from school. We got on like brothers. We used to spend our afternoons and evenings together, talking and discussing books we had read. He was an intelligent and hard-working boy who

---

[14] 'Gina', No. 154, dated 1934. [15] 'Mars', No. 153, dated 1934.
[16] 'Leib', No. 130, dated 1934. [17] 'Yahudiya', No. 56/392.

was eager to learn. He had no father; his parents were his stepfather and his mother, who had a smallholding in Młodzieszyń (near Sochaczew).[18]

Antisemitism did not always constitute an obstacle to closer contacts. One author, Jakób Gelfer from Otwock, described his love affair with a girl who 'hated all Jews' except him.[19] Another young writer, A. Szac from Bereza-Kartuska, remembered his great passionate love for a 'free-thinking Catholic girl'.[20]

Jula Wald was also not averse to flirting with *goyim*, despite the fact that she considered herself to be an 'Orthodox Jew'. She did, however, make certain that her friendships did not overstep the 'limits of decency', even though she did not conceal the fact that she derived great pleasure from them. Below I give two quotations, but these are not the only examples to be found in her diary:

> I nearly died laughing today because of this lunatic, Mr Koziński; he is a real eccentric and he is beginning, as they say, to be after me seriously, and for my part I must say I feel quite flattered, but I also feel a bit worried in case he should 'fall in love' like Mr Wilczyk, of whom I don't even know if he is dead or alive, for this would cause unnecessary trouble for me. For my part, I am also beginning to lose my heart to him as from the moment I laid eyes on him, I liked his face and especially his blue, innocent eyes looking at me—but I don't know, this is how I am and I always have to be involved with someone . . .

The above confession is dated 1919. But in 1924, a few days before her marriage to an unloved, young Orthodox stranger, Jula wrote:

> The other piece of news from Stefa made me laugh. Mr Wacek Koziński loves me and he values and respects me so much that for several years he did not tell me as he was afraid of offending me, and it was only when Stefa pressed him that he confessed it to her, but requested that in Heaven's name she should not tell me this before the wedding—funny but nice.[21]

All the love affairs between representatives of different faiths described in the memoirs did not last. In most cases the reason for their disintegration was the pressure of social opinion, where antisemitism or the fear of it played a significant role. Ludwik Stöckel, the son of Jewish landowners from Tłuste, described his first love in the following way:

> I also realized that there was no sense in going out with her, because sooner or later people would start to talk. And then Marysia would say something disdainful about me to her friends, because a relationship with a *yid* would not be convenient for her.[22]

---

[18] No. 48/384, dated 1934.
[19] 'Refleg', No. 176, dated 1934.
[20] 'Modestus', No. 196, dated 1934.
[21] No. 331.
[22] No. 98, dated 1934.

This negative social pressure was double-edged. The traditional culture of both faiths opposed mixed marriages. The memory remained alive of the legal limitations in this matter imposed in the Russian sector, restrictions which persisted until the First World War. New legislation in independent Poland also made such liaisons difficult.

ATTITUDES TO POLISHNESS

What I find particularly astonishing is the fact that despite the painful experience of antisemitism, the writers of these memoirs retained considerable faith in Poland as a country. The intensity of this trust followed the patterns of political ideas. Orthodox Jews trusted Polish institutions completely, even though the influence of attitudes which were menacing to Jews could be clearly observed within them.

The Zionists were somewhat more critical, but one exception among them was fifteen-year-old Blima Bader from Kołomyja, who concluded her autobiography by exclaiming 'If only the war would break out at last!', in the belief that after the war a more just state would emerge.[23] Still more critical were the Communists, but even their attitude to the state was reasonably respectful, a fact which we may find rather surprising nowadays.

The level of emotion in relationship to Polishness or Polish culture was quite a different thing. Such attitudes did not even exist for Orthodox Jews. By definition, Orthodox Jews were virtually precluded from experiencing a sense of Polish nationality or cultural identity. Jula Wald is exceptional, as in some respects she was the most integrated of them all and, despite having a provincial outlook, treated Polishness and Jewishness without any antagonism between the two. She was a Polish Jewess with a strongly developed sense of citizenship, even though her mentality was pre-political. In her all these features were combined in a 'natural', unselfconscious, and unproblematic way.

The Zionist attitude to Polishness and Poland was more complicated, but at the same time more carefully thought out. Members of this group had the difficulty of experiencing a sense of Polishness as well as of Jewishness. Yet Jews and Poles were strictly exclusive categories: the decision was based on one's birth and not on one's awareness. Cultural integration, which for many signified social advancement, posed a host of identity problems. Criticisms of the Polish state inherent in the political choice of Zionism coexisted with admiration for Polish culture and with a rejection complex.

As a rule, the young people who wrote their autobiographies in Polish

---

[23] No. 238/574, dated July 1939.

first encountered the Polish cultural heritage in school, whether it was state-run or Jewish. Their familiarity with this area was furthered by the reading of classical Romantic and Positivist authors, whose works were not only on the reading lists but enjoyed genuine popularity. Eliza Orzeszkowa was a favourite, and her works are discussed in several of the diaries.

School and literature inculcated a certain stock of national symbols which fill the pages of many memoirs, sometimes in astounding juxtapositions. N. Misztejn from Kowel writes: 'I imagined that it was not Poland, not the Diaspora—only the dearly beloved (in the manner of Kasprowicz) motherland, Palestine.'[24]

The schools also instilled the Polish concept of patriotism, which was then transferred to Zionism, the ideology most commonly followed by the young writers. Hinda Fink from Sanok wrote:

I was also interested in the struggles of the Polish nation during the years of bondage, their sacrifices, and the single goal they elected for themselves and to which they completely dedicated themselves in order to become an independent nation in the shortest possible time. And at such times, for the first time, I began to wonder why it is that we Jews are the only ones who make no attempt to fight for our motherland in a similar way. At the same time I was very influenced and shaken to the depth of my soul by something we were reading in class at that time entitled, *A Child from the Old Town*.[25] When under the influence of this book, I temporarily became a sort of patriot and I would have liked to defend my motherland together with these children of the old town.[26]

Similarly, Regina Glaser from Kołomyja wrote in her diary:

Love for Poland was being instilled in the children and they were being taught that one had to live and die for it. At such times, something akin to a feeling of envy would awaken inside me. Why is it that only we Jews do not have a country of our own? . . .

Thoughts about Palestine did not awaken in me just because of the Zionist books I had read or the debates or propaganda, oh no! They rose up as a result of the love for Poland which was being inculcated. I felt respect for Poland because I had been born here and because I attended this school, but the love I felt was for Palestine.[27]

In the case of the majority of these writers, the road to a Jewish national consciousness passed through a stage of assimilation or acculturation. The discovery of Zionism would result in a rejection of the concept of assimilation, but a complete turn-around was not always possible, and this caused

[24] No. 961, dated 1939.
[25] *Dzieci starego miasta*, a 19th-cent. patriotic novel by Józef Ignacy Kraszewski.
[26] 'Yahudiya', No. 56/392.
[27] 'Gina', No. 154, dated 1934.

problems for some. Zygmunt Horwitz from Zakopane, who was born into an assimilated family and had spent his childhood among the uplanders, declared:

Aside from Zionism, I really had nothing in common with Jewishness. I considered the Hebrew language a hobby and I thought only in Polish, I got to love this nation and its language, its history. Even today, Sienkiewicz's trilogy gives me the most immense pleasure . . . Jewish history, on the other hand, represented distant events, something smacking of legend, at least for me who had been brought up far from the atmosphere of Jewry and Jewishness. I was partially assimilated and the organization converted me.[28]

But the bitter words written by Abraham Rotfarb from Warsaw make a deep impression; he was born into an Orthodox family and discovered Polishness in his Jewish school Khinukh Yelodim:

I am a poor assimilated soul. I am a Jew and a Pole, or rather I was a Jew, but gradually, under the influence of my environment, under the influence of the place where I lived, and under the influence of the language, the culture, and the literature, I have also become a Pole. I love Poland. Its language, its culture, and most of all the fact of its liberation and the heroism of its independence struggle, all pluck at my heartstrings and fire my feelings and enthusiasm. But I do not love that Poland which, for no apparent reason, hates me, that Poland which tears at my heart and soul, which drives me into a state of apathy, melancholy, and dark depression. Poland has taken away my happiness, it has turned me into a dog who, not having any ambitions of his own, asks only not to be abandoned in the wasteland of culture but to be drawn along the road of Polish cultural life. Poland has brought me up as a Pole, but brands me a Jew who has to be driven out. I want to be a Pole, you have not let me; I want to be a Jew, but I don't know how, I have become alienated from Jewishness. (I do not like myself as a Jew.)
I am already lost.[29]

Zionism, which was the crowning achievement of the genesis of national consciousness, developed under the influence of Polish traditions and under the threat of antisemitism. Taking this into account, one is surprised neither by the ideological borrowings nor by the shifts within the national consciousness occasioned by the pressures of social hostility and accompanied by the writers' feelings of having cast aside their best intentions. The nationalism and chauvinism of some Poles and the xenophobic tradition of both societies often resulted in analogous attitudes on the part of Jews. In the autobiographies examined I found two whose authors exhibited what could be seen as incipient Zionist chauvinism. Hela from Kołomyja describes how she participated in a boycott of girlfriends who had chosen a Polish instead of a Jewish

[28] No. 128, dated 1934.   [29] 'A. Harefuler', No. 245/584, dated 1939.

grammar school: 'All my friends, including myself, went to the Jewish school, and only five or so attended the state school. We considered them as delinquents and renegades and we did not speak to them or have anything to do with them.'[30] N. Milsztejn from Kowel, together with her whole class, put pressure on her girlfriend to break off relations with her Christian friends:

Nojma left primary school and had many friends. It was quite common for her to exchange a few words or to cross the street with a *goy*. This used to antagonize the whole class and later the whole grammar school. Her friends, including myself, used to defend her and we tried hard to persuade her that she should stop doing this. And finally we managed it. It was also Nojma who introduced the tradition of speaking Polish into our class. I did not like that at all, because I hated all *goyim* . . .
I remember that day as if it were yesterday, when after I had spent a long time explaining to Nojma how terrible her crime was, she threw her arms around my neck and through her tears admitted that I had been right.[31]

These two authors came from culturally assimilated families, and both of them were representatives of a second generation with Zionist convictions. The evolution of such ideas on the road towards chauvinism can also be viewed as a distortion in the genesis of national consciousness. Clearly, it was not unconnected with Polish antisemitic attitudes and the popularity of totalitarian political concepts.

A GENERATION IN CRISIS

With few exceptions, the YIVO collection consists of memoirs of unhappy people, a normal feature in this genre of literary creation. Within our group the authors tend to put pen to paper at certain critical points in their lives: when they meet with their first defeats and when their desires collide with cruel reality. They might have just left school, and were unable to find a job or a niche for themselves; they were in a state of conflict with their parents; they could not accept the rules of the organization to which they belonged; or they felt lost and without any prospects for the future. Sometimes they may have had problems with making friends or were unsuccessful in love. They felt isolated and lonely. A very touching autobiography by Sara Kopyto from Płock, written in May 1939, is an example of loneliness caused by physical disability. Sara was a hunchback, and her entire monotonous life was one long struggle with the social implications of this physical deformity.

---

[30] 'Pinkas Horowitz—for Hela', No. 231/571, dated 1939.   [31] No. 961, dated 1939.

For her, the crowning success of these struggles was the first time (and perhaps the last, in view of the date) she went out with a man.[32]

Some hoped that YIVO would solve at least some of their problems, to which requests for advice and help placed at the end of the text bear witness. Sometimes the choice of a pseudonym would hint at such expectations; for example, Sara Frydman from Wołkowyska provided an inscription which read 'She who is perplexed' for her memoir.[33]

The source of many worries was poverty and unemployment, giving the young people no possibility of escape from their trapped lives. This generation was starting life during a period of great crisis. The autobiographies describe families suddenly going bankrupt, and the growing poverty among the poor. At the age of thirteen Aleksander Guttenplan from Borysław walked all the way to Kraków and back to Lwów again looking for work. In the end he became a travelling chiromancer.[34] The son of an unemployed *melamed* (teacher in a traditional Jewish school), the Communist Józef Grzywacz, after many attempts at casual work, including that of a street photographer, drifted into the criminal world. His brother, whose dream was to play in a jazz band, drank a bottle of iodine when unemployment stood in the way of his matrimonial plans.[35] Markus Lieber used to spend the nights in his classroom and later slept on top of the oven in a bakery, so that he could complete his secondary education.[36] Mojżesz Tendlarz, whose father was a city councillor in Parczew, despite having graduated from secondary school, was forced to earn his living as a member of an itinerant orchestra performing folk music.[37] Ewa Tanenzapf from Sołotwina (Stanisławów province) described the gradual ruin of her family, with her rabbi father having to retrain as a ritual slaughterer and forced to practise his profession illegally.[38] All these young people were fighting for the right to an education, and whenever circumstances made it impossible to receive formal education, they continued to study at home.

Frequent generation conflicts are also reflected in these memoirs. Sometimes this took the form of a feeling of rejection and lack of parental love. Many authors express grave doubts about the system of values with which they have been indoctrinated. This is the way in which a young worker in a Kraków Jewish children's home describes her 'father's trial', which was carried out by her brothers on the day of their eviction:

But somehow today father is not in a hurry to begin the Sabbath service. He has propped his head up on his hands and he is listening to his children's reproaches. Unmindful of God's commands to honour one's mother and father, they accuse

[32] No. 71/407.
[33] No. 239/575.
[34] 'Garner', No. 39, dated 1934.
[35] 'Heniek', No. 115, dated 1934.
[36] 'Mars', No. 153, dated 1934.
[37] 'Mojżesz', No. 175/511, dated 1939.
[38] 'Eter', No. 176/512, dated 1939.

only him. They place the whole burden of guilt and responsibility on his shoulders.

'This is all your fault! You are an oaf. You have never done anything. You told us to believe in God and you promised that everything would be all right. Nothing but God exists for you. Instead of working like all the other people's fathers, all you can do is pray. The children have to work for your keep. You sent your youngest, fifteen-year-old son to work in a factory, but as for yourself, you went around with your arms folded behind your back, telling jokes . . . You did not care that your children and wife are suffering. You had to eat chicken broth when your children were eating salted potatoes. You told your sons to get up at six so that they could say their prayers before going to school. But what have you given us? You had to have thirteen children!

'It's all your fault! You are a selfish egotist. For you no one else exists. As long as you are content and left in peace.'

Father's head is sinking lower and lower. He is on trial. His children are accusing and judging him.

Mother, as she is in the habit of doing in such situations, keeps wiping her eyes and nose in her clean, Sabbath apron. She has quite forgotten that it is she herself who will have to wash it and she should not really be making it dirty.

This is how things are nowadays! I did not reproach my father in this way. I did not even dare to raise my voice in his presence. But was I better off for it? Did not my father have thirteen children? But was it his fault! And what about his father? Did he also not have many children! And yet they had had a good life. The world was different then. Children respected their parents. There were no such children in the past.[39]

Conflicts between Orthodox parents and their children's secularizing generation tended to develop gradually. These autobiographies reflect this process of transition from naïve and fervent childish belief to atheism and the loss of faith in traditional authority. This is how Abraham Rotfarb from Warsaw tried to recreate the state of his consciousness of earlier years:

I disliked *apikoresim* [Jewish non-believers] very much. Among them I included any Jew who was well dressed in the European fashion, everyone who did not attend the *ḥeder*, and also every Zionist. The word 'Communism' aroused fear in me and I imagined it to be worse than being a bandit. A Communist could no longer be considered an *apikores*, but something worse than a *goy* . . . As for myself, I was very religious. For example, I would never go to bed without a cap. But I did this more out of fear of *shedim* [demons] than for the sake of the ritual itself. As a rule, religion inspired me with fear.[40]

And Zosia from Kraków described the religious indecisions of her childhood in the following way:

No, God is not really good. When after my sister's death my mother grieved so terribly and asked God to let her die, father used to say: 'Don't sin! One has to live

---

[39] Miss Zosia, 'Żen-ka', No. 152, dated 1934.   [40] 'A. Harefuler', No. 254/581, dated 1939.

as long as the Lord our God commands. He gives us life and he takes it away. It is his possession.'

But this God is heartless. He takes children away from their mothers! And mothers from their children! And one has to go on living without one's nearest and dearest! ... And why does he allow people to die at all? If he were good, he would not do this ...

Actually, why should he like Jews best of all? After all, there are such bad Jews and such good *goyim*.[41]

But not everyone rebelled against religion. An anonymous Orthodox Jew from Bołszowiec did not experience any such uncertainties. He had, however, felt obliged to stand up to his godless friend, as he describes below:

My friend did not reflect for long and he told me that everything that I believe is due to my having been given incorrect information. God does not exist. I told him that since every family has a head and every administrative district has a head and every province has a head and every region has a head and every state has a head, how can the world be without a head? This surely cannot be so.[42]

Jula Wald also belonged to a group of people with unshakeable faith, and this despite the fact that on numerous occasions she had to face strong temptation in the form of handsome, seductive clients in her father's inn:

A rabbi from B. came to L., and despite the fact that he made hardly any impression on me, Hanka and Cela and I went to the synagogue to hear his *kiddush*, and to tell the truth I did not even think about going, but daddy said, 'Why don't you go?', so I went, which I don't regret at all, for when I stood and listened, I was torn by strange feelings and I never suspected that the sight of a group of Jews respectfully gathered around one rabbi would be capable of awakening in me feelings which had been dormant before! In spite of myself I began to tremble when I remembered that many times people had tried to talk me into having myself baptized. Was I supposed willingly to give up this sight which gives me such a wonderful feeling? Oh no, never![43]

Just as emphatically she rejected progressive suitors:

It has been my great desire, if I ever get married, to marry no one but an Orthodox Jew ... the reason I want an Orthodox Jew is because he will never be such a ... rogue; truly, I have heard so many dreadful stories about those progressive boys that nothing in the world could persuade me to settle for one of them. I would sooner marry a *goy*, because the sort of things they get up to I could just about forgive a *goy*, but never a Jew.

While remaining under their parents' care, the children were forced to

[41] 'Żen-ka,' No. 152.   [42] No. 234/570, dated 1939.   [43] No. 331.

compromise. Despite their feelings of dissatisfaction, they took part in prayer meetings, imposed limits on their political aspirations, and gave up many entertainments which were considered to be 'too worldly' or 'unworthy of a Jew' (such as football or sport in general). They could escape by finding independent jobs, if they were not employed in the family business, away from home. The aim of all the hopes and dreams of many of these authors was to escape to a bigger town. Even Jula Wald, although she referred to herself as an Orthodox Jew, made a move to Kraków the main condition of her marriage articles, and she wrote at the same time that, in equal measure, the move and the marriage were for her a means of escaping from her father's domination.

Sometimes Orthodox parents were against their children receiving a secondary education, but in general they accepted primary schooling, even if the school was not a Jewish one. Some children, however, were certainly prevented by their parents from taking their formal education as far as they wished. Dawid Moses Schleifer from Kałusz solved this problem by enrolling in a correspondence course.[44] The majority of his contemporaries felt quite helpless in a similar situation. The only solutions available to them were to read books or borrow class notes and textbooks from their more fortunate friends.

Self-instruction, which had deep roots in the Jewish tradition, continued to be popular. Frequently this was seen as an important factor in the choice of political options. Ajzyk Rozen from Tomaszów Mazowiecki, a Socialist by conviction, joined Betar (a right-wing Zionist youth movement) because they offered a more interesting programme of self-instruction.[45]

SYSTEM OF VALUES

Unquestionably, learning and education held an important place within the system of values of these young writers. The reason for this may have been the extreme difficulty of achieving this goal on account of material hardship, opposition from Orthodox parents, and restrictions imposed by the government (in the 1930s there was a shortfall of half a million school places in the country). A similar situation existed in the labour market, particularly throughout the period of crisis, when a large part of society found itself unemployed and competition for jobs readily shifted to the plane of ethnic animosity.

The generation born after the First World War was very politicized. Only a tiny minority affirmed no political views. The majority advocated some

[44] 'Damaszek', No. 135, dated 1934.   [45] 'A.R.' No. 94, dated 1934.

kind of ideology, be it Zionism, Socialism in one of its variants, or Orthodoxy. Youth organizations played an important part in this, and also performed various other functions. They gave some meaning to people's lives, killed the boredom of living in small towns, provided social contacts, and constituted a venue where one could meet groups of contemporaries, form friendships, and start love affairs. The joining of a party, which usually occurred as early as primary or secondary school, was seldom motivated by conscious political choice. It was decided by peer pressure or by other, non-ideological considerations. Lejzar Gieguziński, another diarist, describes how he ended up joining one of the Zionist organizations almost in spite of himself:

The main thing that happened to me in that class was that I was made to join the youth organization. It happened on a Friday, and the boys and girls who already belonged to this organization asked me to come the next day, Saturday, to a meeting. At first I laughed at them and went home, but the next day after dinner, not having anything better to do, I went to the meeting . . .

After the meeting an older boy came up to me and asked me if I knew anything about the ideology of this organization. I did not know what to answer, firstly because I had no idea what the word 'ideology' meant and secondly because I really didn't know anything about it. However I said that I did. Then he asked if I wanted to join. I didn't know how to reply to this question either, but I said yes. So this is how I joined the organization at the age of nine, not having any idea what it all meant.[46]

Lipman Bosak from Kraków writes how he was talked into joining Hashomer Hatsa'ir (the Zionist scout organization) by the two friends with whom he was apprenticed to a locksmith:

Often, when there was nothing for us to do, we would sit and talk. I would join in the conversation, but only up to the point when the organization came under discussion. I was totally uninitiated in this subject. They talked about Palestine, about some sort of Socialism, they chatted about the ideal conditions to be found in something they called co-operatives, and all this time I would sit in silence. I did not understand many of the words they were using, for how was I supposed to? Was I expected to find out about all this from my friends, the Vistula boys, or perhaps from the criminal detective novels which I was devouring at the time? They could not understand why I never said anything on this subject. Finally the younger one asked me:

'Do you belong to any organization?'
'Yes.'
'Which one?'

---

[46] No. 185/512, dated 1939.

'What do you mean, which one? To ours.'
'I don't understand. Which ours?'
'Well, to ours, the Vistula boys.'
Both of them burst out laughing.
'Why are you laughing?' I asked.
'Why indeed. You don't belong to any Jewish scout organization?'
I did not have the faintest idea what they were talking about.
From that day onward, during breaks at work, they gave me 'awareness lessons' about all these things which I had known nothing about. It was also at their instigation that at the age of fourteen I joined the Jewish scout organization.

The Zionist scout organization changed Lipman's life. Previously he had been living in isolation and his only companion was his widowed mother, an impoverished pedlar of second-hand clothes, struggling to survive. In the following description the author underlines the changes which, thanks to his membership of the organization, took place in his personality:

At first I would sit on the sidelines. I would think about my life, and it seemed to me that I was unhappy. But this was only a transitional phase. Then I seemed to lose my feeling of depression, my sadness disappeared, and in its place appeared happiness. Shyness gave way to freedom. I found myself a member of a whole group. Surely, it must be difficult to find another life which contains so much charm, which would be as interesting ... Every one of the brothers and sisters who has lived that life, and whose motto is work and duty, has come out prepared for the struggle for survival.

There is so much I owe this organization. Laziness, work-shyness, indifference, all completely disappeared. They disappeared under the influence of the Socialist system which I got to know here in this organization.[47]

Further advantages gained by active party membership are outlined by Dawid Moses Schleifer from Kałusz, who was a member of Tse'irei Agudas Yisroel:

In general, I owe this organization my mental and intellectual development and my entire knowledge of ancient Hebrew literature, and thanks to this I have become a one hundred per cent religious Jew, who did not allow himself to be seduced by any contemporary pernicious influences; for this reason I shall always remain grateful to it and in the future I shall remain a member in perpetuity.[48]

But not everyone shared the enthusiasm of the writers quoted above for the organization in which they ended up as members. Expressions full of criticism can also be found, and the censure is not confined to those who joined accidentally. Markus Lieber from Krasne became a Zionist in order to be able to spend nights on the party's premises. He wrote:

[47] 'Eliezer Achimeir', No. 111, dated 1934.   [48] 'Damaszek', No. 139, dated 1934.

As the price of being admitted to the club I joined the organization, and immediately became the secretary. I did not like the job, however, so I resigned. Next, I was asked to go on a training course, preparatory to going to Palestine, but I did not feel like going. In those days one could get a certificate much more easily, and I could easily have gone to Palestine. I did not want to do it because I was exhausted by school work and I did not feel strong enough to perform physical labour, and in addition I felt that I was capable of doing something more interesting than manual work.

In the end he allowed himself to be talked into going to a training camp, but because of all the quarrels and conflicts he returned totally disillusioned with the whole movement.[49]

Sara Kopyto from Płock, who was recruited by a friend, gave up her activities in Po'alei Tsion (a Zionist-Socialist organization) because of her disability. This is how she stressed the social role of the party in a conversation with a friend:

'I too would like to work for some idea and to be part of a larger group, but there is one thing I am worried about and which frightens me, and that is that the comrades will not like to look at me and will persecute me, for nowadays everyone is only interested in feasting their eyes on what is outwardly beautiful; so, my dear friend, I am giving up the idea, because having to live in such circumstances I would experience terrible suffering. But, my dear Hala, I advise you to join the organization, for why should you lose time being with me? Not for anything in the world do I want you to sacrifice your entire youth in my company—get to work and devote your free time to something useful.' For a while she did not want to join without me, but I explained to her that I would work along with her and take an interest in everything like a properly joined-up comrade, so she let herself be convinced and joined Po'alei Tsion.[50]

Young people with leftist tendencies had one great ideal, that of social justice. If they belonged to the Zionist left, then they saw the realization of their aspirations in Palestine. This country was idealized in the eyes of all the Jewish nationalists. Sara Frydman from Wołkowyska presents her vision of the motherland, albeit in a somewhat childish manner, in the following passage:

If one were to be a film actress, then only in Palestine ... I would like to work for my motherland. I do not want to be rich, but happy. Happiness for me means living in Palestine in a little house surrounded by fields and woods, near a river, and working for the motherland. To love and to be loved.[51]

[49] 'Mars', No. 153, dated 1934.
[50] No. 71/407, dated 1939.
[51] 'She who is perplexed', No. 239/575, dated 1939.

Her imagination painted a picture nearer to the image of a Polish rural village than the Jordan valley. Others saw the problem of emigration in a more sober light, for example Hersz Wolf Sztolcman from Sochaczew, who wrote, 'I would finally like to go to Palestine, to be able to work and study at the same time, but the obstacle in my way is money.'[52] Ludwik Stöckel from Tłuste directed the planning of his entire future towards this goal and recreated the motives for his decision in several pages of his autobiography, for example:

> I knew that Palestine does not need any lawyers. Pharmacology is a profession which could also be useful in Eretz, but I did not like it all that much. I was much more attracted by law ... So, despite the fact that it is an unproductive profession, I still decided to take it up ... Besides, I think that the more educated people a nation has ... the stronger it will be, from both the moral and the spiritual points of view. Particularly for us Jews, a large amount of expertise is an absolute necessity. But this in no way means that, for example, I should take into consideration right now the fact that my final goal might end up to be a life of work on the land. Because this is the inevitable outcome of my ideas. Our nation needs farmers. So I am going to be a civilized farmer![53]

Emigration was not an easy decision to make. As a result, the love for Palestine evinced by many of the writers remained platonic, so to speak, unconsummated in action. In any case, in the 1930s emigration became practically impossible. Even those who had managed to go before that time did not always succeed in finding happiness. Markus Horowitz from Kraków had a brother Dow, who lost his life in a skirmish with Arabs in 1923; a second brother, Cwi, was deported by the British because of his Communist activities, and when he arrived back in Poland a sentence for desertion awaited him. A fifteen-year-old sister ran away from home and joined the scouts. But due to the state of her health she had to come back six months later. The source of all these family disasters was Ozjasz Thon, whose lecture (which was probably read about 1920) set off an 'emigration psychosis' among the young people who attended it:

> When I was about five years old, I remember that I was taken to some kind of Zionist meeting where Dr Thon was giving a speech. I remember this name because soon after the meeting my brothers and sister went to Palestine and our parents kept on 'blessing' Thon, saying that it was because of him that they had decided to go.[54]

Friendship and love held an important place in the value-system of the young autobiographers, even though they tended to take second place to idealism and political commitment. There is a clear division between girls,

---

[52] No. 48/384, dated 1934.
[53] No. 98, dated 1934.
[54] 'Mordechaj Natanson', No. 90, dated 1932–4.

dreaming of a great love, and boys, who preferred male friendships and frequently express critical opinions about the fair sex. For example, Munio Fuchs from Kosów Łacki complains that 'I do not look for girls as I don't like to chase after them and also I am quite shy and I don't know what to talk to them about ... and finally, I know all about how false women are.'[55]

Such priorities were doubtless typical of people of the age-group to which the writers belonged, but it may be that, to some extent, they also stemmed from Jewish tradition, where contacts between boys and girls were not looked upon favourably and the ideal of romantic love had not taken deep root. Many of the young people wrote openly about their repressions and complexes, which frequently complicated their lives. Abraham Rotfarb remembered Moniek, a Communist friend of his who came from an Orthodox family, and whose sexual problems drove him to suicide;[56] luckily, this was not a common phenomenon. Puritanism formed part of the ethos of contemporary Christian bourgeoisie as well; it was common to both societies.

The autobiographies reflect the changes in customs connected with the advent of sexual education and information. Jula Wald still belonged to the generation which knew nothing about this subject and in which it was not considered respectable even to have such knowledge. However, her curiosity drove her to seek random bits of specific 'knowledge' in the crude jokes told by drunken customers, the confidences of the Catholic housemaid, and the allusions made by her girlfriends and sisters.[57] But the slightly younger writers already knew about the subject, and even used to discuss it in the youth organizations.

Sometimes the memoirs contain very intimate confessions on the subject of sexual initiation. Such material is invaluable for research into contemporary society. Frequently, the descriptions are stylized in the manner of great film romances. I quote two extracts from the memoirs of Sara Kopyto from Płock. The first depicts a realistic scene describing a first meeting:

I felt that someone was following me and then I heard his voice.
  'Excuse me, but I would like to speak with you.'
  'With me? ... Yes, what can I do for you?'
  'Please forgive me for taking the liberty of speaking to you without being introduced. I hope you will not refuse me and will make my acquaintance.'
  'What harm can it do to get acquainted?'
He extended his hand and introduced himself as Henry, but I did not manage to catch the surname.

---

[55] 'Lonek from Kosów', No. 184/520, dated 1939.
[56] 'A. Harefuler', No. 254/581, dated 1939.
[57] No. 331, dated 1916–24.

But in the second scene, in the park, the conversation definitely suggests a film dialogue:

His resolute voice broke the silence.

'What a lovely spot you have chosen. Sitting here one is overcome by a feeling of bliss.'

I looked at him with indifference and said:

'So you are feeling the same thing as I am? . . .'

'I can see that you are still young; nevertheless, your great moral suffering has ravaged your face and no one attempts to understand you. But I noticed this the first time I saw you and something in me immediately responded to it and impelled me towards you. So, I am asking you to put your trust in me and tell me all about your suffering and your pain which are destroying your beauty. Let me experience the suffering together with you and perhaps, together, we shall manage to get something more out of life.'

My answer came slowly; I looked down on the ground, as I did not dare to raise my eyes.[58]

It may well be that some of these 'stylized' romances were nothing but fantasy, but there is no way of verifying this.

To summarize, the system of values revealed in the Polish-language section of this collection is idealistic. Ideology and political involvement held a prominent place in it. The next position was held by the yearning for friendship and great love. The young writers, even the Orthodox ones, wanted to be modern. The new, secularized generation wanted to break with traditional models, but they were not always successful in achieving this. Echoes of Jewish traditions sometimes resounded in their hopes and dreams. Modernity, whether in the realm of civilization or customs, was not always easily accessible to them. It is for this reason that traditional values frequently played a compensatory role.

SUMMARY

I have attempted to trace certain threads which form part of the fabric of the substantial Polish-language section of the YIVO collection of autobiographies of Jewish young people. The collection lends support to the thesis of the polyglot nature of interwar Jewish society.

The memoirs show the extent and universality of the secularizing process which was a consequence of cultural assimilation. The other side of the coin was the continuing disintegration of traditional culture, which took a more violent turn among the Jews than was the case in Christian culture. The generation conflict, which inevitably played a part in these occurrences, only increased the feeling of alienation among young people.

[58] No. 71/407, dated 1939.

This feeling of alienation is revealed in a singular manner in the system of values of young people in the throes of breaking with tradition. The value-system was very idealistic and compensated for the loss of tradition. Politics held a prominent position; the most popular trends were varieties of Jewish nationalism, ranging from the Zionist left to Revisionism. One may expect that in the Yiddish section of the collection these proportions will prove to be quite different: interest in the Bund and Folkism must have predominated in this group. None the less, it is interesting that Zionism expressed itself so frequently in the Polish-language section.

THE MEMOIRS AS HISTORY

For reasons of space I am able to give here only a few hints as to how these documents can be exploited as a historical source. Memoirs certainly form very tempting material, not only for the historian but also for the sociologist, ethnologist, and even psychologist. This collection of autobiographies contains much information on the fate of individuals and families, customs, national consciousness and its evolution, and the motives which led people to adopt certain positions. Many pages are filled with descriptions of historical facts, which have been only lightly touched upon above. These relate to the First World War, wartime suffering and wandering, the formation of the independent Polish state, the Ukrainian wars, the pogroms of the early postwar years, and the later ones which were connected with the economic crisis and totalitarian tendencies. Three writers who spent their childhood in Soviet Russia describe post-Revolutionary repressions and hunger. Day by day, Hanna Jakubowska's contemporary diary[59] presents the Bolshevik invasion in Płock in 1920. Young Communists describe the reaction of their groups to the dissolution of the Polish Communist Party. Memoirs of Orthodox Jews portray the internal power-struggles which were going on in the community councils. Wilhelm Kittenplan[60] describes the arrival in Kraków of refugees from Nazi Germany.

The examples presented above in a perfunctory fashion do not give an adequate picture of the richness of factual data or the vividness of description that are to be found in these autobiographies. It is to be hoped that a selection from the Polish-language section of the collection should be published in Poland. If this were to occur, it would be valuable for both Polish and Jewish researchers. This would, I believe, be the very first publication to examine the Jewish community of young people from the inside, from the point of view of their expectations and desires, and of the calamities which befell their lives. It would also make it possible for once to

[59] No. 106. [60] 'Kitka', No. 3630.

present a picture which would not be stereotyped, something which has so far always, characterized descriptions of Jews in Poland. A look at one's own history through someone else's eyes would be a revelation.

Polish–Jewish Relations as Reflected in Memoirs of the Interwar Period

SZYJA BRONSZTEJN

INTRODUCTION

THE Jewish population—or 'people of the Mosaic faith', as the 1931 census expressed it—made up 9.8 per cent of the inhabitants of Poland. They were not evenly distributed throughout the country: 76.4 per cent lived in towns.[1] A quarter of Polish Jews lived in one of the five largest cities—Warsaw, Łódź, Vilna, Kraków, and Lwów—where they made up 30.6 per cent of the total population. In some voivodships the proportion of Jews in the total urban population was even higher: in the Polesie voivodship it was 49.2 per cent; in Wołyń 49.1 per cent; in Lublin 42.9 per cent; in Nowogródek 42.6 per cent. There were quite a few towns and small towns in interwar Poland where Nowogródek Jews constituted more than 50 per cent of the total number of residents. Apart from the voivodships where the above-mentioned cities were situated, Jews were also to be found in other parts of Poland in considerable numbers: they made up 13 per cent of the total population of the Lublin voivodship, 12.3 per cent of the Białystok voivodship, 10.1 per cent of the Polesie voivodship, and 10 per cent of the Wołyń voivodship.[2]

It was not only the pattern of their residence in Poland which distinguished Jews from other residents of that country, but also differences in religion, tradition, and lifestyle, their different social and professional structures, and the specific mode of dress of a substantial part of the Jewish community. If we also bear in mind the growing tensions in Polish–Jewish relations before the outbreak of the Second World War and the fate to which the Nazis subjected Jews during that war, then it is understandable that in virtually all the memoirs published on the interwar period after the war, Jews or the entire Jewish community in various places are mentioned to a greater or lesser degree.

[1] As against a figure of only 22.1 per cent among the non-Jewish population.
[2] In the western areas the percentage of Jews was not very high, e.g. in the Silesian voivodship it was 1.5 per cent, in Pomorze 1.8 per cent, and in the Poznań voivodship 2.1 per cent.

The aim of this essay is to describe both the sporadic and the permanent contacts or links which united Poles and Jews, and also the differences, contradictions, and even antagonisms between the members of these two peoples. The study is based on everyday events noted by the actual participants in and witnesses of the facts and episodes described. On the basis of the information contained in the memoirs, I hope to demonstrate how the disposition, behaviour, way of reacting in various circumstances, and attitude of the Jews to the vital interests of Poland influenced Polish–Jewish relations. These relations should not be perceived as incidental results of specific situations, but as phenomena that were determined by a long history and diverse conditions.

In this essay the memoirs of about 150 people contained in a hundred books published in Poland after the Second World War are referred to.[3] Seventy-five per cent of the authors were not Jews. All the episodes, facts, events, and information cited here have been previously published, but are spread over many thousands of pages. By bringing them together, I hope to obtain a full, comprehensive, and more objective picture of the problem being examined.

In this group of memoirs there is a spectrum ranging from incidental references to Jews to whole sections of books; and episodes and issues which are referred to incidentally in some books are developed and complemented in others. This allows a fuller picture of the events and processes to emerge. In several instances single small facts recalled in various memoirs enable an event to be totally reconstructed. Some authors, wishing to provide appropriate documentation for their arguments, cite official documents and press publications.[4] Facts and assessments are also cited from the memoirs and recollections of other authors.[5] The form of the narration naturally depends on the literary ability of its author. The language reflects the usage and influence of the period at which the memoirs were written and published.[6]

The anecdotal character of the memoirs provides an ideal medium through which the climate of a given period may be perceived. The texts contain reflections of everyday life, cares and worries, weaknesses and humour, moments of celebration and feasts, the great careers of ordinary people as well as the often difficult existence of great and well-known personages. These memoirs draw us closer to the period being studied.

---

[3] In three cases the memoirs are published in journals.

[4] Bolesław Drobner does this most frequently, in *Bezustanna walka*, ii. *Wspomnienia 1919–1935* (Warsaw, 1965).

[5] For example, J. Wittlin, *Pójdź ze mną! Dziennik—pamiętnik*, i (Kraków, 1985), cites A. Wat's memoirs; similarly, S. E. Nahlik, *Przesiane przez pamięć* (Kraków, 1987), cites the memoirs of M. Naszkowski, A. Hutnikiewicz, and W. Szolgin.

[6] For example, A. Fiderkiewicz, *Burzliwe lata* (Warsaw, 1963), writes about Sanacja and Piłsudski as Fascists, a Fascist dictatorship, etc.

They are without doubt presented subjectively, something which gives us an insight into the unique viewpoint of the direct observers and witnesses of those times.

There are often varying views on the same people formulated by different authors. This is a natural result of the nature of the acquaintance in each case.[7] Likewise, convergent or even identical events are interpreted differently by different authors, depending on the social group to which they belonged, their political views, or what impression the events made on them.

The assessments made by these authors clearly depended on their differing experience of life. Remarks by statesmen, information in party programmes, and archival or statistical materials cannot replace the experiences and feelings of common people found in these memoirs, such as the feelings of a child who notices that her friends behave in a different way towards her depending on the company and place they are in.[8]

The facts recalled in these memoirs have not only been filtered through memory, but have probably also been subjected to self-criticism and self-censorship. The judgements expressed are still a valuable component in the descriptions of the events being recalled. As in sociological research the questionnaire method is used to acquaint oneself with the subjective assessment of various facts, so in historical research recollections can be used to evaluate various events according to the accounts of their direct participants. A reasonably objective account of the facts given in the memoirs, particularly those which appear many times, can often be attained. The information gleaned as a result can provide a valuable supplement to other historical materials.

THE STRATIFICATION OF THE JEWISH POPULATION

When examining Polish–Jewish relations, the far-reaching stratification of both communities should be kept in mind. A Warsaw taxi-driver recalls that 'The stratification of the people of Warsaw into various milieux was visible and perceptible. Besides the Jewish national group which separated itself from the rest there were also working-class, artisan, industrial, commercial,

---

[7] S. E. Nahlik writes that they were taught Polish in Form 6 of the grammar school by 'Dr Henryk or Herman (but it's all the same as we nicknamed him Herszek) Balk, a kind of arrogant know-all, a Jewish intellectual of the first generation ... that loathsome individual did not hold on to his place longer than a year in our school ... But the fact that Artur Hutnikiewicz in his memoirs [see n. 5] refers most positively to Balk proves how varied opinions can be' (*Przesiane przez pamięć*, 1943).

[8] See Halina Korn-Żuławska, *Wakacje kończą się we wrześniu* (Warsaw, 1983), 62–4.

intellectual, and aristocratic milieux.'[9] But Poland did not end in Warsaw. According to the 1931 census, 60.6 per cent of the population of the whole of Poland made its livelihood out of agriculture.

Among the Poles there were differences conditioned by more than a hundred years of subjugation to the partitioning governments, and by the various ways of opposing those authorities so as to maintain their national identity. It should also be noted that a considerable percentage of the non-Jewish population, 28.3 per cent, was made up of people belonging to other national minorities in Poland.[10]

The Jews likewise did not constitute a uniform community. They were considerably differentiated both professionally and socially, by the extent of their wealth, and by their political views, traditions, Jewish national awareness, and the extent of identification with Polish nationalist aspirations. In the pages of the memoirs are to be found remarks about Jewish industrialists and factory-workers, owners of retail stores and small shopkeepers, artisans and door-to-door salesmen, writers and politicians, remarkable barristers and famous doctors, prostitutes and the lumpenproletariat, students of the holy books in the *ḥadarim* and *yeshivot*, as well as those who, wishing to break away from their community or obtain a state position, changed their faith.

The social and professional stratification meant that the material situation of these people was very varied. Alongside people possessing legendary fortunes,[11] there was a large proportion of the population living on the verge of total poverty. The authors of these recollections cite examples which prove that the Jewish proletariat lived in conditions no better than those of the Polish proletariat,[12] whose fortunes were not to be envied. In periods of crisis cases of suicide by the ruined owners of famous commercial firms were not unknown.[13] If there was a Polish Jewish community it was a community of circumstances and not of interests.

Against this background of frustration caused by economic conditions, of the undeniable social inequality of Jews and Poles, manifested in the failure to employ Jews in the state administration or army, and of the growing

---

[9] Marian Sękowski, *Pamiętnik warszawskiego taksówkarza* (Warsaw, 1978), 57.

[10] Calculated on the basis of J. Tomaszewski, *Rzeczpospolita wielu narodów* (Warsaw, 1985), 35. Other nationalities apart from the Jews made up 25.5 per cent of the total population.

[11] Maria Kamińska writes about the enormous fortunes of her uncle, Maurycy Poznański, her Grandmother Silberstein, and other Łódź industrialists: see M. Kamińska, *Ścieżkami wspomnień* (Warsaw, 1960), 273–4.

[12] Zdzisław Kaliciński, Franciszek Kotula, Stefan Otwinowski, Kazimierz Rudnicki, and Henryk Vogler provide evidence for this.

[13] Leopold Marschak writes about the suicide of the merchant Starkman: *Byłem przy tym . . .* (Warsaw, 1976), 169–70. Hanna Mortkowicz-Olczakowa explains the causes of the suicide of her father, Jakub Mortkowicz: *Pod znakiem kłoska* (Warsaw, 1962), 241.

wave of antisemitism in the 1930s, the desire to emigrate grew stronger and revolutionary tendencies increased. This was particularly so in the case of the young Jewish intelligentsia. In turn, this radicalization of attitudes resulted in the accusation that the Jews were 'Red yids', and intensified antisemitism.

The link with Polish culture and the culture of partitioned Poland, formed over many years and conditioned by historical development between particular Jewish groups, was a varied one. Undoubtedly there was a certain proportion of Jews who were emotionally and sentimentally involved with Polish culture and Polish national aspirations. However, the greater part of them continued to remain under the influence of German and Russian culture.

At the end of the nineteenth century the Jewish masses driven out by the Tsar and arriving in Poland, the so-called 'Litvaks' (Lithuanian Jews), were saturated with Russian culture. Analysing the situation of the Jews in Vilna and the specific widespread character and strength of antisemitism there in 1934–7, Ludwik Krzywicki writes that at the beginning of the century 'the Jews by their behaviour gave the city above all a Russified profile'. The author goes on to emphasize that the Jews were impressed by the wealth of Russian culture, and that the Jewish youth were drawn by the ideological momentum of the Russian intelligentsia, by the fearless struggle of a handful of heroes against the Tsar, and by the great earning potential in trade with Russia. Even 'after independence had been long established, the Vilna Jews were more persistent in their use of Russian than native Russians. This has not been forgotten in Vilna to this very day and had a great influence on the widespread antisemitism there.'[14]

The numerical preponderance of the so-called 'Litvaks' among Jews in the central and eastern areas of Poland undoubtedly had a negative influence on Polish–Jewish relations. Regardless of any assessment of the role the 'Litvaks' played in the development of the economy of the kingdom of Poland, and regardless of their personal attributes and shortcomings, it has to be said that the Litvaks' bond with Russian culture did not endear them either to the Poles or to assimilated Jewish families. 'At home', Maria Kamińska recalls, 'we didn't speak readily about the Litvaks, the Jews who spoke Russian.'[15]

The influence of German culture on the Jews living in Wielkopolska (Greater Poland) has been explained by Krzywicki as follows:

the Jews had a loose connection with Poland, individual Jews joined in the Polish independence movements and embraced Polish culture, but the masses remained

[14] Ludwik Krzywicki, *Wspomnienia*, iii (Warsaw, 1959), 328.
[15] Kamińska, *Ścieżkami wspomnień*, 275.

closed in their self-chosen cultural ghetto, and when they had to make a choice between Polish culture, poor in many respects, and German culture, overflowing in rich cultural achievement and providing possibilities for greater remuneration, they did not hesitate a second over which way they had to go. One may regret that that is how things were, but it should be of no surprise to anyone that it was so.

The author then suggests that Poland needed a third estate, with which the Jews could have been culturally assimilated as had happened in Germany, and adds: 'The Poznań gentry and the extremely Catholic middle class, just beginning to emerge, looked down on the Jews and were thus unable to draw them into Poland.'[16]

Ludwik Hirszfeld, without restricting himself to the Wielkopolska area, assesses the causes of Jewish attitudes to the Germans in a similar manner: 'The Jews on the whole lived in the towns. The bourgeois German culture was more akin to them than the landed Polish culture. They willingly went to study in Germany, took on German dry-nurses, went to German baths, and consulted German doctors. One could say now that the Germans were the failed love of the Jews.'[17] Here one may add that for many years after Poland became independent the Jews of former Galicia felt a great sentiment for Austria, recalling how good life had been under Franz Josef.[18]

JEWISH SEPARATION

The Jewish people, on account of the role they played in the national economy and in its culture and arts, formed an integral part of Polish society. However, in spite of their internal differences, the overwhelming majority of Jews lived their own separate lives, alongside the Polish populace, to some extent as a separate community. Many facts prove this.

Antoni Słonimski, when considering the lack of knowledge of the Polish language displayed by the leading Yiddish poet Itzik Manger, in spite of the fact that he had lived in Warsaw for several years, writes: 'It is an example of that particular ethnic border which ran through the town somewhere around Bielańska Street, separating Śródmieście (the central district of Warsaw) from the Jewish district. Those were two separate worlds.'[19]

Jewish workers—tailors, cobblers, cab-drivers, painters, varnishers, and others—were members of separate union branches,[20] as were shop and office workers. There was a separate union for Jewish writers and journalists.

[16] Krzywicki, *Wspomnienia*, iii. 332–3.
[17] Ludwik Hirszfeld, *Historia jednego życia* (Warsaw, 1946), 346.
[18] Cf. Franciszek Kotula, *Tamten Rzeszów* (Rzeszów, 1985), 263.
[19] A. Słonimski, *Alfabet wspomnień* (Warsaw, 1975), 139.
[20] Cf. Kamińska, *Ścieżkami wspomnień*, 291.

The Jews had a Lawyers' Association alongside which an Association of Court and Legal Articled Apprentices also functioned.

Jewish students were not members of the Bratnia Pomoc (Self-help Organization). They ran their own organizations: for example, they had their Wzajemna Pomoc (Mutual Help) at the Free Polish University in Warsaw,[21] and at the Jagiellonian University in Kraków the organization corresponding to the Bratniak (a student club) was the Ognisko.[22] The same happened in other university cities, where there were large groups of Jewish students, such as Lwów and Vilna.[23]

Part of the Jewish intelligentsia played a prominent role in the activities of the Polish Socialist Party (PPS) or sympathized with that party. Jewish workers, like certain sections of the intelligentsia, belonged to and worked with dedication in the Communist Party.[24] At the same time a very active Jewish socialist party with a relatively large membership functioned—the Bund, whose activity was independent of the various Zionist parties. When the Feraynigte Party, which had fewer members than the Bund, decided to join with the Party of Independent Socialists, the latter recognized autonomy in cultural issues for the organizational cells of the Feraynigte in several Polish towns where the two organizations had united. 'The agreement also gave the Party of Independent Socialists the right to set up a separate Jewish national section.'[25] It should also be mentioned that in the Communist Workers Party of Poland (KPRP) a 'Jewish Office' existed and functioned,[26] and some Polish communists even learnt Yiddish in order to facilitate their contacts with Jewish comrades.[27]

The Jewish *petite bourgeoisie* usually spent their holidays in different places, nearer to the larger cities, from those frequented by their Polish counterparts. 'Podkowa Leśna, Otrębusy, Komarów were the summer resorts of the Polish rich, as Otwock, Falenica, and Świder were for the rich Jews;'[28] a Warsaw taxi-driver recalls. It was not any different in other towns: the village of Pleśna, situated in the White Valley on the Tarnów-

[21] Cf. Teofil Głowacki, *Górny bieg* (Warsaw, 1983), 98.
[22] Cf. Henryk Vogler, *Autoportret z pamięci: Część pierwsza* (Kraków, 1978), 88.
[23] Cf. Jerzy Putrament, *Pół wieku, Młodość* (Warsaw, 1962) 153.
[24] Much attention is devoted to these activities in many of the memoirs used here.
[25] Drobner, *Bezustanna walka*, ii. 68–9.
[26] Roman Jabłonowski recalls this several times in *Wspomnienia 1905–1918* (Warsaw, 1962) 276, 303.
[27] Józef Kowalczyk, *Ze wspomnień redaktora* (Warsaw, 1978) 43, says that Jerzy Czeszejko-Sochacki learnt Yiddish and 'soon became well known in the party as a conscientious reader of Jewish-language publications' Maria Kamińska writes that Olga Cywińska 'was fluent in Yiddish and spoke it willingly' (*Ścieżkami wspomnień*, 287); Maksym Tank, *Kartki kalendarza* (Warsaw, 1977), 48, writing about a communist called Władek (he does not give his surname) from Zagłębie Dąbrowskie, points out that 'in prison he learnt Yiddish and Ukrainian'.
[28] Sękowski, *Pamiętnik warszawskiego taksówkarza*, 61.

Stróża line, was very popular among the Jewish circles in Tarnów.[29] Henryk Vogler recalls holidays spent away from Kraków: 'I remember summer in the countryside, perhaps Zborni, perhaps Jordanów, maybe in Niepotomice, as it was in those places that I spent my first secondary-school holidays with my family.'[30]

The Jewish intelligentsia, with the exception of the assimilated intellectual élite, organized their own clubs in the medium-sized and large towns, and it was there that they spent their free time. In Rzeszów, as Franciszek Kotula writes, 'somewhere about 1930 the Jews, the progressive ones—university graduates, doctors, lawyers, merchants—opened their own casino [club]. They probably modelled it on the official casino in the Communal Savings Bank ... It was only open to members and their guests.'[31] Jerzy Jerzmanowski recalls a similar club in Kielce.[32] Entertainment and cultural activities were organized in some of the towns by clubs of the Makabi sports association. Maksym Tank writes about that sort of activity in Vilna. It is worth mentioning that the Jewish cultural community in Vilna, which in the interwar years formed a world centre of that culture, did not attract particular interest in the non-Jewish community. The remark by Jerzy Putrament in *Po prostu*, that it was only in 1937 that 'probably for the first time an attempt was made in the Vilna press to do some reporting on the undoubtedly very active Jewish literary milieu in the city',[33] is proof of this.

Most of the Jewish youth interested in sport belonged to and were active in such clubs as the Makabi, whose members were mainly middle-class youth, the Bund's Association for Physical Education, the Jutrznia, the Association for Physical Education Gwiazda, which was based on the Po'alei Tsion Left (a Zionist-Socialist Party), and also the Jewish Workers' Sports Club, connected with the Po'alei Tsion Right. It should be noted that the three workers' clubs mentioned belonged to the Union of Workers' Sporting Associations created in 1925, and some members, e.g. Grünbaum, Natan Tylman, Lucjan Blit, and Maurycy Orzech, played no mean role in the development of the Union.[34] Naturally, some well-known sportsmen and sports activists played in general sports clubs. In some of the memoirs mention is made of the names of the football-players Sperling and Gintel from Cracovia, of Singer, the boxing trainer of the Danzig 'Gryf', and of the tennis-player and activist of the 'Lublinianka', Dr J. Arnsztajn.[35]

---

[29] See Władysław Czapliński, *Szkoła w młodych oczach* (Kraków, 1982), 128.
[30] Vogler, *Autoportret z Pamięci*, 63–4.
[31] Kotula, *Tamten Rzeszów*, 352.
[32] Jerzy Jerzmanowski, *W starych Kielcach* (Łódź, 1984), 253.
[33] Putrament, *Pół wieku, Młodość*, 314.
[34] Cf. Tadeusz Jabłoński, *Młodość mego pokolenia* (Warsaw, 1977) 275–6.
[35] Cf. Brunon Zwara, *Wspomnienia gdańskiego bówki* (Gdańsk, 1984), 271.

In his memoirs Ludwik Hirszfeld examines the reasons for the separation of the Jews in Poland. The author considers that in contrast to the West, where 'the Jews wanted to integrate with the nations in which they lived and did not want to be a separate nation', the eastern Jews were a nation 'and wanted to be one. The masses considered themselves to be a nation with a separate destiny and separate values. The lower classes—primitive, agitated, growing rapidly, persecuted, and nostalgic—felt themselves to be a separate nation and were treated as such by the Poles.'[36] Hirszfeld maintains that the freedom which the Jews found in Poland, the 'right to practise their religious customs and rules, enabled them to develop independently of their surroundings . . . Special days in the Jewish calendar, kosher food, ritual slaughter, a different mode of dress, circumcision, the different architectural style of their synagogues and temples, and their different religious customs created a sharp dividing-line between the Poles and the Jews.'[37] The author sees the adoption of Christianity as a possible way to bring these two communities together, and that was what he did himself.

Another eminent Polish scholar, Szymon Askenazy, had a different understanding from Hirszfeld's of the bond that Jews felt with Poland and with what was Polish. Without negating and indeed often emphasizing his Jewish origins in an ostentatious manner, Askenazy, wishing to stress his Polishness, 'often used to say', as Janusz Pajewski relates,

that just as the Polish Tartars, while preserving Islam, their own Islamic customs, and tribal feelings, had become good Poles, as Armenians had become Poles, so should Jews follow in their tracks without renouncing either the faith or the traditions of their predecessors. He was one of the first, acting as an example for others, who knew by heart and liked to recite long passages from the Polish national epic *Pan Tadeusz*, which opened the doors to Polishness for him.[38]

Jewish distinctiveness and difference ought not to be identified with being foreign. When there are no internal tensions, good material conditions, no professional competition, comfort of life, then distinctiveness forms part of the social scenery, is an accepted condition of unity in variety. Distinctiveness can become something foreign when it is in isolation, when there are no professional and personal contacts and no cultural interaction and diffusion of cultures, and when the economic environment turns hostile.

In interwar Poland even the most religious and Orthodox circles of the Jewish community neither lived nor were able to live in total isolation from the rest of the population. The following episode can be cited as an example. When one Saturday night the rabbi's son in Góra Kalwaria fell ill

[36] Hirszfeld, *Historia jednego życia*, 345–6.
[37] Ibid.
[38] J. Pajewski, *Przeszłość z bliska: Wspomnienia* (Warsaw, 1983), 92.

with croup, without delay a surgeon, Dr Józef Czarkowski, who had only just started practising and was there on holiday, was called in. Czarkowski, seeing the despair in the eyes of the father, carried out the necessary treatment, even though he did not have the proper instruments. The doctor was paid a very high sum and the rabbi, as he recalled later, told him as he was leaving: 'You will always be known by me as "Golden hands", and soon you will come to understand what that means.' 'Yes, I really did. Soon patients, fellow believers of the rabbi, started to flock to see me.'[39]

Cultural interaction in the interwar period could not have been as intensive as it is now. However, there is no doubt that there was a Polish cultural influence on the Jews, mainly due to schooling, the Polish press (the Jewish Press being also widely available), films, and interaction outside of the Jewish districts stemming from ordinary neighbourly relations. Further influence arose from contacts with progressive students, co-operation with trade-union organizations, and co-operation within political parties.

In examining Jewish separateness as a condition determining Polish–Jewish relations two issues should be taken into consideration. First, the entire interwar period lasted barely twenty years, a relatively short period of time in which to counteract the indisputable influence of German and Russian culture on the Jews, which had lasted more than a century. Secondly, Poland was a multinational state in the interwar years. There were therefore specific relations between Poles and other national minorities, apart from the Jews, as there were between these minorities and the Jews.[40] In conditions favouring social integration, different from those that existed in eastern Europe in the interwar period, the representatives of the various national groups do not upset anyone by their specific characteristics. 'Wherever nations arise from different races', Hirszfeld wrote,

> each one of them contributes their habits. The Italians macaroni, the English roast beef, and the Jews garlic. And no one sees anything wrong in this since there macaroni is not regarded as a symbol of Italianness nor garlic of Jewishness, but quite simply as being macaroni and garlic. Here, however, in this foul Europe, in the melting-pot of nations, even unimportant habits become national symbols. Here it is not tolerance which prevails but idiosyncrasy. The nations are falling sick from their minorities. Not only from the Jewish minority.[41]

It has to be said, however, that—leaving aside the fully assimilated aristocratic lines of non-Polish origin, and the assimilated German or Armenian intelligentsia—the attitude of the Poles to other minorities was

---

[39] Cited on the basis of Jan Kruszewki, *Przed pół wiekiem w stolicy* (Warsaw, 1969), 146–65.
[40] S. E. Nahlik cites examples of the extreme antisemitism of some Armenians in Lwów; *Przesiane przez pamięć*, 230, 308–9, 314.
[41] Hirszfeld, *Historia jednego życia*, 352.

quite different from that to the Jews. This was a result of the factors cited in our introduction, which distinguished the Jews from the other peoples of Poland.

ATTITUDES TO THE JEWS

Attitudes towards the Jews, as the memories show, were dependent mainly on the affiliation of individual people, their families, or entire groups of people to various social classes. This could be the position of superiority of a state official in relation to his suppliant, or of the customer towards the shopkeeper seeking his custom. 'I was brought up', Józef Świdrowski recalls, 'with a feeling of the superiority of the Poles over the Jews, although it is difficult to say what that superiority was supposed to be based upon. The Jews whom I came into contact with in Szmulowizna (a Warsaw suburb) were small tradesmen and craftsmen, who spoke a jargon among themselves and used the Polish like foreigners.'[42] One might add that these shopkeepers and craftsmen were often seen as being on the verge of poverty and working hard so as to be able to keep their families, but they were also sometimes regarded quite simply as schemers, crooks, or even usurers.

Some authors regarded the Jews whom they mentioned as equal partners without going into their national affiliation. That is how workers wrote about their colleagues. 'Jewish workers and working women', Zdzisław Kaliciński recalls, 'struggled with unemployment and poverty just like the Polish proletariat. They were united by joint strikes and by the political struggle on a joint front with the trade unions and the Jewish Bund.'[43] Workers who were employed by Jews remember them in varying ways. Some saw them objectively, as belonging to another social class but at the same time as people who were conscientious and just, if there were no conflicts or misunderstandings between them. Others, however, saw them as exploiters and as people who were alien both by their class and by their nationality.[44]

Political prisoners recall their fellow sufferers in a friendly manner[45] and also as their intellectual friends. The gradation of friendship which we

---

[42] Józef Świdrowski, *Moja droga w świat* (Warsaw, 1980), 110.

[43] Zdzisław Kaliciński, *O Starówce, Pradze i ciopokach* (Warsaw, 1983), 207.

[44] This opinion is expressed by Piotr Haberko, chiefly with reference to the Jews but also concerning the Germans and Czechs, in *Moje huty szkła, Wspomnienia z lat 1905–1965* (Wrocław, 1980).

[45] Cf. the memoirs written by Bereza Kartuska prisoners in the volume of collected essays *Bereziacy* (Warsaw, 1965).

encounter in Jarosław Iwaszkiewicz's works is interesting in this respect. He writes about Mieczysław Grydzewski as a friend; when recalling Marek Eiger he says that they were bound by a close friendship, and in another place calls him his friend. However, he defines his relations with Tuwim as a 'poetic friendship',[46] suggesting a greater degree of emotional distance.

It is quite natural that the attitude of neutral observers to the Jews—those who were not emotionally involved and simply observed from the side—was quite different from that of those waging a relentless competitive war. In recalling the eastern 'Kresy' (borderlands) Czesław Bobrowski writes: 'I did not discover in the end any traces of antisemitism either in what I heard or in attitudes. Perhaps that was to a certain extent due to the fact that in those areas there was no conflict between the Polish and Jewish tradesmen and artisans, as there were few Poles involved in these activities.' A photographer from Łuck who was fiercely competitive with Jewish photographers in the town viewed these matters somewhat differently.[47]

Polish traders complained about Jewish merchants, accusing them of lowering prices. In Żyrardów, for example, 'the shopkeepers sometimes complained that they depressed prices, sold poor-quality goods, that a suit made by a Jewish tailor smelt of onions'.[48] J. Segory, the owner of a lacquer workshop in Danzig, went so far as to draw credit from an NSDAP member in the competitive struggle with the Jews. In the autumn of 1938 Stanisław Borowski from Białystok applied 'as an Aryan to an Aryan firm,' as 'he intended to open a shop to go into competition with the large Jewish enterprises in that town'.[49]

In considering competition between Jewish and Polish enterprises, one should not forget that economic relations between these two communities were not restricted to the merchant–client relationship or that between provider and recipient of services. There were also cases of joint enterprises being set up. Franciszek Kotula recalls that the Jew Julek Haar opened a car and agricultural-machine repair workshop in Rzeszów with the Pole Ferenc.[50]

In the specific circumstances of strong competition, difficult living conditions caused by the economic crisis, and the ruthless struggle to survive, someone who was an outsider could quickly become an enemy. This was manifested not only in the economic and social boycott, but also by anti-Jewish excesses and even pogroms, the existence of which

[46] Jaroslaw Iwaszkiewicz, *Książka moich wspomnień* (Kraków, 1968), 180, 187, 225, 228.
[47] Czesław Bobrowski, *Wspomnienia ze stulecia* (Lublin, 1985), 17–18; of Bolesław Gawel, *Lata włóczegi* (Olsztyn, 1977), 128, 130–1.
[48] Paweł Wiktorski, *Lot nad kołyską* (Warsaw, 1984), 147.
[49] Zwara, *Wspomnienia gdańskiego bówki*, 255.
[50] Kotula, *Tamten Rzeszów*, 173.

cannot be passed over in silence or denied 'as the authors of some of the memoirs do'.[51]

We shall restrict ourselves to considering the attitudes of two groups of people towards the Jews: the rural population and some circles of the Catholic Church. Andrzej Burda described the attitude of the peasants to the Jews from the village of Ryszotara near Kraków as friendly and says that 'in the countryside, good will was something quite natural in the common lives of people bound by the land'. In rural areas, as he writes, the Jew was the seventh and indispensable figure of the pastorale, the Christmas play; he gave advice, mediated, and mitigated.[52] The rural Jews not only acted as advisers and farmed, but, like Hirsz Zelwiański in one of the Białystok villages, they earned extra money by treating sick cattle.[53] Jerzy Putrament similarly devotes many friendly words to the blacksmith Jankielewicz, living in the village of Dokudów in the Vilna area.[54]

However, the countryside was not free from antisemitic occurrences. Józef Wittlin recalls that the political propaganda of the governor of the Lwów voivodship during the holidays in the countryside had little effect, as he 'was a Jew, which in these parts did not excite the admiration of the local clerical and nationalistic population'.[55] There was a far more tense situation in the villages of the Limanowa district. What is described by Walenty Gawron in his memoirs was no longer a battle over trade but real war, made even more bitter by the demagogic propaganda of Father Stojałowski: 'Priests got involved in it,' he relates. 'In Limanow on market-day [in 1938] three priests used to walk around the stalls and stop the Catholics buying from the Jews.'[56]

The National Democratic sympathies of a considerable part of the Catholic clergy and the clergy's participation in antisemitic acts are well known; and they are referred to in Słonimski's poem:

> Already excellent 'Catholics'
> Only not yet Christian.

All the more reason for recalling the Catholics already become Christians.

Jan Dobraczyński, recalling his father, writes: 'My father was also supported by the Jews, because although he was an ardent Catholic, he was always a guardian of charitable institutions and a friend of Janusz Korczak.'[57] Bolesław Drobner relates very movingly how Father Józef Niemczyń-

---

[51] e.g. Jan Dobraczyński, *Tylko w jednym życiu: Wspomnienia* (Warsaw, 1977).
[52] A. Burda, *Lata walki i nadziei* (Kraków, 1970), 13, 191.
[53] Cf. Józef Rybiński, *Słońce nad miedzy* (Olsztyn and Białystok, 1983), 178.
[54] Putrament, *Poł wieku, Młodość*, 228.
[55] Wittlin, *Pójdź ze mną!*, 44.
[56] W. Gawron, *Wspomnienia z Limanowszczyzny* (Warsaw, 1986), 277.
[57] Dobraczyński, *Tylko w jednym życiu*, 90.

ski, the parish priest in Kraków Podgórze, voluntarily appeared in court in 1938 as a witness and testified against the Catholic deputy Kuśnierz, who was indicting Drobner.[58]

Cases of Jews being honestly and justly treated by representatives of the right-wing nationalistic (Endecja) intelligentsia ought to be emphasized; prominent in this group are university professors. Władysław Czapliński recalls that Professor Władysław Konopczyński's seminar at the Jagiellonian University was relatively well attended by Jews despite his being a member of the Endecja. 'Moreover, I never saw any kind of antisemitic behaviour by the Master towards his students; we also knew that Jozef Feldman, who came from a Jewish family, was his student, and prepared for his Doctorate of Philosophy and later *habilitacja* [the post-doctoral thesis which entitled a university teacher to tenure] under him . . . We quickly understood that Konopczyński valued Feldman's work highly.'[59] The former prosecutor Kazimierz Rudnicki recalls how a well-known philologist and professor of the Jagiellonian University, who 'did not hold any radical views', vigorously requested the release of one of his students, Salomon Jaszuński, 'a future star of the Polish academic world, who had been arrested as he was a member of the Polish Communist Party (KPP).'[60]

Naturally, not all the Endek professors were free of rabid antisemitism. Wacław Sobieski, a professor of history and sometime rector of the Department of Philosophy of the Jagiellonian University, is one example. Czapliński, in recalling him, shows surprise: 'Where it originated in that fundamentally good person I don't know.'[61]

A remark made by Bolesław Drobner about a judge who led the investigation into the Kraków events of November 1923 shows that political views do not always permit assumption concerning the character and behaviour of the individual. He wrote: 'Podobiński really was a National Democrat, but his attitude towards the socialists was one of exceptional courtesy and impartiality.'[62]

Some of the Polish intelligentsia made contact only with those Jews who were fully assimilated. For example, Czesław Bobrowski writes: 'Of course I saw the enormous group of Jews in Lublin—there was no way one could not see them—but, with a few exceptions, I only knew families which were fully assimilated.'[63] For the author the Jews constituted a world which, as he observes, 'I lived alongside without knowing it'. And it was only during a stay 'in charming Kazimierz, where there was a certain

---

[58] Drobner, *Bezustanna walka*, iii. 19.   [59] Czapliński, *Szkoła w młodych oczach*, 250.
[60] Kazimierz Rudnicki, *Wspomnienia prokuratora* (Warsaw, 1956), 90.
[61] Czapliński, *Szkoła w młodych oczach*, 252.   [62] Drobner, *Bezustanna walka*, iii. 85.
[63] Bobrowski, *Wspomnienia ze stulecia*, 33. It is worth mentioning that according to the 1931 census Jews made up 34.8 per cent of the total population of Lublin.

symbiosis between the Jewish and non-Jewish population, that I saw the world of Jewish carters, carriage-drivers, workers of the tannery, and above all brokers living from day to day.'[64]

However, attitudes which perceived the Jews as intruders, nuisances, enemies, as a group which ought to be separated, removed from the general community, expelled, were not alien to the Poles. The Jews were blamed for all the bad things which went on in Poland. Right-wing clerical circles led in this prejudice. The National Democrats, and later other right-wing parties, included antisemitism in their programmes. It is impossible to deny the existence of an ugly and virulent antisemitism, which in Poland was particularly intense in the 1930s.

Immediately after Poland became independent certain events took place which, as Maciej Rataj wrote, recalling the anti-Jewish excesses in Lwów on 22 November 1918, were foul and horrible. The author considers, and he is certainly right, that if General Czesław Maczyński 'had shown more energy on that day, he would have been able at least to limit, if not prevent, the excesses. I saw General Maczyński going by car through the market-place and smiling condescendingly at the scene. I can neither forget nor forgive him that day and that smile.'[65]

It is a fact, that if the army had wanted to it could have prevented or restricted the anti-Jewish demonstrations. The example of Tarnów is proof of that. 'As early as November,' Czapliński writes, 'the first days of freedom were spoilt by anti-Jewish demonstrations. When they became dangerous the army was called in to help and the news that the army was approaching was in itself enough to calm down the hotheads.'[66]

Recalling the situation which arose following Poland's independence, Bolesław Drobner states that in January 1919, when the newly born state was beset by various unavoidable difficulties, the Endecja wanted to put the blame for all shortcomings on such leaders as Piłsudski or Daszyński, while presenting themselves as the saviours of the homeland. 'An incredible mess has been made,' he wrote, 'and thus it's all the Jews' fault again, so the Jewish influence must be destroyed and then there will be paradise on earth led by Christian democracy—the antisemites.'[67]

The attitude of some of the Jewish youth during the Polish-Soviet war in 1920, and the manner in which the government reacted to what it regarded as treason in a moment of national crisis, undoubtedly had an influence on Jewish-Polish relations during the first years of independence. Acknowledg-

---

[64] Bobrowski, *Wspomnienia ze stulecia*, 35–6.
[65] Maciej Rataj, *Pamiętniki 1917–1927* (Warsaw, 1961), 26.
[66] Czapliński, *Szkoła w młodych oczach*, 132.
[67] B. Drobner, *Moje cztery procesy* (Warsaw, 1962), 115.

ing that the war was seen by the Poles above all as a national and not a class conflict, Czesław Bobrowski writes:

Naturally it could not be like that everywhere. When I was in the army, I heard about paramilitary units made up mainly of national minorities, which were created on the other side of the front. To what extent one should have seen in this aspects of a revolutionary current, and to what extent enmity to the Polish state felt by the Belorussians and so-called 'Litvaks', i.e. Jews who had only recently come to Poland from the Russian empire—it is difficult to say. In any case it nourished antisemitism, and a typical by-product of war was, quite simply, acts of brutality against the Jews.[68]

Describing the government's propaganda, Maria Kamińska wrote:

On the walls enormous posters appeared: skulls, skulls, and more skulls all piled up, and on them an enormous wild cutthroat was sitting with a knife between his bared teeth. He had a Red Army cap on his unkempt head. The face of a degenerate—hideous and vicious. One is struck by the fact he is an exclusively Semitic figure. People stop, terrified. 'A Jew, a Bolshevik,' you can hear them saying. One or two whisper astutely: 'Trotsky.'[69]

Both Kamińska and Bolesław Drobner recall the camp in Jabłonna outside Warsaw where Jewish volunteers to the Polish Army were held in 1920. The Polska Partia Socjalistyczna (PPS: Polish Socialist Party) protested vigorously against this in a statement issued by the Central Executive Committee on 5 September 1920. 'That protest', Drobner writes, 'was successful, as on 17 September 1920 the camp in Jabłonna was closed down.'[70]

Jews were often teased with various pranks, sometimes quite recklessly. The memoirs record examples of mischievous jokes as well as evil tricks. Not only children, but sometimes even adults committed these acts. 'We were capable, for example, of getting hold of a cat', Zygmunt Kaliciński writes,

And sticking walnut-shells to its paws and letting it loose in Icchok Pałasz's shop. Pałasz used to sell cakes, sweets, fruit, and soda water. The cat ran around as if it were mad, all over the floor, and on to the counter, where delicacies were lying under the glass, clattering on it with the shells. Hania, Pałasz's daughter, screamed her head off, and old Icchok shouted at her, at the cat, and at us.[71]

Door-knocking half-way through Lent was somewhat more malicious. It

[68] Bobrowski, *Wspomnenia ze stulecia*, 40.
[69] Kamińska, *Ścieżkami wspomnień*, 200.
[70] Drobner, *Bezustanna walka*, iii. 22–3.
[71] Kaliciński, *O Starówce, Pradze i ziopokach*, 159.

was a practice well known in Mazowsze, when exactly half-way through Lent people went round in the evening from house to house knocking on doors and throwing pots full of ashes into the house. Kaliciński writes: 'we beat on the doors indiscriminately, sometimes knowing well that it was Jews and not Catholics who were living there. The doors opened with shouts of: "Hoodlums! Bandits! Hooligans! I hope a pot like that hits you on the head!"' The author adds that the whole aim was to provoke that kind of reaction. 'After all, we knew which homes were Jewish and which were Polish.'[72]

Pranks were also played on the Jewish feast-days. During the Feast of Tabernacles, stones would be thrown at the temporary shelters in which Jews ate and sometimes slept during the festival. If it was discovered who had done it, the elder Jews would go and complain to the boys' parents and then the belt was used, as the older people, although they may well have done similar things in their childhood, did not encourage such pranks.'[73]

The same author writes about far more unpleasant pranks carried out on the Day of Atonement. 'The Jews could be most upset by letting a black bird into the Synagogue on the Day of Atonement. It was a very ominous sign. That is why when it happened even the gendarmerie under Austrian rule or the police under Polish rule would intervene.'[74]

Piotr Haberko, who had no love for the Jews, recalls the rowdy pranks of plasterers working in the Rogów glassworks in southern Poland, who were irritated by the unnecessary and meddlesome conversations of a bookkeeper.

> They had just prepared the mortar under the large sand-block weighing about 150 kilos. When Giechman started to talk to the leader of the group of workers, they let the block fall with full force and the mortar splattered all over the place and splashed the bookkeeper's trousers. This effectively put an end to his pointless and meddlesome talks with us. He later complained about my plasterers and their having ruined his clothes. I explained to him that there was nothing malicious in it, but they quite simply could not hold such a heavy weight.[75]

If this example was an individual rowdy prank, the event described by Brunon Zwara was of a far more dangerous character. After completing military preparation exercises in Starzew and visiting Kraków and Wieliczka in 1938, Danzig scouts arrived in Częstochowa.

> There was a great commotion there because of us. It was our friends' fault, who, bumping into Orthodox Jews on the streets, pulled their long side-curls for a joke. Uproar resulted among the Jews of Częstochowa. Seeing the long cloaks of the scouts, they shouted that the Nazis had arrived. Of course they were only harmless

[72] Kaliciński, *O Starówce, Pradze i ziopokach*, 202–3. [73] Kotula, *Tamten Rzeszów*, 159.
[74] Ibid., 386. [75] Haberko, *Moje huty szkła*, 101.

jokes as both the older leaders and the young scouts had no intention of persecuting the Jews, as they themselves well knew what it meant to be attacked and beaten up. The authorities, however, treated the matter with all seriousness and the numerous police patrols on the Avenue of the Most Holy Mary were proof of this.[76]

The antagonism towards Jews displayed by non-Jewish men did not make the latter blind to the attraction of Jewish women. Paweł Wiktorski recalls that during manœuvres in the Suwałki region

> We billeted Lieutenant Kuligowski in a Jewish house, in whose window we caught sight of a pretty face. We went in and checked it out. Are there stores of onions in the house? Yes. The lieutenant does not like them. Are there portraits of bearded patriarchs? Yes. The lieutenant does not like them either. Is there a girl like the rose of Sharon? Yes. That is what the lieutenant likes.[77]

Edward Kwiatkowski, a Legionnaire and former chairman of the Union of Legionnaires in Lublin, who was appointed mayor of Kazimierz Dolny after the May *coup* which brought Piłsudski back to power in 1926, 'himself said that he was a continuer of the traditions of Kazimierz the Great: he had fallen in love with a Jewess, a young painter from Warsaw, and intended to marry her'.[78] However, they never got married because Kwiatkowski committed suicide, having been accused—wrongly as it later turned out—of breaking financial regulations. If that had not happened, it would have been one of the rare mixed marriages of the interwar period.

In the memoirs several such marriages are mentioned. Ludwik Krzywicki writes that a professor of the Main Trade School, Jan Cieśliński, had 'a Polish wife, who was an Orthodox Jewess'.[79] Ludwik Hirszfeld, writing about the fate of Professor Centnerszewer in the Warsaw Ghetto, recalls that he had an Aryan wife.[80] Jerzy Jerzmanowski recalls that Nachtman, a judge from Stopnica in the Busko-Zdrój district, although himself a native Pole, had a wife who was a dentist and came from a Jewish family.[81] Bolesław Gaweł writes about two of his friends from Łuck who married Jewish girls.[82]

There is also an example from Rzeszów, where a pig merchant, Jan Czechnicki, fell in love with one of the daughters of the local publican, a Jew. The very religious Jews would not agree to the marriage, which had to

---

[76] B. Zwara, *Wspomnienia gdańskiego bówki*, 242.
[77] Wiktorski, *Lot nad kołyska*, 347.
[78] K. Bielski, *Spotkanie z Kazimierzem* (Lublin, 1965), 51
[79] Krzywicki, *Wspomnienia*, iii. 297.
[80] Hirszfeld, *Historia jednego życia*, 330.
[81] Jerzmanowski, *W starych Kielcach*, 155-6.
[82] Cf. Gaweł, *Lata włóczęgi*, 142-5.

wait until the death of her father.[83] Paweł Wiktorski recalls the tragic conclusion to such a love:

> There were also other reasons for their suicide, which are difficult to believe today. She came from a Catholic family and he was a Hasid. Her parents did not allow her to marry a Jew, his did not want to permit their son to marry the daughter of a Gentile. The young couple went for their last walk along the railway line towards Bednarska Droga and on the way back threw themselves under the train.[84]

In some circles, where jealousy also undoubtedly played a role, even flirtations were frowned upon. Jerzy Jerzmanowski recalls such a case in Kielce, the romance between an associate judge, Stanisław Styczien, and the attractive articled clerk to the Kielce Regional Court, Zofia Freiman.[85]

The memoirs referred to provide proof that not all of the conflicts and quarrels between Jews and non-Jews were a result of national differences or antisemitic motives, and that among the Jews themselves there were also at times misunderstandings, quarrels, antagonisms, conflicts, and political battles.

The antagonism between the two Jewish Socialists, one of the left, the other of the right, Bolesław Drobner and the editor of the Kraków *Naprzód*, Emil Haecker, certainly did not have a nationalist basis but an ideological one. The well-known case between the latter and a Kraków lawyer, Włodzimierz Lewicki, a Ukrainian by birth, which had clear antisemitic motives, was quite different.

Maria Ludwika Mazurowa, Bolesław Leśmian's daughter, complains that the Skamander poets, the main avant-garde literary group in Poland in the 1920s, 'were jealous of [her father's] fame and made no mention of the successive volumes of poetry which were published. The main responsibility for this silence lay with *Wiadomości Literackie*. It was a power in those days and the whole nation respected its views.'[86] Opinions are divided as to whether that really was the case. There is no question, however, for all those who recall this matter that it had nothing to do with the nationality of the participants.

Jerzy Putrament recalls that his father began to feel particularly uncomfortable in Kołomyja in 1922, when the later famous General Mond, the highest-ranking Jew in the Polish army, became regimental commander. His father 'took whatever chance he could and arranged to leave Kołomyja'.[87] He does

---

[83] Cf. Kotula, *Tamten Rzeszów*, 177–8.
[84] Wiktorski, *Lot nad Kołyska*, 138.
[85] Cf. Jerzmanowski, *W Starych Kielcach*, 124–5.
[86] Maria Ludwika Mazurowa, 'Podróże i praca twórcza Bolesława Leśmiana', in *Wspomnienia o Bolesławie Leśmianie*, ed. Zdzisław Jastrzebski (Lublin, 1966), 27.
[87] Putrament, *Poł wieku, Młodość*, 39–40.

not make any suggestions, however, as to Bernard Mond's background, as Grot-Rowecki does,[88] but writes that Mond was a Legionnaire and his father had previously served in the Russian army.

Some of the authors show affection towards some Jews, which resulted from recollections of their childhood and youth. 'I went down to old Moszkowa,' Jarosław Iwaszkiewicz writes, 'whom I recognized straight away, to buy some bad sweets. I looked at the old Jewess with emotion. My mother always used to do her shopping in her shop. She did not know who this strange tall young man was, who saw in her the "sweet-providing angel" of his childhood.'[89]

Jerzy Jerzmanowski recalls that in the 1920s an old-boys' meeting of the Kielce Civic Association Russian Grammar School took place:

In the hall of the Resursa Obywatelska [a local patriotic association] the supper had brought together an impressive number of important men. During the reception an uninvited guest slipped in—Icek (the school's second-hand bookseller). He was different from how we remembered him. He had grown old and had an enormous grey beard. None the less the familiar face sat at a table together with 'his pupils'. He sat between his contemporary and Żeromski's friend, Zygmunt Wasilewski, the editor of *Myśl narodowa* (a right-wing antisemitic paper) and Felicjan Sławoj-Składowski, the future Prime Minister, twenty-one years Żeromski's junior. For over an hour Icek was the main attraction. For a long time he recounted impressions and gifts he had received, as more than a hundred of 'his pupils' had been at the banquet.[90]

When dealing with attitudes to the Jews, Władysław Czapliński writes: 'In the sphere of religious life there was still a long way to go towards bringing both religions closer together in the spirit of the second Vatican Council. On Good Friday, people still prayed "Pro perfidos Judaeos", and popular hymns were sung with lines about Jews being the killers of Christ, the worshippers totally forgetting that Christ was also a Jew.' Further on the author adds that in spite of the severe tension which also occured in business competition between the two communities, 'there was great respect and esteem towards individual people of Jewish nationality'. Czapliński says that among the people whom his father respected there were also merchants of medium wealth, respected representatives of the best Jewish traditions of commerce.[91]

Stefan Otwinowski's parents came from the nobility. He recalls that his mother liked to utter 'words of truth' to a Jew, the hospital attendant in Grodzisk Mazowiecki, Arbuz. 'Her convictions were', as he writes, 'rather

---

[88] Stefan Rowecki (Grot), 'Notatnik—pamiętnik 1939', *Odra*, 9/288 (1985), 8.
[89] Iwaszkiewicz, *Książka moich wspomnień*, 134–5.
[90] Czapliński, *Szkoła w młodych oczach*, 26.
[91] Ibid.

reactionary in comparison with my father, and she thought that Jews had it too good in Poland. That is what she "thought", but her every deed was based on the premiss that the Jewish poverty in the town, which moved the heart of honest people certainly no less than Polish poverty, must be alleviated.'[92] His father, although expressing reservations about the willingness of the Jews to make sacrifices for the Polish cause, was more pro-Jewish:

The Jews are good Poles. Jews can be the best—Poles, even those who speak badly about Poland ... There has not yet been a general Jewish movement, which would shed the necessary amount of blood for this land, but let us not forget that we the gentry have observed that right and duty of sacrifice to the exclusion of others besides the Jews.[93]

It can be seen from remarks in some of the memoirs that there was an understanding of the real situation of the Jews. Kazimierz Rudnicki writes:

The impressions of life alongside the peaceful, poor, and, in my world of the time, very numerous Jewish proletariat, renewed again after a dozen or so years when I met literary characters like Mendel Gdanski, Chawa Rubin, and Meir Ezofowicz, have protected me in life from the venom of racism. I did not consider the Jews to be the chosen race, but I also did not regard them as a cursed nation.[94]

CONCLUSION

Relations were undoubtedly best between the non-Jewish liberal intelligentsia and the Jewish intelligentsia. Tadeusz Kudliński recalls the 'Poets' Conventions' in Płowowice, to which 'Aryans and non-Aryans' came for discussions.[95] Antoni Słonimski, comparing these meetings to Wyspiański's *Wesele* [The Wedding, a famous late nineteenth-century play in which the Jewess Rachel acts as the intermediary between the world of the past and the present], writes: 'The editor of *Czas* was also there, but the only poet was Beaupré, there was Rachel and the host, a Jew, and even a lot of Jews.'[96]

The Belarussian poet Maksym Tank noted in his *Kartki kalendarza* [Pages of the calendar], that at a soirée of Belarussian poetry and songs in Vilna on 15 March 1936 'Nearly the entire Vilna Belarussian colony and

[92] Stefan Otwinowski, *Niedyskrecje i wspomnienia* (Kraków, 1957), 85–6.
[93] Ibid. 86.
[94] Rudnicki, *Wspomnienia prokuratora*, 79.
[95] T. Kudliński, *Młodość mojej stolicy* (Kraków and Wrocław, 1984), 429.
[96] Słonimski, *Alfabet wspomnień*, 157.

many representatives of the Polish, Jewish, and Lithuanian intelligentsia were there.[97]

Economists also worked together. Czesław Bobrowski recalls that some members of the editorial board of the *Gospodarka narodowa*, including himself, 'maintained close relations with Michał Kalecki ... Furthermore, in the latter half of the 1930s I had frequent contacts with Henryk Tennenbaum, an economist, who has been forgotten today but who was the best expert in prewar industry.'[98]

Many non-Jews worked in Jewish institutions such as hospitals[99] or schools. Jewish students were very often friends with their Polish teachers.[100] The co-operation with the Polish progressive youth group in producing the young people's supplement to *Nasz przegląd*, the *Mały przegląd*, is well known.[101]

Tokens of friendship were also exchanged between ordinary people. An example of good neighbourly relations is cited by Franciszek Kotula: 'Jews who got on well with Polish families knew that it was fish which was the required dish for the Christmas Eve meal, and they very often brought fish cooked in a Jewish way in a jar as a present.'[102]

The ways in which the Jews were different—particularly their religion, their great numbers in some towns and in certain areas, and their predominance in the service professions—given the economic situation of Poland in those days, very often gave rise to animosity against them on the part of the Poles. 'However, the difference between aversion', S. E. Nahlik observes, 'and systematic repression is enormous.'[103] Poland in the 1930s was literally sick with the Jewish issue. In this study I have not examined the deterioration of the Jews' plight in this period, or the consequences of it for their relations with the Poles. That is a broad problem which requires separate treatment.

Student disturbances and unscrupulous competitive battles were sad symbols of Polish–Jewish relations in the second half of the 1930s. Undoubtedly 'Endecja' circles were the inspiration behind these events, which, with the help of indiscriminate antisemitic propaganda, were aimed at winning over the largest number of adherents. 'There were moods in our community', Ludwik Krzywicki ascertains, 'which favoured the spread of antisemitic

[97] Tank, *Kartki kalendarza*, 93.
[98] Bobrowski, *Wspomnienia ze stulecia*, 78.
[99] Tank, *Kartki kalendarza*, 216, writes about this; see also Aleksander Pacho, *Narodziny lekarza* (Warsaw, 1970), 269.
[100] Cf. Konrad Bielski, *Most nad czasem* (Lublin, 1963), 156.
[101] Kazimierz Koźniewski describes this co-operation at length in *Zamknięte koła: Wspomnienia z lat 1929–1945* (Kraków, 1984) 87–9.
[102] Kòtula, *Tamten Rzeszów*, 390.
[103] Nahlik, *Przesiane przez pamięć*, 310.

agitation. After all, the Jews were disliked by the most ignorant elements in the towns, and also by merchants and craftsmen.'[104]

There was, however, another Poland, the Poland of Tadeusz Kotarbiński and Maria Dąbrowska, of Adam Próchnik and Leon Kruczkowski, Stanisław Kulczyński and Edward Lipiński, bishop of the Greek Catholic diocese of Stanisławów, Grzegorz Chomyszyn and Jerzy Andrzejewski, who together with several other friends left the *Prosto z mostu* team, in protest at the growing antisemitism of that paper. That other Poland contained a multitude of people who had had enough of thoughtless and senseless action and who understood that this was not the way to heal the social and economic situation of Poland.

Today it is difficult to try to guess how Polish–Jewish relations may have developed further if there had not been the brutal intervention of Nazi Germany. Now in a different Poland, richer for its tragic experiences, these links remain only in memory, a recollection of a once common home.

[104] Krzywicki, *Wspomnienia*, iii. 293.

Shtetl Communities: Another Image

ANNAMARIA ORLA-BUKOWSKA

INTRODUCTION

IF 20 per cent of all Jews—the second largest Jewish community in the world at that time—lived in Poland during the interwar years, then the history and heritage of a plurality of Jews in the world today stem from that territory and time. Yet, as Jerzy Tomaszewski recently pointed out,[1] the history of Jews in Poland in the twentieth century has received much less attention than the earlier period. For obvious reasons, most studies concerned with the present century focus on the Second World War and less on the events preceding it. The interwar years cover a very short time-span, but it was an extremely important and crucial period. Poland was being pieced together and re-created as one nation, and, although the effects of the rule of the three governments which had partitioned Poland did persist to some extent, the history of the country's Jewish population was now being shaped by a sovereign Polish state.

Writings about the interwar years deal primarily with history and statistics in a way which presents a monochromatic picture derived from facts, documents, and censuses. This image needs to be filled in by means of first-hand anthropological and cultural research. In her foreword to *Life is with People* Margaret Mead noted how such work captures 'the essence of a culture just as it was changing forever into something new and strange'.[2] During her travels in Israel, Agata Tuszyńska noticed that: 'In coincidentally met company in Haifa, Tel Aviv, or Jerusalem will always be found someone from Lublin, Białystok, or Warsaw: the grandson of the rabbi from Przysucha or a relative of the innkeeper from Lubartów; a son of a friend from Nowotki Street or the daughter of the tailor from the Biłgoraj market square.'[3] In order to understand the 'new and strange' modern Jewish culture, the context of its predecessor needs to be borne in mind.

[1] J. Tomaszewski, *Najnowsze dzieje Żydów w Polsce: W zarysie (do 1950 roku)* (Warsaw, 1993), 7.
[2] M. Mead, *Life is with People*, ed. M. Zborowski and E. Herzog (New York, 1952), 9.
[3] A. Tuszyńska, *Kilka portretów z Polską w tle: Reportaże izraelskie* (Gdańsk, 1993), 42.

Another tendency in existing literature is to centre on Jews in large municipalities. This focus probably stems from a mistaken impression that most Jews, stereotypically considered urban, lived in sizeable cities. The rising importance of socialist and nationalist movements in the 1920s and 1930s must be acknowledged, assimilation was indeed increasing, and by 1931 a quarter of Poland's Jews lived in the five major urban centres of Warsaw, Łódź, Vilna, Kraków, and Lwów.[4] But in 1921 the majority of Jews in Poland still lived in the smallest towns, where, if modern movements were taking hold, it was a very slow process. Ten years later most of the city dwellers had arrived but recently; their roots were planted in the *shtetl*.

Jews lived everywhere in Poland between the two world wars (the country was about 50,000 sq. km larger than at present). They lived in the lowlands and in the mountains, scattered in smaller and larger groups in most towns and villages, especially along well-worn trade routes. For example, they constituted 5 per cent of the population of the mountainous region of Polish Oravia.[5] In the late nineteenth century, about 40 per cent of Galician Jews lived in rural areas.[6] Of Poland's 630 towns in 1931, 76 per cent had a population of under 10,000. In the interwar years about 40 per cent of all Polish Jews continued to live in villages or townlets, and Jews from towns of a population less than 20,000 comprised 62 per cent of all urban Jews.[7]

Memoirs (*pinkas*es and others) have been published in which Jews write of *shtetl* life, but they show only one view. As fundamental a work as *Life is with People* also focuses on the Jewish profile. For their part, sociologists in Poland have written about images and stereotypes of Jews, or descriptions of Jewish life from a Polish Catholic view. Historians have also transgressed:

Meanwhile the most recent history of Poland and the history of Jews are generally treated separately. Polish historians analyse the history of the Polish state or nationality, usually making no mention of the fate of national minorities, at most considering the relations between them and Poles ... Jewish historians outside Poland are most often interested solely in the history of Jews, disregarding the fact that they lived in a particular country, coexisting with other nationalities. They often limit themselves to an analysis of the relations between Jewish society and other citizens.[8]

---

[4] Tomaszewski, *Najnowsze dzieje*, 162.

[5] A. Krzewniak, 'Żydzi na polskiej Orawie', *Płaj: Zeszyt krajoznawczy towarzystwa karpackiego*, 5 (1993), 46.

[6] A. Bartosz, *The Jews in Tarnów Region* [pamphlet published by the Regional Museum in Tarnów] (Tarnów, 1993), p. [2].

[7] J. Marcus, *Social and Political History of the Jews in Poland, 1919–1939* (New York, 1983), 16.

[8] Tomaszewski, *Najnowsze dzieje*, 5.

Even in fiction, Polish Christian authors tended to portray no more than one or two token Jewish characters, while Polish Jewish writers often completely overlooked the Gentile population among which their characters would have lived. Works that recall the life of Polish Catholics and Jews together in communities are practically non-existent. Some Jewish biographical and autobiographical material does mention contact with the Gentile population. Extremely rare are accounts by Polish Catholics of coexistence with Jews; histories of Polish towns often make only passing mention of Jews, who frequently constituted a majority of the population.

Because of the Holocaust, it is impossible today to write an equally balanced account of Catholics and Jews from the same community. More important from a sociological point of view is the fact that, though it is still feasible to interview Polish Catholics who have never left their birthplace, recollections by Jews from a particular *shtetl* must be coloured by their experiences outside it and by the fact that nearly all live in large Western cities. It is possible, however, to attempt a reconstruction of *shtetl* community life by synthesizing what has been written and said by Polish Catholics and Polish Jews. Below I attempt to sketch *shtetl* life from such observations and descriptions, focusing above all on the interactions between and coexistence of Jews and Gentiles. Without in any way diminishing the importance of such historically and emotionally intense experiences as pogroms and the Holocaust, this essay, in the interests of achieving an accurate, rounded picture, will concentrate on everyday culture and life from an anthropological perspective.

The following account is based on memoirs written by *shtetl* Jews, scholarly works which deal with Gentile or Jewish life (or both) in such communities, and interviews conducted by myself and other students of the Jagiellonian University. Quotations and anecdotes given below with no specific source are from the 27 interviews recorded in 1991 by the present author in the community of Frysztak, and several hundred interviews completed between 1988 and 1990 for Project Galicia, which encompassed nearly all of the towns and cities of considerable Jewish population lying within the area of Austrian Galicia which is still part of present-day Poland.

SHTETL COMMUNITIES

Structure and Organization

Whereas the phenomenon of two or more traditional cultures occupying the same territory and divided along ethnic, religious, and class lines occurs everywhere in the world, the *shtetl* community was of a singular character.

Though it was an anachronism in the twentieth century, it took the force of the Holocaust to wipe it out. Its inhabitants were predominantly traditional, Hasidic Jews living among and with traditional Catholics, primarily peasants. The local community was the centre of their cosmos:

> Despite the multiple impacts from without, until the late nineteenth century a very large proportion of the shtetl population grew up in ignorance of the world beyond ... The whole world was commonly assumed to be just one shtetl after another ... 'the whole world consisted of Slonim, Warsaw and a few towns in between ... As far as we were concerned people lived only in Slonim and in a few places around there. We had heard of Moscow, but it was just a name. People didn't live there.' Space and time ... were fluid, vague concepts, always less real than people and God.[9]

The term 'town' in this context should not call to mind the usual image. Most Polish towns had been founded in the Middle Ages, never expanded much beyond their original limits, and never experienced significant population growth. Very often, even now, a few small farms can be found within town borders, and at least a rooster, goat, or cow might be kept in the yard. 'In a small shtetl the Jews and the peasants may be close neighbors. In a large one, most of the Jews live in the center and the peasants on the outskirts, near their fields. The other inhabitants are the animals who share the streets, the yards, and on occasion the houses.'[10] A town meant a settlement with a charter, a mayor and town council, a square where the weekly market-day and a certain number of annual fairs were held. It was the nucleus of a community which included the nearest villages, which were part of the parish, whose Jews attended synagogue on the more important holidays, and which belonged to the administrative unit governed by the town. Notwithstanding the fact that, after the economic depression of the early 1930s, many Polish towns lost their charter and were officially reduced to village status, they continued to fulfil the main functions they had performed before.

The town had a square, sometimes only a widened, irregular area in the centre, sometimes a well-planned quadrangle accessed by streets at each corner. Here were usually located the post office, bank, and town hall, possibly a small hotel for travelling Jews, a cultural centre, and a holding cell. The town possessed a restaurant, bakeries, a blacksmith, tailor, cobbler, butcher, and a doctor and lawyer. In larger towns there might be a carpenter, metalworker, tanner, hat-maker, and jeweller. There were very often dim roads leading to and through a *shtetl*. If there was a railway

---

[9] M. Zborowski and E. Herzog, *Life is with People* (New York, 1952), 158.
[10] Ibid. 62.

nearby, it was a key mode of transportation, though it too could be cut off in severe winter. The better houses on the market square might be brick and stucco, sometimes two storeys high, with the ground floor serving as a store and the upper one forming the living quarters; some might have plumbing.

Though nearly every village had a schoolhouse with the minimum number of class-grades mandated by law (four, later increased to six), in town there was a school offering higher classes. In larger towns there might be a high school at which pupils from outlying areas boarded. But few children attended the higher classes: school took time away from study of the Talmud for Jewish boys, it took away labour from the farm, and meant a long walk each way for peasant children. Usually only the most determined from among the rural population continued their education in town.

Religious education was also obligatory, and solutions to this issue were various. In some schools religion was the last class of the day and Jewish children were sent home early, or else a Jewish teacher might be hired, or the pupils would be sent out to play, which in winter meant sitting in the back of the classroom. Another problem was posed by classes held on Saturdays. Where big cities might provide special Sabbath schools with lessons on Sunday, in *shtetl*s and villages there was no such accommodation. Occasionally Jewish children were expected to attend but excused from writing; more often they were entirely exempt from attendance on Saturday. Some teachers used that day for a review or summary of the previous week's work, others introduced new material but did not question Jewish children on it until they had a chance to catch up. A *shtetl* could also have ten or more *ḥeders*. As the *melamed* was usually poor, one room in his home functioned as the living-room, kitchen, bedroom, and study room. All Jewish boys attended *ḥeder* on five and a half days each week, except for holidays.

Usually in diagonally opposite corners of the market square there stood the two most significant structures, whose silhouettes dominated the centre: the church and the synagogue. Within close range of each were the cemeteries. But it was also customary to find, in the quarter dominated by the synagogue, a *mikvah*, the *kahal* building, a *beit-midrash* (study house), and often a small hospital or clinic, an orphanage, or a home for the poor. It is important to note that during most of the interwar period *shtetl kehillot* were dominated by wealthy members of the community who were ardently Orthodox Hasidim. In the late 1920s this orientation was being questioned by Zionist and socialist movements, which were repelled for a time by rules which denied voting privileges to persons who were not religious. As Tadeusz Olszański noted, Zionist ideas 'must have barely reached—and only a few—élitist centres like Drohobycz, Nowy Sącz, or Zakopane; they did not get as far as Kołomyj or Stryj, let alone the villages'.[11] Joachim Schoenfeld confirmed this: 'The Zionist organization in our shtetl, however, was anemic and dormant due to the opposition of the Chassidim. They represented the majority and held the upper hand.'[12]

A majority of the Jewish population in Poland made their living in trade, but this principally meant peddled trade rather than retail. Necessity—and tradition, for it was a privilege granted by kings—made market-day the key to the rather primitive economic structures which predominated in Poland. What made a *shtetl* a *shtetl* was its market-place and its market-day. This was its pulse, a meeting-ground, the centre of action, a place relatively empty for six days of the week but transformed on the seventh. Jewish merchants were so important that no town held its market-day on Saturday. High peasant wagons arrived with horses, cows, chickens, fruit and vegetables, grain, dairy products, eggs, and flax. Jewish stalls were set up in their area with furs, hats, jackets, trousers, shoes, boots, and coloured linen. The open market-place was divided into sections by commodity, and each section had its characteristic odour. The pedlar, tailor, cobbler, and blacksmith also travelled to any town within reach:

> Costermongers were out through the week every day attending a market in a different shtetl . . . [They] had their own, or hired, horse-drawn wagons on which they loaded their merchandise for sale, with stalls ready to be put up. Others left for the market with empty containers and boxes to be filled up with merchandise bought at the market from the peasants . . .
>
> In the afternoon the merchandise bought during the day was packed and brought home to the shtetl, where it was sold to the wholesalers or exporters . . . On the other hand, the ones who were not buying but were selling merchandise at the markets replenished their stock at the wholesalers and loaded their wagons for the next trip. After a few hours' sleep, and upon rising in the early morning, they left for another shtetl where on that day the market was held.[13]

Winter snow and cold did not keep people away. A resident of a town with a population of 1,800 describes Thursdays:

> At four a.m. already . . . Here in town, setting up stalls, the arrival of the Jews from Kołaczyce. The arrival of Jews from Niebylec, from Krosno. And each had his stalls. All sorts of goods . . . The carter waited there somewhere below Frysztak . . . The fair ending, everyone loaded things on to wagons and rode back . . . It usually ended at about one or two in the afternoon . . . But during the fair there was

---

[11] T. A. Olszański 'Żydzi w Karpatach, wstępny przegląd demograficzny', *Płaj: Zeszyt krajoznawczy towarzystwa karpackiego*, 5 (1993), 14.

[12] J. Schoenfeld, *Shtetl Memoirs: Jewish Life in Galicia under the Austro-Hungarian Empire and in Reborn Poland, 1898–1939* (Hoboken, 1985), 118.

[13] Ibid. 28.

publicizing. Publicizing. Jews yelled what goods they had. Praised their wares . . . And if he said, let's say, 20 złoty for the merchandise, he sold it for 5 . . . The whole marketplace . . . was crammed with stalls. On both sides . . . Here everyone traded . . . Over there was a cattle market. And there was trade in horses, cattle . . . horse trading was the biggest. After the fair ended, the peasants took off for the inn. After the fair ended, everything was merry, returning home with a song.

Although the majority of local residents were self-employed, earnings were quite modest. *Shtetl* communities often exhibited an almost feudal division of social roles, where the Polish nobility owned land and filled government positions, Jews were traders and merchants, and Polish peasants produced agricultural goods; such an economy did not allow for a high income. One Catholic villager observed that 'Only a few individuals were rich; the majority led a very humble life at a low level.' Frequent small purchases had to be made because few could afford more than 4 oz of salt or a quarter litre of kerosene for lighting. A Jewish villager commented that potato pancakes, a favourite, were made dry because oil was too expensive and used only at Pesach and Hanukkah.[14] The local intelligentsia and wealthy rarely included more than 1–5 per cent of the population.

But there could not be a town without its villages. During this period peasants were self-sufficient to a great extent, but there was always a need to go to town: on market-day to sell and then buy, on holy days for services, and for weddings and funerals. Because there was no public transport, most villagers walked to town:

It was six kilometres. I had to be in town once if not twice each week, because I went to church every Sunday. By foot one walked for an hour. Sometimes in the summer one went through the fields. But in winter that was impossible because of the heaps of snow; the path was not clear, so one walked along the road.

If town residents were generally poor, the entire village lived in poverty. Water was always taken from the well and most people went barefoot.

While towns often had a Jewish majority with few Catholics, the villages had a Christian majority with few Jews; yet nearly every rural settlement included at least one or two Jewish families. The local inn or mill (flour or timber) would be owned by a Jew, likewise often a nearby quarry, forest, or small factory. Yet: 'It would, however, be a misconception to disregard Jewish farmers. There was among them a small group of landowners, certainly and above all in Galicia, where there was even a bilingual (Polish/Yiddish) agricultural periodical.'[15] 'Above all, there were in Poland Jews working their own, not large, farms—the same kind of peasants as their

---

[14] T. Knobel Fluek, *Memories of my Life in a Polish Village, 1930–1949* (New York, 1990), 15.
[15] Tomaszewski, *Najnowsze dzieje*, 167.

neighbours . . .'¹⁶ Toby Knobel Fluek, for instance, was born and grew up in a rural village in eastern Poland. Her family had been there for generations; ten of the 250 families in the village were Jewish. Her father was 'a born farmer, and knew little else'. He worked with his hired help in the fields, cutting, tying, and threshing wheat with primitive tools.¹⁷ A Gentile farmer recalls: 'There were five Jewish families in Cieszyna. Right there by the bend, at the crossing, there was a Jew. His name was Lejzor. He ran an inn . . . it was called *At Lejzor's* . . . Another had the mill, that was Faust . . . But he had probably three morgs [16,800 sq. metres] of land. So he had a horse, and worked, and farmed.' Ilex Beller describes how 'The *peasant* Jews lived in cottages scattered around the countryside. They were innkeepers, blacksmiths, farmers and millers,' and Abraham the dairyman, who delivered milk and kosher butter to the very religious Jews, owned a run-down cottage, two cows, a goat, several chickens, and a lean horse.¹⁸ A woman now living in Israel recounts: 'I remember my grandfather, but he was atypical, because he worked the land. I remember the goat which overturned the Seder table because my brother and I let her in as the prophet Elijah.'¹⁹

With no synagogue or *ḥeder* in such a village, services for the Sabbath and holidays were held in one of the homes, and one person in the village fulfilled all ritual functions or went to the nearest *shtetl* for a shochet or rabbi.²⁰ 'For Rosh Hashanah and Yom Kippur we had a *Baal T'fila* (leader in prayer) come from Podkamien to conduct the services in our house.'²¹ But there was a stigma attached to being a *dorfisher*, a villager. In *Life is with People* a typical *proste* Jew is characterized as being loud, coarse, quick-tempered, strong and broad, and dressed like a peasant.²² Certainly, even on the Sabbath some work had to be done on the farm. A neighbour of some Jewish farmers reports: 'He gave the horse its feed, chased the cow into the field, milked it. Because it was written, even in the Old Testament . . . They asked Christ, "If an ox falls into a well, should one wait until Sunday to pull it out, because it is not allowed on Saturday."'

Interaction and Coexistence

'I went to his place, he came to mine. We lived near each other just past the

---

[16] J. Tomaszewki, *Rzeczpospolita wielu narodów* (Warsaw, 1985), 151.
[17] Knobel Fluek, *Memories of my Life*, 6.
[18] I. Beller, *Life in the Shtetl: Scenes and Recollections*, trans. A. D. Pannell (New York, 1986), 102.
[19] Tuszyńska, *Kilka portretów z Polską w tle*, 40.
[20] Knobel Fluek, *Memories of my Life*, 3.
[21] Ibid. 39.
[22] Zborowski and Herzog, *Life is with People*, 144–5.

main road ... My neighbour was a Jew. I travelled there with the Grinbaums with eggs, and traded in eggs, leather, and butter. I travelled with them, rode through the villages with them. A lot of Jews went to school with me.' So recounted a Roman Catholic from Dubiecko, describing his everyday contact with Jews in that *shtetl*. When questioned about how those relationships were shaped overall, he replied, 'it depends. There were those who hung around and associated with Poles, and there were those who only traded with them. In general it was average.'

The buying and selling of various products was the occasion of the most frequent contact between Jews and non-Jews. In the *shtetl* itself these transactions took place in the market-place or in the shops located in nearly every Jewish house on the square. The streets were lined with small 'general stores crammed with a medley of merchandise calculated to appeal to the taste and needs of the peasant customer'.[23] In one place one could buy groceries, shoe-leather, fabric, cigarettes, wine, spices, raisins, and string. And the most important customer was the first one of the week, who often appeared on Saturday evening: 'They didn't hide from me. Like when I went on Saturday right after the holy day, when the first star shone ... when I went to him, to that friend, he wouldn't let me go, so that I would buy, because it was luck for the whole week until the next Saturday.' Joachim Schoenfeld notes that the first coin earned had to be spat upon for good luck: 'It was a good *potshontek* [początek—beginning].'[24]

The types of products and services that Jews and Gentiles bought from each other were diverse. A Catholic woman fondly remembered how 'the bread in the Jewish stores was better than in the Catholic ones.' A Jewish village girl recalled that 'Mother also baked for the other villagers to get a little extra income. For Easter, the peasants used to order large braided white breads called *Paska*. For the intellectuals—the priest, the engineer—Mother baked round sponge cakes.'[25] Again, 'Mother baked the wedding cakes for the gentiles ... the large cake was necessary, because the peasants invited everybody from the village to their weddings.'[26] Shoemakers might be either Catholic or Jewish. Those who sewed for a living might have clients from any religious background: 'She made the clothes for the intelligentsia and the wealthier people ... Surcie made some blouses for the peasants too, and they in return worked for us in the fields.'[27] 'My mother often made the black velvet vests. She would trace a design on the fabric and use bright-colored threads for the embroidery.'[28] A Catholic woman

[23] Ibid. 63.
[24] Schoenfeld, *Shtetl Memoirs*, 43.
[25] Knobel Fluek, *Memories of my Life*, 23.
[26] Ibid. 59.
[27] Ibid. 8.
[28] Ibid. 58.

from Kolbuszowa describes a family with which she was associated on several levels:

And there was Josef Syskind; he had children, among whom one was my school friend, a very nice girl, Anka, and the second was a blonde ... sweet Rose ... She brought me beautiful books ... And when I embroidered for them ... when I brought them a set, a tablecloth and six napkins, Salcia said to her husband, 'Listen, she said 6 złoty for it, isn't she going to have too little?' And Josef says, 'Salci, however much you give her, it will always be too little, because she has left her eyes there. She had to sew a lot in order to embroider it like that'.

This same woman sewed for other Jewish women in town. Also, as a seamstress who continually needed to buy material, buttons, and trim, she found that she could always enter into an arrangement with the shopkeepers: 'When, for instance, I needed various trimmings for dresses, I went over to, for instance, Mrs Rajckow or Grabszyc.'

It is well known that Jews allowed purchases on credit and often loaned money outright. But the reverse also happened: 'There was a Jew here, Wagszal. I know that somehow he was friends with my father, that Wagszal. So father always lent Wagszal money.' A peasant who built tile stoves for heating and cooking made one for a poor Jewish man in his village; three months later the client offered him a watch and 5 złoty, which was accepted. But most recall how one could always buy on credit, at no added interest, from the Jews. The Catholic tile-stove maker noted one incident in particular when he bought roof tiles on credit in August for a large sum of money; in November 'I sold the heifer ... and straight from the cattle market I went to return the money ... He did not count any interest at all. If you took merchandise from him, the percentage was counted already in the goods. He produced more and gave more. It was better than in a bank now.'

Since more people lived in the villages than in the town itself, and villagers rarely made the trip more than twice weekly, 'Most of the tradesmen in the shtetl were peddlers. Long before daybreak they would be on the road ... The peasants would give the Jewish peddlers a warm welcome. They were old acquaintances and often had been in school together. In addition to bringing merchandise the people needed, the peddlers also brought news of the big city.'[29] 'His wife's grandfather was a wandering pedlar. He sold haberdashery among the villages in the Lublin area: suspenders, buttons, handkerchiefs, thread. All his life he walked and traded with the Poles.'[30] Toby Knobel's uncle made a living buying eggs from peasants which he then sold to city merchants: 'All day he walked along the

---

[29] Beller, *Life in the Shtetl*, 84. [30] Tuszyńska, *Kilka portretów z Polską w tle*, 49.

dirt roads, at times ankle-deep in mud . . .'[31] But in spite of spending most of the day away from home, these pedlars kept kosher; they would take their own pot, drink only hot water or tea, and eat dairy produce. 'Usually the peasants would serve you a meal. The food wasn't too good and we could only eat dairy there. They used wooden dishes and cutlery and we would sit around their long table together with them.'[32] Many Catholic peasants recollect the pedlars, tailors, and especially the Jewish women who came almost daily with their pails to milk the cows and take kosher milk back to town.

Keeping kosher meant selling what was *tref*. This worked to the distinct advantage of both parties as one sold what he could not eat, while the other bought what he liked at a lower price. 'The rabbi examined chickens and roosters and everything for them. Everything. When he observed that it was *tref*, they didn't eat it. More than once I bought a chicken, rooster, or some goose from them. They brought it to mama. More than once mama bought it . . . They sold it cheaper.' Polish Catholics were also well aware that the hindquarters of a calf could be had at a good price.

The inn on the road, often at a crossing, was also a place of contact between Jews and Gentiles as it was the social centre for Gentiles and a place where travelling Jews could get kosher food. Such an inn could be found in practically every village: 'In Frysztak itself there was no inn. But there was one here in that building . . . Then there was one in Glinik, in the village—there was a roadside inn. There was one in Kobyle, an inn by the road. And possibly in Twierdza there were a few inns.' When the clamour of the market was over, the restaurant on the square did not gain many patrons: 'At any rate, peasants didn't go to Aksman's there to get drunk. They only went to Jewish restaurants . . . They felt more at home there. Because a Jew knew how to talk differently.' According to one Jewish account, innkeepers, living out of town among the peasants, were not envied by other Jews.[33] However, the prayerhouses in Podwilk and Zubrzyca Górna were situated in the nearby inn. Further, 'The Oravians very warmly recall the Jewish innkeepers, from whom they could always obtain a loan or credit.'[34]

Undoubtedly, the closest alliances, true friendships, were formed among schoolchildren. 'The relationship between Jewish and non-Jewish students in our school was a friendly one. Jews and non-Jews visited each other's homes and very often did their homework together.'[35] Particularly on Monday, after their absence on Saturday, the Jewish children would borrow

---

[31] Knobel Fluek, *Memories of my Life*, 16.
[32] Zborowski and Herzog, *Life is with People*, 253.
[33] Schoenfeld, *Shtetl Memoirs*, 33.
[34] Krzewniak, 'Żydzi na polskiej Orawie', 47–8.
[35] Schoenfeld, *Shtetl Memoirs*, 116.

notes and ask what material had been covered. Or, as someone who attended the one-room schoolhouse for Cieszyna and Stępina recalls: 'Next to him [a Jewish boy]? There sat Poles. And it often happened that one of those Poles didn't know the answer; then he would prompt them. Yes, or he let them peek.' As a child, a retired schoolteacher had gone to school with Jewish children and noted: 'There were few Jews, but Jewish girls were very amiable girlfriends. We liked each other a lot, those Jewish girls and I.' That same teacher later had a training period in a *shtetl* and related how, though she already had a contract at another school, 'an old Jew came to my aunt and asked, "My lady, perhaps this lady could also stay here another year and continue teaching . . . She treated all the children the same and we would like her to continue teaching here."'

After school was over for the day Jewish and Catholic children did homework and played together. One woman's brother had a Jewish friend: 'He went to that one Jewish family. He went there regularly and borrowed books for himself.' Another woman from town reminisced about her best friend, who, although from an Orthodox family, visited the Catholic girl often: 'She came to my house, where we did our Polish homework . . . I had a lot of girlfriends, but that one—she lived closest to me and she would come. We always left school together and then later did our homework . . . Every day, every day. I went to her place there, she to mine.' A peasant from the village recalled: 'Jankiel, that was my best friend . . . Well, and there was Solomon as well. If he came over, we played together.' In Drohobycz a student of Bruno Schulz's relates: 'My best friends were Poles, the majority of them in any case. I played ball with them, played with them, went to school with them.'[36] The same man who once romped with Jankiel and Solomon recollects:

Come Sunday they came to us as friends . . . and we played together, normally and sportingly . . . Mostly outdoors . . . we made a hoop from a piece of wood, and let it go on the road. Four stood here on the road, four there, and we took some sticks. We let the hoop go to see which side was able to push it past, just like the matches they play today . . . It was a kind of game, that's how we played.

A Catholic woman spoke of her friend:

Her name was Hajka Szmit . . . We knew each other from the last years of school . . . For the fifth, sixth, and seventh elementary grades I went to the school in Frysztak. Well, there I became friends with her and I liked her a lot . . . She came to my home, and [I to hers] when no one was home, because they were kosher Jews. A few times at least I was at her home for fish on Saturday . . . inviting a *goy* on Saturday for fish was a great honour.

[36] Tuszyńska, *Kilka portretów z Polską w tle*, 117.

Of course, boys will be boys: 'We played together ... in school and sometimes near the house too. And as it is between youths, fights resulted. That's how we played near here.' Later the same man related how the Catholic boys would elbow a Jewish boy between them in school. When asked if the Jewish youth fought back, he replied: 'Of course! He was no coward! It was normal. Normal youths. Normal like everyone else.' Except for the *sheyneh*, most Jewish boys did find time to play and they fought, even though that was un-Jewish. There were fights between the *proste* and *balebatish*, and sometimes between Jews and *goyim*: 'It would all start with insulting songs and would be returned with insulting songs. Then the fighting began until their parents stopped it.'[37]

Learning a trade and being apprentices to a craftsman often involved close daily contact between Jews and non-Jews. Knobel's sister had two apprentices, a Jewish girl and a Gentile girl, who came to the house five times a week for a year.[38] A woman from Frysztak remembered:

My sister, she went to a Jew ... She knew Hebrew, they spoke Yiddish. And that Jew, from whom she learnt how to sew, he would say 'Janka, in front of you I can't say anything you wouldn't know' ... And she had a girlfriend, a Jewish girl who came from Cieszyna, from that village ... The two of them went to him. He liked her, he liked my sister.

The Jew was so close to his Gentile apprentice that he entrusted the money in the workshop to her.

The Jews who travelled to a different town each weekday for market hired peasant drivers with wagons to transport them and their goods. Many of these Gentile men recollected how departures took place so early in the morning that the Jews recited their morning prayers on the wagon *en route*. But there were also cases of Jewish animals being hired:

Here there was a Jew who had a horse. When it was necessary to go somewhere, or for some other reason, for instance to pick up the priest, he gave his horse. The driver was Catholic, but the horse was Jewish, and with a Jewish buggy ... They preferred Jewish because Jewish gave good luck ... Later my sister became sick, and they had to take her from here to Niewodna ... and then that Jew—Schtekel was his name—that Jew gave his horses and drove them himself.

In Radymno a man noted that 'Cabmen were Jews. They had a horse, and drove people to the station, to or from the train.'

The employment of a *shabbes goy* is well known, although sometimes such a servant lived with the Jewish family for the entire week. The Roskieses

---

[37] Zborowski and Herzog, *Life is with People*, 343–4.
[38] Knobel Fluek, *Memories of my Life*, 11.

portray the peasant woman who worked for many years in a Jewish home. 'Each morning she would recite the *Moyde ani* prayer with the children ... and make sure that they kept all the rules and regulations of Jewish law.'[39] When asked if her Jewish friend had a Gentile servant, a Catholic woman replied, 'Everywhere probably—everywhere Jews had servants.' More important was the intermingling that occurred in this sphere:

On the other hand, Jewish children acquire from the shtetl servants a large part of their impressions about the non-Jewish world. These impressions are available not only to the children of the rich, for women of modest circumstances who work in a store or at the market often have the help of a peasant girl in the house ... Sometimes the servant will take them to the home of her parents, making sure that nobody gives them forbidden food. Sometimes she even takes them to church.[40]

One Jewish woman recalled how 'Our neighbour Katerina and her children helped us with many chores. Katerina used to sift the wheat in the barn. Her son often shredded it. And her daughter, Jewka, used to run errands for us on the Sabbath when we could not do any work ... Mother gave Katerina some money and stitched over her hand-sewn linen shirts.'[41] Sometimes such help was more casual. A man who, as a boy, came through town on Saturday mornings on his way to school describes such a situation:

There was a store. The Weiners lived there, and ran that store. My parents were their clients from time to time. So it happened that when on Saturday I walked to school, Mr Weiner or Mrs Weiner ... would ask me to come: 'Józek, come light the fire there.' So I went—gladly because it wasn't any real work. I lit it and looked to see if it had lit, and Mrs Weiner, for doing that for her, gave me buns called *szabasówki* ... a sort of sweet bun. It was very tasty, elegant.

This interviewee further pointed out that to be chosen for such a task was considered an honour.

Jews who lived in villages very often employed landless peasants or youths to work their fields. 'Wasyl, our neighbor, worked in the fields for us, cutting the oats and hay with a scythe. Since some fields were about two kilometers away, Wasyl used his horse and buggy to get the wheat and hay to our barn.'[42] In areas where there was both an estate owned by a Catholic lord and a large Jewish holding, some peasants noted that the pay was better at the latter. Many Jewish farmers worked side by side with their help. Others teamed up with a Gentile farmer in order to make the work easier. A farmer from Cieszyna stated:

---

[39] Sh. Anski, quoted in D. and D. G. Roskies, *The Shtetl Book* (Hoboken, 1975), 78.
[40] Zborowski and Herzog, *Life is with People*, 155–6.
[41] Knobel Fluek, *Memories of my Life*, 49.   [42] Ibid. 50.

That Lejzor who had the inn and store—he had a fabric store . . . he was a richer Jew. But as for him standing out, to show that he was richer, that he didn't need anybody—no. He just hitched together with Woś. They also had some land, so one came and both of them worked in the field, ploughed, sowed. Their farming together was normal. The farming over, later both of them rode home together . . . This one gave one horse, that one the other. So they turned out the manure, ploughed, then later sowed.

Although there were five Jewish farmers in the village, each of them always teamed up with a Gentile.

Both religious communities included numerous craftsmen of all types, among whom skill was more important than faith. Franciszek Grela was a highly regarded tile-stove maker, particularly known for building a 'Sabbath oven' in which to keep Saturday's food warm and slowly cooking. Once, a very wealthy Jew who owned the forests surrounding the village sent a driver to fetch Grela when, after a period of disuse, the smoke was failing to go up the chimney. After assessing the situation, the craftsman asked for some straw and lit a flame big enough to clear away the cobwebs. The Jew asked what he owed:

And I say, 'For that I can take nothing. I only ask that you take me home by horse.'
'Oh no. I will give you some Sabbath vodka to drink.'
Nice vodka it was, the raw liquor with syrup. And in a liqueur glass like a finger. Well, he poured some for me, so I drank.
'This is Sabbath vodka, we always drink one like this on the Sabbath.'
The liqueur glass had a sort of long stem, crystal.

It was generally the case in Galician towns that, where Jews comprised a large percentage of the town population, they held positions on the local town council. Although the mayor would be a Roman Catholic, the deputy mayor was a Jew. Sometimes—for example, on the death of the mayor—his deputy would succeed and fill the position until the end of the term. The daughter of a Catholic town-council member recalled one such case:

I remember that when that mayor died they wanted to make my father the mayor. I remember as if it was today how the Jews came on Saturday, still dressed—because, you know, they went to synagogue in those fur-trimmed hats. They all implored my father . . . so, so solemnly dressed, if I may say so. Well, they asked my father to become the mayor, but my father refused because he felt that it might—how can I put it?—well, that he would have to offend someone or something, take someone's place.

Joachim Schoenfeld spoke of the Polish mayor in his town: 'Anyway, he was no anti-Semite, knew everyone in the shtetl, spoke Yiddish fluently, and even dispensed medicines to poor Jews at no charge. He was the pharmacist in the city.'⁴³ Rymanów Jews also 'took part in the political life, and were often members of the town council and various types of delegations appointed by the town.'⁴⁴ Villages also had their political leaders, who often included prominent Jews in their number. In any case, meetings held to decide matters of importance to the village were attended by all members of the community.

More than anything, Jews and Catholics were neighbours and treated each other as such. Sometimes they even lived under the same roof:

There were Jews and Catholics living in that house ... Of course. How did that look? ... there was a wooden house in which there was a hall. They traded in cattle. In one room there were Catholics. Going further down the hall, in the next room there were Jews. And through this corridor one went also to the barn. Yes, because they bought up cattle, so they led the animal in and at once put it in the barn. And later at the markets they led them out and traded them ... The Catholic family was the Pietrzyckis. In the second—the last name I don't remember—in the second lived, let me see, Abram. Abram. And right under that same roof, except with a separate entrance, there lived a Jew by the name of Chava. They lived very much in unity, those who lived there.

Sometimes, though, Jews and Catholics lived more separate lives:

Jews don't use the bridge very often. It leads only to the village, and who but a peddler has any reason to spend time with the peasants? Except when it's *shabes* ... what better opportunity is there to make a dash for the village? Some of the peasants are friends from way back and let us climb the trees. They know that we'll pay them later on in the week.⁴⁵

A woman whose family was one of two non-Jewish ones on the marketplace remembers how her 'Mother conversed with them; they came over, sat on the porch.' 'We used to hear all sorts of stories, but we were good friends with all our Gentile neighbors.'⁴⁶ A literate Jew might help an illiterate peasant with reading, or with writing a letter to family in America; friends of the miller would be presented with the best flour just before the Easter or Christmas holidays. 'During the winter evenings, Mother would invite our neighbors, the peasant women, to a feather-plucking party. They sat around the table telling jokes and stories, having a good time while the work was done.'⁴⁷

---

⁴³ Schoenfeld, *Shtetl Memoirs*, 123.
⁴⁴ J. Konieczny, 'Historia społeczności żydowskiej w Rymanowie', *Płaj: Zeszyt krajoznawczy Towarzystwa Karpackiego*, 5 (1993), 64.
⁴⁵ Roskies and Roskies, *The Shtetl Book*, 7.
⁴⁶ Zborowski and Herzog, *Life is with People*, 153.
⁴⁷ Knobel Fluek, *Memories of my Life*, 55.

Yes. They were normal neighbours like Christians. When there were holidays the Jews here, after all, when they had their holiday pastries or *matzah*, or something like that, they always brought them to us. They brought us those *matzot*. They also had their special baked goods. It was called laykakh cake. It was like sponge cake, only better . . . That they brought to us.

Jews also recall these exchanges: 'On Pesach the Jewish students gave their non-Jewish colleagues some matzo and received from them pisanki [decorated eggs]. At Christmas time the non-Jewish students treated their Jewish colleagues to kutyiah (a traditional meal) made from boiled wheat with honey, nuts, and poppy seeds.'[48] Ilex Beller tells of how Purim pastries such as *homantashen* were carried from one family to another and to the village officials.[49] One interviewee remembered a different treat: 'But most of all they liked liver baked in ashes—in the oven it was hot, she sifted even more ashes, put the liver in, baked it, then washed off the ashes. It was delicious! I ate it myself at Mrs Birnbaum's.'

Because of kosher laws, edibles were generally offered by Jews to Gentiles. A Catholic woman whose Jewish friend often visited could only suggest tea or water, and never tried to proffer food because it was *tref*. Not to offer food to a guest was impolite, not to eat what was offered was also an insult, but in a Gentile home one could eat only parve food and only from uncontaminated vessels. The farmer whose Jewish neighbours always teamed up with the Christian horses, noticed that when two Catholics worked together they ate at one of their homes, but a Jew would always want to eat at his own home: 'Well, because it would be what was called *tref*. That was their religion, which did not allow him to eat at a Pole's.'

The status of neighbour also carried some responsibility of care in time of need. 'We took care of each other very much. I remember when my mother was sick, all the Jewesses swore, all of them, to save my mother . . . I was a little girl, but I remember it like today, the group of Jewesses, how they saved my mother.' The respondent from Radymno stated: 'When they lived next door, then when there was something bad, let's say that someone had died, the Jews sympathized. My mother died, or someone at home, or else someone had some bad luck—and they sympathized. It even happened at times that they came with some material help.' A woman who lived on a small farm just within the city limits tells of how, while her mother and sister were in church and she was alone, their cow began to calf. She went across the road to the home of a Jew who traded in livestock.

In fact I had no other choice. I ran to him here because he traded in cows. Ran to those who were there. I just told them, 'Come, because my cow is calving and there is no one at home, neither mother nor father.' They were praying then. You see,

---

[48] Schoenfeld, *Shtetl Memoirs*, 116.   [49] Beller, *Life in the Shtetl*, 38.

they gathered like that, in a home—on whatever day . . . I can't say anything against them because about five or six came running. And they calved it! Of course! . . . You couldn't see the cow for the Jews gathered around it.

Small towns and villages, with their wooden buildings, were often susceptible to fires, and then everyone was expected to come and help put out the flames. 'In the memory of the residents of Oravia remains the active participation by the Jews in the extinguishing of the church fire in Podwilk, and their financial participation in its rebuilding.'[50] And when a fire broke out at a Jewish farmer's home.

All the families went to help to Jankiel's father's when the old house was burning . . . And people flocked there to save everything—they drenched it, and saved it . . . I too was there when it was burning, to carry things out . . . People flew in, they saved everything. Nothing there was burnt, nothing inside the house. Only they laughed about how he knew that there was going to be a fire because the down comforter was tied up in a sheet.

'That was a wedding. Who didn't come? Even the peasants from all around the shtetl. It lasted 3 weeks.'[51] 'And they, for instance, at Faust's, the brother of Faust's wife—Neche—he went everywhere with those boys. Everywhere to Catholic weddings. And when his sister got married, the boys were there at the wedding to see what it was like.' As a rule, not everyone was formally invited, but many watched the wedding, which took place outdoors, and then gathered outside the house, where the bride's father would come out with trays of food to treat everyone; in town, the family of the bride might come the next day with cakes. The woman whose sister was apprenticed with a Jew recalled:

When it was her wedding the town was full of Jews from the top of the hill to the bottom . . . She even sent her invitations for the wedding. Whenever one of the Jewish girls here got married, we got invitations. Mother went and she went . . . I saw the reception, of course. She was dressed in white and sat in a corner. And she had *laykakh*. And there was vodka, and she hosted . . . They had very beautiful weddings . . . And then together we went to the home of the young couple. And such a lot of people; there was a crowd because they always took their vows on the main road . . . There were many Polish people there at that wedding.

Funerals in the *shtetl*, however, were never attended by members of the other group. Catholics noticed that women and some of the male Jews stayed away from the cemetery. When a neighbour died, the custom was to stand reverently outside the home when the body was carried out.

[50] Krzewniak, 'Żydzi na polskiej Orawie', 47.
[51] Zborowski and Herzog, *Life is with People*, 270.

There were few secrets in the *shtetl*. Control was inseparable from a strong feeling that individuals were collectively responsible for one another. Schoenfeld described how this worked when an influx of maskilic Jews threatened the status quo in his shtetl. These non-Hasidic Jews went to the Christian butcher to buy food, including pork, on fasting-days.

Some time later the butcher asked a [local] Jew to tell him on what day of the year it was that Jews were allowed to eat pork. And so the secret of these *trefniakes* ... became known and an uproar ensued in the *shtetl*. The parnassim (the board of the Jewish community organization) supplied the Polish authorities with a list of the unwanted immigrants, insisting that all the revolutionaries be ordered out of the shtetl.[52]

Notice should be taken of the fact that the Jewish authority appealed to the Polish authorities for assistance in this matter. As for the Catholics, Oravian innkeepers utilized this method: 'During the time of the mass, the inns were closed and all the guests chased off to church.'[53] The servant, often fluent in Yiddish, could 'become more a stickler for religious observance than some of the household, and will see to it that the boys do not eat before praying, sharply remind any child who is careless about wearing his cap ... and take pride in keeping the ... pots rigidly separate.'[54] Further, where there was no *mikvah* nearby, a few women would have a peasant drive them, and if one of the women did not turn up, the driver would ask why not.[55] On the other hand, relationships within certain trades and, later, the influence of reformed Judaism, led to more, albeit still rare, ties between Jews and non-Jews in the form of activities such as card-playing or discrete visits to a non-Jewish friend where a Jew could drink vodka and eat sausage. Joachim Schoenfeld tells of how

Usually a group of 5 or 6 students mounted their bicycles in the late afternoon on Saturdays and went for the 45 minute ride [to Czernowitz to see a play]. However, in order to hide the fact that they were riding their bicycles before the Sabbath was over, the bicycles were taken on Friday to the house of a non-Jewish colleague, who lived outside the city on the way to Czernowitz.[56]

It might be expected that in the area of religious observance any intermingling would be absolutely precluded, but Catholics and Jews went to each other's place of worship, bathed in the same *mikvah*, and shared the same holiday treats. Furthermore, Jewish funds were often lent for the building

---

[52] Schoenfeld, *Shtetl Memoirs*, 121.
[53] Krzewniak, 'Żydzi na polskiej Orawie', 47.
[54] Zborowski and Herzog, *Life is with People*, 155.
[55] Ibid. 286.
[56] Schoenfeld, *Shtetl Memoirs*, 111–12.

of a new church; while in Śniatyn the synagogue was built and decorated by Jewish and Gentile craftsmen.[57] In Polish Oravia, 'The priest going from house to house for Christmas visits did not actually go into the Jewish homes, but in front of each one he found some sort of gift for himself.'[58] There were three Jewish farming families in the Łemko village of Zyndranowa:

> I remember quite well how older boys went from house to house on Christmas Day carolling. Please try to imagine how much those people grew accustomed to our Łemkos, since they were angry if the boys did not come to them. They wanted the boys to visit them on the occasion of our holidays, to come into their homes so that they could rejoice together with us and show respect for our holidays ... on our holidays they never went out into their fields. There was mutual observance.[59]

It should be noted that shops would be closed and work would be halted on any major Christian holiday such as Christmas or Easter. Further, on Corpus Christi, or when the bishop came to town, the Jews and their rabbi would participate in the procession. All the same, on any normal Sunday stores would be open, to the gratification of the peasants for whom this was one of two weekly trips into town.

National holidays, such as 11 November (Independence Day) or 3 May (Constitution Day), tended to take on a somewhat Christian character. Thus, Jews would take part in the celebration but would stand aside when the procession stopped by the church or a cross in town. However, on those days the Jewish community would also hold special services in the synagogue. A woman whose father was a town councillor recounted how her father and other representatives were invited to and attended these services.

In the *shtetl* the most important holiday was the Sabbath, and Catholics could not help noticing the extraordinariness of this day. 'Słońce nisko, szabas blisko'—'Sun low, Sabbath near'—they would say. As nearly everything the non-Jews might need was purchased at Jewish stores, any last-minute shopping had to be done before the synagogue assistant began knocking on the doors and shutters, giving the signal to close up. If a peasant was driving Jews home from market in another town, he was well aware that their journey had to end before sunset. If a Gentile girl was engaged for the Sabbath, she knew that her working day was about to begin. On Friday night the streets would be filled with Jewish men and boys heading for synagogue; on Saturday, after morning services there was walking and visiting: 'The walk was, I remember, on Saturday. It was still

---

[57] Schoenfeld, *Shtetl Memoirs*, 81.
[58] Krzewniak, 'Żydzi na polskiej Orawie', 47.
[59] T. Gocz, 'Żydzi w Zyndranowej', *Płaj: Zeszyt krajoznawczy Towarzystwa Karpackiego*, 5 (1993), 89.

their Jewish holy day. And they walked here, all the way to the cemetery and back. It was impossible to get across. It was that crowded.' With the rise of the third star on Saturday, the shops reopened for business and everything returned to normal.

Although their liturgical calendars differed vastly, Gentiles living with Jews knew their holidays very well, and what they might need for them. 'The peasants knew that Sukkot was coming and brought to the marketplace lots of reeds and cornstalks for sale'; they also knew to bring the willow-twigs for the morning prayer of Hoshanah Rabbah.[60] Sukkot, however, also gave birth to many folk sayings: 'Because precisely when there were the *kuczki* [booths in which Jews were supposed to live for the period of the holiday], there was rainfall. People said, "Oh, *kuczki* are coming. Time to finish up the work, because there'll be non-stop rain."' A Jewish observer affirmed, 'It is so common to eat these meals in a downpour.'[61] It was common to 'sell' goods to a non-Jew for a token sum, and then buy them back for the same price after Passover.[62] But Pesach was also well known as the season at which wheat had to be specially handled. One Polish farmer described in great detail the entire process, from the purchase of the grain, to the treatment of the mill where it was ground, to the procedures taken with the oven where the *matsah* was baked. It was not insignificant for such farmers that Jews paid double the going rate for the wheat.

Catholics and Jews alike, particularly as children or youths, were inquisitive and interested in each other's religious practices. The seamstress from Kolbuszowa, on seeing Jews standing by the river [on the Jewish New Year], asked her Jewish friend what they were doing and was told that it was a form of confession, that bad deeds were being thrown into the water. The same woman expressed how she felt about Jewish prayers: 'I was very fond of listening to those prayers. I don't know if you can call it singing or a kind of searching, a kind of lamentation.' Conversely, a Jewish man from Drohobycz remembered that 'I often even went to church. I didn't pray, but only went to look, just as they would come to the synagogue. They helped us too—for instance, with lighting the fire on Saturday.'[63] A woman from Rymanów was very curious about the synagogue interior, just as her girlfriends were about the church, and so one Rosh Hashanah she was invited to the gallery, where she looked through the windows with the rest of the women.[64] Another Catholic woman recollected how

---

[60] Schoenfeld, *Shtetl Memoirs*, 100–1.
[61] Zborowski and Herzog, *Life is with People*, 398.
[62] Ibid. 115.
[63] Tuszyńska, *Kilka portretów z Polską w tle*, 117.
[64] A. Małeta, 'Żydzi w pamięci mieszkańców Bobowej', *Płaj: Zeszyt krajoznawczy towarzystwa karpackiego*, 5 (1993), 85.

one Jewish child wanted to stay on for religious instruction in school because she liked the priest. More than one Catholic took an express interest in the appearance of the rabbi presenting the Torah when the bishop came to town.

There was even contact between peasants and the local rabbi. Respecting his authority and aware of the tradition of settling legal matters with the rabbi, 'Even a judge would sometimes ask two quarreling Jews, "Why don't you go to the rabbi?" Often a Gentile would suggest to a Jew with whom he had a dispute that they submit the dispute to the rabbi for a decision.'[65] A man in Radymno spoke thus of the rabbi: 'He was a very pious person, because if the rabbi said something, it was sacred. Because when a Catholic sometimes went to complain to the rabbi about some Jew, and [the Jew] was wrong, then he said "I will take away your seat in the synagogue. You will not have a seat." That's how I recall it.' Sometimes Christians approached the rabbi simply for counsel:

The prosteh yiden [lowest socio-economic class of Jews] and the peasants considered my grandfather a holy man, in fact they used to call him Holy Rabbi . . . and the Gentiles always came to him for advice, they never went to court. He was a very wonderful person and the peasants were extremely loyal to him. Once in a big storm he . . . went to shul . . . to say evening prayers. When he didn't come back . . . my grandmother went to the peasant and asked him to look for my grandfather. It didn't take five minutes and in the big storm the whole town of Gentiles was out looking for the Holy Rabbi. They found him in shul studying with some men.[66]

A more striking form of contact was intermarriage or a change of faith, which was considered a catastrophe by the Jewish family. Non-Jewish youths, however, often flirted with Jewish girls, who were considered particularly beautiful, and at least one Catholic man spoke of a neighbouring Jewish girl who disclosed that she would prefer a Polish boy from the village. Though more permanent unions were unacceptable, some did occur. Perhaps because Jewish women enjoyed more freedom and, therefore, had more contact with non-Jews, most such marriages involved a Jewish bride who changed her faith and married a Catholic. Apart from mourning as if the girl had died, reactions by the family could be extreme. A woman from Kolbuszowa told of one Jewess who drowned herself in the well in the market square because her daughter was engaged to marry the Gentile lawyer in town.

Also, the business of selling livestock sometimes resulted in a Catholic witnessing ritual slaughter by the *shochet* or a Jew seeing a butcher at work; reactions from either side were nearly always negative. Contact also occurred

[65] Schoenfeld, *Shtetl Memoirs*, 17.
[66] Zborowski and Herzog, *Life is with People*, 221.

in the military, but seldom. The armed forces in Poland were primarily Catholic, and wealthier Jews very often paid bribes to get their sons out of mandatory service, since keeping kosher in the garrison often meant a starvation diet. Those Jews who were drafted were often extremely unhappy, and one Polish man recalled saving a Jewish soldier who wanted to drown himself rather than continue serving.

Language is always considered a factor defining ethnicity, and can exert an isolating influence. However, German was the official language of the Prussian and Austro-Hungarian partitions, so that most Poles who attended school before the end of the First World War had at least a rudimentary knowledge of that language and could therefore understand some Yiddish; they certainly noticed the similarities between the languages. Ilex Beller observed that the Jews in Grodzisko Dolne spoke German when under Galician rule, but 'They also spoke enough Polish to communicate with the peasants who lived in the surrounding countryside ... Even the few Catholics in the village spoke Yiddish.'[67] This is confirmed by a *shtetl* observer cited in the Roskies' book: 'especially in the *shtetlech*, there were a good many gentiles who spoke Yiddish well and used Yiddish even among themselves. There were even some who knew so much about Jewish matters that if not for their gentile appearance, they would be mistaken for Jews.'[68] In Kolbuszowa a Catholic woman was still able to recite various songs in Yiddish. Another woman revealed: 'They spoke in Yiddish, so I learnt to speak Yiddish with them ... I spoke like a Jewish girl with them, to that degree ... I knew it perfectly.' The reaction of some of the shopkeepers was telling: 'I know that when I came in and they [the shopkeepers] had some secret, not to be spoken in front of the little girl, [they would say] "Moydele nol vida."' More than one respondent recited Yiddish words and demonstrated knowledge of the Hebrew alphabet, which some had been able to read and write. As for Jews speaking Polish, non-Jews assessed their ability as very good; at times they indicated that older ones spoke it worse or that women knew the Gentile language best. Schoenfeld counters that opinion: 'Most of the Jews with the exception of the younger generation and, of course, the intelligentsia, spoke only Yiddish.'[69] But a woman in Israel notes that her grandmother 'was very elegant and intelligent, but she played with peasant children' and therefore used their dialect and terminology.[70]

Language was not the only element that Christians and Jews appropriated from one another. There were common superstitions such as giving salt and bread to assure luck, touching a button when meeting a chimney-sweep, and

---

[67] Beller, *Life in the Shtetl*, 10.
[68] Sh. Anski, quoted in Roskies and Roskies, *The Shtetl Book*, 78.
[69] Schoenfeld, *Shtetl Memoirs*, 8.
[70] Tuszyńska, *Kilka portretów z Polską w tle*, 41.

not shaking hands over a threshold.[71] There was a Yiddish saying: 'A peasant proverb is like a quote from the Torah.'[72] Mutual respect for magic powers meant that a peasant woman might be called in to deal with a case of the evil eye, just as peasants often consulted the rabbi. '[In] many places even the Orthodox employ a peasant woman if they need, and can afford, the luxury of a wetnurse. Undoubtedly this practice has contributed to the mingling of Jewish and non-Jewish superstitions and magic practices, so that it is often difficult to tell which group has borrowed from the other.'[73] Folk motifs in art were also transferred: 'In decorating her home she will draw chiefly from peasant art. Any household embroideries are apt to be copied from peasant themes.'[74] Even the Jewish calendar was not immune: 'Urbanized though its people are in occupation and in habits, they share with their agricultural neighbors the feeling that the year begins with the springtime rebirth of nature... To us in the shtetl, Pesakh was considered the beginning of the year. People were hired from Pesakh to Pesakh, new clothes were bought, and so forth.'[75]

CONCLUSION

'In the shtetl everyone was busy with his own way of making parnusse (living) and didn't, wouldn't, or rather couldn't care less if there existed a world beyond the marketplace or the store.'[76] This was a cosmos, and the most significant people were those who lived in it; the most meaningful interpersonal relationships were among its inhabitants. It is true that the primary tie between Jews and non-Jews was economic, but there were more personal friendships. The closest such attachments undoubtedly occurred among school children and women. A connection was also easier between *proste* or rural Jews and Catholics; assuredly, the different lifestyle of village Jews facilitated more bonding there. But contact was daily and everywhere, and even where the market-place was the basis of cultural intermingling, it epitomized interdependence, reciprocity, and a working equilibrium.[77]

In all cases, the essence was two halves forming a symbiotic whole. 'Experience is seldom perceived as unmixed, for the shtetl is not given to absolute and categorical contrasts—things are seldom all black or all white.'[78] Life was seen as a complex of contrasts which were complemen-

---

[71] Schoenfeld, *Shtetl Memoirs*, 42–4.
[72] Roskies and Roskies, *The Shtetl Book*, 50.
[73] Zborowski and Herzog, *Life is with People*, 326.
[74] Ibid. 364.   [75] Ibid. 383.
[76] Schoenfeld, *Shtetl Memoirs*, 110.
[77] Zborowski and Herzog, *Life is with People*, 67.
[78] Ibid. 91.

tary, not conflicting.⁷⁹ 'Moreover, while each group harbors a stereotype of the other, each sees the other as an essential partner in the life of the community. One is the man of action, the other the man of thought.'⁸⁰ Thus does *Life is with People* define the relationship between the *sheyne* and *proste* Jew. The same can be said of that between the *shtetl* Jew and the peasant Gentile. 'The cultures did affect each other; the gentile servant learned to keep kosher just as the Jewish boys read of the valor and prowess of Polish real and fictional heroes.'⁸¹

Most literature in this field focuses on one of the two cultures and tends to treat the Jewish community as an island; but 'What Jews wanted in particular was, not isolation from the Christians, but insulation from Christianity.'⁸² Separatist thinking perpetuates the myth that Jews and Christians in a *shtetl* community lived side by side but absolutely unconnected; it encourages the stereotypical view that ethnic groups live more in conflict than in peace. A skewed image is formed which ignores the reality that ethnic groups, living in a traditional culture and occupying shared territory, will find a place in each other's world and together create their own. It may be that by calling attention to the differences scholars overemphasize the lines that divide at the expense of those that connect. A peasant farmer recognized the latter kind:

And when he was leaving he said 'With God.' 'With God' and he left . . . and if he said 'With God', that means that he recognizes God, and after all we all believe in one God. Whether it was a Jew, or a Pole, or a Catholic, everyone in one God. Only that there are different faiths, rituals, but God is the same.

While it is true that they will periodically find themselves in confrontation, most of the time they will live in co-operative symbiosis.

Yet contemporary researchers very often split apart those mutual dependencies, and, as a result deny themselves the possibility of understanding the course of historical processes.⁸³ That which was becomes lost in memory, and then, lost from memory, passes into fiction. There is a great need for more research into and emphasis on the intercultural contact between Polish Catholics and Polish Jews. While sources are still available, social anthropologists and ethnographers should paint a portrait of that Poland which includes all its shapes and colours. As the Jewish writer Grigori Kanowicz discerned: 'those little towns are our second Old Testament. All of us came from there, Polish writers too—Schulz, Stryjkowski. For many it is an exotic landscape.'⁸⁴

⁷⁹ Ibid. 264. ⁸⁰ Ibid. 146–7. ⁸¹ Ibid. 17.
⁸² Roskies and Roskies, *The Shtetl Book*, 34.
⁸³ Tomaszewski, *Najnowsze dzieje*, 6.
⁸⁴ Quoted in Tuszyńska, *Kilka portretów z Polską w tle*, 109.

The Civil Rights of Jews in Poland 1918–1939

JERZY TOMASZEWSKI

THE Polish republic, beginning in November 1918, consolidated territories that had previously formed part of Russia, Austria-Hungary, and Germany, and took over the legislation of these territories. In effect, at this time different laws, established by the previous ruling nations, were valid in different regions of the republic; uniform laws, consistent with the principles underlying the new state, were then gradually established. By the time of the Second World War this had been generally accomplished, but in some legal areas (e.g. family law) regional differences still obtained.

One of the problems that the sovereign republic had to resolve was the legal status of Jews. In Russia they were subject to various discriminatory laws; in Austria-Hungary the Yiddish and Hebrew languages were outlawed in public life. The legislation established in the Prussian partition had less significance, since there was only a small Jewish population in that area.

It was very difficult to settle the question of which Jews were Polish citizens. The present study is confined to the question of civil rights and discriminatory laws alone. It omits the very important problem of achieving uniformity in the laws that regulated the status of Jewish religious communities, and does not touch upon the quarrel concerning conceptions of national and cultural autonomy.

On 1 February 1919, in a circular sent to subordinate administrative organs, Minister of the Interior Stanisław Wojciechowski wrote: 'I feel compelled to remind you that the Jewish population enjoys the Polish civil rights just as the aboriginal Polish population does and must not be subjected to violence or abuse of law. In independent Poland the citizens are not divided into categories.'[1] This was, however, only a declaration, which could not in itself abolish various existing discriminatory regulations; nor

[1] Archiwum Akt Nowych w Warszawie [archives of contemporary records, referred to below as 'AAN'], Komitet Narodowy Polski w Paryżu [Polish national committee in Paris], vol. 2066, p. 119.

could it answer the question of who in fact had the right to be granted Polish citizenship. The legal basis for this could only be established by international treaties, by a constitution, and by bills due to be passed by the Sejm.

The peace treaties signed by Poland (with Germany on 28 June 1919, with Austria on 10 September 1919, and with the Soviet Republics on 18 March 1921) regulated civil rights according to the laws valid in these countries. General principles were settled by the so-called Little Treaty of Versailles (also known as the Minorities Treaty) of 28 June 1919, which stated:

Poland admits and declares to be Polish *ipso facto* and without the requirements of any formality German, Austrian, Hungarian, or Russian nationals habitually resident at the date of the coming into force of the present Treaty in territory which is or may be recognized as forming a part of Poland but subject to any provisions in the Treaties of Peace with Germany and Austria respectively.[2]

The quoted passage did not mention the Polish–Soviet treaty, which was concluded only in March 1921. In practice, the most difficult problem in the rights protected at Versailles appeared to be that of how to interpret the term 'habitual residency' *stałe zamieszkanie*).

The treaty with Germany recognized as habitual residents those who had been living in territories which formed part of Poland before 1 January 1908. The treaty with Austria resolved that:

Toute personne ayant l'indigenat (pertineza) sur un territoire faisant antérieurement partie des territoires de l'ancienne monarchie austro-hongroise acquiera de plein droit et à l'exclusion de la nationalité autrichienne, la nationalité de l'État exerçant la souveraineté sur le dit territoire.

The Polish–Soviet treaty recognized as Polish citizens the persons included in the records of habitual residents of the former Polish kingdom, or registered in a district office (*gmina*) or in a state organization (*soslovnoye obshchestvo*) in the territories of the former Russian Empire attached to Poland.[3]

All the treaties permitted individuals to opt for citizenship of another country. Identical provisions were contained in the bill of citizenship enacted on 20 January 1920. That bill in addition granted the right to acquire Polish citizenship to all Polish nationals, wherever they had hitherto been living (which encouraged political emigrants to return home), and

---

[2] *Dziennik Ustaw Rzeczypospolitej Polskiej* [referred to below as *DzURP*] (1919), No. 110, item 728.

[3] *DzURP* (1920), No. 35, item 200; ibid. (1925), No. 35, item 200; ibid., No. 17, appendix; ibid. (1921), No. 49, item 300.

defined the principles of acquiring Polish citizenship (by process of naturalization) for persons not included in any of the above-mentioned categories.[4]

Every person who had the right of residence in a territory which was previously part of the territories of the former Austro-Hungarian monarchy will obtain the full right to the nationality of the state which is exercising sovereignty over the said territory, to the exclusion of his right to Austrian nationality.

Practical application of the provisions of the treaties proved not to be easy, especially in the former Russian territory. The reasons were both objective and political. In many eastern regions (and to a lesser extent in central areas) the documents, such as records of habitual residents, community records, etc., that could establish the right of an individual to acquire Polish citizenship were destroyed during the war, and interested persons were frequently not able to submit any sufficiently reliable documents. The administrative organs, on the other hand, aware of the radical, social and national moods prevailing among the non-Polish population living in these regions, often interpreted the provisions of the treaties over-rigorously and demanded that persons applying for Polish citizenship submit numerous documents. The authorities were also prompted by the fact that a considerable number of refugees from Russia, who had not been granted the right to acquire Polish citizenship, stayed in Poland at that time. Since only Polish citizens were enfranchised, as long as the Russian refugees were not Polish citizens they were deprived of the vote, so that possible 'revolutionaries' among them might not be proposed as candidates or vote in elections. This situation, however, coexisted with the obligation upon persons of undefined citizenship to perform duties to the benefit of the state, such as, for example, military service.

Some specific groups among the population (especially Jews) which habitually lived in the territories attached to Poland raised additional difficulties. Their habitual residence was not formally confirmed by the appropriate documentation since, upon moving to another locality of habitual residence, they had neglected to inform the respective administrative organ and had thus not obtained the appropriate registration. It may be that by neglecting the formalities they wished to bypass some restrictions of the Russian law.

In effect, the category of people of undefined citizenship grew quite large (according to some estimates it comprised about 600,000 Jews).[5] These people were given provisional certificates defining their citizenship as that of

[4] Ibid. (1920), No. 7, item 44.

[5] This figure, considered to be an exaggeration, was quoted by the National Party during its propaganda campaign in the 1930s. The same figure was quoted by Gen. Felicjan Sławoj Składkowski at a session of the budget committee of the Sejm on 27 Nov. 1928: AAN, Prezydium Rad Ministrów [praesidium of the Council of Ministers, referred to below as 'PRM'], vol. 3A15, p. 23.

'the former Russian Empire', which put them in a legal no-man's-land since the Empire had ceased to exist in 1917. This situation produced numerous inconveniences, for example when someone in this category wished to purchase a piece of land or a house, or to engage in certain professions.

The question of granting Polish citizenship to Jews and other minorities of undefined citizenship became the subject of a long-term legal dispute accompanied by political struggles. Thus, from a copy of a decision by the Supreme Court of 19 October 1922 found in the files of Deputy Yitzhak Grünbaum we learn that Beniamin Nisman and his wife Nina, inhabitants of Węgrów, had been crossed off the electoral register pertaining to elections for the Sejm and Senate since they could not submit any document proving that they were Polish citizens. The Supreme Court did not consider whether, by virtue of the Polish–Soviet treaty of March 1921 (the Riga treaty), they had the right to acquire Polish citizenship, but stated that 'By enlisting as a soldier in the army, Beniamin Nisman acquired Polish citizenship, even though he had not earlier been granted it' (whereby his wife too, became a Polish citizen, and ordered that the husband and wife be entered into the electoral register.[6]

Probably encouraged by this decision, on 28 November 1922 Nisman applied to the County Office (Starostwo) in Węgrów requesting that he and his family be recognized as Polish citizens. However, the decision of the head of the office (starosta) of 23 April 1923 was to disallow the application, and on 22 October 1925 the governor (wojewoda) of Lublin Province rejected Nisman's appeal against this decision. Nisman then appealed to the Supreme Administrative Court, which on 22 April 1927, overturned the previous decisions.[7] Since further documents concerning this case are not available, we do not know how the story ended, but probably its final conclusion was positive. We should, however, note that the long drawn-out nature of the application clearly illustrates how the procedure was delayed and how the local administration was reluctant to settle a case that seemed to have already been decided by the Supreme Court in November 1922.

In his circular of 26 June 1924, ordering that problems associated with civil rights should quickly be settled, Minister of the Interior Zygmunt Hübner carried on the attempt to put the matter into order.[8] His successor in this office, Cyryl Ratajski, ordained on 28 February 1925 that the rural population living in the provinces of Nowogródek, Polesie, Wołyń, Białystok,

---

[6] Central Zionist Archives in Jerusalem [referred to below as 'CZA'], vol. A127/95.
[7] A copy of the Supreme Administrative Court decision is preserved in CZA vol. A127/75.
[8] This circular could not be traced, but it is mentioned in a circular dated 13 Jan. 1926. The latter circular and others quoted in this essay may be found in CZA, vol. A127/95.

and within the administrative district of Vilna be acknowledged *en masse* as Polish citizens. The rural population in these provinces was mostly comprised of Belarussians, Lithuanians, Poles, and Ukrainians, with only a small number of Jews, who chiefly lived in towns. It was only on 13 January 1926 that the next minister of the interior, Władysław Raczkiewicz, ordered a similar procedure to be adopted in the towns. His circular contained examples of documents that were to be regarded as sufficient proof of entitlement to citizenship.

We can guess that the minister's instructions were being put into effect very slowly, since on 9 July 1926 his successor Kazimierz Młodzianowski wrote in a circular: 'I receive complaints informing me that these authorities [i.e. the administrative authorities] bureaucratically delay answering requests for the granting of Polish citizenship, and that they demand from people documents that are not necessarily required and could not be obtained by the people even if they earnestly tried to get them.' The minister insisted that the procedures be quickened and simplified, both in the countryside and in the towns. On 28 August of that year he wrote with even greater emphasis: 'The registration has not been started everywhere; it is delayed, and the local authorities are seeking difficulties.' In order to simplify the procedure of granting citizenship to persons who did not come under the provisions of the existing regulations, the minister authorized the governors (wojewodowie) to decide in individual cases.[9] In his circular of 28 August he stressed that persons enlisted in military service and those who had settled in Polish territories before August 1914 and had undertaken paid work, should be given priority. This permitted the granting of citizenship to those Jews who had not fulfilled earlier registration formalities at the proper time.

The very fact that successive ministers wrote circulars dealing with the same question points to the indolence of local authorities in executing instructions to recognize the citizenship of national minorities. As we can infer from the circulars, one of the methods that the local authorities adopted in order to delay decisions was to demand still more documents, or even the complete set of documents indicated as examples in the circular of 13 January 1926, when one of them alone would have been sufficient. Therefore, on 12 January 1927 Deputy Yitzhak Grünbaum applied to the ministry of the interior asking it to instruct the local authorities once again about the procedure to be adopted when granting or recognizing Polish citizenship. Thus, on 6 August 1927, the ministry issued a new circular, signed by the Director of the Administrative Department.

[9] The decision of 29 Aug. 1926 contains the statement, 'The offices of Provinces [Województwa] are to decide cases of the granting or refusal of Polish citizenship': *DzURP* (1926), No. 93, item 545.

In 1928 most of the cases seem to have been finally settled. According to the reply of the then minister of the interior, Felicjan Sławoj-Składkowski, to the question posed by Deputy Stanisław Ratajczyk and his associates in the Sejm on 9 March 1933, about 1.6 million people had been recognized as Polish citizens.[10] Although Jewish deputies continued to raise this matter in the Sejm, by this time the remaining group of people of undefined citizenship was certainly not numerous and included chiefly those, who, by virtue of the Riga treaty, had been granted the right to acquire Soviet citizenship.[11]

The question of the citizenship of Jews emerged anew in 1938, when some extreme nationalist groups proposed that Jews should be deprived of Polish citizenship—on the model of the Nuremberg Laws enacted in the Third Reich. Similar proposals were tabled in the Sejm by two deputies, connected with the Sanacja camp, but they were not even put on the agenda of the Sejm committees. Proposals originating in the consular department of the foreign ministry were of greater importance.

On the initiative of the director of this department, Wiktor Tomir Drymmer, on 31 March 1938 the Sejm passed a bill providing for the deprivation of Polish citizenship. The bill stated: 'A Polish citizen staying abroad may be deprived of Polish citizenship if . . . being resident abroad for at least five years after the formation of the Polish state, he has lost his ties with Polish statehood.'[12] Later on, at a conference of Polish consuls in Berlin, W. T. Drymmer explained: 'The bill's aim was to elevate the dignity of a Polish citizen by excluding all those who had not been deserving and, above all, to exclude dangerous elements (such as representatives of national minorities, especially Jews, who are destructive elements).'[13] It is, however, worth noting that the bill's wording was general, and did not formally discriminate against any group of citizens.

In February 1939, the consular department began to think about how to revise the bill of Polish citizenship so that the so-called 'immigrant' Jews, probably those recognized as Polish citizens in 1928, might be deprived of their citizenship. The idea was approved by Foreign Minister Józef Beck, who demanded, however, that the planned bill 'should not be openly anti-Jewish'.[14] But the bill was never prepared.

An equally difficult task appeared to be that of securing equal rights for all Polish citizens, irrespective of religion and nationality. Declarations on

[10] AAN, PRM, vol. 3A15, p. 15.
[11] CZA, vol. A127/95.
[12] *DzURP* (1938), No. 22, item 31.
[13] AAN, Ambasada RP w Berlinie [Polish embassy in Berlin], vol. 3278, p. 119.
[14] AAN, Ministerstwo Spraw Zagranicznych [ministry of foreign affairs, referred to below as 'MSZ'], vol. 9908, p. 53.

this issue had been made by Polish politicians since November 1918, when Poland had committed itself to compliance with the relevant provisions of the Minorities Treaty, and the 1921 constitution guaranteed equality of rights, stating: 'No citizen may be restricted in the rights granted to all citizens because of his faith or religious views', and adding: 'No bill may contradict the present constitution, nor violate its provisions.' But the final article of the constitution stated: 'All the existing regulations and legal institutions inconsistent with the provisions of the present constitution shall be submitted to the legislative body, within a year at the latest, so as to bring them into conformity with the constitution by means of appropriate legislation.'[15]

The latter provision gave rise to numerous complications. Until the constitution was accepted, the existing discriminatory laws, if they had not been abolished on the occasion of previous amendments of the law, continued to be valid. For example, in the former Austrian partition the injunction stipulating that Yiddish and Hebrew should not be spoken at public meetings, as they were forbidden in state offices, was still observed (though probably inconsistently), and even Jewish deputies were obliged to comply with it. These regulations were in conflict with the formal wording of the constitution, which had not, however, repealed them automatically: new bills had to be passed to abolish them. The constitution had thus not annulled the existing discriminatory regulations against Jews. Although, on 23 March 1921, the government published an explanatory note in the *Monitor Polski* (the Polish official gazette)[16] indicating which regulations had been abolished by bills enacted after 1918, the note was not precise, and above all it did not have legal force. As it turned out, the regulations restricting the use of Yiddish and Hebrew were still binding, something confirmed by the General Prosecutor's office in a letter to the ministry of the interior on 27 June 1923, although the office considered meetings and lectures organized by citizens and their associations to be private and thus not liable to the injunction, which forbade only public use of these languages.[17] Although to some extent favourable, this was no more than a new interpretation of the existing regulations.

It was only on 9 January 1922 that the Council of Ministers passed a draft bill repealing the discriminatory laws against Jews in the former Russian partition.[18] The draft mentioned in detail the respective articles of existing laws, such as the civil code, the criminal code, the bill defining the organization of provincial administration in the Kingdom of Poland (the

[15] *DzURP* (1921), No. 44, item 267, arts. 38, 11.
[16] *Monitor Polski* (23 Mar. 1921), No. 67.
[17] AAN, PRM, vol. Rkt 64/4, pp. 48–9.
[18] Protokóły Rady Ministrów [protocols of the Council of Ministers, referred to below as 'Prot. RM'], vol. 17, pp. 89, 97.

semi-independent state, dynastically linked with the Tsarist empire, whose autonomy was almost entirely abolished after the 1863 uprising), the mining law, the regulations for the sale of lands apportioned to peasants by Russian agricultural reforms, the customs law, the excise law, and the bill of criminal procedure. This list was probably derived from the numerous motions that had been submitted by Jewish and socialist deputies to the Sejm since 1919, but it did not include all the existing laws concerning Jews.

The Sejm did not endorse the bill, and thus on 27 March 1923 the Council of Ministers again passed a draft bill abolishing the old Russian regulations discriminating against Jews.[19] Before the Sejm proceeded to consider this draft, a cabinet crisis broke out and a new cabinet, avowedly nationalist, was formed under the lead of Wincenty Witos. On 7 October, the new cabinet resolved to withdraw the previous draft and amend it.[20] Somewhat earlier, the same cabinet had decided to establish the *numerus clausus* at universities, thereby the numbers of Jewish students were to be strictly limited.[21]

When Witos's adminstration collapsed, the primary task of the new cabinet formed under Władysław Grabski was to reform the currency and put the finances of the state in order. The new situation prompted Deputy Maksymilian Hartglas to table a motion demanding the abolition of the Russian regulations discriminating against Jews. The political committee of the Council of Ministers at first resolved to propose a firm decision,[22] but within a short time, on 2 July 1924, the Council of Ministers endorsed the previous draft abolishing old Russian regulations which discriminated against Jews.[23]

We can surmise that the main reason for delaying a decision on the question of civil rights for Jews was that several politicians considered it would be improper if the discriminatory laws against Jews were abolished while similar Russian laws discriminating against the Catholic Church were still valid. The latter question continued to be discussed since Church circles were making demands beyond those which successive cabinets were inclined to approve.

But there was a difference between these two questions in that the discriminatory laws against the Church were not applied in practice, while those against Jews were. It is difficult to estimate to what extent this was so: accounts found in the literature give a variety of pictures. There is a dearth of information describing how often Jews were refused mining rights, not

---

[19] AAN, Prot. RM, vol. 21, p. 779.
[20] Ibid., vol. 24, p. 183.   [21] Ibid., vol. 22, p. 778.
[22] AAN, Komitet Polityczny Rady Ministrów [political committee of the Council of Ministers], vol. 2, p. 39.
[23] AAN, Prot. RM, vol. 26, p. 73.

permitted to purchase peasant-apportioned land, or excluded from candidacy in elections to appoint the heads of provinces. There are also reports of circumstances under which people were forbidden to convert from the Christian faith to Judaism,[24] but the available data are so sporadic that we may suppose such incidents to be rare. Thus the administrative organs did not widely apply the discriminatory regulations; those involved might also find ways of bypassing them or bribing the officials.

The Yiddish and Hebrew languages were, however, still banned in public life. Władysław Grabski's cabinet initiated bills permitting the Belarussian, Lithuanian, and Ukrainian languages to be used in courts and state offices; Yiddish, Hebrew, and German were not included in these measures. Although, at a session of the Council of Ministers held on 9 July 1924, Grabski declared that bills regulating the use of these languages should also be passed, he did not manage to initiate them before he resigned in the autumn of 1925.

The Supreme Court and the Supreme Court of Administrative Law differed in their opinions. A decision of the former of 16 February 1924 stated that the constitution had automatically abolished all the anti-Jewish regulations whose abolition had not required the establishment of new laws. The latter maintained that since the constitution required a formal abolition of the discriminatory regulations, they were valid until the Sejm endorsed the appropriate bills.[25]

In 1925, Poland signed a concordat with the Vatican. This removed one of the greatest difficulties that delayed the abolition of the regulations discriminating against Jews. Meanwhile, however, because of current political and economic problems—such as the breakdown of the złoty in August 1925, the collapse of Grabski's government, and then Józef Piłsudski's *coup d'état* in 1926—this question ceased to be of primary importance. In effect, it was not until early 1929 that the legal committee of the Sejm proceeded to consider the Jewish deputies' motion proposing the abolition of the regulations. The motion was discussed by the legal committee on 12 February, and then by the constitutional committee on 22 March.[26] In principle, the constitutional committee accepted it, though it was argued that the discriminatory regulations had in any case been applied only sporadically and that the bill should be extended to include all similar regulations discriminating against other religious or national groups. Eventually, the committee adopted the extended proposal, and then Deputies

---

[24] According to the question presented by the Sejm Member Maksymilian Hartglas and colleagues on 30 Nov. 1928: AAN Ministerstwo Wyznań religijnych i Oświecenia Publicznego [ministry of cults and education], vol. 390, pp. 180–1.

[25] See the question referred to in n. 24.

[26] CZA, vol. A127/106.

Maksymilian Hartglas, Antoni Lange ('Wyzwolenie'; 'Liberation'), and Herman Lieberman (Polska Partia Socjalistyczna) submitted a draft bill to the constitutional committee. The draft consisted of two basic articles:

Art. 1. It is hereby declared that all restrictions of the civil rights of Polish citizens imposed because of their religion or nationality and included in the hitherto valid laws ceased to be valid on the day when the constitution of 17 March 1921 came into effect, i.e. on 1 June 1921.
Art. 2. All decisions taken by authorities based on the restrictive regulations that are abolished by the present bill and that had not yet come into force or had not been executed are no longer in force.

This wording removed all doubts about the possible exclusion of certain regulations from the legislation. Moreover, it formally included the former Austrian discriminatory regulations, still valid, against minority languages. But it violated the legal principle, commonly observed, that *lex retro non agit* (restrospective legislation shall be avoided).

The deputy minister of justice, representing the government, questioned the necessity of the bill, arguing that numerous new regulations coming into force in many domains of life replaced the laws established in partitioned Poland and thereby abolished the former discriminatory regulations. He also stressed that the courts had fully respected the principle of equality of all the citizens and had acted in conformity with decisions of the Supreme Court. Nevertheless, he did not oppose the draft, beyond proposing the deletion of article 2 and formulating article 1 as follows:

The regulations restricting the civil rights of, or granting privileges to, Polish citizens in virtue of their origin, race, or religion and included in the laws enacted before Poland regained its statehood, if they are in contradiction with the legal status established by virtue of this fact or are inconsistent with the articles of the constitution that provide for the legal equality of all citizens, are no longer in force even though these special regulations have not been explicitly abolished by the bill.

In comparison with the original draft, the government's proposal was narrower in scope. It was opposed by deputies of the Christian Democratic Party, the Polish Peasant Party Piast, and some deputies of the Non-party Bloc for Co-operation with the Government, who wanted the regulations in question to be specifically abolished. Professor Bohdan Winiarski of the National Party proposed that the draft should be re-examined by the legal committee with a view to establishing whether it was necessary to pass such a bill. But since deputies of the national minorities, the left-wing deputies, and some deputies of the Non-party Bloc voted in favour of the government's draft, it was finally approved.

The legislative procedure, however, took so long that the bill could not be passed before the dissolution of the Sejm on 30 August 1930. It was only the parliament elected in November 1930, dominated by members of the Non-party Bloc for Co-operation with the Government, that endorsed the government's draft providing for the abolition of the special regulations which restricted the civil rights of citizens of the republic depending on their origin, nationality, race, or religion.[27] The draft submitted to the constitutional committee by the vice-minister of justice on 22 March 1929 was only slightly amended, in the final version of the bill, although this included an important addendum abolishing the regulations discriminating against the language spoken by some Polish citizens.

This conclusion of the discussion about the abolition of the discriminatory regulations was probably convenient for the government. The earlier parliaments, dominated by democratic parties, had been unable to settle this crucial constitutional question, even though Jewish deputies were supported by the left-wing groups. It was only the parliament dominated by supporters of the May *coup d'état*, elected by a procedure that violated law, that managed to abolish the discriminatory regulations in a short time.

In the second half of the 1930s, however, proposals restricting the civil rights of Jews again emerged in the Polish parliament. The motion proposing that ritual slaughter (*shehitah*) should be forbidden, tabled by a group of deputies including Janina Prystorowa (wife of the Speaker of the Sejm, the former premier Aleksander Prystor), was given widest publicity. Formally, the motion intended to regulate the procedure of slaughter and was presented as being motivated by humanitarian reasons. But economic reasons lay behind it, since the aim was to remove Jewish merchants and craftsmen from the slaughter of and trade in cattle and meat. We may also think of political reasons. The motion was supported by the opposition nationalist circles, but the ministers were embarrassed and protested. Speaking at a session of the administrative committee of the Sejm, a representative of the ministry of cults and education, Revd Żongołłowicz, proposed that the motion should be modified and argued that banning *shehitah* would violate the constitution, which guaranteed freedom of religion.[28] In the opinion of the minister of agriculture, the proposal threatened the interest of farmers, since such a bill might prevent religious Jews from eating meat.[29] Eventually, on 17 April 1936, the Sejm passed a bill restricting *shehitah* in proportion to the number of Jews, Muslims, and Karaites living in individual regions.

At the beginning of 1938, Deputy Janusz Dudziński (elected as a candidate

[27] *DzURP* (1931), No. 31, item 214.
[28] See AAN, files of Fr. Potocki, vol. 13, pp. 4–7, 10–11.
[29] See Cz. Bobrowski, *Wspomnienia ze stulecia* [Memoirs from the Century] (Warszawa, 1985), 93–4.

of the pro-government National Unity Camp) tabled a draft amendment to this bill, stipulating a total ban on *shehitah*, to be imposed from 1 January 1939. A representative of the ministry of cults and education again protested, arguing that this would violate the freedom of religion, and the ministry of agriculture indicated possible economic consequences.[30] The administrative and self-governmental committee approved the motion, but the parliament was dissolved before proceeding to endorse it. The motion was again put under discussion by the Sejm in the spring of 1939, but this time the debate was interrupted by the outbreak of war.

On 25 March 1938, however, the parliament passed another bill concerning the manufacture and trade of devotional and religious cult-articles. The bill stated that:

Permission to manufacture and trade in devotional objects and articles of worship to be used by believers of the Christian, Jewish, and Muslim religions may only be given to a person who is a believer in the respective religion, or to a corporate body whose management, supervisory board, and all other authorities are composed of believers of the respective religion.[31]

The bill aimed to eliminate Jews from the profitable production and trade in Catholic devotional articles.

It was characteristic of the bills that they formally affected all citizens and thus were not discriminatory. Actually, they were directly opposed to the religious or economic interests of Jews. It is worth noting that the bills were proposed by deputies close to the nationalist opposition, which wished to get the government into political trouble.

It was only in the spring of 1938 that some politicians of the ruling camp became disposed to accept openly anti-Jewish laws. Motivated by social, economic, and political reasons, the consular department of the foreign ministry headed by Wiktor Tomir Drymmer began to promote a mass emigration of Jews, who were viewed as a political force trying to restore democratic rule in Poland against the intentions of the state.[32] In May 1938 the National Unity Camp passed a resolution proposing that Jews should be more energetically encouraged to emigrate and should be gradually removed from Polish economic life. The resolution actually suggested a sort of legal discrimination against Jews.[33]

In February 1939 the consular department of the foreign ministry set up a more detailed programme. In order to force Jews to emigrate, it proposed that the laws and the state policy should be changed so as to dismiss Jews from offices held in institutions controlled by the state and to remove them

[30] AAN, files of Fr. Potocki, vol. 13, pp. 4–7, 10–11.
[31] *Dz URP* (1938), No. 19, item 149.
[32] AAN, MSZ, vol. 1004, pp. 8, 13.
[33] Ibid. 135.

from cultural life; it also proposed that the bill regulating the grant of Polish citizenship be amended, a *numerus clausus* established in certain professions, and a special emigration tax imposed on Jews.[34] On 15 February 1939, these proposals were in principle accepted by Minister J. Beck,[35] but the planned bills were never drafted in detail, nor were they endorsed.

The fact that a great number of Jews were Polish citizens and sought the abolition of discriminatory laws induced sharp political struggles in Poland in the interwar period. Although the parliament elected just after the formation of the Polish state was definitely dominated by democratic parties, practice appeared to differ from theory. The nationalist right wing, represented chiefly by the Popular National Union, later transformed into the National Party, attempted to exploit the complicated status quo in the eastern borderlands so as to limit the number of Polish citizens of non-Polish nationality. The proposed bills abolishing the restrictive regulations against Jews were blocked in various ways. Although the nationalist right wing was in power for a relatively short period (in the second half of 1923) and had not enough time to set up its policy towards the national minorities (including Jews), its representatives in the Sejm and Senate hampered the legislative procedure, and their followers within the administrative apparatus paralysed the execution of decisions taken by the ministry of the interior, which wished to regulate the question of civil rights.

Some progress was achieved in the years 1924–5, before the May *coup d'état*. Thanks to the initiatives started during this period, the question of Polish citizenship for national minorities could more easily be settled after the May coup, though some individual matters remained unsolved. On the initiative of Jewish deputies and representatives of the left-wing groups a proposal to abolish the discriminatory laws was soon prepared and then supported by the government.

Thus, the most important changes in the legal status of the Jewish population occurred after the May *coup d'état*, when the authoritarian regimes were able to break the resistance of the nationalist right-wing of the opposition and purge the local administrative apparatus of its supporters and followers. This success, however, hid the seeds of future failures, since at the end of the 1930s the same authoritarian government was able to ignore the democratic opposition and adopt some elements of nationalist conceptions. Although, before September 1939, Poland avoided the establishment of any openly discriminatory laws, some initiatives born at the beginning of 1939 might well have led in this direction. We cannot now assess how real this danger was, since the outbreak of the Second World War interrupted any normal development of the Polish republic.

[34] Ibid.   [35] AAN, MSZ, vol. 9908, pp. 53–4.

The Jewish Question in Polish Religious Periodicals in the Second Republic: The Case of the *Przegląd katolicki*

FRANCISZEK ADAMSKI

As is well known, the Jewish question in the reborn Polish state had several different aspects: national, international, political, economic, cultural, religious, and moral. This was due to the high percentage of Polish citizens of Jewish nationality, whose religion was alien to the official one, who had a different mentality and way of thinking, a different lifestyle, and a different everyday culture. Some of these characteristics had been formed under the age-old influence of the spirit of Judaism, others had been acquired during the Jewish wanderings among the peoples of Christian Europe. Wherever they settled, the Jews represented something of a problem, and its seriousness was conditioned by their proportion in the total population and the host country's economic structure, religion, legislation, and historical continuity. In the case of Poland, which had regained independence after 120 years of foreign rule, there were some unique circumstances that added to the weight of the problem.

That is why the issue was constantly present in popular thinking; this was reflected in the press, at that time the most influential mass medium of communication and propaganda. Most factions and political orientations of the time represented a more or less united front concerning the Jewish question. Its thrust was anti-Jewish and its force was determined by party divisions in the case of the secular press and by the degree of formal allegiance to the Church hierarchy in the case of the religious press. Even a cursory glance at just a few of the titles makes this clear. It may therefore be useful now, from a perspective of more than fifty years, to take a more probing look at the individual periodicals, with a view to uncovering the deeper message of these publications. By this means different facets of the 'Jewish question' and the nature of Polish antisemitism will emerge.

I take the view that the religious press was less antisemitic the closer it was to the episcopate and the more representative of the hierarchy's opinions. The periodicals in this category gave a deeper and less narrow-minded presentation of Jewish problems, putting them in perspective and writing about them in a less virulent and hate-filled tone. It is not my intention to play down the evil nature of certain passages that undeniably appeared in Church periodicals. But I wish to demonstrate a distinctiveness in their attitude that set them apart from the general (and most familiar) current of anti-Jewish propaganda.

We cannot here undertake an analysis of all the titles that might be called religious and classified according to their closeness to the hierarchy. For the purposes of this paper, I have chosen just one representative title which deserves special attention for its century-old tradition, its status as an official Church publication, the broad range of topics that it covered, and presumably—in view of its durability and the clarity of its articles—the extent of its influence.

Przegląd katolicki was first launched in 1841 by the Revd J. Szelawski as a monthly under the title *Pamiętnik religijno-moralny* and then from 1862 continued under the editorship of the Revd Michał Nowodworski as a weekly bearing the title *Przegląd katolicki: Pismo tygodniowe poświęcone sprawom religijnym, kulturalnym i społecznym* [A weekly journal devoted to religious, cultural, and social matters]. From the very beginning the periodical was the property of the Warsaw archepiscopal curia; it had both clerics and lay authors on its staff, and it set itself the task—as the editorial statement in the first issue put it—'of spreading truth and virtue and destroying falsehood and vice'. The editors' main concern was to 'elevate Catholic culture both among the clergy and among lay people'. *Przegląd* was from the outset recommended to the clergy by the Warsaw ordinary, but above all, as the author of a retrospective article later put it, 'it recommended itself by its contents: theological and philosophical treatises and above all a very rich chronicle'.[1] The periodical comprised sixteen quarto pages, each of them divided into two columns of print. From the start it had trouble with censorship. The First World War brought the closure of *Przegląd*, but a new epoch in its life began a few years after the rebirth of the sovereign Polish state. In his letter of appointment to the editor-in-chief, the Revd J. Kłopotowski, dated 21 June 1922, Cardinal Kakowski wrote: 'There is an urgent need for a periodical that would defend and spread the principles of our holy faith while also guarding all great endeavours that bear the stamp

---

[1] N. J. St Czarnecki, 'Z dziejów Przeglądu katolickiego', *Przegląd katolicki* [*PK*] (1934), No. 13, p. 212.

of Catholicism or lie in the province of Catholic life.'[2] In the days of the Second Republic *Przegląd* appeared regularly as a weekly from 6 July 1922 to mid-August 1939.

There were four sections in the paper: (1) Church, Religion, Morality; (2) Philosophy, Pedagogy, Law; (3) Culture, Literature; (4) Politics, Social Problems. In addition, every number devoted a few columns to a comprehensive chronicle of news items placed under such rubrics as 'Notes and Observations', 'Press Review', 'Political Review', 'Cultural and Social Review', 'Political and Social Notes', and 'From Literature'. Owing to this abundance of material, *Przegląd* became one of the most interesting periodicals in interwar Poland. It obviously caught on and was probably a strong influence on its many readers,[3] which was no doubt the intention of the Church hierarchy. Together with the Jesuits' *Przegląd powszechny* and the organ of Catholic Action, the *Ruch katolicki*, it formed the vanguard of the Catholic periodicals of the time. Yet, unlike the others, owing to its standard, editorial shape, and varied contents, it reached a vast audience. It was because it was so many-sided in its approach and so 'orthodox' with respect to the hierarchy, and because it had enjoyed such an unquestionable position on the map of Polish religious, cultural, and social life since the middle of the nineteenth century (especially during the Second Republic), that the Church made strenuous efforts to resume publication of *Przegląd* after 1945. This, however, became possible only in the days of Solidarity, and this time its size was much smaller,[4] and it was subjected to particularly rigorous censorship.

During the Second Republic, Jewish problems enjoyed a privileged place in the columns of *Przegląd*. This is seen in the frequency of articles on the topic, the amount of space allotted to them, and the fact that they appeared in each of the weekly's major sections and under each rubric of the chronicle. Altogether, Jewish problems were raised 133 times in the period between the world wars and had 266 columns devoted to them—approximately 1 percent of the total space. The accompanying table demonstrates that the reader of *Przegląd* was able to read about virtually all the major problems pertaining to the 'Jewish question,' an issue which aroused such strong emotions in the reborn Polish state. Discussion centred on the Polish–Jewish conflict, whose underlying causes and the means to their elimination were given close attention.

[2] Ibid.
[3] Unfortunately, I have not been able to find any data on the circulation of *PK*.
[4] At present *PK* has a circulation of 40,000 copies and an average size of six four-column pages.

Table 1 Analysis of Jewish Topics Treated in *Przegląd katolicki* (1922–1939)

Topic	Frequency of appearance			Columns allocated
	Articles and essays	Notes, reviews, news items	Total	
Essence of Judaism and relation to Christianity	19	—	19	39
History and philosophy of Judaism	3	—	3	13
Negative Jewish attitude towards Christianity	8	—	8	13
Pride of the Jews	8	—	8	13
Jewish personality	4	—	4	12
Positive qualities	2	—	2	3
Negative qualities	2	—	2	9
Programme of Jewish world policy	6	3	9	23
World domination	2	1	3	5
Revolutionary attitude	3	—	3	12
Harmful to Poland	1	2	3	6
Jewish settlement in Poland	15	3	18	63
Numbers	3	1	4	14
Legal privileges	7	1	8	33
Jews as aliens, traitors, bad citizens, etc.	5	1	6	16
Jews in Polish economic, social, and cultural life	19	9	28	48
Dominance in some sectors of the economy	5	1	6	9
Dominance in lucrative liberal professions	2	—	2	2
Penetration into Polish culture	2	2	4	4
Jews as carriers of Communist ideology	5	5	10	16
'Judaizing' sects	5	1	6	17
Necessity and means of solving the 'Jewish question'	25	9	34	64
Need for anti-Jewish legislation	5	1	6	27
Ways to oust Jews from economy and culture	9	5	14	12
Zionism and emigration	7	3	10	15
Opposition to primitive antisemitism	4	—	4	10
Echoes of antisemitism	—	24	24	11
Reports	—	8	8	3
Tendentious comments	—	13	13	6
Vicious comments	—	3	3	2
Others				
Statistics, ritualism, conversions, etc.	1	4	5	6

THE IDEOLOGICAL AND HISTORICAL ROOTS OF THE CHRISTIAN-JEWISH CONFLICT

This issue, commonly simplified and trivialized, received an authoritative interpretation in *Przegląd*. After a public lecture on the topic by the Revd Professor Eugeniusz Dąbrowski at Warsaw University, readers of *Przegląd* received a long and detailed report of the event.[5] They learnt that Judaism had from the start carried on a 'relentless struggle' against Christianity, that the first persecutions had been the work of Jews (St Stephen and St James the Apostle were the victims of Jewish hatred), that the Jews had opposed the spread of Christianity not only in Palestine but also throughout Asia Minor, Greece, and Italy, and that Tertullian had clearly pointed to them as the instigators of the persecution. After the Edict of Milan of CE 313 the Jews, no longer able to hinder the triumphant progress of Christianity, instituted the ghetto. Jewish historians, *Przegląd* wrote, were thus wrong to claim that the ghetto was the fruit of Christian nations' hatred for the Jews. The ghetto was called into being by rabbinical teachings, which sought to prevent distortion of Judaic doctrine by imposing strict isolation.

In the Middle Ages Jewish–Christian relations became even more tense following the publication of a 'Jewish libel against Jesus Christ' entitled *Toledot Jeshu* [The history of Jesus]. After the French Revolution, European Jews gained equal rights with other people and began to concentrate commerce and capital in their own hands; at the same time anti-Jewish movements arose as a result of the Jewish attitude towards ethical norms. In later years liberal Jews as a rule embraced the extreme views on the historicity of the Gospels and distorted Christ's ideas. It was in this spirit that the fundamental Jewish works on Christianity were written.[6] When dealing with the Jewish attitude towards Christians, well-known Jewish thinkers always stressed that Christianity was just a variant form of Judaism. They claimed that in the sphere of ethics Christianity had had nothing new to offer to the world. In Jewish eyes Christianity was still hateful as 'a form of idolatry', while in the opinion of Maimonides, which was widely shared by Jews, the Christians by adopting many heathen features, had themselves become heathens.

The following question thus arose, *Przegląd* continued: What were the causes of this Jewish attitude towards the Christian doctrine, which otherwise commanded general admiration for its sublimity? *Przegląd* tells its

---

[5] Leon Radziejowski, 'Judaizm wobec chrześcijaństwa', *PK* (1934), pp. 767–8.
[6] The author meant such writers as Joseph Salvador (1796–1873), Heinrich Graetz (1817–91), Abraham Geiger (1810–74), Claude Montefiore (1858–1938) and Joseph Klausner (1874–1958).

readers about various theoretical interpretations of this phenomenon. One of them draws on the racial-anthropological theories of Gobineau and Chamberlain, in whose opinion 'the Semites are organically incapable of accepting the lofty teachings of the Gospel'. By contrast, the Gospel itself is the product of the Aryan spirit. According to Chamberlain, Christ was an Aryan because he came from Galilee, whose population was not Semitic.[7] According to *Przegląd* this analysis fails to explain the Jewish opposition to Christianity, because present-day anthropologists believe that the terms 'Semitic' and 'Aryan' make sense only in linguistics. From a Christian standpoint, the Jews' alleged inability to accept Christianity contradicts the spirit of the Gospel, whose message is universal.[8] Nevertheless, it was true that through a long period of living in special circumstances the Jews had acquired to some extent a peculiar mentality of their own.

According to another interpretation, the main cause of the quarrel between Judaism and Christianity lay in the religious tendencies which became entrenched among the Jews after their exile to Babylon in the sixth century BC. There came into existence then 'a new type of Jewish religiousness, which continues until today'. These new directions, *Przegląd* tells us, which shape the mentality of the modern Jews have been called Judaism. When the Jews returned from the captivity and set about rebuilding their 'national homeland', the covenant between God and Israel began to be looked upon as a kind of 'business contract' ensuring worldly benefits to the followers of monotheism. The belief that Israel was the chosen people lay at the foundation of Judaism. The religious and moral conditions of God's promise were completely forgotten. Hence the Messianic ideas of the Old Testament no longer had anything to do with Judaic Messianism. The Jews became extremely nationalistic and imagined that the Messiah would restore their independence within the borders of the kingdom of David and Solomon. Judaism sees the Messiah proclaimed by the prophets as a victorious leader marking out the frontiers of Jewish dominion by the sword: Judaic Messianism, then, is strictly nationalistic and at the same time utterly materialistic. What the Jews look for in their future state is extensive material wealth fit to be admired and envied by other nations. Christ, who proclaimed the God of all nations and confronted Jewish nationalism with his own universalism, was bound to meet with determined opposition and hatred from the Jews, especially as Christianity countered the material

---

[7] Even though such claims have no scientific basis, they were followed by people like F. Delitsch and A. Rosenberg. The latter, in his book *Der Mythus der XX. Jahrhunderts* (Berlin, 1899), repeats the fiction of Christ the Aryan and preaches the need to 'cleanse' the Gospel of Old Testament influences.

[8] Christ commanded his Apostles to 'go and make disciples of all the nations' (Matt. 28: 16–20).

dominance of Judaism with its own spirituality, the Kingdom of this world with the Kingdom of God, and expounded no differentiation by race, calling instead for purity of the heart. Another change effected in Babylon concerns ritualism, which was of minor importance in Mosaism but grew to extreme limits in Judaism.[9] The spirit of ritualism is alien to Christianity: Christ points out to the Pharisees the absurdity of their conduct.

It follows from these arguments that Christianity strikes at the essence of Judaism and so must be rejected by it. The doctrinal, ethical, and social principles of Judaism have in time produced a special type of Jewish mentality for which Christianity as an ideology or philosophy of life is unacceptable. 'The very spirit of Judaism, then, engenders antisemitism. It is and always has been intolerable to the nations whose lot it is to live with Jews in their midst,' the author of the report concludes.

I have devoted some space to this review of the ideological and historical roots of the Jewish–Christian conflict as presented by *Przegląd katolicki* in order to bring out the editors' unswerving determination to give an orthodox theological interpretation of the age-old ideological battle between Christianity and Judaism and seek what they believed were the objective causes of the hostile attitudes and mutual antipathies. In the eyes of its authors, the explanation of the problem in *Przegląd* was free from propaganda and superficial arguments that might further poison the already envenomed atmosphere of mutual dislike or even hatred.

JEWISH SETTLEMENT IN POLAND AND ITS SOCIAL CONSEQUENCES

Of course, this aversion and hostile attitude of the Christians to the Jewish community also had other, more mundane, causes. After the destruction of Jerusalem the Jews scattered all over the world, but in later times they took a particular liking to Poland. According to the statistics frequently quoted by *Przegląd*,[10] at the peak of the economic crisis in the early 1930s more than 3 million out of a world total of 15 million Jews were living in Poland. Poland was thus the home of 20 per cent of all Jews, and they accounted for 10 per cent of the population of the Polish state. At this time the United States had 4 million Jews, the Soviet Union 2.7 million, Germany 640,000, and France 160,000 (no more than a third of the Jewish population of

---

[9] This refers to the minor rules of ritual regarding the Sabbath, prayer, and intercourse with non-Jews that made it virtually impossible to live 'without sin'.
[10] See e.g. the note 'Za dużo Żydów w Polsce', *PK* (1932), p. 437; H. Sukiennicki, 'Ludność żydowska w Polsce a emigracja', *PK* (1937), p. 195; Revd Dr J. Kryński, 'Nieco ze statystyki żydowskiej w Polsce', *PK* (1935), p. 210; 'Żydzi w szkołach polskich', *PK* (1929), No. 26.

Warsaw), while Palestine was home to 150,000 Jews. The distribution of the Jewish population in Poland was uneven. At the beginning of the 1920s they formed 33.1 per cent of the population of Warsaw, as much as 44.5 per cent of the town of Łódź, and 14 per cent of the Lublin voivodship.[11]

Their occupational distribution was also uneven. They formed as much as 41 per cent of the total number of professional people. They had a firm hold over the Bar and the lawcourts, which were 41.5 per cent Jewish; they constituted 34.5 per cent of all artists and 31.8 per cent of doctors, and as much as 60 per cent of commerce was in Jewish hands.[12] The meaning of these statistics was quite unequivocal; the short note in *Przegląd* ends with the following remark: 'It is good to know how many Jews we have in Poland, how they are distributed, and what they do in this country, because this information, apart from having import in itself, is of invaluable service in our efforts to rid the country of Jews, as we reveal the effects of these actions in various areas.'[13]

We can thus see that the data on the number, distribution, and occupational structure of the Jewish population published from time to time by *Przegląd* had a very clear purpose: the persistent aim of 'ridding Poland of Jews'. In this *Przegląd* even invoked Sombart's words: 'a small percentage of Jews is beneficial because they encourage competition and rivalry. But too high a percentage (as in Poland) stems the growth of the people among whom Jews have settled.'[14] The Jews were thus blamed for the state's failures in various sectors of the economy, while the state authorities were accused of legal discrimination in favour of Jews. *Przegląd* dealt with the topic of 'Jewish privileges' on six occasions, devoting $19\frac{1}{2}$ columns to the subject. This indicates how much importance the editors ascribed to it.

A no less important cause of dislike on the part of the Christian population, was the Jews' active 'pushing into Polish culture', otherwise referred to as 'Jewish domination (*zażydzanie*) of the intellectual culture of Poland'. Passages on this topic appearing in *Przegląd* were usually quoted from other sources and merely supplemented with self-explanatory headings and phraseology. For example, it was claimed that the pro-government press was dominated by Jews, that Jewish journalists 'have a stranglehold on public opinion and are throttling it without mercy',[15] that the Jews had gained control over the theatre, which 'because of the large Jewish audience and its tastes promotes nakedness, vilifies 'antiquated' ethics, and pushes new, liberated ethics'. The readers were told: 'The pillars of such cabarets

[11] 'Żydzi w Polsce', *PK* (1937), No. 37 ('Press Review').
[12] H. Sukiennicki, 'Ludność żydowska w Polsce a emigracja', *PK* (1937), p. 195.
[13] J. P. 'Żydzi w Polsce', *PK* (1937), No. 33.
[14] A. Małyszko, 'Żydzi a handel', *PK* (1933), p. 437.
[15] 'Żydzi w prasie', *PK* (1936), p. 492.

as *Qui pro quo, Morskie Uko, Banda, Rex* are Jewish and cabaret songs are written by Tuwim, Hemar, and Wlast.'[16]

Przegląd feared that with their activity in culture, literature, and art the Jews were assimilating the Poles while they themselves remained Jewish. Within Jews were helped by the fact that 'the Poles have an ability to assimilate easily; that is to say, they do not assimilate the Jews but assimilate to the Jews in the sphere of cultural life'. It had come to the point where 'the cadre of our intelligentsia has become so assimilated to the Jewish intelligentsia that they do not even see their own false position. This concerns not only the liberal but also the Catholic and "antisemitic" intelligentsia.'[17]

No less important was the circumstance that the Jews settling in Poland, unlike those in other countries, did not accept the language of the host country as their own but held on to Yiddish, a German dialect. And despite the fact that 'the Polish people regard it as a dishonour to Polish culture and a betrayal of Polish sovereignty, the Jews find it convenient to stick to their jargon, which they need in order to communicate among themselves in a language unintelligible to their neighbours'.[18] In this way the Jews were defending themselves against assimilation to Polish culture. As cultural strangers they found it easier to batten on the Poles.

THE PROBLEM OF 'JUDAEO-COMMUNISM' THREATENING POLISH NATIONAL INTERESTS

The last major cause of the divisions between the two communities was referred to in the press as 'Judaeo-Communism' (*żydokomuna*), an unequivocally derogatory term. *Przegląd* dealt with this issue on ten occasions, devoting to it about sixteen columns, which shows the importance attached to the problem. The idea was expressed in the titles of the articles themselves: 'Jews in the Russian Communist Party', 'Jews and the Revolution', 'Jewish Communists and the Bund', 'Democracy and the Volksfront', 'The Jewish Role in Communism', etc. Let us recall that at the dawn of independence Poland had successfully fought off an invasion by the first Communist state and that it was under constant threat of infiltration by subversive Communist ideology. Under these circumstances, *Przegląd's* presentation of the role of Jews in the rise of Communist ideology, their contribution to the creation of the Communist state, and their involvement in efforts to bring Communist ideology into Poland must have put the

---

[16] 'Zażydzenie kultury umysłowej w Polsce', *PK* (1933), p. 437.
[17] 'Żydzi asymilują Polaków', *PK* (1937), No. 30.
[18] Jerzy O., 'Żydzi polscy a żargon niemiecki', *PK* (1920), No. 46.

generally anti-Communist Polish society on their guard against Jews and incited anti-Jewish animosity. We can even say that from the political and national point of view this was the strongest card of the proponents of a campaign to 'rid Poland of Jews'.

The matter was taken up in *Przegląd* by well-known publicists, both clerics (the Revd Dr Stanisław Trzeciak) and lay people (A. Romer, Jakub Pollak, and others). From the extracts printed from Father Trzeciak's book *Program światowej polityki żydowskiej* [The Programme of Jewish World Policy] the reader learnt that Jews were striving for a world revolution and that the Bolshevik revolution had been a successful first stage. Apart from the obvious fact of Jewish participation in the preparation and carrying out of the Bolshevik revolution, the thesis was substantiated by quotation from the notorious 'Protocols of the Elders of Zion', where one can read, for instance:

By secret means available to us we shall use the gold exclusively in our possession to create an economic crisis; we shall make the multitudes of workers take to the streets simultaneously in all the countries of Europe. They will delight in spilling the blood of those whom in their simplicity they have envied since their earliest years and whose property they will be able to loot. (Protocols, III, para. 43).[19]

At this point the author goes on to list the strikes and riots organized by Jews in Europe apart from their participation in the Bolshevik revolution, and then expresses the view that the Jewish nation wants to seize power all over the world and that revolution is a means to that end. Since Israel is not strong enough to achieve this, they 'mould the characters of the goyim so as to strengthen their own masterful forces and weaken the native peoples'.[20] The text further claims that the principles laid down in the 'Protocols of the Elders of Zion' were used to prepare and carry out the revolutions in Russia, Mexico, and Spain. The point of the article is quite transparent: the Russian Revolution was financed and carried out by Jews. They made similar attempts in Spain and Mexico, but, luckily for Europe, these failed.

The tenor of these extracts from Father Trzeciak's book is reinforced by the information about Jewish membership in Communist Parties published in the 'Political Review' and 'Press Review' columns of *Przegląd*. In 1928 Jews accounted for as much as 16 per cent of the membership of the Russian Communist Party. In Poland they could not come out into the open but instead, as Jakub Pollak wrote, 'The ground has been prepared owing to the work of the Communist Bund. The Bund itself ought to be regarded as a Communist outpost: one often does not know where the Bund ends and

---

[19] Given in the Revd Dr St. Trzeciak, 'Rewolucja a Żydzi', *PK* (1936), p. 132.
[20] Ibid.

Bolshevism begins.[21] The author then lists dozens of Bund activists and leaders whose names appear in the *History of the Communist Party of the Soviet Union* as Communist activists. In another place the links between Polish Jewry and the Communist movement are asserted even more strongly. Pollak writes:

The members of the Bund in Poland passionately sympathize with the Communists, defending and protecting them and pouring abuse on their critics. The Bundists have demonstrated recently that they simply make it easier for Jewish Communists to publicly address the Jews ... they provide cover for criminals and allow them to speak under party pseudonyms—and that verges on criminal activity.[22]

The mass participation by Jews in the Communist revolution (and its earlier theoretical preparation by other Jews in the form of the ideology of the proletarian state), according to *Przegląd*, had a clearly defined goal. It was part of a Jewish global policy that aimed at conquering the world by first encircling it. The essence of the encirclement had allegedly been expressed by the English Jew Oscar Levy, who said: 'We Jews are nothing else today but the demoralizers and demolishers of the world. We are its incendiaries and executioners.'[23] A more precise expression of the same sentiments is found in the (bogus) text of an appeal to world Jewry allegedly issued by the Alliance Israélite Universelle and published by *Przegląd* in 1928 (No. 51). Here I reproduce only the few sentences printed by *Przegląd* in bold type:

Scattered among other nations, who have been hostile to our interests and to our rights from time immemorial, we want above all to be and to remain Jewish. Our nationality is the religion of our forefathers and we recognize no other nationality. We live in foreign lands and we do not care about the ambitions of these countries, which are totally alien to us. Our cause is holy and its success assured ... Catholicism, our eternal enemy, lies in the dust, mortally stricken in the heart. The net that Israel has cast over the globe is widening and growing and the momentous prophecies of our sacred books are finally nearing fulfilment. The day is not distant when all the wealth and all the treasures on earth will fall to Israel.

To achieve this goal, it was claimed, Jews were uniting internationally in the Zionist movement initiated by Theodor Herzl. Zionism, we read in *Przegląd*'s report on the Sixteenth Zionist Congress in Zurich in 1930, saw the Jewish nation in a new and in some degree mystical way as 'all those who share a common tradition of the past and aspire towards common goals in the future. [Zionism] aims at a rebirth of the lost language and culture and

[21] J. Pollak, 'KPP a Żydzi', *PK* (1932), p. 230.
[22] J. Pollak, 'Komuniści żydowscy a Bund', *PK* (1932), p. 624.
[23] 'Na marginesie książki ks. dra St Trzeciaka: Problem światowej polityki żydowskiej, Warszawa 1936', *PK* (1936), p. 829.

at creating a native homeland for the reawakened people'—of course at the expense of other peoples.²⁴ A nation that was inevitably to fall victim to Jewish encirclement was Poland. This idea was emphatically expressed by the Revd K. Jastrzębiec in an article with the telling title 'The Wandering Jew'. The article reported on a Nazi exhibition called 'Der ewige Jude' held in Munich in 1938. Jastrzębiec wrote:

> I stand in front of a board on which in huge lettering appear the names of countries most seriously threatened by the Jewish element, those in which the springs of the Comintern have been set and which are being turned into fiery confluences of world Jewry. First comes Bolshevized Russia, second Spain, third Poland. That is my most painful experience of the exhibition 'Der ewige Jude'.²⁵

All the same, *Przegląd* did not confine the programme of the Zionist movement to 'encirclement' and 'subjugation of the world'. At the beginning of the 1930s it carried a long text by the Revd Dr T. Macior entitled 'At the Sources of Zionism'. The author presented his reflections on the recently published book of L. Belmont *Mojżesz współczesny: Rozdroże Teodora Herzla* [The Modern Moses: Theodor Herzl at the Crossroads]. This time Zionism received a favourable appraisal because 'its goal was also to call into being an independent sovereign Jewish state open to every Jew wishing to have a native country'.²⁶ This idea provides a convenient transition to the next part of the present study, where we shall reconstruct the ways of solving the 'Jewish question' suggested by *Przegląd*.

WAYS OF SOLVING THE 'JEWISH QUESTION'

Scrutinizing the texts on this topic, one obtains the impression that *Przegląd* deliberately brought into prominence the many facts and circumstances engendering the Polish–Jewish conflict in order to be able to commit itself more resolutely to the search for ways of solving the Jewish question. It is only fair to say that texts showing situations of conflict are very rarely found isolated from the main idea, which is to indicate possible solutions. Only those texts whose authors enlarge on ways of 'ridding Poland of Jews', as they put it, have a clearly antisemitic note. Such texts are decidedly in the minority. Their authors are never members of the clergy (or at least they are not so designated), and such texts mostly appear as short notices under rubrics such as 'Notes and Observations', 'Cultural and Social Review', and 'Press Review'. The author's intention is usually revealed in the title:

---

[24] 'XVI Światowy Kongres Syjonistów w Zurychu', *PK* (1930), No. 29.
[25] J. K. Jastrzębiec, 'Żyd wieczny tułacz', *PK* (1938), p. 151.
[26] *PK* (1931), No. 18.

'Struggle to Rid the Bar of Jews', 'Let Us Call for a Boycott of Jews', 'Jewish Blindness', 'Doctors against the Jews', 'The Need to Introduce Anti-Jewish Legislation', 'Trial of Judaeo-Communists'. It is significant that such texts appeared in the journal in the last years before the outbreak of the war, when short notices attacking, ridiculing, or accusing Jews were published on average every two months.

Still, it cannot be said that these texts set the tone for *Przegląd*'s approach to the Jewish question. As has been said earlier, more serious articles, those carrying more weight and appearing in the major departments of *Przegląd*, expressed a number of reservations and showed the complexity of the situation while at the same time concentrating on the 'way out'. Efforts to devise such a solution had been made from the earliest years of independence. In 1925, in a programmatic article, the Revd S. Wesołowski wrote:

As by historical coincidence we have been doomed to coexist with the Jews, we have long been of the opinion that sooner or later we ought to find some just and rational *modus vivendi*, with the reservation that the rights of the Polish people, the ancient masters of this land, should in no way be restricted or infringed, and that we should be able to protect our ideals and religious sanctities against the destructive influence of a materialistic and anarchistic Jewry ... Every society, including ours, has not only the right but also the duty to guard the *holy* faith, the inviolable dignity of God's Church, and moral purity.[27]

The two-column article ends with an ideological declaration: 'A war with the Jews we do not want; all brutal excesses by the rabble we condemn; but we shall always guard and defend our rights and all that which is the inviolable sanctity and the property of the Christian soul.'

What can be felt in this and many other programmatic texts is an unswerving determination to put a definitive end to Jewish 'excesses', of which, as we have shown, *Przegląd* often informed its readers. This was to be attained not through retaliation or street brawls. When publishing *in extenso* the government exposé by Edward Smigły-Rydz which discussed the social and political situation in Poland, the editors used bold type for those sentences which set forth the official attitude towards the Jewish question:

With regard to the Jewish population our position is this: we value too highly the standard and content of our cultural life and the public peace, law, and order that no state can dispense with to approve acts of licence or brutal anti-Jewish reactions which hurt the prestige and dignity of a great nation. On the other hand, the

---

[27] *PK* (1925), pp. 454–5.

instinct for cultural self-defence is understandable and the Polish society's tendency to economic independence is natural.[28]

Thus, in the opinion of *Przegląd* legal and cultural self-defence and liberation from Jewish economic domination were crucial for the solution of the 'Jewish question'. Quite uncompromising proposals along these lines can be found in *Przegląd* as early as the mid-1920s. A three-column programmatic article bearing the significant title 'Will Poland Free itself from Jewish Rule?', published in 1926, unequivocally advocated the following actions: restriction of Jewish privileges, prosecution and punishment of Jews guilty of bribery and other crimes, strong support for Polish commerce and craft products, exclusion of Jews from occupations requiring absolute honesty (such as the legal and medical professions) and from the civil service and local government.[29] The topic remained open throughout the existence of the Second Republic: in a 1939 text on 'How to Put the Jewish Question on a Realistic Course' we find the very same suggestions and proposals, plus the requirement that Jews should be prohibited from teaching in Christian schools and that public performance of works by Jewish authors or belonging to Jewish culture should not be allowed.[30] The author contended that it was impossible to continue a situation where

> Jews in Poland are mere spectators of our state-building efforts; benefiting from our independence, they gather profits from this state of affairs and give Poland virtually nothing in return. They are spectators of our national effort: they share in the profits of the Polish economy and yet at the same time they slander Poland in the arena of international politics, alleging that they are wronged and persecuted in the Polish state.[31]

In its efforts to change this state of affairs, *Przegląd* keeps reaffirming that 'we are opposed to all persecution and all violence against the Jews'.[32] In a three-column programmatic text by A. Romer published in the late 1930s, at the height of the Polish–Jewish crisis, we can read:

> Love of one's neighbour is an absolute obligation, so there can be no question of leniency towards any manifestation of hate or brutality directed against the Jews. Still, we regard the Jewish question as one of the most burning global problems and indisputably a problem of the foremost importance in Poland. Having regained our independence, we must secure it by placing our social structure on a sound footing.[33]

---

[28] 'Ideowo-polityczna deklaracja płk. A. Koca', *PK* (1937), p. 132.
[29] Ks. Mat. Jeż., 'Czy Polska wyzwoli się spod panowania Żydów', *PK* (1926), p. 227.
[30] Jerzy Szczęsny Rogala, 'O wprowadzenie kwestii żydowskiej na tory realne', *PK* (1939), No. 21. [31] Ibid.
[32] L. J. R., 'Sprawy żydowskie w Polsce', *PK* (1928), p. 765.
[33] A. Romer, 'Zaostrzanie sprawy żydowskiej', *PK* (1938), No. 16.

This consisted in the cultural, economic, and legal equalization of Jews with other citizens, which would mean a reduction in the proportion of Jews in some important occupations and major spheres of social, economic, and cultural life to a level commensurate with their numbers in the population as a whole. The change would of course worsen the Jews' social and economic position, but, Romer went on to write,

World Jewry should take the matter of Jewish emigration from Poland in their own hands so as to protect Polish Jews against the spectre of economic catastrophe that they would then face ... We cannot afford to continue the hospitality once extended either voluntarily or under compulsion to Semitic immigrants. It is not our fault that they labour under the curse of homelessness and that a nation of more than ten million cannot bring itself to end its dispersion and win a home for itself by its own force.[34]

The objective was not merely to get rid of the Jews. In advocating the adoption of anti-Jewish policies, *Przegląd* argued that these would also be in the interests of Jews themselves. It stressed many times that the consequences of liberating the Polish economy from Jewish influence

will have to be borne by the Polish Jews, because in the long run they can endure neither the struggle for survival with the ever strengthening current of Polish competition nor the improved economic structure of the country. It is high time, then, that the Jews, in the interest of the fraternal coexistence of nations, changed their policy thoroughly and started to withdraw from the public life of other nations.[35]

As might have been expected, that part of Zionist doctrine which postulated the reconstruction of an independent and sovereign Jewish state was regarded as conducive to such a solution of the Jewish question. Hence, Palestine-related problems are frequently dealt with in *Przegląd*. Besides many short news items and notes on Jewish settlement in Palestine, *Przegląd* published ten longer articles on the subject. When the matter was first broached in the early 1920s, *Przegląd* wrote about the attitude of the Holy See towards the 'Palestinian question'.[36] It showed that the problem had Arab, Christian, and Jewish aspects. The fact that the Arabs made up 88.5 per cent of the Palestinian population of 754,000 and that Palestine was the home of their national shrines gave them certain ethnic and religious rights. No less was the claim of the Christians, for whom Palestine was their Holy Land and had in fact been in their hands for 700 years (between the third and tenth centuries). Palestinian Jews formed a mere 11 per cent of the population, but they represented the Jewish diaspora of more than 14

[34] Ibid. [35] Ibid.
[36] Ks. dr. Wł. Szczepański, 'Pius XI wobec problemu palestyńskiego', *PK* (1925), No. 5.

million, who looked upon Palestine as their long lost, and as Herzl put it, 'unforgettable', native land. The British Mandate in Palestine after the breakdown of the Ottoman Empire 'had been implemented at the suggestion of the Jews, who were promised Palestine as their national home by Lord Balfour and granted enormous and totally unjustified privileges there by Lloyd George, to the prejudice of Arab and Christian rights'.[37]

The reader was informed of the state of affairs in Palestine, the Jewish immigration movement, the Jews' growing control of the land, their settlement in the towns, organization of the economy, and also of the attitude of the Holy See, which 'does not totally condemn the Zionist movement, but neither does it accept political Zionism, some sort of Israeli kingdom in Palestine, to the prejudice of the local people'. In an editorial on 'The Catholic Church and Palestine' the reader was told that 'the Jews unashamedly domineer over others, meting out the same treatment to Arabs and Christians, and the whole "Palestinian Utopia" must be viewed in the light of the economic position of the Jewish settlers'.[38] The economic struggle of the Jewish settlers was thus seen as the cause of their taking unfair advantages of their legal privileges at the expense of the majority of the population of the area.

As is known, the plight of the settlers (and the attendant political complications) did not encourage large numbers of Jews to immigrate, nor did it give any hope for the resettlement of about a million Polish Jews, which in the opinion of the Polish Zionist leader Yitzhak Grünbaum himself could have remedied the situation in Poland.[39] Even though the idea of 'ridding' Poland of at least a third of her Jewish population was entertained (despite the Vatican's unfavourable attitude towards the colonization of Palestine), it was recognized that such a solution was a fiasco. The emigration, as we know, proceeded with difficulty. According to the information in *Przegląd*,[40] the Jewish population of Palestine was 66,574 in the year 1920 and only 200,000 in 1933. The truth about Palestine appeared in black colours. At the beginning of 1939 *Przegląd* published a strongly critical article that amounted to a final dismissal of the 'Palestinian gamble'. The author, Jan Żelewski, wrote:

Enormous sums have been collected and spent on the 'Palestinian project', yet what have the Jews accomplished with these huge amounts of money? In twenty years they have colonized an area of a thousand square kilometres, whereas the mandate covers 116,000. Only 400,000 Jews have settled there—that is, the number that there are in Warsaw. The annual emigration from Poland in times of prosperity

[37] Ks. dr. Wł. Szczepański, 'Pius XI wobec problemu palestyńskiego', *PK* (1925), No. 5.
[38] 'Kościół katolicki a Palestyna', *PK* (1925), p. 9.
[39] As cited in A. Romer, 'Zagadnienia kolonialne a sprawa żydowska', *PK* (1936), No. 36.
[40] Ks. dr. J. Kruszyński, 'Nieco ze statystyki Żydów w Polsce', *PK* (1935), p. 210.

amounted to 10,000, while their annual population growth has been 50,000. What, then, has Poland gained from the Palestinian project?

The proposal to set up Jewish colonies (in Madagascar) as a means of solving the Jewish question was approached, but only tentatively, and few believed it made sense. *Przegląd* wrote about it three times, indicating that such a solution of the Jewish question was unrealistic. Nevertheless *Przegląd* continued to stress the importance of the question for the Polish people and the Polish state in the months immediately preceding the outbreak of the Second World War.

To conclude, let us emphasize the political, social, and moral significance of the approach of the *Przegląd katolicki* to the problem at hand. The material, which could be only partially presented here, demonstrates that *Przegląd* played an important part in the (frequently one-sided) public commitment to a solution of the 'Jewish question'. The topics listed show the importance to it of these problems. All the topics analysed here were extensively discussed in *Przegląd*: the journal provides an almost exhaustive review of the major aspects of the 'Jewish problem, of which Jews were accused: of themselves doing better in the Polish state than its native hosts and inhabitants were able to do, and of achieving this at the expense of the Poles; this had to lead to a conflict. The reflection of the conflict in the pages of the *Przegląd katolicki*, a leading journal of a Catholic nation, is of unquestioned importance for the political and cultural history of the two nations. As such, it merits an even more thorough sociological analysis than has been attempted here.

The Image of the Jew in the Catholic Press during the Second Republic

ANNA LANDAU-CZAJKA

INTRODUCTION

THE Catholic press during the interwar period consisted of numerous periodicals, from dailies to monthlies. They were published both by religious orders—which included the Jesuits, Pallotines, Michaelites, and Franciscans—and by lay organizations. The number of titles in 1936 alone totalled 199. The print-runs of some of these were huge: in fact they accounted for 27 per cent of the total output of periodicals in Poland.[1] The Catholic press thus exercised considerable influence.

Catholic journals were aimed at readers from various social groups and classes, and their circulation levels varied. Some of the titles were published in small editions and were concerned chiefly with local parish affairs. There was a significant amount of reading material aimed at children and young people, sometimes in the form of separate titles, sometimes in the form of supplements to periodicals for the adult reader. There were also journals intended specifically for priests, or chiefly concerned with missionary matters.

Clearly it would be impossible to discuss, even in broad terms, the whole of the Catholic press, or even a majority of its titles. In this essay, therefore, I shall look mainly at selected periodicals (and almanacs, which had a no less important influence) aimed at a non-clerical readership, and shall concentrate on those with a large print-run and circulation and which, in terms of content, were not restricted to purely local affairs. The range includes those aimed at the popular market and printed in large numbers through to those aimed at a more intellectual readership, with a considerably smaller print-run; some concerned themselves chiefly with religious problems, while others discussed political, social, and cultural issues.

The following periodicals served as a basis for this study: *Przegląd*

[1] A. Paczkowski, *Prasa polska w latach 1918–1939* (Warsaw, 1980), 293.

katolicki [Catholic review, weekly], *Królowa apostołów* [The queen of apostles, monthly], and *Kalendarz królowej apostołów* [Almanac of the queen of apostles], which were published by the Pallotine Fathers; *Posłaniec serca Jezusowego* [Messenger of the heart of Jesus, monthly], *Kalendarz apostolstwa modlitwy* [Almanac of the apostles of prayer], *Sodalis Marianus* (monthly), and *Przegląd powszechny* [General review, monthly], published by the Jesuits; *Rycerz Niepokalanej* [Knight of the Virgin, monthly] and *Mały dziennik* [The small daily], published by the Franciscans; *Ruch katolicki* [The Catholic movement, monthly], the organ of Catholic Action; *Kultura* (weekly) published by the Central Institute of Catholic Action; *Kalendarz królowej korony polskiej* [Almanac of the queen of the Polish crown], published by the Michaelities; *Przewodnik katolicki* [The Catholic guide, weekly], published by the bookshop of St Wojciech in Poznań; *Pro Christo* (monthly), published by the Marian Order.

Often from the title alone one can tell what kind of reader they were intended for. *Rycerz niepokalanej, Posłaniec serca Jezusowego, Królowa apostołów, Mały dziennik*, and the almanacs were all popular, mass-circulation journals. *Ruch katolicki, Kultura, Sodalis Marianus*, and *Przegląd powszechny* were aimed chiefly at a more intellectual Catholic readership. *Pro Christo*, the most radical of the journals and the one most criticized by other periodicals for an outlook which too frequently departed from Christian principles, was intended for young people.

I shall discuss the attitude of the Catholic press towards the Jewish question, the way in which these periodicals protrayed the Jewish community, and their attitude towards it, but not the official programme of the Catholic Church towards the Jewish question. My aim is to show how the Catholic press shaped the image of the Jewish community in the eyes of its readers.

The Jewish question was of interest to the Catholic press irrespective of its attitude towards the Jewish minority. Several articles in each issue of all the periodicals we have mentioned were generally devoted to the subject, although, with a few exception (e.g. *Pro Christo*, or to a large extent *Mały dziennik*), this issue does not seem to have been central to the Catholic press in the interwar period.

Still, as we might expect, Catholic journalists, rather more than their non-Catholic colleagues, dealt with the religious separateness of Jews and with Jewish religion and religiosity, and pondered on the relationship between Judaism and Catholicism. It should be remembered that before the war the official attitude of the Catholic Church towards other faiths—even Christian ones—was considerably different from what it is today. A large majority of the Catholic journals at that time expressed the view that Catholicism should be the dominant faith in the Polish state, and that full equality of rights for members of other faiths was undesirable. We also encounter quite frequently the view that Catholics should, as far as possible, distance themselves from members of other creeds, since such contacts might serve to unsettle or undermine their Catholic faith. In this respect the attitude displayed in the periodicals towards Jews was merely an extension of that displayed towards all dissenters, and was a result of their stance *vis-à-vis* questions such as whether a Pole should necessarily be a Catholic, whether all religions should have the same rights and place in the Polish state, and, if so, whether equality of rights was possible. Journalists considering these problems did not merely concentrate on Jews, but on all non-Catholics in Poland. Jews were seen as a group distinct from Poles, but members of the Orthodox faith or Protestants were just as distinct: the criterion of differentiation employed by the journalists was between Catholics and non-Catholics. If, as happened fairly often, a call was made for these two communities to be separated, then, for example, Catholics of Jewish descent and those who were ethnic Poles were classified on one side, whereas Polish Protestants would be on the other. In this case the only important criterion would be religion, not ethnic or racial background. This was the position held by Catholic journalists chiefly in regard to appeals for separate single-faith schools to be created for those of the Catholic, Orthodox, Evangelical, and Jewish faiths.

Opinions of this kind, probably the most logical from the viewpoint of prevailing Catholic doctrine, are nevertheless encountered infrequently. A variation of this standpoint was to treat Jews as adherents of another religion, but also to distinguish clearly between Judaism and other non-Catholic religions. It was emphasized on these occasions that Judaism was the one non-Christian religion of any significance in Poland, and what was most important, that it had been unreservedly hostile towards Christianity from the very start of the Christian era. Accusations appeared in print to the effect that the Jews had murdered Christ, persecuted Christians, spread atheism, sometimes even that they had killed Christian children to use their blood in *matsah* (unleavened bread), although the Catholic Church had officially acknowledged such charges to be unfounded already in the eighteenth century. The Jews were thus a religious minority, but different from others, and since their religion and Christianity were mutually incompatible it followed that there must be antagonism between the two communities professing these faiths. The stigma of the crucifixion of Christ would remain for centuries to come with the Jewish people: that was the reason for all their misfortunes. Just as the Catholic religion and its adherents were to enjoy a secured primacy within the state, as the one true religion of the majority, so conversely, Jews should be isolated, or at least treated with suspicion and reserve as the adherents of a faith which was false and hostile and which even at times induced its believers to commit sinful acts. These twin viewpoints clearly determined the attitude towards the Jewish minority. What was the difference, after all, between not acknowledging the true faith and being the adherent of a faith directed against Catholicism and its believers? What was the difference between not believing in Christ and being responsible for his crucifixion?

There was a third trend of thought in articles on the Jewish question. This treated Jews not as a religious minority but as a distinct nation, ethnic group, or race. The issue of faith was relegated to the background, with most interest centring on ethnic-national differences. The authors' views were varied, but similar themes were discussed. They wrote of restoring trade and business to Polish ownership, of limiting the number of Jews eligible for government employment, and discussed the Jewish community's international links, its relationship to Communism and Freemasonry, and the political rights of Jews in Poland.

Of course, all these aspects of the Jewish question could not be separated in discussion. The author who emphasized the religious differences of Jews often also drew attention to their racial or national distinctiveness. In spite of such differences in emphasis, there was not in fact a very wide spectrum of attitudes towards Jews displayed in the periodical literature. Some periodicals brought out by the same publisher, or even by the same religious order, and intended for more or less the same group of readers, could display quite a variety of views. For example, the *Rycerz Niepokalanej* was tolerant towards Jews while the *Mały dziennik* was basically antisemitic. In general terms, one may say that the journals least tolerant of Jews were those aimed at the 'man in the street' (though the *Rycerz Niepokalanej* is an exception), whereas those which were most positively disposed were aimed at a more educated readership (though here again the anti-Jewish *Kultura* may be mentioned as an exception).

BAPTISM OF JEWS

One of the fundamental issues raised in all Catholic journals (with the exception of *Mały dziennik*, which covered day-to-day events rather than religious questions) was that of Jewish religiosity and the eventual conversion of Jews to Catholicism. Discussion revolved around the basic question of whether baptism should be available to all who wished it, and, if so, how baptized Jews should be treated. Opinions on the subject varied greatly. They ranged from outright approval for Jews wishing to become Catholics and willingness to recognize converts as full and equal members of the Catholic Church, to treatment of baptized Jews with the greatest suspicion and dislike, and a refusal to grant them equal status.

All authors in the periodical literature supported the official position of the Catholic Church, which was that Catholics should pray for the conversion of Israel. It was often emphasized, though, that the Church had been trying to convert Jews for many centuries without visible success. The majority of writers considered that efforts to convert Jews should be continued. However, some recommended caution when baptizing Jews: more often than not conversion was undertaken for completely worldly and material ends. So the motives of the candidate for conversion should always be thoroughly investigated beforehand. *Posłaniec serca Jezusa* stated that 'the Church cannot close its doors to anyone—it can only exercise greater or lesser caution. As far as Jews are concerned, it has been forced to exercise such caution by sad experience.'[2] In the author's opinion the Church's representatives should first satisfy themselves that the candidate's intentions were pure and that prospective converts had a knowledge of Christian principles. The journal *Kalendarz królowej polski* reminded its readers that the Church had attempted to convert Jews from its earliest days and that the meagre results of these efforts could only be attributed to the Jews' blindness.[3]

Many writers considered that under present circumstances the conversion of Jews, or at least admitting them to the Church through baptism, was impossible, since Jews were by divine judgement unresponsive to the workings of God's grace. Only by dint of prayer that the sentence imposed on that people by fate would be lifted could the way be cleared for Jews to enter the Catholic Church. No human means or persuasion would have any effect. We read in *Ruch katolicki*:

> The divine hand of rebuke lies heavy on the Jewish people. The eyes of that people are blind ... The Jewish question cannot be resolved. The Jewish soul, the Talmudic soul, obstinately spurns each hand which is stretched out towards it in friendship. For the Christian peoples there remains only armed struggle against fanatical Jewry. There is one more thing, namely the prayers of the Good Friday Church for the ignoble Jews, that our Lord and master may remove the screen around their heads so that they too may recognize Christ.[4]

This theme—of conflict or struggle with the Jews, but at the same time of praying for the conversion which would bring an end to the struggle—recurs quite frequently. Baptism of Jews was seen as an indispensable

---

[2] 'O nawracaniu Żydów do wiary katolickiej', *Posłaniec serca Jezusowego* (May 1939), 186.

[3] 'Nasz stosunek do Żydow', *Kalendarz królowej polski* (1929), 197–200.

[4] Father S. Kowalski, 'Posłannictwo i tragedia narodu żydowskiego', *Ruch katolicki* (July 1936), 314.

condition for the conclusion of hostilities between Christian and Jew, and conversion was considered possible only with divine intervention. The goal which Catholics had set themselves—complete conversion of the Jews—was shown to be still a long way off, so that this distant aim did not clash in any way with current policies and actions towards the (as yet unconverted) Jews. Father M. Wiśniewski wrote in *Pro Christo*: 'our immediate aim in this respect must be to free ourselves from Jewish domination, and subsequently to convert the people of Israel'.[5] The same author wrote: 'young people must know that the mainspring of scheming against Poland is the "Talmudic Jew" . . . They should pray together with all Catholics for the conversion of Israel, but before that comes about they should ensure that the Jew does not ruin the Christian spirit.'[6]

In a similar vein a writer for *Sodalis Marianus* stated that the highest imperative of the Church's love towards Jews should be the complete separation of Christians and Jews and the creation of ghettos: 'We should implement the dictates of justice, which demands the establishment of ghettos, and not withdraw from those dictates in the name of any love whatsoever. Only then, with the door open, will the secret of its hidden love be revealed. The Christian Church will reveal the baptismal font in its churches.'[7]

The most pronounced opponent of baptism for Jews was Father M. Wiśniewski of *Pro Christo*, who has already been mentioned. He maintained that conversions would be almost exclusively attempts on the part of Jews to break into Polish society, and he advised that the problem should be approached with the greatest possible caution, actually suggesting a complete halt to the baptizing of Jews in Poland for the time being. The only sincere type of conversion, in his view, would be one which took place abroad, without any visible advantage to be gained for the convert in Poland. Furthermore, converted Jews should not be full and equal members of the Polish community.[8]

Many Catholic writers looked with sympathy and approval on those Jews who wished to be baptized or had already been so. They referred to biblical examples, maintaining that good Jews had accepted baptism from the earliest days of the Church, while only the unworthy had remained recalcitrant. In recounting the story of an elderly Jew who converted on his deathbed, the author stated: '—good Jews, like St Joseph, St Peter, and St Paul . . . believed in the messiah, and the evil ones, such as Ananias and

---

[5] Father M. Wiśniewski, 'Apostolstwo świeckich', *Pro Christo* (Feb. 1927), 94.
[6] Id., 'Na maginesie Ligi Katolickiej', *Pro Christo* (May 1927), 330.
[7] 'Nawet Żydów, Stachu!', *Sodalis Marianus* (Feb. 1939), 87.
[8] Father M. Wiśniewski, 'O świętą jedność w Chrystusie', *Pro Christo* (Oct. 1934), 730.

Caiaphas, murdered him'.⁹ The reader was told that Jews who wanted to be christened were acting in accordance with holy instructions. The oft-repeated charge of deicide should no longer be levelled at them. It was explained that the best, most worthy Jews were indeed being christened, so that there was no need to regard them with suspicion. *Posłaniec serca Jezusowego* printed a series of stories about converted Jews, presenting their many and varied positive characteristics and their worthy deeds. *Rycerz Niepokalanej* stated that 'one can find among the Jews, too, souls who are worthy and seek the truth, and these often convert'.¹⁰ One of the authors of *Pro Christo* even suggested that all the best Jews should be christened and the worst rendered harmless.¹¹

Many Catholic writers warned against being too credulous in accepting into the Church Jews who were not true believers. But an equal number of writers expressed themselves decidedly against any kind of persecution or inferior treatment within the Catholic Church of converted Jews. The journal *Królowa apostołów* stated that new converts should be valued and accepted into Catholic society, and that their strength of spirit and the power that came from the grace of Jesus in their souls should be recognized. Although cases occurred where Jews turned to Catholicism for ulterior motives, there were also many who were good and believing Catholics. The author of the article emphasized strongly that 'the idea of cutting oneself off from someone completely only because he is a Jew by descent, and despite the fact that he might be an exemplary human being and Catholic, cannot be reconciled with Christian principles'.¹²

Even within the columns of a single periodical one could find radically different views on the subject of baptized Jews. Articles appeared in *Pro Christo* maintaining that a distrustful attitude towards baptized Jews went counter to the Church's teaching. J. M. Chudek wrote:

Some of the more radical, nationalist journalists, who are not always able to agree with Catholic ethics, have lately begun to disseminate the curious view that a Jew can never become a true Catholic . . . However, whenever the former Talmudist has accepted God's grace, the most marvellous Christian virtues have flowered in his spirit and that often to a most heroic degree.¹³

A priest of Jewish origin, J. Unszlicht, stated that 'it would be strange, after all, if the race which gave Jesus and Mary to the world did not also produce their most ardent worshippers'.¹⁴

---

[9] 'Do nieba', *Kalendarz apostolstwa modlitwy* (1922), 187.
[10] 'Okpieni', *Rycerz Niepokalanej* (Sept. 1926), 260.
[11] 'Św Tomasz Akiwnu a kwestia żydowska', *Pro Christo* (Jan. 1938), 34–6.
[12] 'Katolicy i Żydzi', *Królowa apostołów*, (Nov. 1936), 38.
[13] J. M. Chudek, 'Seweryn z Lubomli', *Pro Christo* (Apr. 1928), 256.
[14] Father J. Unszlicht, 'Jak nawracać Żydów', *Pro Christo* (Sept. 1926), 698.

Father J. Urban, in his review of the biography of a converted Jew, emphasized those parts of the subject's life story in which he encountered unfriendly behaviour from Catholics. 'It is a curious thing', wrote the author of the review in conclusion,

that our society, within which live some three million Jews, avoids going deeper into the Jewish problem, indeed closes its eyes so as not to see it, or else limits itself to antisemitic slogans which are for the most part ineffective, even in those quarters to which they are directed; and yet no account is taken of the possibility that there may be among the Jews individuals for whom a place should be found in our community. Sometimes, because one is afraid that an ear of corn may grow on one's soil, one tears up all the wheat.[15]

Baptism was widely regarded as the essential element in the ethnic assimilation of Jews. Neither command of the Polish language nor absorption of Polish culture was sufficient proof of assimilation if not accompanied by baptism, sincerely undertaken. As an author argued in *Przegląd powszechny*, assimilation without conversion was simply not worth considering. 'If a Jew is a real Christian, then he can become a positive element in the Polish nation . . . but one cannot hope that a Jew who is not converted can be a completely healthy and safe member of a Christian society.'[16] In another article in the same periodical it is argued that assimilation can never be complete unless it is accompanied by a complete breaking off of contacts with Jewish circles and rejection of any common cause with Jewish nationalists (Zionists). In other words, a merely formal change of faith would not be sufficient; a condition of acceptance would be an unarguably genuine baptism, leading to a complete break from one's former companions in faith.[17]

A few journalists, holding the view that the distinctiveness of the Jewish people was chiefly racial and not primarily religious, did not acknowledge the possibility of assimilation through baptism. This was a view held by some authors writing in *Pro Christo*. They maintained that, while admittedly the mission to convert the Jews was a Christian duty, there was no duty to assimilate Jews, still less to attempt to transform the converted Jew into a Pole. Converted Jews, it was explained, should remain Jews, continuing to live and work among Jews. These authors considered that the Polishness of converted Jews would always be suspect in the eyes of ethnic Poles, and that such converts lacked the fundamental Polish national temperament. The Catholic Jew therefore found himself in a kind of limbo. It was maintained

---

[15] Father J. Urban's review in *Przegląd powszechny* (Apr. 1929), 130.

[16] Father J. Rostworowski, 'Sprawa Kościoła: Nowe głosy w kwestii żydowskiej', *Przegląd powszechny* (June 1936), 386.

[17] E. Kosibowicz, 'Rzut oka na dzieje "żydowskiej kwestii"', *Przegląd powszechny* (Jan. 1934), 143–62.

that the idea of assimilation had been foisted on the Poles by Jews and had brought the Polish community untold harm.

At this point it is worth drawing attention to a discussion which took place in the columns of *Kultura* during 1936, and which touched on the divergence between the Catholic Church's official position (that the Jewish question was a religious problem and mass conversion would bring an end to the present conflicts) and the opposing view, which held that the Jewish question was one of racial differences, so that conversion alone would not materially change the situation. The discussion elicited a very interesting article by Zofia Kossak, who wrote that it was a basic error to treat the Jewish problem as purely religious. It was rather a racial-national-economic problem. In contrast to the views of the majority of Catholic authors, she stated that in this case the interests of the Pole as a member of the nation were not compatible with his interests as a Catholic. One only had to imagine the mass baptism of Jews to realize that basically nothing would be changed. Baptism might alter the Jews' way of thinking, but not their race. To call the Jewish problem a religious issue was, in her opinion, quite simply sinful. One should rather admit that the struggle against the Jews was being waged for the right to exist in one's own territory—not because one was a Catholic, but in spite of it.[18] By way of reply, Father P. Kuczka stated that the struggle against the Jews was a religious struggle *par excellence*, since the Jews were enemies of the Church. The position of the Pole and that of the Catholic were congruent in this case, since it was the duty of each to resist the enemy. Father Kuczka wrote:

the Jew who accepts baptism from us wants to be considered a Pole, and we usually look upon him as one. Yet it is generally accepted that one's nationality cannot be changed at will ... If, however, an individual wishes to change his national identity, then he is either betraying his own people or else dissembling—that is, lying. So the Jew who accepts baptism and describes himself as a Pole commits either one offence or the other, and whoever lends his hand in support also commits an offence.[19]

From the above discussion it emerges clearly that, irrespective of their attitude towards the conversion of Jews and to neophytes, Catholic journalists in general considered that the only road which could lead Jews to the Polish community, or at least render them less alien to that community, was baptism. No one expressed the opinion that the attempt to convert Jews should be abandoned. These attitudes were derived from the received doctrine that Catholicism was the only true religion and the sole route to salvation; they were also a consequence of the decidedly hostile attitude towards the Jewish religion.

[18] Z. Kossak, 'Nie istnieją sytuacje bez wyjścia', *Kultura* (27 Sept. 1936), 1.
[19] Father P. Kuczka, 'Wolno bronić się przeciw napastnikowi', *Kultura* (8 Nov. 1936), 4.

The only periodical which held that desire to know God might in itself suffice as a means to salvation—even where no baptism had taken place—was the *Rycerz Niepokalanej*. The question was asked whether a Jew could be saved if he wished to know the true God, but, being unsure in which religion he would achieve his goal, continued to live in accordance with the precepts of his own religion. The editor answered: 'let us assume that a certain Jew seeks the truth, but does not acknowledge Catholicism. God will redeem him in so far as he observes the precepts of the Jewish faith, and will require him to perform an act of contrition which will include the desire for holy baptism.'[20] Elsewhere the *Rycerz Niepokalanej* expressed the view that every Jew, in so far as he desired baptism, could become a temple of God. These were answers which were far removed from the views of the majority of Catholic writers, who considered that fulfilment of the requirements of the Jewish religion did not bring an individual closer to God, but rather distanced him.

JEWS AS ENEMIES OF THE CATHOLIC RELIGION

Efforts should be made to convert Jews not only so that they may come to know the true faith, but also because, as followers of the Mosaic faith, they had been enemies of Christianity from its very beginnings. Jews were, above all, the perpetrators of the death of Christ, which, according to Catholic doctrine, burdened all generations of Jews down to the present. This accusation was levelled by many Catholic writers, particularly in those periodicals which were hostile to the Jewish community, such as *Pro Christo*. According to this publication, Jews had of their own volition drawn down upon themselves the curse which, according to divine will, had weighed upon them ever since. All Jewish activities from the time of Christ's crucifixion had been directed by the Devil, and all their efforts had been directed to the destruction of Christianity:

when, nineteen centuries ago, the sons of Israel called in one voice, 'Crucify him, crucify him', drawing down the blood of Christ on themselves and their issue, until the ending of the world, the Jews sold themselves to Satan. From that time onwards they have been consumed by an inextinguishable hatred for Christ and everything he represented or which led to Him. Damned from that time by God, they seemed to be a curse imposed upon the whole world.[21]

Elsewhere we read, 'On this deicidal nation hangs the irrevocable curse of

---

[20] 'Trudności religijne', *Rycerz Niepokalanej* (Apr. 1936), 118.
[21] M. Niezabitowska, 'Masoneria', *Pro Christo* (Apr. 1926), 309.

God.'²² Finally, one of the writers in *Pro Christo* presented the whole Jewish people as a compliant tool in the hand of Satan, created uniquely for the struggle with the Catholic Church. 'Today the chosen people no longer exist, but there exists a people cast out—the seed of the God-killers. And today it seems that the only justification for the existence of Jews is that they are an instrument by which the rebellious angel carries out his designs—to oppose God and his Church.'²³

Other journals did not write of the links between the Jews and Satan, but did emphasize that a curse lay on the whole Jewish race. All the activities undertaken by Jews carried the stigma of excommunication, which hung over the nation of God-killers. All the setbacks and misfortunes which Jews encountered resulted from this, and so it did not lie in the power of mankind to change the situation. 'The Jewish people, after the destruction of Jerusalem, were cast out from Palestine and scattered throughout the world. God punished them, as we Christians believe, because they tortured and crucified our Lord.'²⁴

Catholics should therefore avoid Jews and not allow them to have free association with Christian peoples. After all, each follower of the Mosaic faith was indirectly responsible for the death of Christ, and because of this had become a dangerous enemy of the Catholic Church and its adherents—an enemy, we may conclude, by divine judgement. Working on this assumption, it was impossible to believe in the good intentions, or even neutral attitude, of Jews towards Christian peoples, since their hatred for Christians came not from material circumstances but directly from God. (Jews who did not feel this hate in themselves were converting and thus ceasing to be Jews, so the threat of excommunication did not weigh upon them.) The Church regarded any kind of relationship with Jews as dangerous for a Christian because 'it recognized the threat of excommunication hanging over this people, the germ of rejection and, as it were, of censure which the Jewish spirit drew down upon itself on the first Good Friday of human history, from that moment almost irreversibly infecting everyone who came in contact with it and became imbued with it.'²⁵

Although everything that had happened to the Jewish people following the crucifixion of Christ was in a certain sense unavoidable—it resulted from the plans of Satan, or else was the sentence of divine providence—before that the Jewish people had had freedom of will and had used this freedom to sentence Jesus to death. The Jews had decided to crucify Christ

---

²² A. Dobrowolski, 'Jeszcze w sprawie nawrócenia Israela', *Pro Christo* (Jan. 1927), 48.
²³ L. Czerniewski, 'Katastrofa świata', *Pro Christo* (Oct. 1932), 595.
²⁴ J. Trzecieski, 'Kto wywołał antysemityzm, czyli ruch przeciw Żydom', *Kalendarz królowej apostołów* (1929), 195.
²⁵ 'Romantyczny asemityzm', *Sodalis Marianus* (Feb. 1939), 77.

as a false prophet, since he had not given them what they had expected from the true Messiah—material wealth and sway over the whole world.²⁶ Jews were enemies of Christianity before it had even come into existence: 'The first enemies of the Church were Jews. They wasted the opportunity that Christ presented, and thereafter expected it to be far easier to destroy his work in embryo form. They threw themselves into this with a bitter determination of which only they are capable.'²⁷

The Jews were thus presented to the reader as the slayers of Christ, a tool in the hand of Satan, a people cursed by God who had been in conflict with the Catholic Church and its faithful from the dawn of Christianity. Such a people were not deserving of sympathy, whatever their fate. The Catholic Church, claiming that Christ was the true Messiah, threatened the foundation of the Jewish anticipation of world rule—hence the spontaneous hatred of Jews towards the Church and their desire to destroy it. Father Unszlicht asserted that in the opinion of some Catholics and Talmudists the denial of Christ was the essence of the Jewish spirit.

The only sympathy that the Catholic could entertain towards Jews had nothing to do with their persecution or discrimination, but centred on the tragic fact that, having had among them the chance of salvation, they had rejected it and gone on to commit deicide.²⁸ The only hope for the Jews would be for them to undergo mass baptism, and until that happened the greatest reserve should be shown towards the people responsible for the death of Christ.

The Jewish religion, then, was presented as something opposed to Christianity. The Catholic press in general wrote of the Mosaic faith as though it were the greatest threat to Catholicism, as a religion whose main objective and preoccupation were the destruction of Catholicism, with the eventual aim of world domination. In many articles Catholic writers took the trouble to set out the main tenets of the Jewish religion and the Talmud, reflecting on the fate of the people who had once been God's chosen race and today—as the authors claimed—were cursed by him.

In writing about the Jewish religion, the authors argued that it was not the same as it had been in antiquity. They contrasted the religion of the ancient Jews, based upon the laws of the prophets, with that of contemporary Jews, based on the instructions of the Talmud. These writers explained that one should not project a dislike for contemporary Jewish religion back to the period when the Jewish race was still the chosen people of God. 'One should look at the history of the Jewish people through the prism of their relationship to God and his manifestation. One should distinguish between

[26] Father Patryk, 'Sekta tzw. "Badaczy Pisma Św."', *Pro Christo* (Dec. 1932), 733–42.
[27] 'Kościół Chrystusowy wobec swoich wrogów', *Rycerz Niepokalanej* (July 1929), 195.
[28] J. Nawrocki, 'Błędy Żydów', *Pro Christo* (Oct. 1926), 733–6.

Jews before and after Christ. Until the death of Jesus Christ, this was God's favourite people,' stated the *Rycerz Niepokalanej*.[29]

Other authors showed that the Jews had lost the title 'chosen people' before Christ, although their mission came from God and was exceptionally important for the history of all mankind. However, throughout history the Israelites had repeatedly defied God's will, so that the whole people, instead of moving nearer to God, had slipped lower and lower, and the result of this defiance of God was the setbacks which they had encountered. In the pre-Christian era the Jews had forfeited their title of 'chosen ones', shifting to a demand for material domination of the world. They submitted themselves not to the will of God, but to the temptations of the Devil. The Jews had rejected and betrayed the true Messiah, not because they had not read the writings of the Old Testament, but because they had distorted them and had failed to behave in keeping with their injunctions.[30]

The motif of betraying the ideals of the Old Testament is encountered frequently. It was an attempt to reconcile a definite aversion to all manifestations of the Jewish religion with the assertion that the Old Testament, in spite of being the Jews' holy book, was still holy for Christians also. If one believed that the Jewish religion was completely false and inimical, one would find difficulty in conceding that the Old Testament was the common inheritance of both faiths. So Catholic writers more often wrote that the religion of contemporary Jews was in no way based upon its real tenets. J. Dobraczyński commented:

from the moment he concluded his pact with the Jewish people, the Jews became a tool in the palm of the Creator, an evil, unruly, and base tool ... Numerous prophets served to remind the Jews of their mission ... But as punishments and rewards have not managed to tie the Jews permanently to the pact, so death will be the prophets' reward ... Indeed, the Old Testament as a historical record is one great reproach directed towards the Jews, it is the most antisemitic book.[31]

The Jews were once, it is true, the only people to know the true God. One priest wrote: 'unfortunately even that people was often disloyal to the Lord's plans and in the end their faith became merely dry formalism ... The Jewish spirit did not recognize any higher, spiritual ascent to God, maintaining only the appearances of compliance with the Decalogue and the Mosaic ceremonials.[32]

In the minds of Catholic writers the situation of contemporary Jews was entirely different. The Jews had lost their position as the chosen people and no longer lived according to the tenets—even in a debased form—of the

[29] 'Trudności religijne', *Rycerz Niepokalanej* (Apr. 1939), 116.
[30] Kowalski, 'Posłannictwo i tragedia' (above, n. 4), 312–16.
[31] J. Dobraczyński, 'Od Jahwy do Mesjasza', *Kultura* (21 Mar. 1937), 6.
[32] Father K. Mazurkiewicz, 'Kryzys w świecie starożytnym', *Ruch katolicki* (June 1933), 269.

Old Testament. There could be no comparison between the Jews of biblical times, the chosen race of God, and contemporary Jews. To confuse the two would be to forget, as Father Charszewski lamented in *Przegląd katolicki*, the most important aspect of the Jewish question, that of religion. From this oversight, the author pointed out, resulted the most appalling confusion of views; any antisemitism which left out this aspect descended to the level of anti-Christianism:

In the only true Christian interpretation which fits historical reality, the biblical Jew and the Talmudic Jew are like a sunny day compared with a moonless, overcast night. The spirit of the first is reflected in the Bible, but that of the second in the Talmud—the fruit of the original disintegration of the Jewish spirit.[33]

The main factor determining the behaviour of contemporary Jews, it was generally claimed, was the Talmud and its injunctions. 'There is a great difference between Jews of the old belief and contemporary Jews. The old patriarchs awaited the coming of the Messiah whom we honour in the person of Jesus Christ. Today's Jews reject Christ as the Messiah, and so their religion is, as it were, a house without a foundation,' explained a columnist in *Przewodnik katolicki*.[34] He went on to claim that the basis of contemporary Jewish activity was the Talmud—a repository of Jewish wisdom in which one could find things that were beautiful and sensible, boring and funny, and sometimes dangerous. It was important to pay attention to those passages in which Jews continued to claim for themselves the role of 'chosen people' while other races, the *goyim*, were considered to be the 'footstool' of the Jews.

This was an untypical assessment of the Talmud, since the overwhelming majority of writers did not attribute to it any positive features at all. The Talmud was represented as the main cause of the faults inherent in the Jewish race, as a book which preached the necessity of Jewish world domination. It was a work both dangerous and criminal, and it contained blasphemy, painful to the Christian spirit. As the *kalendarz królowej apostołów* explained to its readers, 'the whole Talmud may be summarized as encapsulating the aim of the Jews to achieve world domination and their methods of achieving their goals—Marxism and the destruction of Christian principles'.[35] Elsewhere we read of the principles of the Jewish race: 'As to their principles, the proof is their holy book, the Talmud: one may steal, commit arson, bear false witness, falsify, kill. He who is not a Jew is an

---

[33] Father I. Charszewski, 'Antysemityzm przeciwchrześcijański', *Przegląd katolicki* (21 Dec. 1922), 387.
[34] 'Nie będziemy płacić na obrzędy cudzej religii', *Przewodnik katolicki* (15 Mar. 1936), 168.
[35] 'Nasz stosunek do Żydów' (above, n. 3), 197.

animal, a pig, who should neither be buried nor rescued if he is drowning.'³⁶

Distaste for Jews and the need to defend the Christian community against them were the direct result of that people's espousal of the hostile ethic of the Talmud, many authors claimed. Jews themselves, admitting that their principles were hostile towards other peoples—treating them like cattle or like slaves who were to serve the chosen people—earned the illwill and rejection of others. The Talmudic ethic, it was explained, was the antithesis of the Christian, and contact with it had a demoralizing effect on Catholics. One could hardly be surprised then that the Christian peoples defended themselves against a people, immersed in such immorality. As one author of wrote in *Kultura*:

> The Talmud is the element which gave birth to 'antisemitism'. The Talmudic principles, in which the Jewish masses are steeped, provoked a reaction from exploited *goyim*. Putting double standards into practice ... theft and deceit, bearing false witness as long as the Jew profits from it at the cost of the *goy* (which the Talmud accepts as permissible and just)—these are the elements which hamper cohabitation between Jews and the rest of the community in the diaspora. And so it is not 'antisemitism' so much as 'anti-Talmudism'.³⁷

In this same periodical J. Dobraczyński held that there were striking analogies between the Talmud and *Mein Kampf*. Similarities existed, the author maintained, in statements on a whole range of different matters—confidence in one's own superiority, inability to extend forgiveness, racism, willingness to employ force.³⁸ One of the most anti-Jewish authors in *Pro Christo* even suggested the complete removal of all Jews from Poland on the grounds that they were adherents of an immoral, even criminal, religion:

> Since the Talmud is an immoral work, and Jews not only support its tenets but rear future generations upon it, then they must be opposed collectively as an immoral sect and denied equal rights with Christians. After all, no one in his right mind would demand that a gang of bandits should be given equal rights with honest and decent Polish citizens.³⁹

It is true, however, that although the Jewish religion itself aroused the aversion of the majority of Catholic journalists, many admired the tenacity of Jews in adhering to its precepts and their scrupulous observation of its requirements. On several occasions Jews were held up as an example to

---

³⁶ 'Żyd', *Kalendarz królowej apostołów* (1927), 107–8.
³⁷ S. J. Nowak, 'Antysemityzm czy antytalmudyzm?', *Kultura* (12 July 1936), 4.
³⁸ J. Dobraczyński, 'Niepokojące analogie', *Kultura* (14 May 1939), 1.
³⁹ Father M. Wiśniewski, 'Rozwiązanie sprawy żydowskiej w świetle rozumu i wiary', *Pro Christo* (Sep. 1933), 513–19.

Catholics, as writers drew attention to the generosity with which they contributed towards the building of synagogues, and their scrupulous observation of the Sabbath and holy days. *Rycerz Niepokalanej* put its readers to shame by pointing out that there were more synagogues in Warsaw than Catholic churches: 'What does that prove? That the Jews stand firm in their faith, that they live it. Should we not all be blushing with shame at this moment?'[40] *Posłaniec serca Jezusa* was inclined to explain the successes of the Jewish community in the economic sphere as a prize awarded by providence for careful observance of prescribed holy days.

These remarks in praise of Jews for their strict adherence to their belief stood in obvious contrast to the others presented above. After all, one cannot at one and the same time regard a given religion as hostile and immoral and adherence to it—the more fervent the better—as a virtue which is rewarded by God and brings the faithful to a higher moral level. It seems that praise concerning the religious faith of Jews was in the first place intended to shame readers, showing them how much less attached to Catholicism they were than the Jews—poorly rated on other grounds—were to their own religion.

The Jewish religion had to be opposed because of its immorality and its false doctrine. An additional reason was that, as some Catholic writers pointed out, the adherents of the Mosaic faith were actively involved in a struggle with Christianity, in particular with the Catholic Church. The cruellest manifestations of this struggle were, a small number of writers claimed, ritual murders or the killing of Christian children to make unleavened bread. The view that such practices had occurred in the past and were still to be found is very rarely encountered in the Catholic journals, since the Catholic authorities had dismissed such stories as being without foundation as early as the eighteenth century. Yet in spite of this official position, a few journalists in *Pro Christo* attempted to assert that the killing of children to make *matsot* had taken place, or, more circumspectly, repeated rumours to that effect. W. Zajęty, in his 1927 article 'Ritual Murder among the Jews', stated without equivocation that such cases were an everyday occurrence. In an article of 1929, whose tone was much calmer, A. F. Kowalski wrote that there could be no definite verdict on whether or not ritual murder existed. One had to treat the allegation with scepticism, but also take account of numerous testimonies, including papal testimonies, to the effect that such events had taken place.

Drawing on the assumptions of the Mosaic religion, one could conclude, as numerous writers tried to convince their readership, that its main enemy, and hence the main goal of its attacks, was the Catholic Church. The Jewish

---

[40] 'Religijność u Żydów i u nas', *Rycerz Niepokalanej* (July 1927), 211.

religion, based on the Talmud, had formed in opposition to Christianity, and combating it was the Christians' chief aim:

In the light of implacable reality, which science confirms and elucidates, the religion of contemporary Jews is a degeneration of the religion of pre-Christian Jews ... In its further development, however, the idea of the AntiChrist evolved, and this became the soul of the new Jewish religion, just as Messianism or Christism was the spirit of the old. Fertilized by this satanic, damnable idea, the Old Testament religion degenerated radically. It was a sacrilegious violation of that religion which gave forth to the world the bastard religion of contemporary Jews.[41]

Jews opposed the Catholic Church in order to demoralize its people and by so doing to enslave them. The greatest barrier to the Jews' plans was the Church, which had for centuries opposed the Jews and unmasked their conspiracies, and in addition was educating its faithful along lines which would prevent the Jewish race from bringing them under its control. From the very first the Jews had harmed the Catholic people. As J. Rostworowski wrote in *Przegląd powszechny*, 'from the first great encounter with the person of Christ, Jewry has not ceased to wage a stubborn fight with the Church and to harm it at whatever cost ... Jews introduced into the Christian community a contagion whose effects are inestimable.'[42] In a further article in the same journal Father J. Urban called the Jews the eternal enemies of the name 'Christian'.[43] Father J. Hetnał, writing in *Przewodnik Katolicki*, asked his readers, 'Who always fought Christianity most intensely?', and replied: 'The Jews. In their hatred they crucified Christ, and even today they are consumed with that same hatred for his followers.'[44]

In their struggle with the Church, it was claimed, the Jews made use of various organizations, most of all the Freemasons. The goal which Freemasons were aiming at had been set for them by Jews, explained the *Kalendarz królowej apostołów*. The aim of the Freemasons was the complete extinction of Christianity, and so, in the first instance, of the Catholic Church. Then they would found the new order, in which Jews would take complete and unlimited control over the world. The author of these claims wrote: 'As Christ and Christianity are their greatest enemy, how could the Masonic programme not appeal to the Jews, who also brand

[41] Father I. Charszewski, 'Religia Żydów współczesnych', *Przegląd katolicki* (22 Feb. 1923), 115.
[42] Rostworowski, 'Sprawa Kościoła' (above, n. 16).
[43] Father J. Urban, 'Sprawa Kościoła', *Przegląd powszechny* (Nov. 1920), No. 443, pp. 314–46.
[44] Father J. Hetnał, 'Socjaliści są pachołkami żydowskimi', *Przewodnik katolicki* (12 June 1938), 403.

Christ and Christianity as their greatest enemy?'[45] Father P. Kuczka wrote an article for *Kultura* which the editors included with the caveat that it contained views which did not represent those of the journal. In it he maintained that the Jews wished to achieve world domination and were hindered in their aims chiefly by the Church and nationalist movements. This explained the profound Jewish hatred for Christianity. 'This is why the Jews fight with such determination against the Catholic Church, supporting and financing Communism, the atheist movement, sectarianism, and sowing demoralization by various means and lack of confidence in the clergy; while on the other hand they fight with equal intensity against the nationalist movements.'[46]

In *Pro Christo* Father Patryk explained the Jewish hatred for the Church in other terms. Jews refused to acknowledge the true Messiah because he had not granted them world domination. The Catholic Church, by declaring that Christ was indeed the one Redeemer who had been awaited for thousands of years, undermined the basis of Jewish ideology and their plans for world domination, and so deprived Jews of the justification for considering themselves to be the race chosen to rule over others:

This is the origin of the elemental hatred of the Jews for the Church, their desire to subvert it, to root out its influence on human souls. The Jews are attempting to destroy the Church with the help of sects which produce and fashion in thought the Jews' own guiding principles ... in this way the Judaic spirit is penetrating Christianity.[47]

An author in *Przegląd powszechny* expressed yet another view, that the Jews had transferred their hatred for the Romans to the Christians at a later stage. The struggle between the Jews and the Christians was not exclusively religious, since it was a continuation of a war between the Aryans and the Semites. Since the first centuries of Christianity the Jews had always and everywhere sided with its enemies: they had allied themselves with the Vandals, the Tartars, the Turks, the Moors, etc. Yet the twentieth century, bringing with it full emancipation of the Jews, had allowed them in their struggle against the Christian peoples to abandon the slogans of a religious struggle, which had only been a pretext, and wage an openly racial war.[48]

All these arguments were an attempt to convince the reader that the struggle waged against the Jews was a just one. It did not contravene the commandment to love one's neighbour because it was essentially the self-defence of a nation against a threatening foe. The struggle with the Jews

---

[45] 'Masonerja', *Kalendarz królowej apostołów* (927), 71.
[46] Kuczka, 'Wolno bronić się ...' (above, n. 19), 733.
[47] Patryk, 'Sekta t.zw. "Badaczy Pisma Św."' *Pro Christo* (above, n. 26).
[48] J. Trepka, 'Niebezpieczeństwo semickie', *Przegląd powszechny* (June 1919), 408–19.

ought to be prosecuted so that the Polish people might profess the Catholic religion in peace and protect its most holy religious and moral values from destruction.

Only *Rycerz Niepokalanej* treated the Jewish religion with some degree of tolerance, even conceding that it contained elements of religious revelation. In the story of the monkey employed to determine which was the superior religion, the animal drew from an urn cards containing the names of the founders of the various religions. It bit, tore, and threw them all away except the card with Moses' name on it, which it allowed to fall to the ground without any obvious sign of disapproval; but it displayed pleasure only when it drew out the card with Jesus' name on it. The author of the tale admitted by this means that the Mosaic religion had certain elements in common with Christianity, or at any rate gave his readership to understand that it did not deserve their ill will—in contrast to other non-Christian religions.[49] The *Rycerz Niepokalanej* did not commend the ridiculing of other religions even when it perceived in them certain comic traits. The editors answered one reader's question by saying that one could calmly demonstrate certain comic or illogical elements of various religions, but laughing at them only infringed the injunction to love one's neigbour, and certainly did not lead to the desired goal of conversion.[50]

THE REASONS FOR DISTINCTIVENESS: RACE OR PSYCHOLOGY?

Although the attitude to Jews as adherents of the Mosaic religion was similar in all the Catholic journals under discussion (since it was the product of received doctrine), fundamental differences appeared when the discussion turned to Jews as a distinctive race. There was no consensus in the periodicals as to whether Jews should be regarded as representatives of another race, and how this should affect their treatment.

The great majority of journalists expressed themselves decidedly against the racist argument, which was inadequate as an explanation for dislike of Jews. Some maintained that pure races as such did not exist in the contemporary world, and so Jews could not be treated as alien from the biological point of view. The *Mały dziennik* maintained that the theory of the inequality of races, propagated in Germany, was sceptically received by anthropologists.[51] In *Pro Christo* we read: 'Standing firmly on Catholic principles, we cannot admit theories of racial struggle and racial hatred.'[52]

[49] 'Pan Bóg i przez nierozumne zwierzę okazuje prawdziwość wiary św', *Kalendarz rycerza Niepokalanej* (1927), 76.
[50] 'Trudności religijne', *Rycerz Niepokalanej* (Oct. 1933), 306.
[51] 'Judaizm a chrystianizm', *Mały dziennik* (7 Feb. 1937), 5.
[52] S. Kaczorowski, 'Zagadnienie żydowskie', *Pro Christo* (June 1933), 336–43.

In an article quoted earlier, Father Charszewski argued that false racial theory ignored the difference between pre-Christian and contemporary Jews. This pseudo-scientific antisemitism, claimed the author, treated all Jews with hatred indiscriminately—both those of ancient times and those of the present day.[53] A writer in *Kultura* argued: 'No one doubts that the ethic of racism is the greatest negation of Catholicism.'[54] Anti-racist sentiments expressed by the Vatican were cited. All opponents of racism were agreed that to view the struggle against Jews as a racial conflict had nothing in common with good sense, Christian love for one's neighbour, or scientific fact. Such authors also argued that it was wrong to remind people of their Jewish origins and background, particularly in cases where they were good Catholics, and in general that one should not judge people on the basis of race.

Voices were heard, however, in support of the racial theory. It is interesting that the same periodical would often publish the opinions of both supporters and opponents of racial theories. Writers who emphasized the racial distinctiveness of Jews generally referred to the age-old antagonism between the Aryan and Jewish races, a hostility which had not sprung up recently, as the result of political or economic conditions, but which had endured for centuries. One author, writing under the pseudonym 'Swastika', wrote:

Despite the fact that religion and upbringing can play a large role . . . nevertheless, it is beyond doubt that the most significant factor in the shaping of a human being is the blood which forms his race . . . Jewish blood rejects Aryan blood and the Aryan spirit; that same instinct of self-preservation bestowed on Aryans the intelligent and just notion of fencing themselves off from Jews and maintaining the purity of their race—in other words, without any admixture of Jewish blood . . . We should count as a Jew not only the follower of the Talmud . . . but every human being who has Jewish blood in his veins . . . In Poland only a person who can prove that there were no ancestors of Jewish race in his family for at least five generations can be considered to be a genuine Aryan.[55]

The author went on to state that there was nothing in racial theory, understood in this sense, which ran counter to Catholic teaching or to Christian morality: the racial struggle against the Jews was not based on the fact that they were a semitic race, but on their being a 'degenerate offshoot' of it and 'scabs in the physical and spiritual sense'.

In the article by Zofia Kossak, quoted above, the author wrote:

Jews are so terribly alien to us, alien and unpleasant, that they are a race apart. They irritate us and all their traits grate against our sensibilities. Their oriental impetuosity, argumentativeness, specific mode of thought, the set of their eyes, the

[53] Charszewski, 'Antysemityzm' (above, n. 33).
[54] W. Zbierowski, 'Rasizm a katolicyzm', *Kultura* (30 Apr. 1939), 1.
[55] 'Zagadnienie rasy, jego uprawnienia etyczne i granice', *Pro Christo* (Aug. 1934) 619–28.

shape of their ears, the winking of their eyelids, the line of their lips, everything. In families of mixed blood we detect the traces of these features to the third or fourth generation and beyond.[56]

Pro Christo printed articles written by Father M. Wiśniewski in which the author, although admitting to a dislike of Jews, declared his opposition to criticism of Jews on the basis of race: 'We are equally convinced that it is not sufficient to use racial grounds in the struggle against you. Racial antagonisms have no place. Racial differences, just like those of nationality, are the product of culture.'[57] Articles, such as those cited earlier, which gave a thorough endorsement to racist theories appeared very infrequently, even in journals which attempted to stir their readership to take up the fight against Jews. But there is a noticeable underlying acceptance of racist theories in numerous comments on 'the peculiarities of Jews' and 'the influence of the Jewish race'. Also noticeable in a number of Catholic journals—especially in *Przewodnik katolicki*, *Pro Christo*, or *Mały dziennik*—is the tendency to search for evidence of Jewish ancestry among opponents.

In this context special mention should be made of the controversy which broke out between Catholic writers as to whether Christ was a Jew. Those who shared the opinion that Jews as a race are inferior to others opposed this view vigorously. J. Dobrowolski, writing in *Kultura*, argued: 'those who refer to the Jewish descent of our Lord do so without justification, since, although he was a man, he was and is above all a God, and his conception was a miracle.'[58]

The opinion of the majority of authors, however, was that Christ's affiliation to the Jewish nation was beyond doubt. They put it forward as one of the crowning arguments against representing the Jews as an inferior race. Racial hatred towards Jews was, in their view, contrary to the spirit of Christianity. 'The racial differences which separate us from the Jews cannot be the reason for hostile attitudes; for Christ our Lord and his most holy mother belong to that race,' explained Father Kowalski in *Ruch katolicki*, at the same time putting forward the idea that separate laws might be introduced for Jews and that they might be treated differently (i.e. in an inferior manner) from other people.[59]

This question was thoroughly investigated by Father Granat in *Przegląd powszechny*, where he set out the whole debate over the racial and ethnic identity of Christ. He stated that there was not the slightest doubt that Jesus was a Semite by blood and race and that he was a Jew, although he

[56] Kossak, 'Nie istnieją sytuacje' (above, n. 18).
[57] Father M. Wiśniewski, 'Na miłość Boską: Nie zwlekajcie', *Pro Christo* (Apr. 1934), 247.
[58] J. Dobrowolski, 'Znów szantaż', *Pro Christo* (Apr. 1934), 262–8.
[59] Kowalski, 'Posłannictwo i tragedia' (above, n. 30).

was free of the numerous and disgusting flaws of contemporary Jews. Despite the fact that by his character Jesus was superior to all past and future generations, he felt vividly the common link with his people. The theory of Aryanism was only an attempt to reconcile racist concepts with Christianity, claimed the author:

The Polish nationalist, to whom tomorrow's Poland belongs, if he wishes to develop in the main current of Catholic thought, must accept the real Christ ... Although Christ the descendant of David and Abraham is for many racists an outrage and an idiocy, we should not be ashamed of the Gospels! To the question of whether or not Christ was a Jew, we should give a straight, clear, and firm reply in the affirmative.[60]

The majority of Catholic authors, as we see, rejected racism and other forms of treating Jews based upon race. What distinguished Jews from Christians was not their blood, but the character or psyche which resulted from their religion or customs. It was a psyche completely different from that of Catholics, such as to rule out completely the possibility of the two peoples, Polish and Jewish, inhabiting the same territory. Jews were different not only because of their religion and customs, but also because of the way they thought, their morality, culture, and principles; as a people, their faults and even their positive characteristics were different. At the same time their mental traits, and their morality in particular, were thought to be considerably inferior to those of Christians.

A journalist in *Kultura* explained the difference in the psychological make-up of Jews by reference to their religion and history, concentrated as they were on material and not spiritual life. Among the Jews, the author maintained, religion played a chiefly 'biological' role in preserving the Jewish-nation; it lacked metaphysics, which was a fundamental shortcoming in the development of the Jewish spirit. 'This characteristic feature of the Jewish psyche—reducing everything to the most shallow level and showing lack of understanding for phenomena and values which are truly spiritual ...'[61]

Przegląd powszechny attributed this distinctiveness of the Jewish mentality to their centuries-long wandering exile, during which the spiritual type of unproductive trader-middleman had become prevalent. The ruling passion had become financial profit and wealth. This had been accompanied by a religious fanaticism, embodied in the Talmud, a conviction of the superiority of the 'chosen people'.[62] In the same issue of *Przegląd powszechny* Father Granat sketched the outline of the contemporary Jew,

[60] Father W. Granat, 'Narodowość Chrystusa i ghetto ławkowe', *Przegląd powszechny* (Feb. 1938), 169–85.
[61] A. Rogalski, 'Kultura polska wobec inwazji żydowskiej', *Kultura* (26 June 1938), 1.
[62] L. Wilczkowski, 'Wojna z Żydami', *Przegląd powszechny* (Sept. 1937), 234–50.

in whose national character the cunning of the slave is intermixed with the superciliousness of power, the mysticism of money and the temporal with a religious belief in the worldly, Messianic mission, in which anarchy of the spirit and the sowing of disintegration amid Christian communities are reconciled with passionate attachment to a long-past glory and some fossilized, Talmudic formulae. The psychological type of the contemporary Jew is repugnant to us, not because of his physical so much as his moral peculiarities.[63]

Nevertheless, the author did not deny the Jewish people certain noble features, and recognized the possibility of national and religious rebirth.

Pro Christo observed that there was an unbridgeable gulf between Poles and Jews, who represented two completely distinct cultures. Anti-Jewish pronouncements had to be understood in this light. But more frequent than reflections on the psyche of the whole nation were comments reproaching Jews for their generic faults, and for the commission of deeds which were not in keeping with Christian morality and law. Above all, the authors dwelt on Jewish membership of international organizations, chiefly Freemasonry and their participation in the Communist movement. Father Wiśniewski in *Pro Christo* listed the main aims which linked Jews and the Masons; causing Poland to secede from Rome; non-religious, pagan schools; legalization of atheist groups; release of political prisoners from jail; abolition of the death sentence and of courts martial; complete freedom of expression in the printed word, and freedom of assembly; dissemination of Bolshevik propaganda among the masses; equal opportunity for national minorities in the economic, political, and national spheres.[64]

The Jews were also seen as disloyal to the Polish State. Particular emphasis was laid on the links Jews had with Communism. In the unending stream of articles on court cases involving Communists, attention was drawn to the number of Jews who had been accused. Authors would often also give the Jewish names of leaders of the Communist movement in Soviet Russia. The majority of writers seemed to assume that although not every Communist was a Jew, every Jew was certainly a Communist. The *Posłaniec serca Jezusowego* explained, 'this is, after all, quite logical. Communism grew out of the Jewish spirit and in its deepest roots possesses all the features of the degenerate materialism of Jews, dreaming of the creation of a promised land on earth.'[65] On the other hand Father R. Moskała, writing in *Przegląd powszechny*, considered it an exaggeration to claim that Communism was a movement planned by Jews from all over the world. The fact that Jews occupied the most senior ranks of the Communist movement was not

---

[63] Granat, 'Narodowość Chrystusa' (above, n. 60), 178.

[64] Father M. Wiśniewski, 'Posunięcia masonerii', *Pro Christo* (Mar. 1926), 225–36.

[65] 'Żydzi rozsadnikami komunizmu', *Posłaniec serca Jezusowego* (Apr.—1938), 220.

evidence that they had organized the Revolution, only that they had benefited from it:

> Moreover, the lack of moral sense, of delicacy and conscience, which characterizes Jews was most closely suited, and could be adapted to, Bolshevik methods ... Whatever truth there is in this matter, Russian Bolshevism is glaring proof of what terribly poor material in the moral sense Jewry is.[66]

Most frequent, however, were articles explaining to the reader frankly that there could be no co-operation of any kind with Jews since they acted in all areas to the detriment of Poland. Perhaps the flavour of such pieces is best captured in a poem which appeared in *Przegląd powszechny*, in which the author lists in rhyme, all the threats which Poland faced at the hands of the Jews:

> Jewry is contaminating Poland thoroughly:
> It scandalizes the young, destroys the unity of the common people.
> By means of the atheistic press it poisons the spirit,
> Incites to evil, provokes, divides ...
> A terrible gangrene has infiltrated our body
> And we ... are blind!
> The Jews have gained control of Polish business,
> As though we were imbeciles,
> And they cheat, extort, and steal,
> While we feed on fantasies,
> Our indolence grows in strength and size,
> And we ... are blind![67]

All Catholic journals tended to attribute a range of negative characteristics to the Jews, and this tendency grew in the second half of the 1930s. Before that period Jews were perceived chiefly, although not exclusively, as enemies of the moral order and of good customs, corrupters of youth, and atheists engaged in conflict with the Church. Much space was taken up with what was seen as the destructive influence of Jewish children and young people on their Polish colleagues at school. Through their contact with Jews, Polish children abandoned their deepest principles and disregarded ethical rules. The warning was given that Jews, as a race which matured earlier, spread immorality among their colleagues in school. Writers deplored the fact that Jewish pupils were granted certain privileges, such as free Saturdays or wearing a *yarmulkah* (head covering) in class. This had a damaging effect on young Poles: it was not possible to introduce a new school programme on Fridays and the *yarmulkah* was a nest for lice. 'And we may add that Jewish

---

[66] Father R. Moskała, 'Nasz sąsiad wschodni', *Przegląd powszechny* (May–June 1920), 387.
[67] 'A myśmy ... ślepi!', *Przegląd powszechny* (7 Dec. 1922), 36.

children are a very turbulent, unruly, slovenly element; in primary schools they have a bad moral effect on Catholic children and corrupt them.'[68]

Jews were said to corrupt young people in the cities, the common people in the market, and officials, who were tempted with bribes.[69] Jews had also gained control of the banks, industry, and land, and in the process had made Christians their servants and slaves. They scorned physical work and abandoned their own lands in order henceforth to live at somebody else's expense—'Like the louse, the bed-bug, the locust, the typhus germ, and the cholera and plague bacillus'.[70] In order to achieve their goal, Jews were ready to swear to be worthy and honest and to forswear theft, forgery, plunder, perjury, arson, usury, contraband, and murder. There were no crimes of which Jews were not capable. They were often compared to parasites, feeding on the Polish organism.

From 1933 onwards the criticism directed towards Jews in Catholic periodicals grew in strength. In addition to the faults which had already been laid at their door, attention was drawn to the Jewish menace in the fields of economy and culture, something which had been referred to earlier but with less alarm. In 1936 the majority of these periodicals published either in whole or in part a pastoral letter from Cardinal August Hlond, the Polish Primate, in which we find some confirmation of the negative opinion of the Jewish community which prevailed in Poland. One passage in the letter read as follows:

It is a fact that Jews oppose the Catholic Church, are steeped in free-thinking, and represent the avant-garde of the atheist movement, the Bolshevik movement, and subversive action. The Jews have a disastrous effect on morality and their publishing-houses dispense pornography. It is true that Jews commit fraud, usury, and are involved in trade in human beings. It is also true that the influence of Jewish young people on their Catholic peers is generally, on the religious and ethical level, a negative one. But we must be fair. Not all Jews are like this. There are very many Jewish faithful who are honest, just, compassionate, and charitable.[71]

A majority of Catholic writers during this period displayed sympathy with the first rather than the second part of this extract. Jews were generally regarded as a harmful and destructive element which Poland could well do without. If a country in which Jews took up residence could not handle them satisfactorily, then the community would grow sick and weaken. Apart from the charges listed above, Jews were accused of disloyalty or hostility towards the Polish state, and of accumulating wealth and privileges without

[68] 'Listy o szkole: Przywileje żydowskie w szkole', *Przewodnik katolicki* (19 June 1927), 14.
[69] Trzecieski, 'Kto wywołał antysemityzm' (above, n. 24).
[70] 'Żyd' (above, n. 36), 107.
[71] 'Głos Prymasa Polski', *Rycerz Niepokalanej* (May 1936), 140.

regard for prevailing law. Such problems were mainly discussed in periodicals interested not only in religious matters but also in contemporary events, in particular the *Mały dziennik*, *Pro Christo*, and *Przegląd powszechny*. Other publications carried less on these subjects.

The authors attempted to convince their readers that from the moment of their settlement in Poland until the present, Jews had harmed and were harming the country, and were not fulfilling the duties of loyal citizens. As their *Przewodnik katolicki* stated tersely, 'Wherever something is taking place which is harmful to our country, just scratch around a little and you will find a Jewish culprit.'[72] They had been responsible in the past for, among other things, the election of August the Strong and the Saxon governments, and the weakening of Poland which had led to the partitions. In 1846 Jews had acted as informers, telling the German police where insurgents were concealed. In 1863 they had provided the insurgents with inferior weapons, and in addition had informed on them to the Muscovites. During the war of 1920 they had sided with the enemy.[73] Following the creation of an independent Poland, they had acted against its interests, speaking out abroad about supposed wrongs they had suffered and arousing in the international arena an uproar over so-called pogroms.[74] The Jew's greatest fear was always the creation of a large, strong Poland, and so, claimed the *Przegląd powszechny*, they made every possible effort to ensure that she remained small and weak.[75] Jews could not be good citizens, the writers stated, because they remained just as alien to the Polish community now as they had been at the time they arrived on Polish territory. Even declarations of loyalty had little meaning: 'We must remember that in moments which are decisive for the Polish nation the Jewish element will always be either passively indifferent within the state, or else acting against her interests both within and without,' commented *Przewodnik katolicki*.[76] If there were ties which linked Jews with Poland, then they were based exclusively on clearly understood interests, mainly of a financial nature: so writers in the *Mały dziennik* informed their readers, referring also to the limited enthusiasm which Jews had shown towards the Polish acquisition of the Teschen district from Czechoslovakia in 1938. 'We do not hold it against the Jews. Once again they have demonstrated that they are foreigners whom only circumstances and "geszeft" [a pejorative reference to Jewish commercial activities] tie to Poland. When, however, there is a need to take risks or

---

[72] 'Gawęda Janka Obleciświata', *Przewodnik katolicki* (26 Mar. 1933), 198.
[73] 'Żydzi w roku 1920', *Mały dziennik* (16 Aug. 1938), 3.
[74] 'Żydzi polscy w oświetleniu ankiet zagranicznych', *Przegląd powszechny* (Feb. 1921), 152–8.
[75] Trepka, 'Niebezpieczeństwo', (above, n. 48).
[76] 'Hasło: "Swój do swego po swoje"', *Przewodnik katolicki* (25 Aug. 1929), 13.

make sacrifices for our country and our people, then they clearly show a cool indifference at the very least.'[77] *Przegląd powszechny* expressed deep scepticism as to whether the majority of the Jewish community possessed any sense of civic duty, of sacrifice, and of uncompromising links in their life and fortunes with Poland.[78]

In the immediate prewar period the attacks on Jews grew in strength. They were reproached for numerous desertions, for mass refusal to undertake army service, for shirking in the rear, for having crossed to the side of the enemy in former conflicts, for too small a financial contribution, and for removing capital from Poland. There were even accusations that Jews, together with the Freemasons and the Communists, had conspired to cause war between Poland and Germany because they wanted such a conflict to smother the antisemitism that was growing everywhere.[79] Readers were assured that in the event of war it was not only the co-operation of Jews but their very loyalty which was in doubt; they had always been parasites rather than fellow citizens of the Polish state.

Articles offering an alternative view—in which attention was drawn to the loyal and patriotic attitude of Jews—were exceedingly rare. They always concerned individuals, and only exceptionally was it pointed out that there were more Jews of this kind, whom the Poles should value and esteem.[80] In a very few pieces the author emphasizes the positive features of the Jewish community. In one of the issues of *Pro Christo* the readers' attention was drawn to the high moral level of the Jewish working class, which, after all, represented the majority of the community. Opinion of the Jews in general was harmed, the author explained, by those elements which do not practise the Mosaic religion, but these were a minority among Jews. Enforced isolation (in ghettos) had engendered many positive features in Jews, such as unity and a capacity for self-defence, and an unbroken effort to maintain ethnic solidarity.[81] A parish priest writing in *Przegląd katolicki* put forward the Jewish innkeeper as a model for Catholics, pointing out that formerly, when the inns had been in German and Jewish ownership, their owners had not allowed people to sit and play cards during holy services. Now, however, that the inns had passed into the hands of Polish Catholics, the owners themselves encouraged young people to stay.[82] On occasion there was reference to the Jews' attempts to combat the white slave trade, and to their kindly treatment of servants. *Przegląd powszechny* recom-

[77] 'Zaolzie i Żydzi', *Mały dziennik* (7 Oct. 1938), 3.
[78] Father E. Kosibowicz, 'Sprawa Kościoła', *Przegląd powszechny* (Mar. 1927), 370–82.
[79] 'Nauki z ubiegłych dni', *Mały dziennik* (6 Oct. 1938), 3.
[80] 'Żyd Powstaniec', *Przewodnik katolicki* (27 Dec. 1931), 879.
[81] 'Dysputy', *Pro Christo* (Nov. 1928), 829–33.
[82] 'Pogawędki proboszczowskie', *Przegląd katolicki* (24 Nov. 1929), 9.

mended the pedagogical works of Janusz Korczak and the poetry of Julian Tuwim. But these were exceptions.

All the articles critical of Jews were intended to convince Catholics that a real danger threatened them from that quarter. The fear was that Poland would be turned into a 'Judeopolska', by which was meant the taking over by Jews of political and economic power and the seizure by a secret, international Jewish government of world hegemony. Such themes were common to the nationalist and the Catholic press. The latter, however, directed most of its attention to the religious aspect of the Jewish danger, explaining that Jews sought world rule and in particular control over Poland because they were driven by the false idea that they were the chosen people. Two elements of deformed Judaism shed light on Jewish aims—the search for a promised land on earth and the economic conquest of the whole world.[83] Jews, since they did not believe in anything better than life on earth—i.e. a life beyond the grave—concentrated on securing for themselves the best possible material conditions in the real world,—and that led them to seize control of ever more areas of life. Even the Jewish non-believer was steeped in this desire for world domination.

The second explanation for Jewish expansion that Catholic journals gave was the link between Jews and Freemasonry, as mentioned above. Freemasonry was presented as an organization of Jews aiming to establish Jewish rule on earth and to draw into its orbit as many non-Jews as possible. Many authors warned that apart from the Freemasons there was another, completely secret, Jewish organization, the assumptions and goals of which were consistent with the principles of the Freemasons—the drive towards world domination and the destruction of Christianity.[84]

The majority of authors did not enquire why the Jews should want to seize power in all countries, but took this as axiomatic. Readers were told that this was not a danger which would threaten Christian nations, and Poland in particular, sometime in the distant future. The Jewish invasion, the discrimination in favour of the Jewish community in Poland, the creation of a 'Judeopolska'—these were all phenomena taking place at that very moment. Father Hetnał in *Przewodnik katolicki* warned dramatically that 'native Poles who have inhabited these lands for centuries ... are sinking in increasing numbers to the level of servants and slaves of the Jews'.[85] The *Kalendarz apostolstwa modlitwy* expressed its view even more plainly: 'A terrible danger hangs over Poland. Day by day, hour by

---

[83] Father J. Urban, 'Rewolucja, Żydzi i księgi święte', *Przegląd powszechny* (July 1922), 97–108.

[84] M. Skrudlik, 'Masoneria, jej cele i działalność', *Kalendarz królowej korony polskiej* (1936), 126–38.

[85] Hetnał, 'Socjaliści' (above, n. 44).

hour, we are gradually ceasing to be masters of our own land! Poland is becoming a Judeopolska!'[86]

The *Mały dziennik* teemed with titles and headings which were intended to alert the reader to the real threat from Jewish power: 'The secret Jewish army awaits the orders of the great inspector to seize control of the world'; 'Europe is aflame. The peoples want to cast off the yoke of the Semites'; 'Jews, Jews—everywhere Jews'; 'If we don't declare war on them, the Jewish rope will strangle us.'[87] Each Pole, it was stressed, must realize that the fate of the world depended upon the attitudes of contemporary Christians and their relationship to Jews. After all, the danger did not threaten only Poland. In spite of their isolation Jews were always hatching plots to seize control of all Christian states. Already the whole press (except the Catholic press), publishing concerns, the radio and film industry were in their hands. This was the way in which Jews took control, argued the writers—by means that were not generally noticeable, demoralizing and drawing to their side unwary young people. As one of the contributors to *Pro Christo* wrote, 'Jewish rabbis, in order to achieve their goals of world domination more quickly, commanded their subordinates to demoralize the "goy" intentionally.'[88]

The power of the Jews was frequently described as 'huge', 'terrible', or 'almost indestructible'. This was supposed to bring home to readers that the struggle with Jews was not a simple matter, and would certainly become an exceedingly important problem. Jews were everywhere, in every country, in all areas of life, in all positions. Father J. Rostworowski wrote in *Przegląd powszechny*: 'Should we not tremble to the very core of our being before the terrible power of international Jewry, which, having caught the world in its spider's web, is now trying to destroy the Christian culture it contains?'[89] *Przegląd katolicki* indeed regretted that 'The Christian world is falling increasingly into the Jewish snare, like Gulliver in the Lilliputians' net. Jews in positions of power have managed to gain increasing control of the press, finance, trade, and industry. Their aim is to rule by money, which today is master throughout the world.'[90]

Poles, like the representatives of other nations, worked hard only to find their efforts exploited by Jews. Jews grasped all their moral and material wealth, the Catholic authors wrote. Religious Jews took control of the banks, industry, and the land, turning Christians into their servants and

---

[86] 'Rodacy! Do walki!', *Kalendarz apostolstwa modlitwy* (1924), 110.

[87] *Mały dziennik* (21 Aug. 1938), 9; (22 Nov. 1935), 2; (30 Oct. 1938), 5; W. Kaszubski, ibid. (11 Dec. 1938), 6.

[88] S. Żelechowski, 'Żydzi a kinematografia', *Pro Christo* (Oct. 1929), 714.

[89] Father J. Rostworowski, 'Nacjonalizm, jego uprawnienia i etyczne granice', *Przegląd powszechny* (Feb. 1923), 114.

[90] 'Kronika kościelna zagraniczna: Niemcy', *Przegląd katolicki* (2 Mar. 1924), 141.

slaves, while secular (non-religious) Jews carried on their destructive work and achieved positions of such influence that the governments of small and medium-sized states were not even capable of independently promulgating laws to protect the interests of native inhabitants.[91] Jews exploited all existing organizations and movements to achieve their aims. The effect of this was the destruction of Christian civilization, since 'Only with the complete victory of anarchy throughout the world can the Jews grasp their eventual goal, absolute power over a humanity grown wild.'[92]

The allegation that there existed a secret Jewish plan to gain power over Christian nations was one of the most frequent and most widely repeated accusations of Catholic writers, one which appeared in almost all the periodicals we have been discussing. Only one of the contributors to *Przegląd powszechny*, in a review of Z. Krasnowski's *Światowa polityka żydowska* [Jewish world politics], insisted that the suspicion that there existed a Jewish world government, some common political leadership, betrayed a complete lack of awareness of the antagonisms which divided Jews, a conscious omission of the opinions of Orthodox Jews, and that it was unethical for a Catholic journalist to make such an allegation. But this was an isolated view.[93]

Almost all of the issues discussed here—the emphasis on the religious, national, and sometimes racial distinctiveness of Jews, the allegation of their destructive role in the Polish state, their lack of loyalty towards the country of their hosts, their plans to usurp power in the economy, culture, and politics—these served as a basis upon which to consider the problem of what kind of attitude to take now and in the future towards the Jews in Poland. From the overwhelming majority of comments we can see most clearly that Catholic writers, with a few notable exceptions, had precious little sympathy for Jews; they assumed that Polish Catholics and Jews would, for many reasons, inevitably develop into hostile camps. They presented the situation obtaining in Poland as one of conflict between Jews and the Christian community, a struggle in which only one side could win. Although for Poles to engage in conflict with the Jews would contravene the Christian principle of love for one's neighbour, nevertheless the majority of writers considered it essential to mount a defence against the threat which they posed.

[91] 'Nasz stosunek do Żydów' (above, n. 3).
[92] Trepka, 'Niebezpieczeństwo' (above, n. 48), 412.
[93] A. Romer, Review, *Przegląd powszechny* (July–Aug. 1934), 153–6.

The Jewish Press in the Political Life of the Second Republic

ANDRZEJ PACZKOWSKI

IN the first half of the twentieth century the fundamental instrument of social communication in the Western world was the press. This was true not only for societies that took the form of modern states, regardless of their internal systems, but also for ethnic and stateless groups. Newspapers and periodicals are among the most important sources of documentation for understanding social, public, and political life. As a rule, historians appreciate this, but they treat the press almost exclusively as a source of facts or opinions; they rarely examine it as a separate, autonomous element of social life, and most scholars who deal with the history of the press ignore the importance of this independent role. Alongside descriptions of events and political opinions to which the press gives a certain permanence, in itself the press constitutes a social fact of considerable significance. The purpose of this essay is to describe the Jewish press in Poland during the period 1918–39 as a socio-political and cultural phenomenon. Rather than concentrating on individual publications, the discussion will centre on the entity which they formed as a whole.

Recent works dealing with the Polish section of the interwar diaspora do not generally focus on the press, even though it is used copiously to support arguments.[1] Marian Fuks, in his book on the Warsaw press, devotes much attention to the period 1918–39,[2] but the work is not very accurate[3] and is largely a description of individual titles, albeit given in an interesting and detailed way. Only recently have detailed bibliographies

---

[1] Joseph Marcus, *Social and Political History of the Jews in Poland, 1919–1939* (Berlin, 1983); Celia S. Heller, *On the Edge of Destruction: Jews of Poland between the Two World Wars* (New York, 1980); Paweł Korzec, *Juifs en Pologne: La Question juive pendant l'entre-deux-guerres* (Paris, 1980).

[2] Marian Fuks, *Prasa żydowska w Warszawie, 1823–1939* (Warsaw, 1979), chs. VIII and IX, 159–293.

[3] Some of the errors have been pointed out by Andrzej Notkowski in his review in *Przegląd historyczny*, 72/4 (1981), 723–46.

by Paul Glikson[4] and Yechiel Szeintuch[5] emerged. The authors themselves regard these as 'introductory': the works contain not only press publications but also almanacs, reports, and even brochures. The available lists do not allow us either to decide what constitutes a newspaper and what does not, and fail to give reliable information on circulation numbers or print-runs.

During the interwar years nothing on the subject emerged from within the Jewish community. The only available material from that period either originates from official sources or was prepared by antisemitic 'experts on Jews'.[6] All these works deal with a limited period and amount to statistical lists rather than descriptions of the press. In more recent monographs covering the whole of Poland the authors have consciously omitted the Jewish press.[7] No history of any of the more important Jewish publications has been written; only Pakentreger's small but fascinating article deals with some of the numerous examples of the provincial press in the town of Kalisz.[8] Although Paul Glikson details 118 items on the history of the Jewish press in Poland in his introduction, the overwhelming majority of these do not deal with the period under discussion.

The Jewish community in Poland was one of the largest in 1931, second in size only to the American and, with its 3.1 million people, equal in number to that of the Soviet Union.[9] The size of this community created an environment conducive to a modern, mass-scale press: only 4 per cent of the Jewish community was employed in agriculture, over three-quarters lived in towns, and up to a quarter resided in large cities of over 200,000 inhabitants. As a separate group, however, the Jewish community exceeded 200,000 people only in Warsaw and Łódź. Next in size was Lwów, with 100,000 Jews: there were thus only three large urban centres for Jewish life in Poland. There were four towns with a medium-sized (40,000–60,000),

---

[4] P. Glikson, *Preliminary Inventory of the Jewish Daily and Periodical Press Published in the Polish Language, 1823–1982* (Jerusalem, 1983).

[5] Y. Szeintuch, *Preliminary Inventory of Yiddish Dailies and Periodicals Published in Poland between the Two World Wars* (Jerusalem, 1986). Both Glikson and Szeintuch reproduce material published previously by Izrael Szajn in *Biuletyn Żydowskiego Instytutu Historycznego* [*BŻIH*] (1971), 107–32 and in J. S. Fishman (ed.), *Studies on Polish Jewry, 1919–1939* (New York, 1984), 422–83.

[6] The most important are Pawel Czajkowski, 'Prasa żydowska w Polsce', *Przegląd judaistyczny* (1992), No. 3, and 'Zygmunt Urbański' [pen-name for a group of workers of the Ministry of the Interior who dealt with the national minorities], *Mniejszości narodowe w Polsce* (Warsaw, 1933); see also the statistical analyses in *Biuletyn Informacyjny Ministerstwa Spraw Wewnsętrznych* [*MSW*], 1924–5.

[7] Wiesław Władyka, *Krew na pierwszej stronie: Sensacyjne dzienniki II Rzeczypospolitej* (Warsaw, 1982); Daria Nałęcz, *Zawód dziennikarza w Polsce, 1918–1939* (Warsaw, 1982); Andrzej Notkowski, *Polska prasa prowincjonalna w II Rzeczypospolitej (1918–1939)* (Warsaw, 1982).

[8] Aleksander Pakentreger, 'Prasa żydowska w Kaliszu (1918–1939)', *BŻIH*, (1974), 97–108.

[9] In subsequent points I refer to material in J. Marcus and Szyja Bronsztejn's *Ludność żydowska w Polsce w okresie międzywojennym: Studium statystyczne* (Warsaw, 1963).

Jewish community. Over two-thirds of Jews lived in small communities, and among these there was considerable territorial scattering, so that most small communities were enclaves surrounded by Poles or other ethnic groups. In contrast to Poles or Ukrainians, whose urban communities were usually surrounded by rural environments, the Jews lived within ethnically alien groups. Territorial boundaries were usually rather clear-cut and corresponded roughly to the former frontiers of Germany, Russia, and Austria-Hungary, with population concentrations distributed over large areas.

Some 60 per cent of the population consisted of very small entrepreneurs, most of whom did not employ other workers. Among those who did hire such workers, as many as 75 per cent owned enterprises in industry and mining; of these there were generally fewer than five hired workers in each enterprise. Less than half of the 500,000 non-agricultural employees worked in medium-sized or large establishments; the rest were employed in small factories. A large part of the Jewish population, therefore, belonged to the very poor lower middle class. The intellectuals and large entrepreneurs (a category that can also be classed as 'enlightened'), along with their families, probably numbered no more than 400,000–500,000 people.

The Jewish population was also less well educated than other urban groups. Although rapid inroads were made in the battle against illiteracy, in 1931 11.3 per cent of the town populations were still unable to read or write, with illiteracy higher among older people and among women; it was also higher in the countryside. The Jewish community in Poland was generally quite young: about 30 per cent were under 15. Both the age and illiteracy indexes show that in the middle of the period under discussion, among the 3.1 million members of the Jewish community no more than 1.8–1.9 million were potential readers of the press. In addition, sex, demography, and income also affected whether people read the press. Thus, the Polish Jewish newspaper readership was relatively small and largely scattered (with a small number of larger centres), and was overwhelmingly poor.

In addition, the Jews in Poland were a multilingual community: in the 1931 census 10 per cent declared that they normally spoke a language other than Yiddish, and there was almost universal use of Polish, especially among the younger generation that attended school after 1918.[10] Some regularly spoke German (in Bielsko-Biała even Jewish periodicals were published in German), while in the eastern regions Russian was quite prevalent (the first Jewish periodical appearing in Białystok in 1919–20 was called *Golos Bielostoka*). If the Jewish readership of German or Russian press publications was minor, those who read the Polish press were considerably more numerous.

[10] This question is discussed by C. S. Heller, 'Poles of Jewish Background: The Case of Assimilation without Integration in Inter-war Poland', in Fishman (ed.), *Studies on Polish Jewry*, 242–76.

The Geography of the Jewish Press in Poland, 1938

Key:

— — —   boundaries of the partitioning states

●   localities where the Jewish press appeared in Yiddish and Hebrew

△   localities where the Jewish press appeared in Polish

▽   localities where the Jewish press appeared in German

The Distribution of the Jewish Polish-language Press, 1918–1939

Key:

— — — boundaries of partitioning states

· · · · · · boundary of the former kingdom of Poland

These publications were much more varied, easily accessible, and, as a rule, cheaper than the Jewish ones. Thus, at least some members of the Jewish community, even among those who declared their mother tongue to be Yiddish or Hebrew, were families with the Polish press.[11]

Factors affecting this readership included socio-professional structure, type of settlement or education, political and social activity, and participation in institutional political life. There was a high degree of political mobilization within the Jewish community and participation in organized political activity was widespread, among both the older and the younger generation. Political participation took different forms. Only some Polish parties were linked to international groupings (the illegal Communist Party and the Polish Socialist Party), while many Jewish parties and political groups were connected with corresponding international centres. In this way political involvement and interests were stimulated not solely by events that occurred in the Jewish political environment in Poland, but also abroad, in the political centres of the diaspora. The system of religious communities also distinguished the Jewish community's public life from that of the Poles. Although the state authorities put an end to the projects to create national Jewish autonomy in Poland, the self-government system (*kahal*) established in a decree of 7 February 1919 soon extended beyond the domain of religion, and of interest also to anti-religious parties such as the Socialist Bund. The institutions of the *kahal* were based on the principle of election, which naturally gave rise to contention and political polemics. There were about 600 such *kehillot* in Poland, and even if the majority were too small to become the scene of political battles, there was considerable tension among the larger ones. In the years 1919–39 the Jewish community in Poland took part in six parliamentary elections, five elections to municipal councils, and several elections to the boards of religious communities. One group even participated in successive elections to conventions held by the Jewish parties. Political antagonism, in which the press must have played a large role, was rather frequent.

Joseph Marcus[12] devotes much space to the existence and functioning of what he describes as the 'civic society'. Here we can present only a few facts that testify to the dimension and trends of participation and activity. In 1928, for example, there existed in Poland 1,350 local organizations of merchants, petty traders, or artisans, and these had a total of 330,000 members. In 1930 about 800 Jewish co-operatives (which mostly forwarded financial advances to their members) had about 260,000 shareholders. In

---

[11] The multilingual aspect of the press is discussed below.
[12] Marcus, *Social and Political History*, esp. chs. 8 and 16. See also Rachel Ertel, *Le Shtetl: La Bourgade juive de la Pologne—de la tradition à la modernité* (Paris, 1968), esp. chs. IV, VII, and VIII.

1929 4,650 councillors elected from Jewish lists took part in municipal councils—amounting to 32 per cent of all the councillors, with the exception of the Poznań and Pomorze voivodships, where the number of Jews was minuscule. At least 6,000–7,000 people sat on the boards of the *kehillot*. The ballot lists of the Jewish parties for the parliamentary elections, whether as separate groups or coalitions, gained up to a million votes from 1922 to 1930. In 1930 there were about 700,000 votes, and in 1939 about 460,000. In Warsaw during the elections to the municipal councils held at the end of 1938 the Jewish lists won 76,600 votes, in Łódź 54,000. At the end of the interwar period over 30,000 members belonged to Bund trade unions, while the unions connected with Po'alci Tsion Right had around 23,000 workers. In 1932 there were about 250 registered Jewish unions, associations, and institutions in Warsaw.[13] The range of organized social and political life influenced the size and character of the press published and read by the Jewish community.

There is still another important element affecting research on the press, which became apparent during an investigation of press handling of Polish emigration.[14] The Jewish community in Poland, its publications, and the contents and information provided in its press can be regarded as similar in many ways to communities of ethnic minorities abroad. Thus, Poles viewed their kinsmen in foreign countries as less immediately interesting: the world was divided into 'Poland' and 'non-Poland'. On the other hand, until 1930 Poles living in the United States were as interested in their old homeland as they were in their adopted country and the ethnic group to which they belonged; they were also interested in other centres for Polish *émigrés*, such as Brazil or France. Similarly, if the Jewish press coverage is indicative of the interests of the Jewish community, then the interest in what was happening to fellow Jews outside Poland was very keen. At least four main areas were covered in the Jewish press: Poland, Jews in Poland, the worldwide Jewish community, and Palestine, the old homeland. In 1938, for example, *Nasz przegląd* [Our review], the largest Jewish Polish-language daily, had as many as thirty-seven correspondents abroad (part-time rather than special staff): seven sent information and commentaries from towns on the eastern coast of the Mediterranean, from Salonika to Beirut and Jerusalem, four wrote from the United States, and two were in Australia.[15]

---

[13] Marcus, *Social and Political History*, and 'Urbański', *Mniejszości narodowe w Polsce*. See also the *Mały rocznik statystyczyny, 1939*; and Adam Próchnik, *Pierwsze pietnastolecie Polski niepodległej* (Warsaw, 1983).

[14] Included in A. Paczkowski, *Prasa polonijna w latach 1870–1939* (Warsaw, 1977); id., *Prasa i społeczność polska we Francji (1920–1940)* (Wrocław, 1979).

[15] *Nasz przegląd*, 263 (18 Sept. 1938) (anniversary number). For the sake of comparison, one of the largest Polish dailies at the time, *Ilustrowany Kurier Codzienny*, had its own correspondents in 16 foreign cities.

Without a detailed and well-verified bibliography, the size of the Jewish press in Poland from 1918 to 1939 cannot be stated absolutely. The main difficulty is not so much inaccuracies in the data provided by Główny Urząd Statystyczny [GUS: Main Statistical Office] but rather that it classified publications according to the language they were written in. From the beginning of the Second Republic, however, a number of Jewish publications were written in Polish. According to data furnished by the Ministry of the Interior, in 1932 these comprised 14.2 per cent of the Jewish press and 19.6 per cent of one-off editions.[16] This is not insignificant: a list made by Izrael Szajn included a total of 172 titles.[17] The GUS data should thus be supplemented by about 10–15 per cent. The state and growth of the Jewish press are best illustrated by the following list of the number of Yiddish and Hebrew press publications between 1922 and 1937:[18]

1922	176	1934	79
1923	60	1935	102
1924	72	1936	123
1932	93	1937	130
1933	80		

The crisis of 1923, so evident in this list, affected the entire Polish press, although Jewish publications suffered particularly badly. This was the outcome of both economic and political problems: there was very high inflation and an increasingly unstable political situation. If 1924 is taken as the first normal year—the beginning of a slight boom, and less volatility in the currency market—then it can be said that the Jewish press increased by 80.6 per cent, a rate which lags behind the growth of all press publications in Poland (139.8 per cent). This difference was mainly brought about by the greater decline of the Jewish press during the Great Depression of 1929–33; both crises seem to indicate that the Jewish press was much more sensitive to the impact of economic decline than the press in Poland as a whole. Perhaps the structure of the Jewish press, dominated by more popular publications and therefore more dependent on a fluctuating readers' market, was responsible. For instance, in 1930 daily newspapers and periodicals that were issued more than once a month constituted 66.7 per cent of the Jewish press and 45.1 per cent of the Polish-language press. Since the dynamics and growth of the press in Poland during that period were determined by periodicals that appeared irregularly, the structure of the Jewish press caused it to suffer from a slower pace of development. One main factor may

---

[16] 'Urbański', *Mniejszości narodowe w Polsce*, 311.
[17] The list (pp. 108–32 of the article) is probably incomplete and includes a number of errors.
[18] The GUS publications for the years 1925–31 give yearly data only. Unless another source is cited, I take data presented below from official GUS publications.

have been the multilingual capacity of Polish Jews: so many of them read Polish professional and specialist publications that the need for Yiddish texts of this type was limited.

It can be concluded from the statistical data that during the first years of the reborn Poland the number of titles published by the Jewish press grew very rapidly. In 1922 Yiddish and Hebrew publications comprised as much as 14 per cent of the press issued in Poland, and practically 23 per cent of the Warsaw press. The rate of growth from 1919 to 1922 for Jewish publications was considerably higher than that of the Polish press or of other nationalities. This activity was a natural aftermath of the existing political and social situation.

The Polish struggle for the frontiers, particularly dramatic in the east, was accompanied by a great intensification of nationalism. Anti-Jewish pogroms in 1918–19 along the front lines reached proportions similar to those of 1881 and 1905–6 in those areas. In the course of several years, the population was mobilized by three mass election campaigns (parliamentary elections in 1919 and 1922 and municipal councils in 1919). After the Balfour Declaration and the end of the First World War, interest in Palestine and emigration to Erets Yisrael grew significantly. Violent controversies broke out between the Polish and Jewish communities, and within the latter there was contention about the purpose, possibility, and range of Jewish autonomy. Tidal waves of unrest, strikes, and rebellions passed through large parts of Europe, foreshadowing the spread of the Bolshevik revolution within the heart of the old Continent, if not throughout all Europe. The polemical and political nature of the Jewish press in Poland emerged clearly at this time,[19] but the data from later years show that polemics also remained important afterwards. At least two factors account for this: the pronounced differences in political views within the Jewish community, and the constant threat from Polish antisemitism (socially sanctioned, and in certain periods state-instigated), as well as from other minority groups. The polemics in the Jewish press were directed not only against political rivals but also against the hostile or unfriendly surroundings. In the 1930s the need to conduct a press struggle—propagandist and polemical—was increased by the threat to the European diaspora from the developing, and in some countries victorious, Fascist and Nazi nationalisms.

---

[19] At the beginning of the 1930s the proportion of political journals in the press of the main national minority groups was as follows (the two percentage figures refer to number of titles and total print-runs respectively): Jewish press (1932)—67.6%/78.7%; German press (1932)—42.5%/43.9%; Ukrainian press (1930)—25.3%/33.2%. The Jewish information is from Urbański, *Mniejszości narodowe w Polsce*; the German information is from Karol Kaschnitz, *Prasa niemiecka w Polsce* (Warsaw, 1933); the Ukrainian information is from Marian Feliński, 'Prasa ukraińska w Polsce', *Sprawy narodowościowe* (1930), No. 1.

One of the effects of this sudden upsurge in publications during the first years of the Second Republic was the predominance of the Jewish press in Warsaw as compared with other centres, especially the small provincial towns. It is true that the capital always enjoyed a predominance, with at least 40 per cent of the Yiddish and Hebrew press over the whole interwar period being published in Warsaw. Warsaw's zenith was in the period 1919–20 when about two-thirds of the Jewish press originated in the capital, and only about a tenth appeared in provincial towns and small townships.[20] After the 1923 crisis the proportions changed. Data from the Great Depression indicate that the provincial Jewish press was more stable than titles issued in Warsaw and other large urban centres. However, Warsaw did in fact exhibit greater stability than the other urban centres. In the 1930s, in contrast to the Jewish press in all of Poland (regardless of language), the Jewish Warsaw publications increased. In those years, Jewish titles in Warsaw amounted to half of total press publication in the capital. The production of the Yiddish and Hebrew press over the period 1922–37 was distributed geographically in the following proportions (figures are percentages):

1922: Warsaw 65.3; Łódź, Kraków, Lwów, and Vilna 24.4; remaining towns 10.3
1937: Warsaw 43.8; Łódź, Kraków, Lwów, and Vilna 17.7; remaining towns 38.5

The tempo of growth for the provincial Jewish press was quicker than that of provincial publications in other languages. The difference may reflect a greater openness to modernization within the Jewish community compared with citizens of the Polish state as a whole. This may be an oversimplification, but the reason for the difference is certainly worth investigating, especially by comparing all nationalities living in Poland at that time, rather than using only the distinction between Jews and non-Jews.[21] In any case, the increase in the number of provincial Jewish press publications was quite distinct, although some adjustments should be made (e.g., additions to the data for Warsaw and the large towns) by including Jewish Polish-language titles. The increase in publications was characterized not only by more titles, but also by the appearance of publishing activity in new places. At the beginning of the 1920s the Hebrew and Yiddish papers were published in about twenty localities, but at the beginning of the 1930s forty Polish towns boasted their own Jewish press.

At this time the small towns in the north-eastern frontier areas became

---

[20] With the exception of the large towns, Łódź, Kraków, Lwów, and Vilna.
[21] The division given here would tend to play down differences between the German and Polish populations, and perhaps assimilate them with the virtually peasant Ukrainian and Belarussian communities.

important centres for the development of a provincial press. To a great extent, it was a press of the *shtetl*. In 1938 there existed at least eight small towns in which the only press was Hebrew and Yiddish; in eleven other towns such publications were equal in number to those in Polish.[22] This does not necessarily indicate that the Jews were more avid readers of newspapers than the Poles, but it does demonstrate the scope of the political and intellectual activity among members of the Jewish community, even in areas with small population concentrations.

Kalisz was certainly not an average *shtetl*: it was considered a sizeable town, with a population of about 69,000 in 1931, and with a considerable Jewish community of almost 20,000. It was located on the border between the old Prussian and Russian partitions, in a relatively prosperous area. Local cultural and political life was well developed, and in 1927 Kalisz was the centre of a region where ten Polish journals, including five dailies, were published. This town is the only Jewish publication centre to have formed the subject of a separate study, by Aleksander Pakentreger.[23] From 1927 to the start of the war it had two or three permanent Jewish journals; altogether, it was home to at least ten such publications, including a variant of the Warsaw *Undzer expres*. Two weeklies, the Zionist *Kalisher vokh* and the *Kalisher lebn* (from 1937, entitled *Dos naye lebn*), operated in a spirit of amicable rivalry, constantly polemicizing against each other. From time to time they were joined by a third publication: from 1934 to 1936 it was the weekly *Dos yidishe vort*, which was founded to provide a public forum for debate on the question of filling the vacant post of the rabbi of Kalisz, but may also have served as a spin-off of a Warsaw sensationalist journal. Regardless of the controversies (or perhaps because of them), the two main publications of the Kalisz Jews were important for maintaining the internal ties of the community and those between Kalisz and neighbouring *shtetl*s. The publications helped with the organization of many local social initiatives, and served as platforms for the consolidation of opinion. Despite the presence of the press from the larger urban centres, the local publications also provided information about the world and the larger diaspora. It is a pity that in her 'historical voyage' through the Polish *shtetl*s Rachel Ertel did not deal with any town which possessed its own press.[24]

[22] These are rough data taken from the press catalogue of PAR 1938–9 (PAR was an advertising agency: Polska Agencja Reklama Franciska Krajny, Poznań. The small towns were: Ostrowiec Świętokrzyski, Międzyrzec, Zamość, Tomaszów Mazowiecki (which had two Jewish journals), Prużana, Dubno, Kowel, and Równe. In such towns as Wilno, Częstochowa, or Grodno the number of Jewish journals was almost equal to those in Polish. In Białystok there were even more Jewish than Polish journals.

[23] 'Prasa żydowska w Kaliszu (1918–1939)'.

[24] *Le Shtetl*. The author did not notice that there were two Polish-language Jewish journals in Nowy Sącz, although Szajn lists them in his bibliography.

The rate of growth of the Jewish press in Poland after the initial expansion between 1919 and 1922 was greatest in the medium and small towns. It was the intellectual and political activity of this press that contributed to the increase in the number of titles. Although the Jewish press lost the clear superiority it enjoyed during the first years of the Second Republic, it continued to account for a very large proportion of the total output of presses representing the national minorities:

1919	44.9%	1931	38.2%
1922	69.6%	1934	27.1%
1924	33.6%	1937	29.7%
1928	40.0%		

Originally, the Jewish press owed its position to the downfall of the German press, which did not begin to revive until 1924–25; in the 1930s, however, its main rival was the Ukrainian press, which developed rapidly from a base of only a few publications. The addition of the Polish language press would only slightly alter those proportions, which remained similar throughout the interwar period.

Although there are no monographs dealing with the reading public in the small and medium-sized towns, it is clear that at least some publications from Warsaw and other large cities must have been imported into these areas. According to information gathered by the Ministry of the Interior, which gives data for the entire press rather than for Jewish publications alone, in 1932 half of the print-runs of the nine Yiddish dailies published in Warsaw were sent outside the capital[25] (i.e. about 83,000 copies). While there are no precise circulation data, at least some copies must have reached the towns and small townships of the central voivodships. The Polish-language Jewish dailies in the capital must also have forwarded part of their editions to the provinces. Given these probabilities, one can estimate that on every day except Saturday about 100,000 copies of Jewish-press publications arrived in the smaller and larger *shtetl*s. This is a significant figure: it probably comprises about a third of all Jewish journals in Poland.[26] There is only fragmentary information on the appearance of a system of provincial editions of journals published by the large centres. Warsaw, Kraków, Łódź, and Poznań, but this became a widespread phenomenon in the 1930s. From 1938 to 1939 provincial editions of various titles constituted practically 40 per cent of the entire Polish daily press. A number of large journals also

---

[25] A. Paczkowski, 'Nakłady dzienników warszawskich w latach 1931–1938', *Rocznik historii czasopiśmiennictwa polskiego*, vol. XV, (1976), No. 1, p. 73, and tables.

[26] 'Urbański', *Mniejszości narodowe w Polsce*, claims that the total daily print-run of all publication from the Jewish press was 289,000.

published so-called 'franchised editions' (*nakłady listowe*), although statistics have not yet been compiled on these. It is more than likely that the Jewish press also had such a system. Although the role played by provincial editions of titles originating in the large towns was considerable in helping to integrate the community in the national political sphere—and this may even have been foremost in the plans of the publishers—it was not the only function performed by such a press. In many *shtetl*s it was also the distributor of modern cultural forms and stood at the vanguard of mass secular culture.

Marian Fuks describes the reasons for the existence of a Jewish Polish-language press.[27] It would be difficult to add anything new to his arguments, but there are certain problems with the territorial distribution of these publications. For example, one of the Warsaw dailies described by Fuks as Jewish is not included in Szajn's bibliography. This publication, known as *Ostatnie wiadomości* [Latest news], was founded by Samuel Jackan, one of the pioneers of the Yiddish press in Poland, and until 1938 the publication was owned by Jews. Originally one of the most popular publications in the capital, as well as having many provincial editions, *Ostatnie wiadomości* did not advertise the fact that it was part of the Jewish press, and the editor's office always employed a large number of Poles as editors-in-chief. In the absence of any polls of the reading public, it will probably never be possible to determine whether Poles or Jews were the principal readers of the publication. To take a further example: how does one classify a journal categorized by Szajn as part of the Jewish press but which appeared from 1919 to 1929 in Łódź in Polish and was called *Głos Polski* [The voice of Poland]? If the Nuremberg norms were applied (and there were people willing to use this standard in Poland at the time), how can a publication edited by Ignacy Rosner, Stefan Grostern, or Jozef Wassercug (Wasowski) be classified? One of the newspapers, the Łódź-based *Republika*, was completely owned by important textile industrialists from this Polish 'Manchester', who were overwhelmingly Jewish. One thing that can be said of the *Ostatnie wiadomości* or the Łódź *Expres ilustrowany* is that these publications did not contain antisemitic accounts. Is this a sufficient criterion by which to recognize such newspapers as Jewish? This would mean that in Poland in the years between the First and Second World Wars only those journals that openly declared their Jewish affiliation should be regarded as Jewish.

Galicia was well represented in the Jewish Polish-language press, as, of course, was Warsaw. According to Szajn's bibliography, 50 per cent of all publications of this type appeared in the capital, and 32 per cent in both

---

[27] Fuks, *Prasa żydowska*, ch. IX.

parts of Galicia. In contrast to this, 1930 data provided by GUS show that only 6.5 per cent of the Yiddish and Hebrew periodicals were published in Galicia. The second and third largest (the largest was the Warsaw *Nasz przegląd*) and oldest Polish-language dailies were published in Kraków and Lwów (*Nowy dziennik* [New journal] and *Chwila* [Moment]). It should be noted that all three were regarded as leading Zionist publications and had nothing in common with the assimilationist trend, which had fallen into disrepute in 1912, dying off as a political movement under the impact of the 1918–20 pogroms.

An examination of the Jewish Polish-language press shows that there were significant differences in political culture between the former Russian and Austrian partitions: for example, in all the parliamentary elections Galician Zionists presented lists separate from their former ideological comrades in the Russian partition. An indication of the growth of acculturationist tendencies, not necessarily associated with the loss of Jewish national identity, was the fact that among the 72 press publications issued in the Warsaw ghetto as many as 24 appeared in Polish (as well as three publications by the assimilationists).[28] Certainly, the Jewish Polish-language press in this period had a secure readership. Journals of this type were relatively permanent; their circulation did not differ from Yiddish publications, and in certain periods they increased their readership when the Yiddish ones did not.[29] The remnants of acculturation to the languages of the partitionary powers proved less lasting, but as late as 1922–5 the Russian-language Jewish weekly *Svobodnaya mysl* still appeared in Białystok, while the German-language publications in Bielsko-Biała were issued until the end of the interwar period.

With the present state of research, it is impossible to compile statistics of press readership among the Jewish population in Poland. First, only fragmentary data about circulations have been established and published, and second, it is not possible to identify the reading public of the Polish press as a whole, or of the Jewish Polish-language press. From the scattered circulation data, it can be ascertained that in 1925 there was a total print-run of 87,000 for Jewish daily publications,[30] in 1930 200,000, in 1932 290,000, and in 1938 350,000. It is highly probable that the number for 1925 is too low, but even with such flawed information it is possible to obtain a picture of dynamic

---

[28] These figures are based on the census in Fuks, *Prasa żydowska*, 299–302.

[29] According to data gathered by the Ministry of the Interior, 'the [annual] number of Polish-language periodicals [printed] grew between 1929 and 1932 from 85,000 to 105,000 [i.e. by 23.5 per cent]. On the other hand, the Jewish-language print-run fell by 6% ('Urbański', *Mniejszości narodowe w Polsce*, 313).

[30] This includes dailies in Polish; all data are taken from Ministry of the Interior sources.

growth that exceeded that of the Polish journals.[31] What characterized the daily press in the period under discussion was an increase in print-runs rather than more titles. This fact shows the other side of the coin, the relatively weak growth in the number of different publications among the Jewish press. On the estimation that in 1938 the Jewish population in Poland amounted to about 3.3 million there was one copy of a Jewish journal published for every 10 people (regardless of age), or 10:100.[32] In 1932 a similar index for the German minority was 13:100, and in 1938 for the native Polish population, 8:100. And the end of the 1930s the same index in the United States was 31:100, in Great Britain 38:100, and in France 27:100.

The legal system that regulated the existence of the press exerted an important influence on the extent of press activity. In the Second Republic, the press system evolved gradually; after the *coup* of May 1926 the free press was replaced by a system of control, but this never acquired a totalitarian character. Control was exercised from the very beginning of the reborn Polish state, as from the very first weeks the publishers had to reckon with the possibility of confiscation. Throughout the entire interwar period—during the 'Sejmocracy' as well as after the May *coup*—two categories of the press were subject to a particularly strong control and seizure of contents: the Communist press (in all languages) and Ukrainian journals. Contrary to Fuks's argument,[33] the Jewish press was not the object of special harassment. Searches, closing of printing shops, suspension of journals, and confiscations took place with regard to the Polish press as well (albeit to a lesser degree) prior to May 1926, and to a similar or even greater extent during the Piłsudski government. We have relatively little systematic information about the scope of the seizures, that most universal technique for the controlling of content. Table 1 reproduces the only data published in Poland which cover the entire press.

Even Michal Pietrzak, author of a work on administrative and judicial control and repression of the press,[34] does not find evidence of an especially negative attitude towards the Jewish press, although he is critical of the

---

[31] According to Ministry of Interior data, the number of Polish dailies issued in the mid-1920s was about 750,000, and at the end of the 1930s about 1,800,000 (A. Paczkowski, *Prasa codzienna Warszawy w latach 1918–1938* (Warsaw, 1983), 285). The number of copies of German dailies issued in 1925 was about 56,000, and in 1932, about 98,000. However, the reading public among this particular minority imported press, including dailies, from neighbouring Germany. The Ukrainian dailies did not exceed 5,000–10,000 copies; the Belorussians did not publish a daily newspaper.

[32] Counting only the population over the age of 15 (*c.* 2.3 million), the index was 13:100; subtracting the non-literate adult population (about 30,000), a more realistic figure would be 14.5:100.

[33] *Prasa żydowska*, 177, 179, 190, 191.

[34] *Reglamentacja wolności prasy w Polsce (1918–1939)* (Warsaw, 1963).

Table 1 Journals seized in Poland, 1928 and 1931[a]

Press	Jan.–Feb. 1928		1931	
	No.	%[b]	No.	%
Jewish[c]	68	5.4	145	6.9
German	103	8.2	82	3.9
Ukrainian	223	17.9	334	15.9
Other ethnic minorities	68	5.4	—	—
Polish	790	63.1	1539	73.3
TOTAL	1252		2100	

[a] Figures include partial confiscation as well as seizures of entire issues
[b] Of total seizures.
[c] In all languages.

Source: Ministry of the Interior documents. See Notkowski, *Przegląd historyczny*, 7214 (1981), 734.

press policy pursued by the successive governments of the Second Republic. The Jewish press was subject to control for different types of content than in the case of the Polish or Ukrainian press: the basic object of confiscations in the Jewish press were articles and information on discrimination against Jews, or the passivity of the authorities in regard to antisemitic excesses, or pieces containing criticism of decisions by the authorities on various Jewish issues. In the Polish press confiscation affected anti-government statements, and the more celebrated publications of the opposition were subjected to constant harassment: in certain cases every second or third number was seized for several years. The Ukrainian press, always less numerous than Jewish publications and with considerably smaller print-runs, was seized for statements regarded as separatist or outrightly irredentist. In the domain of ethnic relations, the Polish-language press of the Jews was regarded as unquestionably opposed to the state authorities.

Attacks by antisemitic armed bands against editors' offices or Jewish printing-shops had their counterparts in similar attacks organized by pro-government societies on offices of opposition publications or in the assault of anti-government journalists by 'unknown perpetrators'. Yet a definite anti-Jewish bias may be deduced from the fact that antisemitic numbers of the press (not only Polish) were seized rarely and only in the most extreme cases, and some journals devoted exclusively to antisemitic propaganda appeared without hindrance. There were other forms of harassing the Jewish press, such as difficulties connected with obtaining credit or in the process of distribution.[35]

[35] These problems were encountered by Warsaw Jewish journals, as described by Eugeniusz Rudziński, *Informacyjne agencje prasowe w Polsce, 1926–1936* (Warsaw, 1970), 109.

After May 1926 the Jewish press obtained very little officially generated revenue in the form of fees (always generous) for carrying advertisements of state enterprises or court announcements[36] (this 'advertisement manna' was also denied to the opposition press). The Jewish press received no income whatever from these sources during 1922-3, which was a particularly critical period for the press; the National Democratic opposition press was also deprived of such subsidies. Altogether, apart from the radical left-wing Communist and pro-Communist Jewish press, the legal conditions under which the remaining (or main) segment of the Jewish press functioned were no different from those in which the opposition press had to suffer. The main difference lay in the consistency with which the Jewish press was regarded as oppositional for practically the entire Second Republic, while the Endek press was only really in this position after 1926.

The Jewish press as a whole was incomparably more open to contacts with Polish society, as well as with other publishing milieux, than that of other national minorities. This can be seen from the appearance of Polish-language journals whose task was to inform Polish public opinion (and the government) about the mood and sentiment of the Jewish community. It is also evidenced in the Warsaw and Łódź journalists' syndicate, which included autonomous Jewish sections, while journalists from the Jewish press were also members of many other local syndicates; only at the end of the 1930s did some of the syndicates (in Vilna, Pomerania, Wielkopolska, where similar steps were taken against the Germans in the 1920s) introduce into their constitutions or interpretations thereof the principle of *numerus nullus* (total exclusion of a given group). Leading journalists of the Jewish press enjoyed high professional esteem, but these writers never held chief posts in the all-Polish associations. The exchange of journalists between the Polish and Jewish press was insignificant, except for journals which did not openly declare the nationality of their owners. The publishers of the main Jewish journals belonged to Polski Związek Wydawców Dzienników i Czasopism (the Polish Union of Publishers of Daily Newspapers and Periodicals), and if their enterprises met the requirements of size, they became members of the board of trustees. The overwhelming majority of the German journalists and publishers, and probably all the Ukrainian ones, kept their distance from national organizations dominated by the Polish press.

The above is no more than an outline: it is too general and schematic to show the full spectrum of political orientation, world outlook, or personality

---

[36] The subject is briefly examined by A. Notkowski, 'Prasa w systemie propagandy rządowej w Polsce (1926–1939)', in *Studium techniki władzy* (Warsaw, 1987), 31. Financial contacts existed between the Ministry of Foreign Affairs and the Jewish Telegraphic Agency as well; see Rudziński, *Informacyjne*, 252–3.

of the journals and their authors. Nor does it portray the diverse opinions of the various categories of reader. The description has been largely confined to an indication of quantitative relations brought out by statistics, passing over the messages, as well as their spiritual underpinnings, that are contained in the actual texts. Nor has this sketch touched upon the process of the accumulation, in and through the press, of new scales of value grafted on to the old, or even ancient ones constantly recreated by reading of the Scriptures. And no attempt has been made to deal with the important context of the press in other Jewish communities in central eastern Europe, the Soviet Union, and the United States: after all, only full comparisons make it possible to see the differences and extract what is universal.

The Jewish press in the Second Republic can be characterized as a holistic, relatively developed system; it engaged in its own internal polemic, was comprised of separate facilities (such as the Jewish Telegraphic Agency) or independent institutions (journalists' organizations), and reflected a wide gamut of political opinions and cultural differences:

- It was open (in the best sense) to the ruling national group of the state and to all acculturated or potentially acculturated Jews.

- Through its organizational connections and the materials the press disseminated, it was part of a wider phenomenon, the international diaspora and the question of Palestine.

- When the polemics it expressed were directed outside the Jewish community, it was part of the all-Polish political spectrum, as well as contributing to political life in local or regional sections.

- It aided the Jewish community's participation in public state life and assisted in the constitution of representative bodies at various levels; as a whole, it functioned in a public and legal manner.

- In the period under discussion, its presence in the life of the community became consolidated, with the tendency to expand; it won new readers, increased circulation, and appeared in areas where there had been no press publications before.

- The Jewish press even included such modern editorial components as sensationalist afternoon newspapers, supplements, and illustrated magazines, as well as provincial editions. It was a press for a society that was in the process of being transformed from a traditional one to a modern urban force.

Polish Political Parties and Antisemitism

JERZY HOLZER

IN Polish political life the processes of assimilation and Polonization were the traditional means of solving the Jewish question, a view inherited from the democratic movements of the nineteenth century and from Warsaw positivism.[1] These points of view were characterized by a tolerance of Jews as individuals, as well as by a dismissal of Jewish religious and cultural traditions as manifestations of backwardness. Although the liberal middle class, a weak stratum in Poland, accepted the fact that Jews were religiously distinct, it was felt that, because of 'Europeanization' and Polonization, as reflected in the emergence of 'progressive' synagogues, culturally the difference was only relative. The Socialists, on the other hand, rejected Judaism along with all religions, and advocated their own vision of assimilation in a radical way. Thus, they did not accept a separate Jewish socialist movement, although the pressures of reality gradually forced them to come to terms with the use of Yiddish for purposes of propaganda and with local party organizations that recruited Jews specifically.[2] The substance of these concessions is revealed in a statement by the anti-nationalist and revolutionary socialist party in the early twentieth century, the Social-Demokracja Królestwo Polskiego i Litwy (SDKPiL: the Social Democracy of the Congress Kingdom and Lithuania): 'The fact that this unavoidable assimilation takes place in Yiddish does not alter the situation at all.'[3]

An alternative to the assimilationist position was the isolationist one, which called for cultural separation and religious hostility, and condemned

---

[1] See A. Cała, 'The Question of the Assimilation of Jews in the Polish Kingdom (1864–1897): An Interpretive Essay', *Polin*, i (1986), 130–50.

[2] For example, the Polska Partia Socjalno-Demokratyczna (PPSD: Polish Social Democratic Party), reacted aggressively to the establishment of the Jewish Social Democratic Party in Galicia, although it had previously accepted the establishment of the Ukrainian Social Democratic Party without a problem. See W. Najdus, *Polska Partia Socjalno-Demokratyczna Galicji i Śląska 1890–1919* (Warsaw, 1983), 215, 439 n.

[3] *Przegląd Socjaldemokratyczny*, 7 (1902), 21–5, following F. Tych (ed.) *Socjaldemokracja Królestwa Polskiego i Litwy: Materiały i dokumenty*, ii. *1902–1903* (Warsaw, 1962), 88.

all contacts with Jews. Isolationism had a significantly longer tradition than assimilationism, although more as a feature of everyday behaviour by Poles than as a social and political concept. As long as Jews remained deprived of political rights as a social group, they were socially and politically isolated. Only the lifting of various restrictions created conditions which made it possible for Jews to enter the orbit of Polish cultural and economic life. Isolationism now began to be synonymous with the goal of thrusting Jews back behind the ghetto walls.

At the lowest level of ideological consciousness, the economic premises of this isolationism were declared openly (buttressing conservative customs). Such declarations were linked either with instances of conflict among various social groups—for example, in Galicia between peasants and Jews who were known innkeepers, moneylenders, and tenants of estates—or with competitive situations within the trade and craft sectors, and later in the realm of intellectual work. At a higher level of ideological consciousness, feelings of cultural difference and conflict of interests were channelled into a doctrinal justification of antisemitism, part of the nationalist worldview. Enhancing the isolationist position was the assimilation of some Jewish circles to cultures other than the Polish: Russian, for example.

Devoid of doctrinal nationalistic justification, characterized by conservatism on the one hand, and the exposure of economic conflicts on the other, antisemitism could be found in the Galician peasant movement, in the following of the radical priest Fr. Stojałowski, in Stapiński's Polskie Stronnictwo Ludowe (PSL: Polish Peasant Party), and in the PSL Piast.[4] Economic antisemitism was also important in the propaganda of the Peasant Movement in Wielkopolska (the area around Poznań). Characteristic of this movement is its initial attack on the National League for allowing itself to be influenced by the Jews of Warsaw.[5] It was only in the pre-nationalist, and subsequently the nationalist, movement within the Russian partition that antisemitism occupied a central place in the party programme and in its practical activities. Within the Prussian partition, it took second place to anti-German feeling, since the Jews were as a rule Germanized. In Galicia, on the other hand, the nationalist movement endorsed assimilationist processes that were relatively broad in scope. Polonization was most common—which, given the national conflict between the Poles and Ukrainians, changed the balance both quantitatively and, to an even greater degree,

---

[4] The wording was discrete, however: see S. Lato and W. Stankiewicz (eds.), *Programy stronnictw ludowych* (Warsaw, 1969), 68, 72; also A. Garlicki, *Powstanie Polskiego Stronnictwa Ludowego: Piast 1913–1914* (Warsaw, 1966), 149, 220.

[5] See J. Marczewski, *Narodowa Demokracja w Poznańskiem 1900–1914* (Warsaw, 1967), 80, 120. Similar accusations were levelled against the National League by the Upper Silesian *Katolik*: see M. Orzechowski, *Narodowa Demokracja na Górnym Śląsku [to 1918]* (Wrocław, 1965), 82 n.

qualitatively (since it primarily encompassed the educated Jewish social stratum).[6]

The antisemitism of the nationalist movement in the Russian partition had a threefold basis. First was the emotional aspect, to which feelings of cultural difference were fundamental. Dmowski, for example, fostered a very strong antisemitism.[7] Second was the especially strong competition among the petty bourgeoisie and the intelligentsia in these regions. Finally, the third aspect was the instrumental exploitation of antisemitism. In the Polish kingdom, while the Jews were the sole ethnic group of significant size, they were nevertheless politically vulnerable so that attacks on them met with relatively easy success. The need for a nationalistic training ground of this kind became even greater when the National League and National Democratic Movement began to seek compromise with the Russian authorities.

During the First World War Polish political life became even more affected by antisemitism. This was intensified by the conscious activities of the German occupying forces in Poland, and thus in part of the kingdom and frontier areas. The Jews were treated as a separate ethnic group which, because of the close similarity in language, could potentially shore up German policies in the east. Second, the war was accompanied by financial speculation, and since Jews as a group were employed mainly in trade and services they aroused hostility. Third, toward the close of the war, the Jews were caught in the conflict between the state and national groups, between Poles and Ukrainians, Poles and Czechs, Poles and Germans.

The radicalization of antisemitism was expressed in spontaneous mass reactions, including pogroms (as in Lwów in 1919) and other forms of violence. However, it did not emerge in programmatic declarations or in more serious political discussions. At the First Congress of the Związek Ludowo-Narodowy (ZLN: Popular National Union) in May 1919 (held while the right and centre were still in the process of merging under the hegemony of the National Democracy), the need to Polonize towns was discussed only in general terms, without any clear formulation of an organized campaign other than the economic boycott, under the slogan 'each to his own'.[8] At the Second Congress, after the divisions that led the ZLN to become more unambiguously national democratic in character, antisemitic slogans accompanied declarations about the need to maintain

[6] R. Wapiński, *Narodowa Demokracja 1893–1939: Ze studiów nad dziejami myśli nacjonalistycznej* (Wrocław, 1980), 129 n.

[7] He ended by fearing the judaization of Poles, attributing to Jews an individuality that was so powerful that it prevented assimilation: 'and it is they who would be capable of the spiritual—and, in part, even physical—assimilation of our majority' (R. Dmowski, *Myśli nowoczesnego Polaka* (Lwów, 1904), 215).

[8] Statements from the First Congress; see *Gazeta Warszawska*, 128–30 (12–14 May 1919).

principles of legal equality *vis-à-vis* Jews.⁹ In the programme endorsed at the time, the theme of Polonization of the towns, industry, and trade, and of assuring a Polish face to social, economic, and cultural life, was raised several times; at the same time, exceptional legislation and the oppression of groups differing in faith or nationality were opposed.¹⁰

The Narodowa Partia Robotnicza (NPR: National Workers' Party) justified its antisemitism in a similar way, arguing the view of the harmful predominance of Jews in certain branches of production and commerce and the need to support Polish and Christian elements.¹¹ A somewhat different tone, however, was adopted by the Christian Democratic Party. Although they too employed nationalistic arguments and appeals to economic interests, in their primary argument on the opposition of good and evil, Christianity represented the good and Judaism the evil. The Jews were thus a danger to faith and morals.¹² It is worth noting, however, that in the first years of the Second Republic, antisemitism disappeared completely from the official pronouncements of the peasant or people's movement and played no important role in the practical activities of particular people's parties.

The antisemitism of the Endecja (National Democrats) and the Chadecja (Christian Democrats) intensified between 1922 and 1923. It was stimulated by successive political events: parliamentary elections in 1922, presidential elections, the campaign against Narutowicz, and the president's murder. The party platform of the Christian Union of National Unity, the Chjena, which was an electoral bloc comprising Endeks, Chadeks, and a section of conservatives, not only included traditional economic and cultural antisemitic arguments, but, as a result of the alliance of the left, the Jews, and the Germans, also contained especially virulent political threats.¹³ From then on, the 'anti-Polish belligerent Jewry' thesis, applied to domestic and

---

⁹ See the statement issued by the Second Congress of the All-Polish People's National Union, which took place on 26 and 27 Oct. 1919 in Warsaw: *Sprawozdanie z II Zjazdu Wszechpolskiego Związku Ludowo-Narodowego* (Warsaw, 1919), 18 n.

¹⁰ See the Programme of the Popular National Union of the Polish Republic, which was carried by a Congress of 8,000 delegates from all over Poland (27 Oct. 1919): *Program Związku Ludowo-Narodowego Rzeczypospolitej Polskiej uchwalony przez Zjazd 8000 delegatów z całej Polski w dniu 27 października 1919r. w Warsawie* (Warsaw, n.d.).

¹¹ See the Programme of the National Workers' Party, resolved at the Second Council of the NPR in Kraków, 4-6 Sept. 1921: *Program Narodowej Partii Robotniczej uchwalony na II Kongresie NPR w Krakowie w dn. 4, 5, i 6 września 1921r.* (Katowice, 1922).

¹² H. Mianowski, *Czego chce Polskie Stronnictwo Chrześcijańskiej Demokracji?* (lecture given at the conference on 7 Sept. 1919) (Kraków, 1919), 18; S. Adamski, *Zasady i dążenia ChNSP* [Chrześcijańsko-Narodowe Stronnictwo Pracy] (Poznań, 1921), 5 n. Antisemitic views were particularly vociferous in the journal *Przewodnik Chrześcijańskiej Demokracji*, which appeared from Apr. 1922 to Apr. 1923.

¹³ *Gazeta Warszawska* (15 Oct. 1922).

international politics, constituted one of the main propaganda motifs of the ZLN, the Christian Democratic Party, and small right-wing groups.[14]

Aside from those indiscriminate attacks in the popular press that could incite pogroms, public statements were dominated by demands for a separation that would have isolated the Jews and made any contact with Polish society impossible, and which would have been supported by an economic boycott.[15] The extent to which Jewish isolation was to result from social acts, as opposed to the exceptional decrees directed against Jews, was not clear. In any case, the ZLN's governing council of June demanded the legal enforcement of the *numerus clausus* (whereby the number of Jewish students was restricted) in all institutions of higher education, and in February 1925 this demand was supported by the Second General Academic Conference in Vilna, not only by the Endecja's Młodzież Wszechpolska (All-Polish Youth), but also by the Chadecja's Odrodzenie (Renaissance).[16]

The *coup* of May 1926 did not generate any great changes in the views and behaviour of particular political movements. Nor did the establishment of the Obóz Wielkiej Polski (Great Poland Camp) or the Stronnictwo Narodowe (SN: National Movement) constitute a turning-point. The Jewish question appeared rather sporadically in their public statements, but the way it was stated in the party platform bore similarities to the stance of the ZLN.[17] In political practice, however, particularly in propaganda, antisemitism became increasingly dominant, and 'henceforth all cases were evaluated through the prism of the Jewish question'.[18] More fundamental

[14] Proceedings of the ZLN Governing Council in *Gazeta Warszawska* (15 Jan. 1923), and again ibid. (18 June 1923); the proceedings of the council of Polskie Stronnictwo Chrześcijanskiej Demokracji (PSChD: the Polish Christian Democratic Party) (10 Dec. 1925) in *Biuletyn polityczny*, 2–3 (1927), 212–13; programme of the Polish Christian Democratic Movement carried at the Second All-Polish Congress of the movement, 31 May and 1 June 1925: *Program Polskiego Stonnictwa Chrześcijańskiej Demokracji uchwalony na ii Ogólnopolskim Kongresie Stronnictwa z dn. 31 maja i 1 czerwca 1925* (Warsaw, 1926); *Pro Patria*, 9 (15 Oct. 1924). The secret Service of Polish Patriots (Pogotowie Patriotów Polskich), founded in Nov. 1922, was noteworthy for its aggressiveness: *Biuletyn polityczny*, 2–3 (1927), 632.

[15] The ZLN organ *Myśl narodowa*, however, adopted an extreme stance favouring pogroms, particularly in the numerous writings of Adolf Nowaczyński.

[16] *Gazeta Warszawska* (1 Mar. 1925).

[17] Leaflets from the series 'OWP [Obóz Wielkiej Polski], Wskazania programowe' [The Camp for a Greater Poland, programmatic guidelines], which appeared in 1927, did not take up the Jewish question directly at all. In its programme of 1928 the National Movement confined itself to demanding separate primary and secondary schools for Jews and the *numerus clausus* at institutions of higher education, since demands for a national state and support of Polish industry or trade related to the Jewish question only indirectly. See the programme of the National Movement carried by the Movement's Governing Council on 7 Oct. 1928; *Program Stronnictwa Narodowego uchwalony przez Radę Naczelną Stronnictwa dn. 7 października 1928r.* (Warsaw, 1928). See also Sz. Rudnicki, 'Narodowa Demokracja po przewrocie majowym: Zmiany organizacyjne i ideologiczne (1926–1930)', *Najnowsze Dzieje Polski 1914–1939*, 11 (1967), 52 n.

[18] Sz. Rudnicki, *Obóz Narodowo-Radykalny: Geneza i działalność* (Warsaw, 1985), 113.

changes took place by the end of the 1920s. The general trend can be summarized as follows. On the one hand the national camp, i.e. political forces with roots in the National Democracy, changed from ideological and tactical antisemitism to supporting the organized use of physical force against the Jews. These groups openly called for exceptional legislation to eliminate almost all Jewish rights. On the other hand, groups which had previously believed in assimilation began to take an antisemitic position, joining the parties already advocating antisemitism in the form of Jewish segregation and an economic boycott. Thus, the entire political wing representing 'restrained antisemitism' was prepared to accept exceptional legislation limiting the rights of Jews in certain areas of economic and cultural life. In effect, antisemitism as an element in political life was openly espoused and increasingly radical.

We need not discuss the causes for these changes in Endecja in detail here, since they have been covered extensively in the literature. Scholars of the national camp agree that two elements contributed to the change: the growing extremist views and activities in this camp, which was linked to a generational change in leadership, and the effects of the great socio-economic crisis that began in 1929.[19] Scholars also describe on the one hand the presence of deep phobias and antisemitic psychoses (hence the phenomenon of 'Judaeocentrism') and, simultaneously, the instrumental use of antisemitic incidents provoked to achieve confrontation with the ruling Sanacja, which was answerable for public order.

New ideas appeared in the programme as early as 1931-2. These were advanced particularly within the Youth Movement of the Great Poland Camp. The racist justifications for antisemitism were more clearly supported for the first time. Racism meant consistent opposition to all assimilationist concessions: assimilation was to be rejected even if that meant combining Polonization with Christianization. Ultimately, the transformation of social antisemitism to antisemitism as an element of state doctrine was almost completed. In the previous period, even demands for *numerus clausus* were accompanied by the vocabulary of equal rights for Jews (opposition was centred only on their special privileges). Now the demand was for outright abrogation of citizens' rights for Jews, denying them higher education (the principle of *numerus nullus*), limiting their access to primary and secondary education (even though it be separate), a prohibition on residence in certain parts of the country, and a law that they live in specific areas of cities (ghettos). Exceptional legislation was also intended to cover earlier limitations on economic and professional activities.[20]

[19] Wapiński, *Narodowa Demokracja*, 190 nn.; Rudnicki, *Obóz*, 113 nn.
[20] See *Wytyczne w sprawach żydowskiej, mniejszości słowiańskich, niemieckiej, zasad polityki gospodarczej* (Warsaw, 1932). This text, published by the Academic Division of the OWP, has been discussed by Wapiński and Rudnicki, among others.

In the years that followed, these ideas became more widespread and were gradually accepted as axiomatic by all sections of the 'national camp'. The Obóz Narodowo-Radykalny (ONR: National Radical Camp) led the way, with its declaration of 15 April 1934 in favour of depriving Jews of Polish citizenship and treating them as temporary co-residents.[21] This declaration was not fully developed as part of a political programme, however, and discussions of the Jewish question were limited to generalizations. It was only later that increasingly virulent anti-capitalist statements linked to antisemitic ones appeared in the press of the ONR. Finally, in the so-called green programme of the Falanga, an ONR faction directed by Bolesław Piasecki, the confiscation of Jewish property and the expulsion of the Jews from Poland were recognized as political aims. Exceptional legislation was thus only one stage in the path to this goal.[22]

The principal faction of the national camp, the SN, followed in the footsteps of the ONR. Although it expressed antisemitism later than the ONR did, there were no major differences in their attitudes on the Jewish question, except for the SN's avoidance of anti-capitalist slogans and the continued perception of economic antisemitism as part of a programme of economic Polonization. After all, the chief creators of the SN concept were the youth, and while there were internal disagreements and conflicts with the leaders of the ONR, both groups were of the same generation and had similar ideological backgrounds.

In 1938 the most active of these young ideologues, Jędrzej Giertych, took the view that the Germans had been Poland's enemy in the past (although Jews and Freemasons had already then been seen, alongside the Germans, as enemies). Now, he believed, the Jews constituted the most important problem for Polish politics of the period; they were the main enemy and the mainspring of anti-Polish activity. Giertych regarded the task of breaking Jewish power in Poland as fundamental. As events progressed, all secondary powers would be swept away until only two camps would be left in the field of battle: the national or Polish, and the Communist or Jewish. Giertych threatened the Jews with terror (as a response to alleged Jewish terror) and foresaw the use of reprisals in the event of war, although he did not state precisely who the enemy would be in such a war.[23]

There was a rather different development of views in those parties which, although they may not have been free of antisemitism, had rejected the extremism of the national camp in their programme and practical activities in the 1930s. The Christian Democrats continued to maintain the position

[21] 'Zasady Obozu Narodowo-Radykalnego', *Sztafeta* (13 May 1934), supplement.
[22] *Zasady programu narodowo-radykalnego* (Warsaw, 1937).
[23] J. Giertych, *O wyjście z kryzysu* (Warsaw, 1938), 132, 144, 149 nn., 177, 234 nn.

held in the 1920s, in which the Jews were perceived primarily as representatives of another faith, and consequently of an alien morality and culture. Although they often resorted to arguments about the economic competition between Poles and Jews, racism was rejected as incompatible with Christian morality. Assimilation was admitted as an exceptional phenomenon, and only when accompanied by a 'sincere acceptance of Catholicism'. In October 1933 the Governing Council of the Polish Christian Democratic Party had already declared itself in favour of treating Jews as citizens of the state; in February 1937 the Executive Committee of the Governing Body appealed for the Jewish question to be solved by legislative means. It is difficult to say whether these were similar views that were differently formulated, or whether a real evolution of position was hidden behind this—from opposition to an acceptance of exceptional legislation. The use of force and violence was consistently rejected, however.[24] From the end of the 1920s the National Workers' Party was in favour of the reduction of Jewish numbers in Poland through a policy of encouraging emigration.[25]

It was symptomatic of a greater preoccupation with the Jewish question, or of a peculiar psychosis in its background, that the centrist Stronnictwo Pracy (Party of Labour) paid more attention to this issue in its programme than did the two parties from which it had emerged, the Christian Democrats and the NPR. Many arguments were used to exaggerate the significance of the Jewish question: the excessive number of Jews, their unequal social and territorial distribution, their political and social tendencies that were harmful to Polish interests. The Party of Labour expressed the need to support Polish economic and cultural output, to extend Polish publicly owned and private property, and to develop Polish industry, trade, crafts, free professions, and co-operative movements. These demands retained a traditional ring, harking back to a time when antisemitism was primarily a social movement. There was a further demand, however, for the introduction of legislation that would accelerate the processes of nationalizing economic, political, cultural, and social life. This was a euphemism that disguised the hidden demand to limit Jewish rights and opportunities by exceptional legislation.[26] In May 1938 the Governing Council of the Party of Labour formulated a statement pointing out the impossibility of assimilating Jews, the harmfulness of attempting to do so, and the need to rid Poland of them through emigration, although the use of force continued to be opposed.[27]

Like the peasant political movement of the 1920s, Stronnictwo Ludowe

[24] *Warszawska Informacja Prasowa* (1933) 742 n.; ibid. (1937), 117.
[25] *Podstawy programowe Narodowej Partii Robotniczej* (Warsaw, 1928).
[26] *Stronnictwo Pracy: Program* (Warsaw, 1937).
[27] *Warszawska Informacja Prasowa* (1928), 211.

(SL: the Peasant Party) was silent with regard to the Jewish question in its first manifesto of 1931. In its 1935 programme, however, it devoted an extensive section to the issue, which took up a tenth of the entire programme.[28] The party members were indeed against the use of force and supported the recognition of equal citizens' rights for Jews, but nevertheless they adopted an approach to the Jewish question once peculiar to the National Democrats. The Jews were a barrier to the development of the Polish middle class, for they controlled the socially important functions of trade and credit mediation. There were too many of them in Poland. Assimilation was an unrealistic concept, and the Jews were in any case an alien nation in Poland. In order to oust them 'throughout economic life', it was necessary to support the Polish element (the greatest role here was ascribed to co-operatives), as well as to support 'with all one's power' the emigration of Jews from Poland. Such declarations appear to have been the result of conflicting views. Some party members believed that concentrating on the Jewish question drew the attention of the village away from other important problems. Others were ready to sanction even exceptional legislation limiting Jewish rights.

The Polska Partia Socjalistyczna (PPS: Polish Socialist Party) remained hostile to antisemitism, but in an indirect way it attested to the spread of antisemitism in political life. Aware of the increasing popularity of this feeling in Poland, and recognizing the growth of Jewish national consciousness, some socialists modified their assimilationist views. Contacts with socialist Zionist circles in Poland and Palestine were manifestations of a more critical attitude to assimilation. One of the most popular publicists, Jan Maurycy Borski, openly criticized assimilationist concepts as outdated. He treated antisemitism as a constant element of Polish life, even in the event of a socialist victory. Only the emigration of Jews from Poland remained part of the programme.[29] The PPS met Borski's statements with an embarrassed silence, although Zygmunt Zaremba did attack him for succumbing to the prevailing climate of antisemitism.[30]

Particularly serious changes took place within the ruling Sanacja. It continued to maintain its dual stance until the beginning of the 1930s, viewing favourably all manifestations of Jewish assimilation, but also tolerating expressions of cultural and national separateness, as long as the latter were accompanied by a readiness to co-operate loyally with the state authorities. There was a sense in which the Sanacja position could be seen as particularly advantageous for the Jews, since it allowed them to choose between two options to express their hopes and expectations for the future.

[28] Lato and Stankiewicz, *Programy stronnictw ludowych*, 313–18; see also 299–309.
[29] J. M. Borski, *Sprawa żydowska a socjalizm: Polemika z Bundem* (Warsaw, 1937).
[30] Z. Zaremba, 'Różnice czy błędy', *Światło*, 4–5 (1937).

Other views were beginning to emerge within the Sanacja, however. These were a result of the influence of elements from the Endecja, Chadecja, and other small Catholic and conservative-national groups. They included Zespół Stu (the Group of a Hundred), for example, which broke with the National Democrats and became a local Lwów group, the Catholic People's Movement, and the Christian Social Union, founded in 1934 after the schism in the Chadecja.[31] Antisemitic tendencies appeared in the Left National Workers' Party, an offshoot of the NPR that co-operated with the Sanacja. An independent extremist antisemitic group of national socialists, outside the framework of the Sanacja, was not formed until 1933, but this group did not play any role in political life.[32]

In the second half of the 1930s the Sanacja as a whole changed its stance with regard to the Jewish question. The changed view was enunciated in Prime Minister Składkowski's speech of June 1936, in the declaration of Obóz Zjednoczenia Narodowego (OZON: the Camp of National Unification) in February 1937, in General Skwarczyński's speech of 21 February 1938, and, in a more expanded form, in the resolutions of the Governing Council of the Camp of National Unification of 21 May 1938, and in the description of these resolutions by Bogusław Miedziński.[33] Although the terminology had undergone a certain radicalization in the course of two years, the basic idea was preserved. In its founding declaration, the OZON adopted an approach to the Jewish question borrowed from an earlier phase of National Democracy. The need for cultural and economic self-defence was emphasized. In the May 1938 resolutions of the Governing Council the Jewish question was treated with all the gravity of a weighty political issue. The Jews were described as an extra-state group with independent nationalistic (and therefore political) aims that weakened the normal development of a

[31] J. Majchrowski writes about the Zespół Stu: *Szkice z historii polskiej prawicy politycznej lat Drugiej Rzeczypospolitej* (Kraków, 1986), 15. The Catholic People's Movement was a continuation of the Polish Catholic People's Movement, whose programme includes antisemitic economic and religious-moral arguments, presented in A. Bełcikowska, *Stronnictwa i związki polityczne w Polsce* (Warsaw, 1925). The programmatic statement of the Christian Social Union appears in the *Warszawska Informacja Prasowa* (1934), 302.

[32] Majchrowski, *Szkice z historii*, 84 nn.

[33] See the ideological-political declaration of the chief of the camp of National Unification, Adam Koc, and the speeches of Stefan Starzyński, chairman of the municipal organization of the Camp of National Unification: *Deklaracja ideowo-polityczna szefa Obozu Zjednoczenia Narodowego Adama Koca i przemówienia przewodniczącego organizacje miejskiej Obozu Zjednoczenia Narodowego Stefana Starzyńskiego* (Warsaw, 1937); the speeches of General Stanisław Skwarczyński, chief of the Camp of National Unification, at the Congress of the Praesidium of Regions of the OZN in Warsaw on 21 Feb. 1938: *Przemówienie szefa Obozu Zjednoczenia Narodowego gen. Stanisława Skwarczyńskiego na Zjeździe Prezydiów okręgów OZN w Warszawie w dniu 21 lutego 1938r.* (Warsaw, 1938); B. Miedziński, *Uwagi o sprawie żydowskiej wraz z uchwałami Rady Naczelnej OZN z dnia 21 maja 1938r.* (Warsaw, 1938). See also J. Majchrowski, *Silni–Zwarci–Gotowi: Myśl polityczna Obozu Zjednoczenia Narodowego* (Warsaw, 1985), 127–37.

Polish national state. The use of force continued to be consistently opposed, however, and emigration was seen as the most important means of solving the Jewish question. The assimilation of Jews was not completely rejected, but was seen as a peripheral phenomenon, affecting only a few individuals. The May resolutions left no doubt about the aims behind the introduction of exceptional legislation, though the extent to which this legislation was to be applied remained unclear. In any case, it was to include the limitation of Jewish participation in certain professions and the 'regulation' of access to higher education for Jews.

The official position of the Camp of National Unification was restrained compared with the views voiced by some Sanacja groups. Związek Młodych Narodowców (ZMN: the Union of Young Nationalists) adopted an extreme stance in its declaration of May 1934. At the time it was still at a crossroads, halfway between the Youth Movement of the Great Poland Camp, from which it had emerged, and the Sanacja, with whom it aimed to co-operate. The ZMN called for work and bread in Poland for Poles above all, openly recommending the expulsion of three and a half million Jews.[34] It is worth noting, however, that in the political declaration of the National State Movement of December 1937 (and heir of the ZMN) the Jewish question was referred to only marginally, in the context of the need to Polonize trade.[35] More attention was devoted to the question in practical activities. Extreme antisemitic views were voiced by a group from the journal *Jutro pracy*: 'the Jewish problem was central to the group's interests'.[36] Its propositions were not clearly formulated, however, beyond the appeal for a complete boycott of Jewish trade. Was the nationalization of economics and culture as demanded by *Jutro pracy* to tie in with the introduction of exceptional legislation, and if so to what extent? The group had no answer to this. The arguments against the Jews included some that related to negative racial characteristics. Racism was also clearly in evidence in the journal *Polityka*, which was an organ of the young conservatives. Although this group condemned the use of violence and the confiscation of Jewish property, it did not reject projects for exceptional legislation, particularly in the form of the *numerus clausus* at institutions of higher education and for the free professions, and it also demanded that the state administration take practical measures to restrict Jews (in the realm of government contracts and employment opportunities in state institutions).[37]

Those groups that had traditionally renounced antisemitism in the second half of the 1930s began to adopt some of the movement's ideas. Among the

[34] See *Awangarda Państwa Narodowego* (1934).
[35] Ibid. (1938).
[36] Majchrowski, *Silni–Zwarci–Gotowi*, 186.
[37] *Polska idea imperialna* (Warsaw, 1938), 42–8.

conservatives was the newly established Conservative Movement, whose founder, Janusz Radziwiłł, adopted the slogans of economic and moral battle against the Jews, though he condemned persecution.[38] Continuing the tradition of *Naprawa*, the Union of Social Activists recognized the need to nationalize economic life.[39] The head of the small Polish Radical Party was Tytus Filipowicz, a one-time socialist and future member of the Democratic Club. The party adopted as its slogan 'the dejudaization of Poland', and worked against Jewish aims to dominate in all areas of Polish life.[40] Antisemitic concepts even appeared in the enunciations of the Sanacja left. The Polish Democratic Union demanded the nationalization of enterprises belonging to Jewish capital.[41] For the Union of the Patriotic Left, the Jewish question was a problem of state whose solution lay in changes to the economic structure and the encouragement of Jewish emigration.[42]

Polish politics reflected a number of changes with regard to the Jewish question. First, from an issue that was clearly in the hierarchy of political problems, the question began to occupy a prime position. Second, the vast majority of Polish parties and political groups at the beginning of the interwar period rejected antisemitism but were silent on the subject of the Jewish question, whereas by the close of the period an equally large majority of groups and parties admitted their antisemitism. Third, the beginning of the interwar period saw the first stages in a process that transformed antisemitism from a social movement isolating Jews into a movement whose aims included the imposition of exceptional legislation and the more or less brutal enforcement of emigration. Fourth, in its most extreme form antisemitism changed from an isolationist movement (later including legal discrimination against Jews) into a movement advocating physical force and terror. It is as if antisemitism constituted a kind of psychosis at the end of the Second Republic, disabling a healthy political sense and obscuring an awareness of the genuine threat to the life of the Polish state, and to its ethnic and organic life.

[38] *Warszawska Informacja Prasowa* (1937), 385; ibid. (1938) 234; *Tezy programowe Stronnictwa Zachowawczego* (Lwów, 1938).

[39] *Warszawska Informacja Prasowa* (1936), 344.

[40] *Założenia ideowe PPR* [Polska Partia Robotnicza: Polish Workers' Party] (Warsaw, 1936). See also T. Filipowicz's speech given in the Civic Hall, Warsaw, on 26 Feb. 1936, and the directives of the Polish Radical Party: *O polską myśl polityczną: Przemówienie wygłoszone w sali Resursy Obywatelskiej w Warsawie dnia 26 lutego 1936r. oraz wytyczne programowe Polskiej Partii Radykalnej* (Warsaw, 1936).

[41] *Warszawska Informacja Prasowa* (1937), 281.

[42] *Rodowód i prawdy Lewicy Patriotycznej* (Warsaw, 1937).

The Polish *Kehillah* Elections of 1936: A Revolution Re-examined

ROBERT MOSES SHAPIRO

PREFACE
LUCJAN DOBROSZYCKI

Jewish elections and the work of Jewish deputies of the state, municipal, and self-governing elective bodies in the Second Polish Republic undoubtedly comprise one of the most intrinsically important chapters in Polish Jewish history. Yet there is no comprehensive study of the various kinds of elections in which Jews took part, both as citizens and as members of a distinct ethnic group, in the years 1919–39. During that period Jews were able to capture about a hundred seats in the five parliamentary elections, in addition to a much greater number of seats in the cities and towns throughout Poland. The way Jewish representatives were elected and the role they were to play in the general elective bodies differed drastically from the well-known

---

The present paper is based on research conducted with the support of the YIVO Institute for Jewish Research, National Foundation for Jewish Culture, Memorial Foundation for Jewish Culture, Institute of Contemporary Jewry at the Hebrew University in Jerusalem, IREX International Research and Exchanges Board, Kosciuszko Foundation, Fulbright–Hays Program, and the Government of Israel and the Holocaust Studies Program at Yeshiva University. The original version of this paper was published in 1988 by Yeshiva University together with the accompanying preface by Dr Lucjan Dobroszycki.

The following abbreviations are used in the references

AAN	Archiwum Akt Nowych (Warsaw)	MSW	Ministerstwo Spraw Wewnętrznych
BŻIH	*Biuletyn Żydowskiego Instytutu Historycznego*	NF	*Nayer folksblat*
Dz. URP	*Dziennik Ustaw Rzeczypospolitej Polskiej*	Pinkas hakehillot: lodz	*Pinkas hakehillot: Polin*, i. *Lodzh vehagalil*, ed. Danuta Dąbrowska and Abraham Wein (Jerusalem, 1976)
Dz. Urz. MWRiOP	*Dziennik Urzędowy Ministerstwa Wyznań Religijnych i Oświecenia Publicznego Rzeczypospolitej Polskiej*	SN	*Sprawy narodowościowe*
		SZMN	*Sprawozdanie z życia mniejszości narodowych*
LV	*Lodzher veker*		
MRS m. Ł. 1935r.	*Mały rocznik statystyczny m. Łodzi 1935* (Łódź, 1937)	YT	*Yidishe togblat*

pattern in the United States and most west European countries. In Poland, Jewish representatives were elected by Jews according to lists put out by Jewish political parties, organizations, and groups, with a clear mandate to serve the overall interest of the state and to defend the Jewish minority and its legal and actual rights. This, of course, was not the case for the few Polish Jews who saw themselves as Poles of Jewish descent; nor is it true to say that Jews *qua* Jews never voted for a non-Jew. They often did so, either because of the candidate's personality or simply in order to stop another, less desirable, non-Jew. As a rule, this was the case when a Jewish voter was confronted, on one side by a candidate from one of the antisemitic parties like the National Democrats or Christian Democrats, and on the other by a person affiliated with the Polish Socialist Party or Piłsudski's Non-party Bloc. The latter two were usually more sympathetic to the needs of the Jewish constituency.

For Jews as much as for anyone else in Poland, involvement in the elections and observance of the frequently tempestuous debates in the elective chambers was a constant factor in the struggle of everyday life. This becomes even more striking when we go on to consider another, strictly Jewish, body, the *kehillah*, an entity dating back to the days of the first Jewish settlements in Poland. Although in modern times it had lost many of the ancient prerogatives, between the wars the *kehillah* in Poland was still an institution of public law, whose authority derived from free elections. And it is exactly on the subject of elections to the *kehillah* that we can learn much from Dr Shapiro's enquiry. He has chosen the year quite deliberately, since it was of special importance; its outcome drastically altered the composition of the boards of many local *kehillot*. The Bund, the Jewish Socialist Party, which often stayed away from the *kehillah* because it considered it reactionary, took part in the 1936 elections, and gained a plurality in many cities and towns. In order to comprehend this fact more fully, one must remember that this party, which did so well in the *kehillah* election, was never able to elect a single deputy to the Parliament. Dr Shapiro gives us ample proof why, in 1936, the Bund was so successful on a local level. More than that, his essay—based on primary sources found in Poland's state archives and elsewhere—shows us the wealth of materials available for the study of Jewish history. However, one has to have a command of all the languages involved—Yiddish, Polish, Hebrew—to undertake this research. Fortunately Dr Shapiro, a young American Polish Jewish historian, is up to the task. His 'Polish *Kehillah* Elections of 1936: A Revolution Reexamined' is just a small fraction of a much larger dissertation which he completed in 1987 at Columbia University: 'Jewish Self-government in Poland: Łódź, 1914–1939'.

Yeshiva University/ YIVO Institute for Jewish Research

SOCIAL AND POLITICAL BACKGROUND

THE more than three million Jews who lived in Poland between the First and Second World Wars were organized in nearly 900 religious communities which were recognized by the state as public legal corporations with the power to levy taxes on their membership. All Jews were automatically members of the local Jewish religious community or *kehillah*,[1] the latest incarnation of the centuries-old heritage of communal autonomy which was a hallmark of Jewish life in the diaspora. Although the *kehillah* was nominally an exclusively religious institution, it touched nearly every aspect of life within the largest Jewry in Europe before the Second World War. The *kehillot* were governed by bodies whose election involved the entire array of Jewish political parties. Yet the Polish state used various means to affect the outcome of Jewish communal elections, in much the same way as it interfered in municipal politics and government.

Poland had been reborn as an independent republic at the end of the First World War, which had wrought the simultaneous collapse of its powerful neighbours—Germany, Russia, and Austria-Hungary. War-ravaged and predominantly agrarian, the new Poland faced numerous obstacles on the road towards unification of its long-partitioned regions, inhabited by various national minorities comprising over a third of the country's population. Proportional representation made the parliament a reflection of the splintered political spectrum, precluding the formation of stable majorities in the Sejm. Parliamentary instability both reflected and exacerbated the chronic economic crisis. To bring order out of the chaos of 'Sejmocracy', Poland's first head of state, Józef Piłsudski, seized power in a *coup* in May 1926. Although the forms of parliamentary democracy remained in place, the Piłsudski regime, known as the Sanacja, sought to create a government without the discredited political parties. After the 1928 parliamentary election failed to produce a majority for the Bezpartyjny Blok Współpracy z Rządem (BBWR: Non-Party Bloc for Co-operation with the Government), which proposed to amend the constitution in an authoritarian direction, the opposition became increasingly hostile. Efforts to use the courts and the Sejm's investigative powers to reveal corrupt use of the state apparatus and funds to benefit the BBWR set the stage for the 1930 election. Resorting to trumped-up charges to justify mass arrests before the election, Piłsudski employed both fair means and foul to win an absolute majority in the Sejm, although still not enough to force through constitutional amendments. A month before Piłsudski's death in May 1935, the constitutional revisions

---

[1] Polish Jews also referred to the *kehillah* by the Yiddish names *kehile* and *gmine*, the latter taken from the Polish *gmina*.

were adopted through a shabby parliamentary ploy. To complete the victory over the political parties, laws were prepared which sought to extinguish the parties' influence over the political arena. This is not to say that Poland became a police state, for civil liberties and freedom of expression remained, albeit under increasing restriction as the decade wore on.[2]

The symbolic significance of local municipal and Jewish communal elections grew substantially in the wake of the parliamentary election laws of July 1935 that eliminated proportional representation and severely hampered the ability of political parties to field candidates.[3] A widespread opposition call to boycott the Sejm election of September 1935 produced an officially reported turnout of only 46.5 per cent of eligible voters, many of whom cast blank ballots. In Warsaw a mere 23 per cent of those eligible voted.[4]

Faced with such rejection during the 1935 parliamentary elections, the Polish government was reluctant to schedule city council elections in which the opposition parties would be free to field their own candidates against the regime's. The government did feel confident enough to schedule elections in the hundreds of *kehillot* that nominally were merely religious institutions. To the Polish regime's dismay, the Jewish Socialist parties achieved numerous successes against the more reliably conservative elements portrayed as the surrogates of the Sanacja on the street in Jewish communities.

The remarkable *kehillah* elections of late summer 1936 saw much of the Jewish electorate turn to the Socialists in protest against the increasingly pervasive and violent antisemitism in Poland. Both the conservative Orthodox Jewish party Agudas Yisroel and the principal Zionist factions lost voter support. This apparent shift to the left on the Jewish street adumbrated the results seen in subsequent municipal elections, when many Polish voters used their ballots to demonstrate their rejection of the regime of Piłsudski's heirs. Thus, the Jewish communal elections of 1936 indicated the direction in which much of the Polish and Jewish electorate was headed during the final years of the Polish Republic. The success of the Socialists among the Jewish parties contending both in the communal and in the city council elections served to reinforce the impression of a more general shift to the left.

On 30 May 1936 the Polish Minister of Religions directed that elections were to be held in all Jewish communities where the four-year term of office had elapsed, with voting in minor *kehillot* on Sunday, 30 August, followed a week later on 6 September with elections in the major *kehillot*.[5] Conducted on the basis of a slightly amended election regulation, the elections would

---

[2] Antony Polonsky, *Politics in Independent Poland 1921-1939* (Oxford, 1972).
[3] Ibid. 397-8; *Dz. URP* (1935), No. 47, pp. 795-815.
[4] Polonsky, *Politics*, 399-400.
[5] *Monitor polski* (1936), No. 135, item 246; *Dz. Urz. MWRiOP* (1936), No. 4, item 86.

embrace nearly every Jewish community in Poland.⁶ The proclamation of new *kehillah* elections came at a time of intensifying anti-Jewish agitation, legislation, and outright violence. Pogroms became more common as both the Catholic Church and the Polish state overtly condoned economic antisemitism and anti-Jewish boycotts, although rejecting physical violence against Jews or their property.⁷ Government decrees in 1935 on *kehillah* finances and kosher slaughter had already undermined the fiscal autonomy and viability of the *kehillot*, leading Sejm deputy and Łódź *kehillah* president Lejb Mincberg of the Agudas Yisroel party (sometimes referred to simply as 'the Agudah') to threaten mass resignation by the board of one of the few *kehillot* with a 'stable Orthodox majority'.⁸ Agudas Yisroel did not look forward to contesting for power in every *kehillah* in Poland after it had failed to prevent adoption of the law severely restricting kosher slaughter, a measure that had been proposed by Madame Prystorowa, a member of the government caucus and wife of one of Piłsudski's closest associates. Moreover, the Agudah was itself riven with internal dissension.⁹

An important factor in the electoral equation was the Bund's ultimate decision to participate. As a Jewish secular Socialist party, the Bund had always been extremely ambivalent and torn over whether to take part in the elections of a formally religious body with an undemocratic election law that disenfranchised women and the young.¹⁰ Although the Bund had taken part in the 1924 and 1928 *kehillah* elections, it boycotted the 1931 elections in protest against the introduction of the notorious 'paragraph 20' that permitted omission from the voters' rolls of 'persons who publicly come out against the Mosaic faith'.¹¹ Responding to vociferous charges by Zionist Sejm deputies that paragraph 20 was being employed arbitrarily against opponents of Agudas Yisroel, the Minister of Religions declared to the Jewish Telegraphic Agency that it was the government's policy to prevent politicization

⁶ Jewish male residents over 25 years old were eligible to vote: Decree of the Minister of Religions, 7 July 1936 (*Dz. URP* (1936) No. 57, item 418). The full text of the *kehillah* election regulation was published by the Warsaw *kehillah*, with annotations by the community's legal adviser: Jakob Grynsztejn (ed.), *Regulamin wyborczy do gmin żydowskich* (Warsaw, 1936).

⁷ Emanuel Melzer, *Maavak medini bemalkodet* (Tel Aviv, 1982), 39–117.

⁸ *YT* (10 Nov. 1935), No. 34, p. 7; (11 Nov. 1935), No. 35, p. 4; (18 Dec. 1935), No. 67, p. 6; (23 Dec. 1935), No. 71, p. 6.

⁹ Gershon C. Bacon, 'Agudath Israel in Poland, 1916–1939: An Orthodox Response to the Challenge of Modernity' (diss. Columbia, 1979), 336–8.

¹⁰ On the Bund and the *kehillot* see the article by the former secretary of its central organization, Emanuel Nowogródzki, 'Der "bund" un di kehiles', *Unzer tsayt* (Oct.–Dec. 1972), Nos. 10–12, pp. 67–77.

¹¹ See the Oct. 1930 decree of the Minister of Religions amending the *kehillah* electoral regulation: *Dz. URP* (1930), No. 75, item 592, art. 20. The amended regulation also substituted the phrase 'religious groupings' for 'groupings and parties' which were to be taken into account in the formation of election commissions. Moreover, the state could withhold confirmation of individual commission members without giving any reason: art. 14.

of religious institutions. The government could not tolerate exploitation of the Jewish communities by 'anti-state factors and organizations' for the purpose of conducting their subversive activities. The minister specified that

Naturally, this only concerns Communist organizations and does not apply to the Bund and related organizations, whose programme does not include the slogan of struggle with religion. [However,] the application of the ordinance will be left up to the communal organs themselves, [as] the government has no intention of interfering in internal Jewish affairs and by no means desires to override the principle of autonomous governance of religious and cultural affairs by Jewish society.[12]

It should be recalled that the *kehillah* election regulation of October 1930 was issued in the midst of a hard-fought parliamentary campaign, taking place in an atmosphere of administrative terror as thousands of members of opposition parties were arrested.[13]

For Bundists who had looked on the *kehillah* as a rostrum from which to reveal the 'reactionary swindle taking place on the Jewish street and to expose Adam-naked the characters of this game',[14] the *kehillah* had now lost its value as a public platform and retained only the trappings of democracy and autonomy. The Bundist weekly in Łódź declared, 'This appears already to be a characteristic of Fascism in Poland: retention of certain democratic pretences and forms around the completely dictatorial police-state substance of the regime.'[15]

Although the *kehillah* remained formally a religious body with an undemocratic electoral law, the 1936 election campaign took place at a time when the Bund was perceived as leading the way on the Jewish street in the fight against the intensified anti-Jewish violence and economic boycott.[16] The Bund had achieved a resounding success on 17 March 1936, with its call for a nationwide half-day strike to protest against the Przytyk pogrom[17] and

[12] Interview published in *Nasz przegląd* (1 Apr. 1931), quoted at length by J. Tomaszewski, 'Walka polityczna wewnątrz gmin żydowskich w latach trzydziestych w świetle interpelacji posłów', *BŻIH* (1973), No. 1, pp. 91–2.

[13] Polonsky, *Politics*, ch. VII.

[14] *LV* 11 (13 Mar. 1931), quoted in J. Hertz, *Di geshikhte fun bund in lodzh* (New York, 1958), 357.

[15] Ibid.

[16] *Historisher zamlbukh* (Warsaw, 1948), 73. This work contains articles and documents on the history of the Bund in Poland. Although the book was confiscated by Polish censors, a copy is in the Bund Archives at YIVO.

[17] Przytyk was a predominantly Jewish rural market town near Radom in central Poland. After the authorities failed to deal with anti-Jewish boycott propaganda and related violent attacks on Jews in several small towns, a pogrom broke out in Przytyk on 9 Mar. 1936, during which masses of peasants attacked Jewish stallkeepers and Jewish homes. Scores of Jews were injured, and three Jews and one Christian Pole were killed. The subsequent trial outraged Jewish public opinion, since Jews who had defended themselves were given heavier sentences than their attackers. See Jerome Rothenberg, 'The Przytyk Pogrom', *Soviet Jewish Affairs*, 162 (May 1986), 29–46.

the general atmosphere of anti-Jewish agitation. The strike date coincided with the Sejm's consideration of the bill on humane slaughter that threatened to ban kosher slaughter and ruin the livelihoods of tens of thousands of Jewish families.[18] In the minds of masses of non-Socialist, religious Jews, the Bund's initiative in organizing the protest strike of 17 March identified the secularist, Marxist Socialist party with the effort to defend basic precepts of Judaism.[19]

Seeking to build on the success of its March protest strike, the Bund called for a 'Workers' Congress to Fight against Antisemitism' to be held in Warsaw on 13 June 1936. The election of delegates had already taken place in 300 towns when the government suddenly withdrew permission for the congress at the last moment.[20] In the draft resolutions prepared for the aborted congress the Bund bluntly rejected what it considered to be the contention shared by antisemites and Zionists, that Jews were aliens whose only option was to emigrate:

Here were we born, here we work and struggle, here we live with our anguish and joy, here is our homeland. No persecutions by reactionaries can abolish the fact and awareness that we are citizens with roots here, who bear their duties [along] with others and who demand their rights equally with others.[21]

The congress would have protested

against the Jewish communities which allow themselves to operate elementary schools not in the Yiddish language, which allow themselves to manage the moneys of the Jewish masses in an unheard-of manner and, while faithfully executing their servile role in Jewish life, do not support the most important elements of Jewish secular culture—the Yiddish secular school.[22]

The Bund leadership had little desire to waste time and effort on state-controlled *kehillot* with limited responsibilities and franchise.[23] Accepting Henryk Ehrlich's position that the 1936 communal elections were merely a trick to divert the Jewish masses from real problems and threats, the Bund central committee decided to abstain.[24] Yet, only two weeks later, the party

---

[18] Although Jews and Judaism were not mentioned in the bill on humane slaughter, it was expressly structured so as to deal a fatal blow to the involvement of Jews in the meat industry. The law required that cattle be rendered unconscious before slaughtering, which would have precluded kosher slaughter. See Shapiro, 'Jewish Self-government', 450–9; and Moses Moskowitz, 'Anti-*shehitah* Legislation in Poland', *Contemporary Jewish Record*, 23 (May–June 1939), 32–42.

[19] *Yidisher arbeter-klas in yor 1936* (Łódź, 1937), 12–19, 35–6, 54–9, 66–137.

[20] Ibid. 193–202.

[21] From the preface of a confiscated publication dated 3 July 1936, *Tsum kamf kegn antisemitizm*, repr. in *Historisher zamlbukh*, 73–4.

[22] Ibid. 77.

[23] Nowogródzki, 'Der "bund"', 71.

[24] Melzer, 'Yahadut polin bemaavak medini al kiuma beshnot 1935–1939' (diss. Tel Aviv, 1975), 108.

council of representatives of the local Bund organizations voted in favour of running, compelling the central committee to reverse its position on 29 July.[25] Victor Alter, who had led the central committee minority originally favouring participation, explained that the reversal did not reflect a change in the central committee's evaluation of the *kehillot*, but was an accommodation to the combative spirit of local Bundists who sensed that the mood among the Jewish masses might be conducive to class struggle on the Jewish street.[26] Another observer suggested that the local Bund organizations were anxious to hold on to the numerous cottage workers (*chałupnicy*) and artisans who were gravitating to the Bund and who were strongly in favour of running in the *kehillah* elections.[27]

With the Bund's participation, the 1936 Jewish communal elections would be a measure of the relative strength of the entire Jewish political spectrum, except for the Jewish Communists, who vehemently attacked the Bund as social Fascists who collaborated in a reactionary religious institution.[28] The Bund's principal concern was how to deal with the biased *kehillah* electoral machinery, which could use paragraph 20 as a potent weapon. Local Bund organizations in Pińsk and elsewhere were advised by the party central committee to avoid provoking the Orthodox Jews, who could use paragraph 20 to strike Bundists from the voters' rolls as atheists.[29]

In a 'strictly secret' circular letter to provincial authorities, the Ministry of Internal Affairs declared that the participation of the Bund in the *kehillah* elections prompted 'grave fears concerning a change in the character of those institutions' which by law were to be centres of Jewish religious life. In the ministry's view, 'Entrance of representatives of the Bund into these institutions, and possibly even here and there attainment by them of a majority, would change the character of the community, introducing into it many secular elements, and even making it a convenient instrument of political struggle.' Such a result would place before the government the 'necessity of intervention, and even dissolution of several communal boards'. To preclude such an eventuality, the ministry directed preventive action against the Bund's campaign. While 'mass application [of paragraph 20] would not be a clever move', its use for 'knocking off certain inconvenient more important individuals would permit avoidance of the later need to apply repressive measures'. Application of paragraph 20 was possible 'through appropriate moulding of or influence on electoral organs'. The

[25] *SN* (1936), Nos. 4–5, pp. 510–11; *Yidisher arbeter-klas in yor 1936*, 221–2; Nowogródzki, 'Der "bund"', 72–3.
[26] *Folkstsaytung* (1 Aug. 1936), quoted in Nowogródzki, 'Der "bund"', 72–3.
[27] *SN* (1936), Nos. 4–5, pp. 510–11.
[28] Nowogródzki, 'Der "bund"', 73–4.
[29] Confidential report on the activity of the Bund in Brześć n/Bugiem to the Political Department of MSW in Warsaw, dated 20 Aug. 1936 (AAN MSW 1064, mf. 25635).

circular concluded with the request that the matter be held in the strictest secrecy, even to the point of returning the document to Warsaw immediately after reading.[30]

Inspired by the aforementioned circular, the governor of Kielce province ordered postponement of the Radom *kehillah* election almost on the eve of voting on the ground of 'inflammation of local elements'.[31] Expressing concern about the possible entry into the Radom *kehillah* council and board of 'elements undesirable for both the state authorities and the self-government of the religious community',[32] the Kielce provincial governor had ordered postponement of the Radom election. The eight contending lists[33] included almost exclusively Zionists and leftist labour lists, but there was no Agudas Yisroel list. This created a situation in which the *kehillah* organs would include 'elements unfavourably inclined towards the authorities, with whom co-operation would be impossible', and who would want to make of the Jewish religious community 'an instrument of political struggle and would certainly contribute to the deepening of the frictions which have existed for several years among Radom Jewry'.[34] However, on 14 September 1936 the Ministry of Internal Affairs notified the Kielce governor that the reasons given for postponing the Radom *kehillah* election were inadequate and that the election was to be rescheduled as soon as possible.[35]

ELECTION RESULTS

The government's premonition about the Bund's prospects was confirmed by the results of the Jewish communal elections on 30 August and 6 September 1936. The Bund had generally run in a bloc with the Po'alei Tsion Left (PZ-Left) and the Jewish trade unions. Although no overall tabulations were published, the Bund's strength was clearly demonstrated in the town of Nowy Dwór Mazowiecki, where the Bund's list received a plurality[36] of 34

---

[30] AAN MSW 1064, mf. 25635, letter dated Warsaw, 22 Aug. 1936. The text of the letter is appended below.

[31] This is based on the folder of 'Korespondencja w sprawie wyborów do gminy wyznaniowej w Radomiu. 1936', AAN MSW 1066, mf. 25637.

[32] Letter of 10 Sept. 1936, from Provincial Administration in Kielce to the Political Department at the MSW, Warsaw (AAN MSW 1066, mf. 25637), labelled 'Secret!'

[33] Like Polish municipal elections, *kehillah* elections were proportional as voters cast their ballots for lists of candidates which won council seats in proportion to their share of the vote.

[34] Letter of 10 Sept. 1936 (n. 32 above).

[35] Letter of 14 Sept. 1936 from MSW, Warsaw, to Kielce governor, labelled 'secret' (AAN MSW 1066, mf. 25637). The Radom *kehillah* election was held on 22 Nov. 1936, and resulted in 6 of 18 council seats going to the Bund–PZ-Left bloc. In the May 1938 *kehillah* election labour groups would win 8 of 18 council seats in Radom: *SN* (1938), No. 3, p. 323; Melzer, 'Yahadut polin', 111.

[36] The highly fragmented Jewish political spectrum rarely produced absolute majorities. The party receiving the largest single vote total claimed a relative majority since it had won a plurality of the vote.

per cent of the votes cast even though it had been invalidated.[37] The results in Warsaw were even more striking, leaving the Vilna *Vilner tog* 'truly amazed'.[38] Voter turnout for the Warsaw *kehillah* was almost double what it had been in 1931, as over 40,000 ballots were cast for 35 lists in 1936.[39] The Bund list won a plurality of 26.6 per cent of the votes. Including PZ-Right and PZ-Left, Socialist lists received over a third of the votes cast in the Polish capital's *kehillah*.[40] The relative success of the Bund seemed to be a widespread phenomenon, as its lists won 30 per cent of the votes in Grodno, 30.5 per cent in Piotrków Trybunalski, 25 per cent in Kutno, and about a third in Lublin. The Bund won a fifth of the Vilna *kehillah* council seats, coming in second to the Zionist camp but ahead of the Religious Bloc.[41] On the other hand, there were places like Kalisz and Tomaszów Mazowiecki where the Bund captured only a single council seat.[42]

Data from 45 of the 83 major *kehillot* showed that the Bund won 11.8 per cent of the council mandates.[43] Together with the PZ-Right and PZ-Left, Socialists had obtained 20.9 per cent of the council seats, while the various Zionists held 29.1 per cent. Agudas and other Orthodox lists together received 31.9 per cent of council seats. Another tabulation of data from 97 minor and major communities in the central provinces provides slightly different proportions.[44] According to the tabulation in Table 3, the Bund held only 8.8 per cent of the mandates, while the three Socialist parties together held 16.2 per cent, reflecting the fact that the Socialists did less well in the numerous small *kehillot* where there was no significant proletarian element. The Agudah won 21 per cent, while the Non-party Orthodox lists obtained 15.5 per cent, thus giving a total of 36.5 per cent for Orthodox lists

---

[37] *Yidisher arbeter-klas in yor 1936*, 224. The invalidated Bund list won 243 of 713 votes cast.

[38] *Vilner tog* (9 Sept. 1936), quoted in Nowogródzki, 'Der "bund"', 74.

[39] Eligible voters increased by 36% to 94,300, while the voter turnout jumped from 29.5% in 1931 to 42.9% in 1936: Melzer, 'Yahadut polin', 109; Ruta Sakowska, 'Z dziejów Gminy Żydowskiej w Warszawie 1918–1939', *Studia Warszawskie* 14/4: 177–9; *Yidisher arbeter-klas in yor 1936*, 224–5. The figures for total votes cast, eligible voters, lists fielded, and votes received by individual lists vary among the cited sources. I have used Melzer's data as the most conservative. Sakowska gives the total eligible to vote as 96,000, with 45,510 votes cast (47.4%). *Yidisher arbeter-klas in yor 1936* gives the individual vote totals received by 35 valid lists, of which only 15 won mandates; 20 lists receiving no mandates attracted 5,105 votes, about 12.6% of the 40,532 votes cast for valid lists.

[40] See Table 1. The relative success of the Bund was somewhat diminished by the effect of linkage of several minor lists with the principal Agudah and Zionist lists to form blocs of approximately equal strength.

[41] *Yidisher arbeter-klas in yor 1936*, 223–4; *Pinkas hakehillot: lodz*, 226; Melzer, 'Yahadut polin', 111.

[42] *Pinkas hakehillot: lodz*, 125, 217.

[43] See Table 2. *Kehillot* with over 5,000 Jews could be designated 'major' by the state. Such major communities directly elected a council that in turn chose the *kehillah*'s governing board.

[44] See Table 3.

Table 1 *Kehillah* Council Election, Warsaw, 6 September 1936

List No.	Votes		Mandates	List No.	Votes		Mandates
	No.	%			No.	%	
1	341	0.8		26	147	0.4	
2	66	0.2		27	637	1.6	1
4 Bund	10,767	26.6	15	28	231	0.6	
5 PZ-Right	2,046	5.0	2	29	311	0.8	
6 PZ-Left	915	2.3	1	30	169	0.4	
8	365	0.9		31	262	0.6	
11	207	0.5		32	560	1.4	1
12	331	0.8		33 Stueckgold/ Adas Yisroel	1,249	3.1	2
13	340	0.8					
15	683	1.7	1				
16	738	1.8	1	34	237	0.6	
17 Mizrachi	2,205	5.4	3	36	494	1.2	
18 Agudas Yisroel	5,256	13.0	10	37	231	0.6	
				38	71	0.2	
19	692	1.7	1	40 Lifszits	904	2.2	1
20	467	1.2		41	476	1.2	
22 Prylucki–Folkists	972	2.4	1	42	50	0.1	
				44	8	0.0	
23	301	0.7					
24	821	2.0	1				
25 National Bloc (Zionists)	6,982	17.2	9				
				TOTAL	40,532	100.0	50

Source: Yidisher arbeter-klas in yor 1936, 224–5.

(excluding Mizrachi). The various Zionist lists held 26.1 per cent (31.6 per cent including PZ-Right). In the case of the province of Polesie, where the *kehillah* elections were held on 25 October and 1 November 1936, there are data on the allocation of mandates in 19 of the province's 21 *kehillot*.[45] In this eastern border province, leftists won 20.6 per cent and the Orthodox and Agudas Yisroel only 17.5 per cent; General and Revisionist Zionists won a total of 35.5 per cent, while various non-partisans held 27 per cent of the seats. Such tabulations demonstrate that, although the leftists led by the Bund were a major force, the Socialists did not dominate the mass of smaller *kehillot*.

Both the Bundists and the Zionists had directed their campaigning mainly against Agudas Yisroel as the embodiment of the government camp on the Jewish street. The Agudah had responded by trying to mobilize the Orthodox masses to defend the religious *kehillah* from the various free-

[45] See Table 4.

Table 2 *Kehillah* Council Mandates in 45 Major Communities, September 1936

Parties	Mandates	
	No.	%
Non-partisans	115	16.8
Orthodox	113	16.5
Zionists	107	15.6
Agudas Yisroel	105	15.4
Bund	81	11.8
Mizrachi	62	9.2
Po'alei Tsion Right	50	7.3
Revisionists	30	4.4
Po'alei Tsion Left	12	1.7
Folkists	9	1.3
TOTAL	684	100.0

Source: *SN* (1936), No. 6, pp. 657–8.

Table 3 Kehillah Mandates in 97 Towns in the Central Provinces (Excluding Warsaw), 1936

Parties	%
Agudas Yisroel	21.0
Zionists	17.2
Non-party Orthodox	15.5
Other non-partisans	9.5
Artisans	9.5
Bund	8.8
Mizrachi	6.2
Po'alei Tsion Right	5.5
Revisionists	2.7
Po'alei Tsion Left	1.8
Merchants	1.1
Folkists	1.0
Veterans	0.3

Sources: MSW, *SZMN za I kw. 1937r.*, 141–2; *SN* (1937), Nos. 1–2, pp. 123–4.

thinkers and atheists.[46] However, on 8 September 1936, two days after the voting, the editor of the Agudah daily *Yidishe togblat* dramatically declared that the *kehillah* election had been a 'plebiscite which ought to determine who has the right to speak in the name of Jewish society and who [does]

[46] Bacon, 'Agudath Israel', 337–9.

Table 4 Mandates in 19 *kehillot* in Polesie, October–November 1936

Parties	Mandates	
	No.	%
Non-partisans	44	27.0
Zionists	44	27.0
Orthodox and Agudah	29	17.5
Revisionists	14	8.5
Po'alei Tsion Right	14	8.5
Bund	14	8.5
Po'alei Tsion Left	5	3.0
TOTAL	164	100.0

Source: *SN* (1936), No. 6, pp. 658.

not'.[47] The Agudas daily's lead article on 10 September, entitled 'The Warning Signal', bemoaned the fact that

> The whole truth is that the Bund received very many votes from the simple masses of the people, from the Jewish poor who still keep the Sabbath, still eat kosher, go to pray on the Sabbath, and put on *tefillin* every day. The very Bund whose slogan is 'to uproot everything', which wants to destroy *Yidishkayt*, managed to infiltrate with its influence the Jews of the synagogue and house of study and win them for its deadly poisonous ideas.[48]

While the Mizrachi organ, *Yidishe shtime*, considered the Bund's success astonishing, it was an 'unexpected victory for the Bund, but not for Bundism'. The religious Zionist periodical held that the voters had not chosen the Bundist ideology but its position as a symbol of protest.[49] The venerable thinker and journalist Hillel Zeitlin wrote in *Moment* on 10 September 1936 that the years of irresponsible conflict and mud-slinging in Jewish politics had led the Jewish voter to reject all the bourgeois parties.[50] Zionist newspapers, *Chwila* in Lwów and *Haynt* in Warsaw, blamed the Bund's success on the relatively weak Zionist campaign and failure to get Zionists to go to the polls; in contrast, the Bund had conducted a very well organized and intensive campaign, and also benefited from the radicalization of the Jewish electorate.[51]

[47] *Yidisher arbeter-klas in yor 1936*, 227–8. This book was published by the Bund and gleefully includes extensive quotes from the non-Socialist bourgeois Jewish press.
[48] Quoted ibid.
[49] Quoted ibid. 231.
[50] Quoted ibid. 228–30 and by Nowogródzki, 'Der "bund"', 74.
[51] Melzer, 'Yahadut polin', 109, citing articles appearing on 8 Sept. 1936 in *Chwila* and *Haynt*.

Writing in a Palestine Hebrew daily, the veteran Polish Zionist leader Yitzhak Grünbaum declared that the *kehillah* elections had not amounted to rejection of the principle of *aliyah*, emigration to the Land of Israel. The vast majority of mandates had gone to groups which supported the ideal of *aliyah*. Rather, it was the Agudas Yisroel which was the major loser, since oppressed Jews found that the Agudah's claimed ties to the government did not ease Jewish misery and had failed to prevent adoption of the law on slaughter. The Jewish masses had perceived in the Bund the only unflinching opponent of antisemitism. Moreover, Grünbaum believed, the Bund had benefited from the support of the Communists in the Jewish trade unions affiliated with its election bloc. On the other hand, the Zionist campaign had been sluggish and listless, concentrating on local issues and opposition to the Agudah instead of emphasizing Palestine, *aliyah*, and the battle against antisemitism.[52]

Bundists considered their 1936 electoral success as reflecting a fundamental trend that had begun with the widespread boycott of the parliamentary elections of September 1935, despite the involvement of the Agudas and much of the Zionist camp. As to the value of Communist support, Bund leaders pointed out that the extreme leftists had actively attacked the Bund's participation in the *kehillah* elections. At union meetings and in Yiddish leaflets, the Communists had called for a boycott of the *kehillah* election. Only on the Friday evening preceding the Warsaw election of Sunday, 6 September, did the Jewish Communists finally call on their adherents to halt their boycott. The practical value of such a late turn-about was minimal, but it was a symbolic victory which added to the Bundists' feeling of political satisfaction.[53]

Only three weeks after the elections in major Jewish communities, the impression made by the Bund's success was underscored by the Socialist victory in the Łódź city council election of 27 September 1936. There were three contending Jewish blocs, led by Agudas Yisroel, the Zionists, and the Bund. In an election that saw a relatively high voter participation of 74.5 per cent in contrast to only 30.9 per cent during the 1935 ballot for the Sejm, Jewish lists received less than a fifth of the valid votes and won eleven

[52] Y. Grünbaum, *Milḥamot yehudei polania 5673–5700* (Jerusalem and Tel Aviv, 5701 [1941]), 399–404, reprinting an article that originally appeared in *Haolam* in Sept. 1936. On a visit to Warsaw from his new home in Jerusalem about a month before the Warsaw *kehillah* election, Grünbaum provoked a firestorm of criticism from all sectors of the Jewish press when he told a press conference that the 'excess Jews' in Poland would be compelled by loss of livelihood to leave finally for Palestine. The same kind of criticism was voiced after the appearance on 8 Sept. of an article by the Zionist Revisionist leader Jabotinsky in the Polish conservative daily *Czas* proclaiming the need for the evacuation of Poland's Jews along with those endangered in other countries: Melzer, 'Yahadut polin', 136–9.

[53] Melzer, 'Yahadut polin', 110; *Yidisher arbeter-klas in yor 1936*, 232–4; Nowogródzki, 'Der "bund"', 74.

Table 5 Łódź City Council Election, 27 September 1936

List	Votes		Mandates	
	No.	%	No.	%
PPS and Trade unions (PPS, German Socialists, Communists)	95,115	37.1	34	47.2
National Camp (Endeks)	77,919	30.4	27	37.5
Bund and Jewish Trade Union (including PZ-Left)	23,692	9.2	6	8.2
United Jewish Election Bloc (Agudah, Artisans, Folkists, Revisionists, assimilationists, economic groups, etc.)	14,947	5.8	3	4.2
United Zionist Bloc (General Zionists, Hitachdut, Mizrahi, merchant and economic organizations)	10,601	4.1	2	2.8
Other lists that won no mandates	34,233	13.3	0	0
TOTAL	256,507[a]	99.9	72	100

[a] Misprinted in the source as 156,567.

Source: *Yidisher arbeter-klas in yor 1936*, 239–40. These figures differ somewhat from those published in *SN* (1936), Nos. 4–5, pp. 511–12.

mandates, down from seventeen in 1934.[54] The Bund-led bloc, which included the PZ-Left and the Jewish trade unions, received a stunning 48.1 per cent of the votes cast for Jewish lists and won six council seats. The Agudas bloc collapsed from ten mandates in the former council to only three in 1936, and the Zionists also declined from four to two seats (see Tables 6 and 7). The overall shift to the left among the Jewish electorate may have been even greater than is apparent at first glance, as an unknown number of Jews voted for the Polish Socialist Party–Trade Union bloc.[55]

The Agudas Yisroel leadership in Łódź had succeeded in delaying the Łódź *kehillah* election until 15 November.[56] Preparations for the election proceeded under the shadow cast by Bundist victories in the Warsaw *kehillah* and Łódź municipal elections. Despite allegations that thousands of

[54] *SN* (1936), Nos. 4–5, pp. 511–12; R. Leslie (ed.), *The History of Poland since 1863* (Cambridge, 1980), 187–8; *MRS m. Ł, 1935r.*, 181. See Table 5.

[55] The Polska Partia Socjalistyczna (PPS: Polish Socialist Party) and Communists had actively called on Jews to vote for the PPS list in order to prevent a win by the antisemitic Endeks. There were contemporary Jewish estimates that up to 40,000 Jews may have voted for the PPS list: *SN* (1936), Nos. 4–5, pp. 511–12; M. Teper, *Ersht nekhtn iz dos geven* ... (Warsaw, 1961), 64. The latter source is a memoir by a former Łódź Jewish Communist activist. If 40,000 Jews had voted for the PPS, then Jews would have comprised about a third of the voters, matching their share in the city's population. Moreover, it would mean that over two-thirds of Jewish voters cast their ballots for Socialist lists, which thus drew about half of their votes from the city's Jews.

[56] The *kehillah* council elected in May 1931 had not taken office until Nov. 1932, so the term would end in Nov. 1936: *Moment* (1 July 1936), 4. Elections were also postponed to November in Lwów, Brześć n/Bugiem, Kobryń, and Pińsk, while the 18 minor *kehillot* in Polesie were to vote on 25 Oct.: ibid. (3 Nov. 1936), 2; *SN* (1936), No. 6, p. 658.

Table 6 Łódź City Council, Elected 27 May 1934

List		Mandates[a]
Endeks (including Ch.D.)[b]		39
Sanacja		10
Socialist Bloc		7
PPS	4	
German Socialists	1	
Bund	2	
Agudah and Folkists		10
Zionists		4
Bourgeois Germans		1
PZ-Left		1
TOTAL		72

[a] The Łódź city council had 72 seats; (=23.6%) city councillors were elected on the Jewish lists (Bund, Agudah and Folkists, Zionists, and PZ-Left).

[b] National Democrats (Endeks) were the principal right-wing Polish opposition party, while the Christian Democrats (Ch.D.) advocated government on Christian principles, including extensive social-welfare programmes for the working class.

Sources: Hertz, *Bund in lodzh*, 376–82; Melzer, 'Yahadut polin', 111–14; Teper, *Ersht nekhtn*, 64.

eligible workers had been omitted from the voters' rolls, along with nine leading Socialists, the Bundists felt confident of success and remained in the campaign.[57] To prevent the Bund from getting ballot-list number four, with which it had triumphed in Warsaw, the Agudah submitted several fictive candidates' lists. The remaining twenty-one valid lists included no fewer than twelve submitted by Agudas Yisroel, four by Zionists, two by Folkists,[58] and one each by the Bund–PZ-Left–Jewish Trade Unions bloc, the assimilationist 'Social Economic Bloc', and the 'extreme leftists'. Whether the latter means that a Communist list was submitted is unclear.[59]

Fearing another major Socialist success in the proletarian centre of Łódź, the Ministry of Religions decided to postpone the *kehillah* election there indefinitely. On 30 October 1936 the Łódź city governor (*starosta*) notified the *kehillah* board that the action was 'in consideration of the public

[57] Hertz, *Di geshikhte fun bund*, 407–8; *Moment* (16 Oct. 1936), 10.

[58] The Folkists were a movement of secular Yiddishists committed to the development of democratic autonomous institutions to serve the needs of the Jewish nation.

[59] *Moment* (16 Oct. 1936), 10; (20 Oct. 1936), 2; (26 Oct. 1936), 2. The contending lists of candidates were to be submitted to the *kehillah* election commission by the respective parties between 18 and 22 Oct.

Table 7 Jewish Lists in the Łódź City Council Election, 1936

List	Votes		Mandates
	No.	%	
Bund and Jewish Trade Unions	23,692	48	6
United Jewish Election Bloc	14,947	30	3
United Zionist Bloc	10,601	22	2
TOTAL	49,240	100	11

Source: *Yidisher arbeter-klas in yor 1936*, 239–40.

interest' (*z uwagi na interes publiczny*)'.[60] The Lwów *kehillah* election was also postponed at about the same time, although it was eventually held in May 1937, when the Zionists won.[61] No new *kehillah* election would be held in Łódź before the outbreak of the Second World War.

Electoral success did not necessarily translate into power, as the government intervened to eliminate undesirable or uncooperative municipal and Jewish communal councils. Thus, the Socialist majority in the Łódź city council was unable to obtain government confirmation for its candidate for the post of city president. On 1 April 1937 the Łódź city council elected the previous September was dissolved.[62] A similar fate had overtaken the Warsaw *kehillah* council and board, paralysed by the wrestling of roughly equal factions of Agudah, Zionists, and Socialists.[63] When the Government Commissioner for Warsaw acted on 5 January 1937 to dissolve the Warsaw *kehillah*'s council and board, the justification given was that those bodies did not guarantee 'positive work for the good of society', as the *kehillah* council had discussed and voted on resolutions of a political nature, twice obliging the state observer to dissolve its sessions.[64]

By the beginning of 1937 government-nominated commissioner regimes governed the *kehillot* in such major cities as Warsaw, Lwów, and Kraków, while the Łódź *kehillah* election remained indefinitely postponed, leaving in office the Agudas-dominated council and board elected in 1931.[65]

No new *kehillah* election was ever held in Łódź. Yet there were two

[60] *Moment* (30 Oct. 1936), 2; (1 Nov. 1936), 4; H. Banner, *Gmina Żydowska w Łodzi: Krótki zarys dziejów ustrojowo-gospodarczych* (Łódź, 1938), 34.

[61] *Moment* (3 Nov. 1936), 2; *SN* (1937), Nos. 4–5, p. 469; F. Friedman, 'Di nayeste geshikhte fun idn in poyln', in *Haynt yoyvl-bukh (1908–1938)* (Warsaw, 1938), 136.

[62] Hertz, *Di geshikhte fun bund*, 407.

[63] Bacon, 'Agudath Israel', 342; *SN* (1936), No. 6, pp. 658–9.

[64] Bacon, 'Agudath Israel', 343–4; *SN* (1936), No. 6, pp. 658–9; *Moment* (3 Dec. 1936), 1; Nowogródzki, 'Der "bund"' 75; MSW, *SZMN za I kw. 1937r.*, 143–4.

[65] *SN* (1936), No. 6, p. 659.

Table 8 Jewish Lists in the Łódź City Council Election, December 1938

List	Votes		Mandates	
	No.	%	No.	%
Bund, PZ, and Jewish trade unions	31,682	57.9	11[a]	64.7
Zionist–Democratic Bloc	11,987	21.9	3	17.6
Jewish National Bloc[b]	11,019	20.1	3	17.6
TOTAL	54,688	100.0	17	100.0

[a] Including 8 Bundists, 2 PZs, and 1 Communist.
[b] Agudas Yisroel, Zionist Revisionists, Artisans, and others.
Sources: J. Marcus, *Social and Political History of the Jews of Poland, 1919–1939* (Berlin, New York, and Amsterdam, 1983), 468–9; Hertz, *Bund in lodzh*, 426–32; Melzer, 'Yahadut polin', 266; Sh. Milman, 'Undzer heymshtot lodzh', in *Lodzher yizker-bukh* (New York, 1943), 45; *SN* (1939), Nos. 1–2, pp. 132–3.

elections in autumn 1938 that could serve as indicators of the attitudes of the Jewish public. Łódź *kehillah* President Mincberg won official nomination for re-election as the sole Jewish candidate to the Sejm in the city with the country's second-largest Jewry. Mincberg argued that Jews as a minority could not risk abstention; Jewish deputies had managed to blunt assaults on Jewish rights and interests.[66] On 6 November 1938 Mincberg was re-elected to parliament with 57 per cent of the votes cast, as the overall turnout in his district rose to 51 per cent of those eligible. The number of votes he obtained doubled from 17,844 in 1935 to 34,085 in 1938.[67]

The opposition looked to the municipal elections for a truer reflection of the popular will. As in 1936, three Jewish blocs contended in the Łódź city council election on 18 December 1938, although voter participation declined somewhat from 74.6 per cent to 68 per cent. The Bund-led bloc won an absolute majority of 57.9 per cent of the votes cast for Jewish lists, while Agudas Yisroel's bloc received only 20.1 per cent (down from 30.4 per cent in 1936) and the Zionists had 21.9 per cent (21.5 per cent in 1936). The Bund list received eleven mandates and the Agudah and Zionists three each to the 84-seat city council.[68] The leftwards shift of the Jewish electorate was further emphasized by the fact that two of the Zionists elected were of the radical Al Hamishmar faction, while the third was a leading member of the non-Marxist labour Zionist party Hitachdut.[69]

[66] *NF* (24 Oct. 1938), 8.
[67] Ibid. (3 Oct. 1938), 7; (31 Oct. 1938), 7; (7 Nov. 1938), 1; *SN* (1938), No. 6, p. 652; *MRS m. Ł. 1935r.*, 181.
[68] On the 1936 and 1938 city council elections in Łódź see Tables 7–9.
[69] *SN* (1939), Nos. 1–2, pp. 132–3. In Warsaw the main Zionist list in the 1938 municipal election was composed of the Al Hamishmar faction and the Po'alei Tsion Right.

Table 9 City Council Elections in Łódź: 1936–1938

Lists	Votes[a]		Mandates	
	1936	1938	1936	1938
PPS and Trade Unions	95,000	82,000	34	33
OZN	—	29,000	—	11
SN (Endeks)	78,000	40,000	27	18
Bund, Jewish Trade Unions, and PZ-Left	23,692	31,000	6	11
United Jewish Bloc[b]	14,947	11,019	3	3
Zionist Bloc	10,601	11,987	2	3
Others	34,000	45,000	—	—
TOTAL	256,240	250,006	72	79

[a] There are minor discrepancies and inconsistencies in the totals cited in the various sources, particularly due to rounding off to the nearest thousand.
[b] Agudah, Artisans, Revisionists, assimilationists, etc.
Sources: Hertz, *Bund in lodzh*, 401–3, 426–32; *SN* (1936), Nos. 4–5, 511–12; ibid. (1939), Nos. 1–2, 132–3; *Yidisher arbeter-klas in yor 1936*, 239–40, 243–4; Marcus, *Social and Political History*, 468–9; Melzer, 'Yahadut polin', 266, 269.

Bundists saw the results of the 564 municipal elections between December 1938 and May 1939 as proof of their power on the Jewish street.[70] The Bund polled a plurality of Jewish list votes in 51 of the 89 cities where it had fielded valid lists.[71] Bund-led lists won a majority of the votes cast for Jewish lists in Warsaw, Łódź, Vilna, Białystok, Lublin, and nine other of the 35 cities with over 10,000 Jews.[72]

However, political analyst Leopold Halpern, writing in the Zionist *Haynt*, disagreed with any Bundist claim to primacy in Jewish politics. The Bund's city council successes had come in existing Bundist strongholds, while entire provinces and regions were largely Zionist sweeps (Galicia, Wołyń, Eastern Upper Silesia (Zagłębie)). Even in Congress Poland there were places where Zionists dominated. No party, especially the Bund, could claim that the

---

[70] Between Dec. 1938 and May 1939 elections were held in 564 of Poland's 604 cities. Jews won 17.3 per cent of the 10,040 city council seats, a marked decline from 1929, when the figure was 31.4 per cent: *SN* (1929), No. 6, p. 847; *Haynt* (28 May 1939), 2, 6. During 1938–9 about 15,000 villages elected 560,526 councillors, including 5,138 Jews (0.9 per cent): *Haynt* (26 May 1939), 2.

[71] Bund lists were invalidated in about 20 cities: *Naye Folkstsaytung* (18 Aug. 1939), 9; (25 Aug. 1939), 9.

[72] Ibid. (11 Aug. 1939), 7. On the Warsaw election see Table 10. Other cities with over 10,000 Jews where the Bund won a majority of votes for Jewish lists: Radom, Grodno, Tarnów, Kalisz, Kowal, Piotrków, Tomaszów, Włocławek, Zamość. There were no Bund lists in Lwów, Stanisławów, Równe, Brześć, Kielce, Kołomyj, Tarnopol, Borysław; and three-quarters of Bund district lists were invalidated in Siedlce and Chełm. Cities where the Bund ran but failed to win a majority of votes for Jewish lists: Kraków, Częstochowa, Będzin, Sosnowiec, Łuck, Przemyśl, Drohobycz, Rzeszów, Stryj, Włodzimierz Wołynsk.

Table 10 Jewish Lists in Warsaw City Election, December 1938

List	Votes		Mandates	
	No.	%	No.	%
Bund and Jewish trade unions	47,224	61.7	17[a]	85.0
PZ-Left	2,060	2.7	—	—
Zionist–Democratic Bloc (Al Hamishmar, PZ-Right)	14,481	18.9	1	5.0
Jewish National General Bloc (Et Livnot, Agudah, Mizrachi, Revisionists, Merchants' Association)	12,808	16.7	2	10.0
TOTAL	76,573	100.0	20	100.0

[a] One of the Bund-led list's 17 mandates went to a Communist trade unionist.

Sources: Marcus, *Social and Political History*, 429–30; Melzer, 'Yahadut polin', 264.

election results gave it hegemony over Jewish life. In Halpern's view, the Bund's series of successes were an 'unnatural phenomenon'.[73]

Nevertheless, regardless of attempts to minimize the significance of the Bundist success in the 1938–9 city council elections, it is clear that it continued a trend begun during the *kehillah* elections of 1936, when much of the Jewish electorate turned to the Socialists in protest against the ever worsening anti-Jewish agitation, violence, and discrimination. With Agudas Yisroel's policy of accommodation revealed as impotent and the Zionists unable to open the gates of British Mandatory Palestine, many Jews desperately turned to the Bund as a champion of Jewish interests even though its prospects for real success were minimal in an increasingly authoritarian Poland.

APPENDIX

MINISTRY OF INTERNAL AFFAIRS DIRECTIVE ON
PREVENTING BUND VICTORIES IN *KEHILLAH* ELECTIONS

Warsaw, 22/8/36

STRICTLY SECRET

TO: Chief of the Social-Political Department in the Provincial Administration in [*list of twelve provinces and the capital*].

Entrance of the 'Bund' into the electoral campaign to the Jewish religious communities causes grave apprehensions concerning a change in the character of these institutions, which under the binding legislation and internal statutes ought to be centres of Jewish religious life. Entrance of representatives of the 'Bund' into these institutions, and possibly even here and there capture by them of a majority,

[73] Leopold Halpern, 'A por faktn un tsifern vegn di shtotrat valn', *Haynt* (6 June 1939), 4.

would change the character of the community, introducing into it many secular elements and even making it a convenient instrument of political combat.

That sort of result of the Bundist campaign would place the state authorities before the necessity of intervention, and even of dissolution of several communal boards.

To avoid that eventuality, earlier counteraction of the Bundist campaign is indicated. There exists the possibility of application of paragraph 20 of the electoral law of the religious communities. Mass application of that paragraph would not be a clever move, but knocking off with its aid certain inconvenient major individuals would permit avoidance of the later need to apply repressive measures. Application of paragraph 20 is possible through appropriate moulding of or influence on electoral organs.

Giving these observations for [your] personal information, I request handling of the matter as strictly secret and return of this letter immediately after reading.

Respectfully yours,
[*Illegible*]

Source: AAN MSW 1064, mf. 25635.

Jewish Artisans

ZBIGNIEW LANDAU

WHEN considering the situation of artisans in interwar Poland, one must bear in mind several methodological problems which make precise study very difficult. The difficulties are of various types but together they make any quantitative approach a very hard task. Above all, the term 'artisan' is quite vague. Of course we can attempt a theoretical definition, but in practice any definition is subject to serious flaws. There is no precise way to distinguish between handicraft work, small-scale industry, and cottage work. The manufacturing techniques and organization were similar in all; the only point of contrast lay in the economic basis of each sector, but even here differences were not great. Theoretically, it could be argued that artisans produced in response to a concrete order, while small capitalist entrepreneurs produced for an anonymous market, but while these differences had been clear in the more distant past, the distinction became blurred during the Second Polish Republic. The difference between an artisan and a cottage worker lay in the fact that while the former worked on his own account, the latter was required by others to process the materials entrusted to him. Frequently, however, artisans combined both functions, working sometimes on their own account and sometimes as cottage workers. This is not surprising since the manufacturing techniques were identical in either case.

Under these circumstances, to state who was and who was not an artisan is a matter of arbitrary decision. It was generally laid down by legislation which crafts were performed by artisans, while the Treasury imposed separate taxes on handicraft works. Yet during the period between 1919 and 1939 there was considerable fluctuation in the list of crafts designated for tax purposes as the work of artisans, and in the imposition of tax on workshops.

It is not only the theoretical definition of handicraft work that creates difficulties, but also the practical application of such a definition. Even if we adhere to the categories laid down by legislation or the Treasury, we remain hampered by the shortage of statistical evidence, which makes it impossible to estimate the number of handicraft works. Statistical data supplied by the Organization of Handicraft Workers include only information on the number of licences granting the right to engage in a craft. In order to obtain a licence, a craftsman had to complete his apprenticeship or graduate from a technical college. Many artisans could not satisfy these requirements and did not possess licences, but they nevertheless ran handicraft works. The government was quite flexible and the legal requirements were not always enforced. For instance, all those who worked in handicrafts when the new legislation came into force in 1927 were allowed to maintain their workshops regardless of whether they possessed the required qualifications. As a result, the number of licences was much lower than the number of people who actually ran handicraft works. Similarly, the financial statistics include only those workshops which paid taxes, although it is well known that many small artisans evaded payment. Under these circumstances the statistics furnished by the artisans' organization and the financial evidence indicate no more than the minimum number of workshops. Reliable information is simply not available.[1]

It is even more difficult to estimate the number employed in handicrafts or deriving their living from such an occupation. Generally, those running handicraft workshops were not interested in revealing the full number of workers employed since this would result in higher taxation. In view of the persistent level of unemployment in the Second Republic, to find workers not registered by the appropriate authorities was no problem for artisans. Besides, workshop-owners were frequently recorded as workers, so their real number is beyond the reach of any statistical evidence and we simply do not know how many people made a living from handicrafts. Since we do not know the number of workshops, estimates of the economically active and passive population deriving their living from handicrafts are subject to an increased level of error. But we have to draw conclusions from the existing evidence, however imperfect we know it to be. All of these difficulties increase further when we attempt to establish separate data relating to Jewish handicraft workers. Many statistical records embrace the whole craft, and division must be arbitrary.

These problems make it impossible to provide a complete history of handicrafts in the Second Polish Republic, and *a fortiori* preclude such an account for Jewish artisans. The scale of the difficulties involved may be demonstrated by the fragmented nature of information included in the standard monograph on the subject.[2] Postwar studies have hardly advanced beyond Bornstein's conclusions, despite several attempts.[3]

---

[1] Z. Landau, 'Rzemiosło polskie w latach 1936–1939', *Drobnomieszczaństwo XIX i XX wieku: Studia*, ii (Warsaw, 1988), 181–224.

[2] I. Bornstein, *Rzemiosło żydowskie w Polsce* (Warsaw, 1936).

[3] Cf. e.g. J. Tomaszewski, 'Gospodarka drobnotowarowa', in Z. Landau and J. Tomaszewski, *Druga Rzeczpospolita: Gospodarka, społeczeństwo, miejsce w świecie* (Warsaw, 1977), 157–90; S.

Let us nevertheless attempt to make some generalizations. The First World War brought about the destruction of many handicraft workshops and the pauperization of artisans. Mass migrations, military operations, and evacuations affected Jewish handicrafts to a higher degree than the rest of handicraft activities in Poland. This was mainly due to the territorial distribution of these workshops, which made them vulnerable to military operations. Jewish handicraft works were not spread regularly over Polish territory. For historical reasons, they were most frequently located in the former Russian and Austrian partitions. In the eastern provinces of interwar Poland, Jews accounted for 73 per cent of all artisans, in the central provinces 52 per cent, in southern Poland 41 per cent, while in the western provinces the figure was a mere 0.2 per cent.[4] These data refer to the turn of the 1930s, when there had already been some territorial shifts in the structure of the Jewish population. It was only in the eastern, southern, and central territories of interwar Poland that the military operations of 1914–20 took place, during the First World War and the Polish–Soviet war. Simultaneously, the destruction of industry led to growing unemployment and caused Jews to seek employment in handicrafts. Most Jews were without financial means to start capitalist production, could not find employment in industry, and had no funds for buying land and for farming activity. This goes a long way towards explaining the gravitation of Jews in the direction of small-scale activities like handicrafts and petty trade. Handicraft activity (e.g. tailoring or shoemaking) usually required moderate financial resources. Moreover, independent handicraft employment made it possible for Jews to celebrate the Sabbath and to perform other religious obligations which would have been very difficult while working in industry. Conversely, this was the reason why many entrepreneurs were not willing to employ Jews. Therefore they were often forced to look to artisan work.

The situation of Jewish artisans during the postwar inflation, the stabilization of the currency in 1924, and the years of prosperity (1926–9) is now practically impossible to reconstruct. There are no statistical records, and the descriptive materials are impossible to aggregate. Thus, only hypotheses may be formulated. It seems that in general inflation was favourable for artisans. A flight from currency raised the demand for handicraft products and services. A serious destruction of industrial works further extended the scope of artisan opportunities. In 1921, when industry was at an initial stage of reconstruction, several crafts exceeded the 1913 level of works in opera-

Bronsztejn, *Ludność żydowska w Polsce w okresie międzywojennym* (Wrocław, 1963); J. Żarnowski, *Społeczénstwo Drugiej Rzeczypospolitej 1918–1939* (Warsaw, 1973); J. Marcus, *Social and Political History of the Jews in Poland 1919–1939* (Berlin, 1983). (I do not know the literature in Yiddish and Hebrew.)

[4] Bornstein, *Rzemiosło*, 49.

tion. There was a considerable difference in the level of funding required to start a handicraft workshop and that needed for an industrial factory. In this connection, according to the 1921 population census there were 1.3 million independent artisans and their families, 8,600 white-collar workers, and 341,000 blue-collar workers.[5] Assuming that the 1921 distribution of works into Jewish and non-Jewish categories was not much different from that of 1 January 1929, at least 40 per cent of the works belonged to Jewish artisans.[6] It is probable that in practice the Jewish share was higher, since government records do not take into account the illegal artisan activity which was more widespread among Jews than in society as a whole. This was due to the more difficult situation of Jewish artisans, who had limited access to government credits and orders. Thus, many Jewish artisans simply could not afford to buy a handicraft licence or an industrial certificate.[7] Many of them also had no formal qualifications.

The hyperinflation of 1923 and the depression of 1924–6 created increasing difficulties for artisans, all the more because they faced ever more serious competition from reconstructed industry. Many independent artisans therefore joined the ranks of cottage workers, whose earnings were usually much lower than those of artisans. Moreover, they did not benefit from the extensive labour legislation and social-security system of interwar Poland.

The years of prosperity, 1926–9, brought a recovery of handicraft activity. Nevertheless, we do not know how many works there were or how many people were employed at that time. The 1928 estimates of the Ministry of Industry and Trade showed 319,400 works, while the Central Statistical Office recorded only 197,800 handicraft licences. Taking into account illegal works, the total number should be raised to about 450,000,[8] of which perhaps 180,000–200,000 belonged to Jews.

As a proportion of industrial production, the share of artisan workshops decreased from 14.7 per cent in 1924 to 10.5 per cent in 1928.[9] This was due to the growing rate of completion of industrial factories, whose production increased very rapidly in the years of prosperity. The situation of artisan workshops was further aggravated by the extension of cartels, which not only monopolized the market but also boosted prices for raw materials

---

[5] L. Landau, 'Skład zawodowy ludności Polski jako podstawa badania struktury gospodarcze', in *Wybór pism* (Warsaw, 1957), 161–2.

[6] According to the Ministry of Industry and Trade information on the issue of handicraft licenses. Cf. Bornstein, *Rzemiosło*, 49.

[7] I. Bornstein, 'Akcja zapomogowa dla kupców i rzemieślników na opłacenie podatków', *Zagadnienia Gospodarcze* (1935), Nos. 1–2, pp. 101–2.

[8] W. Hauszyld, 'Rzemiosło i przemysł ludowy w Polsce w ostatnim dziesięcioleciu', in *Bilans gospodarczy dziesięciolecia Polski Odrodzonej*, i (Poznań 1929), 528; *Mały rocznik statystyczny*, (1931), 46; Z. Landau and J. Tomaszewski, *Od Grabskiego do Piłsudskiego* (Warsaw, 1971), 81.

[9] Calculated according to *Rocznik Ministerstwa Skarbu, 1927–1930* (Warsaw, 1931), 110–11.

processed by artisans. The competition between artisans made it impossible for them to raise their prices proportionately. Thus, handicraft earnings failed to grow despite a booming economy, while the structural unemployment of the Second Republic constantly pushed many towards casual jobs in handicrafts. Since the unemployed worked illegally, they could offer lower prices because their costs did not include overheads such as taxes, insurance, or rent. Thus, intense competition radically limited the growth of handicraft earnings. Whether or not the same thing happened to Jewish artisans in particular is impossible to state in view of the complete lack of separate evidence for that group. However, one may risk the hypothesis that the situation of Jewish and non-Jewish artisans was more or less the same: had there been any difference, one would expect it to receive specific mention in the sources.

The influence of the Great Depression, which in Poland lasted from 1930 to 1935, on Jewish artisans was different from its impact on industry. While industry reacted by reducing the number of existing factories and the level of employment, in the handicraft sphere the opposite occurred. The many workers leaving industry undertook handicraft activities, frequently unlicensed. The number of industrial certificates bought by artisans also increased sharply. While in 1929 197,000 certificates were issued, six years later the number had grown by 75 per cent.[10] According to various provincial data, between 48 per cent and 79 per cent of artisans possessed handicraft licences.[11] In view of widespread illegal handicraft activity (estimated at about a third of all works), the authorities took certain steps to legalize the unofficial workshops. However, there were problems with the legalization of many Jewish artisans who had no formal qualifications. Educating young artisans was also problematic since there were not enough master craftsmen among the Jewish artisans authorized to teach apprentices. For instance, in Warsaw in 1932 only 7 per cent of registered Jewish artisans were masters, while in the Włocławek Handicraft Chamber (the officially recognized organ of artisan self-government) only 8 per cent had this status (for other chambers there are no data). Among non-Jewish artisans the proportion of masters was about 45 per cent.[12] Production of qualified handicraftsmen among the Jews was therefore quite limited, and Jewish artisans were more frequently forced to undertake illegal activity.

A rapid inflow of new workers to handicraft occupations resulted in a far-reaching pauperization of artisans. The declining demand for handicraft

[10] *Mały rocznik statystyczny* (1931), 46; ibid. (1937), 93.

[11] C. Ptasiński, *Struktura zawodów drobnoprzemysłowych według spisu z dnia 9 grudnia 1931* (Lublin, 1936), p. xxiv.

[12] I. Giterman, 'Perspektywy rzemiosła żydowskiego w Polsce', *Zagadnienia Gospodarcze* (1935), Nos. 1–2, p. 9.

products and services was satisfied by an increasing number of people trying to make their living in legal or illegal handicraft activities. This was particularly the case with Jewish artisans in the areas where they were numerically dominant. And that was the situation in many provinces. While the average proportion of Jewish artisans among owners of handicraft works in Poland was about 40 per cent, in Polesie it was 81 per cent, in the Nowogródek province 77 per cent, in the province of Białystok 76 per cent, in Wołyń 73 per cent, in the province of Vilna 60 per cent, in Warsaw 56 per cent, in Lublin 57 per cent, in Kielce 53 per cent, in Stanisławów 49 per cent, in Tarnopol 46 per cent, in Lwów, 41 per cent, in Kraków 31 per cent, while in the Poznań province it was a mere 0.4 per cent, in Pomorze 0.3 per cent, and in Upper Silesia Jewish artisans were hardly recorded at all.[13] It should be pointed out that in all provinces except Poznań province and Pomorze the share of Jews in handicrafts greatly exceeded the proportion of Jews in the total and urban populations. In Polesie Jews accounted for about 13 per cent of the population, in the Nowogródek province 9 per cent, in the Białystok province 15 per cent, while only in Warsaw did their numbers exceed 33 per cent.[14] On average, in the 1930s the share of Jews in handicrafts was almost four times higher than their proportion of the total population and in the provinces with the highest percentage of Jewish artisans (Polesie, Nowogródek) nine or ten times higher. Such a high percentage of Jews in handicrafts made the bad economic situation more perceptible among the Jewish population, and also helps to explain the growing hostility between artisans of various nationalities. Jews defended the position they had achieved because handicrafts were their basic sphere of economic activity in towns, while pauperized Poles, Ukrainians, or Belarussians sought chances to make a living in the same field. Under these circumstances, the economic difficulties stimulated the growth of antisemitism among the urban petty bourgeoisie and among those peasants who left the countryside and sought employment in towns. The growth of antisemitism in its turn undermined the economic welfare of many Jewish artisans.

According to estimates made by Bronsztejn on the basis of the 1931 census, there were 328,000 Jews employed in handicrafts. This figure seems rather too low since the author leaves out Jewish workers employed in larger handicraft works.[15] These data refer to the economically active population only. Any estimate of the total number of Jewish artisans should therefore be supplemented by adding those economically passive people depending on artisan owners and workers in handicraft workshops, although this would involve a speculative guess at the relation between the economically active and passive groups. All that one can say is that among all the independent

[13] Bornstein, *Rzemiosło*, 48.   [14] Ibid.   [15] Bronsztein, *Ludność*, 218–19.

entrepreneurs using hired manpower the ratio of the economically passive population to 100 economically active people was 137, while among those who did not hire manpower it was 186.[16] However, there is no way to determine how many of the 328,000 people employed in handicrafts were independent artisan owners and how many apprentices or workers. We must therefore take into account the whole industry (statistically including handicraft), in which the ratio was 159 economically passive per 100 economically active Jews. This ratio was higher than among the non-Jewish population, and was a major reason for a lower standard of living among Jewish artisans in relation to other handicraftsmen. This question will be discussed below.

If the ratio of 159 economically passive to 100 economically active people is adopted, the total number of Jews dependent on handicrafts may be estimated at about 850,000. This would mean that about 27 per cent of all Polish Jews (and 36 per cent of the urban Jewish population) made their living from handicrafts.

However, if the estimate made by Tartakower is considered more reliable, the ratio should be 215 economically passive Jews to 100 economically active ones in the whole industrial sector (the figure given for non-Jews is 168).[17] In that case the total number of Jews depending on handicrafts would exceed 1 million, or 33 per cent of all Polish Jews. Bornstein estimated the number of Jews living on handicrafts even higher, at 1.5 million people.[18] This would account for about 45 per cent of all Jews in Poland. (But even Jewish economists have though the latter estimate too high: most of them estimate the share of those making a living from handicrafts to be about a third of the total number of Jews in Poland.) No wonder Polish Jews attached such importance to maintaining their position in this sector of the economy.

The proportion of Jews varied in the different crafts. Traditionally there was a group of crafts in which Jews dominated, while in others non-Jews prevailed. Among 67 registered crafts, Jews dominated in 17, non-Jews in 15. Jewish artisans prevailed in cap-making, haberdashery, bronze-working, goldsmithery, shoe-upper making, wig-making (from 75 per cent to 92 per cent of these activities), while in pottery, basketry, wheel-making, file-making, stonework, well-making, tile-stove setting, stucco work, sculpturing, carpentry, pork butchery, block smithery, metalwork, and instrument-making, the participation of Jews was insignificant. Generally speaking, Jews prevailed in textile crafts (65 per cent of issued licences) and in

[16] Ibid. 84.
[17] A. Tartakower, 'Zawodowa i społeczna struktura Żydów w Polsce Odrodzonej', in I. Schiper, A. Tartakower, and A. Hafftka, *Żydzi w Polsce Odrodzonej: Działalność społeczna, oświatowa i kulturalna* (2 vols.; Warsaw, 1936), ii. 376.
[18] According to A. Hafftka, 'Żydowski stan rzemieślniczy w Polse Odrodzonej', in *Żydzi*, ii. 556.

personal services such as hairdressing and manicures (53 per cent), while their share was lowest in wood-processing crafts (23 per cent) and metalwork (30 per cent).[19]

As mentioned above, the Great Depression of 1930–5 resulted in the severe pauperization of all artisans, but especially of Jews. There were several reasons for this. Firstly, the average size of Jewish workshops was smaller than that of non-Jewish ones. In Warsaw in 1936 non-Jewish works employed in average 3.5 persons, while the Jewish figure was 2.1. Non-Jewish works were larger in all crafts.[20] The situation in the Łódź province was similar. Here 52 per cent of non-Jewish and 62 per cent of Jewish workshops operated without hired workers.[21] These data may be treated as representative of the whole of Poland.

Secondly, Jewish artisans faced more difficulties because they supported a larger number of economically dependent members of their families. This considerably limited their investment input and ability to make bulk purchases of raw materials (at reduced wholesale price), forcing the artisans to look for expensive loans, and so on.

Thirdly, Jewish handicraft was concentrated in the poorest regions of Poland (eastern and central provinces), where the depression was particularly severe. The pauperization of society influenced the situation of handicraft works. The impoverished population could no longer afford handicraft products or services, and increasingly turned to making the necessary products themselves. This led in fact to a subsistence economy.

Fourthly, Jewish artisans were disadvantaged in the placement of government or local-authority orders. In most cases these orders went to non-Jewish works.[22]

During the Great Depression, handicrafts in Poland were affected by massive unemployment. This was due to the fall of demand but also to the influx of new workers to the handicraft sector. It was estimated that in 1932 as many as 52 per cent of artisans were out of work. In some crafts and in some regions this situation was even worse. It also differed in relation to independent artisans, apprentices, or hired workers. Clearly an artisan owner would defend his position by reducing the number of his employees, but ultimately even he could be left jobless.

In reports of Handicraft Chambers the size of unemployment among artisans is strongly stressed: the Kielce Chamber in 1930 already shows that 30 per cent of its

[19] Bornstein, *Rzemiosło*, 50–1.

[20] B. Sikorski, 'Rzemiosło warszawskie II Rzeczypospolitej', in *Warszawa Drugiej Rzeczypospolitej 1918–1939*, iii (Warsaw, 1971), 78.

[21] IX Sprawozdanie Izby Rzemieślniczej w Łodzi za rok 1938 (Łódź, 1939), table 'Stan zatrudnienia w rzemiośle w 1938 r.'

[22] J. Borenstejn, 'Zagadnienie pauperyzacji ludności żydowskiej w Polsce', in *Żydzi*, ii. 401–2.

shoemakers are jobless. Only the owners are still working while all apprentices are dismissed. In Kraków unemployment among shoemakers has reached 80 per cent of works, in tailoring 50 per cent. In Stanisławów and in the small towns of its province almost all apprentices have been dismissed ... In Lublin perhaps 10 per cent out of 1,200 shoemakers may earn some money, while the rest are jobless ... In Warsaw only a third of shoe-upper makers are still employed. Among 15,000 shoemakers only 4,000 are still working.[23]

In 1931—that is, early in the Great Depression—unemployment in tinsmithery amounted to 80 per cent, in hat-making, coppersmithery, bronze-work, and photography, 75 per cent, in wheel-making, 70 per cent, in shoemaking 60–70 per cent, in upholstery 65 per cent, in clock-and watchmaking, engraving, shoe-top making, bookbinding, coopering, basketry, cap-making, and furriery 60 per cent, and so on.[24] In most of these crafts Jews played an important role. Thus, the growing unemployment seriously undermined the standard of living of Jewish artisans. It must also be remembered that artisans had no unemployment insurance. A loss of orders meant living on reserves, if there were any, or selling out, or living on loans, which were more and more difficult to get. Unemployed artisans were sometimes helped by various charitable organizations, but the extent of this aid was rather limited.

Loss or decline of earnings inevitably led to a decrease in the standard of living, which even before the depression was quite low (except for a small number of the wealthiest artisans). Data concerning earnings of Jewish artisans and apprentices are fragmentary and cannot be aggregated, so that it is not possible precisely to calculate the level of income of this part of the Jewish community. Undoubtedly growing competition and the decline in orders had diminished handicraft earnings below the level of economic profitability. Small-scale producers such as artisans reacted to the decline in earnings in a different manner from that of industrial capitalists. An artisan could not simply close his workshop, because this would terminate his income altogether. He would try at all costs to keep his workshop in operation by accepting even lower earnings. At the same time, if he failed to renew his facilities and reserves he gradually consumed accumulated capital. All this meant depreciation of handicraft assets.

Despite the shortage of income statistics, it seems obvious that the standard of living of apprentices was worse than that of industrial workers who were still employed. In 1933 average weekly wages in large and medium-sized industrial works were zl 27.4, in small-scale industrial production zl 22.8, and in handicrafts, zl 18.4; only in cottage industries and in public works was it lower (zl 14.0 and 14.1 respectively).[25] In handicrafts as

[23] Ibid.   [24] Ibid. 402.
[25] Z. Landau and T. Tomaszewski, *Robotnicy przemysłowi w Polsce* (Warsaw, 1971), 426.

many as 44 per cent of workers earned less than a very low minimum subsistence level, while in large and medium-sized industry this figure was 20 per cent, in small-scale industry 31 per cent. On the other hand, the proportion was even higher in cottage work (56 per cent) and public works (58 per cent).[26]

The standard of living of independent artisans may be evaluated only on the basis of indirect information concerning consumption per capita in 1933 as compared with 1929. It was estimated that among the urban lower middle class (including artisans) it decreased by 22 per cent in real terms. In the same period the consumption of office workers did not change, that of the free professions diminished by 8 per cent, of landowners by 18 per cent, of industrial workers by 25 per cent, and of peasants by 56 per cent.[27] It must be remembered that these are average data: the situation of Jewish artisans was worse than average.

The years 1936–9 brought some improvement in the situation of handicrafts in Poland, although they did not recover to the level obtaining before the Depression. Of major importance were the constant pressure of the unemployed (registered unemployment still exceeded 400,000 people) and the growing competition of industrial products. This was particularly the case in shoemaking, which, together with tailoring, employed the largest number of Jewish artisans. Tailors faced the growing competition of the clothing industry, which utilized very cheap domestic labour. Apart from that, the situation of artisans generally improved, more rapidly in the years 1936–7 and less so in 1938 and 1939, when agriculture experienced a slight recession.

The improving economic condition was not accompanied by a sense of stabilization among Jewish artisans. After Józef Piłsudski's death, some of his followers who belonged to the ruling Establishment ('Sanacja') took over the National Democratic idea of the need to eliminate Jewish artisans from the Polish economy. Official statements suggested the imperative Polonization of economic life, especially in towns. This was emphasized in the programme of Obóz Zjednoczenia Narodowego (OZON: the Camp of National Unity), which stated that 'it is intended that Polish society develop an instinct of cultural self-defence and a desire for economic independence'.[28] On 21 May 1938 the Supreme Council of the Camp of National Unity formulated more precisely the objectives of the organization in

[26] 'Stan rzemiosła w Polsce: Opracowany w zarysie przez Związek Izb Rzemieślniczych Rzeczypospolitej Polskiej za okres 1936 roku' (manuscript; Warsaw, 1938), 173.

[27] M. Kalecki and L. Landau, *Dochód społeczny w 1933 r. i podstawy badań periodycznych nad zmianami dochodu* (Warsaw, 1935), 29.

[28] *Deklaracja ideowo-polityczna Szefa Obozu Zjednoczenia Narodowego Adama Koca i przemówienie przewodniczącego Organizacji Wiejskiej Obozu Zjednoczenia Narodowego Andrzeja Galicy* (Warsaw, 1937), 18.

relation to Jewish economic activities: 'The economic independence of the Polish rural and urban population is one of the most urgent tasks faced by the nation and by the Polish state ... In order to realize this objective the share of the Jews in our economic life must be reduced.'[29] This thesis was more and more frequently repeated in the announcements of government officials. The Minister of Industry and Trade, Antoni Roman, speaking before the Budget Commission of the Sejm on 17 February 1939, stated that the development of small-scale economic activities was first of all aimed at the Polonization of economic initiative.[30] Vice-premier and Minister of the Treasury Eugeniusz Kwiatkowski predicted that at the last stage of the 15-year plan, in the years 1948–51, 'an ultimate Polonization of Polish towns should take place'.[31] If one also bears in mind the well-known 'Why not?' uttered by Prime Minister Felicjan Sławoj Składkowski in connection with the economic boycott of Jewish business, the prospects of Jewish handicrafts in Poland must have appeared bleak. Handicrafts supported about a third of the Jews living in Poland. Driving them out of handicraft activities could only result in their further pauperization, while the chances for emigration of such a numerous community were at that time non-existent.

[29] B. Miedziński, *Uwagi na marginesie sprawy żydowskiej wraz z uchwałami Rady Naczelnej OZN z dnia 21 maja 1938* (Warsaw, 1938), 33–4.

[30] 'Zagadnienie średniej i drobnej wytwórczości: przemówienie pana ministra przemysłu i handlu Antoniego Romana w Senacie', *Polska Gospodarcza* (1939), No. 7, p. 266.

[31] E. Kwiatkowski, *O wielkość Rzeczypospolitej: Przemówienie wygłoszone w Sejmie w dniu 2 grudnia 1938 r.* (Warsaw, 1939), 59.

Some Aspects of the Life of the Jewish Proletariat in Poland during the Interwar Period

D. GARNCARSKA-KADARY

THE peculiar nature of the Jewish proletariat in Poland and its sheer magnitude require considerably wider treatment than that accorded to the working class in general. This applies to the whole of Poland. While taking into account the various attitudes of sociologists and analysts of social structures in this field[1] and of the actual economic living conditions of the Polish population during that period, I propose to include the following groups of workers in the Jewish proletariat: not only wage-earners, i.e. manual workers, cottage workers, and white-collar employees, but also non-hired elements, such as craftsmen working without any hired help (referred to as 'self-employed' in the statistical nomenclature) or those whose self-employed status had not been confirmed. In addition, I incorporate in this group certain elements which had been temporarily engaged in street trade[2] and those who were working in various sectors of the economy but not as hired labour (porters, barbers, cart-drivers, washerwomen, etc.).

The Jewish proletariat, perceived in this way, differed from the Polish working class in general by its very social composition. In 1931 it numbered 684,500 actively working people, which amounted to 61 per cent of the total economically active Jewish population. This figure was composed of 57.3 per cent hired labour and 42.7 per cent non-hired workers.[3]

The Jewish proletariat comprised 60–1 per cent of the active workforce of the Jewish population during the entire first decade of independent Poland, but its numbers rose dramatically during the following decade.

[1] A. Hertz, 'Proletariat', in *Świat i życie, Zarys encyklopedyczy współczesnej wiedzy i kultury*, (Lwów and Warsaw, 1934); W. Sombart, *Proletariat* (Warsaw, 1907); F. Gross, *Proletariat i kultura, Warunki społeczne i gospodarcze kultury proletariatu* (Warsaw, 1938), 32.

[2] S. Bauman, 'Handel uliczny w Warszawie', *Biuletyny*, *WSH* 8 (1930), 313–52; R. Mahler, 'Żydowscy sprzedawcy obwarzanków w Warszawie w świetle ankiety', *Zagadnienia Gospodarcze* (1935), 108–20.

[3] *Statystyka Polski*, ser. C, vol. 94d, table 34.

The occupational structure of the proletariat is a function of the economic structure of the country and the whole nation in question. The economic structure of the Jewish population emerged under the influence of historical factors which were dissimilar to the circumstances of the majority of the remaining citizens of the country. The fact that about 80 per cent of the Christian population lived in the country, and, conversely, 76.4 per cent of the Jewish population inhabited the towns, suggests an inverted economic pyramid for the two groups. While in 1931 66.7 per cent of the Christian population made a living from farming, including a third of the whole working class, 78.8 per cent of the Jews were engaged in industry and trade and only 4 per cent made a living from farming.[4] The part played by the Jewish population in Polish commerce was very great, although it already declined significantly during the first decade of the Republic (from 64.5 per cent to 52.7 per cent). This sector, which included 38 per cent of the total economically active Jewish populace, did not belong to those which hired workers. On the contrary, there were large numbers of bankruptcies among Jewish traders, with stallholders and their children regularly joining the ranks of the unemployed.

The two predominant fields of activity in the occupational structure of the Jewish proletariat and in the structure of the entire Jewish population were industry and commerce. In 1921 these areas included 72 per cent and in 1931 as much as 81 per cent of the total working proletariat. The dramatic increase of workers in the first decade occurred almost exclusively in the industrial sector (an increment of 213 per cent). In 1931 this single sector accounted for 72 per cent of all Jewish wage-earners, as compared with 48.3 per cent in 1921.[5]

The industrial occupational structure of the Jewish proletariat reveals its anomalies and weaknesses better than anything else. These facts are well known.[6] I shall therefore limit myself to the recollection of what I consider to be the most important elements of this anomaly.

From the point of view of its distribution, the process of confinement of this group to the second and third branches of production within the industrial sector gradually intensified. But its presence in the branches which comprised the foundation for the development of Polish industry as a whole—i.e. in mining, steel manufacturing, and metallurgy—decreased. Jewish labour was never widely represented in these branches, both because

---

[4] *Mały rocznik statystyczny* (1939), p. 24, table 18; p. 31, table 27; pp. 258–9, p. 1–2.

[5] *Statystyka Polski*, vol. 31, pl. XX, pp. 316–17; sec. C, vol. 94d, table 34.

[6] B. Garncarska-Kadary, 'Shikhvot haovdim hayehudim bepolin bein shtei milkhamot olam (nituaḥ statisti)', *Galed: Ma'asef letoledot yehudei polin*, 3 (1976), 141–89; ead., 'Hatemurot bemivneh hasotsi'ali-miktso'i shel shikhvot ha'ovedim hayehudim bepolin vehamediniut hamemshaltit legabei hayehudim (1918–1939)', *Galed*, 4–5 (1978), 111–52.

Table 1 Distribution of Employment among Non-agricultural Workers in Poland, 1931

Employment	Percentage[a]		Total percentage[b]
	Non-Jews	Jews	
Garment industry	7.1	39.5	44.8
Textile industry	13.3	11.7	11.3
Food industry	9.3	10.5	14.2
Occupation not stated	15.4	14.0	18.2
TOTAL	45.1	75.7	

[a] These columns give the percentage of the total Non-Jewish and Jewish industrial workforce, respectively, in each of the categories listed.

[b] This column gives the percentage of the total industrial workforce employed in each of the categories listed.

of Jewish workers' distaste for this kind of work and because of anti-Jewish prejudice. But even in the first decade of independence its involvement in the metallurgical and steel industry declined from 7 per cent in 1921 to 4.6 per cent in 1931. In 1921 there were still 11 per cent of all working Jews in the steel industry in Warsaw, but by 1931 this had fallen to 7.7 per cent of the total Jewish industrial workforce.[7] In Łódź, the biggest centre of the textile industry, the percentage of Jewish workers in this branch decreased from 51 per cent to 40 per cent, while the percentage of those employed in the manufacture of garments was rising.[8] It is worth noting that within these major branches of industry of both cities we would not find any Jewish workers in Warsaw's great steel works and only very few in the textile factories in Łódź. Jewish cottage workers were found mainly in small plants in the textile and metallurgical industries (70 per cent of the total), and also worked as locksmiths, tinsmiths, and makers of precision instruments were employed in knitting workshops or hand-weaving plants.[9]

The branches with the highest concentration of Jewish industrial workers in 1931 are shown in Table 1.[10] Jewish workers were heavily concentrated in the garment industry, particularly in Łódź and Warsaw. Two further branches, the textile and the food industries, and the undefined occupations lagged behind the garment industry. Fewer than a quarter of all Jewish wage-earners and cottage workers worked in all the remaining ten branches of industry. In fact their concentration in the above-mentioned three branches was even greater, since of the 225,000 hired industrial workers over 60 per cent were employed in tailoring and food supply.

[7] *Statystyka Polski*, vol. 49, table 34.
[8] See nn. 5 and 7.
[9] *Statystyka Polski*, vols. 49, 67.
[10] Ibid.

Table 2 Distribution of Employment among Industrial Jewish Workers in Warsaw, 1914–1931 (% of total Jewish industrial workforce)

Size of workshop	1914	1921	1931	All Poland 1931
1–5 workers (category 8)	24.3	53.9	85.8	83.4
6–30 workers (categories 4–7)ᵃ	45.5	35.4	12.2	13.4
Over 30 workers (categories 1–3)ᵃ	19.4	7.7	2.0	3.4

ᵃ The division into categories is estimated; groups 1–3 are given by Heller, *Żydowskie przedsiębiorstwa*, i. 338–9, based on incomplete data.

Such a narrow, one-sided Jewish proletarian structure produced various consequences. One phenomenon, possible the most painful of all, was the employment structure of Jewish workers, which to all intents and purposes entailed a state of near isolation in work ghettos. This situation worsened considerably in the years 1921–31. We do not have any direct comparative data available, but if we adapt the criteria used in the 1931 census to classify workplaces according to the size of their workforce, and apply them to the data obtained from a 1921 poll carried out by the Jewish Defence Committee, we find that in 1921 the numbers of hired workers employed by the smallest workshops was 60.6 per cent, and in 1931 83.4 per cent, of the total number of Jewish workers employed in the industrial sector.[11] The process of splitting up the Jewish workforce and of driving it into the smallest workshops is best illustrated by the example of Warsaw. Table 2 shows the comparative data of results from the 1931 poll carried out by the Jewish Defence Committee in Warsaw.[12] These data show the direction of development in the field of Jewish employment in the most economically developed centre and the one with the largest Jewish proletarian population. The same tendencies came to light in Łódź, and the message of the figures is clear. The fact that 83–5 per cent of workers could find work in only the smallest workshops had far-reaching consequences. It categorized the entire Jewish working class as second-rate. Small workshops typically employed a very large proportion of young people, sometimes between a quarter and a half of the workforce.[13] This phenomenon could be observed throughout the period under discussion. Work in small workshops carried with it a total

---

[11] Ibid.; E. Heller (ed.), *Żydowskie przedsiębiorstwa przemysłowe w Polsce według ankiety z 1921 r.*, i–iv (1922–7).

[12] Heller, *Żydowskie przedsiębiorstwa*, i. 338–9; *Statystyka Polski*, vol. 49, 67.

[13] S. Berkowicz, 'Udział młodocianych robotników żydowskich w przemyśle odzieżowym i drukarskim', *Zagadnienia Gospodarcze* (1935), 29–35; Sh. Bergson, 'Der anteil fun yiddishe yungtlekhe in der bakleid-industriye', *Dos virtshaftlekhe lebn*, 2 (1934), 17–21; R. Kantor-Likhtenshtein, *Yugnt-arbet in yiddishn druker-vezn* (Warsaw, 1932); Y. Leshtshinsky, 'Di yiddishe arbeter-yugnt in poylin', *Virtshaft un lebn*, 5 (1929), 11–31.

absence of any social rights, unemployment benefit,[14] or the possibility of striving for better working and living conditions; for the vast majority it meant long working hours and starvation wages. Seventy per cent of all sales employees worked in retail and itinerant businesses. Whereas 90 per cent of Christian transport workers worked in the state industry—the railways, shipping, and the airlines—90 per cent of the Jews employed in the transport sector worked in small forwarding agencies as porters or loaders, and so on, and nearly 30,000 'self-employed' ones offered their services at the railway stations or in the streets as porters, drivers, loaders, or cabbies.[15]

One may draw certain conclusions from the direction which the changes in the structure of the Jewish proletariat were taking, in comparison with analogous ones in the whole working class in Poland during that period. Jewish labour was apparently being shunted into a side-track, on the periphery of industrial activity and outside the mainstream of the working class in general, as if its development was subject to some other laws, not merely the effects resulting from problems in the labour market. Additional and subjective factors also played a part in this situation; these included official government policy and the attitude of a significant part of Polish society towards the Jewish population and Jewish labour.

During the interwar period a great gulf was opened up among the Jewish masses between exigency and striving on the one hand, and opportunities on the other. It was clear that the Jews' situation would be alleviated only if new job opportunities could be created. With the help of its organizations and social institutions, the Jewish proletariat strove to achieve changes in the employment structure so that work would become available in all branches of industry, but first and foremost they sought the opportunity to break into manufacturing industry and find employment in large factories. But the chances of achieving this were slim. The process of elucidating this conflict leads us to the sources of the singular structure of the Jewish proletariat, which reach back into the historical past of Polish Jewry. It is precisely the interwar period which throws a particularly bright shaft of light on these sources, which very clearly reveal the influence of anti-Jewish prejudice upon the formation of Jewish proletarian structure. The endless repetition by historians of Tartakower's views from the early 1930s[16] to the

[14] Z. Landau and J. Tomaszewski, *Robotnicy przemysłowi w Polsce. Materialne warunki bytu, 1918–1931* (Warsaw, 1971), 222; M. Ciechocinska, *Położenie klasy robotniczej w Polsce, 1929–1939* (Warsaw, 1965), 91–6; M. Bornstein-Lychowska, *Polityka społeczna państwa polskiego, 1918–1935* (Warsaw, 1935), 147–8 etc.

[15] *Statystyka Polski*, sec. C, vol. 94d, table 34.

[16] A. Tartakower, 'Proletariat żydowski w Polsce', *Żydzi w Polsce odrodzonej*, 2 (1934), 570–89.

effect that Jews tended to avoid working in big factories and in manufacturing industry because of psychological or religious considerations is naïve. A greater degree of familiarization with the history of this proletariat's fight for the right to work from the end of the last century onward, and particularly in the interwar period, may shed some light upon the extent of the boycott of Jewish labour and also upon the realities of the special and distinct character of the labour market which was a direct result of these circumstances.

Very briefly, at this stage I would like to discuss the hitherto insufficiently investigated problem of the social distribution of recruitment of Jewish hired workers during the interwar period. It seems clear that a systematic investigation of the provenance of the young people entering the job market would provide adequate proof of the social changes which were affecting the working class. Scholars researching the Polish working class maintain that even in the 1930s about 70 per cent of the workforce appearing annually on the labour market were migrants from the country areas, while the remaining 30 per cent were from the so-called hereditary working class.[17]

The dynamic growth of the Jewish working class was due to the fact that, in addition to members of the hereditary proletariat, emigrants from new backgrounds and social strata were systematically joining its ranks. A poll carried out in 1926 by the Jewish Economic Institute and 'Tsukunft' among Jewish working-class youth disclosed that a large majority (63 per cent) came from working-class or artisan backgrounds, but even at that time this group included a significant proportion of children from the families of bankrupt industrialists. Just over a third of the young people investigated came from merchant, petty-bourgeois, middle man, or *melamed* backgrounds, or others of this sort. By this time one can also count among these working young people children of the clergy and free professions (3.7 per cent).[18] This slow course of social displacement inside Jewish society in the mid-1920s appears to have been a continuation of the productivity drives which were intensified before the First World War. The accelerated tempo of these processes can already be observed in the late 1920s, and they take on an entirely new character in the 1930s. This state of affairs also finds expression in a policy of recruitment of people with technical qualifications, and can be elucidated by following up the fates of young people through their primary, secondary, and higher education, and by studying the declarations of the young people themselves. Below are given just a few examples.

During the school year 1927–8 the Warsaw Experimental Psychology Institute carried out studies in eight boys' technical training schools, among

---
[17] *Młodzież sięga po prace* (Wyd. Instytutu Spraw Społecznych; Sprawy zatrudnienia i bezrobocia, 13; Warsaw, 1938).
[18] Leshtchinsky, 'Di yiddishe arbter-yugnt in poylin'.

them two Jewish ones. In all 1,500 pupils were included in this study, 312 of them Jewish.[19] The only aspect of interest to us in this contest is the social background of these pupils. The most numerous group of young people learning a trade from both communities was made up of children whose parents had no permanent jobs—41 per cent of the Jews and 44 per cent of the Christians; there is thus little difference in this group. Of the Jews, most of the young people had arrived from small towns, and their parents were chiefly melameds and stall holders. The next most numerous group among the Jews were children of artisans (27 per cent as opposed to 13 per cent among the non-Jews). The remainder of the Jewish group came from the families of merchants, white-collar workers, and others (including almost none from a farming background, as opposed to the comparatively large 16 per cent of non-Jews whose parents were farmers).

In the 1930s 67–70 per cent of all pupils from technical training schools in Łódź, Warsaw, and Białystok came from commercial and industrial families, about 20 per cent came from working-class families, and the remaining 10–13 per cent were children from educated or clerical homes.[20] In the Małopolska region, of the 1,500 Jewish pupils at technical training school, 30 per cent came from merchant homes, 20 per cent from Orthodox and clerical environments (rabbis, members of the rabbinical courts, ritual slaughterers, *melamed*s, rabbis' staff, etc.), 10 per cent were children of industrialists, members of the free professions, or white-collar employees, 7 per cent were children of day labourers or invalids, 3 per cent the children of farmers, and only 20 per cent had parents who were artisans or manual workers.[21]

The fact that ever more children from educated homes, both secular and clerical, as well as from industrialist and merchant backgrounds, were entering the ranks of the working proletariat was a new development, indicating a radical change in the social mentality among Polish Jewry, for a long-standing bias against hired labour had become established among these strata of society. It appears that these families must have begun to falter in the basic principles of their philosophy of life. A very important element of this process, but certainly not the only one, must undoubtedly have been the pauperization of the broad strata of Jewish society, which finally engulfed these groups as well. It should be mentioned that in the 1930s it

---

[19] Y. Yashunsky, 'Poylishe un yiddishe fakhshul-yugnt in shein fun psyckhotekhnik', *Virtshaft un lebn*, 11/3 (1930), 50–62.

[20] Ibid.; D. Lwowitsh, 'Tsvantsik yar tetikeit fun "ORT" in Lodz', *Lodzer yizkor bukh* (New York, 1943), 95–100.

[21] C. Klaftenowa, 'Zagadnienie produktywizacji i szkolnictwa zawodowego wśród Żydów', *Miesięcznik żydowski*, 8 (1931), 126. The remaining 10 per cent unaccounted for in the source probably comprised children from other social groups.

was in general no longer the case that children from artisan and stallholders' families inevitably went to technical training schools, since the parents could no longer afford to support their children during the three to four years of study and to pay their tuition fees. As a result, we find fewer and fewer children from artisan homes, especially from the families of manual workers, and more and more whose parents would still be likely to afford it, as they belonged to the educated and more affluent strata of society. This, in turn, testifies to major changes in their philosophy and awareness of life. And the profound alterations in the spheres of interest of the younger generation also bear witness to this.

Again I give only a sample of the relevant evidence. During the 1930s a significant drop in interest in and aspirations to continue their secondary and further education was noted among the young. During 1922–38 the numbers of Jewish pupils in higher education decreased by a half, and in secondary education by about 40 per cent (up to 1936–7).[22] It is likely that the student disturbances and the 'ghetto benches', where Jews were compelled to sit, in institutions of higher education were also responsible, to some extent, for this state of affairs.[23] Nevertheless, the decisive factor in all this was the situation in which Polish Jews found themselves and the lack of prospects facing Jewish youth. In this context, in 1936 a questionnaire was circulated among 350 Jewish females who had finished primary education in Warsaw schools in 1933. The following results were obtained:[24] about 25 per cent were continuing their education in grammar schools or attended evening courses, about 45 per cent were already waged workers, and the remainder were looking for work. A similar study was carried out in the same year among 294 pupils who had attended a Lwów state grammar school during 1925–35, thus including those who may already have graduated or were still attending school. These were the results: among the pupils attending the school during the years 1925–31 15.5 per cent had not continued their higher education, among those from the years 1932–3 the number had already risen to 47.5 per cent, among those from 1933–4 to 77.2 per cent, and among those from 1934–5 more than 80 per cent of candidates for the secondary school certificate had not begun further education.[25] The questionnaire also asked about the present situation of the pupils from the Lwów state grammar school. Asked to state their present occupation, the

---

[22] M. Mirkin, 'Di yiddishe akademiker in poyln', *Yiddishe ekonomik* (1938), 273–572; *Mały rocznik statystyczny* (1939), 334.

[23] Y. Leshtchinsky, *Erev hurban: Fun yiddishn lebn in poylin, 1935–1937* (Buenos Aires, 1951); E. Melzer, *Maavak medini bemalkodet: yehudei polin, 1935–1939* (Tel Aviv, 1982).

[24] *Biuletyn ekonomiczno-statystyczny: Materiały i cyfry z życia ludności żydowskiej w Polsce*, 4/4 (1937), 14–15.

[25] Ibid. 1/2 (1936), 41.

majority replied that they were: manual workers (joiners, electricians, locksmiths, or attending technical training school); among the thirty pupils from 1933–4, eight worked in industry and the remainder were unemployed;[26] from the 68 who continued their education in the law faculty, 38 had reached the apprenticeship stage, but not a single one had a job in the profession. Eight people graduated from the polytechnic, but not one of them managed to find work in the field in which he was qualified, and all but one were unemployed. Four former pupils who had subsequently graduated in philosophy and six who had graduated with various medical qualifications were in the same situation. One, who qualified as a doctor in Leipzig, was lucky to have a job ... in a printing shop as a printer.[27]

This deep crisis affecting Jewish youth and the intelligentsia resulted in a massive decline in the numbers pursuing an academic career and of education in general (but by no means caused by a lack of willingness or talent). This young generation was forced to reappraise its previously held views and attitudes regarding its goals in life. In practice, such reappraisal led to the acceptance of manual work. The revision of previously accepted concepts and the process of reaching similar conclusions also affected the parents and reached every Jewish home, where until recently, nothing but distaste and prejudice towards hired labour had been the rule.

One should not forget, however, that such prejudices were not an exclusive trait of the Jewish bourgeoisie. Such attitudes were no less noticeable among the Polish gentry and bourgeoisie or the peasantry.[28] The answers given to a poll carried out in 1927 and repeated in 1932 among workers in Warsaw, Łódź, and Zagłębie Dąbrowskie, testify to the views held by these workers on the subject of hired labour. In response to the question of what occupation the parents would wish to secure for their children, fewer than 4 per cent of the total (in Warsaw a mere 3 per cent) were resigned to the prospect of their children becoming manual workers.[29] As a rule, all parents, no matter how poor, were striving and dreaming about being able to ensure a better future than their own for their children, so that their children would find a better position in the social hierarchy. Even though every nation has its peculiar traditions and different hierarchies of values, very few have valued waged manual labour highly, especially before the Second World War, when such workers generally had to work very hard and were always down at heel (especially the Jews); certainly, poverty had never been admired by anyone.

[26] *Biuletyn ekonomiozno-statistyczny: Materiały i cyfry z życia ludnośći żydowskiej w Polsie*, 1/2 (1936).
[27] Ibid.
[28] S. Ruchlinski, 'Warstwy pracujące', *Wiedza i Życie*, 5–6 (1938), 369.
[29] J. Żarnowski, *Społeczeństwo drugiej Rzeczypospolitej, 1918–1939* (Warsaw, 1973).

The situation in which Polish Jews found themselves in the interwar period brought the question of their very survival into sharp focus. In the face of this new harsh reality, practically all the activities of the social, political, and economic Jewish organizations were directed towards finding jobs and promoting the idea of hired labour through press publications. The youth organizations, particularly the workers' scout and kibbutz movements, which attracted the best young people, became the places where new ideas and concepts affecting Jewish youth were forged. These young people understood rather sooner than their parents that manual labour could not only make it possible for them to earn their daily bread, but could also become a defence against frustration and hopelessness. Of course, in the end both the older and the younger generations joined this struggle for the right to work. The 1926 Jewish Workers' Congress with its motto of fighting for the right to work was yet another expression of the existence of solidarity between parents and their children.[30] The struggles connected with this fight were described by the Jewish workers' press, and the subject of the joys of working was taken up by the participants in a biography competition organized by YIVO in 1934.[31] One can also see from these biographies that, quite often, awareness of the necessity to work did not suppress aspirations towards education and creative knowledge.

An analysis of the recruitment patterns of the Jewish proletarian community during the interwar period suggests that, as a rule, the internal development of the Jewish proletariat in Poland at this time followed a different road from that of the Polish workforce as a whole. The coming into being of a Polish state, the development of a state machine, an army, administration, courts of justice, media to influence the masses, as well as educational institutions—all resulted in a significant part of the historically derived white-collar workforce and ideological and cultural élite having to leave the working community. On the other hand, the opportunities for social and career advancement in various walks of life resulted in the total disappearance of these white-collar workers from the ranks of the Polish working class. Undoubtedly a certain number of them still continued to influence and serve this class, but this was done from the outside, via various social institutions. But the opposite was true in the Jewish labour sector. The latter were forced to use their energies and abilities within the working-class environment, because all doors to administrative,

---

[30] N. Lemberger, *Der yiddisher arbeter in kamf far rekht oyf arbet* (Warsaw, 1926); E. Mus, *Kamf far rekht oyf arbet* (Warsaw, 1926).

[31] M. Kligsberg, 'Di yiddishe yugnt-bavegung in poylin tswishn beide velt milkhomes (a sotsialistishe shtudie)', in *Shtudies vegn yidn in poylin 1919–1939* (New York, 1974), 138–228; M. Weinreich, *Der veg tsu unzer yugnt: Yesoydes, metodn, problemen fun yiddisher yugnt-parshung* (Vilna, 1935).

civil-service, military, or academic careers were closed to them and because white-collar refugees and students were joining the ranks of the working class *en masse*.

The lives of the Jewish proletariat were accompanied by a feeling of loneliness, isolation, and social injustice. This feeling continued to grow during the hours spent in miserable workshops and in the poverty at home, sowing the seeds of discontent and rebellion, but most of all it encouraged Jewish workers to organize themselves. To organize workers who were scattered throughout scores and hundreds of small workshops and ateliers, where people worked 10–12—or more—hours a day, would appear to be a daunting task. However, as it turned out, a large sector of the Jewish proletariat was eager to organize, since by this process they were able to achieve what it was impossible for them to have in the workshop, a workers' collective. By joining these organizations they could at least find allies and work together in order to express their grievances. This is attested by the fact, *inter alia*, that the growth of persecutions, antisemitism, and boycotting of Jewish labour was accompanied by a similar growth in the ranks of the Jewish labour movement.

Data obtained from reports of individual trade unions are probably not entirely accurate and definitely not complete, as they did not include the many groups of Jewish workers who belonged to the general Polish class-orientated trade unions. In general, one can surmise that in the 1920s 18–28 per cent of Jewish workers belonged to Jewish trade unions, but towards the end of the period under discussion, about a third of all Jewish workers were involved in the Jewish labour movement, which was divided among different political factions (but periodically unified in the National Council, which united the Bund majority, the trade headquarters being under the control of the Po'alei Tsion Left, Communist groups, and others, and from 1934 onwards also separate trade unions controlled by the Po'alei Tsion Right).[32] Compared with the general situation in the Polish labour movement, the level of organization in the Jewish labour movement, despite its scattered nature, was quite high.[33]

The realities of the Jewish labour market and boycotting of Jewish labour weighed heavily upon the Jewish labour movement. Mass unemployment, the fight for the right to work, and the exhausting battle for each individual job frequently caused the movement to resort to extremes and lapse into sectarianism and excessive militancy, in this way often working against its

---

[32] Y. Sh. Herts, 'Di profesionele fareinen fun di yiddishe arbeter', in *Di geschikhte fun bund*, iv (New York, 1972), 227; L. Estrin, 'Nokh di profesionele kongresn', *Arbeter-Zeitung* (13 June 1929).

[33] L. Hass, 'Układ sił i zasięg oddziaływania ruchu zawodowego wśród klasy robotniczej', *Polska klasa robotnicza*, 4 (1973), 139–222.

own interests. The stigma of political rivalry, mainly between the Bund, the Socialist left, and the Communists, also contributed to this militancy, which expressed itself (for example) in the gravity and frequency of labour conflicts and in the numbers and urgency of strikes—sometimes directed against bosses who themselves were no better off than their workers.[34]

There are no comprehensive data giving the total numbers of labour disputes and strikes carried out by individual workplace, or even by specific trade unions, despite the fact that the Jewish labour press supplied daily strike information. The only way to draw any conclusions on this subject is indirectly. The largest trade union was that of the garment-workers, which represented nearly 40 per cent of all Jewish workers. The frequency of labour disputes and strikes associated with this organization should give a typical picture of this sphere of activity.

In late 1935, at the third conference of the Jewish Garment Workers' Union in Poland, a report containing data related to labour disputes and strikes which had been collected by the union headquarters during 1927–35 was read. This report makes it clear that it had not taken account of strikes in individual workshops, which were far more common, nor even of those organized in specific branches of the garment industry. The data include only strikes which had been organized by the headquarters and only those which involved all branches of the garment industry. It appears that during the ten months up to October 1935 this particular union headquarters had managed to organize 49 strikes in 28 branches, in which roughly 12,000 workers participated. The total number of working days lost in this manner was 203,993.[35]

Statystyka Pracy [Labour statistics] points out a phenomenon which came into being during the years of crisis, namely, that strikes in large factories were rare, while they showed an increase in small workshops. During 1935 80.5 per cent of all strikes took place in small workplaces, and 560,630 working days were lost.[36] It appears that the working days lost through strikes organized by just one Jewish union headquarters during ten months made up 36.4 per cent of all days lost in the entire sector of light industry in Poland during the year. Even though this constitutes indirect proof, it seems sufficient to allow the conclusion that the frequency of strikes in the Jewish sector was much greater and that they tended to last longer than in the non-Jewish sector. Further evidence of this can be seen in the number of strikes in small textile workshops (mainly those producing

---

[34] See the statement in M. Weinreich's autobiography (n. 31 above).

[35] *Driter tsuzamenfor fun profesioneln klasn farein fun bakleidung-industri-arbeter in poylin, dem 25–26 yuni 1932 in Varshe. barikht un diskusie-materialn.*

[36] A. Komarnicka, 'Okupacja zakładów pracy w latach 1933–1935', *Statystyka pracy*, 15 (1936), table 3, p. 191.

knitwear) in the Łódź district, which repeatedly outnumbered the strikes in large textile factories.[37]

It should be noted that during the 1930s almost all Jewish strikes were of a defensive kind. The protests were against reduction in pay, redundancy, increase in working hours, etc.[38] Even in the 1920s, during periods of economic upturn, hardly a week passed without strikes in Jewish printing shops, bakeries, garment workshops, etc. During 1927–9 the press carried daily stories of strikes which 'ended successfully' in most instances. But somehow these successes did not reach the workshops; the same struggles were resumed time and time again, once more the press would give news of 'successes', but still the individual worker in his workshop continued to get the same pay, had to work not eight but twelve or more hours, and had no choice but to work without even the most basic social benefits. These were truly sisyphean labours. And the sometimes heroic struggles of two or three generations of the Jewish proletariat did not produce any noticeable changes. During the 1930s their working conditions and standard of living were not much different from those of their fathers at the end of the nineteenth century. But the Polish working class as a whole had made giant strides forward in the sphere of social rights and living conditions since those times.

What were the reasons for this? The Jewish proletariat, because of its peculiar circumstances, was confined to the ghetto of the Jewish labour market in the small workshops. The discriminatory economic policy towards the Jews was aimed at small manufacturing industry, driving it further and further towards the edge of the country's economic life. Both the attempt to create Jewish employment and the struggle of the Jewish working masses were pushed to the periphery of Polish economic and social life.

During this difficult period, and on this perimeter of Polish social life, a different, new life began to flourish. The influx of refugees from new strata and social classes, including white-collar and educated youth, into the ranks of the Jewish proletariat had an amazing, revitalizing effect on the general mentality of this group. Every person coming from this kind of new background, with his individual preferences, traditions, and psychological make-up, brought these values to the working environment and there, in this new atmosphere, underwent his own peculiar metamorphosis and assumed new powers.

The potential of this concentration of energy within the Jewish working class found its expression in the birth of wide cultural and educational activity. Jewish labour parties—and these included a number of shades of

---

[37] L. Kieszczyński, *Ruch strajkowy w przemyśle włókienniczym okręgu łódzkiego* (Łódź, 1969), 144.

[38] Ibid.; *Fierter tsuzamenpor fun profesioneln klasn fareinen fun bakleidung-industri-arbeters in poylin, october 1935, tsentral-forvaltung*.

red—competed with one another in the field of cultural and educational activity, no less than in the intensity of the strikes which were organized by their trade unions. It is the former of these two areas that was rather more creative and interesting.

Special institutions were being founded, like Arbeterheym (Workers' House) or the Society of Workers' Evening Courses, whose objectives were education and cultural and publishing activity, and which were both organized by the Po'alei Tsion Left; there was the Tarbut Society, which was run by the labour Zionist party Hitachdut, the Bund-inspired Kultur-Liga (Cultural Alliance), the choral society Hazamir, and Tsysho, the Jewish Society of Secular Schools, and others. These institutions ran popular secular schools for working-class children, evening classes, workers' universities, etc. And out of sheer necessity the Jewish trade unions provided job centres, medical and legal aid, sanatoriums for children suffering from TB, summer camps, etc. In other words, they were involved in organizing a wide range of cultural and educational activities.

The problems faced by these Jewish institutions in their attempts to supply such cultural and educational services were of a varied nature, and it is impossible to give an exhaustive account of the subject here. I touch very briefly on one aspect, the activities of the popular libraries and the reading habits of the Jewish proletariat.

Purchasing books was becoming more and more difficult because of the ever-increasing pauperization and unemployment among the Jewish population. A shrinking of the Jewish book market had been noted, particularly during the period of crisis, even if in the same period there was a rise in the cheap and specialized Hebrew and Yiddish periodical press.[39] The libraries and their lending facilities thus provided the only means of satisfying the desire for books, particularly among the proletariat.

In addition to the private lending libraries, the most popular contemporary facilities for the mass reader were the libraries bearing the names of Shalom Aleykhem, I. L. Peretz, Bronisław Grosser, and Ber Borochov, as well as a few Jewish public libraries. In 1934 the findings of a study investigating the state of libraries and reading habits in Warsaw and several other centres for the year 1933 were published. In 1933 the economic crisis reached its nadir, while these libraries relied on monthly or annual subscriptions from their readers for their income. However low these subscriptions might have been, it must have taken a high degree of abnegation to spend the 50 groszy on the library subscription rather than to buy bread. One has to take this into

---

[39] The numbers of Hebrew and Yiddish books appearing in 1934 reached 79% of the number published in 1930. But periodical publication in these languages rose by 22%. See M. Linder, 'Dos yiddishe drukvezn in poylin in di yorn 1933–1934 (a tsushteyer tsu undzer kultur statistik)', *YIVO bleter*, 10 (1936), 305.

Table 3 Readership of Grosser's Library and the Judaic Library Reading Room, Warsaw, 1933 (%)

Occupation	Grosser's Library	Judaic Reading Room
Manual and office workers	50.2	38.0
Schoolchildren and students	38.6	33.9
Rabbis and *yeshivah* students	—	12.5
Free professions and teachers	6.3	8.7
Artisans, small tradesmen, etc.	4.9	6.9

account in order to grasp the full impact of the data cited below. There were fifty working Jewish libraries in Warsaw, with a total collection of 265,400 titles; forty of them were public libraries. What is of interest to us here is the proportion of workers and young people among the readers. Such data exist for two Warsaw libraries with extremely different profiles: B. Grosser's was a popular working-class library, while the other, the Judaic Library attached to the Tłomackie Street synagogue, was just the opposite—exclusive and intended for the Jewish cultural élite.

During that year 1,570 readers were using the B. Grosser library, while 9,855 readers used the reading room (which was free) in the Judaic Library.[40] There is a striking concurrence in the social composition of the readers in two libraries of such different character. From this one may be justified in drawing a number of conclusions reaching deeply into the traditions and culture of the Jewish people. The very fact that waged workers and their children (from Jewish schools in this instance) made up the vast majority of the readers in both types of libraries testifies to the high cultural level of the Jewish proletariat and the strength of its national ties.

The Warsaw data given above are by no means exceptional. To take another illustration, the most popular cultural institution in Białystok was the Shalom Aleykhem Library, boasting a collection of 42,000 titles. Of its 1,861 permanent subscribers at the beginning of 1935, 40 per cent were workers, 15 per cent artisans, 45 per cent schoolchildren, students, and members of the free professions.[41] But even more interesting is the social composition of the readers in the Judaic Library attached to the Jewish community council in Białystok, where workers and artisans also comprised 40 per cent of the readership, while 25 per cent were teachers, journalists, and other types of writer; 21 per cent of the readers were unemployed and

---

[40] B. Temkin, 'Di yiddishe bibliotekn in varshe in likht fun tsipern', *Dos virtshaftlekhe lebn*, 6–7 (1934), 20–4.

[41] Y. Sh. Hertsberg, *Pinkas bialystok: Grunt-materialn tsu der geshikhte fun di yidn in bialystok biz nokh der ershter velt milkhome* (New York, 1950), 345–8.

without a specific occupation.[42] Such examples are legion. On the other hand, we have very little information on the frequency of borrowing books. The following information from a report from the Grosser Library in Warsaw may throw some light on the subject. During the first three months of 1931, when the library had only 1,190 permanent subscribers, its turnover of books among readers was 6,847.[43] From this it appears that, on average, each reader had read nearly six books, or two books per month; this is quite a lot for a manual worker. It should be added that all the popular libraries which were generally under the protection of Jewish labour parties, were also very much involved in wide-ranging cultural activities such as literary evenings, choirs, dramatic circles, and so on.

A far-reaching intellectual revolution occurred among the Jewish working population during the interwar period. Its significance was far greater in small towns than in large industrial centres. This is attested by studies carried out among the Jewish proletariat, which included subjects like religious activity among the workers (numbers of people attending prayer meetings), or participation in cultural functions and political action. A new type of young person emerged, who modelled himself on the youth branches of the workers' and scout organizations. These new young people had nothing but contempt for the 'sophisticated' youth: they had very different and much wider interests, and a different lifestyle. Studies carried out among printing workers in Warsaw revealed, *inter alia*, that 59 per cent of them attended workers' university lectures on a regular basis; more than 79 per cent regularly read books, and 94 per cent also read the press; 80 per cent of the printers in the study went to the theatre and 90 per cent to the cinema. However, many fewer joined in group outings (41.6 per cent) or played sports (46.6 per cent).[44]

It is difficult even to attempt to assess the significance of these facts, if the unbelievably low levels of income are taken into account (this is so even if printers were paid a little more than others). Such a lifestyle can be found among the very poorest working-class families. The household budgets of working-class families reflect this phenomenon best of all.

In conclusion, I would like to quote the statement of a young worker from Ostrowiec, which to me seems ideally to characterize the typical daily life of Jewish workers in interwar Poland. This worker (in a shoemaker's shop) describes the extreme poverty of his family, and claims that his earnings played a very important part of its budget. In his own words:

---

[42] Ibid., H. Lonski, 'Di Strashon Bibliotek in Wilne', in *Wilne, a zamlbukh gevidmet der shtot Wilne* (New York, 1935), 273–87.

[43] Ch. Sh. Kozdan, 'Di shul un kultur tetikeit', in *Geshikhte fun Bund*, iv. 333–433.

[44] Kantor-Likhtenshtein, *Yugnt-arbet in yiddishn druker-vezn*, table 36, pp. 70–1.

I was already earning six zloty a week. One zloty I would keep for myself and five zlotys I gave to the family. I had to keep myself all week for this one zloty. 15 groszy went on my party membership [he belonged to Tsukunft], 25 groszy were for the cinema—this was a first priority—and 10 groszy for the newspaper *Yunger Veker*. The remainder I used to buy myself a piece of herring to go with my piece of dry bread...[45]

[45] Kligsberg, '*Di yiddishe yugnt bavegung*, 168.

The Expulsion of Polish Jews from the Third Reich in 1938

KAROL JONCA

THE German anti-Jewish pogrom of the *Reichskristallnacht* on 9–10 November 1938 has obscured the events linked with the tragic expulsion of Polish Jews from the territory of the Third Reich on 28 and 29 October. The expulsion of 15,000–17,000 Jewish citizens of the Polish state was closely linked with the intensification of Nazi racist politics throughout 1938 (and in previous years), and was characterized by a violent increase in the wave of anti-Jewish terror in Austria (incorporated into the Reich in March 1938), attacks on Jewish homes, the deportation of German Jews to concentration camps (from Breslau on 25 June), the public identification of Jewish firms in July, and the vigorous promotion of emigration policies. Other events reinforced the terror; they included a decision to expel Jews with criminal records from the Reich and those who were Polish citizens (20 September), an order concerning the passports of German Jews (the 'J' Note of 5 October), and the increasingly rigorous enforcement of anti-Jewish directives in the economic life of the Reich. These are only some examples of the process of removing Jews from German socio-economic life. The action to expel Polish Jews ordered on 26 October 1938 by Reinhard Heydrich, chief of the security service, augured future 'violent solutions', and indeed the 'final solution' to the Jewish question in the Reich.

The Polish decree of 6 October 1938, which demanded the submission of foreign passports for checking (by 29 October), constituted the pretext for Heydrich to issue a decree on 26 October for the immediate expulsion from Germany of Jewish citizens of the Polish state. In vain did a Polish *aide-mémoire* of 27 October assure Berlin that the Polish authorities did not intend any mass action as a result of this decree. The 'Polish wave' of explusions against the background of Nazi anti-Jewish policies deserves some attention. Nazi Germany had no intention of coming to terms with the fact that the Austrian *Anschluss* of March 1938 increased the number of Jews in the Reich by 200,000 at a single stroke. A confidential circular from the Berlin Ministry of Foreign Affairs issued to German missions abroad informed them that 1938, 'a year of destiny', had not only seen the realization of the 'Great German idea', it had also brought closer 'the solution of the Jewish question', for anti-Jewish policies constituted both a condition and a consequence of the events of 1938. In the opinion of the Berlin Ministry of Foreign Affairs, the sudden increase in the number of Jews in the 'Great German Reich' as a result of 'the development of external political events' had simply imposed the necessity of finding a 'radical solution to the Jewish question'.[1] It is true that the Ministry's circular continued to identify this radical solution with the intensification of emigration 'of all Jews residing within the territory of the Reich'. This acceleration was to be achieved by extending economic restrictions and by eliminating 'the powerful economic position of the Jews' in Germany.

The sudden anti-Jewish repression begun in March on Austrian territory by the Vienna-based staff of Adolf Eichmann, who had been sent by the Nazis to Vienna to head an office (Zentralstelle für jüdische Auswanderung) to encourage Jewish emigration, found an echo in Poland. It was feared that a proportion of those Viennese Jews who came from the territory of Galicia, fearing German repression, might wish to return to their former homes, which were now within the territory of the Polish state. The Warsaw *Gazeta Polska* estimated their numbers to be as high as 30,000.[2] It is difficult to decide whether it was solely a desire to prevent the eventual influx of Jews from Austrian territory that prompted the submission of a draft act withdrawing Polish citizenship for the Sejm's deliberation. In any case, at the Sejm session of 15 March the rapporteur justifying the introduction of such an act did not mention the possibility of Jews returning, or the intention to prevent their return by establishing legal barriers. The representative of Obóz Zjednoczenia Narodowego (OZON: Camp of National Unity), Jan Hoppe, cited the resolution of the Senate's War Commission, which called on the government 'in the interests of state security to introduce in the current session the draft of an act withdrawing Polish citizenship from those Polish citizens who, residing abroad, have lost contact with the Polish state or who have acted against the interests of the Polish state'.[3] In the discussion, whose participants included deputies Morawski, E. Hutten-Czapski, Witwicki, Sommerstein, and Snopczyński, citizens residing abroad

---

[1] *Akten zur deutschen auswärtigen Politik*, series D (*1937–1945*), v (Baden-Baden, 1953), 780–5, 'Runderlaß des Auswärtigen Amtes, Berlin, den 25. Januar 1939, die Judenfrage als Faktor der Außen politik im Jahre 1938'.

[2] *Gazeta Polska*, 77 (19 Mar. 1938), 6.

[3] *Sprawozdanie stenograficzne Sejmu Rp* (1937–8), session 80 (25 Mar.), 20–39, here at p. 20. Particular attention is drawn to the research results of Prof. Jerzy Tomaszewski concerning the deportation of Polish Jews from the Third Reich'. J. Tomaszewski, 'Żydzi w Zbąszyniu [7]: Ustawa o pozbawieniu obywatelstwa', *Folks-Sztyme*, 2 (1985).

for political reasons were mentioned (W. Witos), and Deputy Sommerstein alluded to certain incidents in Austria affecting 'not only the Jewish population living there, but . . . also Catholic circles, bishops, and archbishops'.[4] The Jewish question and the influx of Jews into Poland were not a subject of discussion in the Sejm, nor were these topics used as an argument to justify the passing of an act for the withdrawal of citizenship. The Sejm act had another dimension, as did the report of the Germany Embassy in Warsaw sent to the Ministry of Foreign Affairs in Berlin. At a time when the anxiety of European public opinion was being aroused by the Nazis' severe anti-Jewish repression in Vienna, the discussions taking place in the Polish parliament and the citizenship act benefited German propaganda. It was significant that the Berlin Ministry of Foreign Affairs made the report of the German Embassy, signed by Councillor Johannes Wühlisch, available to the Ministry of Internal Affairs of the Reich.

On 29 March the German Embassy in Warsaw informed Berlin of the acceptance by the Sejm of the second and third readings of the bill, which would make it possible to withdraw citizenship from certain categories of Polish citizens residing abroad. Let us look more closely at this document (No. 1 at the end of this essay), which would be significant for policies threatening the interests and fate of Polish Jews living in Germany. The draft act, as the German Embassy in Warsaw related, was directed against Polish citizens abroad involved in activities aimed against the Polish state, citizens who had failed to maintain contact with official Polish state bodies or with 'Polishness' (*zum polnischen Volkstum*) for at least five years, or those who had been involved in some other way in activities abroad harmful to Poland. The German Embassy commented particularly on the fact that, owing to the influx of 'unwelcome Jewish elements from Austria', work on the draft act had been accelerated in the Sejm. In the opinion of the embassy, these were principally Jews who came from the region of Galicia and who had not maintained contact with Poland, as well as other Jewish emigrants who had resided abroad for many years. The embassy's report emphasized arguments raised by the Sejm rapporteur to the effect that Poland was not interested in such elements, or in other citizens who harmed Poland's reputation and acted against her interests. Also quoted was the statement of the rapporteur, who made it quite clear that the act would not be implemented against political enemies, against the former Prime Minister Witos, and 'other post-Brześć *émigrés*' (politicians who had fled to Czechoslovakia after Piłsudski's political clampdown in 1930). Commenting on the course of the Sejm debate, the author of the report, Councillor Wühlisch, stressed that the act was directed above all at Polish Jews living in Vienna

---

[4] Stenographic record (see n. 3), 36.

(25,000–30,000 people). This, as we have mentioned, was not made clear at all during the debate. Also absent from the debate was the councillor's suggestion that the act could be extended to Jewish citizens of Poland living in the remaining German territories (outside Austria). After expressing his opinion, Wühlisch added that 'one can assume that, at present, this act is directed against Jews living in Vienna'. Without entering into the details connected with enactment of the legislation, it is important to note the justification of the act put forward many years later by a former senior functionary of the Ministry of Foreign Affairs in Warsaw, Wiktor T. Drymmer:

There were, throughout the entire world, several thousand Polish citizens of whom we had justified suspicions that they had not been born in Poland, had never been to Poland, and did not know the Polish language. With the aim of regulating this situation, which had eventually to be resolved, a decree of the President of the Polish Republic was formulated by me in agreement with the interested departments in March 1938 on the withdrawal of Polish citizenship from those Polish citizens who, in the space of five years, had not demonstrated the ties linking them with Poland or with Polish society beyond the borders of the Polish Republic. The act was criticized—some accused it of being antisemitic, others of being anti-communist. From my time in Poland during the war period, I know that it was accepted by the Jews with perfect equanimity.[5]

The act, accepted by the Sejm of the Polish Republic on 31 March 1938, aroused the interest of the central authorities of the German Reich. On 21 April, at a meeting held at the Berlin headquarters of the Central Security Department of the Reich at Prinz Albrechtstraße 8, its consequences were discussed. Participants at the meeting, called by SS-Gruppenführer Dr Werner Best in the name of the SS Reichsführer and the chief of the German police, included Hans Globke and Councillor Walther Springorum from the Ministry of Internal Affairs of the Reich and Prussia. In the course of the meeting the possibility of expulsion (*Abschiebung*) of the Polish Jews beyond the Reich's borders was considered for the first time, even though the official note stated that 'this would be too difficult, since every foreign state demurs at accepting such stateless people and none can be compelled to accept them'.[6] The participants at the meeting could not then produce a single example of the withdrawal of citizenship from Jews by the

---

[5] W. T. Drymmer, 'Zagadniene żdowskie w Polsce w. latach 1935–1939', *Zeszyty historyczne*, 13 (1968), 65. Tomaszewski cites Drymmer's statements of 1938, taken from the records of the Polish Ministry of Foreign Affairs. Among these, particularly noteworthy are Drymmer's words at the conference in the Polish embassy in Berlin on 24 and 25 May 1938: Tomaszewski, 'Żydzi w Zbąszyniu (7): Ustawa'.

[6] Politisches Archiv—Auswärtiges Amt [henceforth PAAA Bonn], Rechtsabteilung 6382/H adh. I, i/2, fos. 6–9.

Polish government, and were limited to considering probable consequences of a rigorous application of the terms of the newly passed act by the Polish authorities. Fears were expressed that, given the lack of a bilateral agreement, the Polish government would neither be inclined nor obliged to withdraw its decision on the deprivation of citizenship. Given this situation, it was decided to request the Polish government, through the German Embassy in Warsaw, to clarify its intentions regarding application of the act. Dr Wilhelm Stuckart stated in his letter to the Ministry of Foreign Affairs that the German government would not tolerate the continued presence of some 72,000 Jewish citizens of Poland within the territory of the 'Great German Reich' if Polish authorities made their return to Poland impossible by withdrawal of Polish citizenship. The Ministry of Internal Affairs of the Reich informed the Ministry of Foreign Affairs in Berlin that it awaited a firm declaration from the Polish government 'without delay'; otherwise, the appropriate German bodies would be instructed to forbid the renewal of residence permits in Germany for Polish citizens.[7]

In Warsaw the German ambassador, Adolf von Moltke, personally delivered his government's note to Under-Secretary of State Count Jan Szembek, who in the course of conversation mentioned similar reservations expressed by the French government, resulting no doubt from comparable fears as to the consequences of the Polish act. Szembek explained to the German ambassador that the intention of the Polish legislation was

solely the regulation of an awkward situation created for the Polish government by the institution of *Heimatrecht* [the right to one's homeland], which was binding in former Austria-Hungary and thus in the Galician parts of Poland. Since the 'right to one's fatherland' is inherited, many people living beyond Poland's borders, some of whom have never been to the country, nevertheless continue to possess Polish citizenship today on the basis of peace treaties.[8]

Though Szembek could not yet offer the ambassador any binding assurances, he stated that it was likely that withdrawal of citizenship would be applied only in exceptional circumstances. It appears from Ambassador Moltke's reports to Berlin that the question of the return of Jews to Poland was not discussed in the conversation.

On 21 June 1938 the German ambassador in Warsaw informed the Ministry of Foreign Affairs in Berlin that the optimistic view of Under-Secretary of State Count Szembek, that citizenship would be withdrawn only in exceptional cases, might not be justified in the light of confidential information obtained in Warsaw. Ambassador Moltke, citing 'strictly confi-

[7] Ibid., fo. 23, letter from Dr W. Stuckart to Auswärtiges Amt, Berlin, 6 May 1938.
[8] Ibid., fos. 34–5, letter from Ambassador von Moltke to the Ministry of Foreign Affairs in Berlin, Warsaw, 25 May 1938.

dential sources', informed Berlin that 'the authorities here have no professed intention of returning passports to their owners', but added that at the same time there were far-reaching differences of opinion regarding the interpretation of the act. It is difficult to ascertain to what extent the official reply contained in the Polish government's note of 22 June 1938 satisfied Berlin.[9]

The German government intensified anti-Jewish restrictions within the territory of the 'old Reich' during this period. In July 1938 it ordered that Jewish enterprises and shops be publicly marked as such. On 21 July the President of Police in Breslau ordered that the sign *jüdischer Betrieb* should be displayed on Jewish shops and businesses.[10] Similar instructions were given in the other provinces of the Reich.

Meanwhile, in Gestapo headquarters in Berlin preparations were being made to strike at Polish Jews residing within the territory of the Reich. At a conference organized on 20 September 1938 in the Gestapo headquarters it was decided to remove from Germany Polish Jewish citizens who had committed criminal offences. Various methods were to be used to pressurize them into 'voluntary' departure from German territory.[11]

The deteriorating situation of Jews who were Polish citizens in Germany was made worse by the 'Decree concerning the travel passports of Jews' of 5 October 1938, signed by Dr Best.[12] The decree made the validity of Jewish passports dependent on the stamping of the passport with a 'J'. No new passports were to be issued to Jews for use within Germany. Passports were replaced with 'identity cards', and only passports belonging to German Jews would be stamped.[13]

It is notable that on the following day, 6 October, the Polish Minister of Internal Affairs, Felicjan Sławoj Składkowski, ordered people to submit foreign passports granted by the Foreign Office of the Polish government for inspection, beginning on 29 October.[14] This order did not mention

---

[9] PAAA Bonn, Rechtsabteilung 6382/H adh. I i/2, fos. 38–41, letter from Ambassador von Moltke to the Ministry of Foreign Affairs in Berlin, Warsaw, 21 June 1938, and the diplomatic note of 22 June 1938 (fo. 42).

[10] Wojewódzkie Archiwum Państwowe we Wrocławiu (Provincial State Archive in Wrocław) [henceforth WAP Wrocław], zesp. Polizei Präsidium Breslau, sig. 843, fo. 382, by order of the president of police in Breslau, 21 June 1938.

[11] E. Ben Elissar, *Le Facteur juif dans la politique étrangère du IIIe Reich (1933–1939)* (Geneva, 1969), 305.

[12] Archiwum Państwowe w Legnicy (State Archive in Legnica) [henceforth WAP Legnica], zesp. City of Lubin, sig. 607, fo. 44, Verordnung über Reisepässe von Juden, vom 5. Oktober 1938.

[13] U. Knipping, *Die Geschichte der Juden in Dortmund während der Zeit des Dritten Reiches* (Dortmund, 1977), 84; also R. Bruss, *Die Bremer Juden unterm Nationalsozialismus* (Bremen, 1983), 219.

[14] Decree of the Minister of Internal Affairs of 6 Oct. 1938, issued in agreement with the Minister of Foreign Affairs concerning the inspection of Polish foreign passports: *Dziennik Ustaw RP* [henceforth *DU*] (15 Oct. 1938), No. 80, item 543.

Jews, and the obligation to present passports concerned all Polish citizens residing outside the Republic. Refusal or delay in granting the appropriate stamp could take place in two situations: (1) if there were some suspicion concerning the authenticity or validity of a passport; or (2) if there were circumstances justifying the withdrawal of citizenship or confirmation that the passport was forfeit. There was a striking convergence of dates on which the decrees regarding travel passports were announced: 5 October 1938 by the German Minister of Internal Affairs, and 6 October by the Polish minister for 'continuing passport control to be conducted abroad'. The German ambassador, von Moltke, citing his 'strictly confidential' channels of information, reported to his government in Berlin about the intentions of the Polish minister in conjunction with the Polish Ministry of Foreign Affairs. It does not appear, however, that the German and Polish decrees were the result of identical political premisses.

The German decree of 5 October 1938 was announced on the wave of intensifying anti-Jewish restrictions in the summer of that year. There was a clear connection between the act directing public marking of Jewish shops and enterprises in July and other anti-Jewish acts of the German government. The Polish act depriving non-resident Poles of citizenship on 31 March and the order of 6 October were intended to prevent the immigration of Jews to Poland, as has recently been convincingly argued by Jerzy Tomaszewski.[15] Polish decrees could also be applied to Polish political emigrants who did not relinquish their activities against the Sanacja government—despite assurances expressed in the Sejm during the March debate on the draft of the decree. Political *émigrés* included the former prime minister Wincenty Witos, Wojciech Korfanty, Karol Popiel, and other politicians whose activities within the opposition right-of-centre *Morges Front* were not at all to Warsaw's liking. Although some in the government camp were admirers of Endecja's ideas and proposed initiatives against the Jews, nevertheless, according to Andrzej Ajnenkiel, in many areas the government in Warsaw worked together with Jewish organizations and parties. Although Ajnenkiel's statement is accurate in itself, it does not remove all doubt about the true intentions of the policies of Sławoj Składkowski's ministry. Jerzy Tomaszewski for one disagrees with Ajnenkiel.[16]

[15] J. Tomaszewski, *Wysiedlenie Żydów obywateli polskich z Niemiec 28–29 października 1938r.* (Studia nad Faszyzmem i Zbrodniami Hitlerowskimi, 14; Wrocław, 1991), 167.

[16] A. Ajnenkiel, *Polska po przewrocie majowym: Zarys dziejów politycznych Polski 1926–1939* (Warsaw, 1980), 594 ff. Cf. also Tomaszewski, 'Żydzi w Zbąszyniu (7): Ustawa', passages 7, 8, and 9. Tomaszewski had earlier published a report about the case of Polish Jews in Germany on 25 Feb. 1936 by Dr Stefan Odrowąż-Wysocki, who foresaw the consequences of the anti-Jewish policies of the German authorities and, among other things, the possibility that Polish Jews would return from Germany: J. Tomaszewski, 'Polska dyplomacja wobec położenia Żydów polskich w III Rzeszy na początku 1936', *Biuletyn Żydowskiego Instytutu Historycznego*, 1 (1983), 94.

There is certainly no doubt that the Polish decision on the withdrawal of citizenship and passport inspection was made at a very convenient time for the Germans, and was used as a pretext for taking reprisals against Polish Jews on the territory of the Reich and incorporated Austria. Ambassador von Moltke, it should be remembered, provided the Berlin Ministry of Foreign Affairs with German translations of the full texts of the Polish acts.

The postwar trials of the principal Nazi war criminals before the International War Tribunal brought many secrets of Nazi anti-Jewish policy into the open. The direction of Nazi policy was evidenced, for example, by the minutes of the meeting that took place on 14 October 1938 in the Air Ministry under the chairmanship of Hermann Göring. Göring presented this policy succinctly: 'All possible means should now be used to resolve the Jewish question, since it is necessary that they [the Jews] should be ousted from the economy. All means should be employed, however, to ensure that the resolution of the Jewish question is not reduced to preventative acts [realized by] incompetent Party comrades.[17] Göring decidedly rejected the view that 'Aryanization' was the business of the Nazi Party. This should be dealt with by state organs—with the proviso, however, that the state, as Göring stipulated, should profit from the emigration of German Jews. For the first time, Göring went on record as being in favour of separate ghettos for Jews in city centres. Despite encouragement to escalate anti-Jewish policies, Ministerial Councillor Schmeer, who was present at this meeting, warned against arbitrary attacks on Jews and proposed the establishment of Jewish labour colonies. He foresaw the accelerated emigration of Jews from Germany if such restrictions were imposed. Another ministerial councillor was in favour of mitigating anti-Jewish policies in Austria. This, however, did not meet with the approval of Göring, who suddenly cut the meeting short. No concrete political steps were decided upon and no conclusions were drawn concerning the law to be applied against the Jews. No doubt the participants of the meeting with Göring wanted to await a suitable moment to act against the Jews in the economic and socio-political sphere. In the chain of significant events after 14 October, the most suitable moment turned out to coincide with the assassination of Ernst vom Rath on 7 November 1938 in the German embassy in Paris by the young Herschel Grynszpan.

The German government interpreted the announcement on 6 October 1938 of the instructions of the Polish Minister for Internal Affairs as a measure preventing the return of Jews to Poland, and acted swiftly to forestall the

[17] *Der Prozeß gegen die Hauptkriegsverbrecher vor dem Internationalen Militärgerichtshof, Nürnberg 14. Nov. 1945–1. Oktober 1946* (Nuremberg, 1948), xxvii.

passport control planned by Polish diplomatic agencies in Germany. Barely two days after the German Minister of Foreign Affairs, Joachim von Ribbentrop, had presented a proposal for a 'global solution' to German–Polish relations to the Polish ambassador, Józef Lipski, the Germans commenced a political action which followed a pattern reminiscent of that adopted in recent months towards Austria and Czechoslovakia. On 16 October the Berlin Ministry for Foreign Affairs presented an *aide-mémoire* to Warsaw through the German ambassador von Moltke which bore all the marks of an ultimatum. At the same time, and without waiting for a reply from Warsaw, the chief of the Nazi Security Service, Heydrich, directed an order to the presidents of provinces and presidents of the outposts of the security police forbidding the residence of Jewish citizens of Poland within the territory of the Reich. Events unfolded with lightning speed, much to the surprise of the Polish authorities. The course of events was as follows: on 26 October the Ministry of Foreign Affairs in Berlin informed Ambassador von Moltke in Warsaw by cable that the German government would not be a passive spectator of the development of events connected with the Polish directive of 6 October regarding passport control. Therefore, 'as a preventive measure, as soon as possible Jews of Polish citizenship will be removed from the Reich'. The German government would desist from the immediate implementation of resettlement if the Polish government were to give up the realization of its directive with regard to Jews residing within the Reich, or if the government issued a statement that passport control would be necessary only directly before a return to Poland. The German Ministry of Foreign Affairs, conveying this information to the Polish government via Ambassador Moltke, demanded 'a cable today regarding the Polish reply'.[18]

That same day, 16 October, Ambassador Moltke presented the German *aide-mémoire* to the Polish Ministry of Foreign Affairs. Its contents were perturbing, since the wording left no doubt as to German intentions for immediate action involving the removal of Jewish citizens of Poland from the Reich. The Polish Ministry of Foreign Affairs did not bend in the face of this blackmail, nor did it provide the reply demanded that same day.

The Polish *aide-mémoire* of the following day, 27 October, directed to Berlin contained the assurance that the directive of 6 October was

general in character and will not be specifically applied to a particular group of Polish passport-holders. The basic aim of the directive could be reduced to checking the passports solely of those people who, of their own accord, declare their

[18] PAAA Bonn, i/2, fo. 62, telephonic instruction to Warsaw, Berlin, 26 Oct. 1938: 'Die deutsche Regierung kann einer solchen Entwicklung nicht tatenlos zusehen. Die in Deutschland befindlichen Juden polnischer Staatsangehörigkeit werden deshalb vorsorglich sofort in kürzester Frist aus dem Reich verwiesen werden.'

intention to enter the Republic. The Ministry of Foreign Affairs does not expect that this type of application, and thus the control of passports, will take on a mass character.

Referring to the question concerning Jews contained in the German *aide-mémoire*, the Polish Ministry of Foreign Affairs noted that it was precisely the Jewish Polish citizens who had settled in Germany years ago who were the subject of many interventions by the Polish diplomatic and consular agencies, whose aim was to protect them from the consequences of Reich legislation. The Polish ministry maintained that, unfortunately, these interventions had not been effective. At the same time, the ministry expressed its readiness to participate in talks with the German side in order to clarify the material situation of the persons named and to regulate the problem.[19]

Berlin did not wait for the answer of the Polish Ministry of Foreign Affairs. On 26 October, the day that Ambassador von Moltke presented the German *aide-mémoire* in Warsaw, the chief of the Nazi Security Service in the name of the SS Reichsführer and chief of the German police, Heinrich Himmler, in agreement with the German Ministry of Foreign Affairs, demanded the arrest of Jewish Polish citizens and their deportation to Poland. This order emphasized that it was intended to counteract the results of the Polish order of 6 October and that the further residence of Polish Jews in Germany would no longer be tolerated.[20] Following Heydrich's order, Dr Best informed presidents of provinces and Gestapo centres in the name of the SS Reichsführer that Polish Jews were prohibited from residing within the Reich because the Polish government had not given a comprehensive explanation of the application of regulations concerning passport control. It was therefore necessary to begin, with full mobilization of all forces of the security police and regular police force, immediate imposition of residence prohibitions against Polish Jews, to conduct arrests (*Abschiebungshaft*), and to take those arrested in collective transports to the Polish border immediately. Best stressed that 'collective transports should be conducted in such a way that their despatch across the Polish border can take place before 29 October 1938'.

In a lightning action on the night of 27–8 October, the day before Minister Sławoj Składkowski's directive was to go into effect, police authorities throughout the entire Reich detained around 15,000–17,000 Jewish citizens of Poland and withdrew their German residence permits. Next, collective transports of Jews who had been detained, including children separated from their parents, were delivered by train to the German–Polish

---

[19] PAAA Bonn, i/2, fo. 60, *aide-mémoire*, Warsaw, 27 Oct. 1938.

[20] WAP Wrocław, zesp. Rejencja Opolska [henceforth RO], I/12466, fos. 271–2; also Elissar, *Le Facteur*, 305–6.

border. It was not necessary to hunt out the Polish Jews scattered throughout the Reich, since each one's place of residence was known to the police. Police instructions of 22 August 1938 had obliged every foreigner to submit a 'declaration of residence' (*Aufenthaltsanzeige*) containing this information.

Sybil Milton has drawn attention to the fact that many Polish Jews affected by the deportation had lived in Germany for many years, and the younger generation had been born and raised in a German milieu and spoke only German.[21] As a result of the rapid deportation action, without agreement of the Polish authorities, the Germans managed to expel a number of people into Polish territory. Although the Polish border authorities accepted the first transports, they categorically refused to accept subsequent ones. In this situation, the Germans commenced unloading further transports in the vicinity of the official border crossings on the Berlin–Poznań line in Zbąszynek (Neu-Bentschen), near Chojnice (Konitz) in Pomorze, near Wschowa (Fraustadt), and near Bytom, Upper Silesia, and then began to drive thousands of Jews across the 'green border'—i.e. illegally—into Polish territory. It was only then that, after some resistance, the Polish authorities agreed to accept them.[22] The incidents at the German–Polish border at Neu-Bentschen are reasonably well known; less known are those that took place at Bytom, Chojnice, and Wschowa.

Surviving records of the president of the German police of the Upper Silesian industrial region, Dr Palten from Gliwice, reveal that the action to drive Polish Jews across the Reich's border had been planned and carried out on the German side by the police, security-service units, and SS individuals. On 28 October the police transported 4,200 Polish Jews to the German–Polish border at Bytom and, in the words of the police president, 'shoved them' into Poland. The following day, a further 1,800 Jews were 'shoved' over. The 1,700 Jews the police did not succeed in expelling to Poland on the night of 29–30 October were transported back into the depths of Germany. Panten informed the president of the Opole Regency that he intended 'to send those stateless Jews still residing in this region to a concentration camp.'[23] He abandoned this aim the moment the deportation was suspended. According to Palten, the Jews were driven across the

---

[21] S. Milton, 'The Expulsion of Polish Jews from Germany, October 1938 to July 1939', *Year Book Leo Baeck Institute*, 29 (1984), 170; also K. Jonca, '*Noc Kryształowa' i casus Herschela Grynszpana* (Wrocław, 1992), 94.

[22] Details in Tomaszewski, 'Żydzi w Zbąszyniu', passages 19 and 22; also Z. Bujkiewicz, 'Obóz w Zbąszyniu dla Żydów wysiedlonych przymusowo z Niemiec w 1938,' *Przegląd Lubuski*, 3–4 (1985), 39; R. Thalmann and E. Feinermann, *La Nuit de Cristal 9–10 Novembre 1938* (Paris, 1972), 41. These last two authors hold the Polish government of the time 'to a large extent responsible' for the deportation of Polish Jews from the territory of the German Reich.

[23] K. Jonca, 'Noc Kryształowa' na Śląsku Opolskim na tle polityki antyżydowskiej Trzeciej Rzeszy', *Studia Śląskie*, 37 (1980), 112–17.

German–Polish border during the night, under a police escort augmented by a detachment of security police and the Bytom SS-Standarte.[24] In a few cases the Jews put up some resistance, which was immediately crushed following the recommendations of the Ministry of Internal Affairs communicated by telephone to the chief of the Opole police, Dr Emanuel Schafer. According to these recommendations, in the event of a refusal to accept the Jews by the Polish authorities they should be 'taken to the green border and from there, using police force (excluding, of course, the use of firearms), driven into Poland'. It is not difficult to picture the nightmare of 'driving' thousands of people illegally over the border near Bytom (as had happened at Neu-Bentschen Zbąszyń). Some of the people driven across the border lost their suitcases and luggage, some of which was not released by the police—the luggage of Jews deported from Leipzig to Bytom, for example, having been transported in separate carriages. Directly before being led on foot to the German–Polish border, the Jews were detained in primitive conditions in the synagogue in Bytom, which had been requisitioned in advance for the length of the action by the president of police. The costs incurred by the stay of several thousand Jews in the synagogue were charged to the Jewish Relief Organization in Bytom. The latter was also made to bear the costs connected with the return journey of those Jews whom the police failed to drive across the 'green border'. As has been mentioned above, Jews deported from Leipzig (1,464 adults and 196 children, including 97 under the age of 4) and the German cities were driven into Polish territory near Bytom. The deportation of Polish Jews from Leipzig is known to us from the reports of the American consul David H. Buffom, who on 28 October cabled the Secretary of State, Cordell Hull: 'a general expulsion of Polish Jews from Leipzig to Poland is to take place here. Radical means to achieve this were applied this morning at five o'clock. The authorities combed schools, houses, shops, and even a home for aged women'.[25] The dramatic 'expulsion' of Polish Jews near Bytom lasted two days (or rather, two nights), and in the end, after the 'action' had been suspended, the president of police, Dr Alten, could not accurately state how many Jews had been expelled to Poland. Neither the German police nor the directors of the transport possessed lists of names of those deported. From the statement of the police president it emerges that in the course of those two nights around 6,000 Polish Jews were 'expelled', while during the night of 30 October around 1,700 Jews were transported from Bytom back into the depths of Germany.[26]

[24] Jonca, 'Noc Krystalowa', 94.
[25] Milton, 'The Expulsion', 181–3.
[26] WAP Wrocław, RO I/12466, fos. 279–80, telegram of 29 Oct. 1938; also Tomaszewski, 'Żydzi w Zbąszyniu', Doc. 18, 'Na granicy śląskie'.

No less dramatic was the expulsion of Jews near Chojnice, where 1,500 Polish Jews who had been brought from Berlin and Königsberg fell victim to the *Polenaktion*.[27] Similar incidents took place near the border-point at Dworski Młyn. Around 4,000 Polish Jews were loaded by the Germans on steamers and other boats, in which they were taken to Gdynia, where only 1,500 people were allowed to disembark by the Polish authorities.[28] Jews from Bremen were brought to the German–Polish border at Wschowa, and there they were driven across the border. The police list of people detained comprised 80 names, including traders, tailors, commercial travellers, and so on.

Among those deported to the German–Polish border at Neu-Bentschen were Polish Jews living in Hamburg (around a thousand people) and in Hanover, who were forced, after a train journey of several hours, to make the 7-kilometre march to the illegal crossing-point on foot, where they were driven across the 'green border' into Polish territory. In order to prevent their return, German guards fired to frighten them, and the shots naturally created panic as intended. For several hours the Jews waited in the cold and rain without shelter for permission to proceed to Zbąszyń.[29] The grim situation on the German–Polish border is described in the account of the Polish State Police Border Commissariat in Zbąszyń:

I report that on 28 October 1938 at 20.00 hours the German authorities expelled 654 people across the border via the Zbąszyń–Rogatka road, and that they were stopped by police on the Polish side at a distance of 1 km. from the border. Immediately the alarm was raised, alerting the entire border commissariat in Zbąszyń ... At 21.00 hours news was received that a second group of around 300 people had crossed the border near the railway line and was marching towards the railway station in Zbąszyń ... Next, at intervals of 30–60 minutes, further groups of the deported arrived along the Klasztowa–Nędznia road and the Zbąszyń–Zbąszynek railway line. It was claimed that those expelled were Polish citizens of Jewish nationality and that they had resided in Germany either from birth or for a few years. Since the police forces and border guard were insufficient on their own, the German authorities had summoned an army company who, with bayonets fixed to their guns, turned on those sitting, beating them and trampling on them. Using their bayonets and the butts of their rifles, the soldiers forced the deported to cross over on to Polish territory. On 28 and 29 October this year up to the hour of 17.39, 6,074 people were expelled to Poland, including those expelled on the Trzciel road. There were no further collective expulsions after 17.39. On 31 October there was one case of suicide on the railway line and on 1 November of this year a death

---

[27] Milton, 'The Expulsion', 188 ff.
[28] Ibid., 171.
[29] WAP Poznań, zesp. Starostwo Powiatowe Nowy Tomyśl, sig. 937, fos. 1–2 and annexe V.

due to a hernia and twisting of the bowels. A further 54 people were sent to hospital . . .[30]

The expulsion of Polish Jews at Neu-Bentschen–Zbąszyń caused numerous personal tragedies over the next few days, weeks, and months and was the subject of reports and commentaries by the European press agencies. Among the victims of the *Polenaktion* was the Grynszpan family, who had been deported from Hanover. In Polish Zbąszyń, as soon as they had crossed the border, they contacted their 16-year-old son Herschel in Paris to inform him of what had befallen them. The establishment of facts connected with the expulsion of the Grynszpans and the transport of Jews from Hanover played a significant role during the inquiry into the assassination committed by Herschel Grynszpan on 7 November 1938, and we shall return later to some aspects of this inquiry.

At this point we turn our attention to the diplomatic activity on the Polish and German sides and to the second wave of expulsions of Polish Jews from the Reich in 1938–9. It is worth mentioning that the Polish government decided to detain a group of Germans (including some Germans of Jewish descent) and to deport them from Poland with the aim of inducing the German authorities to suspend their deportation action. But after a few days the Polish action was abandoned and the detainees were returned to their places of residence (which included Łódź). In a conversation with the representative of the German Ministry of Foreign Affairs, the embassy counsellor of the Polish government in Berlin, Stefan Lubomirski, told him unambiguously that the Polish government would be forced to take measures against citizens of the German Reich residing in Poland. In this context he added that it was important to settle the question of expelled Jews who were Polish citizens.[31] Polish–German talks on this issue took place on 2 November in Berlin, but soon ended in impasse. On 8 November the Polish ambassador to Berlin, Józef Lipski, in a conversation with the German secretary of state, Ernst von Weizsäcker, suggested the need to renew the conversations. They were resumed on 4–7 January 1939. On 20 January the delegations negotiated an agreement, just before the return visit of the Minister for Foreign Affairs, Ribbentrop, to Warsaw. On 24 January Ambassador Lipski sent the text of the German–Polish agreement (which took effect on that day) to Ribbentrop. The two sides had agreed the following points. (1) The Reich government would allow those Polish citizens who had been expelled from the Reich on 26–9 October 1938 back into Germany on a temporary basis in order to settle their personal and

---

[30] Text by Tomaszewski, 'Żydzi w Zbąszyniu', doc. 19, 'Zbąszyń w końcu października 1938', *Folks-Sztyme*, 27 (1985).

[31] PAAA Bonn, i/2, fo. 084, Note, Berlin, 4 Nov. 1938.

financial affairs, provided they submitted an application to do so within four weeks from that date; (2) Joint offices would be opened in Nowy Tomyśl and Świebodzin (Schwiebus), where applications would be considered from those deported for permission to re-enter Germany; the Polish and German governments would assign to these offices staff authorized to give the necessary passport annotations (namely a German entry visa and the Polish stamp); (3) The Polish government would permit the citizens who had been deported to Germany to return to Poland. The Polish government also agreed on a few technical details with the German government regarding the entry of Jewish citizens of Poland into Germany and their return to Poland. According to the agreements of 24 January, the German authorities agreed to allow a first party of 1,000 Jews temporarily into Germany, for a period of eight weeks.

On 24 January 1939, the day the agreement came into effect, Prime Minister Göring, as the 'plenipotentiary for the Four-year Plan', provided the Minister of Internal Affairs of the Reich with a set of guidelines regarding the intensification 'by all available means' of the emigration of Jews from the Reich. The Reichszentrale für die jüdische Auswanderung (Reich Central Office for Jewish Emigration) which was established under the aegis of the Ministry of Internal Affairs, had as one of its tasks the direction of 'the privileged emigration of Jews' and the acceleration of individual emigration. The directorship of the Reichszentrale was entrusted to the chief of the security service, Heydrich. In Berlin, from 30 April 1939, as part of the anti-Jewish programme of restrictions aimed at encouraging a speedier decision to emigrate, German Jews were forced to leave their homes and move to the so-called *Judenwohnungen* or *Judenhäuser* in the centre of the city. The basis for this 'ghettoization' was provided by a decree on the leasing of residences.[32]

Despite the visit to Germany of the Polish Foreign Minister, Beck, and his talks with Hitler and Ribbentrop, and Ribbentrop's subsequent visits to Warsaw in the spring of 1939, there was a cooling of political relations between Berlin and Warsaw. This was reflected in the renewed intensification of policies aimed at Polish Jews residing within the Reich. Once more the central German authorities wished to repeat the action of expelling Polish Jews, using similar methods. Reinhard Heydrich issued a directive in Himmler's name on 8 May to centres under his command prohibiting residence within the Reich for all Polish Jews 'not possessing a valid passport entitling them to return to Poland', and 'their expulsion to Poland using police force'. The prohibition also affected those Jews whose stamps

---

[32] C. Engeli and W. Ribbe, 'Berlin in der NS-Zeit (1933–1945)', in W. Ribbe (ed.), *Geschichte Berlins*, ii (Munich, 1987), 1001.

certifying Polish citizenship had been cancelled or not extended. Heydrich ordered that the action should be conducted 'using mass transports'. 'The aim', as we read in the order, 'is that the Polish Jews in question should leave the Reich by 31 July 1939 or that they should be sent to concentration camps with the aim of carrying out *Abschiebungshaft*.[33] At the same time Heydrich recommended to the German border police 'that all possible police methods should be used in order to force the expulsion of the Polish Jews across the green border to Poland. The expulsion of Polish Jews into the Protectorate of Bohemia and Moravia should be avoided.' Heydrich's resolutions broke the settlement embodied in the joint German–Polish agreement of 24 January 1939. According to information from the Berlin Ministry of Foreign Affairs, there were around 26,000 Polish Jews living in Germany at the beginning of June 1939, of whom around 10,000 had not had their passports stamped at a consular office. These people, as well as the 3,000–4,000 women and children who had not been expelled in October 1938, were now threatened with expulsion from Germany to Poland according to Heydrich's order.

Before long a number of Polish Jews were arrested in Breslau. On 8 June 2,000 Polish Jews who had been deported from a variety of locations arrived at the illegal border crossing at Zabrze (Hindenburg). They camped in the open air 'in the neutral zone between the two countries', as reported by the press. On 26 July Dr Kroning, of the headquarters of the SS Reichsführer, informed the Berlin Ministry of Foreign Affairs that the action had not been thought through, since only 'a relatively small number of Jews had been successfully expelled across the German–Polish border'. According to his information, the action should have involved another 10,000 Jews.

In one contingent numbering several thousand Jews sent by rail to Neu-Bentschen on 29 October 1938 and then expelled across the German–Polish border, there were 484 Jewish citizens of Poland who had been arrested by the German police in Hanover. Among them was the family of the tailor and tradesman Sendel Grynszpan from Hanover, his wife Ryfka (Rosa), their 22-year-old daughter Esther Beile (Bertha, Barbara), and their 19-year-old son Markus. Their names and fate were to find their way into the pages of European papers in connection with the assassination committed on 7 November by Herschel (Herzsch, Hermann) Feibel Grynszpan. Sendel Grynszpan left all his belongings at Burgstraße 36 in Hanover. Herschel's parents and sister informed him of their personal tragedy in a postcard sent from Polish Zbąszyń (Document 3.1 below). It reached him on 3 November at the house of his uncle in Paris at Petites Écuries 6. 'On reading this card

---

[33] PAAA Bonn, i/2, fo. 020, express letter, Berlin, 8 May 1939.

I learnt of the danger in which my parents found themselves,' Herschel said in evidence after he was detained following the assassination in the German embassy. 'I decided then to perform an act of revenge on some representative of the Reich with no intention of killing anyone, but I wanted to cause a stir which could not be ignored by the world, as the behaviour of the Germans had enraged me.'[34]

The account written by Herschel's sister in German on a postcard from Zbąszyń did not, it is true, contain a detailed description of the expulsion of Polish Jews across the 'green border' at Neu-Bentschen (Zbąszynek). However, the description of the detention of the Grynszpan family by the German police and their deportation from Hanover must have angered the young Herschel. The next postcard written by Herschel's sister, signed by his mother and with a note from his father, was sent from Zbąszyń on 7 November, the day of the assassination. It could not have reached Herschel Grynszpan until later, and so could not have affected his decision to carry out the assassination (Document 3.2). 'On Saturday we were set down in the open country. The way and means by which we were driven across the woods and fields made a nerve-rending sight,' wrote his sister. 'Then we were forced to settle in barracks. Those who have money can arrange for private accommodation. There is a committee from Warsaw here. These people do what they can for us . . .' Father Sendel, adding a few words on the card meant for his brother, Abraham Grynszpan, described the situation of those resettled as 'very sad' and asked for help (Documents 3.2–3). Abraham was unable to respond to this request since, suspected by the French police of co-operation in the assassination, he was arrested together with his wife Chawa on 7 November and handed over to be dealt with by the public prosecutor. Chawa's brother, Abraham (Bernich) Berenbaum (Beerenbaum), hurried to provide the resettled family with financial help. Based in Paris, he travelled to Poland to make contact with the Grynszpans in person. Berenbaum's evidence, given after his return to Paris before the investigating magistrate, Jean Tesnière, placed the responsibility for the fate of the expelled Jews and the death of some of them firmly on the shoulders of the German authorities.

During the months of preparation for the trial of Herschel Grynszpan, both the French defence and the German authorities insisted that the witnesses of events at Neu-Bentschen–Zbąszyń and even of the expulsions from Hanover should be interrogated. The list of witnesses was to include not only members of the family of Herschel Grynszpan, but also German officials from Hanover and from the border station at Neu-Bentschen. On 8

---

[34] Ibid., fo. 172, Documentary report Grimm; also Zentrales Staatsarchiv Potsdam, Promi. group, file 50.01, No. 982, fos. 53–5.

December 1938 Jean Tesnière examined Abraham Berenbaum, who as a result of his journey from Paris to Zbąszyń had come to know the material situation of the Grynszpans in Zbąszyń and the circumstances of their resettlement in person. On 16 January 1939 the Polish magistrate Julian Kuzdrowicz questioned the parents of Herschel Grynszpan in Zbąszyń at the request of the French investigative bodies.[35]

The Germans had every reason to fear that the circumstances accompanying the resettlement of the Polish Jews from Hanover would be closely scrutinized during the trial of the young assassin. The examination of witnesses in Hanover and the collection of material intended to exonerate the German authorities in regard to the methods employed in the course of the resettlements continued throughout February and April 1939 (Document 2). There should be no illusions about the value of the 'evidence' of those Jewish witnesses, who, after the pogrom of 9–10 November 1938, lived in constant insecurity as to their fate and on the margins of German social life. Collecting documentation, a high-ranking official of Goebbels's Ministry of Propaganda, W. Diewerge, was finally able to inform the Berlin Ministry of Foreign Affairs that the accounts of twenty-three witnesses did not contain any ambiguous material and were advantageous to the Germans. As we shall see below, the Germans were not content with the evidence of these witnesses from Hanover, but hunted out further testimony, and with the help of the German embassy in Warsaw they prepared a separate evaluation of the social life of Jews in Poland. On 13 February 1939 the public notary Heinrich Keybote drew up the record of the survey of the house at Burgstraße 30 in Hanover, which had been occupied by the Grynszpan family until they were resettled. Those members of the board of the religious commune present at the survey, Dr Max Israel Schleissner, Richard Loewe, and others, gave evidence to the survey that they had visited the Grynszpans' residence and had 'found it completely in order. It is not at all damaged ... The photographs submitted convey the true state of the house.' A statement was also attached to the record from the criminal commissar in Hanover, Schulke, and the criminal assistant Westermann, together with the evidence given by the Grynszpans' neighbours, 49-year-old Lina Oettgen, and Paula Eibe, a 22-year-old Jewess. Furthermore, the board of the Jewish commune supplied the German authorities with a separate document containing their view of the resettlements. The extensive document prepared by Commissar Schulke contained specific information concerning 'collection of those assigned for deportation', the deportation to the border, the despatch of the transport in Neu-Bentschen, and so on. The commissar emphasized: 'It does not fit the facts in any way whatsoever to

[35] PAAA Bonn, i/6, fos. 2–9, procès-verbal, 16 Jan. 1939, Zbąszyń.

allege that some Jew of Polish citizenship was driven from his house at night, barefoot, or without clothing.' In the opinion of the commissar, the deportation action took place 'quite in accordance with proper procedure', the transports arrived at the border station 'without friction', and after arriving in Neu-Bentschen the transports were registered in accordance with regulations and orders. The driving of Polish Jews across the 'green border' was not mentioned either in Commissar Schulke's statement or in any other official German document. They say only that the action was conducted according to proper procedure and that the treatment of those deported was quite correct. The evidence of the neighbour Paula Eibe was cited: '... no one from the Grynszpan family was handled badly, let alone mistreated.' The president of the Jewish commune in Hanover was quoted to the effect that members of the commune's board had not noticed that anyone among those detained had been maltreated.[36]

The German professor of international law Friedrich Grimm was to represent the 'civil side' (including the brother and father of the murdered Ernst vom Rath) during Herschel Grynszpan's trial. In the spring of 1939, during preparations for the trial, Grimm gave his expert opinion to the Berlin Ministry of Foreign Affairs, in which he drew attention to the role that would be played during the trial by the expulsion of Polish Jews from Germany during 27-9 October 1938. Grimm, who had gained access to the documents of the inquiry taking place in Paris, recalled the words of the accused Grynszpan that 'he committed an act in order to avenge his parents and the whole of Jewry on the German authorities' specifically because of this deportation action. Grimm reminded the ministry that the defendants had delegated a relative of the assassin to go to Zbąszyń. To his statement submitted to the Ministry of Foreign Affairs Grimm attached a copy of the postcards sent on 31 October and 7 November 1938 by Herschel Grynszpan's family from Zbąszyń to his address in Paris.

At the end of April and beginning of May 1939 Professor Grimm visited Neu-Bentschen himself, and from there went to Kraków, Radomsko, Łódź, and Warsaw to collect information about the deportations, deportees, and situation of Jews in Poland. In Neu-Bentschen Grimm talked with a functionary of the Gestapo office there, Criminal Secretary Wallasch, who gave him information about the expulsion of Jews to Poland. According to Wallasch, the transportation of Polish Jews was carried out in an exemplary and organized fashion, peacefully, humanely, and with no petty difficulties or unpleasant incidents. In Grimm's view, Wallasch's objective account would undermine both the accounts given by the expelled Jews themselves

---

[36] Ibid., i/3, fo. 236, Paula Eibe's statement of 23 Feb. 1939. Other statements cited here have also been taken from this volume.

(including the closest relatives of the accused) and the press reports placing responsibility on the Germans for the inhumane, forced deportation of Polish Jews from the Reich (Document 4). (A more detailed account of the report of the German criminal secretary is omitted here.)[37]

After returning from his Polish trip, Professor Grimm prepared an extensive report (dated 6 May 1939) based on the evidence, accounts, and information gathered on the deportation of Polish Jews from Hanover to support his thesis about the proper (*korrekt*) and humane treatment of expelled Jews by German functionaires. In the report are sections giving information about where Jews were housed after being collected by police from their homes, their treatment during deportation, their provisions, medical care, pregnant women, and the treatment of Grynszpan's parents and siblings. Of Herschel Grynszpan's family Grimm wrote that they were treated 'properly throughout' (*durchaus anständig*), and that the deportation of the father was carried out in accordance with procedure (*korrekt*).

Professor Grimm's conversations with the staff of the German embassy in Warsaw no doubt generated the reflections which Ambassador Moltke sent to Berlin on 15 June 1939. In this eight-page document 'the case of the murder by the Jew Grynszpan' is indeed discussed, but the killing that took place in Paris is used only as a pretext to describe the 'problem' of Jews in Poland; there is no analysis of the murder of vom Rath. The ambassador focused attention (to cite the titles of some sections of this document) on 'Jews as criminals', 'Jews as communists', 'Jewish collective responsibility', 'antisemitism in Poland', 'guidelines for solving the Jewish question', and also Polish countermeasures connected with the German expulsions at the end of October 1938. The theses of this document were quite transparent. The ambassador demonstrated that Jews were at the top of the list in Polish criminal statistics and that in Warsaw 'Jews maintain their own school for training thieves. The Jews practise their craft with such impudence . . . that they have established an insurance company here for thieves in which they have insured several thousand thieves in the event of legal punitive measures.' Ambassador Moltke noted with more than a little satisfaction that 'the Polish nation has long been antisemitic and therefore Poland also enjoys the reputation of setting a standard for pogroms'.[38]

A week later, on 22 June 1939, Ambassador Moltke sent another extensive document to the Ministry of Foreign Affairs in Berlin concerning the

---

[37] Wallasch's statement; also annex IV. This was taken from the collections in Zentrales Staatsarchiv Potsdam, Promi. group, file 50.01. No. 982, fos. 53–5.

[38] PAAA Bonn, RA, Strafrecht No. 21, vol. v, fos. 352–9, and Zentrales Staatsarchiv Potsdam, zesp. Promi. group, file 50.01. Two copies of this statement have survived in the collections cited here in Bonn and Potsdam; cited here according to the Potsdam records, No. 982, fos. 68–75.

Grynszpan family. This document contained the intelligence reports of agents from Radomsk about Herschel Grynszpan's relatives. In June 1939, when the ambassador was preparing the report, the assassin's closest family, his father Sendel and wife Ryfka, and the brother and sister of the assassin who had been deported with them, still resided in Zbąszyń. The father maintained contact by letter with Herschel, who at that time was incarcerated in a Parisian jail.

The extensive documentation concerning the expulsions gathered by the Germans was not in the end presented to any court. Indeed, the inquiry was completed by the French magistrate Jean Tesnière and the records of the case given to the court, but the trial did not take place—either before war broke out or during the war. After Herschel Grynszpan was handed over to the Germans in 1940, preparations for a trial were begun in Berlin, but it had still not taken place before the war ended. Herschel Grynszpan thus survived the Holocaust.

APPENDIX: DOCUMENTS

No. 1
Political Archive—Foreign Office, Bonn
German Embassy, Warsaw, 29 March 1938
To the Foreign Office

Today, after the second and third reading, the Polish Sejm accepted the plan for a law that should make it possible, in certain circumstances, to take citizenship away from Polish nationals who reside outside of the country. The revocation of citizenship can occur when the national in question works against the Polish state, remains out of contact with Polish officials or the Polish people for a long time (5 years), or in some way damages Polish prestige in a foreign country. The revocation of citizenship will be carried out by the Interior Minister by the authority of the Minister for Foreign Affairs. An appeal against the decision to revoke can be made to the highest Administrative Court.

According to the very acrimonious debate which preceded acceptance of the bill in the Sejm, it can be understood that the implementation of the plan is to be accelerated with regard to the influx of unwanted Jewish elements from Austria. It deals next with Jews who came from formerly Austrian, now Polish, Galicia and had no previous contact with Poles. Further, it deals with Jewish emigrants who have lived outside the country for many years and have maintained no relationship with their home towns. The rapporteur explained that Poland has no more interest in such elements, just as they have none in other Polish citizens who damage Polish prestige or work against the interests of the Polish state. From the side of the government it was expressly declared in the course of the Sejm's debate that the law would in no way be used against the so-called *Brester Emigranten* (Witos and others).

It is to be understood that this law will be directed next against those Jews living in Vienna, whose numbers are estimated at 25,000–30,000. It must also be considered that it can be turned against the numerous other Jews of Polish nationality in Germany.

After the bill is accepted by the Sejm, it must be passed through the Senate. I reserve further accounts until notification appears in the Polish legal paper and the law gains legal power.

Sincerely,
Wühlisch

No. 2

Political Archive—Foreign Office, Bonn

1. *Condition of the Synagogue community of Hanover*

On the occasion of the displacement of the Poles of Jewish race, I was with Dr Max Israel Schleisner and Rabbi Emil Israel Schorch in the preparation house on 29 October 1938 where the incarcerated Poles were located. In addition, we received permission from the Gestapo to supply the Poles and give them coats, blankets, and linens. We did not notice any mistreatment of any of the prisoners. Also, no complaints from either side were registered during our presence of many hours in the preparation house. All of us, especially the chair of our central office, Mr Emil Israel Sichel, can attest that no complaints were received about any mistreatment on the part of police officials. This is based on the innumerable letters from Zbąszyń and Polish cities where relatives live, and from the caretakers and agents of the displaced persons. The initial complaints mostly concerned the haste of the arrests and the lack of opportunity to take along enough linen and clothing.

2. *22 February 1939*

The departure of the Jews took place in three stages. (1) Collection and housing of the deportees at City Hall on 27 and 28 October 1938. (2) Transport to the border on the 28th and 29th. (3) Surrender of the transport in Neu-Bentschen [Zbąszynek] and the continuation of deportation on the 29th. No Jews of Polish nationality were ever taken from their homes barefoot or without clothing at night. The transport to the Polish border in a special train also went forward successfully without discord. After arriving, the transport registered in Neu-Bentschen, according to the rules and commands of the manager of the deportation there. To my knowledge, at no time was there any inhuman treatment by police escorts.

3. *23 February 1939*

In no case did mistreatment of Polish Jews occur during their arrest; for had even the slightest such thing happened at that time, we would have certainly been notified by our clients.

4. *23 February 1939, Statement by Paula Eibe*

I can also say with certainty that no one from the Grynszpan family was handled badly, let alone mistreated.

No. 3

Political Archive—Foreign Office, Bonn

1. Postcard; postmark: Zbąszyń, 1 November 1938

Dear Hermann,
You have certainly heard of our misfortune. I am writing to tell you what happened. On Thursday evening rumours were circulating to the effect that all Polish Jews were being deported from a certain city. Still we resisted believing it. On Thursday evening at 9 o'clock a Schupo [Schutzpolizei] came to us and told us that we should take our passports and turn ourselves over to the police district. So we all went together to the police district escorted by Schupos. Almost our whole city quarter was there together. A police car brought us directly to City Hall. Everyone was brought there. No one told us what it was about. No one has yet told us what it is about. However, we knew that we were finished. Someone stuck an identification order in our hands. We must leave Germany by the 29th.

We were not allowed to go home again. I begged to be allowed to go home, at least to fetch some things. I then left with a Schupo escort and packed the most necessary pieces of clothing in a suitcase. That is all that I saved. We don't have even a penny. Couldn't you or [*illegible*] send something to Łódź for us? More to follow. Regards and kisses from all of us. Bertha

2. Postcard; postmark: Zbąszyń, 7 November 1938

Dear Hermann,
We have received your dear letter. Up to now, no change has materialized in our sad situation. I'll continue my description. They did not let us go home again from jail. Friday evening at 9.30 we all departed from Hanover. There was such weeping and wailing. It would have reawakened the dead. But our crying was to no avail.

Saturday morning they let us out along the line for a stretch. The way and manner in which they pursued us through field and forest was a nerve-racking spectacle.

Since then they have forced us to settle into the barracks. Those who had money could get private accommodation. A committee from Warsaw was present here. These people did for us what they could. We were badly fed, slept on sacks of straw, and were given blankets.

But believe me, dear Hermann, one cannot hold out any longer. We still haven't taken off our clothes since we left. Aunt Sure has stayed behind, she is stateless. Uncle Schlomo is in the hospital. He has had an eye operation. He too has stayed behind. All our hope is with him. May God keep him healthy! Everything is subordinated to the surveillance of the Israelite community. We haven't received any money from you. What do they think will happen to us? We'll run out, we can't go any further. If you answer, I beg you to send a reply-paid card so that we can send back an answer.

Many heartfelt greetings and kisses from us all,
(signed) Rosa

3. *Postscript from father*

Dear Brother and Sister-in-law,

We find ourselves in a very sad situation. We are poor and in misery. We don't get enough to eat. You too were in need before. I beg you, dear brother, to remember us. We don't have the strength to bear this. You must not forget us in this situation. We send you our heartiest greetings,

(signed) Sendel

No. 4

Potsdam Central State Archives
Prom. Collection 50.01. Catalogue No. 982, fos. 53–5

Professor Dr Grimm   Berlin, 2 May 1939

Report on my consultation with Criminal Secretary Wallasch from the Gestapo office at Neu-Bentschen on 1 May 1939.

I had a consultation with Secretary Wallasch on 1 May. I informed him as thoroughly as possible about the necessity for the German defence in the Grünspan trial for clarification regarding the practices for the deportation of the Jews on 29 October 1938 at Neu-Bentschen.

I shared the present state of affairs in the trial with him and the probable tactics of the opposition. I also showed him how it affects the advocacy of the German standpoint.

Secretary Wallasch, who took part in the whole affair, reported the following to me about it:

On 10 October 1938 Government Counsel Liphart from the Gestapo office at Frankfurt an der Oder personally took over the direction of the arrangement. Without doubt, everything proceeded well, correct in every way, and with certainty.

Subsequently the attempt was made to make regular transfers to the Poles of as many Jews as possible by rail. For this purpose many carriages from the special trains would have to be attached to the scheduled passenger trains. These carriages were received by the Poles without any difficulty.

On the other hand, the Poles hesitated to expedite special trains in this way. It was necessary to disperse the majority of the Jews to Poland over the 'green border' land route. Now this did not happen by indiscriminately driving the Jews through field and forest over the border; they were in fact on two roads which ran parallel one or two kilometers on the left and right sides of the tracks leading to Polish territory.

What is more, they were transported on the regular border crossing on the road, where they were taken over by the Polish border personnel without difficulty. There were thus generally no difficulties at the Neu-Bentschen border. At the border near Neu-Bentschen the voluminous baggage of the Jews was transferred to trucks.

Those Jews fit for marching went on foot; older and weaker people were likewise transported to the border by truck. The SA and SS were not brought into action at all, but dispatching was exclusively carried out by the police. No mismanagement whatsoever occurred, nor was there any incident of any nature. There was no shooting and there were no deaths. Everything at Neu-Bentschen went off without a hitch.

The majority of the Jews were later transferred by the Poles into a camp. Between 60 and 70 Jews were incarcerated for 8 weeks in a customs house.

Criminal Secretary Wallasch promised to draw up as complete a report as possible and to furnish me with photographs and sketches when able.

It would also be practical to invite State Counsel Liphart to Berlin one day for a consultation so that the operation at Neu-Bentschen, Bentschen (Zbąszyń) be explained as exhaustively as possible under the given conditions.

No. 5
Provincial State Archive in Poznań
Collection: District Starostwo Nowy Tomyśl sig. 937
fo. 1, Extract from the report of the Commissariat of State Border Police in Zbąszyń, Zbąszyń, 2 November 1938

No. 1623/38. The deportation of Jewish citizens of Poland—statement

To (according to distribution),
I report that on 28 October 1938 at 20.30 hours the German authorities transferred across the border by the Zbąszyń–Rogatka road 654 people, who were detained by the police on the Polish side at a distance of 1 km. from the border. The entire border commissariat in Zbąszyń was immediately alerted and the detained were moved to the border and surrounded by a police cordon and the border guard. At 21.00 hours the news was received that a second group of around 300 people had crossed the border by the railway line and were marching in the direction of the railway station in Zbąszyń. Three policemen were sent to the spot and, together with border guards, they stopped the deported persons at the Zbąszyń–Nądnia level crossing. Next, at intervals of between 30 and 60 minutes, further groups of the deported arrived by the Klastawa–Nądnia road and the Zbąszyń–Neu-Bentschen railway line. It was ascertained that the deported were Polish citizens of Jewish nationality who had resided in Germany either from birth or for a few years. At 21.00 hours on 28 October 1938 it was ascertained that the whole border was manned close to the border line with larger armed detachments, such as border guards, police, and others whom it was impossible to identify in the darkness. In order to demonstrate their strength, the leaders of the detachments gave orders loudly, and kept detachments in close order at the border. By tramping their feet and rattling their weapons, the detachments aimed to discourage any action aimed at resettling the expelled.

At 22.13 hours on 28 October of this year around 900 deported Jews arrived by train from Germany; on 29 October at 0.56 hours around 1,050 deported arrived by train; at 9.09 hours 300 persons, at 01.53 500 persons, at 13.03 500, and at 17.39 500 persons.

There were group expulsions throughout 29 October by the Zbąszyń–Rogatka road next to the railway line, and by the Klastawa–Nądnia road; the largest group of 700 people was expelled at 09.30 hours by the Zbąszyń–Rogatka crossing. This group sat down by the Polish border on the German side and refused to enter Polish territory. Since the police and the border guard were not a sufficient force, the German authorities brought in an army detachment, who, with bayonets fixed to their rifles, turned on those seated, beating and trampling them. With their bayonets and rifle butts the soldiers forced the deported to cross into Polish territory.

On 28 and 29 October up to 17.39 hours around 6,074 persons were deported to Poland, including those deported along the road. After 17.39 hours there were no further group deportations.

Those deported by train were detained in the carriages pending a decision from the authorities and, from 02.00 hours, were directed to ex-army barracks by road. At the same time, registration of the deported and document inspection was organized that night. Persons not possessing documents or without a valid permit, or those in possession of Viennese passports issued before 12 March 1938, were stopped and sent to Germany by train as follows: on 30 October at 03.25 hours 24 persons without passports, 75 persons with Viennese passports, and 6 persons who were German citizens of Jewish nationality from the Poznań province were expelled from Poland. At 07.00 hours 23 German citizens of Jewish nationality were delivered from the Łódź province. The Germans moved those expelled on the same day at 09.09 hours. They were taken back into Germany by train at 10.39; at 13.03 a further group was moved to Poland comprising 26 German citizens, 21 without passports, 2 persons with permits that had expired, and 17 with German passports issued before 12 March 1938. A document was received together with the deported from the Police Commission in Neu-Bentschen stating that the German authorities had suspended deportation on 29 October in the evening, and if expulsions from the Polish side continued the German authorities would regard this as breaking the terms of the agreement. The persons who had been detained—26 German citizens of Jewish nationality, 21 persons without documents, 2 with invalid documents which had expired, and 17 with Viennese passports—were housed in separate accommodation and put under guard.

On 31 October one suicide took place on the railway line, and on 1 November there was a death due to a hernia and twisting of the bowels. A further 54 people were sent to hospital, 2 of whom were suffering from nervous shock.

There were 5,799 persons registered.

It has so far been ascertained that among the deported Polish citizens of Jewish nationality there is one Polish citizen of Polish nationality; there are also a few persons of Jewish descent but who profess the Christian faith. Two Polish citizens of Jewish nationality with passports issued by the Polish authorities had been studying in Vienna.

After passport control and registration had taken place, 2,336 persons departed to join relatives or families in Poland.

On 31 October at 15.30 hours all departures from Zbąszyń were suspended and roads leaving the town were manned with police sentries. Sentries were also posted at the railway station, and everyone leaving the town was subject to strict inspection.

No. 6
Provincial State Archive in Poznań
Collection: District Starost Nowy Tomyśl, sig. 938, fo. 172

No. 1624/38	Zbąszyń, 4 December 1938
Jewish displaced persons	To the District Starost in
leaving of luggage	Nowy Tomyśl

Pursuant to the Vicestarosta's [deputy prefect] recommendation by telephone today concerning the unclaimed luggage left by Jewish displaced persons at the German border in Neu-Bentschen, I hereby inform you that on 1 December I spoke with the German customs house in Neu-Bentschen and one of the customs officers explained to me that the customs house in Neu-Bentschen had sent to Zbąszyń 10 carriage-loads of luggage left at the German border on 28 and 29 October 1938. In answer to my question concerning what had happened to the luggage that the displaced persons had lost in Neu-Bentschen and its environs, the German customs officer explained that the police had driven about all day by car collecting luggage; the luggage that was found filled half a carriage at the customs house in Neu-Bentschen and was sent to Zbąszyń.

Director of the Border Commissariat
Olasik, aspirant

The Jewish Boycott Campaign against Nazi Germany and its Culmination in the Halbersztadt Trial

ALFRED WIŚLICKI

FROM the time that Germany came under Nazi control, the Jewish community in Poland felt it had to protest vigorously and take concrete action. One way to do so, besides political propaganda, was to boycott German goods. Although this campaign was directed against a limited number of products, it could be expected to have a noticeable effect in Germany. The idea of opposing the increasing advance of Nazism and antisemitism by an economic boycott was suggested by the Polish delegation during the World Jewish Congress of August 1932 in Geneva. The Polish representatives insisted: 'The Jews can only respond by taking active boycott measures, and only historical necessity forces the nation to fight back with methods borrowed from its enemies.'[1]

When Adolf Hitler was appointed Reichskanzler in 1933, the Jewish population of many countries became involved in the boycott campaign. In the same year a Convention of Jewish Boycott Committees from various countries was held in Amsterdam. The chairman was Dr Untermayer, a brilliant lawyer from the United States, and speakers included Rabbi Stephen Wise and Rabbi Sacerdoti from Italy. The Polish delegation officially represented 'all the Polish Jews, who are determined to fight for human rights until victory. An economic struggle with Germany is a new and unprecedented stage in Jewish history.'[2]

The next World Jewish Congress, which concentrated on the struggle against the persecution of Jews in Germany, was held in London in 1933, and the Polish delegates were the deputy Wacław Wiślicki and the senator Rafał Szereszewski.[3] At the congress it was decided to establish a World

---

[1] *Nasza obrona* [a periodical dedicated to the anti-Nazi economic campaign, printed in Polish and Yiddish], 1 (Nov. 1933).
[2] An interview with Deputy Wacław Wiślicki in *Nasza obrona*, 1 (15 Nov. 1933), 7.
[3] Ibid. 2 (Feb. 1934), 1–3.

Committee, headed by a leading representative of the American Jews, and with Wacław Wiślicki as vice-president.[4]

A 'Centralny Komitet Antyhitlerowskiej Akcji Gospodarczej' (CK AAG: Central Committee for Anti-Nazi Economic Action) had already been set up in Poland at the beginning of 1933 to co-ordinate and develop a boycott campaign. The Central Committee and the campaign were organized by the Central Headquarters of the Union of Jewish Merchants, with the deputy Wacław Wiślicki as chairman.[5] The Central Headquarters' action included publishing a periodical, *Nasza obrona* [Our defence], which first appeared in November 1933 and then in February 1934. It was edited by Leo Finkelstein.

Head of the CK AGG was the senator Rafał Szereszewski, and the vice-president was the deputy Wacław Wiślicki. The Committee included the engineer Stanisław Szereszewski, and was made up of representatives of the Central Headquarters of the Union of Merchants, the Central Headquarters of Retail and Small Merchants in Poland (headed by B. Zundelwicz, a lawyer), the Central Headquarters of the Union of Jewish Craftsmen, and the Association of Jewish Engineers.

The Central Committee decided the outlines and nature of the boycott, and tried to exert moral pressure to influence consumers. It also helped set up boycott committees and published lists of alternative foreign suppliers. News about the progress of the campaign was provided by *Nasza obrona*, which also explained the purpose of the boycott.

The campaign, in the words of the lawyer Apolinary Hartglas, 'has united previously competing groups, large and small, into a single whole; it creates discipline and a feeling of national, Jewish responsibility, which will also be one of the fruits of our victory'.[6] The campaign also had enemies. The editorial in the first issue of *Nasza obrona* warned: 'We have many opponents. Some claim that our whole effort has no point, is unnecessary and harmful ... Our answer is: show us how else to act against this unprecedented attack on our dignity. We are not going to back down from the fight.'

The boycott campaign made rapid progress in Poland. Local Committees appeared in Kraków (led by Dr Fischlowitz), Łódź, Lublin (H. J. Zybler), Poznań, Rozwadów (Dr Trauenstein), Kielce, and other towns. In Warsaw a Committee of Jewish Academicians was set up, with Władysław Nemes as its secretary.[7] Moreover, the campaign produced results. According to data presented in *Nasza obrona* (Nos. 1 and 2), at least thirty important factories

---

[4] I cite these facts from memory.
[5] Ignacy Schiper, *Dzieje handlu żydowskiego na ziemiach polskich* (Warsaw, 1937), 736.
[6] *Nasza obrona*, 2 (Feb. 1934),
[7] Władysław Menes, MA, now lives in Israel.

involved in the textile, chemical, mechanical, electro-mechanical, and food industries terminated their contacts with German suppliers. The Union of Physicians reported that the import of pharmaceuticals and drugs from Germany fell by 85 per cent in 1934. In every case the imports were replaced by Polish goods or those from other countries.

For obvious reasons, *Nasza obrona* did not publish the names of the firms taking part in the boycott, except for the jeweller J. Schreibman, the Amazonka food works in Włocławek owned by Ch. Janower, and the Warsaw wholesaler Ch. M. Heller.[8] I know personally that equipment and machines for the Celuloza Nadniemańska factory near Grodno, which was then under construction, were not purchased in Germany despite attractive terms. It should be added that the German suppliers informed the relevant Reich authorities about the boycott of their products. The embargo involved increasingly wider areas of trade and industry, although there were some firms which refused to join in.[9]

For various reasons, including the boycott by Jewish tradesmen and industry, German exports (as well as those from Austria) to Poland declined from zl 210.8 million in 1930 to zl 145.6 million in 1934 (the zloty at that time was a hard currency), while the boycott in other countries helped to some extent to reduce German exports from zl 29.4 billion in 1931 to zl 8.7 billion in 1934.[10]

Dr Hjalmar Schacht, chairman of the Reichsbank, claimed that the boycott was a threat to the German economy. Although the decline in exports of around 70 per cent compared with the pre-Nazi level was mainly caused by a shift in the German economy to armaments production, the boycott certainly played a part.[11] Consequently, Germany began to exert pressure to limit the effects of the boycott campaign in Poland. In 1934 this led Józef Beck, the Polish Foreign Minister, to assure the German ambassador that he would insist that the Minister of the Interior use his powers of censorship to prevent any articles about the boycott from appearing in the Polish press. He was to be true to his word.[12]

In a period of German–Polish *rapprochement* and increasing antisemitism in Poland, the government and political organizations acted to weaken and ultimately end the boycott. In 1935 Colonel Walery Sławek, head of the parliamentary club Bezpartyjny Blok Wspólpracy z Rządem (BBWR: the Non-Party Bloc for Co-operation with the Government), threatened Deputy

---

[8] *Nasza obrona*, 1 (Nov. 1933).
[9] *Nasz przegląd*, 1 (25 Sept. 1939).
[10] *Mały rocznik statystyczny* (1939), 163, 166.
[11] Apolinary Hartglas, 'Bojkot', *Nasza obrona*, 2 (Feb. 1934), 1.
[12] Emanuel Melzer, 'The Anti-German Economic Boycott by Polish Jewry in 1933–1934', *Gal-Ed*, 6 (1982).

Wiślicki, verbally and in writing, with parliamentary and club sanctions unless he resigned from the Boycott Committee and stopped the campaign, which was contrary to official policy towards Germany.[13] Wacław Wiślicki 'resolutely rejected this request on the grounds that as a Jew and human being he was opposed to the brutality of barbaric political systems'.[14]

Faced with a continuation of the boycott, the authorities decided to bring a single case to court as an example. The boycott was to be destroyed in a court of law, where the complex issues involved could not be examined in full.

Naum Abraham Halbersztadt, the owner of an electrical shop at 26 Ogrodowa Street in Warsaw, was accused of libelling the leader of the German nation and was tried on 23 September 1935 in the Warsaw Regional Court. The following report appeared in *Nasz przegląd*:

It has been several years since the Regional Court has seen a trial of such spontaneous and enormous interest. This unusual case of a 56-year-old Jewish merchant, Halbersztadt, has attracted a large audience to the courtroom, one which follows the trial with rapt attention. Halbersztadt had received a business letter from the Dresden-based Elektrolental Einheit Fischer et Rittner GmBH. He returned it to the sender unopened, and on the back of the envelope wrote in German: 'I have asked you on innumerable occasions not to bother me: *solang Hitler mit senem Gesinde* [as long as Hitler with his lackeys] remains in the saddle, no decent person can have any contact with Germans.'[15]

The letter, as the prosecution indicated during the trial, was intercepted by the German Post Office and returned to Poland with a demand that the sender be punished for offending the German nation. This was the basis of the charge against Halbersztadt. According to the indictment, his words rendered him liable to three years' imprisonment under Article 111 of the Penal Code, for libelling the head of a foreign state.

The defence lawyers included Aleksander Margolis and Igel Edelman. Witness for the prosecution was René Michalski, head of the Foreign Department of the Ministry for Post and Telegraph. Witnesses for the defence were Deputy Wacław Wiślicki, the former deputy Dr Henryk Rozmaryn, from Lwów, and the newspaper editor Marek Turków, who were called on to establish the defendant's emotional state at the time of the crime and his reasons for committing the offence.

[13] I saw Col. Walery Sławek's letters and my father's reply. After the war, my mother and I were unable to find them because all the papers left behind in our home in Warsaw were lost. Walery Sławek burnt his private papers before his suicide, and the Archive of the Central Headquarters of the Union of Merchants was destroyed during the war.

[14] From a speech by the engineer M. Zajdenman, at a memorial meeting on the first anniversary of the death of Wacław Wiślicki, *Przegląd handlowy*, 11 (1936), 11.

[15] *Nasz przegląd* (24 Sept. 1935).

At the outset of the trial, the prosecutor unsuccessfully objected to defence witnesses being called, claiming that their evidence was irrelevant to the case. The trial began with the judge asking the accused if he pleaded guilty. Halbersztadt answered: 'I wrote the words, but I do not admit to being guilty. I simply wished to condemn everything that is happening in Germany. I was not aware that this is forbidden in Poland ... My words referred to the present regime in Germany.' The judge asked if the accused has suffered personally; Halbersztadt replied that he had not. When the judge asked him if he believed that the situation of the Jews in Germany was unfavourable, he replied, 'Of course.'

The first witness for the defence was Deputy Wacław Wiślicki, who made the following statement:

> I should be here on trial myself. When I discovered that a Jewish merchant had been accused, I felt that I ought to be tried instead of him. What the defendant did is the result of our campaign and of the action organized by the Anti-Nazi Committee, which had received permission for this from the late minister Pieracki. I am one of the organizers of this campaign, which is being conducted all over the world as well as in Poland.
>
> We called for an economic boycott of Germany, and I believe that the conduct of the accused is a reflection of the dignity and honour of the Jewish nation.

Wiślicki went on to mention that the worldwide boycott campaign had held a convention in London, where as important a person as Lord Melchet had been present, and that the United States Attorney-General Untermayer was energetically leading the American boycott. He continued: 'The Jewish citizens in Poland could not act differently from the whole world. Those who did not join in our campaign were regarded as traitors to the Jewish cause. We can already claim today to have had some success in the campaign.'

Wiślicki then referred to statements made by Dr Schacht, economic supremo of the Third Reich, about the difficult economic situation in Germany, and also gave two examples of the boycott campaign. These were that a certain Rudolf Lauche from Leipzig had written to a Jewish merchant in Warsaw, threatening that if the merchant refused to buy his goods, Lauche would find a German Jew to take hostage in order to force the Polish Jew to comply.[16] Another German trader, Friedrich Böhler from Hamburg, had advised a Jewish merchant to restore trade relations because the Polish government would eventually be toppled and replaced by a Nazi one,[17] an event which had fortunately not yet taken place.

---

[16] A letter by Rudolf Lauche published in *Nasza obrona*, 1 (Nov. 1933), printed in the appendix below (Document No. 1).

[17] A letter by Friedrich Böhler published ibid. (see Document 2 below).

The judge then asked the witness what sanctions were taken against those who did not observe the boycott. Deputy Wiślicki answered that the boycott applied to both Jewish and Christian firms, and that sanctions included the complete exclusion of offenders from professional and local government life.

The next witness, Deputy Henryk Rozmaryn, stated that he had 'played a prominent part in the boycott, and the entire Jewish community considered the campaign the most realistic and possibly the most effective way to take action'. He claimed that throughout the world—in London, Geneva, or the United States—the call for the boycott was supported not only by Jewish but also by working-class organizations, and that the struggle against racism was a battle for survival against an enemy using every means at its disposal. This meant that the Jewish community had to use more than fine words in the struggle for its existence and future.

The final defence witness was the editor Marek Turków, who explained that he was 'participating directly in the campaign, which is constantly encouraging the boycott and singling out all traitors to the cause'. The defence also produced as evidence the diplomatic protocol of the Ministry of Foreign Affairs, which stated that although Adolf Hitler had assumed the office of Führer and Reichskanzler on 8 August 1934 it was not announced until 23 November 1934. This meant that the letter returned to Halbersztadt in September 1934 was written before Hitler was confirmed in office, and therefore could not be considered as libel against a head of state.

The prosecuting lawyer replied that this argument was invalid: what mattered was the defendant's intent. He insisted that the accused had no justification for his crime.

When the court reached its verdict in the name of the Republic, it stated that 'friendly relations between Poland and the Third Reich require that Halbersztadt be found guilty of the crime committed'. He was sentenced to eight months' detention, but the judge refused the prosecution's demands for actual imprisonment and ordered him to report regularly to a police station. In this way ended the brief Halbersztadt trial, which in reality had been directed against the boycott of Nazi Germany by the Jewish merchants in Poland. The trial illuminated various contemporary attitudes and provides historians with valuable material and ideas.

The prosecuting lawyer's approach reflects that of the state authorities themselves: they felt it important to accuse a Jew of having 'defamed' Adolf Hitler as the head of a foreign state, and believed that 'friendly relations between Poland and the Third Reich' made his action a felony. The whole case clearly showed that the authorities intended to stamp out the Jewish boycott.

The conduct of the defendant and the witnesses on his behalf revealed the determination of a large part of the Jewish community to stand firm. To some extent also, the action of the judge in limiting the extent of Halbersztadt's punishment, despite the prosecutor's wishes, was characteristic of the attitude of the Polish intelligentsia.

The pressure exerted by the state and further Nazi influence hampered the activities of the boycott committees, making it impossible for them to conduct a propaganda and press campaign. But the boycott continued right up to the outbreak of war. Wacław Wiślicki's speech in court was the culmination of his public and political career. He was already suffering from a weak heart, and he became fatally ill after the trial. Wiślicki died ten days later, on 3 October 1935.

This paper is concluded with a personal recollection. Nazi Germany did not forget Wacław Wiślicki—or the boycott campaign. At the beginning of October 1939, soon after the Germans occupied Warsaw, we returned to our home, which was in an area where the defence of the capital had been conducted. (We had spent the entire siege with relatives, in the town centre). Here we were visited by a member of the Gestapo in an SS car. He was wearing a black uniform with the inscription 'Leibstandarte Adolf Hitler' on his cap-band, and was accompanied by a German translator who spoke poor Polish. The Gestapo officer asked if the Wiślicki family lived in the house, adding as an afterthought: 'Jude?' The evening and the police curfew were approaching, so the German then left. Before doing so, he ordered that the house, which had been damaged by bombing, should be cleared up. He also left a guard at the door and said we would be taken away the following day. They never found us: we escaped through the ruins and made our way to the east, knowing that the Germans would be watching for us in Warsaw.

There was no doubt that they wanted the family of Wacław Wiślicki.

APPENDIX: DOCUMENTS

No. 1

Letter from the Rudolf Lauche Factory for the Manufacture of Natural and Artificial Perfumes and Dyestuffs, Leipzig, to the Firm Amazonka in Włocławek, Poland, dated Leipzig, 4 September 1933

We have received your letter dated the first of this month and have taken note of your reasons for abrogating your agreement with us. As adults and intelligent men, you know as well as we do that they have no validity. Nevertheless, we were interested to learn how deeply lies and atrocity propaganda against the German Reich have taken root. You will not take offence that we make use of all the means at our disposal to deal with these flagrant lies and slanders. We have decided to take the following measures.

We shall take one of your co-religionists in Germany into protective custody for as long as you fail to withdraw the slanders contained in your letter of the first of this month. We advise you to modify your opinion of the treatment of Jews in Germany as quickly as possible, since otherwise you yourselves will be responsible for whatever measures are taken against your co-religionists.

In addition, we should like you to be informed that we have passed your letter on to the relevant authorities.

Yours faithfully
Rudolf Lauche Company

No. 2

Letter from the Friedrich Böhler Shipping Company, Hamburg, to the Ch. M. Heller Company, Warsaw, dated 8 August 1933

You have returned to me the information briefing which was sent to you on 11 August regarding shipping traffic between Hamburg, Gdynia, Danzig, and Poland and have allowed yourself to make disparaging remarks about the current government and state of affairs in Germany. As a foreigner you can have absolutely no idea of the nature of our present government and of conditions in Germany. You should come to Germany and see for yourself.

It is, of course, not my task to discuss politics with you, but to conduct business. I must therefore, much as it pains me, ask you to abstain from this subject, but should like to make it clear that it is only because your sentiments and your level of understanding are of so primitive a cultural level that you have allowed yourself to be so carried away as to make your observations.

Although I recently sent a circular of this type to some 1,500 companies in Poland, you are, I regret to say, the only one which has opposed our present government in this despicable way.

Perhaps one wonderful day you in Poland will experience a change in conditions similar to that which has taken place in Germany. I shall be interested to see whether then, in your own country, you will still indulge in observations of the type you have expressed to us.

I am sending a copy of this letter to the Board of Trade so that action can be taken.

Heil Hitler
C. Friedrich Böhler Nfl.

What Shall We Tell Miriam?
A Tale for the Present

RAFAEL F. SCHARF

THERE must be many Miriams and Sarahs and Shulamiths and Samuels and Benjamins and Daniels all over the world where Jews have set foot. They are, or will soon, be asking their parents and grandparents questions about what life was like in the country where they were born in that incredibly distant past before the Second World War, and even before the First World War. What were the people like, our grandparents and great-grandparents? How did they live, what did they do, what did they think, what did the places look like, how did they smell? In the words of the historian Ranke: 'Wie es wirklich gewesen.' Posing such questions is a part of a natural cyclical process: indifference, then curiosity. It is important to tell them about these things, for our sake and theirs. Who will if we won't? Ours is the last and vanishing generation of living witness. But *how* to do it? The young have little patience. Of course, it would be simple enough to use the precept of Hillel, *tsé ulemad*—send them to the library to read and learn. How realistic is this counsel? Perhaps one might recommend a specific reading list that could be tailored to the particular circumstance. Nothing would give a better picture than some of the works of Mendele, Sholem Aleykhem, Peretz, Opatoshu, Sholem Asch, Agnon, the Singer brothers, and later Stryjkowski. On the Polish side, there is Julian Ursyn Niemcewicz, Józef Korzeniowski, Ignacy Kraszewski, Syrokomla, Gomulicki, Konopnicka, Orzeszkowa, and Klemens Junosza.

There is, however, a more personal way, by describing life in that long-ago world through the story of one's own family. My family, for example, is not untypical of the many aspects of Jewish life around Kraków in western Galicia, the 'Austrian' part of Poland at the end of the nineteenth century and the first decades of the twentieth.

On my father's side, I am descended from a long line of rabbis or *melameds*. My father was the youngest of fifteen children, not all from the same mother and not all surviving to adulthood. To give a thumbnail sketch of the family, one would need a very large thumb indeed.

My grandfather, a white-bearded patriarch, by trade an innkeeper (like Tag in Stryjkowski's *Austeria*), was in his youth an 'oak' of a man. I only remember him as bent in half, toothless, shrunken with incessant toil, worry, and the blows of fortune. He died comparatively young—certainly he was less than 'three score years and ten'—and the saying at the time was 'a yingerer sol nysh shtarben' (let never a man die younger than he).

Our family name was Scharf, and there were so many of us in that part of the land, in the villages and towns like Chrzanów (where we began), Kalwaria, Alwernia, Żywiec, Bochnia, and the environs of Kraków, that it is a wonder there was room for anybody else. (Incidentally, the great majority of the Jewish population inhabited localities of less than 20,000 people.) This vast clan was seething with activity and appeared to be in a state of perpetual motion, travelling with trunks, cases, parcels by train or horse-drawn carts in feverish pursuit of their affairs, large and small, and to family gatherings: weddings, circumcisions, funerals. I remember the colourful, noisy crowd passing at various times through our dwelling in Kraków, *en route* to their next port of call. They would rest a while, exchange family news, seek advice from my mother or a loan from my father, and refresh themselves with a glass of tea—nothing more. My mother's kitchen was suspect to them, and rightly so. Even though the meat was kosher and ham was never eaten inside the house, the dessert served after a meal of goose could well have been wild strawberries and cream.

The degree of religious orthodoxy in my family covered a wide spectrum. There was my oldest uncle, Motl, almost forty years my father's senior, an ascetic and forbidding figure, a follower, to distraction, of the Rebbe of Bełz. He was not on speaking terms with his younger brother Saul, who was not, God forbid, a *mitnaged*, but a follower of another *tsadik*. As a boy, I refused to visit him because he pinched my cheek so that it hurt for days. Although the pinch was supposed to be a sign of affection, it was really because I was not wearing *tsitsit*.

There was Cousin Hymie, a dreamer and a schemer, frenetically engaged in projects which, if successful, would shed enormous benefits on the whole family, but in the meantime required continuous injections of cash. He was modelled on Sholem Aleykhem's Menachem Mendl, in the way life imitates, or rather parodies, art.

There was Aunt Rachel, an early widow with as many children as there had been years in her happy marriage. She earned her living as a marriage broker, normally a male occupation. Since that involved continuous travel in search of information, developing connections, soothing anxieties, and supervising *bekuks* (the preview prospective couples would be given of each other), she was also a ministering angel to the sick in our widespread family.

She used her uncanny knowledge of folk remedies and deep psychological insights, and long before the name was invented, she understood the nature of psychosomatic illness: 'anredinish is arger wie a krenk [one can talk oneself into an imaginary illness—worse than a real one]'.

Before my time, deeply secreted in our family's common memory, there were tales of the allegedly beautiful Auntie Rosa, her yellowing photograph buried in my mother's drawer of knick-knacks, safe except from my prying hands. She had eloped after a whirlwind love affair with an Austrian officer who had subsequently abandoned her. Rosa ended up in the gutter as a streetwalker. There is no hard evidence for this, but it was felt that the story could not have ended otherwise. Her parents, of course, cast her out and sat *shivah*. Till their dying day, they were consumed by grief and shame.

This motif, which, with slight variations, recurs frequently in Yiddish and Polish literature, from Tevye the Milchiger's daughter Chave to Stryjkowski's Cheremian, shows that such skeletons rattled in many families' cupboards. Traumas of this kind tore at the fabric of the community; no worse thing was conceivable. In the interaction of the group with the surrounding world, forbidden yet tempting, an occasional crossing of the barrier was inevitable. Revulsion against what was seen as suffocating obscurantism also played its part. In the eyes of his contemporaries, however, the convert remained an abhorrent and despised figure. No Jew believed that the change of faith was genuine (a suspicion shared widely by non-Jews as well). How could it be? It was generally considered that, with few exceptions, the convert, indifferent to the old religion and only pretending allegiance to the new, was in it merely for personal advantage of one sort or another.

A case less dramatic than that of Auntie Rosa, but probably not less typical, revolved around my Uncle Jehoshua. His stepmother decided that the parental home no longer had a place for him, and he was packed off to America. This was not an uncommon practice in those days, and the migration was generally beneficial to all. But Jehoshua, who was 14 or 15 years old, was not concerned with the movement of History; he was interested only in his own movements, those of a lost, castaway boy. What were the mechanics of these journeys? In his pocket he had a *Schiffskarte* and was supposed to sail from Liverpool; how he was to get there in the first place was a mystery. In the event, he didn't make it first time around. On the way he met some people who knew his family and considered it terrible that they were sending the boy away and depriving him of his portion of inheritance (of which, no doubt, they had a vastly exaggerated notion). He turned back, and on his return journey he was picked up by some members of a missionary society that believed the conversion of the Jews must precede the coming of the Messiah. They decided that Jehoshua's destiny was to speed the Messiah on his way. A hot meal and a few kind words did wonders. I can still sense the horror in my mother's voice when she told the story, half a century ago—how people, neighbours and friends, came rushing into the house, utterly scandalized, to tell his father and stepmother and the other children that Jehoshua was peddling missionary tracts in the market-place. There was heartbreak, remorse, and dread of scandal. In the end, through bribery, persuasion, or force, the boy was dispatched again, this time effectively, to reach the Golden Shore. Virtually nothing was heard of him for many years after that. Family members suddenly remembered Jehoshua shortly before the Second World War, when some of them needed 'an affidavit' from him—only then did they start casting about for his address, and then it was too late.

My father was an early rebel. Feeling constrained by life in the *shtetl*, he cut his jacket short and changed his hat from the standard Orthodox round black velvet kind to one that was more fashionable and of lighter colour. That transformation probably required more courage than we can imagine. He arrived in Kraków in search of a wife and fortune, and soon succeeded in his first objective beyond his wildest dreams. The second objective somehow became less important.

He retained his attachment to Judaism, for he knew nothing else and felt no need for anything else. I see him on a Saturday afternoon, reaching in the bookcase for a volume of the Talmud and from the way he handled it, the caress, it was clear that the book was holy. Bending over an open volume, he would slowly turn the pages, as if feeling his way through an embarrassment of riches, and then, with a contended familiarity, he would settle down to studying a particular passage. He was no scholar, having had only the required few years of reluctant attendance in *ḥeder*, so he was unable to make his own way through the solid columns of text buried in the undergrowth of commentaries and sprinkled with the poppy-seed of glosses. No matter, he was not looking for solutions to problems or rulings of law, but only to wash away the triviality and harshness of everyday existence. He believed that the book contained the truth and that it was good to touch it. He wished to persuade me to share his outlook, but we did not know how to talk to each other and he realized that an argument with a precocious know-it-all would only lead to an aggravation of spirit. Only once, I remember, he exploded when I asked him: 'What is all this *for*?' 'What is this *for*, fool? The whole of life is for *this!*'

He saw his role at home as that of breadwinner, and genuinely felt that all he had aspired to was for our sake; but bringing up children was not his concern. What little modicum of success he had as a merchant and small-time manufacturer was brought about by continual toil and total immersion in the task at hand. He would provide for all our needs, and he was the one responsible for defining these needs. In this way he sowed the seeds of the next phase of rebellion. The family was already bursting at the seams and moving in all directions. It became a human landscape of great diversity. Some young members of the family became Communists, card-carrying Party members. Now, that was serious business, illegal and dangerous; it could and often did end badly: police searches at home, to the distress of parents, arrests, prison sentences. In spite of, or rather because of, the danger, the Party attracted some very good people indeed. The idea was irresistible: it seemed to offer a solution not only to the Jewish question, which seemed trivial by comparison, but to all other questions of social injustice and exploitation as part of the historically inevitable victory of the proletariat. Brotherhood of nations would come naturally, as a bonus. Such ideas deserved sacrifices, and there were many, including the ultimate, at Stalin's execution wall. My favourite cousin, Mojshe, later Misha, a brilliant linguist and chess-player, was killed this way.

Some of the clan gave their allegiance to the Bund, but most were swept up by the liberating wind of Zionism: the Hashomer Hatsair, Gordonia, Akiba, Betar. By the late 1920s and early 1930s, the *shtetl* was left behind, and most members of the family had migrated to larger towns, mainly Kraków. There they embraced, penetrated, and intermingled with other families, so that virtually everybody became a relative: the black-bearded Schwarzbards and red-bearded Rotbarts, the ubiquitous Landaus, Grosses and Kleins, Schusters and Schneiders, Wolfs and Schaffs, Sperlings and Spatzes, Spiras and Schapiras, Kohns, Kohens, and Kahanes (as well as the Loewys), Sonntags, Montags, Freitags, and Sonnabends, Zuckers and Pfeffers, Gruens and Brauns, Golds and Silbers, Nussbaums, Gruenbaums, Rosenbaums, all the other -baums, and Aschkenases and Gumplowiczes. This list includes only those families which I know personally had a bond with the Scharfs.

It was an interesting mixed community. I heard a story of a man who went to Kraków and on his return told his friend: 'The Jews of Kraków are remarkable people. I saw one Jew who spends all his time studying the Talmud, one who spends all his time planning the revolution, one who chases every skirt he sees, one who wants to have nothing to do with women, and one who is full of schemes of how to get rich quickly.' The other man said: 'I don't know why you are astonished. Kraków is a big city and there are many Jews of all sorts there.' 'No,' responded the first man, 'it was the same Jew.'

But I also want to draw another profile of a Jew of those days. It comes from a verse called 'AVI' [My father] by Itzhak Katzenelson, the author of what is possibly the greatest poem written during and about the Shoah (in Yiddish), 'Lid fun gehargeten yidishen folkes' [The song of the murdered

Jewish people]. He writes: 'When did my father learn the Bible by heart? The translations of Onkelos [a Jewish scholar of the first century AD] and Luther? The Talmud, Codes, Midrash, Shakespeare, and Heine? When did he read Gogol, Thucydides, and Plutarch? When did he study the Holy Zohar? When did he sleep?' One can but feel humble. They don't come like that any more. They used to, quite often, over there. Bear in mind that we are not talking about a full-time scholar, with some visible means of support, but of somebody who scraped a living by the sweat of his brow and who did his reading by oil-lamp or candlelight.

If all these people had not lived and died in apocalyptic times, some of that profusion of humanity would have merged with other streams all over the map. Their various talents, energies, and spirit would have enriched the world. As it is, from my closest family (which included hundreds of individuals) there is not a single survivor except for my mother. She survived because of her appearance, language, and Aryan documents, and then only through a chain of coincidences and miracles—but that's another story.

When talking about Polish Jewry before the First World War, it is important to steer a clear course between nostalgia and reality. In mourning the past, it would be wrong to idealize it. The only authentic literature of that time in Yiddish and Hebrew is sharply critical, even though the criticism is tempered by compassion. The writers portray the sordid conditions—poverty, powerlessness, oppression, obscurantism—and rail against them. If you want to know about the position of women in that society, for instance, a short passage from *Debora*, a book by Esther Kreitman, the sister of the Singer brothers and brushed by the same family talent, can tell you more than a dozen learned tracts. Once, when she overheard her father saying proudly of Joshua: 'One day he will be a brilliant Talmudist', she asked: 'And, Father, what am I going to be one day?' Her father looked as if he didn't quite understand the question. 'What are you going to be one day? Nothing, of course (*gornish*).'

It is true that intense poverty was widespread, but it was not a specifically Jewish poverty. On the contrary, urban squalor knew no ethnic boundaries, and the unemployed Gentile labourer suffered the same hardships as the Jew. The countryside could be harsher still: in a bad year, the small landholder and landless peasant led a pitiful existence.

In describing the Jews, one of the Polish peasants in Lanzmann's film *Shoah* said that they stank. When questioned further, he said they stank of leather; indeed, they worked in a tannery and could not have smelt of roses. I have this smell in my nostrils to this day, as so many of my family made their living 'in leather'. There was a notorious case reported in the 1930s in the Warsaw press in which a Polish nobleman, a count (Lubomirski?), left a railway compartment because of the smell of garlic. Moshe Kleinbaum, later Sneh, satirized 'the Count with the sensitive nose', and Tuwim addressed the following stanza to him:

. . . i ty, fortuny skurwysynu,	. . . and you whoreson of fortune
gówniarzu uperfumowany,	Perfumed whippersnapper
co splendor oraz spleen Londynu	Who carries the splendour and spleen of London
nosisz na gębie zakazanej	On a vulgar mug . . .

Since apartments with two bathrooms were rare, the Jewish street had many odours: sweat, the market-place, overcrowded rooms, unaired linen, cooking ('Z kuchni woń ryb smażonych płynęła niemiła [the odour fried fish floated from the kitchen]', says Gomulicki)—the universal smells of poverty, the *Armeleutegeruch*. It was not a specifically Jewish odour, except that along other streets there was a strong whiff of alcohol. In this context, a famous quatrain by Paczkowski is apt:

Dwa są główne powody	Two are the main reasons
Dla których mi Polska zbrzydła:	Why Poland sticks in my gullet:
Za dużo święconej wody,	There's too much holy water,
Za mało zwykłego mydła.	Not enough ordinary soap.

On the other hand, the idea that Jewish life in Poland was always one of unrelieved gloom and oppression is mistaken. There were lights as well as shadows; the rich fabric of the Jewish existence was woven of many strands, and some of its brightest threads could be found on Polish soil. How could Jewish life be so bad and yet so good? The structure of what somebody called 'the Jewish Nation in Poland' was diverse. It had an urban proletariat with industrial workers, tradesmen, and craftsmen (mainly tailors and shoemakers), *luftmenshen* with no visible means of support, a large and amorphous middle class of shopkeepers and business people of all categories, free professions—doctors, lawyers, and scholars—and a plutocracy of manufacturers, bankers, and large industrialists.

The community's religious administration lay in the hands of the *kahal*, which had considerable autonomy and a wide range of competence. There were Jewish and Hebrew schools of all grades, *yeshivot*, and an Institute of Jewish Studies in Warsaw that had university status. A Jewish press flourished in Yiddish, Polish, and Hebrew (in 1939, according to a recent study, there were 30 Jewish daily newspapers and 130 periodicals of all kinds). There were innumerable trade and professional associations: of writers, journalists, doctors, lawyers, engineers, merchants, houseowners (in the late 1930s 40 per cent of town property in Warsaw was in Jewish hands). There was a network of charitable institutions, hospitals, orphanages, provident funds, and summer camps to help the disadvantaged. There were sport clubs for aspiring and actual record-holders in all areas. Above all, there were the political parties with their affiliated youth organizations striving for a better future. Jewish deputies represented the whole spectrum of political life in the Polish parliament.

The community was fragmented and torn by internal strife, but there was also a sense of sharing a common fate that transcended social and political differences. There was a marked spirituality even among the non-religious, a response to what was felt to be the Jewish ethos, a deeply ingrained universal conviction that beyond the daily sweat and strife men had to aspire to higher things. There was a considerable area where the division between the Polish and the Jewish worlds was blurred; living side by side for so long led to a degree of mutual acceptance, tolerance, and harmony. This produced a cross-fertilization, enriching both cultures. Polish literature of the time glitters with illustrious names of Jews (or of undeniable Jewish origin): Leśmian, Tuwim, Słonimski, Peiper, Wittlin, Korczak, to name but a few. This was one aspect of a complex situation, at the end of the spectrum—the other, overwhelmingly, presented a darker picture.

In these lands a civilization flourished with traditions, language, folklore, literature, and music, with roots deeper than the Polish civilization. Did the ordinary Pole realize that in the neighbouring town, or for that matter in the very same street, something was happening that could engage their attention? Hardly ever. The Jewish population was commonly regarded as a 'dark continent', backward and primitive, often evoking feelings of aversion and repugnance. The Poles automatically regarded themselves as superior —each Pole was superior to each Jew, be he a rabbi, writer, merchant, or shoemaker. The Jews in turn would shrug their shoulders: what could be expected from 'them'?

It appears that Jew and Pole did not suit each other. But how can a substantial, visible, competitive minority, intent on its own identity and with its own national aspirations, suit the surrounding nation? Such a question cannot be answered satisfactorily. Perhaps the following two excerpts, by evoking a world that is no more, can provide the best epitaph.

. . . .

przez podlasia zarzecza	through woodland rivers
przez jesień zgarbionych lichtarzy	through an autumn of bowed candlesticks
przez komory gazowe	through gas-chambers
kirkuty powietrzne	graveyards of air
szli do Jeruszalaim	they went to Yerushalaim
i martwi i żywi	both the dead and the living
w swoje powrotne ongiś	into their returning olden time
i aż tam przemycili	a handful of willow-pears
garstkę wierzbowych gruszek	and for a keepsake
i na pamiątkę	a herring-bone
ze śledzia	that sticks to this day
do dziś kłująca ość	

(From Jerzy Ficowski, *Odczytanie popiołów* [The reading of ashes])

And so, as it stood, unprepared and unfinished, in an accidental intersection of time and space, without closing of accounts, without reaching any goal, caught in a half-sentence, as it were, without full stop or exclamation mark, without trial...

(From *Kometa* [The comet] by Bruno Schulz from Drohobycz, in which he describes an imaginary world that comes to an end)

Poyln: Land of Sages and *Tsadikim*

YEHIEL YESHAIA TRUNK

EDITOR'S INTRODUCTION

YEHIEL YESHAIA TRUNK, author of *Poyln: Zikhroynes un bilder* (7 vols.; New York, 1946–53), from which these sketches are taken, was born in 1887 in Osmolin, near Łowicz in central Poland. On his mother's side, he came from a family of village Jews. His maternal grandfather had become the administrator of one of the Sapieha estates, and ultimately succeeded in purchasing an estate of his own, Osmolin, where Trunk spent much of his childhood. On his father's side, he was the descendant of a long line of rabbis. As he relates in the first of the sketches below, his paternal grandfather was the Gaon Reb Yehiel Kutner, and he was also linked, as he describes, with the Vorker Hasidim. This part of his family was connected to the prominent Warsaw family of ironmongers, the Pryweses, who appear in two of the sketches and who, thinly disguised, are the central figures in Isaac Bashevis Singer's *The Family Moskat*. Trunk began his writing career in 1908, strongly influenced by Yitshak Leibush Peretz. He described his first encounter with Peretz in *Poyln*, in a section which has been translated into English by the late Lucy Dawidowicz and printed in her anthology *The Golden Tradition: Jewish Life and Thought in Eastern Europe* (New York, 1967), 297–304. He was introduced to Peretz by his uncle, who had become a follower of the Haskalah, and he describes his approach to the great writer's apartment on 1 Ceglana as 'the most decisive walk in my life. Thirty-odd years later when I passed these streets, my heart still beat excitedly in remembrance of that earlier walk. I have never forgotten the cobblestones, a certain street lamp, a newspaper kiosk, and a dozen other details that caught my eye.'

Trunk had brought with him some of his writings in Hebrew, although he was already beginning to write in Yiddish:

> I did not consider my Yiddish writings as containing the essence of my spirituality. In Hebrew I hoped to express my intellectual moods, my introspections, the subtlety of my observations. In Yiddish I wrote about my milieu and especially my feeling for nature, which was always strong—I had spent my childhood and many months of my later life in the country. Yiddish evoked for me the fragrant fields and orchards among which I had been born and brought up. Hebrew called forth the *gemara* and the intellectuality of my father's family. Hebrew was the language of the Trunks; Yiddish was the language of my mother and my Grandfather Boruch.

Peretz understood the essential nature of his talent: 'You have interesting ideas ... but you don't know Hebrew. You think in Yiddish and translate yourself into Hebrew. No, this has no point. Why don't you write in Yiddish? Doesn't it suit you, a son-in-law of the Prywes', to write in the language of the common herd?' From Peretz Trunk derived not only his decision to adopt Yiddish as the main vehicle of his creativity, but also his commitment to the cause of the common man, which led him, in 1923, to join the Bund, to which he remained faithful all his life.

Trunk's main strength was as an essayist and an evoker of atmosphere. He wrote a number of studies on Yiddish literature, including *Idealizm un naturalizm in der yidisher literatur* [Idealism and naturalism in Yiddish literature] (Warsaw, 1927) and three studies of Sholem Aleichem (S. Rabinovitch): *Sholem Aleykhem* (Warsaw, 1937), *Tevye der Milkhiger* (Warsaw, 1939), and *Tevye un Menakhem Mendl in yidisher velt goyrl* [Tevye, Menakhem Mendl, and human destiny] (New York, 1944). Trunk lived in Łódź for much of the interwar period but moved to Warsaw in the late 1930s, where he was, in 1939, president of the Jewish Pen Club. He left Poland at the outbreak of the war and, after a period in Palestine, settled in New York, where he died in 1961. His most valuable work is undoubtedly *Poyln*, which he described as 'the portrait of my life in the framework of and in relation to the portrait of Jewish life in Poland.' Its significance has been underlined by his cousin, the historian Isaiah Trunk, author of *Judenrat: The Jewish Councils in Eastern Europe under Nazi Occupation* (New York, 1972):

> The seven volumes of *Poyln* by the late I. I. Trunk are a vital literary source for becoming acquainted with Polish Jewry in the seventy years preceding its destruction by the Nazis. Trunk wrote an autobiography, but his life-story, that of a great Jewish writer, is, in fact, an artistic description of Polish Jewry in all its many manifestations. Thus the family chronicle of the Trunks becomes an epic of Polish Jewry, encompassing its many *strata* and segments. It ranges from Torah scholars to the most ignorant boor, from rich merchants and landowners to paupers and wandering beggars. All is there and all is described with empathy, gaiety and the benevolent smile of a great humorist.
>
> Trunk's *Poyln* is not a lachrymose picture of a world that has vanished. He lived during a period of great social change, marked by the gradual decline of the old patriarchal way of life and the rise of new trends and developments. Blessed with a phenomenal memory, he was able, for instance, to describe in great detail the apparel of his grandmother and aunts on the occasion of a wedding in the family, the menu of the feast, the repertoire of the musicians and the wedding entertainer. The pages of *Poyln* are filled with striking figures: aristocrats and simpletons, Hasidic rabbis with their followers, their enlightened (maskilic) opponents, atheists and even converts, Polish peasants and country girls, Polish gentry and their Jewish counterparts. He has resurrected a whole epoch, a whole peculiar civilization which was destroyed before our eyes.[1]

[1] Letter 'To whom it may concern', New York, 8 Sept. 1978, in the possession of Antony Polonsky.

Two volumes of *Poyln* have been translated in Hebrew (Tel Aviv, 1946, 1953). Apart from the material published here, the only other extracts from the work available in English are the account of his meeting with Peretz in Lucy Dawidowicz's *The Golden Tradition* and 'Łódź Memories', in *Polin*, vi (1991), 262–87. Anna Clarke, who translated the extracts printed here, is preparing a one-volume abridgement of the work which we hope will appear shortly.

A.P.

THE KOSHER PASSOVER WINE

The wedding of my parents provided an opportunity for two great Polish *gaonim* to meet after a period of estrangement. One of the *gaonim* was my father's grandfather Reb Yehiel Kutner, the foremost Talmudic authority of his time. He was the last of the legists and his responsa on the most intricate questions reached every corner of the world. Sefardic Jews from distant Morocco spoke to me with awe about the legend of his name. Reb Yehiel was also loved by the simple folk of Kutno. Common townspeople told stories about the youth and origins of their rabbi, the holy *tsadik*.

His mother Devorah was a poor orphan in Płock, where she made a living selling goods in the market. By standing for long days in the cold and in the heat, she saved a dowry. By then no longer a young girl she went to see the then rabbi of Płock, Reb Lajbish Harif. Showing him her few hard-earned roubles, Devorah asked the rabbi to find her a husband, a Talmudic scholar. He did know a great scholar, a poor *melamed* with a brood of small children. 'Is that poor *melamed* without doubt a great scholar?', the girl demanded. Assured that this was the case, she gladly undertook to marry him and raise his children. She and the *melamed* had only one child, Yehiel Kutner, the *gaon*, my father's grandfather. In his turn, he arranged for the wedding of my father. The wedding became a celebrated event and was honoured by the arrival of Reb Avremele of Sochaczew, also a *gaon*.

Like the Kutner, Reb Avremele was a world-renowned Talmudic authority. His youth, though, was spent in a purely Talmudic and thaumaturgical atmosphere. His reputation as a boy genius reached the rabbi of Kock himself, who by then had become hostile to the world and to people. The rabbi of Kock—known universally as the Kotsker—arranged for the wedding of the boy to one of his twin daughters. Having warned the boy early to keep away from lazy good-for-nothing other Hasidim, the Kotsker was glad to see the young son-in-law sit by day and by night labouring hard over the Torah.

The Kotsker lived in a room where the floor was never swept and no window was ever opened. Big fat mice and obese ugly frogs went about freely and openly around him and waited at the table for crumbs that he threw to them late at night. Because of the young boy's presence, the

Kotsker would sometimes leave his room. He would slouch in, wearing his big boots and torn clothes, and stand near the stove to listen to Avremele reciting the Torah. Some time after the Kotsker's death a splinter group chose Reb Avremele as their rabbi. He was undistinguished as a rabbi: his fame came from being a scholar, and in that hierarchy he took his place beside Reb Yehiel of Kutno.

Although they lived not far from one another, these two famous *gaonim* of Poland saw one another but seldom. *Gaonim* do not travel or visit much. They are deep into their books and keep in touch over great questions and responsa, which are famous in the whole rabbinical world. The two held one another in great esteem and were, so to speak, friends from afar. World authorities in Talmudic matters, they would meet only in great *pilpul* battles and then communicate by letters. Once and once only did a black shadow fall between the two.

The incident happened over the following events, and I wish to tell it as it vividly illustrates Jewish life in the Poland of those times. In a very small town not far from Kruszniewica there lived a Jewish brandy-broker. He owned large warehouses of brandy which he sold to all the taverns of neighbouring villages. Every penny he had was in his brandy. He was a simple man, rustic, like all liquor merchants in Poland. Every Passover the rabbi of the *shtetl* would prepare a sale receipt for him. The entire stock was sold to an old lame Gentile. Year by year for many years the Gentile would listen to the rabbi reading in Hebrew the words of the sale recipt. Early in the morning of the day before Passover he would appear already tipsy to legalize by oath the fictitious Jewish sale. For the great act the rabbi put on a silk coat, a cap edged with fur, and a Sabbath belt, and he prayed and shook as though wishing to penetrate into the very soul of the *goy*. In a loud voice in a special *gemara* sing-song he read the formula of the long receipt.

Tipsily, the Gentile nodded his head, received a few roubles, took off to the tavern, took another bitter drop, and fell asleep in the mud of the *shtetl*, always at its deepest at the Passover season. So it went on for many years and the broker felt secure that all was done as it should be.

One year, on the last day of Passover the rabbi realized that he had written the sale receipt incorrectly. According to the letter of the law the whole fictitious act was thus null and void. The poor *shtetl* rabbi shivered and cold sweat ran under his *yarmulkah*. Think of it! The rich merchant is soundly asleep in his bed dreaming no doubt of the thousands his wares will bring him. In fact, in the course of one night he has become a beggar. All because of him, a *shlimazl* of a rabbi whom the simple man trusted completely. Because of the faulty contract, nothing in the warehouses with their hundreds of barrels of brandy may be used. They may not be sold or made even the slightest use of. Instead, the barrels ought to have the plugs removed and all the brandy should be allowed to flow in rivulets into the puddles of the *shtetl*. Even a Gentile must not be allowed near the streams. For should such a Gentile in his happy fervour remove his cap to the unhappy merchant and say 'Thank you kindly, sir'—then will the merchant have had some satisfaction from the act. Oh, some satisfaction indeed, a thank-you from a drunken yokel. But such pleasure or use of the forbidden brandy is not to be had. The pale frightened rabbi saw the might of the merciless Jewish law coming down on the head of the rich merchant, who at this moment was unaware of the dark Job-like news. To be silent and to keep the bitter secret? Honest piety was very strong among Polish Jews of the time. The mere blaze of the sinful thought in his mind made the rabbi see the hell of Gehenna opening under his feet and the flickering fires burn him for millions and millions of years. The angels of destruction lick their lips in delight. They expect to have a sinful rabbi on their spades and to teach him a proper Gehenna lesson. What a treat! A rabbi, an arch-sinner. The thought of not telling the truth did not enter his mind. The very barrels which were in danger of being used to advantage possessed such inherent impurity that they were begging him to be opened up and poured out in the mud.

After a sleepless night the poor rabbi shivered with dread. He was terrified of the coarse broker, who was quick to anger and capable of anything. Early in the morning of the last day of Passover he put on his worn-out fur cap and the threadbare large fur-lined coat, took a stick with a bony knob, piously kissed the *mezuzah*, permitted himself a sigh, and was on his way to the broker.

They wondered in the *shtetl* why the rabbi was out alone without an attendant, in the market, so early in the morning. Probably trouble with the ritual bath, they reasoned. Things will happen, they sighed. The broker opened the door himself. He had just had his first taste of an after-Passover meal. His cheeks were red from the bowl of cabbage bortsch, the fresh home-made bread and butter tasted especially good after the dry *matsah* which he had had to contend with for eight whole days, the poor thing. He also partook of brandy from his warehouses. In high good humour, he waited for a carriage driven by two sharp black horses to take him to a neighbouring landlord. The sight of the rabbi entering his doorway seemingly out of nowhere startled him. A respectful 'Blessed be he who cometh' stuck in his throat. The rabbi was visibly changed. His face the colour of earth, he stood trembling on the threshold.

'A tragedy, Reb Jankel.'

'What tragedy?', asked the broker. He too felt that his heart missed a beat from a terrible premonition.

'A misfortune. Poverty, Reb Jankel, bitter poverty. You are a naked beggar.'

The dealer blinked and looked at the rabbi still standing at the door. Even the rabbi's beard and sidelocks trembled, and he just managed to hold on to his rabbinical stick. The broker was lost. What poverty? Where from poverty? He thought of fire. But how come a fire? If there is a fire, why do the bells not ring in town? And why in a fire would the rabbi run to him?

'Poverty. Not fit for consumption,' the rabbi shrieked in a strange voice. And still at the door he explained the whole of the tragedy.

The dealer began to understand what had happened. His strong hands used to fighting peasants or moving barrels of brandy ached to hold the rabbi and break him up into dust and ashes. The bloodshot eyes burnt with the fires of hell. The rabbi felt sure that his last hour had come. Fearful and in despair, he held on to the thought, nevertheless, that one is required to tell the truth. Making a noise like an ox before slaughter, the merchant lifted his arms. But he kept them in the air away from the rabbi's jacket. First, he felt a healthy man's dislike towards the body so near his hands. The rabbi's beard and sidelocks were in cold sweat emanating an unpleasant odour. Secondly, he knew also that he was lost and unable to find a way in his present predicament through the deep terrible abyss of Jewish law. Using the inner strength of a simple healthy Jew, he strove for self-control and brought out a question—'What is to be done?'

'We have to go to Reb Avremele. Only he, the *gaon*, might perhaps find a way out.'

Without wasting any time, the broker grabbed the rabbi by his tattered silk coat and easily pulled him outside. The two young horses stood harnessed to the *britzkah*, their manes moving in the wind and their feet kicking the ground. 'To the rabbi,' he yelled at the driver, having first bodily lifted the rabbi from the ground and into the vehicle.

The two were silent the whole of the way. There was the smell of post-Passover season from the fields. The sky was mild, the earth covered by fresh grass and by the first spring flowers. Goslings and ducklings played in the thawed rivulets, now free from ice. The peaceful quiet happiness of the awakened spring countryside only worsened the mood of the broker. The fields were different from the ones over which his carriage with the black horses had taken him so often before when he was merry and pleased with life.

They found Reb Avremele in prayer among his books. The two opened the door without stopping to ask permission to interrupt or to be received. The frail *gaon* was startled. He lifted his head from the Talmud and seeing the anxious faces of the two at the door rose from his leather rabbi's chair and went up to the door.

There and then the rabbi explained the problem, in the full terminology of *halakhah* with all the intricacies of the difficulty. The broker stood at the door in his massive heaviness. The strange thorny Hebrew words were flying about. In their exotic sharpness they were cutting into him like evil knives. There was nothing good for him in those words. Through the fault of the rabbi he had become enmeshed in a confusion of other-worldly matters, strange and forbidding.

Reb Avremele was greatly upset on hearing of the impending ruin of an innocent rich man. His expression told the broker plainly that there was for him no mercy but only law and more law. The *gaon* Reb Avremele pulled out great thick volumes from the bookshelves, books upon books, spread them on the table, looked and turned the pages, read, pondered, searched, then ran nervously around the room in quest of a solution but unable to find one. Then again he took more tomes from the shelves. The table was caving in under the weight of the books. He read again, and ran around the room, now become a courtroom.

The guilty small-town rabbi stood at the door with his head down, afraid to look at the broker, whose face was that of a man sentenced to death. Reb Avremele was conducting a heroic war with the rules. And it was not good. The rules would not let go of an unfortunate Jew, they were bound to ruin him for ever.

Abruptly, the books were closed. Reb Avremele sighed heavily and went up to the *shtetl* rabbi.

'It is not good,' he groaned. 'Listen to me. Go to Kutno to Reb Yehiel.' But here he added with the hard sharpness of a scholar: 'If Reb Yehiel says it is all right, mention the critical glossary.' The broker felt that this glossary was the greatest and the most evil of the angels of death. The other thick volumes were giving in to the power of Reb Avremele and were about to let the unfortunate Jew out of their clutches. Not so the stubborn glossary, it was relentless.

In Kutno they told the story to Reb Yehiel, the *gaon*. Before the rabbi came to the end and without consulting any sources, Reb Yehiel pronounced the brandy kosher. The broker was ready to shout with glee and fall at the *gaon*'s feet, but he saw the rabbi's lips moving. He knew that the evil glossary was about to roll out again and it, the stubborn and evil glossary, his angel of death, would not drop the slaughterer's knife even there, in the *gaon*'s room.

Without daring to look at the broker, once again smelling the sulphur of Gehenna should he fail to say what he was ordered to, the rabbi mentioned the glossary. Reb Yehiel showed not the slightest emotion. 'And does the rabbi of Krishnewitz [Kruszniewica] think that I have no knowledge of the glossary? I do have knowledge of the glossary. No matter. The brandy is kosher, well and truly kosher.'

Imagine what went on later, the banquets, the fat roasted geese, and the drinking in honour of the great miracle. But a black cat ran between the two *gaonim* of Poland. Gossipers talked of slighting words used. Like all people who live in the realm of the spirit, Talmudic scholars are very sensitive when it comes to their dignity. The story of the brandy which Reb Yehiel legitimized out of hand with no great *pilpul* battles and without as much as looking at sources resounded all over Poland. And the relationship worsened between the two Torah study residences—Kutno and Kruszniewica.

Let it be said that the two *gaonim* were very discreet about their feelings, and behaved towards one another with respect and affection. They were looking for an opportunity to make peace. For a long time busybodies around them kept the fires going. At last the wedding of my parents provided the occasion and Reb Avremele came in person to honour the wedding of Reb Yehiel's grandson.

THE SPIRIT AND THE LETTER OF THE LAW

The iron merchant Reb Isaiah Prywes was famous for his wealth. He had six sons and only one daughter, Deborah—Dachele to the family. She was an ailing girl with weak lungs, spoilt both by a doting mother and by a stern father. Taken from one warm resort to another, after years of care and anxiety she reached marriageable age. Matchmakers opened their umbrellas and flew all over the country in search of the best catch in Poland. One bold matchmaker went as far as Frankfurt to the Orthodox branch of the Rothschilds themselves. Reb Isaiah turned his nose up at them all. Yet in the end for the sake of his one and only daughter Reb Isaiah surprised all who knew him.

At that time there lived in Warsaw a rich Jew, Reb Meir Mendelson, not nearly as rich as Reb Isaiah. There will always be one Jew in the world to do a different thing, though, and one of the matchmakers among them proposed Reb Meir as the prospective father-in-law to Dachele.

Nor did the matchmaker come with empty hands. 'Reb Meir has real estate in Warsaw. Loaded with money he is, yet not, God forbid, given to ostentation. "Walk humbly with thy God" is his guiding principle.' The broker wanted to impress this upon Reb Isaiah. 'Yet he is no miser. The Jew in question just holds that charity should be anonymous and he bases this on the Talmud.' Filled with the Torah he is, but he knows that the Torah too prefers privacy and shuns public display. Reb Meir comes from a long line of rabbis. His grandfather was no less a person than the famous rabbi of Warsaw, the Ḥemdat Shelomo!' A pause followed to instil in Reb Isaiah's mind the financial and familial qualifications of Reb Meir. Next came the most important point.

'This same Reb Meir has at home—and keeps it private too—a veritable prodigy, his son Hersheleh. Now, a father with less restraint would show off such a wonder, take the boy to the rabbis' court for display. Not so Reb Meir. Prodigies are no news to him. What's a prodigy among our Jewish boys?' Here the broker stopped to make a suggestion. 'Why not use the boy's abilities as a reason for sending a learned teacher of the Torah to him? He could take a good look at him as a prospective groom.' The matchmaker rested his case. He knew well that Reb Isaiah disliked praise for any rich Jew but himself. The Rothschilds of Frankfurt might be excepted, but then Frankfurt was far from Warsaw.

Reb Isaiah stood silent, in thought. From the next room he heard his daughter talk and then cough the deep, hollow cough of weak lungs. Then: 'I will send an examiner, but I will also go myself to see the boy Hersheleh.' The broker ran all the way to Reb Meir and gave him the message at the door. A man given to restraint, hard and taciturn with a firm belief in humility, Reb Meir was unimpressed. Still at the doorway, he asked, 'How much dowry does Reb Isaiah have in mind? In hard cash, that is.' And to the matchmaker's protest, 'What is this you ask ... the very Rothschilds are sending ...': 'What do I care about the Rothschilds? My only concern is the Talmud and an honest deal. I wish to know all the conditions beforehand ... All must be formally written down, as is the custom among Jews. No rabbinical courts after the fact.' And, in a moment; 'Now, if he agrees, let Reb Isaiah send an examiner.'

A few days later the elegant Prywes carriage drove up to the house of Reb Meir in Nalewki. Old and dilapidated, little shops and stalls filling its yards, the place was bustling. Even the staircase was crowded with men and women shouting, moving about, trading. When they saw Reb Isaiah, the traders pressed against the walls to make room for him and for his party.

The door was opened by Reb Meir. Cold and austere, he greeted them with 'Blessed be he who cometh' and invited them into his large library. This room looked more like a rabbi's study than the library of a wealthy man. Books lined the walls up to the ceiling. The windows were seldom opened, and so the air was damp and smelt of leather bindings and paper. A rabbi's large chair, broken and bound with twine, a brass basin for Reb Meir's ablutions, a bare wooden table laden with more books, and the table of the great rabbi, the Ḥemdat Shelomo were also kept in it. In the one drawer of the table Reb Meir kept an annotated list of his tenants, those who had paid up and those who still owed rent. From the ceiling hung a dusty, tarnished lamp engraved with deer. It had several holders but only half held candles and all of those were half burnt out. It was into this library that Reb Meir took Reb Isaiah and his two companions—the one wearing a bedraggled old alpaca coat and a *yarmulkah*, the other being the earnest marriage-broker. For a while the three men sat in silence around the table.

At last Reb Meir offered a question. 'Do your tenants pay their rent regularly?' he enquired. 'Here,' he went on, 'it takes for ever and a day to collect.' Whether tenants can't pay or won't pay, Reb Meir was not going to check their pockets for an answer. 'Many can't and many won't. In the old days people paid up on time. These days, tenants do not treat the matter seriously, even though it is a clear contravention of the law.'

Soon a small pale boy was brought in. In his shyness he kept his eyes on the floor. Matter-of-factly, Reb Meir said, 'This is my boy, Hersheleh. You wanted to examine him, Reb Isaiah. Examine him!' Hersheleh approached the table. The Jew in the *yarmulkah* asked the boy what he was studying. Hersheleh named a chapter. Quickly a question came. Hersheleh considered a moment and then quietly answered it. The examiner questioned again and again—he didn't let up. Right there, at the Ḥemdat Shelomo's table, a sharp dialectic battle ensued. The examiner shouted loudly in his rasping voice, got up from the table, shook his fists, and at one point grabbed his own beard with both hands. With all his knowledge he tried to corner the boy—they were hunter and prey. The pale boy quietly defended his point and did not give in to the examiner.

Throughout, Reb Meir, hard and taciturn, listened. Reb Isaiah likewise listened in silence. He had seen many prodigies before, all had been sharp and impudent. In similar *pilpul*s on the Talmud they had sprung up like fighting-cocks. Reb Isaiah liked the quiet, modest way Reb Meir's boy defended himself against the fierce attacks of the examiner. He thought of his sick daughter who needed gentleness. Then he thought of the web of intrigues he himself wove at home and the competition of his sons for his favours. The competition estranged him from his children and them from him. He felt a chill in his heart like the driving winter snow. Again he thought of Dachele and turned to witness once more the duel between the examiner and the boy.

The examiner was using his best shots but the boy held firm. At last, he quietened and pinched Hersheleh's pale cheek. Reb Meir took his son by the hand and led him out from the library. Silence fell around the table.

Little was said on the way home. Just before they reached the Pryweses': 'Return to Reb Meir's and tell him that I wish to begin the marriage negotiations at once,' Reb Isaiah instructed.

In the days to come Reb Meir remained detached and controlled. In the engagement document he drew up a number of conditions which had to be carried out word for word. He reiterated his unwillingness to go to rabbinical courts after the deed was done. He therefore wanted everything in the contract to be spelt out in small print, which he claimed again was the Jewish custom. Black on White.

'Without further delay and before any official engagement, I want a third of the whole dowry to be deposited by Reb Isaiah with a third party. The remaining two-thirds are to be divided equally between the two fathers, and we each will keep our share locked up securely in an iron cupboard according to the Jewish custom. Second, presents for the bride and groom must all be agreed on and put down in writing. The groom is to be given a gold watch and chain as part of the dowry and as a safeguard against annulment. The dowry, dresses, nightgowns, bedlinen, all, all must be itemized.'

Mother Shevah Prywes was indignant. 'Bedlinen,' she demanded. 'Does Reb Meir think we would not give Dachele bedlinen for her dowry? Who does he think we are?' 'Who indeed?' agreed the matchmaker, noticing the black silk gown and string of pearls she wore on an ordinary Wednesday. 'Tell Reb Meir that I agree to his conditions,' he was advised by a steady Reb Isaiah. Finally, the engagement took place. An enormous gold watch and chain shook on Hersheleh's waistcoat. A large, costly *menorah* of gleaming silver, a tobacco-box brought from abroad, and an otter hat were sent as wedding presents. Reb Meir remained unimpressed. As each gift arrived, he would check his list and find Reb Isaiah short of his commitments. Once he even sent a woman over to ask how a particular dress for the bride was progressing. Each action was justified by a letter of the Law which demanded it. Strict, Reb Meir was.

More than once the engagement was in danger of being broken. In the face of it all Reb Isaiah kept his counsel and peace. He would think deeply for a while and then advise that he agreed and would do whatever Reb Meir saw fit. But it was noticed how stern he grew with his sons. The nearer it was to the wedding, the more frequent became the visits from Reb Meir's messengers. Meanwhile, the best Warsaw dressmakers brought in dresses for Deborah to try—velvets, silks, the richest French brocades. Crinolines, morning dresses, evening gowns. The wedding-dress itself was heavy white brocade with Brussels lace. The dress for *shul* was of rich black silk. Deborah spent hours at interminable fittings and grew paler and thinner. Shevah Prives was glad her husband had chosen a gentle boy for the frail girl, glad he was wise enough to disregard all obstacles. She knew too that Reb Isaiah had taken Hersheleh to the rabbis' court and said afterwards that the hard bargainer Reb Meir was proud but had much to be proud about.

Right up to the day of the wedding, Reb Meir sent messengers with new demands. He was ticking off items from his list of goods and presents. Finally, word came that the bride had arrived in the hall and the groom was waiting. Still severely sober, Reb Meir put on an overcoat over his satin frock and with several relatives made ready for the walk to the Pryweses'. No horse-drawn carriage had been ordered. Reb Meir disapproved of the use of horsepower when one's feet could do as well.

On the way to Reb Isaiah's the group had to pass a large Catholic church well lit by lamps. To the Jews in the street the stone figures on the walls and in the niches of the church looked like pagan images. A shout rang out from Reb Meir's party. 'Look, look,' cried one of the young men. 'Reb Meir, you have dropped a 500-rouble note.' He bent down to pick it up. 'Do not bow down,' ordered Reb Meir sharply. 'Do not bow down to stone images. Young man, continue at once to the hallway where the bride awaits.' Without a backward glance at the 500-rouble note clearly visible in the lamplight, Reb Meir strode forward.

The sound of the wedding band welcomed them in the hall. Reb Isaiah, in rich festive attire, came out to greet his guests. Reb Meir kept his overcoat. Out came the list once more. Hard-faced, Reb Meir pointed out that it was not yet complete. 'There will be no marriage' he said harshly—'if you, Reb Isaiah, do not at once, now, before the *ḥupah* ceremony, honour your obligations. Fulfil them or Hersheleh returns home with me.'

Equally hard-faced, the proud and wealthy Isaiah Prywes glanced at the list and did all that Reb Meir demanded.

THE ALEXANDROV HASIDIM

The Alexandrov Hasidim in Warsaw were a small group. Yet few as they were, and bitterly poor, they retained the old custom and the gaiety of Vorki. The walls of their dark little prayer-house on Twarda watched successful generations in prayer, beginning with the 'Young Vorker', who himself prayed there at one time. Old walls and objects are important for tradition. They bind us to the past, to its fabric and mood. The passage of time brought no great good fortune—the *shtibel*'s Hasidim remained as poor as their fathers and grandfathers. Time, therefore, mattered little. The waters of Vorker gaiety remained as still as in times immemorial.

The old walls seemed to have had a recipe for longevity. Within them men lived to a ripe old age and prayed together with the young. They were old Warsaw Jews and would not acknowledge any mutations in their city. The appearance of new electric tramways was ignored. The streets and old Jewish yards were still called by names long since forgotten by others. It was enough that some old Jewish shops still stood where they used to and that good Polish mead could be bought in Warsaw for the spirit of the Twarda prayer-house to be sustained.

In the very centre of the busiest trading, somewhere in the furthest back yard in three little dark rooms, a part of Vorki lived on. Some of the members of the *shtibel* came to the benediction party on the Sabbath following my wedding. As grandchildren of Vorki, we were welcomed with the affection for the rabbinical stock still smouldering in the old hearts. At the party the Hasidim of Ger sat around tables, noisy and arrogant. They were the cream of the Warsaw rich and looked down with pity and smiling condescension on the Alexandrov sect, those poor old men allowed to enter the party out of consideration for my family.

Some of these old men were concerned about leaving me all alone in a strange environment. Following their advice, my father engaged Itche Ritkes as a tutor for me. For the groom's family to maintain a *melamed* while the boy was still in his father-in-law's home was the accepted thing to do among the rich. Itche was to have been my tutor and companion and form a link with the Twarda prayer-house and its Hasidim.

Itche Ritkes was one of the noblest souls I have ever known. He was terribly poor, and kept his family by selling lottery tickets out in the streets. The first of every month, when rent was due, was like Judgement Day. How can a poor man in Warsaw be expected to find rent money every month? He lived in fear of the rent-collector, who threatened to appear with a couple of Gentiles to remove his few miserable belongings and put them out in the yard. And yet he was a blessed man. His Hasidism and trust in God were profound, with an intellectual base, free of a traditional form. Gradually we came to trust one another.

At first Itche visited me with trepidation. All his life he'd heard tales told of the wealth of the Pryweses, my in-laws. Running around Grzybów in search of clients for lottery tickets, he saw the walls of their houses and heard the savage hammering in the iron yard behind, the basis of their wealth. He knew of their pride and arrogance and observed the subservience shown to them. For the first few days he acted as though disbelieving the privilege of walking on their floors. As for myself, he knew that I was connected to the Alexandrov *shtibel* and was a grandchild of Vorki, but still the only child of a millionaire and a son-in-law of the Pryweses. Up to now he had only observed rich kids from a distance, with that mixture of awe and revulsion which the poor have towards the well-fed. To his mind, the rich lived like migrant summer birds, spared the bitter struggle for existence. Their kids were spoilt rotten from the day of their birth and exempted from learning and work.

This credo of Itche's was no exposition of social protest, but rather a recognition of the intent and act of the Lord. For consider—the Lord has created Jews, who, unlike himself, do not spend their days trying, with scant visible success, to sell lottery tickets and in constant dread of the rent collector who has the power to put their belongings out in the yard. Then, since the Lord manifestly knows what he is doing, it stands to reason that the outcome is right. This being so, why would the Lord suddenly upset the whole apple-cart and burden the rich, in the midst of their ease, with the yoke of studying the Torah or confuse their minds with a difficult problem of the Talmud? But Jews like this, as carefree as birds, do exist – and may they live to the age of a hundred and twenty. For Itche the arrangement was a clear manifestation of order, if it were possible to discern order through judging God by human attributes. The rich enjoy gorging on food—may they thrive on it. The poor have been given other joys—a difficult piece by our teacher, the scholar Samuel Edels, or a Hasidic tale, a rabbinical problem, a story from Vorki, or—wait for it—a Hasidic celebration. There, there is your turn to feast on a piece of herring and a glass of brandy, with exultation and joy. Not for anything would Itche change places with the rich, quite the contrary. He shuddered at the momentary thought of the Almighty taking him away from the Torah and dumping him on a heavy sack of gold.

When he found out that I could read the small print, and also that I could tell some stories of Vorki, Itche forgot my bourgeois origin. My democratic views and respect for the poor seemed to him like a miracle. Even so, instead of seeing these sentiments as an exposition of my revolutionary sympathies with the Socialist Bund, he put a Jewish Hasidic interpretation on them. He liked that best of all. Soon, in the midst of our studies of the Talmud we would find ourselves in long discourses concerning Jewish things close to our hearts.

In the hard, overcast atmosphere of the Pryweses' home Itche was truly a salvation to me. He stood for much that I missed, the people and the objects of my childhood, now a remote dream. Through the heartfelt Folkism of Grandfather Baruch and of Boba [Grandmother] Chayah I felt a spiritual bond with the poor, whose heroism I have always so deeply admired. This young man who came up every morning without the hallmark of my in-laws—a bold knock at the front door—linked me with my past again. Through him I met the other members of the Alexandrov *shtibel*, Liebka Zakon and Jeremiah.

Judged by the standards of the other *shtibel* members, Liebka Zakon might have been called a wealthy Alexandrov Hasid—in a manner of speaking. The exact nature of his wealth—and his bearing and attire were those of a wealthy man—would be difficult to define. For, put in another manner of speaking, Liebka was in fact a down-and-out pauper. Although the rent collector's tone differed slightly from that used to Itche, the none too subtle hint about belongings out in the yard etc. was identical. What, then, made Liebka a magnate? The reversal of the well-known theme of rags on work-days and riches on the Sabbath. To see Liebka in the street on an ordinary morning was to behold a Warsaw great. His expensive coat with a velvet collar, immaculate. The short greying beard brushed, not a hair out of place. Short boots polished to a hard shine. A cloth cap worn jauntily, Warsaw style. And a walking-stick with a polished head which to those ignorant of Liebka's financial standing must have seemed silver. Just so did he walk, his stroll only occasionally interrupted by a genteel little cough.

Elections for overseers at the *kehile* on Grzybowska had started it all. Liebka's name went up suddenly over the sky of Warsaw, like a golden star. The doors of the rich opened to him. Tsirele Prywes poured tea and served him jam with her own hands. One heard nothing but Liebka this and Liebka that. To be a voter one had to pay 15 roubles in municipal tax per annum per year. Liebka's task was to catch voters, to win them over by means fair or foul, and to see to it that Warsaw was at boiling-point.

Now, was Warsaw indeed stirred up and did he really hold Warsaw by its tail and drag voters to the voting-booths? That's the question. The rich and the candidates for inspectorates believed that the *kehile*'s benches were in Liebka's pocket. And he in turn believed that he could do with the bigwigs just as he pleased.

In those days his wallet was well stuffed and he felt rich. But not for long. Soon the inspectors in their top hats were entrenched. Leibka's wealth melted like snow in the spring. The rent collector resumed his admonitions. All forgot him—but he remembered. He looked upon the red *kehile* building as upon his property and the corpulent inspectors in top hats as existing thanks to him. No one noticed Liebka, but it didn't matter. His coat remained pressed and his boots shone. Occasionally, he would pay the *kehile* a visit to see how things were going in his property and how 'the people' were working. Sometimes he would exchange a few words with Eliezer Prywes, Hirshl Grojman, or even Josele Wegmister. Should one of the very rich assimilated inspectors go by, Liebka would quickly take his hat off.

Such, then, was Liebka Zakon for six days of the week.

On the Sabbath and during holidays he underwent a complete change. All his gentility had gone. In *shtibel* and at home he differed but little from the other Hasidim of Vorki. His satin frock was worn and stained, as was his fur hat. In obedience to the commandment on prohibition of work, his beard was unkempt, the white socks and boots untouched by care. No, it was not the same Liebka. On a Sabbath if you mentioned a name like Prywes or Wegmister he might have acted as though he'd never heard the name before. Definitely not the same man.

The highest point of Liebka's existence came at the time of the Third and Last Meal of the Sabbath, at his home. Home was two rooms and a kitchenette, which he kept, the Judgement Day tribute of Warsaw rent notwithstanding. Two old silver candlesticks, a wedding present, adorned the salon. During their years with Liebka they often carried the sign of being pledged to a pawnbroker. But remembrance of the elections and of his general standing among the Warsaw greats produced miracles, and the candlesticks were saved to grace the gatherings of the Hasidim.

No gourmet feasts, these. Some of the guests would bring a piece of Friday *hallah*, a piece of salted herring. Liebka sat at the top of the table wearing his tattered and stained Saturday outfit surrounded by his munching guests. The holy darkness of the Third Meal became thicker and enwrapped them in the mesh of the Princess Sabbath. They sang *zemirot* and psalms of praise. When it was too dark to see anyone at the table, Liebka told stories about Vorki.

Again and again he told of the last days of 'the Young Vorker' in Warsaw, the time of the *tsadik*'s death. The greatest Warsaw doctors declared themselves unable to deal with the fever which consumed the body. But the Hasidim knew that it was the fever of love, love of God and love of Jews. Then the end was near. The nearest in spirit to the *tsadik* stood around his bed. Candles were lit and psalms for the time of agony were read. The *tsadik* moved his lips. Berish Bialer was closest and he put his ear to the lips. All thought that the rabbi was about to disclose some unknown depth from the Torah. What he said was that a new coat should be made for the boy Moshe. Moshe the orphan performed the lowest duties at the 'Young Vorki's' sickbed. Having said that, the holy rabbi surrendered his soul. Reb Berish Bialer then explained that those words of the late *tsadik* were the deepest Hasidic Torah and that the *tsadik* having pronounced them reached the very depth of the Book.

When it was completely dark in the streets of Warsaw, Sabbath was no more and two little candles were lit. Liebka sang the Havdalah, the Hasidim sang 'Hamavdil', and sometimes caught a little dance. But not always. No hurry to face the world of every day, of the struggle for existence, of the rent collector and his threats. Often they would decide to stay on for the Farewell to the Queen. But what on? The pots were empty and the cupboards bare. Liebka looks through the pockets of his everyday suit. Nothing there but a hard worn nickel. Nobody has any money after the Sabbah has just gone.

The shout goes out, 'Jeremiah!' And a weary Jeremiah wakes up from his nap at the corner and immediately brightens up. 'Jeremiah,' says Liebka gravely, 'this Saturday night we wish to partake of the Farewell meal together. And we could do with a barrel of beer.' Without a word, Jeremiah is out of the room and down the stairs. Remarkable. They none of them have any money and Jeremiah is the poorest of them all. Yet as he leaves they all sit there assured that he will return within an hour laden with bread, fish, and meat, with a *goy* carrying a barrel of beer for him.

A few words now about Jeremiah, another member of the Alexandrov Hasidim *shtibel*. Jeremiah was as much a part of the *shtibel* as its walls and benches. He sat around by day and by night in the hope of a celebration, when even the oldest Hasidim of Vorki would have to come to him, Jeremiah. And then he would demonstrate, with ease and generosity, how to procure brandy and herring and delicacies out of the air.

His trade—to use the designation broadly—was to go around the Jewish yards with a little sack on his back looking up at the windows and crying 'Rags and bones'. However, this trade of Jeremiah's existed largely in theory. In practice he spent all his waking hours at the *shtibel* in wait for a celebration. Only late, late at night did he dare go home. By then his wife was sure to be asleep and thus unable to pour upon his head buckets of curses and complaints over his failure to bring home any money. She herself earned a little by selling vegetables, carried in baskets from yard to yard. When she did catch him she would give it to him in a language to sour all past celebrations in his stomach. Meek as a lamb, he would grab his sack and spend an hour or so crying 'Rags and bones'. His duties fulfilled, he was able to dismiss any further demands of his wife as unreasonable. In excellent spirits he could return to the *shtibel* to anticipate further pleasures.

How, then, did Jeremiah provide for celebrations when he was unable to provide for the needs of his own? The answer lies in his character. He made it his business to know where there was anything left from the Sabbath in the kitchen cupboards. He would then go up and demand food with such an air of command that all resistance was useless. Should a Hasidic wife resist, Jeremiah would evoke all the great names of the notables of Twarda who desired a celebration and had sent him over for that purpose. Against such odds, what chance for a Jewish woman to have a say over the food she had cooked? To denigrate the importance of a religious party? Jeremiah stamped his foot and his crossed eyes were ablaze with anger. And were such a Hasidic wife to say that there was nothing left, the doors of cupboards had the propensity in Jeremiah's presence to open on their own, as did the big ovens where the *tshulent*s were put in. Bakers were more difficult to handle than housewives, and here it occasionally came to blows. But blows could not deter Jeremiah in his sacred task: the *tshulent*s came out of the dark interiors. It was the same with beer when it was needed and there was no money, or it was Sabbath and money couldn't be handled: soon Jeremiah could be seen taking a pledge to the pub. If it was late at night, the innkeeper would be woken up and dragged out of bed to open up, and soon the barrel of beer would be rolling to where it was needed.

In justice it has to be said that Jeremiah took almost no part in these celebrations, ate little, and took hardly a glass of the beer he conjured up with so much labour from the air of Warsaw. On one memorable occasion even a funeral became a field for his talents.

A day came when, in spite of the members' firm belief that one should live on and on, Reb Ali, the founder of the *shtibel*, 'went home to his parents'. His death caused a tremor. How times change! Reb Ali had been with them for longer than anyone could remember and now he was gone. On the day of the funeral the struggle for existence was forgotten and all gathered in the house of the deceased. Jeremiah came to the conclusion that on that one day he need have no fear of his wife. Surely even an ignorant Jewess would be capable of understanding that on the day when an Alexandrov Hasid and a Vorker in law dies it would be unthinkable to take a sack and go around yards crying 'Rags and bones'. He was in a state of great agitation.

At the cemetery on Gęsia hours were passing while Reb Ali's body was waiting for its rites. People sat on benches under the trees, talking. Liebka Zakon was there, of course, and, it being a weekday, looked like a magnate. With the cemetery trees around him, he fell to telling stories of Vorki. Yet again he retold the death of the Young Vorker, and talked of Reb Ali, his generosity towards Hasidim. Time went by. Reb Ali was still waiting his turn for a burial in a Jewish cemetery.

The combined effect of the stories of Vorki and the manner in which people sat under the trees ignited a spark in Jeremiah. It was unseemly for Hasidim to sit around so long on empty stomachs. People tend to become melancholy, and who knows how much longer Reb Ali might have to wait for his turn at the cleansing-board? How did Jeremiah find a way among the graves at the Gęsia cemetery? How indeed. For soon he was going around with a large bottle of brandy offering drinks.

The mood became livelier: after all, it was Reb Ali himself who was being buried. Liebka's tongue loosened, and he told more stories. As the hours went by, Jeremiah's bottle was refilled again and yet again. When the word came that Reb Ali's body was at last being taken in, the congregation was nicely warm and well on the way to being inebriated in a Hasidic way. Liebka Zakon, pointing to the sack of bones now on its way to the cleansing-house, said in his resonant voice that anyone can see that Reb Ali was an Alexandrov Hasid since even his funeral was an occasion for joy. Then Reb Ali was buried. Close by the grave stood Jeremiah with a half-full bottle sticking out from his pocket.

When the earth was being shovelled, the sons of Reb Ali, grey-haired and stooped, said *kaddish*. From among the trees of the cemetery on Gęsia came a shout from Liebka to remember that it wasn't just anybody being buried but an in-law of Vorki, so there should be some real religious fervour in the *kaddish*!

EPILOGUE

A few days before the outbreak of the war I decided to visit Kuzmir (Kazimierz), that unique Jewish *shtetl* not far from Warsaw. On my way there I visited my parents, who were spending the summer in Laski, in the country nearby. My parents' cottage stood in the midst of old Polish woods. We spent a whole day outdoors, under the trees. The darkness, the scent, and the rustle of Polish woods has always reminded me of my childhood days in Dłutów. Now that fear pervaded the air, the memories were especially poignant. My father talked to me at length about his own childhood in Kutno. He knew how to talk vividly and picturesquely, and that day he was in very good form and showed great warmth towards me.

Early in the morning he saw me off at the railway station. When the train moved he remained at the platform, looking until he disappeared in the distance. This was the last time I saw my father. He looked at the train for so long; probably his heart told him that it was for ever. He and my mother died together for *kiddush hashem*, in sanctification of God's name.

The little *shtetl* Kuzmir which I visited next was a miniature of Polish Jewry. Even the landscape around it resembled the title-page of a prayerbook for pious women, a *siddur* with shining silver corners. It brought to mind an engraving etched by anonymous Jewish masters of old in their desire to preserve in Polish earth a relief of what was meant by Poylin.

Kuzmir was a *shtetl* on the banks of the Vistula surrounded by hills and cornfields. The landscape was typically Polish, a cradle of legends and of myths. There was much more to it than met the naked eye—it was higher, and deeper, and darker . . .

Between the hills, dark ravines were planted with nut-trees. Their rustle filled the silence. Walking among them, one seldom felt sad, but seldom was one at peace either. One felt completely alone in total silence, and the outside world was like a dream. Coming out of the dark ravines and into the tranquil Polish cornfields, one came out into Kuzmir. In Yiddish literature it has been described over and over again, in word and song, and with much tenderness and feeling. And Jewish painters too never tired of the subject. The famous market of Peretz's mystical-symbolical drama, where on a particular night Jewish fate is played out in reality or in a vision, is no other than the market-place of Kuzmir. The well, the cloister, the school of Peretz's drama were all taken from it.

No wonder, then, that the heart of a Jewish artist responded warmly when his feet touched the ground near Kuzmir. In the tender, sublime sunlight the crooked streets and alleys were revealed with their old-fashioned dilapidated dwellings. These abounded with Jewish picturesqueness. Something about them resembled old and homely *kiddush*-cups. Or cases for *tefillin*, or bags in which they were carried. Or perhaps even Havdalah-boxes or the tattered prayer-books of pious women. They also brought to mind draughty *sukkah*s or Jacob's tents in exile, those tents so often mentioned in the Bible. In the course of many thousands of years, the tents simply aged and wandered with the Jews into Poland. They brought with them the subdued sunlight of the Sinai desert and of Jerusalem the Blessed. Now Jacob's tents displayed their half-broken little windows in the dark-and-light alleys, and the poor little Jewish shops kept their doors opened to the market square around them.

The market was a battlefield, architecturally, of the Jewish and non-Jewish worlds. Or an ancient religious debate between Jews and priests and dukes, the conflict about the unity of God's name. Except that here, in Kuzmir, the tents of Jacob gained the upper hand over the dukes and priests and surrounded the market with *yiddishkeit*.

An old medieval house was all that was left in the market of the dukes and priests. A blackness and whiteness around its pillared walks and recesses copied the cassock of a Catholic priest–inquisitor. The broad front wall of the house was open like the wall of a Gothic church. Dukes and Christian saints in stone helmets and with crosses and weapons in hand stood in the recesses. They gazed at the market, on the tents of Jacob encircling the *shtetl*. They saw the grey Jews milling, only to disappear in the narrow alleys, the Jewish women and girls standing at the doors of the shops . . .

In the middle of the market stood a well, a legendary object from a story-book. Did it come from an old medieval Christian or an old Jewish house? No one will ever know. Wells are silent. So is the water in their damp depth. If inanimate objects have thoughts, then wells keep theirs to themselves.

A tall tapered rock loomed over the *shtetl* rather like the western wall of the temple, a guarding great shadow. In Kuzmir, all was in the in-between land. Commentary, hint, sermon, and counsel were nothing but trees in the garden of knowledge. The hill might be best described as a Jew-mountain of the world, part of a world-concept which has the same dramatic play repeated everywhere and in all dimensions. When the play is performed in historic dimensions it is called the drama of Jews and *goyim*. The hill to me was a *galut*-Jew: a poor Jew of superhuman size, a wanderer from distant parts, weary and stooped. He had stopped near Kuzmir expecting fellow

Jews to welcome him, a visitor like any other to be taken home for the Sabbath.

The mountain was at its most beautiful when the Queen Sabbath was getting ready to enter the *shtetl*. The twilight of the blessed day became even quieter, nobler, and of a deeper gold than during the six days of work. Jacob's tents were taking a rest in the reddish gold. The women came out to the market in their Turkish shawls, the men in their Sabbath attire. The sunset blended with Jewish clothing. It seemed—almost—that it was not poor Jews and Jewesses who were walking about in the market. King David and Queen Esther themselves are taking a stroll dressed in gold and purple, in dark azure, and in threadbare old clothes.

Only slowly did the Queen enter. She came like Mother Rachel—a low *kupkah* on her head, a Turkish shawl over her shoulders, and a silver-cornered *siddur* in her hands. Sunset on Sabbath eve! Observe the Sabbath! In the Jewish houses, Mother Rachel is about to bless her candles. She gives a loving smile to the Kuzmir Jews and greets them—'*Gut shabbes*, Jews.' And in the smile of candlelight Kuzmir lights up both inwardly and outwardly as though from a hidden flame. Slowly, slowly the tall poor-man mountain puts on Friday-night garments, as though it too needed a dark velvet cloak while waiting for Friday-night services.

Often I'd climb the mountain, there to await the arrival of the Sabbath in the *shtetl*. From above one had the best overview of the interplay of the land Poyln and its Jews. Around and around, as far as they could see, lived the *goyim* among cornfields. Close by the poor-man mountain, on another hill, stood the ruins of a castle. Legend had it that the castle had been built by the Polish King Kazimierz for his queen Esther. A host of Polish and Jewish legends turned the ruins into an enlarged version of Kuzmir. For, a true replica of Jewish life in Poland, the life of the *shtetl* took place on a number of planes, real and imaginary.

It may or it may not have been historically true that the benevolent Polish king had a Jewish queen and that her name was Esterke. In the wondrous blend of Ḥumesh and Rashi which formed the imagination of the Jews of Poland, this legend created an organic colour backdrop. In Kuzmir, the legendary expressed itself best by bringing together the dilapidated Jewish *shtetl* and a good Polish king and his Jewish queen. For where else should the king have built a castle for his heart's beloved if not near the *shtetl* Kuzmir? And where else if not behind the extra-dimensional poor-man mountain?

On early Friday evenings, waiting for the arrival of the Sabbath and watching the *shtetl*, I felt that the queen Esterke was standing beside me on the mountain top. Like me, she too was waiting for the Sabbath. And it seemed to me that her shadow, a golden crown on her head and a festive Turkish shawl over her shoulders, had come out from the ruins of the castle. Esterke looks out to the west side waiting for the sun to settle and for the hour of candle-lighting to be called. The sun inclines deeper to the west. Kuzmir, its tents and its Jews, begins to shine in dark gold, the gold of an old *kiddush*-goblet.

It slowly becomes darker. Queen Esterke returns to her castle, to bless the candles. The poor-man mountain where I stand is in shade, as is the queen's castle. The little windows in the houses of the *shtetl* sparkle with lights and the skies tremble with stars. Observe the Sabbath! It is quiet and holy in the tents of Jacob on Polish earth when the Queen-Sabbath-the Blessed arrives, to *mazel* and to blessings.

In March 1941, two days after landing on American soil, I started to write *Poyln*. The first two pages I dictated to my wife Chana. Then the work took hold of me and I took the pen in my own hand. The seventh volume concludes the series. My *Poyln* was written to be a reflection of objective truth and of a subjective poetic vision of one Polish Jew—myself, in all my unimportance. The books were meant to present 'Poyln' in its essence as a great era of Jewish history. The task of describing its entirety or diversity will have to be left to future generations and their various viewpoints.

What, then, is the meaning of the era of the Jews in Poland in the context of the history of the Jewish people? It is perhaps not presumptuous for me to attempt an answer. If the concept of Jewish history can be said to have had a plastic *Gestalt*, then Polish Jewry, individually or collectively, was the mould which formed it. Such was perhaps the dialectic of their fate and the meaning of their demise. Jewish history had reached in Polish Jewry one of the peaks of its arduous uphill climb.

The beginners, the Jews of biblical times, differed but little in culture and in lifestyle from their neighbours Emun, Moab, and Adun. The Jewish vision had had its prophets, but was as yet not shaped into its human collective. That human being was still no more than a cipher in the eternal Torah.

The Jews had to experience thousands of years of historical trials and bloody and bitter experiences before the inspired Jewish thought took on the flesh and blood of the Jewish person. No longer a prophetic ideal, it became the daily habitat of the Jew, his day and his night, his hope and his sorrow, tragedy and comedy, laughter and tears, his strength and also his weakness. The Jewish world-view became the innermost essence of the Jew's existence.

After many years of experiment and trials, the magnificent idea arose of the mystery of Oneness. The human being prevailed over all jungle powers and primeval forces, what we call in today's parlance, 'states' and 'fatherlands'. The human being devoid of power obtained a form and a *Gestalt*. The embodiment of the powerless *homo* was the Jew on Polish earth. This I came to understand after reading Renan. In the years of the First World War I lived in Geneva. Mine was a lonely life, and I had no friends. It was then that Renan's book on Jewish history came into my hands. All my life I'd been a reader of books, interested in literature and in learning. Reading and learning were in my blood, imbibed in my father's house. One tends to read even more in times of loneliness, as there is time then for the soul to take stock. When the ears hear little, the soul is prone to settle accounts. It is probably engaged in settling accounts at other times too, when we are so busy listening to other sounds that we are deaf to the soul's language. When I first read Renan's book on Jewish history, it made a great impact on me.

The great French Hellenist attempted to throw light on the meaning of Jewish history. Renan lost no love on the Jews, great though he perceived them to be. Compared with the clear-sighted sober Greeks, the Jews seemed to be genius-inspired but blind barbarians, tossed about and exploited by history, until Christianity, that most beautiful fruit of their fate, was squeezed out of them. Then, as a tree bereft of its juices is left barren, so were the Jews abandoned, an eternal shadow in the further play of generations.

Thus Renan on the development of Jewish history. He failed to understand —or refused to understand—that it is precisely the later, Christian era which most distinctly and tragically expressed the symbolism of the history of mankind, the hopes, the will, the dreams, and the tragedies of humanity. *Not Jesus on the Cross of Golgotha, but the Jewish folk on the Cross of the world epitomizes the tragic epos of the eternal struggle of the earth with the skies.* And of the history of the Jewish folk, the Jew of Polish earth was endowed with the most beautiful attributes of powerless humanity.

Powerless humanity was revealed by Polish Jews in its splendour and in its grotesqueness, strength and weakness, self-denial and lust. It was looked at from above, from the realms of the spirit, and also from the nether land of bodily passions. It had been the unique achievement of this community to create a Sabbath of powerlessness which totally encapsulated its own experiences, both negative and positive, worldly and spiritual.

The smallest movement of his hands, the muscle-play of his face, the minutest detail of his clothing—all were subordinated to the discipline of a style. They were the manifestations, a strong formal recognition of a distinctive culture, a lifestyle, a unique view of the world, and of an inner responsibility for the world. The form was consonant with the quiet lyric and romantic genre of the Polish Jew, in tune with the rhythm and sing-song of his Yiddish. That language, though stylistically modest, possessed a wonderful ability of self-expression due to a richness of nuances and a variegation of scales.

The multi-faceted Jewish life in Poland was tied together by the style of oneness, in the style of many-sided unity of the godhead, for what is style if not unity in diversity? And, in addition, the old idealistic, prophetic, and future-orientated spirit continued to burn in the souls of Polish Jews. It went hand in hand with a cultural this-worldly orientation, and the spirit bridged the different and opposite forms of the consciousness of Polish Jews.

Internal Jewish conflicts were sharp and bitterly fought. The old generations warred over trifles. A butcher somewhere in a *shtetl* was an excuse for a prolonged fight. Modern times brought new needs, which literature headed by Peretz and socialism with the Bund at its helm carried to the masses, there to unearth new sources of creativity. The conflicts and battles between the old and the new raged like storm-winds inside an old and fragrant wood. The national spirit of the Jewish people flamed up like a prophetic fire in people whose feet were already in the abyss of final destruction. And it seemed—rather than coming to their last days, they were just beginning the Jewish road in the world.

In the last summer before the Second World War, under the black terrible skies, the hearts of Polish Jews were heavy with premonitions of doom. And still, they knew how to turn these forebodings into a feeling of confidence. They learnt through severe trials how to cope with hot and cold without ever giving up hope. Despair which turns into confidence is perhaps a part of the process of the drama of the oneness of the world, a play performed with so much feeling in the depth of the Jewish soul.

PART II

Reviews

REVIEW ESSAYS

Why Did Assimilation Fail in the Kingdom of Poland between 1864 and 1897?

STANISLAUS A. BLEJWAS

IN the aftermath of the January Insurrection, the Warsaw Positivists articulated a democratic vision of a modern Polish nation. Responding to Tsarist Russification policies, the positivists envisaged society as a harmoniously integrated social organism embracing peasants, *szlachta*, the nascent middle class, women, and Jews. The broadening of the concept of nation to include groups previously apart or on society's margin was to be achieved in the case of the Jews through their assimilation into Polish society. At the same time, assimilation was being discussed and prominently advocated by a small number of Polish Jews. This issue is discussed in an outstanding recent book by Alina Cała.[1] Cała shows that the question of assimilation for Polish Jews was much more complex than sympathetic Polish liberals could have imagined, touching the very nerve of individual self-identification for the largest non-Polish autochthonous group inhabiting the Congress Kingdom. Ultimately, it also raised searching questions about democracy and tolerance in Polish political culture and about Polish nationalism.

Cała's work spans the defeat of the January Insurrection until approximately 1897, when new mass political parties and movements like Zionism, the Bund, National Democracy, and the Polish Socialist Party were constituting themselves as changing social, economic, and political conditions compelled proponents of assimilation to battle not only the Orthodox Jewish community, Polish public opinion, and the authorities, but new ideologies. Dividing her work into two parts, Cała examines first the diversity of attitudes and programmatic positions towards assimilation within the Jewish community, then those of Polish society, including conservatives, positivists, and antisemites. Finally, the author reflects upon the failure of assimilation

[1] *Asymilacja Żydów w Królestwie Polskim (1864–1987): Postawy, konflikty, stereotypy* (Warsaw: Państwowy Instytut Wydawniczy, 1989); 408.

to find broad support in either society, and the consequences of this for subsequent Polish–Jewish relations.

Formidable factors inhibited assimilation. The changes brought on by capitalism, especially the development of competing middle classes, the policies of the partitioning powers, the persistence of the deeply rooted religious and cultural distinctiveness (*polskość* and *żydowskość*) of both societies, and the prejudice and discrimination that Polonized as well as Russianized Jews encountered, were daunting obstacles which the accompanying psychological stress of assimilation further burdened. Furthermore, unlike German Jews, those in the Polish lands could assimilate into either Polish, German, or Russian culture, a choice with immediate ramifications for relations with their neighbours. The rapid population increase in the late nineteenth century and the influx of Litvaks reinforced inhibitions against assimilation.

Assimilation was rare until the end of the eighteenth century, and associated with conversion. The Haskalah loosened this link, and by the eve of the January Insurrection a handful of assimilationists were an element on the political scene. Polish society took notice. Democrats favoured equality of rights (*równouprawnienie*), while conservatives toned down their anti-Jewish campaign. Despite this episode of Polish–Jewish brotherhood in the patriotic atmosphere preceding the Insurrection, within the Jewish community, where the question of assimilation was directly pertinent, the 'progressives' were a minority. Orthodox Jewry, which was culturally and linguistically distinct and strongly integrated under rabbinical leadership, and which possessed its own self-governing organs, was resistant to change and ill-disposed to the assimilationists, who were identified with modern and secular currents. Conversely, the assimilationists objected to what they considered to be the fanatical behaviour and backward customs of the Orthodox, and fought them for control of the Jewish community, dominating the Warsaw community from 1867 until the Orthodox revival at the century's end.

Assimilationists were not unified around a single programme. Chaim Zelig Słonimski's Hebrew-language *Hatsefirah*, founded in 1862, offered a moderate programme, popularizing learning and secular social activism as paths to acculturation, while respecting Jewish religiosity and family ties and condemning atheism and the ostentatious violation of the principles of Judaism by assimilationists. While believing that the 'Jewish question' could be solved by close relations with the host society, *Hatsefirah* propagated a minimum programme, suggesting linguistic assimilation and participation in European culture. Articles about Polish culture, such as appeared in the rival *Izraelita*, were not found in *Hatsefirah*, although Cała describes Słonimski in his family life as 'a Polonizing Jew attempting to preserve elements of tradition and religion'. (p. 43).

Izraelita, founded in 1866 and edited by Samuel Hirsz Peltyn, voiced the aspirations of national assimilationists, the 'Poles of the Mosaic faith'. Peltyn, advancing the superiority of Polish culture, advocated cultural and linguistic Polonization while remaining Jewish in religion. *Izraelita* accepted the use of Hebrew for religious worship, and opposed Yiddish, which, it argued, prevented Jews from drawing closer to Poles. *Izraelita*'s programme often paralleled Warsaw Positivism, sharing an initial optimism about the progressive evolution of civilization, the power of learning, and integration into Polish society. The journal also endorsed the restructuring of Jewish society (i.e. a reduced presence in commerce, and increased presence in agriculture, finance, industry, and in the proletariat). Possessing, like the positivists, a deep faith in secular learning, the assimilationists also criticized traditional religious influences in education, in effect isolating themselves from the Orthodox and Hasidic communities, attacking what they considered to be obscurantism and backwardness.

Finally, there were the radical assimilationists, those who broke entirely with Judaism and the Jewish community. They left no programme, and the reasons for their decisions are matter for speculation—perhaps a desire to escape poverty or marry a Christian, frustration with the legal limitations upon Jews, or a desire for social mobility. Moderate assimilationists and Poles of the Mosaic faith condemned such heretics, while the neophytes did not escape the suspicions of Catholics and antisemites.

Assimilationists confronted an array of bewildering questions. Language was a particularly divisive issue, as indicated by the opposition of the Poles of the Mosaic faith to the Yiddish literary revival. Assimilationists prominent in the socialist movement saw revolutionary activity as a road to Polish society and an attempt, as it was for other assimilationists, to find an answer to the ancient question about the role of the Jew in a society. Participation in socialism was, for Jewish socialists, an opportunity to achieve an open society as quickly as possible. In general, as Cała notes, the assimilationists believed in their mission and in the power of education and science, considered themselves progressive and tolerant (although they were not in relation to what they considered to be the community's obscurantist elements), and believed in human brotherhood. But were there Polish Christians who believed that Poles and Jews could live together based upon mutual respect for equality of rights and privileges?

The assimilated Jew challenged the traditional Polish image of the Jew's place in the social hierarchy. Conservative Catholics resisted equality of rights and social integration, the consequences of assimilation, and remained suspicious of the assimilationists. Some, identifying Jews with liberalism and atheism, and seeing a threat to the 'purity' of the Faith, embraced antisemitism. Kraków's *Słowo* was the exception among the Catholic press.

It was the positivists who embraced assimilation almost without reservation. The integration of the Jews into Polish society would strengthen the nation by providing an ally against Tsardom; the Jews, known for their productivity, would fulfil the role of a middle class; and compulsory secular education would liquidate class and religious antagonism, leading to Polonization. The positivists, however, as Cała acutely notes, viewed assimilation instrumentally, from the point of view of Polish national, not Jewish, interests, about which, with the exception of Orzeszkowa, they knew little. Warsaw Positivism, as an expression of Polish national survival, was consistent within the political logic of partitioned Poland. However, to most Jews it might well appear little different from the Russification imposed upon the Poles. In a very careful analysis of the positivists, Cała finds that they were xenophobic regarding difference (*inność*) and separateness (*odrębność*). The fact that some later gravitated toward the Endecja is not as inconsistent as it first appears. The positivists broadened the concept of nation, but at the same time it was a narrow vision. In 1931 Świętochowski reflected on his youthful liberalism of the 1870s: 'Then I admit only to the name of an evolutionist in philosophy and a national humanist in sociology. For this reason, fifty years ago, I defended Jews when they wished to be Poles, and for these same reasons I do not defend them today, when they wish to be Jews, enemies of Poles.'[2]

If the inner logic of Polish liberalism contained within it the seeds of xenophobia, what were the prospects for democracy and future Polish–Jewish relations?

The sentiment within Polish society to hasten national assimilation (i.e. Polonization) of Jews intensified after the pogrom of December 1881, which, not incidentally, also spurred on Zionist sentiments among Polish Jewry. The pogrom also raised the question as to whether assimilation was the answer to the 'Jewish question', stimulating Polish antisemitism, as witnessed by the founding of Jan Jeleński's *Rola* in 1883. Cała explores the antisemitism of Jeleński, Jan Ludwik Popławski, and of Roman Dmowski, who either rejected or doubted the efficacy of assimilation while injecting racism, paranoia, and antisemitism into the emerging mass political culture. Dmowski's legacy was not only the mobilization of resources for the noble aim of independence; it was also the rooting of antisemitism in modern Polish politics.

While assimilation increased towards the end of the century, it failed as an ideology. Understanding why provides a better understanding of Polish culture and the character of modern Polish–Jewish relations. In neither community did the advocates of assimilation speak for the majority of their

---

[2] Aleksander Świętochowski, *Wspomnienia*, ed. Samuel Sandler (Warsaw, 1966), B6.

community. The social and economic emancipation of the well-integrated Orthodox majority, which wished neither to Polonize nor to emigrate, was of colossal significance. The hostility of assimilationists towards a group they regarded as a medieval relic cut them off from a potential base. The assimilationists appreciated neither the Orthodox sense of self-worth and esteem nor their problems, looking upon the Orthodox from the point of view of the positivists. They were confronted by the fact that Jewish culture did not disappear, but blossomed. Furthermore, by the century's end new political alternatives—socialism, especially the Bund, and Zionism— emerged. Polish society for its part was shocked by the emergence of Jewish nationalism and national self-identity, while, as Cała notes, the concept of identity as a Polish Jew only appeared in the new century. While the feudal social structure passed, society had not, despite the traditions of the Commonwealth, matured to the point of accepting the modern concepts of equality of rights and of equal coexistence of different cultures on one territory. One of the unfortunate consequences of the partitions was the embedding of ethnocentricity as a dominant trait in Polish national consciousness. Antisemitism was a xenophobic expression of this ethnocentricity, which, paradoxically, imprinted even deeper the picture of the Jew as a determinant of Polish consciousness, making 'the Jewish question ... an integral part of the Polish complex' (p. 342).

While assimilation appeared to be a progressive approach to the role of the Jew in Polish society, it foundered upon peculiarities unique to the history of Poles and Jews and upon some tenacious inconsistencies. A short review does not do justice to the depth and breadth of this excellent balanced and objective study, which includes an extensive bibliography, an index, and illustrations. Cała's exploration of the assimilation of the Jews in the Kingdom of Poland not only presents the complexities confronting the Jewish communities of the Congress Kingdom; it offers important insights into modern Polish nationalism hitherto unavailable because of the previous official resistance to the study of Polish Jewry. The work is a major addition to the scholarship of Polish–Jewish relations. Its results should be incorporated into new histories of modern Poland if there is to be a fuller understanding of Polish–Jewish relations, and should be made available in other languages.

In the Shadow of the Facts

DARIUSZ STOLA

DAVID ENGEL's book *In the Shadow of Auschwitz: The Polish Government-in-Exile and the Jews, 1939–1942*, appeared in 1987.[1] Although the period since that date has seen a revival of Polish Jewish studies and a growing interest in the government-in-exile, the book has not yet received, as it should have, a review in Poland. It is without doubt one of the most important publications on the subject of Polish Jewish history, and is also of value to those interested in other aspects of the period of the Second World War. This does not mean that one has to accept all the author's views. On the contrary, a number of the judgements he makes are, in my opinion, controversial, unsubstantiated, or biased. In this review I concentrate on those theses and arguments of the author with which I disagree. The areas on which my critique concentrates constitute only part of the book and do not affect my positive general assessment of it. It is certainly the product of extensive and impressive research. The author has worked in eleven Polish, Israeli, British, and American archives in London, Tel Aviv, Jerusalem, and Stanford. His bibliography includes 40 periodicals, 103 collections of documents, and 141 other books and articles in six languages. One would be hard pressed to find another monograph on Polish Jewish history with such a wide source-base. The book's scholarly underpinning is also impressive: endnotes fill 90 pages while the index comprises another 17.

In the preface the author states that his subject is the thinking of Polish leaders in exile on the subject of Jews, and above all the political guidelines followed by the Polish government on this subject. The book is the first part of a work which embraces the war years, and Volume II, *Facing a Holocaust*, appeared in 1993. This first volume ends in December 1942 with the declaration of the Allied governments and the Polish statement which together revealed to the world the news that the Nazis were carrying out the extermination of Jews.

Chapter I describes Polish–Jewish relations in the interwar period. In preparing this chapter the author has relied mostly on the research of other

[1] (University of North Carolina Press: Chapel Hill and London, 1987).

historians, and he refers most often to the work of Emanuel Meltzer, Celia Heller, and above all Paweł Korzec. His picture of Polish–Jewish relations focuses on one of its dimensions, that of conflict. To describe these relations the author frequently uses words such as 'war', 'battle', 'enemy' (in at least eleven places); it is much harder to find 'civilian' terminology. As is evident from the following chapters, this approach conditions the author's hypotheses in the main body of the work. It serves to confirm the durability and strength of the image of the 'Jew-enemy' of Poland among the Polish politicians in exile. For the author, this image is the '*leitmotif* of Polish–Jewish relations during the two decades of Poland's independence' (p. 124).

While it is right to seek to analyse the elements of continuity in Polish–Jewish relations from the interwar period to the war years, this stress on mutual animosity is at least debatable. Why and in what way did these specific opinions of the Nationalist right-wing elements of the Polish political spectrum dominate the thinking of the government-in-exile? Which of the politicians in exile (apart from a few Nationalists) expressed such convictions? I would argue that much more general and of greater consequence was the belief in mutual difference, in the 'foreignness' of Jews, and in the divergent nature of their political aims.

One can cite many examples of Polish–Jewish political conflicts in the two decades between the wars: Polish Jews were more than once unfairly treated in their own country. There is then no need to cite doubtful arguments on this question. Thus Engel goes too far in presenting, as evidence of a *deliberate* anti-Jewish policy by the Polish government, not only the clearly anti-Jewish law limiting ritual slaughter or the law of citizenship of 1938 but also the heavier taxation of the urban population and the issue of Sunday rest, neither of which was specifically directed against the Jews.

Chapter II deals with the first year of the Polish government-in-exile, first in France and then in England, until the Government's publication on 4 November 1940 of its declaration on the Jewish issue. Chapter III, spanning the period until the summer of 1941, is organically connected with the previous chapter, as it presents the breakdown of the strategy of co-operation and the subsequent deterioration of Polish–Jewish relations. The description of relations between the second half of 1941 and the end of 1942 is to be found in the first part of Chapter IV. In effect, Government contacts with Jewish organizations from the German attack on the USSR to the end of 1942 are dealt with much more briefly than the events of the first two years of the war.

This part of the book undoubtedly repays close reading. It is the first systematic analysis of the subject, and has, in many respects, a pioneering character. The presentation of the more important facts, problems, and biases in Polish–Jewish relations abroad fills an important gap. Engel is skilful in presenting the set of considerations which influenced the policies of the government with regard to the Jewish question. These included (1) the need to present a liberal image in the eyes of the West, partly in order to uphold the claim to the 1938 frontier in eastern Poland; (2) the possibility of the Jews proving a help or, alternatively, a hindrance in this context; (3) the Polish belief that the Jews had or did not have real influence on the Allies, the fears of exiled politicians about the reaction of the Poles in Poland to the adoption of a pro-Jewish stance, and suspicions about the real intentions of the Jews.

One might add to this list two other points. In the first place, Sikorski's administration was a coalition Government of National Union. The presence in it of both Socialists and Endeks made it difficult to adopt openly pro- or anti-Jewish positions. Hence the importance of compromise, of tactical considerations, and of the attitude of Stronnictwo Ludowe (the Peasant Party), which had greater flexibility on this issue. Secondly, Jews were not the only or even the most numerous minority in interwar Poland. The position of the Jews was dependent on general attitudes to the question of minorities. For example, the widely acknowledged betrayal of the German minority made more difficult the advocacy of the principle of legal protection of the rights of minorities.

To some events the author pays surprisingly little attention. For example, the appointment of a Jew, Ignacy Schwarzbart (a Zionist), as the only representative of national minorities in the Rada Narodowa (National Council) was an important government decision and should have warranted comment. Apart from the question of budgetary proposals in the spring of 1941, the activities of the Jewish representative on the Council are not sufficiently presented.

At the beginning of the war, it was widely believed in Polish circles that the collapse of Germany and the rebuilding of the Polish state were inevitable, and likely to occur soon. The possibility of the total annihilation of Polish Jewry never entered anyone's head. The question of help for Jews under German occupation, we learn from the book, was not a subject for Polish–Jewish talks. Discussions between the government and Jewish organizations (mainly Western) concentrated on the future, especially on the question of a declaration on Jewish rights in the re-established Poland. In spite of strong demands from American and British Jewish organizations, the government refused to commit itself to a specific declaration supporting Jewish rights, referring to its general declarations on the republican and democratic character of the future Poland.

According to the author, the government was influenced to change its position and issue such a declaration by the weakening of its international position after the fall of France, by its more frequent turning to America, by its increased sensitivity to attacks by the Jewish press in London, and by the participation of Polish Jews in demands for a declaration. These factors may have played a certain role. There are, however, no sources which entitle us to regard them as decisive. The stress that the author has put on this view seems to be based on his belief that those steps that the government took *vis-à-vis* the Jews which can be assessed positively were the fruit of government weakness and effective pressure.

The declaration which Minister Stańczyk made on 4 November 1940 in the name of the Polish government promised the Jews, as Polish citizens, equality of rights and responsibilities and the freedom to pursue their religion and culture. It was, in the eyes of the Poles, a gesture of good will. It was no doubt anticipated that similar conciliatory gestures would be made by the Jewish side, that the declaration would be the beginning of that co-operation and support from Jewish organizations and the Jewish press in Great Britain and the United States which was so needed by the government. Jewish politicians also saw the declaration as a beginning, after which further steps should be made by the Polish side. An improvement in relations between the Jewish organizations and press and the government did not take place. The sincerity of the declaration was called into question, and attacks on individual politicians and the government did not slacken. There was, moreover, no reaction to the Poles' expressed hope for support on the issue of Poland's eastern border.

This constituted a fiasco for the strategy of co-operation and mutual acts of good will; one can understand that in 'Polish London' the supporters of this line of policy lost the initiative. As proof, one might cite the rejection by the Rada Narodowa of Schwarzbart's resolutions calling for the nullification of pre-war discriminatory laws and regulations against Jews. Engel outlines the arguments which were put forward by the Nationalists in the discussion of these matters, but it seems that it was not these arguments but rather the political considerations we have described which influenced their rejection.

More than half of Chapter III is devoted to presenting contemporary Jewish and Polish opinions on the subject of their mutual relations and on the policies of the government. The author's conclusion is that both sides exaggerated. No one could argue with such a moderate and careful opinion, even if it leaves one with a feeling of frustration and curiosity: which of the opposing opinions most approximated to the truth? It seems particularly significant that many of the opinions criticizing the government do not come from the private diaries of Jewish politicians but are contained in political documents and public statements. It would not be hard to point out that besides fully justified reproaches there were many which were patently without real justification. If one wants to understand the reactions of Polish politicians and not succumb to total relativism in assessing the validity of the arguments used by both sides, one should form an opinion on the strengths and weaknesses of these different arguments.

It is strange that the author barely mentions the World Jewish Congress's delegation to the British Foreign Secretary Eden on 1 May 1941. This was perhaps the most important intervention of this organization on the subject of Poland. Members of the Congress presented a long memorandum which, under twenty-five headings, outlined its objections to the behaviour of the government of Poland. The view that most of these criticisms were unfounded is not difficult to uphold—as was done at the time, e.g. in the minute attached to the document by a clerk in the British Foreign Office. For example, the case of the newspaper *Jestem Polakiem* [I am a Pole] was a pretext rather than the reason for the wave of attacks in the press and the British Parliament; the picture of a Jew-baiting newspaper representing a threat to Great Britain and at the same time supported by members of the Polish government did not have much in common with reality. It is a pity that the author confined this information to a note (n. 127). On the other hand, in the main text we can find a very controversial attempt to gauge the real intentions of the government (p. 75). Using a dubious interpretation of the words of one of the ministers, the author suggests that Sikorski's government did not believe in its declaration. Its real stance is to be found in a note whose authorship is unknown, setting out the Endek point of view of the character of the Polish state and the question of minorities.

To the most important political declaration of the government of Sikorski (that of 24 February 1942) the author devotes only one sentence, with the sole aim, it seems, of pointing out the critical reaction to it from the Jewish side. The declaration proclaimed the democratic and republican character of the future state, and its intention to uphold the rule of law and respect the liberties and rights of the citizen, equal rights and responsibilities for minorities, and their freedom of political, cultural, and social development. One is astonished that Engel simply writes off this declaration as 'purportedly democratic'. Why 'purportedly'?

The importance of the appointment of a second Jewish representative to the Rada Narodowa is overshadowed in Engel's presentation by the demands and disputes which accompanied it. This step by the government, which in my view should be seen as a positive move, is (with the declaration of 24 February 1942) presented in a paragraph which states that 'Jewish organizations were encountering further points of friction with the London regime' (p. 122). In November 1941 the president of Poland partially abrogated the law of citizenship of 1938, thus realizing one of the more important Jewish aspirations of the years between 1939 and 1941. Engel's view of the significance of this development is revealed by his relegation of it to a note (n. 130).

Engel explains the negative attitude of Polish politicians towards the Jews by the revival of anti-Jewish sentiments, especially in the form of the image of 'Jew—enemy of Poland'. The negative attitudes of Jewish politicians he attributes to their bad experiences in the past. Without underestimating the prejudice of Polish politicians, which existed and certainly played a part, it has to be said that there was some real basis for their irritation with Jewish behaviour. The fiasco of the initiative embodied in the declaration of 4 November 1940 confirmed the belief that the satisfaction of one Jewish claim would lead to further demands and not to reciprocal gestures. It must be noted also that the boundary between prejudice and beliefs based on experience is not well defined. The inclination to irrational motives is, of course, not related to nationality. One could argue that at this stage of Polish–Jewish history Jewish politicians became, like their Polish counterparts, the victims of their own prejudices. The chance (in so far as it ever existed) of a change of relations was also weakened by the image of 'implacable Polish antisemitism'.

Chapters II and III mostly deal with the attitude of the government towards the Jewish question, while Chapter IV (Russia) examines policy towards Jews, namely Polish Jews in the USSR. It deals, above all, with the functioning of the Polish apparatus of social welfare in the Soviet Union, the recruitment and treatment of Jews in the ranks of Anders's Army, and their evacuation to Persia. Engel presents the achievements of the apparatus of social welfare as well as the complaints which Jews made against it. The balance of judgement of the actions of the Polish embassy in the area of care to Polish citizens in the heart of Russia must be decidedly positive. In such a large-scale and difficult action certain abuses were, it would seem, unavoidable. Jewish representatives in the West, almost from the start of the action in Russia, suspected the government of a lack of good will and often gave voice to these suspicions. The author explains their complaints about the embassy apparatus as a consequence both of bad past experiences and of the poor behaviour of the army authorities.

The suspicious and often hostile atmosphere towards Jews in the ranks of the Polish army in the USSR is well known, and probably no one who has consulted the documents will deny it. There is also evidence of the prevalence of this same attitude among the officers, in recruitment boards, and so on. Engel has focused his attention on the attitude of the Army Command, especially of General Anders. His basic assessment of the aims of Anders can be summarized as follows: not to allow Jews into the ranks of the army, to remove those who had somehow managed to enter it, and not to allow their evacuation from the USSR. The exception was a small group of Jews kept 'for propaganda purposes'. It seems that the author has adopted, without the necessary degree of criticism, the picture of Anders the antisemite.

I do not think that in discussion with a delegation of Polish Jews on 24 October 1941 Anders 'made it clear that he did not want' Jews from eastern Poland under his command (p. 133). Referring to Jews who had 'ostentatiously and gleefully greeted the invading Soviet army' in Poland in 1939, he tried to explain the hostility of many Poles in Russia towards the Jews, but he also stressed several times that he would not tolerate antisemitism and that the same principles should be applied to all Polish citizens.

Documents presented as evidence that, from the middle of October 1941 or earlier, Anders tried to limit the number of Jews in the army (p. 134) say nothing on the subject. Ambassador Kot speaks of 'military men (*wojskowi*) like Pstrokoński', and not of military leaders—as in Engel's translations. Another of Kot's quoted statements says something completely contrary to Engel's assertions: '[Jews] are usually accepted into the army if they volunteer, and when I explained to him [Anders] their ties with America, he promised to stress the need for their favourable treatment. He also asked for Schorr as army rabbi'.[2]

The startling claim that Anders 'sought Soviet assistance in preventing Jewish enlistments' (p. 134) is based on the diary of Anders's ex-adjutant, described by Karol Popiel, not without cause, as a pathological liar. On page 137 he repeats the assertion in a new form, claiming that in January 1942 Anders 'renewed his call to the Soviet authorities to cooperate in the curtailment of Jewish enlistment'.

Anders's note 'Sprawa żydowska' [The Jewish issue, 1 September 1939–1 August 1942] dates from at least a year later than the events to which Engel refers (p. 133). It was written after the attacks on Anders by the Jews, which no doubt contributed in large measure to the hostility to them reflected in its pages.

On page 138 Engel writes:

The Soviet restriction upon Jewish recruitment of Jews did, of course, provide the Poles with a convenient means for covering up their own attitude towards Jews in their army ... To the Poles' great chagrin, however, the Soviet authorities do not appear to have been especially concerned with enforcing the rule that they imposed ...

We also learn that the Poles did not oppose the Soviet restriction because they did not want the Jews in the army, even though this policy undermined their rights to the eastern borderlands. For similar reasons, Anders did not

---

[2] S. Kot, *Listy z Rosji do Gen Sikorskiego* (London, 1955), doc. 2, p. 82.

counter restrictions imposed by the Soviet authorities on the evacuation of Jews: 'Perhaps he feared as well . . . it would be harder for him in the future to reject the many Jews that he did not in the event wish to take along' (p. 146). It seems that the author overestimates the blind hatred of Polish politicians for the Jews. One would also like to have some documentation of 'the Poles' great chagrin'.

The sources do not give as definite a picture as that provided by Engel. It is true that the government did not take an unequivocal enough stance in the Polish–Soviet dispute over non-Polish citizens of Poland, but its motives were more complicated than Engel suggests. Sikorski wrote to Anders:

I sincerely regret that the Soviet government does not want, at any price, to release Jews of Polish citizenship from the USSR. This, though, should not be allowed to inhibit the exodus of the army and the families of soldiers from the USSR. We should not provoke the Soviets with this problem and arouse new frictions. I will notify the British and American governments.[3]

Probably the directive to sacrifice a 'part' was easier to accept as the 'part' left in Russia were the Jews. Sikorski's words do not show the government in a light that would appeal to its apologists, but they also do not fit the picture created by Engel.

The book often cites reports by Jews who were both witnesses and also victims of the events in Russia. According to them, for example, the orders to remove Jews from evacuation transports always came from the Polish command, never from the Soviet authorities (p. 141). We must remember that the NKVD consciously incited such feelings, calculated to exacerbate the Polish–Jewish antagonism which in large measure contributed to the prevalence of the view that the Poles and not the Russians were the main culprits in the tragic fate of Polish Jews in the USSR (which the author mentions on p. 146). One should treat this information as carefully as that coming from the sources that present Anders in a better light. The restrained way that Engel expresses himself on these materials is illustrated by the sentence, 'it is not impossible that the Polish commander, despite his continuous efforts to reduce the number of Jews in the ranks of his forces, wished to see at least some Jews removed from Russia' (p. 143).

More could also be said about the so called Anders order of 30 November 1941. The author is convinced of the authenticity of this document. He concedes (in a note) that Anders himself called it a forgery, but makes it clear that 'ample evidence has been adduced to prove its genuineness'. Yet there are some doubts as to its authenticity. Anders categorically denied its authorship, not only to the Jews but also to his superior, General Sikorski.

---

[3] Quoted in Krystyna Kersten, *Polacy, Żydzi, komunizm: Anatomia półprawd 1939–1968* (Warsaw, 1992), 53.

The issue was investigated by Colonel Bąkiewicz of the Dwojka (Intelligence Corps), who confirmed Anders's words. The inclusion of the order in Kot's book is not conclusive—Kot's hatred of Anders is well known. Statements of other politicians not well disposed to Anders are also unreliable. Strangest of all is the fact that this supposedly secret military document, sent in only four or five copies to division commanders, can now be found in at least three archives: the Hoover Institution, Yad Vashem, and the Ciołkosz Archives.[4]

The fifth and longest chapter, 'Under the Swastika', deals with the government's attitude towards Polish Jews under German occupation. In it, most attention is paid to the government's information policy with regard to news of the Jews' tragic fate. The author briefly compares the situation of Jews and Poles under German occupation in the years 1939–41. He indicates that Jews were placed in the lowest position, in actual practice and within the ideological tenets of the Nazi New Order. On the basis of contemporary reports, he tries to characterize Polish attitudes to Jews at this time. He correctly stresses the difference between our present understanding of the situation and the picture of reality which the politicians in exile created for themselves on the basis of contemporary reports from Poland.

He states: 'The immediate sufferings of the two million Jewish Polish citizens under the swastika do not seem to have moved it [the government] to any serious action' (p. 167). In his opinion, the most important reason for this passivity was fear of the reaction of the Polish population, which, in the view of the politicians in exile, 'had remained largely hostile to Jews even after the German conquest' (p. 166). He then lists three additional factors: (1) the government's concentration on foreign policies and on domestic issues which could contribute to regaining independence; (2) its belief, based on reports from Poland, in the similar and in some respects better situation of Jews as compared to Poles; (3) the lack of pressure concerning this issue from Jewish organizations in the West. One must agree with Engel's identification of the reasons for the behaviour of the Polish government. Yet it is difficult to decide why he ranks them in the way he does. The stress on fears of the reaction of the population in Poland and the downplaying of the remaining factors seem arbitrary.

Three-quarters of this chapter deals with the reception and wider publication of the news of the fate of the Jews, especially in 1942. A large part of this section has lost some of its validity because of the discovery of new and important sources. Our present knowledge leads us to conclusions which are

---

[4] Cable to Polish Consulate in New York, 1 Sept. 1943, Archives of the Polish Institute in London, A.11.49/Sow/21; Kukiel to Strakacz, 31 Aug. 1943, ibid. A.11.755. Engel (pp. 135–6, 275) refers to a copy in the Hoover Institution, Gutman (*Yad Vashem Studies*, 12, p. 271) to a copy in Yad Vashem, Kersten (*Polacy, Żydzi, komunizm*, 42, 72) to a copy in Ciolkosz Archives.

significantly different from the hypotheses presented by Engel. This is especially true of the discussion of the first information concerning the deportation from the Warsaw ghetto in the summer of 1942, contained on pages 186–95.

R. C. Lukas[5] has quoted a telegram of 26 July 1942 from Stefan Korboński to London which was, without doubt, the source of all the news about the beginning of deportations published in the West in July–August 1942. The telegram, cited in Walter Laqueur's book *The Terrible Secret*,[6] from Schwarzbart to the World Jewish Congress of 27 July 1942 was simply a translation of this telegram. The clearest, though not the only, proof of this is the repetition in all versions of a mistake which originated with Korboński: his telegram did not state that 6,000 was the *daily* quota of people deported from the ghetto (which was the case), but that '6,000 people had been deported' as 'the beginning of the annihilation' of its population.

This fact leads to several conclusions quite contrary to those of Engel: news about the start of the deportation was given immediately and in its entirety to Jewish representatives by Minister Mikołajczyk, who also agreed to pass it on to the press. The same occurred with another known Korboński telegram (also cited by Lukas). We see in a different light those articles which appeared at the time in Polish publications in the West and which did not take in the threat of an immediate annihilation of the ghetto's population. Everything indicates that the words used in the telegram from Poland describing the deportation of 6,000 people as 'the beginning of the annihilation' of the population of the ghetto (half a million people) were taken as a metaphorical expression by Korboński and not as a statement of fact. This was not ill will but rather the result of an erroneous (because common-sense) interpretation of the telegram. Yet this case constitutes for Engel one of the strongest proofs of Polish collusion in the concealment of the real dimensions of the Jewish tragedy. The author is familiar with Korboński's telegrams but does not accept that they contradict his conclusions. His discussion of these telegrams is relegated to the endnotes (p. 300 n. 152); they are not mentioned elsewhere. The quotation in the notes is so cluttered with reservations and provisos that its significance does not emerge.

The basic theme of Chapter V is that the Polish government in its statements and publications knowingly and deliberately played down the

---

[5] *The Forgotten Holocaust: The Poles under German Occupation 1939–1944* (Lexington, Ky., 1986), 154. For the Polish version of the Korboński messages see *Armia Krajowa w dokumentach*, vi (London, 1989), 251, 253.

[6] *The Terrible Secret: Suppression of the Truth about Hitler's 'Final Solution'* (Boston, 1980), 109–12.

dimensions of the Jewish tragedy, and in some cases even withheld information. It justified its actions in terms of its fear that the Jewish tragedy might eclipse the suffering of Poles. Several key elements of this theory have not been proven or rest on questionable assumptions. Some do not stand up to the facts. Here are some of the more important (I summarize Engel's argument in italics):

1. *From the start of the deportation from the Warsaw ghetto to the end of November 1942 the Government received from Poland much more extensive information on the subject than it was willing to reveal* (pp. 185–98). The author cites information which was at the time sent from Warsaw, especially the report of 25 July 1942 and the message from Bund, of 2 October 1942. However, he has no proof that this material arrived in London before mid-November, which would not have been strange, given the difficulties of communication (more extensive texts were sent by courier, which sometimes took several months). The postwar memoirs written by Korboński and General Komorowski mention many telegrams to the government. However, to this day, in spite of extensive searches by several historians, only three sent to London can be shown to have arrived before 15 November. They are Korboński's telegrams (from the civilian underground) of 26 July and 11 August and General Rowecki's telegram of 25 August. Korboński's two telegrams, which were sent through civilian channels and amount to barely ten sentences, were shown to the Jewish representatives in the Rada Narodowa, who passed them on. To date there has been no confirmation of receipt in London of other telegrams from Korboński, so it is difficult to speculate as to what they may have contained. Similarly, there is no evidence that the British government in London received any telegrams from the government delegate in Poland.

The case of the telegram sent through the army underground from General Rowecki seems better to fit the hypothesis of a 'conspiracy of silence', as there is nothing to indicate that its contents were ever revealed. However, Laqueur explains this (referring to statements made by Polish personnel) as being due to the restriction of reports from army intelligence to a small group of high-ranking officers.

Engel should be aware that there is no evidence that the reports cited by him ever reached London at that time. In spite of this, he accuses Sikorski of not releasing information on 1 September that 80,000 Jews had already been sent to Treblinka. Sikorski's affirmation on 29 October of the equal rights of Jews in a rebuilt Poland is called by the author 'a rather ironic statement, considering that according to the information *already in his Government's possession*, at least one-third of the country's pre-war Jewish population of Poland would not be alive to enjoy any benefits of victory at all' (p. 197, my italics). As further proof of the Polish conspiracy of silence, he states that radio Świt in a programme on 10 September deliberately omitted to mention the deportation that day of 5,199 Warsaw Jews to death camps.

The author cites as additional evidence for his hypothesis of a conspiracy of silence the telegram from Minister Raczyński to the Representacja Żydów Polskich (RŻP: Representation of Polish Jewry) in Palestine. Here the situation is more complicated. On 12 November the Polish Ministry of Foreign Affairs received a request from the RŻP to confirm information from the press that the Jewish population in Warsaw had been reduced to 100,000 (p. 197 in Engel). In his telegram of 23 November 1942 Raczyński felt unable to confirm this, and promised to investigate the information. Yet we have proof that by 16 November the government had information about the annihilation of the ghetto. The simplest explanation for this fact is certainly the desire for conscious disinformation, and this was the feeling of RŻP.

However, thanks to a discovery by Engel, other possible interpretations come to light. The author states that the text of the minister's telegram was ready on 14 November (p. 302), therefore almost immediately after receipt of the query by the government and, according to our present knowledge, before the arrival in London of accounts of the annihilation of the ghetto. In accordance with Raczyński's telegram, the Minister of the Interior sent a ciphergram to Poland requesting exact information about the persecution of the Jews. The question remains as to why Raczyński's telegram was sent only after ten days, when it was already out of date. There could be many reasons for such a delay (deliberate withholding of information, difficulty in communications, chaos, incompetence, etc.); only after investigating the possibilities could one accuse Raczyński of deliberate disinformation.

If we are to agree with David Engel, then Raczyński's disinformation (i.e. his deliberate delay of the telegram) exposes a serious weakness in the Polish government: the ministers who took part in the anti-Jewish conspiracy of silence either suffered a loss of memory or else were lacking in organization. For on 16 November the Minister of the Interior revealed information about the newly arrived reports of the fate of the Warsaw ghetto to the representative of the RŻP Schwarzbart (who sent them on to the World Jewish Congress).[7] So, Minister Raczyński forgot or did not know that the information which he was hiding from RŻP had been revealed to a representative of RŻP the previous week! The author states that the government withheld information about the annihilation of the Warsaw ghetto until information revealed by the Jewish Agency (on 23 November 1942) forced it to break its silence (pp. 198, 201). The fact that Schwarzbart

---

[7] Schwarzbart Diary, 16 Nov. 1942, Yad Vashem, M2/751.

was made privy to this information a week earlier seriously weakens this theory.

2. *By giving out information not consistent with the facts received in the Bund's letter of 11 May 1942, the government knowingly and deliberately belittled the dimensions of the Jews' tragedy and the threat to them* (pp. 180–2). The letter from the underground Bund was the most complete description of the German extermination of Jews from the summer of 1941 to the spring of 1942. The information contained in it (including references to 700,000 victims of massacres and to the all-embracing character of German action) evoked a significant response in the press of the free countries. However, there is much to indicate that among politicians it was met with almost universal scepticism. A more complete reading of contemporary statements on the subject shows that, with the exception of Szmul Zygielbojm, no significant Polish, Jewish, or British politician publicly accepted the facts revealed by the Bund. On the contrary, some of them (such as Mikołajczyk, representing the government in this matter) clearly distanced themselves from the report. Ignacy Schwarzbart also tried to distance himself from the account provided by the Bund, reasoning that any exaggeration undermined belief in genuine information concerning the Jewish tragedy. We know that the truth of the Bund's information was seriously doubted by such Polish politicians as Pragier, Raczyński, Stroński, and Kaczyński. It was not without reason that the first statements of the Polish government on the subject of mass extermination of Jews claimed that 'the devastation of the Jewish population is *unbelievable* in extent' (my italics). Data officially released by the Polish government referred, according to Mikołajczyk, to 'events which were proved beyond any doubt' and contained figures which were much lower than those given by the Bund.[8] All this casts doubt on Engel's view that 'the dimensions of the Jewish catastrophe were deliberately reduced' by Sikorski (p. 180). On page 202 we read that the government intentionally 'downplayed' news of the annihilation of Jews in the Auschwitz gas chambers. The shocking character of this assertion is somewhat lost in the midst of Engel's other claims.

3. *The downplaying and silence about the news of the extermination of Jews arose from the fear that it would eclipse the suffering of Poles and transfer the sympathy of Anglo-Saxon peoples from the Poles to the Jews* (pp. 191–8). This hypothesis loses much of its validity since, as I believe, Engel has not presented satisfactory evidence that the government concealed and belittled

---

[8] Mikołajczyk statements in *Dziennik polski*, 10, 11 July 1942; Schwarzbart to I. Greenberg, 29 June 1942, Yad Vashem M2/241; M. Lachs to World Jewish Congress, British Section, 10 July 1942, Institute of Jewish Affairs, London, WJC box 1942; government statement of 6 June 1942 quoted in Kazimierz Iranek-Osmecki, *Kto ratuje jednego życia ... Polacy i Żydzi 1939–1945* (London, 1968), 185.

the news of the extermination. It is hard to discuss hypothetical motives for unproven actions.

The theory appears on page 171 as a matter of obvious truth: the government could not allow the fate of the Jews to interfere with the cultivation of popular sympathy for the suffering of the Poles. On page 172 we learn that the position of the government in suppressing information about the Jews came from another more general principle of its policy. That 'fundamental principle' was that the interests and needs of Jewish and Polish society could not be placed on the same plane: 'the Polish government determined that it should concern itself with the welfare of the Polish community alone' (p. 173).

This is perhaps the most important and far-reaching theme of the book relating to government policy *vis-à-vis* the Jews. One would have thought that it would be supported with a strong base in the sources and detailed justification. Unfortunately, the intelligence communiqué referred to in a note (n. 82) has only a very loose relationship to it. The communiqué expresses an opinion on the divergence of Polish national minorities and political aims: this is not a political guideline, nor is it proof of the existence of one to that effect.

The view that disinformation resulted from fear of 'Jewish competition in suffering' is again mentioned on pages 177, 180, 181, 182, and 202. It is introduced as a possibility—a hypothetical explanation—or appears as a fact. At the same time the author suggests that 'the Polish government simply wished to avoid calling special attention to the German massacre of the Jewish population of Poland' (p. 178) and that with premeditation it belittled the magnitude of the catastrophe (pp. 180, 183, 185, 191, 201). Most of the examples given of such belittling and silence rest on a free interpretation of the facts and on the merging of facts and their interpretation.

None of the 195 notes to Chapter V reveals from which sources the author learnt what the motives of Polish politicians were and how he justifies his view that the government issued anti-Jewish political-information directives. We do not learn whether any of the Polish politicians ever made a statement on the subject or whether persons fearing 'Jewish competition in suffering' (and there were some) had enough influence to determine the decisions of Ministers Raczyński, Mikołajczyk, and Stroński, Prime Minister Sikorski, and the whole of the Council of Ministers.

The opinion that the diplomatic and propaganda campaign of the government in November–December, designed to broadcast the annihilation of the Jews, was the result of pressure from Jewish organizations has as much justification as the opposing view, that the campaign was not so influenced. Engel's adoption of the former position seems to be based on the conviction that if the Polish government finally did something positive, it must have done so under pressure. The author resorts to similar argumentation elsewhere. For example: the government had to condemn the German persecution of Jews because if it had not, it 'might conceivably have weakened the government's claim to active Allied sympathy and support' (p. 171); Ambassador Kot nominated Jews to the Civilian Relief Apparatus in the USSR because he *anticipated* Jewish dissatisfaction and wished to forestall it (p. 205). This last opinion is perhaps the further-reaching praise of the pressure strategy. The theory of the effectiveness of the pressure strategy, although never formulated precisely, is touched on more than once in the book. It seems more of an a priori assumption than a hypothesis justified by detailed documentation.

Apart from reacting to pressure, the government, in Engel's view, was induced to take positive steps through cold calculation and tactical considerations. Certainly tactics and calculation played an important part in the decisions of Polish politicians. However, the way in which the author stresses his views sometimes creates an image of the government which seems an inversion of the myth of 'Perfidia Judaea'.

The more we read *In the Shadow of Auschwitz*, the more often we come upon opinions that provoke mixed feelings. Chapters IV and (to a greater extent) V contain statements that are questionable and unsubstantiated. It has not been possible to discuss all of these in this review article. However, in spite of these reservations, David Engel's book has to be acknowledged as a significant contribution to research into Polish Jewish history. *In the Shadow of Auschwitz* is a clear step forward, especially if one considers the way in which the issues the author raises have been discussed in the past. The book contains interesting and convincing theories, and the historian will find in it much information about events and sources not previously known. It is the most complete and factual work which has appeared on Polish–Jewish relations abroad in the critical years of the Second World War. Historians investigating the Polish–Jewish question in these years will have to familiarize themselves with Engel's book. Perhaps those of his theories which evoke our greatest reservations will stimulate new works on the subject of the Polish government-in-exile and the Jews, and create a broader understanding of these complex problems.

Reading and Misreadings: A Reply to Dariusz Stola

DAVID ENGEL

FIRST, my thanks to Dariusz Stola for his generally kind words about *In the Shadow of Auschwitz*, despite his disagreement on certain specific matters. Even more I do appreciate the civil and scholarly tone of his criticism (except for the title of his essay, which, by suggesting that *In the Shadow of Auschwitz*, has obscured 'the facts'—something that the body of the essay does not even argue—seems to me just a bit nasty). Too often, as Michael Marrus has aptly observed, 'Jewish and Polish historians conduct a *dialogue des sourdes* over the issue of relations between Jews and other Poles during the Holocaust.[1] In my own work I have tried to break this pattern; I believe that I have made a sincere effort to listen carefully to both perspectives, and my perception of the events I describe has been affected, I think, by both of them (although ultimately, I hope, neither has been permitted to outweigh the objective documentary record in determining my conclusions). From Mr Stola's concluding comment that 'David Engel's book has to be acknowledged as a positive contribution to research into Polish Jewish history, especially if one considers the way in which the issues he raises have been discussed in the past', I get the feeling that he has sensed this effort and appreciated it. Moreover, from the fact that most of the questions he raises about *In the Shadow of Auschwitz* address themselves to issues that are part of the academic historian's proper bailiwick—viz., whether the evidence adduced as the basis for a particular inference actually justifies that inference, whether additional evidence does not contradict it, and whether cited evidence in fact says what it is claimed to say—I am persuaded that he shares my belief that Polish and Jewish scholars have a primary common interest in bringing to light as many of the documentary traces of Polish–Jewish relations as can be recovered. From such a starting-point Mr Stola has succeeded in raising interpretations of certain parts of the documentary record that differ from my own without the rancour and recrimination that

[1] Michael R. Marrus, *The Holocaust in History* (Hanover, 1987), 96.

have characterized so much writing on the subject of Poles and Jews. From my point of view, this is a most encouraging development.

Mr Stola has presented several portions of what he takes to be the thesis of *In the Shadow of Auschwitz* and has argued that those portions are based upon insufficient evidence. He has also contended that certain facts that seem to him of significance in understanding the attitudes of the Polish Government-in-exile to matters of concern to Jews were not given sufficient or accurate treatment in the book, and in the light of some of these facts he has proposed several hypotheses that he regards as significantly different from my own. His arguments are certainly the result of much serious thinking about the issues *In the Shadow of Auschwitz* endeavoured to probe. However, on close examination it appears that such serious thinking has not been matched by a sufficiently careful reading either of the arguments presented in the book or of the evidence from which those arguments were derived. Indeed, it can be shown that many of Mr Stola's paraphrases of the book's thesis reflect a fundamental misreading of the text and that his notations of lacunae are the result of a failure to pay close attention to the details of both the narrative and the scholarly apparatus. In the ensuing pages I shall offer such a demonstration with regard to the principal points that he has raised. At times the explication may seem rather turgid, but because so many of the issues at stake turn upon close textual and contextual analysis, such a discussion cannot avoid verbosity. I am therefore grateful to the editor of *Polin*, Antony Polonsky, for permitting me as much space as was needed to resolve the matters at hand and beg the reader's indulgence over the lack of terseness in what follows.

I

Let me begin with a few words about the book's aim and perspective. The aim of *In the Shadow of Auschwitz* was stated on p. 11: 'to establish as precisely as possible what the guidelines [formulated by the Polish Government-in-Exile concerning the degree to which it ought to sponsor and defend Jewish interests] were, to describe the manner in which they were implemented during the first three years of the war, and to explain, as fully as the available documentation allows, the thinking behind their adoption.' It will be noted that in order to fulfil this aim it is necessary to produce and prove only certain propositions of fact: required are nothing more than a list of guidelines, a descriptions of actions taken in accordance with those guidelines, a statement of the reasons for the adoption of those guidelines, and evidence that the guidelines were in fact as listed, did in fact generate the actions ascribed to them, and were in fact adopted for the reasons given. Moreover, it should be equally clear as a corollary that fulfilling the given aim requires no *evaluation* of any of the guidelines, actions, or thoughts discussed. As a result, in writing *In the Shadow of Auschwitz* I considered myself free from any obligation to comment upon what I felt about those guidelines, actions, and thoughts—whether I held them praiseworthy or contemptible, well-conceived or misguided, clever or stupid, good or bad. What is more, I was relieved not to be so obligated, especially with regard to the moral implications of any facts adduced. My training as a historian had included no systematic study of ethics, so I did not feel qualified to issue any ethical judgements *ex cathedra*. In addition, intuition and personal experience told me that certain of the moral problems seemingly suggested by the subject-matter with which I was working could not be resolved apodictically by appeal to such estimable but indiscriminate standards as a supposed injunction to be one's brother's keeper; rather they presented complex facets requiring extensive elucidation and debate by moral philosophers. I was thus in no position to do justice to the moral aspect of my subject in a book that had first to analyse a documentary corpus for the most part hitherto unexplored. I determined therefore, to adopt a morally neutral perspective and to confine myself to stating what I believed were factual inferences from the documentary record.

That decision had several immediate implications for the way in which the book would be written, of which, for present purposes, those regarding language and the selection of material for presentation are the most pertinent. Because moral judgement was to be eschewed, words carrying moral connotations had to be avoided. A particular problem presented itself with the word 'antisemitism', which has dominated so much of the discussion of Polish–Jewish relations to date. That term, as Norman Davies has quite properly noted, has lost virtually all denotative precision;[2] as I have shown elsewhere, since the 1930s its primary function has been to suggest that certain attitudes or behaviours with regard to Jews deserve condemnation on moral grounds.[3] Clearly, then, I needed to employ the word sparingly if at all, and I had to forgo any determination of whether any actions or individuals discussed in the narrative ought to be labelled 'antisemitic'. Writing a book about an aspect of Polish–Jewish relations without having recourse to this or other highly connotative, value-laden terms (like 'collaboration', 'treason', 'racism', 'Fascism', or 'democracy', to name a few) required breaking long-ingrained linguistic habits. In the end, though, the effort proved instrumental in enabling me to separate myself from the moral

---

[2] See Davies's reply to Abraham Brumberg in 'Poles and Jews: An Exchange', *New York Review* (9 Apr. 1987), 43.

[3] David Engel, *Semantikah ufolitikah bete'ur hayeḥasim bein polanim leyehudim* (Tel Aviv, 1990), 11–14.

implications of the factual propositions I was presenting. Looking back on *In the Shadow of Auschwitz* almost ten years after it was written (the bulk of the text was composed between March 1983 and February 1985). I find that at several points there is room for an even more radical linguistic purge, but because Mr Stola's criticism did not take notice of any of these passages I shall not discuss them here.

Regarding selection of material, the consequences of a morally neutral stance were also clear. Because of the enormous volume of documentary material pertaining to the subject it was obvious that I would not be able to discuss every single word or deed concerning Jews uttered or performed by someone associated with the exile regime. On the other hand, I had to bring forth enough material to fulfil the book's aim of explicating guidelines, actions, and thought. First priority in selection, therefore, was given to words and deeds that represented actions of a type not taken earlier, allowed new insight into thinking about Jewish matters, influenced the formation or implementation of guidelines, or significantly affected the subsequent tenor of Polish–Jewish relations in general. By the same token, as it was not the aim of the book to offer a moral balance of the guidelines, actions, and thought under discussion, it did not seem necessary, or even pertinent, to consider how the selection of material might conceivably affect any balance that a reader might draw. Moral neutrality did not imply that I should choose material that would be likely to leave readers with a more or less equal amount of favourable and unfavourable impressions of the men of the Polish Government; it meant rather that I could not concern myself with the impressions that any particular piece of material might arouse. The question of whether any given word or deed might be viewed by readers in a morally positive or negative light could not be permitted to affect the selection process one way or the other.

Once these considerations are understood, it should be plain that Mr Stola's basic approach to reading *In the Shadow of Auschwitz* was problematic. That approach, unlike mine in writing the book, was heavily value-laden. Indeed, Mr Stola appears to have come to *In the Shadow of Auschwitz* already having reached, on the basis of his own researches into the matter at hand, certain conclusions not only regarding the facts of the various episodes treated in the book but also with respect to their moral valence. His preconceptions in the latter regard are most evident in his reference on six separate occasions in his criticism to steps taken by the government-in-exile with regard to Jewish matters 'which can be assessed positively'. It should be noticed immediately that the words 'can be assessed positively' represent a proposition of value, not one of fact. Mr Stola is, of course, entitled to offer such propositions of value in his own work (although it seems to me that in order to do so he ought to explicate the ethical premisses from which he has derived them). Should he impose that value-laden approach upon the work of someone else not sharing it, however, he is liable to misread. And that, it seems, is what has happened at several key points in his reading of *In the Shadow of Auschwitz*.

II

Such misreading is notable, among other places, in two generalizations that Mr Stola has offered about how the book treated what he regards as the 'positive' aspects of the Polish Government's approach to Jewish matters. Mr Stola has suggested that *In the Shadow of Auschwitz* does not pay sufficient attention to what he considers 'positive' steps by the government, and he has stated explicitly that it demonstrates a 'belief [on the part of the author] that those steps that the government took *vis-à-vis* the Jews which can be assessed positively were the fruit of government weakness and effective pressure'. He has also focused much of his evidentiary criticism upon the book's discussion of these 'positive' steps, arguing that that discussion is rooted in 'more of an a priori assumption than a hypothesis justified by detailed documentation'. 'The way in which the author stresses his views', he has written, 'sometimes creates an image of the government which seems an inversion of the myth of "Perfidia Judaea".' In other words, it appears that behind Mr Stola's evaluation of the book's factual basis lies his sense that the reader is not apt to come away from reading it with as 'positive' an assessment of the Polish Government as he feels it deserves.

The problem, of course (aside from the issue of whether an action taken under pressure is necessarily of less moral worth, or less 'positive', than it would have been if undertaken spontaneously—a problem for philosophers, not historians, and thus one upon which *In the Shadow of Auschwitz* took no position), is that the category of 'positive steps' that has served Mr Stola as an exordium for his analysis is entirely his own creation. The book itself did not group together the steps in question on any basis at all (let alone that of 'positivity') and advanced no collective hypothesis about them. In writing the book, not only did I not offer any comment of my own about whether any particular step ought to be assessed as 'positive' or 'negative', I did not make any effort to forecast how readers were likely to assess them. Hence in attributing to the book the thesis that 'if the Polish Government finally did something positive, it must have done so under pressure' Mr Stola has actually invented an answer to a question that the book never asked, and has passed it off as a integral part of the book's argument. In the event, from the value-free perspective a question such as 'What was the motivation underlying the Polish Government's "positive" steps *vis-à-vis* the Jews?' is senseless: if the existence of the subject is not admitted, no predicates can follow. Indeed, Mr Stola himself has pointed out that 'the theory of the effectiveness of the pressure strategy' was 'never formulated precisely': in the event that alleged theory was never even implied.

The non-existence of such a theory, even by implication, can be demonstrated by an examination of the actual treatment that *In the Shadow of Auschwitz* gave to the episodes that Mr Stola has grouped together as 'positive'. A careful reading will indicate that not all of these steps were attributed to Jewish pressure. The appointment of Jews to positions in the Relief Apparatus in the Soviet Union, for example, was presented not, as Mr Stola has claimed, as an attempt by Ambassador Stanisław Kot to ward off expected Jewish allegations of discrimination but as an element of a comprehensive strategy aimed both at inviting broad international Jewish co-operation with and support for the Polish relief effort and at countering the Soviet policy regarding the citizenship of Polish Jews in the USSR, which the Government regarded as inimical to the Polish interest. The book showed, in essence, that there were several sets of influences and constraints operating upon the Polish embassy in the Soviet Union, each coming from a different source but each leading to the same conclusion: that the embassy ought to make a concerted effort to integrate Polish Jews into its operations at all levels and to make certain that they benefited from its services as much as possible to the same degree as other Polish citizens. To be sure, mention was made in the book of Jewish complaints about the embassy that were anticipated by the government in London (not by Kot specifically), and it was argued that those anticipated complaints influenced the Government's actions with regard to the embassy's welfare activities; but this was done only because solid documentary evidence of such anticipation was found. That evidence was cited in notes 64 and 66 to the text on page 125. The documents in question, located at the Hoover Institution Archives, have evidently not been checked by Mr Stola. They indicate that on 30 August 1941 Arieh Tartakower, representing both the World Jewish Congress and the Representation of Polish Jewry, wrote to Polish Ambassador Jan Ciechanowski in Washington that 'both the Jewish population in Poland and the World Jewish Congress ... hold that considerations of [both] justice and expediency speak in favour of serious treatment of our desires' concerning the staffing of the Polish relief outposts in the Soviet Union. Tartakower's letter also mentioned that the organizations that he represented had difficulty conceiving how Polish Jewish refugees could be cared for satisfactorily without the participation of Jewish representatives in the process. The cited documents show further that Ciechanowski forwarded a copy of Tartakower's letter to the Polish Foreign Ministry in London on 3 September. On 26 September the secretary-general of the Foreign Ministry,

Karol Kraczkiewicz, sent Ciechanowski an official instruction to inform interested Jewish organizations that 'from the moment when assistance for Polish citizens imprisoned in the Russian interior began to be organized, the Polish Government took pains to ensure adequate assistance for Jewish Polish citizens as well' and that a Jewish Polish citizen, Natalja Aszkenazy, had been appointed attaché to the Polish embassy in Moscow—'*inter alia* out of the conviction that her presence in Moscow will facilitate co-operation ... with the representatives of Jewish Polish citizens'.[4] Kraczkiewicz also told Ciechanowski that 'the Foreign Ministry hopes that the steps taken by the Polish Government will be instrumental in bringing about close and fruitful co-operation between the Polish authorities and Jewish Polish citizens in Russia, as well as with Jewish organizations outside of Russia, and that they will be appropriately appreciated from this point of view by those organizations'. In other words, there is a direct documentary record that during the months when the relief apparatus in the Soviet Union was being established the Polish Government was made aware that Jewish organizations would be scrutinizing the ethnic composition of the relief offices and that the Polish Foreign Ministry regarded it as important that those organizations should look favourably upon the manner in which the government dealt with this issue.

An additional document cited in note 64 reveals that on 6 October 1941 Foreign Minister Edward Raczyński was approached by Sidney Silverman and Noah Barou of the World Jewish Congress office in London with a request that additional Jews be employed in the co-ordination of relief, and suggesting specific candidates. Raczyński agreed to discuss the matter with Ambassador Kot. Documents that were not cited in the book, but that I might have used had I wished to accentuate the role of Jewish pressure, real or anticipated, in influencing the appointment of Jews to the relief offices, show that Raczyński did indeed inform Kot of these suggestions by cable on 9 October; that he followed this cable with a second wire on 31 October, stating that Jewish discontent was mounting and urgently requesting a list of those Jews who had been co-opted into the Relief Apparatus; and that Kot provided such a list on 13 November, stating that he 'would like the Jews' pressure to be directed towards bringing about as quick a realization as possible [of American aid being held up by Soviet authorities pending payment of duty]'.[5] However, alongside this information I found indications in the available documents of much broader considerations that influenced

[4] In reviewing the note in question I have noticed the erroneous statement that the appointed attaché to the embassy was Ludwik Seidenmann. Seidenmann was indeed associated with the embassy, but he was not the person named in the cited document. Should the book see a second edition, this error will be corrected.

[5] Cable, Polish Foreign Ministry to Polish embassy, Moscow, 9 Oct. 1941 (No. 75), Hoover Institution Archives [HIA]—Polish Government [PG], Box 449 (MSZ), file 738/Z, 'Uchodźcy

the behaviour of the relief apparatus towards Jewish refugees, and it was these broader considerations that were given prominence when this issue was analysed in the body of the book. The sentence cited by Mr Stola to prove that I viewed the appointment of Jews to the Relief Apparatus as the outcome of Jewish pressure ('It [the Polish Government] anticipated and attempted to forestall Jewish dissatisfaction over treatment of the refugees in the Soviet Union by appointing Jews to administrative positions in the Civilian Relief Apparatus ...'—a sentence that Mr Stola may or may not agree is well supported by the evidence cited above but that in either case hardly justifies being called 'more of an a priori assumption than a hypothesis justified by detailed documentation'—came rather from the book's conclusion; it was part of a summary discussion about how 'the government clearly saw the need for maintaining good relations with world Jewry and from time to time ... took specific actions toward that end' and was not presented as a summary analysis of the full range of thoughts that impinged upon the staffing of the relief network. Moreover, more than half of the discussion of the operation of the relief network in *In the Shadow of Auschwitz* was aimed at demonstrating that Jewish complaints about discrimination in the distribution of assistance were by and large unjustified and were rooted largely in 'a marked [Jewish] tendency to assume the worst about Polish behavior' (p. 130). In short, a careful, objective reading of the text and context of the discussion in question ought not to have led to the conclusion that that discussion represented an example of an ostensible 'pressure theory' or that it demonstrated a tendency to downplay the significance of 'positive' steps by the government.

Other measures that Mr Stola has termed 'positive' were not represented as the result of Jewish pressure even to a limited extent. Pressure was not mentioned as a factor either in the appointment of a Jewish member to the Polish National Council in December 1939 or in Prime Minister Władysław Sikorski's political declaration of 24 February 1942. Mr Stola has argued, to be sure, that the significance of these 'positive' steps was downplayed in *In the Shadow of Auschwitz* in accordance with a general pattern, but that assertion no more bears up under critical scrutiny than does the assertion of the existence of the 'pressure theory'. The appointment of *two* Jews, Ignacy Schwarzbart and Herman Lieberman, to the first National Council, along with the naming of a Jew to head the Polish consular post in Tel Aviv, was mentioned prominently on p. 54 as an act that gave encouragement to Jews attempting to gauge the new government-in-exile's attitudes towards the

Żydzi—Żydzi w Sowietach'; cable, Polish Foreign Ministry to Polish embassy, Moscow, 31 Oct. 1941 (no. 117), ibid.; 'Wiadomości nadesłane przez Ambasadora Kota telegramem z dnia 13 listopada 1941r.', ibid. See also 'Notatka z rozmowy Kierownika Ministerstwa Spraw Zagranicznych z przedstawicielami brytyjskiego oddziału World Jewish Congress', 6 Oct. 1941, ibid.

Jewish question. Nothing was said about the motivation behind any of these appointments because there is no extant evidence of that motivation.[6] It is also quite off the mark to state, as Mr Stola has done, that 'Apart from the question of budgetary proposals in the spring of 1941, the activities of the Jewish representative on the Council are not sufficiently presented'. In fact Schwarzbart was presented as a central figure in the events leading up to the Stańczyk declaration of 3 November 1940 (pp. 77–80); in the submission of Jewish complaints regarding the treatment of Jews in Polish publications, the Polish army in Great Britain, and Polish welfare agencies in France, Portugal, Palestine, and other countries (pp. 85–93); in efforts to bring about the repeal of previous legislation regarded by Jews as discriminatory (pp. 102–16); and in disseminating information about the killing of Jews in the occupied homeland (pp. 187, 193, 197–8). Schwarzbart's political strategy was also discussed in some detail on pp. 68, 77, 93, 243–4, and 251–2. A perusal of the index reveals that Schwarzbart was mentioned throughout the book more than any other person except Sikorski. I submit that these facts represent quite sufficient treatment of Schwarzbart's activities and that Mr Stola's overlooking them constitutes another example of his failure to read the book carefully.

With regard to Sikorski's statement to the National Council on 24 February 1942, Mr Stola correctly notes that the book devoted only one sentence to it. This relative lack of attention, however, was not, as Mr Stola has suggested, an indication of an intent to 'write off' this declaration in accordance with what he perceives to be a tendency to downplay the significance of 'positive' steps by the government. The statement was not analysed in detail because minimal emphasis was clearly indicated by the guidelines for selection of material that I have outlined above. This declaration made no specific mention of Jews; it contained no words on the subject of national minorities in general that had not been spoken by government officials on a number of prior occasions; it revealed nothing new about the way the Government approached the Jewish question; and by itself it had no noticeable effect upon the future development of the Government's attitude towards Jewish matters or its relations with Jews. In

---

[6] It cannot even be assumed that Schwarzbart was appointed specifically in order to serve as the representative of the Jewish minority. As pointed out in *In the Shadow of Auschwitz*, 244 n. 140, 'neither in Sikorski's initial invitation to him to join the council ... nor in the official act of appointment signed by [President Władysław] Raczkiewicz, was any mention made that Schwarzbart was to be regarded as the official representative of Polish Jewry'. Nor did the official published list of members of the first National Council identify Schwarzbart as a representative of the Polish Jews (in contrast to the official published list of members of the second National Council, which listed Schwarzbart and Szmul Zygielbojm as 'representatives of the Jews [*przedstawiciele Żydów*]'). See Michał Kwiatkowski, *Rząd i Rada Narodowa R. P. w świetle faktów i dokumentów od września 1939 do lutego 1942r.* (London, 1942), 109, 145.

noting this lack of effect, *In the Shadow of Auschwitz* simply pointed out that Jewish leaders were 'unimpressed' with the declaration (not, as Mr Stola has stated, that there was a 'critical reaction to it from the Jewish side'). It also pointed out why they were unimpressed: they regarded the overall composition of the newly appointed second Council, despite the addition of a second Jewish representative to it (a fact duly noted on p. 122), as pointing to 'the reemergence of the right as a force in Polish politics'. They thus doubted the Government's commitment to democratic values, at least as they understood those values. The value-neutral perspective of *In the Shadow of Auschwitz* did not require that I make any determination whether their doubts were well taken; on the contrary, because the word 'democratic' carries strong moral connotations and does not represent a quality subject to objective demonstration or measurement, the value-free perspective demanded that I refrain from using it when speaking in my own voice. Hence the adverb 'purportedly', which indicates neither affirmation nor denial of that which is purported. Mr Stola clearly has not understood any of this. He also has not understood the reason for the Jewish reaction to Sikorski's declaration being mentioned at all—viz., as part of a discussion about why, in the wake of the German invasion of the Soviet Union, when the Polish Government was seriously in need of allies who would advance its position in the Polish–Soviet conflict and hoped to achieve political co-operation with Jewish organizations in the West, such co-operation did not come about. The book was concerned only with assessing the degree to which Sikorski's declaration advanced the possibility of political co-operation in fact, not with 'writing off' its moral significance.[7] In short, there were sound, objective reasons for treating Sikorski's declaration of 24 February 1942 as it was treated.

It should be clear, then, that the various episodes discussed in *In the Shadow of Auschwitz* were analysed not, as Mr Stola would have it,

---

[7] Mr Stola's assertion that the declaration in question was 'the most important political declaration of the Government of Sikorski' seems questionable. One must determine in the first instance to whom and in what sense it was important. Clearly it was not important to many Jews who read it. But there is reason to wonder even how important contemporary Polish spokesmen considered it. A member of the National Council who published a compilation of what he regarded as the most significant documents relating to the government-in-exile in 1942 did not highlight this declaration by allotting it its own chapter, as he did several other political declarations and speeches by Polish leaders. See Kwiatkowski, *Rząd i Rada Narodowa*, 106–8. Moreover, a collection of Polish documents in English translation, published in 1943 expressly in order to 'serve as convincing proof that all that is truly great and creative in Poland has ever been and is today moved by the spirit of humanism and freedom, by liberal and progressive ideals', did not select the declaration in question as one of the eight documents put forth as representing the voice of Poland in exile during the Second World War. See *For Your Freedom and Ours: Polish Progressive Spirit through the Centuries*, ed. Manfred Kridl, Władysław Malinowski, and Józef Wittlin (New York, 1943), esp. p. 7.

categorically, in the light of some a priori determination about what must have influenced Polish actions, but individually, in the light of the context of each particular case and of the specific documents bearing upon it. Such an analysis did indeed lead to the ascription of two steps that Mr Stola has labelled 'positive'—the Stańczyk declaration of 3 November 1940 and Raczyński's note to the Allied governments of 10 December 1942—primarily to Jewish pressure. Examination of the available evidence, however, will show that, contrary to Mr Stola's undocumented assertions, such ascription is far more justified than any other possibility and hardly represents the result of an a priori determination.

With regard to the Stańczyk declaration, the facts (all presented and documented in *In the Shadow of Auschwitz*) are as follows: a public declaration by the Polish Government that Jewish Polish citizens would enjoy equal rights in Poland following liberation was demanded, both in the Jewish press in the West and by Jewish spokesmen in meetings with Polish Government representatives, beginning in November 1939 and repeatedly thereafter; on 2 March 1940 the Polish Foreign Ministry issued an official statement formally rejecting these demands; on 24 August 1940 the Government's political committee determined that the Government should issue no guarantee of rights that mentioned Jews explicitly; on 29 October 1940 the Government reversed its position and instructed Sikorski and Labour Minister Jan Stańczyk to prepare a declaration on Jewish rights in the future Poland; and the declaration was read publicly at a previously scheduled symposium on Polish Jewry on 3 November 1940. These facts prompt an obvious question for analysis: what happened during the two-month interval between late August and late October that caused the Government to change its mind? *In the Shadow of Auschwitz* proposed that the catalyst for this change was the submission, on 8 October, of a memorandum by Schwarzbart to Sikorski 'regarding the advisability of a formal declaration on the part of the Government concerning the Jewish question in the future Poland'. This inference was made, as the book explained, not only from the existence of the memorandum and its chronological proximity to the Government's declaration but also from the following additional facts, all of them documented in the book: Schwarzbart had previously refused to associate himself with the public call for a declaration and had actually tried to dissuade other Jewish organizations from applying pressure upon the Polish Government with that end in mind; the Government had been using Schwarzbart's dissociation from that call as one of its primary justifications for resisting it, but now that justification had been taken away from them; government leaders had previously counted upon Schwarzbart to hold pressure from other Jewish organizations in check, but now they could no longer depend on him to do so; the declaration was ultimately made at a public meeting organized by Schwarzbart; and Schwarzbart was consulted regarding the text of the declaration prior to its issue.[8] In addition, the book pointed out (and documented) that during the interval between August and October the Polish Government had been subjected to growing pressure by the British public, and even by the British government, to repudiate certain practices that had been attributed, rightly or wrongly, to certain Polish circles in Great Britain and that the Polish Government was concerned that such pressure was soon likely to be exerted by the United States as well. Schwarzbart's memorandum addressed the government's disquietude over British and American solicitousness for the Jews directly, emphasizing that 'the more and the better these two democracies appreciate and understand Poland's position, the better our chances for full victory', observing that 'in both these countries, Jewry plays a strong part in political life', and reasoning that 'consequently it ought to be one of the aims of Polish policy to obtain the unqualified support and sympathy of these Jewish communities'. Schwarzbart argued that a declaration on Jewish rights in liberated Poland would be the best way to achieve that aim, and he expressed his conviction 'that the present moment is the right psychological moment for the issuing of a declaration ... which I submit to the Government for its consideration'.

Mr Stola may argue that 'no sources ... entitle us to regard [these facts] as decisive' in influencing the Government to change its previous position regarding a declaration, although if he believes that some other factor was decisive he ought to indicate what it was. As far as I know, I have conducted the most extensive search to date for documents that might have a bearing on this issue, and I have found no other likely possibility. It can, of course, be argued that the Stańczyk declaration was simply the result of a spontaneous change of heart by the Polish leadership that would have come about even in the absence of Schwarzbart's memorandum, broader Jewish pressure, or the overall political context; but no sources justify us in reaching that conclusion either, and in the final analysis such an argument strains credulity. However, even if one wishes ultimately to accept such an argument, it should be clear that the thesis advanced in *In the Shadow of Auschwitz* concerning the origins of the Stańczyk declaration was based upon considerably more than a mere a priori 'belief that those steps that the Government took ... which can be assessed positively were the fruit of Government weakness and effective pressure'.

[8] Had Mr Stola consulted the document cited in note 145 on page 80 he would have learnt that not only was Schwarzbart shown an advance copy of the declaration's proposed text, as reported in *In the Shadow of Auschwitz*, but he actually recommended changes in it that were subsequently incorporated.

The proof that the ascription of Raczyński's note of 10 December 1942 mainly to Jewish pressure was likewise based upon objective documentary foundation can be found in *In the Shadow of Auschwitz* on p. 199. There it was noted that on 27 November Alexander Eastermann and Noah Barou of the World Jewish Congress approached Raczyński 'with a request that the [Polish] government initiate among the Allies ... a declaration that "Germans ... would be held responsible for all deeds leading to the mass murder of Jews ..."'. Had Mr Stola checked the document cited in the attached note he would have learnt that Raczyński immediately reported this request to Mikołajczyk, asking him 'to consider whether it might not be a good idea right now to issue a separate declaration of the Polish Government [apart from any that other interested governments might eventually make on their own] condemning the mass deportations and murders of the Jews carried out in Poland'. In other words, the idea that the Polish Government should take the lead in denouncing the mass killing of Jews began to be discussed in Polish ministerial circles only after Jewish representatives had raised it. *In the Shadow of Auschwitz* did not belabour this point because it hardly seemed an issue requiring extensive elaboration; but it could have noted as well that Zygielbojm also asked the National Council on the same day to adopt resolutions calling upon the Government to intervene with the Allies on behalf of the Jewish cause, only to have his motion rejected,[9] or that Raczyński's diary entry for 29 November indicated that 'Zygelbojn [sic] and Szwarchbart [sic] ... have asked me to organize a protest, which we are doing.'[10] Thus Raczyński himself ascribed his own actions to Jewish initiative.

Moreover, as detailed both in *In the Shadow of Auschwitz* and in its sequel, *Facing a Holocaust* (Chapel Hill and London, 1993), from 23 November the Government was regularly beset with demands for a wide range of actions from a variety of Jewish bodies and spokesmen in Britain, the United States, Palestine, and even the occupied homeland. Government officials discussed all of these demands among themselves, considering carefully, on the basis of what they conceived to be the interest of their Government and the Polish nation at the time, which demands should be accepted, which rejected, and which met part-way. Significantly, from late November 1942 until February 1943 the Government took no action aimed at promoting the rescue of Polish Jewry that was not first demanded by some Jewish group. These facts make it extremely difficult to accept Mr Stola's claim that 'The opinion that the diplomatic and propaganda campaign

---

[9] *Biuletyn sprawozdawczy Rady Narodowej* (2 Dec. 1942), 25–6. See also Yisrael Gutman and Shmuel Krakowski, *Unequal Victims: Poles and Jews during World War II* (New York, 1986), 95–6.
[10] Edward Raczyński, *In Allied London* (London, 1962), 125.

of the Government in November–December [1942] ... was the result of pressure from Jewish organizations has as much justification as the opposing view, that the campaign was not so influenced.' Maintaining the latter possibility is tantamount to arguing that the Polish Government would have done what it did during the period in question even had Jewish spokesmen made no demands upon them, or that the Government's course of action was determined without regard to Jewish demands. The former possibility seems at best improbable; the latter is demonstrably not the case.

Again, Mr Stola may disagree with this analysis (although without some evidence that prior to the last week in November Government officials were actively planning the steps that they eventually took it will be quite difficult to justify such disagreement). But whatever the case it should be clear that the thesis advanced in *In the Shadow of Auschwitz* has a substantial basis in the documentary record.

There is, then, no a priori pressure theory in *In the Shadow of Auschwitz*. Unfortunately, this theory is not the only one whose existence Mr Stola has imagined. He has also ascribed to the book non-existent theses regarding the manner in which the Polish Government dealt with the information on the systematic mass killing of Polish Jewry that reached it in June–November 1942 and the attitude of General Władysław Anders towards Jews in the Polish army in the USSR. The degree of validity of Mr Stola's comments on these two matters will now be examined in some detail.

III

Mr Stola has characterized *In the Shadow of Auschwitz*'s argument concerning the Government's handling of information on systematic mass killing as a 'hypothesis of a "conspiracy of silence"'. He has also stated that the book advanced the 'view that the Government issued anti-Jewish political-information directives' and that it posited 'Polish collusion in the concealment of the real dimensions of the Jewish tragedy' stemming from 'ill will'. And he has read the book's discussion of the handling of the first news concerning the mass deportations from the Warsaw ghetto in July 1942 as if it 'constitutes for Engel one of the strongest proofs' of the thesis that the book purportedly put forth. Here too Mr Stola simply has not understood what he has read.

In the first place, the words 'anti-Jewish', 'collusion', 'ill will', and even 'conspiracy of silence' (which he has effectively claimed, through his use of inverted commas, to have taken from the book itself) are Mr Stola's alone.

Readers may scour the relevant passages for hours on end; they will find no such characterizations in *In the Shadow of Auschwitz*. Indeed, these phrases are so heavy with emotional loadings and judgemental connotations that the value-neutral perspective of *In the Shadow of Auschwitz* could not have permitted their use. Nor did the book ever remotely suggest that the manner in which the Polish Government handled information about the situation of Polish Jewry under Nazi occupation was motivated by ill will or by a conscious desire to damage Jewish interests. In reality the thesis that *In the Shadow of Auschwitz* advanced regarding this matter was far more subtle and complex than Mr Stola has understood—so complex, in fact, that it defies restatement in a single sentence. Instead, that thesis will be explicated here in condensed fashion by retracing the steps that led to its formation. Readers will not, of course, find in what follows a complete recapitulation of the evidence upon which the hypothesis was based, but the subsequent paragraphs should serve as a guide for a correct reading of the book's argument.

The exordium for the view of the Government's handling of information about the Jewish situation advanced in *In the Shadow of Auschwitz* was the documented fact that, as far as could be ascertained from thorough research in all likely repositories, only once between the outbreak of war and the end of 1942 did the Polish Government sponsor (or, more accurately, co-sponsor) a publication devoted *exclusively* to what was happening to Jews in the occupied homeland.[11] On the other hand, careful examination of the relative amount of space devoted to the Jewish situation in other official Polish publications and statements (including actual counting of lines of text) revealed that, with this one exception, the condition of Polish Jewry was always discussed within the context of German persecution of Poles and, except for a one-month interval between 9 June and 9 July 1942 (and especially during the first nine days of July), never received more than a small percentage of the space devoted to the general Polish plight. During that single month the attention given to the Jewish situation in government statements and publications was greater than it had been before, although it still did not depart from the established pattern of presentation within the context of discussions of Polish suffering. After 9 July, however, the relative amount of attention decreased to approximately that which had prevailed before 9 June, remaining at that level until Foreign Minister Raczyński broke the pattern altogether with his note to the Allied Governments of 10 December 1942.

These facts prompted an effort to account both for the existence of the

[11] This was a pamphlet entitled *The Persecution of Jews in German-occupied Poland*, issued in mid-1940 under the auspices of the newspaper *Free Europe*, which was supported in part by funds from the Polish Information Ministry.

observed pattern and for the two notable deviations from it. At first the former problem did not seem like one that would demand much contemplation: it appeared obvious that the Polish Government would devote more attention to the plight of 22 million Poles than to that of 3 million Jews, especially since prior to mid-1942 it was reasonable to conclude from the best information at the Government's disposal that the Jews were actually somewhat better off than the Poles. On the contrary, what demanded explaining was why any departures from this tendency should be noticed at all. In this regard the first explanation that suggested itself was the receipt by the Polish Government of new information that changed the manner in which it perceived the Jewish situation. Indeed, both deviations took place shortly following the receipt of new information—the Bund report (received on 31 May 1942) and the testimony of Jan Karski (who arrived in London around 15 November 1942); it seemed sensible to conclude, therefore, that the augmented recognition of the Jewish plight on both occasions represented the Government's spontaneous response to the discovery of new facts.

However, once put to the test, this working hypothesis quickly proved deficient. For one thing, a comparison of the content of the Bund letter with Sikorski's BBC broadcast ten days after its receipt revealed (as indicated on p. 180) that although the broadcast echoed many passages from the letter, it neglected to mention most of the new information that gave the letter its urgency. Initially my tendency upon observing this fact was similar to Mr Stola's—to attribute the discrepancy to disbelief; in fact, in the book I even discussed the issue of whether the Bund letter was believed by Polish officials in London (p. 176), and I did not rule out the possibility that there had initially been serious doubts as to its veracity. Nevertheless, looking further into the matter, I discovered that by the time of the joint Polish–British press conference of 9 July the discrepancy between the Bund letter and Government accounts of the Jewish situation had narrowed considerably, with the figure of 700,000 Jewish deaths reported by the Bund now acknowledged officially not only by Information Minister Stroński but by his British counterpart Brendan Bracken.[12] At the same press conference

[12] See *Polish Fortnightly Review* (15 July 1942), 8. Stroński included in this figure 'not only those who have been directly executed, but those who have lost their lives since the outbreak of the war'. Bracken and Cardinal Hinsley, archbishop of Westminster, each stated unequivocally that 700,000 Jews had been 'murdered' (Bracken) or 'massacred' (Hinsley). Mikołajczyk, on the other hand, stated that 'the number of massacred Jews exceeds 200,000'. One wonders whether Stroński might have tried to reconcile Mikołajczyk's figure with the number accepted by the British. Whatever the case, Stroński explicitly declared the figure of 700,000 Jewish deaths to be 'correct,' stating further that 'whatever you can say and write about the German horrors in Poland will never be exaggerated'. If, as Mr Stola has stated, 'the truth of the Bund information was seriously doubted by such Polish politicians as ... Stroński' (a statement for which Mr Stola ought to have provided some evidence), such doubt does not appear to have prevented him from publicizing that information at this particular time.

Interior Minister Stanisław Mikołajczyk, although not acknowledging the overall number of 700,000 deaths, quoted the Bund letter's specific casualty figures for, among other places, Lwów (30,000), Vilna (60,000), Stanisławów (15,000), Tarnopol (5,000), Złoczów (2,000), and Brzeżany (4,000). He also declared explicitly, echoing the Bund letter, that 'the wholesale extermination of the Jews' had begun. Hence Mr Stola's statement that 'with the exception of Szmul Zygielbojm, no significant Polish, Jewish, or British politician publicly accepted the facts revealed by the Bund' is untrue. Moreover, his observation that 'Schwarzbart ... tried to distance himself from the account provided by the Bund' must be sharply qualified at least; as reported on p. 184, Schwarzbart and representatives of the World Jewish Congress read from the Bund report at a press conference of their own on 29 June.

There are two possible explanations for the narrowing discrepancy between the Bund letter and official Polish statements about the Jewish situation: either the Poles received new information between 9 June and 9 July that confirmed the details of the Bund letter in their own minds, or their statements following the receipt of the Bund letter were governed by something else in addition to (not necessarily instead of) the degree of credibility they attached to it. In the latter case, it may have been that government officials continued to harbour the same doubts about the accuracy of the Bund report throughout the month in question but chose none the less publicly to certify more of its particulars at the end of the month than at the beginning, or it may have been that they never had any such doubts but chose none the less at first to reveal little of the report's contents, changing their minds later—all because of some consideration other than whether or not they deemed the report accurate. As it turned out, it was not possible to determine with certainty whether either of these explanations was factual, first because no direct documentary evidence could be found attesting to the positions taken by Sikorski, Mikołajczyk, Stroński, and others about the Bund letter or the degree to which its substance ought to be made public, second because the search for additional information that might have arrived in London during the interval in question and confirmed the Bund report was inconclusive. By considering a broad range of circumstantial evidence, however—by looking at other things that happened during the month in question or slightly before or after—it was possible to establish with what seems to me a high degree of probability that belief was not the sole or even the dominant factor that influenced the Polish Government's decisions about publicizing information concerning the situation of the

Jews, neither during the month from 9 June to 9 July nor on any other occasion.

I shall not review all of that circumstantial evidence here, for Mr Stola has not challenged all of it. Instead, I shall discuss only the one item that Mr Stola has questioned—the treatment in *In the Shadow of Auschwitz* of the Government's handling of information about the mass deportations from the Warsaw ghetto from late July to late November 1942. In this case too it will be shown that Mr Stola has neither understood the thesis of the discussion nor paid careful attention to the evidence adduced in its support.

The discussion of how the Polish Government dealt with the news of the Warsaw deportations demonstrated first of all that the Government did not give this news nearly the same degree of public attention that it gave the Bund report in the press conference of 9 July. It did not hold a similar press conference at any time between then and late November; during the same interval the National Council took no notice of the deportations in any resolution, and no Government minister mentioned them publicly. Mr Stola has claimed that Mikołajczyk 'agreed to pass [the information that he received about the deportations from the director of underground civilian resistance, Stefan Korboński, in late July] on to the press', but in fact (unless Mr Stola has made an important new documentary discovery whose details he has not revealed) no press release on the subject emanating from Mikołajczyk's office has been found to date. The only mentions of the deportations from Warsaw in official Polish publications or communiqués that have been located up to the present are two short articles in *Dziennik polski* on 29 July and 19 August and three items in the Yiddish-language edition of the *News Bulletin on Eastern European Affairs* published by the Polish Information Center in New York (appearing on 4, 14, and 20 August). In contrast, neither *Free Europe* nor the *Polish Fortnightly Review*, the government's two primary English-language organs, said anything about the deportations until late November. These facts certainly show that the news of the deportations from Warsaw was not treated in the same fashion as was the news contained in the Bund report; this observation is what set the discussion of the handling of the news of the deportations in *In the Shadow of Auschwitz* in motion.

Another observation reinforced the direction of that motion. That observation was that shortly after 20 August, the last date prior to late November on which any official Polish Government publication or spokesman made mention of the Warsaw deportations, the Government received significant new information about the course and scope of those deportations but did not make this information known—not only not to the press but not even to the two Jewish representatives on the National Council, who earlier had been made privy to at least some of the initial news about them. The information came in the form of a cable from Home Army Commander Stefan Rowecki, dispatched on 19 August and received in London on 25 August. The cable stated that the deportations had been proceeding continuously since 22 July; that initially 5,000–6,000, and at the time of the cable 15,000, Jews were being deported daily; that the majority of the deportees were taken to Treblinka and Bełżec, where they were most likely being killed; and that more than 150,000 Jews had been deported to date.[13] Rowecki's cable was followed by another signal through civilian channels on 31 August, stating that 15,000 Jews were being carried away daily to four places of execution (Czerwony Bór, Bełżec, Sobibór, and Treblinka).[14] Nevertheless, until late November the most that could be gathered from official Polish Government publications and statements about the deporta-

[13] 'Gen. Rowecki do Centrali: Wielka Akcja Likwidowania Ghetta w Warszawie', in *Armia Krajowa w dokumentach*, ii (London, 1973), 298 (No. 329). This document was mentioned in *In the Shadow of Auschwitz*, 194, and cited in note 156 on p. 301. Mr Stola has mentioned a telegram from Rowecki sent on 25 Aug. It would seem that he is referring to 'a radiogram transmitted by the Wanda radio station on 25 August' mentioned in Walter Laqueur, *The Terrible Secret: Suppression of the Truth about Hitler's 'Final Solution'* (Boston, 1980), 113. According to Laqueur, the text of this radiogram was published in *Armia Krajowa w dokumentach*, ii. 210. It appears, however, that Laqueur got two things wrong: the document in question was actually printed on p. 298, not on p. 210, and 25 Aug. was given as the date of *receipt*, not the date of *transmission*. The correct citation and dates were given in *In the Shadow of Auschwitz*. Mr Stola, however, appears neither to have paid sufficient attention to the relevant note nor to have checked the relevant document for himself.

Moreover, Mr Stola's statement that Laqueur explains the fact that the contents of the Rowecki telegram were never revealed by referring to 'the restriction of reports from army intelligence to a small group of high-ranking officers' shows that he has not understood Laqueur's text any better than he has understood mine. The relevant sentence in Laqueur's book (p. 112) is: 'It stands to reason that "military" news, i.e. Home Army affairs, was not widely circulated, *but the information concerning Jews did not belong to this category*' (emphasis added).

The information in this cable also helps to show that by Sikorski's speech of 29 Oct. the Government did indeed possess information that 'at least one-third of the country's pre-war Jewish population would not be alive to enjoy any benefits of victory at all'. The Bund report contained information about 700,000 Jewish deaths by mid-May; Rowecki reported 150,000 Jewish deaths from the Warsaw ghetto alone between 22 July and 19 Aug.; the subsequent cable of 31 Aug. (see below) reported that as of that date deportations were continuing at 15,000 per day. Since Rowecki noted that the rate of 15,000 per day was in force already as of 19 Aug., Government officials could easily have calculated that between 19 and 31 Aug. an additional 180,000 Jews had gone to their deaths. These figures alone total 1,030,000 Jewish deaths as of 31 Aug. of which the Government had been apprised. Moreover, information demonstrably received in London before 15 Oct., labelled 'completely reliable', indicated that the pace of the 'physical liquidation' of the Warsaw ghetto had been stepped up. The Government then surely had a basis for concluding by 29 Oct. that 'at least one-third of the country's pre-war Jewish population [of about 3.3 million] would not be alive' at the end of the war.

[14] 'Depesza z kraju', 31 Aug. 1942, Studium Polski Podziemnej, 56/117. This telegram was also cited in *In the Shadow of Auschwitz*, 301 n. 156. Mr Stola does not seem to have paid any attention to it.

tions from Warsaw was that the German authorities *had plans* to send 100,000 Jews off to 'an unknown destination in the east' (or, according to the Yiddish-language press release of 4 August, 'to "liquidate" the Warsaw ghetto'); that so far 6,000 Jews had been deported; and that the head of the Warsaw Judenrat, Adam Czerniaków, had committed suicide on 23 July. Put another way, no official Polish publication or statement by a member of the Polish Government gave any indication before late November that more than 6,000 Jews had been deported; that deportations had been a daily occurrence since 22 July; or that the destination and fate of the deportees were known—this, despite the fact that such information had been received in London at least by 25 August. In other words, it is certain that during the three months between late August and late November there was a disparity between the information held by the Polish authorities in London about the mass deportation of Jews from the Polish capital and the information that it released to the public.

Notice that *In the Shadow of Auschwitz* established this disparity with certainty only for the period after 25 August; contrary to Mr Stola's claim, it did not state positively that such a disparity existed during the period 22 July–25 August. The book's discussion of the information received during that earlier interval and the manner in which it reached the press actually made a very different point, about which more later. In the meantime, however, it should be pointed out that Mr Stola's statements on this matter—particularly his comments on the significance of the telegrams from Korboński on 26 July and 11 August, both for the elucidation of the issue in general and for their alleged obviation of the analysis in *In the Shadow of Auschwitz*—are for the most part not valid. In the first place, it is not the case, as Mr Stola has implied, that these telegrams represent 'new and important sources' discovered since the publication of the book that have caused the discussion to lose 'some of its validity'; as Mr Stola has himself acknowledged, 'the author is familiar with Korboński's telegrams'.[15] While it appears highly probable that the telegram of 26 July represented the totality of the information shown by Mikołajczyk to Schwarzbart (and also to Zygielbojm, as recent research by Daniel Blatman has

---

[15] As it happens, the two telegrams were published as *In the Shadow of Auschwitz* was being prepared for press. As a result, they could be mentioned, for technical reasons, only in the notes. However, although Mr Stola may not have understood all of the 'reservations and provisos' that, in his words, 'cluttered' note 142 on p. 300, more astute readers will easily comprehend why there was nothing in the cable of 26 July (whose text was given in full) that contradicted the statement in the book that 'it is impossible to ascertain exactly what the interior minister knew of the liquidation of the ghetto on 27 July'. Korboński's telegram of 26 July represents the *minimum* that Mikołajczyk could have known, not the maximum. Readers can be assured that had this not been the case, I would not have hesitated to hold up publication of the book and rewrite the relevant portions as required by the new information. Fortunately, this was not necessary.

demonstrated),[16] and which in turn formed the basis for Schwarzbart's cable to the World Jewish Congress on 27 July 1942, Mr Stola has no way of determining whether that message represented *everything that the interior minister knew* about the deportations from Warsaw at the time. Korboński has testified that he sent more than one signal around this time; he may, to be sure, have testified falsely, but this cannot be proven. It is also certain that a more detailed report was dispatched from Warsaw to London on 25 July, but it is not known how this report was sent or when it arrived.[17] As a result of the uncertainty in the documentary record, *In the Shadow of Auschwitz* reached no conclusion on this matter, stating simply (p. 300) that 'it appears to be anyone's guess exactly what Mikołajczyk knew on 27 July'.

Moreover, the fact that, as Mr Stola acknowledges, 'those articles which appeared ... in Polish publications in the West ... did not take in the threat of an immediate annihilation of the ghetto's population ... [because of] an erroneous interpretation of the telegram' actually lends credence to the possibility raised in *In the Shadow of Auschwitz* that the articles about the deportations appearing in non-Polish publications might have been based upon information supplied through the intermediacy of Schwarzbart or Zygielbojm rather than by the Polish Government directly. As *In the Shadow of Auschwitz* pointed out, those latter articles, in contrast to those appearing in Polish publications, *did* stress the threat of immediate annihilation. If so, then Mr Stola would have to conclude that those articles were based upon a correct interpretation of Korboński's telegram; but if the prevailing interpretation in Polish Government circles was incorrect, the correct interpretation must have come from elsewhere.[18]

Finally, the second Korboński telegram, dispatched on 11 August, actually shows that even as early as that date the Polish Government knew more about the deportations from Warsaw than it made public. That telegram stated clearly that 'from the ghetto 7,000 are taken away daily for slaughter'.[19] Here was confirmation that deportation was a daily occurrence; although the word 'daily' may have been missing from the first telegram, it was not missing from this one. Yet this fact was not reflected in any official

---

[16] Daniel Blatman, 'On a Mission against All Odds: Samuel Zygelbojm [*sic*] in London (April 1942–May 1943)', *Yad Vashem Studies*, 20 (1990), 250.

[17] Mr Stola has claimed that this report was posted. It would be interesting to know on what basis he professes to know this, for the document itself contains no indication of how it was transmitted or when it was received.

[18] Again, it should be noted that *In the Shadow of Auschwitz* did not reach any definite conclusion on this question either, stating clearly (p. 194) that 'on the basis of the available documentary evidence, such a reconstruction of events ... cannot be regarded as more than surmise'.

[19] Quoted in Richard C. Lukas, *The Forgotten Holocaust: The Poles under German Occupation, 1939–1944* (Lexington, Ky., 1986), 157.

Polish publication or statement by a member of the Government until late November.[20] If anything, then, the second Korboński telegram, far from undermining the validity of the discussion in *In the Shadow of Auschwitz*, may actually necessitate moving up the date at which a disparity began to appear between information held and information released from late August to mid-August.

Two facts, then, are clear with regard to the Government's handling of the news of the Warsaw deportations: the Government did not give this news public exposure to the degree that the Bund report had received it, and from at least late August, if not earlier, the Government did not publicize all of the information about the deportations that was in its possession. These facts played an important role in the formation of my thesis that belief was not the key factor that determined how the Government handled information about the condition of Polish Jews under Nazi occupation. Let us assume, for the sake of argument, that none of the information received by the Government in London about the Warsaw deportations was regarded as credible. If this assumption is true, then it seems probable that the earlier Bund report also was not ever regarded as credible; for if the Bund report—which stated explicitly that the Germans had already begun the 'physical extermination of the Jewish population on Polish soil', reported the complete or near-complete liquidation of ghettos in such major cities as Lublin and Vilna, and described the operation of gas vans at Chełmno— had been believed, it makes no sense to suppose that the news from Warsaw, which conformed entirely to the pattern set forth in the Bund report, must have been rejected. But if the Bund report had not been

---

[20] As reported in *In the Shadow of Auschwitz* (p. 195), an article appeared in *Dziennik polski* on 19 Aug. indicating that Adam Czerniaków had committed suicide on 23 July after having been commanded by the German authorities 'personally to organize a list of the Jews, who were to be deported in groups of 7,000 per day'. That article, however, gave no indication that such deportations were still being carried out, or even that they had ever been carried out in the past. Moreover, the article merely repeated information that had been reported in British and American dailies several days earlier—information that had been obtained from sources in Switzerland, not from the Polish Government in London. On the other hand, although the government did not publish information about daily deportations in its own name until the end of November, it evidently did provide this information to Zygielbojm. In a speech marking the third anniversary of the invasion of Poland on 2 Sept. 1942, the Bund representative noted that according to 'the latest news received by the Polish Government in London ... seven thousand people are being sent away every day from the [Warsaw] ghetto': 'Rede oif an internatsionaln Miting in London, 2 September 1942', in *Zygielbojm bukh* (New York, 1947), 347. Of course it cannot be known precisely when or under what circumstances Zygielbojm was made privy to this information (before or after the release of the Polish publications of 19–20 Aug.; at the Government's initiative or at Zygielbojm's). The fact remains, however, that at no time did an official Government spokesman confirm publicly in a Polish publication or in a release to the general press that it had received information that 7,000 Jews were being deported from the Warsaw ghetto every day in continuous fashion.

believed, it is clear that such disbelief did not prevent the Polish Government from confirming publicly most of its particulars at a press conference on 9 July. Some other factor must have convinced the Polish Government that it was in its interest at that time to give publicity even to information whose accuracy it did not entirely accept. But if so, one must ask why that same factor did not lead the Government to give publicity to the information about the daily deportation of up to 15,000 Jews from the Warsaw ghetto and their killing at Treblinka and other locations that was demonstrably in its possession at least from 25 August. Clearly more considerations than the simple credibility of the information must have affected the decision about how to handle this news. Moreover, this must have been so even if the news from Warsaw *had* been believed; in this case, some other factor must have held up its release. It does not seem, then, to be a reasonable generalization that information that was believed was widely publicized while information that was disbelieved was not.

This realization sent me on a search for indications of what other factor (or combination of factors) might have been at work in the cases in question. In this connection I observed several additional facts, all documented in *In the Shadow of Auschwitz*: (1) from early July to December 1942 the essence of virtually every news item about the situation of the Jews in Poland appearing in an official Polish publication had already appeared in a non-Polish publication and was traceable to sources other than the Polish Government; (2) Sikorski, in his capacity as chairman of the St James's Palace Conference on German Atrocities, explicitly refused a Jewish request to include mention of the Jewish situation in the conference's declaration; (3) on 7 July 1942 the Polish National Council modified a motion that originally had dealt mainly with the peril faced by Jews in Poland, eliminating from it all specific mention of Jews; (4) simultaneously with the Bund report, the Government also received new reports about a stepped-up German campaign of violence and repression against Poles; (5) receipt of these reports led the government, beginning precisely on 9 June 1942, to open a campaign for Britain and the United States to warn Germany of certain retaliation and postwar punishment for atrocities committed against Poles; (6) one of these reports contained the observation that 'if Polish reports from the homeland are not entirely believed by the Anglo-Saxon peoples as downright improbable, then the Jewish reports—such as, for example, that in various cities in Poland the Germans have murdered the entire Jewish population, that 50,000–60,000 of them have been murdered in Vilna and 12,000 in Lwów ...—ought to get through to their governments';[21] (7) the Polish campaign

---

[21] 'Jeśli sprawozdania polskie z kraju nie znajdują u narodów anglosaskich w pełni wiary jako wręcz nieprawdopodobne, to przecież powinny dotrzeć do rządów ich sprawozdania żydowskie,

for an Anglo-American warning to Germany came to a successful culmination precisely at the joint Anglo-Polish press conference on 9 July, when Brendan Bracken issued the very declaration the Poles had desired in the name of the British government; (8) prior to Jan Karski's arrival in London in mid-November the Polish Government possessed information that it regarded as authentic to the effect that the population of the Warsaw ghetto had been reduced to 140,000 with ration-cards printed for 100,000 persons only;[22] (9) the Government gave this information to Schwarzbart but *explicitly forbade him to publish it*;[23] (10) Karski's mission required him to report not only to the Polish Government but to Schwarzbart, Zygielbojm, and Jewish leaders in Great Britain.

These facts, taken together with the Government's previously observed pattern of presenting information about the Jewish situation within the context of materials concerned mainly with the plight of the Poles, as well as with several other observations, mainly about the manner in which the Polish leadership in London regarded the role of Jews in the formation of Allied public opinion, led me to the following inferences. In publicizing information about conditions in the occupied homeland, for either Poles or Jews, the Polish Government was primarily concerned with employing that information in a way that would benefit the Polish population. With this aim in mind, it tended to consider carefully whether and how any given piece of information in its possession ought to be disseminated. In making this determination with regard to information about the Jewish situation, it was guided to a significant extent by the notion that the Western Allies might be more sensitive to the Jewish than to the Polish plight. On one hand, this situation could be exploited by the Polish Government in order

---

np. tego rodzaju, że w różnych miastach Polski, Niemcy wymordowali całą ludność żydowską, że w Wilnie wymordowali ich około 50 do 60.000, we Lwowie 12.000 ...': 'Uwagi ogólne'. 'HIA-Stanisław Mikołajczyk, box 9, file: 'Committee on Occupied Poland—Correspondence, 1942–43'.

[22] That this information was held before Karski's arrival is attested both by the fact that Karski's own testimony spoke of 40,000 ration-cards to be printed for the month of October and by the fact that Paweł Siudak of the Polish Interior Ministry told Schwarzbart that the information had been sent by the office of the underground government delegate in early September. For summaries of Karski's testimony see Frank Savery to F. K. Roberts, 3 Dec. 1942, Public Record Office, FO 371/30924.C12221; Martin Gilbert, *Auschwitz and the Allies* (New York, 1981), 93–5. On Siudak's statement see the Schwarzbart diary, 16 Nov. 1942, Yad Vashem Archives, M2/751. The most important passages from this entry have been reprinted in Gutman and Krakowski, *Unequal Victims*, 89–90.

[23] As noted in *In the Shadow of Auschwitz*, 303 n. 175, Schwarzbart informed the World Jewish Congress, to whom he conveyed this information on 18 Nov. 1942, that it was not for publication. Schwarzbart's diary entry for 16 Nov. confirms that he was told not to make this information public (see previous note). That entry also indicates that the Government had not volunteered this information to Schwarzbart; rather a rumour of the existence of the information

to attract the attention of the Allied public and governments to information about the brutal nature of the Nazi occupation regime in Poland, which affected not only Jews but Poles as well. On the other hand, the supposed greater Allied sensitivity to Jewish suffering presented the danger that news about it would overshadow the peril facing the larger Polish population. Hence care was to be taken always to present news about the Jewish situation in the context of information about German atrocities in Poland in general, whereas statements, actions, or publications that focused *exclusively* upon Jews or that encouraged the consideration of the Jewish situation *in isolation* from the plight of all inhabitants of Poland were to be discouraged. On certain occasions, depending upon specific circumstances, it might prove advisable to augment somewhat the proportion of attention devoted to the Jewish situation within the context of statements about conditions in Poland overall, especially if new information about the Jewish situation had recently been reported in the Allied press through other sources. However, the benefit of the majority Polish population required that Allied awareness of its suffering not be overshadowed by the plight of the Jews.

At least two considerations seemed to me to make these inferences highly credible. First, they explained virtually all of the previously observed facts with regard to the government's handling of information about the Jewish situation. For example, both the relatively greater attention given to the plight of the Jews between 9 June and 9 July and the subsequent reversion

had been leaked unofficially to the Jewish representative, and he had confronted Siudak and Mikołajczyk with it. These facts show Mr Stola's statement that 'on 16 November the Minister of the Interior revealed information about the newly arrived reports of the fate of the Warsaw ghetto to ... Schwarzbart' to be inaccurate. Mr Stola, who has indicated that he has read Schwarzbart's diary entry of 16 Nov., appears not to have understood what Schwarzbart related.

These facts also show that it is not the case, contrary to what Mr Stola has argued, that 'The fact that Schwarzbart was made privy to this information ... seriously weakens' the contention that the Government did not publicize all of the information that it held regarding the mass deportations from the Warsaw ghetto until after 23 Nov. In fact, they actually demonstrate the validity of the argument put forth in *In the Shadow of Auschwitz*—that the Polish Interior Ministry did not want the news whose confirmation the Representation of Polish Jewry requested on 6 Nov. to become public knowledge. It is known definitely that on 14 Nov. the Interior Ministry declined to confirm this news even to the Polish Foreign Ministry; it can be reasonably inferred that it did so again on 18 Nov., when, according to an annotation on the outgoing cable-form, the Foreign Ministry put off sending the reply to the Representation's request for several more days (presumably in order to await the anticipated confirmation requested from the homeland). The cable-form is located in HIA-Polish Government, box 700 (MSZ), file 851/e: 'Żydzi—Prześladowania niemieckie', subfile 'Ratowanie Żydów'.

Mr Stola has also stated incorrectly that Schwarzbart was 'a representative of the [Representation of Polish Jewry]'. Actually the relationship between Schwarzbart and the Representation was not terribly clear to anyone who dealt with either body, or even to Schwarzbart and the Representation themselves. This is not the place to try to sort this matter out; suffice it to say that when Polish officials spoke to Schwarzbart they did not assume that they were speaking simultaneously to the Representation of Polish Jewry, which was located in Palestine, not London.

to the earlier pattern after that period now made sense. Between 9 June and
9 July the government felt that the information contained in the Bund letter
concerning the existence of a German programme to kill all of Polish Jewry
and actions undertaken in accordance with that programme could help it in
its campaign to achieve an Anglo-American statement on punishment for
atrocities committed by Germany in Poland. Moreover, towards the end of
this interval there was no reason for the government not to report the
information, for the contents of the Bund letter had already been made
known in the British news media since 24 June. Hence the role played by
Jewish matters at the press conference of 9 July (about a fifth of the
conference's total time) was as it was. However, once the British government
had issued the statement that the Poles desired, the immediate need that had
prompted this action no longer existed: now the Polish Government had to
be concerned lest the peril to the Jews make the Poles' plight pale in
comparison and divert Allied attention from Polish suffering altogether.
Thus when news arrived that the Polish capital was being systematically
emptied of Jews—news that put the spotlight clearly on the Jewish
situation in a way that made it highly possible that the plight of the Poles
might be eclipsed in Allied thinking—the government returned to its
earlier pattern of releasing information sparingly, and then mainly when
that information was also available from other sources. Hence the news that
the government had possessed at least since 25 August about the extent of
the deportations from Warsaw and the fate of the deportees appears to have
been released only following Karski's arrival in London most probably not
so much because Karski brought significant new information (in fact he
added only minor details to what was already known) or because his
eyewitness testimony caused previously disbelieved information to be believed (unlikely in the light of documentary and circumstantial evidence
discussed above), but mainly because Karski had been charged with delivering his information to circles over which the Polish Government had no
control.

The second consideration that recommended the above inferences to
me was the discovery of direct documentary evidence that in 1943 the
argument that the Polish Government must take care not to allow news of
the Jewish plight to make the suffering of the Poles pale by comparison
was advanced by at least two Polish bureaucrats (one of them the highest-
ranking civil servant in the Foreign Ministry) whose opinion on the matter
was solicited. This evidence could not be discussed in *In the Shadow of
Auschwitz* because it pertained to events that occured after the period
treated in the book; it has, however, been presented in *Facing a Holocaust*
on pp. 36–7 and p. 63. To be sure, the evidence does not constitute
direct proof that Raczyński, Mikołajczyk, and other ministers took this

position in 1942, but it does make it appear highly likely that they did—especially when taken together with the circumstantial evidence outlined above.

Two things should now be clear. First, the discussion of Mikołajczyk's handling of the *initial* news of the deportations from Warsaw (the news transmitted—perhaps exclusively, perhaps not—in Korboński's cable of 26 July 1942) was not offered as proof of 'Polish collusion in the concealment of the real dimensions of the Jewish tragedy', let alone as 'one of the strongest proofs' thereof. That entire discussion was offered in order to demonstrate that all treatments of this news that can be traced directly and unquestionably to a Polish Government source differed substantially and consistently in their emphasis from treatments that cannot be so traced. This demonstration was undertaken, in turn, as part of two broader demonstrations—that the government was probably (not certainly) only indirectly responsible for the initial publication of the news in the Western and Palestinian press, and that the government generally endeavoured to avoid making the threat facing Jews appear inordinately greater than that facing Poles.

Secondly, and more important, the notion that *In the Shadow of Auschwitz* spoke of a Polish 'conspiracy of silence' with regard to information about the situation of Polish Jews under German occupation or charged the Polish Government with issuing 'anti-Jewish political-information directives' represents a serious misreading of the text. *In the Shadow of Auschwitz* proposed only that as a result of acting in accord with what it perceived to be the needs and interests of the majority Polish population in the occupied homeland with regard to the publication of information about the deeds of the occupiers, the Polish Government often acted in a fashion that did not accord with the needs and interests of Polish Jewry. Readers may draw their own conclusions as to the morality of such action; they must do so, however, on their own responsibility, for *In the Shadow of Auschwitz* made no judgement in this regard. But to read into this statement an imputation of Polish 'ill will' towards Jews, or 'anti-Jewish' attitudes, or a 'conspiracy' to make certain that Jews did not receive what they needed, is to read without any objective textual foundation: since it cannot be logically inferred that an action that had the effect of harming a Jewish interest was taken out of a conscious desire to harm that interest, it similarly cannot be logically inferred that one who stated that a given action affected a Jewish interest adversely implied by such statement that that action had been undertaken in order to produce that effect.

IV

With regard to the issue of General Anders, Mr Stola has claimed that according to *In the Shadow of Auschwitz* the Polish military leader was determined 'not to allow Jews into the ranks of the army, to remove those who had somehow managed to enter it, and not to allow their evacuation from the USSR, except for 'a small group of Jews kept "for propaganda purposes"'. He has also imputed to me a 'picture of Anders [as an] antisemite in conformity with my alleged overestimation of 'the blind hatred of Polish politicians for the Jews'.

Once again, these readings are Mr Stola's own inventions. Anders was never referred to in *In the Shadow of Auschwitz* as an antisemite; in fact, I never labelled any Polish political or military figure with such an appellation anywhere in the book. Nor did I ever ascribe any of the actions discussed in the book, let alone those relating to Jews in the Polish army in the USSR, to 'the blind hatred of Polish politicians for the Jews'. In the event, I never undertook to determine at any point what any Polish politician felt about Jews in his heart of hearts, for one of the book's main findings was that emotions of any kind (whether hostile or sympathetic towards Jews) played at most a peripheral role in the formation of Polish Government decisions about Jewish matters. And—again despite Mr Stola's use of inverted commas—nowhere will readers find the words 'for propaganda purposes' offered as the explanation for the presence of Jewish soldiers in the Polish armed forces or among the evacuees from the Soviet Union in 1942.

Moreover, Mr Stola's summary of my 'basic assessment of the aims of Anders' is not correct. Far from stating that Anders aimed 'not to allow Jews into the ranks of the army', *In the Shadow of Auschwitz* merely observed (pp. 133–4) that in *mid-October 1941* Anders began 'to seek ways of *limiting* the number of Jews serving with the Polish forces'. Far from arguing that Anders aimed 'to remove those [Jews] who had somehow entered' the army, the book simply noted (p. 134) that 'in many cases excuses were ... found to dismiss Jews who had already begun to serve'. And with regard to the evacuation, the book found (p. 146) that 'in dealing with the evacuation of Jewish *civilians* [not soldiers, whose number was fixed as a result of previous recruitment policies], Anders was forced to operate within a complex field of conflicting constraints and pressures that on balance led him to pursue a visible yet minimal Jewish presence in the departing transports'. Among those conflicting constraints and pressures, moreover, the greatest weight was given to pressure applied by the *British* government to keep the number of Jewish evacuees small—this because the British wished to keep these Jews out of Palestine, the Polish army's destination. An astute reader ought to have understood from the book that had the British and Soviet positions regarding the evacuation of Jews been different, more Jews might have been able to leave the USSR with the Polish forces (although ultimately this is not provable).

Mr Stola has stated further that the picture of Anders that he has read (erroneously) into the book seems to him to have been adopted as a result of uncritical acceptance of the view of sources hostile to the general. Here Mr Stola simply has not paid attention to the evidence presented quite plainly. As noted on p. 134, Anders himself 'ordered that enlistments from the ethnic minorities not exceed 5 per cent of the noncommissioned officers and 10 per cent of the private soldiers'; the published work cited in the attached note gave the text and archival location of this order.[24] Nor is it true that 'the startling claim that Anders "sought Soviet assistance in preventing Jewish enlistments" is based [exclusively] on the diary of Anders's ex-adjutant'. The relevant note referred to research by Kalman Nussbaum, which documented, on the basis of a memorandum located in the archive of the Polish Institute in London, a meeting in November 1941 between Anders and Soviet Colonel Yevstigniev at which the Polish commander complained of the 'excessive number (*nadmiar*) of Jews in the army' that

---

[24] I did not cite the archival location myself because I wished to avoid giving the impression that I had discovered this document. In general, when a relevant document had already been cited in a previous scholarly publication, I credited that publication as my source, except where I wished to call attention to a part of the document that had not been considered there. In this case, the document in question had already been cited and quoted in an extensive study published in Hebrew in 1984 (Kalman Nussbaum, *Vehafakh lahem lero'ets: Hayehudim batsava ha'amami hapolani biverit-hamo'atsot* (Tel Aviv, 1984), 54). To be sure, Mr Stola may not have been able to read this important book. Nevertheless, insufficient linguistic skills do not absolve him of the obligation to be familiar with significant scholarship on the subject about which he writes; certainly they do not entitle him to make the false statement that 'Documents presented as evidence that ... Anders tried to limit the number of Jews in the army ... say nothing on the subject' when he is not capable of checking the cited source. However, the document has now been mentioned in a Polish study that Mr Stola has cited in his review; Krystyna Kersten, *Polacy, Żydzi, komunizm: Anatomia półprawd 1939–1968* (Warsaw, 1992), 33. Mr Stola evidently has not paid attention to this fact.

Regarding Mr Stola's claim that Kot's comments about 'military men ... like Pstrokoński' (actually the text says 'our military men, especially of Pstrokoński's ilk [nasi wojskowi, zwłaszcza typu Pstrokońskiego]') do not implicate Anders, it should be noted first that this document was not used to prove the contention that Anders sought to limit Jewish enlistments but merely as part of a discussion raising the *possibility* that the idea *might have* crossed Anders's mind (perhaps, not definitely) before October; second, that the phrase 'military leaders' was offered not as a translation but as a paraphrase; and third, that Lt.-Col. Stanisław Pstrokoński, the quartermaster of the Polish forces in the USSR, not only qualified as a 'military leader' but was not the only military man to whom Kot was referring. Mr Stola's remarks in this regard are thus neither accurate nor relevant.

had resulted, he alleged, from Soviet manipulations.[25] Whether Jerzy Klimkowski, Anders's adjutant, whose description in his memoirs of a similar meeting was quoted by Professor Yisrael Gutman in his article, was indeed a 'pathological liar', as, according to Mr Stola, the Polish politician Karol Popiel alleged (one wonders what qualified Popiel to diagnose psychopathology, and even more what qualifies Mr Stola to confirm it), the fact remains that in this instance his testimony has been demonstrated to be true by the extant archival record.

Mr Stola's failure to read properly is further exemplified by his comment that Kot's statement to the effect that '[Jews] are usually accepted into the army if they volunteer' 'says something completely contrary to Engel's assertions' about restrictions upon Jewish enlistment. Mr Stola has failed to mention that that statement was made on 5 September 1941, whereas the book stated that the existence of restrictions could be definitely dated only to mid-October. Kot's statement reflected the reality of early September; as *In the Shadow of Auschwitz* stated explicitly (p. 133), 'among those who had enlisted during the first two months of recruitment, an extremely large number—perhaps as high as 40 per cent—were Jews'. Still, the statement shows clearly that the subject of how the Polish armed forces in the USSR ought to deal with Jews was a matter of concern to both Kot and Anders well before enlistment restrictions were enacted, with Kot having to explain to Anders the public-relations aspect of this question. That is how the statement was presented in the text.

Mr Stola is also incorrect in declaring that 'In discussion with a delegation of Polish Jews on 24 October 1941' Anders did not make it clear that 'he did not want "Jews from eastern Poland under his command"', but was referring instead to Jews who had '"ostentatiously and gleefully greeted the invading Soviet army"' in Poland in 1939'. Mr Stola obviously has not checked the record of that conversation; had he done so he would have found that Anders made no such behavioural distinction (in fact, the phrase 'ostentatiously and gleefully greeted the invading Soviet army' came not from the protocol of this meeting but from Anders's memoirs, the second source listed in note 119 to page 133). In the event, the protocol stated that 'in the general's opinion Polish Jews can be divided into two groups, the Jews of the western and central Polish territories and those of the eastern provinces (*Żydów kresowych*); the latter repeatedly behaved as badly as could be during the hard days of Poland's collapse.'[26] In other words, at

---

[25] See previous note. The existence of this document has also been noted in Kersten, *Polacy, Żydzi, komunizm*, 33.

[26] 'Sprawozdanie z rozmowy Generała Andersa z przedstawicielami żydowstwa [*sic*] polskiego na terenie ZSRR', 24 Oct. 1941, HIA-Stanisław Mikołajczyk, box 16, file: 'Polish Army in USSR: Jewish Question'. A facsimile of this document has been printed in Shalom Slowes,

this meeting Anders distinguished among Jews exclusively on geographical foundation; he could not therefore have applied a behavioural test on an individual basis to Jews seeking to join the Polish forces. Furthermore, Anders told the Jewish spokesmen at this meeting that as a result of deliberate Soviet machinations, Jews had taken up so many places in the army that more qualified Poles could not be accepted. It was clear that Anders believed that this situation, in which the percentage of Jews in the armed forces was greater than their percentage in Poland, was unfortunate—a fact that makes it not at all surprising that he would reproach Yevstigniev three weeks later for the existence of this situation.

Mr Stola has also objected to the statement in *In the Shadow of Auschwitz* that 'the Soviet restrictions upon Jewish enlistment ... provide[d] the Poles with a convenient means for covering up their own attitude toward Jews in their army'. He has, however, not offered any basis for his objection; indeed, in view of the fact that Polish restrictions upon Jewish enlistment prior to the imposition of Soviet restrictions have been well documented not only in *In the Shadow of Auschwitz* but in other studies by both Jewish and Polish historians.[27] I do not see how he could. Yet in trying to argue for his objection he has actually presented in his review a highly selective and incomplete quotation from the book's text. His ellipsis omitted the statement that the Soviet restrictions also provided the Poles with a means 'for sidestepping Jewish charges of discrimination', as well as the sentence that 'Polish military officials were advised that minority applicants for induction were to be brought before recruiting boards only if a Soviet liaison officer was present, in order to force the Soviet official to disqualify the applicant in the applicant's presence and to make it clear that it was the Russians, not the Poles, who were preventing Jews from volunteering for Polish military service.' This sentence was supported with a reference (note 148) to a set of instructions issued to division commanders entitled 'The Induction of National Minorities into the Polish Armed Forces (*Pobór mniejszości narodowych do Polskich Sił Zbr [ojnych]*)', in which not only were the provisions described in the omitted sentence specifically stated, but the reason for the adoption was made explicit: 'so that [commanders and those under their command] not create a basis for [propaganda] attacks against the Polish authorities'. That the Soviet authorities generally 'did not oblige the Poles by challenging the induction of minority recruits' (another part of a sentence that Mr Stola cut off in his quotation) is indicated by, among other things,

---

Ya'ar Katyn, 1940 (Tel Aviv, 1986), 227–30. An English translation appeared in *Jews in Eastern Poland and the USSR, 1939–1946*, ed. by Norman Davies and Antony Polonsky (London, 1991), 369–72.

[27] See above, n. 24.

the fact, listed and documented in the book's next sentence, that even in March 1942 Soviet recruiting offices referred Jews to the Polish forces for induction. And 'the Poles' great chagrin' is attested not only by the instructions to division commanders themselves but by numerous communications, including the long letter sent from the Polish embassy in Kujbyszew on 23 March 1942 cited in note 152 to page 138 (which Mr Stola has evidently not checked).

Mr Stola's comments about the manner in which *In the Shadow of Auschwitz* treated the matter of the evacuation of Jews from the USSR do not require extensive treatment, since he simply has not understood the book's thesis regarding this issue. When Mr Stola admonishes that 'We must remember that the NKVD consciously incited ... feelings ... calculated to exacerbate the Polish–Jewish antagonism' and that these actions 'contributed to the prevalence of the view that the Poles and not the Russians were the main culprits', he is actually saying something quite similar to what I have said on page 146—that the Soviets manœuvered Anders 'into a position from which he would unavoidably appear as the principal obstacle to Jewish evacuation, while they could present themselves as generous benefactors of the Jewish interest'. And does not my statement on the same page that Anders was unwilling to challenge the Soviet ban on Jews in the evacuating transports out of fear 'that the Soviets ... would make good their threat to curtail the entire evacuation' in consequence conform with the message from Prime Minister Sikorski that Mr Stola has quoted? Mr Stola would have readers believe that I have attributed the small number of Jews among those Polish citizens evacuated to 'the blind hatred of Polish politicians for the Jews'. I submit that no careful and objective reader can find any basis for such a reading in the text of *In the Shadow of Auschwitz*.

Nor shall I devote much space to Mr Stola's effort to reopen the issue of the genuineness of Anders's notorious order of 30 November 1941. The strained attempt to use the existence of a number of copies of the order as proof of the document's falsehood is a cute bit of academic acrobatics, but it is hardly serious.[28] Mr Stola's assertion that 'Colonel Bąkiewicz of the ... Intelligence Corps ... confirmed Anders's words' that the order was a forgery is false; Bąkiewicz merely reported that he had not found an incriminating copy of the order.[29] Moreover, if Mr Stola finds Kot's

---

[28] It should be noted that Krystyna Kersten, whose discovery of a copy of the order among the papers of Adam Ciołkosz in London Mr Stola has cited as proof of the suspiciousness of the order's authenticity, does not share Mr Stola's position. Cf. Kersten, *Polacy, Żydzi, komunizm*, 42: 'Autentyczność tego pisma z datą 30 XI 1941 roku nie może być kwestionowana—poza tekstami opublikowanymi ... istnieją egzemplarze, których wiarygodność nie budzi wątpliwości.'

[29] See cable, Marian Kukiel to Sylwin Strakacz, 31 Aug. 1943 (L. dz. 1145/WPol/43), Archiwum Instytutu Polskiego—A.12/755/2.

affirmation of the order's authenticity suspect because of 'Kot's hatred of Anders', would not the testimony of Bąkiewicz, a soldier under Anders's command, be similarly suspect? And would Mr Stola include General Zygmunt Bohusz-Szyszko, Anders's chief of staff, among those 'not well disposed to Anders' whose statements 'are also unreliable'? Bohusz-Szyszko explicitly and emphatically confirmed the genuineness of the order in a postwar testimony.[30] In short, the state of the evidence is now such that if Mr Stola wishes to prove Anders's order a forgery, the burden of proof must be on him. And if he wishes to assume that burden, he ought at least to provide a documented thesis as to who perpetrated the forgery and when it was perpetrated.

Finally, I wonder what Mr Stola means by the statement that the picture of Anders that I allegedly presented was adopted 'without the necessary degree of criticism'. Mr Stola has evidently not noticed that the better part of my statements about Anders's actions (not about Anders himself, with whose character and personal feelings I was not concerned) were based upon Anders's own words—in his orders, his communications with London, his personal notes, his memoirs, and his remarks as recorded in official protocols. Use of such sources hardly suggests uncritical adoption of the testimony of those hostile to the general.

V

In conclusion, I shall comment briefly on several other objectionable features of Mr Stola's review.

1. Mr Stola has stated that I 'explain the negative attitude of Polish politicians towards the Jews by the revival of anti-Jewish sentiments', ... whereas 'The negative attitudes of Jewish politicians he attributes to their bad experiences in the past.' As an alternative to this supposed thesis he has argued that 'there was some real basis' for Polish politicians' 'irritation with Jewish behaviour' and that 'Jewish politicians became, like their Polish counterparts, the victims of their own prejudices'. A careful reading of *In the Shadow of Auschwitz*, however, will show that here again Mr Stola has misread and that his position does not differ substantially (except in its use of connotative words like 'negative' and 'prejudice') from the argument advanced consistently in the book. Witness page 213:

[The Polish Government's assessment of its interests *vis-à-vis* the Jews], though

---

[30] The contents of the testimony are described and its archival location given in Nussbaum, *Vehafakh lahem lero'ets*, 73. See also Engel, *Facing a Holocaust*, 86, 240–1, for additional evidence casting doubt on Anders's denial.

heavily influenced by prewar perceptions, appears to have been based even more upon empirical observation of a wide variety of variables, including the character of Polish–Jewish relations under German and Soviet occupation, the exigencies of wartime Polish diplomacy, and the actual results of the interactions between the government and Jewish organizations of the free world. It is fairer to conclude ... that the Polish Government-in-exile's approach to Jewish matters was forged out of the complex interaction of an entire range of factors, both of principle and of self-interest, both hereditary, as it were, and conjunctural, in a fashion that cannot be schematized, but merely narrated and described.

Or consider page 206:

The tests of [the Government's] intentions that Jewish leaders frequently placed before it were often of such a demanding and uncompromising nature that, even had the government been a forthright and energetic promoter of the cause of Jewish civil and national equality in Poland, it is doubtful that it could have stood them successfully. On occasion Jewish complaints concerning the behavior of Polish officials were inaccurate or exaggerated, yet Jewish leaders tended for the most part to dismiss the government's refutations of them as contrived and self-serving ... On the whole ... Jewish leaders demonstrated little sensitivity toward the government's predicament and little tolerance for its attempts to balance conflicting principles and pressures.

Or note page 212:

At the time when Jews needed the Polish Government the most, circumstances presented themselves which, *given the political-cultural baggage that Jews had carried out from the prewar world*, made it extremely difficult for them to take the conciliatory steps that might have induced the Poles to take risks on their behalf ... Specific manifestations of attitudinal continuity ... were revealed primarily in the facility with which Poles adduced proof of ineluctable Jewish hostility toward Poland, *as well as in the frequent readiness of Jews to interpret Polish behavior in the most unfavorable light possible*. [Emphasis added]

In short, *In the Shadow of Auschwitz* found both rational and irrational bases among both Polish and Jewish politicians for the antagonism that they frequently felt towards each other during the first three years of the war.

2. Mr Stola has objected that in 'presenting contemporary Jewish and Polish opinions on the subject of their mutual relations and on the policies of the government' during the first half of 1941, *In the Shadow of Auschwitz* failed to consider 'which of the opposing opinions most approximated the truth'. Evidently Mr Stola has missed entirely the discussion on pp. 99–100, which included, among other items, the following: 'It was ... quite unfair for Jewish spokesmen to charge *Dziennik Polski* and *Free Europe* ... with a general neglect of the problems of Polish Jewry or with presenting Jewish issues in a light unfavorable to Jewish interests ... There were also other Jewish charges that appear to have been factually untrue, such as the

contention that only the Polish authorities in Lisbon were preventing the removal of Polish Jewish refugees from Portugal to Brazil . . .' In the event, whenever the matter in question concerned a proposition of fact rather than one of value, and whenever it was possible to do so, *In the Shadow of Auschwitz* did examine the validity of both Polish charges against Jews and Jewish charges against Poles (see, for example, but not exclusively, pp. 127–9, 130–1, 241–2, 273).

3. Mr Stola has depicted certain statements made by Polish politicians as representing exclusively an 'Endek' position or the views of 'right-wing nationalists'. In the event, however, as *In the Shadow of Auschwitz* showed, those statements reflected a far broader consensus. The arguments presented in the National Council in opposition to Schwarzbart's call for the repeal of certain pieces of pre-war legislation (discussed on pp. 102–6) were presented not merely by the representative of the National Party, Zofia Zaleska, but also by Michał Kwiatkowski of the Labour Party, Władysław Banaczyk of the Peasant Party, and non-party delegates Tytus Filipowicz and Stanisław Jóźwiak. The 'note whose authorship is unknown', cited in the book in connection with the discussion of the internal debates over a Government declaration on Jewish rights—which Mr Stola has stated 'set[s] out the Endek point of view'—actually speaks clearly in the name of the entire Polish Government and reflects a position that was hardly in accord with that taken by the National Party immediately prior to or during the war.[31] And the notion that only 'nationalist right-wing elements' perceived the existence of mutual animosity between Poles and Jews during the interwar period is simply false; although there is no space to discuss this issue here, objective readers will find enough material even in the cursory introductory chapter of *In the Shadow of Auschwitz* to demonstrate that the perception of Poles and Jews as two peoples in conflict was far more widespread than Mr Stola has suggested.

4. Mr Stola has claimed that *In the Shadow of Auschwitz* posited 'fear of

---

[31] 'Notatka w sprawie stosunków polsko-żydowskich', Archiwum Instytutu Polskiego-PRM. 36/6. This document stated, among other things, that 'the Polish Government . . . recognizes the fact of assimilation as a natural process [and] does not intend to subject it to any legal restriction or stimulus', and that 'the Government assumes the firm position that Jews in Poland are equal with Polish citizens before the law'. These statements hardly reflected an Endek position. They were, however, accompanied by statements that 'Poland is a Catholic country, and the Poles in that country have the right to be complete masters in deciding their own fate', that 'the enjoyment of rights must be limited by the acceptance of unconditional loyalty to the state', that 'Jews, who in Poland constitute a limited percentage of the population, may not play a decisive role in the economic life of the state', and that the Government looked favourably upon emigration as an element in the regulation of Polish–Jewish relations. Those attitudes were not exclusively the province of the extreme right wing. Cf., e.g. Jacek Majchrowski, 'Problem żydowski w programach głównych polskich obozów politycznych (1918–1939)', *Znak*, 35 (1983), 383–94.

the reaction of the Polish population' as 'the most important reason' for the fact that during the first two years of the war the Polish Government did not take much action on behalf of Jews in the occupied homeland. Note that Mr Stola has not objected either to the statement that the Government did not take much action or to the proposition that fear of the reaction of the Polish population had something to with this behaviour; he has merely objected to what he has understood to be the 'ranking' of this factor as 'the most important reason' for the government's behaviour. Readers are invited to consult the relevant pages *In the Shadow of Auschwitz* (166-70) to determine whether in fact the book 'ranked' any of the various factors discussed in this regard. They will find that nowhere was 'fear of the reaction of the Polish population' presented as 'the most important reason'; they will also find that more space was devoted to the three other factors that Mr Stola has claimed were 'downplayed' (but whose presence Mr Stola has not disputed) than to the one that Mr Stola has read as the most significant. Any 'ranking' of factors exists in Mr Stola's imagination only.

VI

Mr Stola is not alone in his misreading of much of *In the Shadow of Auschwitz*; a number of critics, both Polish and Jewish, have read into the book propositions that in fact were not there and then criticized the book for putting them forth. On the other hand, some have praised the book for presenting arguments that they found agreeable, even though in fact the book never made them. I suspect that the explanation for this phenomenon is, at least in part, that so many Poles and Jews, even Polish and Jewish historians, feel that what the book says about the Polish and Jewish politicians whose actions it recounts has personal significance for them; they therefore tend to approach the book by asking, among other things, how its findings affect their own self-understanding as members of their respective groups. Some may say that it is precisely the task of historians to provoke such a question in their readers' minds. I disagree. To me the task of historians is simply to provide readers with descriptions of the past that are as accurate as possible; how readers apply those descriptions is not a historian's concern. Moreover, once readers apply those descriptions to a task other than obtaining an accurate factual account of the past they unavoidably remake a historian's work into their own.

Mr Stola's review is witness to this process. In effect, he has written a critique not of *In the Shadow of Auschwitz* by David Engel but of another book, also called *In the Shadow of Auschwitz*, but written by Dariusz Stola in his own imagination. Perhaps this could not be helped; perhaps those literary critics are correct who suggest that a text should be regarded not as a body of words on a page but as an event that occurs in the space between the written page and the reader's mind. I, for one, hope that a text might still have an objective existence of its own. No matter how great the progress represented by Mr Stola's ability to discuss a book from across the Polish–Jewish divide without acrimony and by his obvious dedication to ferreting out the facts of the Polish–Jewish encounter and to understanding them accurately, none of us concerned with elucidating those facts is likely to make serious substantive headway if we cannot read each other's works on their own terms. I hope, therefore, that more historians of Polish–Jewish relations will adopt and refine the value-neutral perspective that I have tried to maintain, for it seems to me that only on this basis will we find our common ground as practitioners of the historian's craft.

I wish Mr Stola the best in his continuing researches. Perhaps he will turn up documents that shed important new light on the subject that concerns both of us, documents that will fill in pieces of the puzzle still missing or authorize correction of inferences that earlier works, including mine, have drawn. Should he do so, I hope that I may be among the first to congratulate him.

BOOK REVIEWS

GERSHON DAVID HUNDERT
The Jews in a Polish Private Town: The Case of Opatów in the Eighteenth Century
(Baltimore and London. The Johns Hopkins University Press, 1992)
pp. xvi + 242.

There is a misleading dryness in the title Gershon David Hundert chose for his study of Opatów's Jews in the eighteenth century. The title hints at a narrow, highly specialized study in local economic history. So do the seventeen tables listing taxes, incomes, debts, and other economic indicators. Some books do not live up to what their titles promise. Hundert's title does little to prepare the reader for the broadness of the study's intellectual horizons and Braudelian richness of the social landscape it reconstructs.

Indeed, the significance of this 'case study' goes far beyond the unpaved Jewish street of Opatów and the town's market-place. Unique in some respects, the Jewish community of Opatów represented a variation of a pattern typical of Polish Jewish history of the early modern period. In the eighteenth century more than half of the world's Jews lived in Poland–Lithuania. Most of the Jews in that Commonwealth lived in nobility-owned 'private' holdings like Opatów, making up at least half of the total urban population. Put in a broad perspective of Gentile–Jewish interaction, Hundert's complex and multi-dimensional reconstruction of Jewish life in Apt (as Opatów was called in Yiddish) greatly enhances our understanding of this historical pattern.

At the heart of the study are economic and power-relations between Jews and their landlords. Rejecting the view that their relationship was based on the nobleman's whim and caprice, Hundert sees it as a rational expression of a long-term economic strategy. Seeking to promote the economic well-being of the town as well as to increase his income, the landlord defended Jewish interests. Although hardly an alliance between equal partners, this commonalty of interest usually prevailed over religious prejudice. It also determined other power-relations: between the town's Jewish and Christian burghers, between Jews and the clergy, and within the Jewish community. While some magnates sought to strengthen Jewish communal institutions as a means of maximizing their revenues, the very duality of power undermined the effectiveness of such efforts. Characteristically, the town's owners, first the Sanguszkos and later the Lubomirskis, were not particularly successful in their efforts to reduce the flood of appeals to their courts from the rulings of the Jewish courts.

During the turbulent eighteenth century Polish towns, including Opatów, entered a phase of rapid socio-economic decline. Hundert shows that the decline of the Christian sector was more extensive and progressed at a faster pace than that of the Jewish sector. The study presents extensive evidence that, contrary to a widespread stereotype blaming the Jews for this decline, 'without Jews the Polish town might have declined even further'. The worsening of economic conditions did eventually trigger a Jewish exodus from Opatów to larger towns, especially Warsaw. The metropolitization process, whose early stages are well reflected in Hundert's sources, marked the beginning of a new chapter in Polish Jewish history.

The discussion of Polish–Jewish economic and political interactions is one of the obvious strengths of *The Jews in a Polish Private Town*. While Hundert never loses sight of the economic roots of social phenomena, his study explores a wide range of non-economic dimensions of Jewish life. Piecing together information from tax registers, legal documents, and the *pinkas* (or minute-book) of the Opatów community, he examines demographic trends, family patterns, the status of women, social stratification, and geographic mobility. The picture he draws is surprisingly intense, full of life and flavour. A complex interplay of Orthodox, Hasidic, and pre-Maskilic influences underlies the stories of a 'local Spinoza' and other religious irregulars. Cases of marital infidelity, political corruption, clashing personal ambitions, and the saga of the Landau family combine to provide the reader with a sense of the spiritual universe and of the texture of the everyday lives of Opatów's Jews. One of the study's most fascinating passages deals with their identity and awareness of the world beyond the city's gates.

Hundert's sources are as impressive as his ability to combine rigour and imagination in interpreting them. They include a large selection of original sources in Polish, Yiddish, Hebrew, and Latin, and a colourful mixture of Polish and Latin, many used for the first time. This wealth of archival information reduces *ad absurdum* a recently made contention (Hillel Levine, *Economic Origins of Antisemitism* (Yale University Press, 1991)) that Polish archives have nothing to offer a student of Polish Jewish history in the early modern period. The scope of secondary sources is no less impressive: a densely printed bibliography of works cited in the study extends over 17 pages.

It is fascinating to watch Hundert work with the sources. He brings his data to life without ever losing sight of their limitations and incompleteness. While he freely moves from the general to the particular, from *structures de longue durée* to a brawl in front of the Opatów synagogue, his conclusions are always carefully documented. The wealth of information, clarity of argument, and linguistic precision make this an important contribution to Polish Jewish history as well as rewarding reading. Readers with a command of Polish will be delighted by numerous Polish quotations, selected with an obvious sensitivity to colour and literary charm.

Jews in a Polish Private Town is also refreshingly free of 'isms'. It relies on a thorough examination of sources and keeps a healthy distance from sweeping generalizations and fancy theories. Hundert is remarkably successful in transcending the various ideological biases of Polish Jewish historiography. In his study, the Polish–Lithuanian Commonwealth of the eighteenth century is neither *paradisus Judaeorum* nor a land of darkness but an arena where Polish–Jewish interactions are shaped by a complex interplay of economic, social, and cultural factors.

MAGDALENA M. OPALSKI

WALENTYNA NAJDUS
Ignacy Daszyński, 1866–1936
(Warsaw: Czytelnik, 1988); pp. 564; illustrations

Ignacy Ewaryst Daszyński was a distinguished Polish Socialist leader with an international reputation. His progressive views, sincere compassion, and devotion to all those at the bottom of the social ladder, as well as multiple and tireless activities in his native Galicia, Austria-Hungary, the Second Polish Republic, and Europe as a whole, earned him respect and recognition at home and abroad. His exceptional rhetorical abilities, in both Polish and German, won him admiration, respect, hatred, and the nicknames 'golden-mouthed' and the 'Polish Jaurès'.

For many reasons (the Second World War, Communist rule, other priorities), Daszyński remained largely forgotten by scholars. His illegitimate son, Adam Próchnik (1892–1942; his mother was a Jewish intellectual, Felicja, née Nossig, 1855–1939), writing as Henryk Swoboda, published the short *Ignacy Daszyński: Życie, praca, walka* [Ignacy Daszyński: Life, work, and struggle] (1934). Even as she pursued other topics, Walentyna Najdus's admiration for Daszyński grew. As early as 1983 she evaluated his political views in the period 1890–1918.[1] She decided, however, to produce a full biography of that exceptional individual.

[1] Walentyna Najdus, 'Koncepcje polityczne Ignacego Daszyńskiego w latach 1890–1918', in H. Zieliński (ed.), *Polska myśl polityczna XIX i XX wieku*, v. *W Kręgu polskiej twórców polskiej myśli politycznej* (Wrocław, 1983).

Prior to her retirement, Professor Najdus was a senior researcher in the Institute of History of the Polish Academy of Sciences. She specializes in nineteenth- and early twentieth-century Polish social and political history, with a focus on leftist movements and individuals. Najdus is the author of many scholarly publications.

Ignacy Daszyński, 1866–1936 is based on extensive archival research in Poland, Austria, Belgium, Holland, Sweden, and other countries, as well as secondary sources. The author was also in touch with the surviving members of the Daszyński family, and with friends and acquaintances. Yet her task was not easy. On the one hand, Daszyński deliberately eliminated biographical detail from his revised memoirs, leaving basically political data only, and on the other, the Second World War deeply affected the family. Numerous records (particularly letters) have been lost for ever.

Najdus presents Daszyński against the background of Polish, Austrian, and European history, with a stress on the social and economic conditions that led to the birth and growth of numerous leftist movements, Socialism included. She examines the former Polish borderlands, where Daszyński grew and matured; his paternal and maternal ancestors; and multi-ethnic and backward Galicia under Austrian rule. The author explains why Ignacy and his elder brother, Feliks (1864–90), turned into political and social rebels early in their lives, and why the 'Polish Jaurès' remained true to Socialism and democracy to the end. The private and public aspects of Daszyński are intermingled. The author describes his appearance, tastes, and attitude towards women, as well as his views and activities.

Then, Najdus turns to the First World War, the disintegration of Austria-Hungary, and the birth of the Second Polish Republic, followed by political and social developments there till Daszyński's death. She examines her character's public and private life in Poland. The author deals with numerous Polish and foreign personalities, devoting much attention to Daszyński's long and changing relations with Poland's man of destiny, Marshal Józef Piłsudski (1867–1935). In her final chapter Najdus provides information about the plight of Daszyński's immediate family during the Second World War and thereafter.

Najdus's Daszyński was a brilliant, passionate, and colourful personality, who tirelessly fought for his ideals (Socialism, democracy, progress, human dignity) for half a century (1880–1930), slowing down only in 1931–6 because of physical and mental exhaustion and declining health (which was never excellent). The 'Polish Jaurès' developed multiple activities. He was a party agitator, leader, involved journalist, distinguished parliamentarian, head of the first government in reborn Poland, deputy prime minister in the Government of National Unity during the Polish–Soviet War of 1920, deputy speaker of the House in 1922–7, and speaker in 1928–30.

Unlike so many people born in mixed ethnic borderlands (Hitler being a prime example), Daszyński was totally free from any ethnic chauvinism. He had friends among Jews, Ukrainians, and others, and was always ready to support a just cause, defend a mistreated individual, or support a group suffering discrimination. For example, he defended Jews in the Austrian parliament, during the First World War, when the chauvinistic Austrian military sought scapegoats for its numerous defeats. The tribune also established links with Jews in Galicia, was sympathetic to their plight and problems, and tried to find a solution to individual or group problems. Local Jews must have trusted him, because otherwise they would not have voted for him.

Daszyński was a reformist Socialist. He was flexible, pragmatic, and could be defined as a real politician. Politics was for him the art of the possible. Evil around him mattered much more than pure doctrinal matters. There was so much to be done in his native Galicia. Although, as Najdus believes, Daszyński was a noble himself, he eagerly fought against the remaining vestiges of feudalism. As tribune he strove for universal male suffrage which was basically accepted in Austria, but not in Galicia prior to 1918.

As the author points out, Daszyński was able to achieve much within the existing system, and worked to improve it rather than destroy it. His mastery of parliamentary rules and tricks could hardly be matched. Daszyński could electrify his audiences and speak for hours without a text. In order to spread his ideas, he visited even the smallest localities. During such visits he eagerly heard people's grievances, and subsequently tried to correct injustices by local or central authorities.

Daszyński was a reformer, never a revolutionary. He had a perfect sense of timing, and knew when a strike, demonstration, or other pressure had some chance of success. Maximalism was alien to him. A limited success boosted the morale of strikers, whereas a defeat led to apathy or other negative consequences. He tried, at any price, to avoid a defeat or bloodshed. A planner, Daszyński tried to think things out, because considered actions were most likely to bring success.

Daszyński was handsome, dashing, and very successful with women. One of his illegitimate children, the historian Adam Próchnik, reached prominence in both scholarship and politics. He much resembled his father. The tribune's marriage with a beautiful actress disintegrated after fifteen years for multiple reasons. In the Second Polish Republic Daszyński developed a liaison with Cecylia Kempner, who was Jewish and attractive. Following his wife's death in 1934, he legalized his relationship with Kempner by marrying her in 1935. Najdus disagrees with the view of Daszyński's children, that Kempner was to blame for destroying their father's first marriage, which in her opinion was beyond salvation anyway. Kempner took good care of Daszyński in his last years. Like so many other Jews, Daszyński's second wife perished in unknown circumstances in occupied Poland.

The tribune continued his activities in the Second Polish Republic. As before, pragmatism prevailed in everyday activity over distant Socialist ideals. He was not satisfied with Poland's borders, but accepted them. On the one hand, he wanted the country's ethnic minorities to remain loyal to the state, on the other, he stood for a large measure of autonomy, particularly for the numerous Ukrainian minority. With regard to Jews, he never changed. Daszyński stood for full equality for those who opted for assimilation, and advocated both understanding and proper respect for those who wanted to preserve their own heritage. He was staunchly opposed to any discrimination based on religion, ethnic origin, or political affiliation. Unlike some other Socialists (e.g. Karl Kautsky), Daszyński considered the Jews to be a separate nation.

Of particular importance were Daszyński's relations with Piłsudski. The tribune eagerly assisted the then little-known and obscure future man of destiny in Austria, and later was both loyal to and supportive of Piłsudski in the first eight years of the Polish Republic. In 1925, for example, he wrote an adulatory book on the great man in Poland. Like many other leftists, Daszyński misread Piłsudski and supported the coup of May 1926, and then did his best to seek national unity. Yet the Marshal, like so many other men of destiny, was not a grateful person. When, in 1930, Piłsudski ordered armed and uniformed officers to appear in the lobby of the House to frighten opposition deputies, Daszyński refused to open proceedings until the officers left. There followed a stormy meeting between the two former friends and allies. Insulted, Daszyński resisted the pressure, but this confrontation resulted in his physical and mental collapse. He never recovered. The vengeful Piłsudski even deprived Daszyński of his speaker's salary, which was a real blow to the old and broken man, generally respected but now almost as poor as in his early years.

Najdus has done an excellent job in writing this large, balanced, and well-documented study of the 'Polish Jaurès'. One admires her painstaking research, perseverance, and above all the final result, and one sincerely welcomes this long overdue biography of Daszyński, whose ideas and activities have placed him among those who should always be remembered.

ADAM A. HETNAL

STEPHEN D. CORRSIN
Warsaw before the First World War: Poles and Jews in the Third City of the Russian Empire, 1880–1914
(East European Monographs, Boulder; New York: distributed by Columbia University Press, 1989); pp. vi + 183

This valuable study is composed of two parts of unequal character and significance. The first—75 per cent of the whole—contains a description of the town of Warsaw at the end of the nineteenth and beginning of the twentieth centuries, with specific consideration given to the situation of the Jewish population. Considering the number of Jews in Poland's capital (their highest concentration in Europe) and their economic potential, this subject will certainly interest the Jewish reader. It does not, however, introduce new facts to a Polish audience. The second part, much shorter, explores the Polish–Jewish conflict in Warsaw during the years 1905–13, the culmination of which was the election to the Russian Duma in 1912. This episode has not hitherto been treated in a scholarly manner, and this part of the book should also arouse attention in Poland.

The author has prepared himself well for his task. He is well acquainted with Polish secondary literature on the political and economic history of the Kingdom of Poland (the 'Congress Kingdom') in this period; he also has the advantage over Polish historians of having made use of Yiddish material. Apart from memoirs and government publications, he has reviewed a large amount of the contemporary Warsaw press, both Jewish and Polish. He did not use archives.

In the second half of the nineteenth century Warsaw grew faster than other cities of central Europe. There was a jump from 200,000 inhabitants to almost a million (excluding the suburbs). The city was enriching and modernizing itself in a market favourable to capitalism, in spite of the difficult political conditions of the backward Tsarist regime. There was also a significant rise in the population of Warsaw Jews (from 73,000 to 337,000) and a slight increase in the proportion of Jews in the town (from 32.6 to 38.1 per cent). The increase in population, both Christian and Jewish, was due in large part to migration. The somewhat higher natural increase of Jews is probably correctly attributed by the author to the fact that the Jewish middle class came to Warsaw in families, whereas the migrating Polish youth were boys going to work in factories and girls occupying domestic positions. Hence, there was a weaker family structure among the Christians and a higher infant mortality rate. The author is unable to estimate the size of the influx of Jews from Russia (pp. 34, 123). They were known as 'Litvaks', were not welcomed in Warsaw, either by the local Poles or by the Jews, and became at the end of the nineteenth century something of a political problem. Their cultural differences strengthened antisemitic attitudes. The author logs the blame for the regrettable increase in Polish–Jewish tension in the early twentieth century at the feet of the numerically superior Polish side. In trying to assess this question objectively, one might wonder today, in the light of comparable experiences, if this conflict could have been avoided. Multi-ethnic communities can coexist peacefully in a feudal structure, in a well-defined state hierarchy with a clear division of economic functions. Capitalism brought the Jews legal emancipation; it also sharpened competition between ethnically different but equally strong groups of townspeople: the bourgeoisie, petty and large, the free professions, and even the proletariat. In the revolutionary years of 1905–17 the political underdevelopment of Tsarist Russia exacerbated this process, which was further complicated by Polish aspirations to independence.

The author is critical not only of the nationalists but also of Polish liberals and socialists; he argues (p. 3) that the programme of assimilation and acculturation of the Jews which they originally launched later became unacceptable to them. Rather, I would claim, this objective was not attainable because of the considerable size of the Jewish population and the cultural differences between them and Christian Poles. Polish liberals may perhaps have been unrealistic Utopians, but they really did not wish the Jews ill. In Bolesław Prus's *feuilleton* of 1909 the author found a sentence about the 'jargon' press which is 'multiplying like yeast bacteria' (p. 67). He sees in this a clear indication of Prus's views—a man who in other respects rejected antisemitism. But Prus in his *feuilleton* voices his comparison to yeast through the mouth of a fictitious speaker whom he ridicules, derides, and mocks.

There are several mistakes in this part of the book. The author should have written 'Duchy of Warsaw' and not 'Grand Duchy' (p. 8); 'Marquis Wielopolski' instead of 'Count' (p. 10). Salomon Lewental was baptized a few weeks before his death (p. 20). Terespol, a border town in the kingdom on the Warsaw–Moscow route, was not in the Ukraine (p. 47). The *Yidishes togblat*, with a circulation of 54,200, had a larger readership than the Polish Warsaw press. It was not at the time the most widely circulated newspaper in Poland (p. 75). *Gazeta grudziądzka* had a circulation of 134,000. Corrsin is correct, in my view, in his observation that both the Jewish and the Polish press in Warsaw contributed to the intensification of inter-ethnic tension (p. 68). Apart from the valuable section about the press, the book does not examine the intellectual and cultural life of Warsaw Jews.

All political histories of Poland written by Poles recount with surprise or outrage the elections to the Duma in 1912, when Jewish votes ensured that the Warsaw representative was not the leader of the National Democrats but an unknown socialist, Eugeniusz Jagiełło. Not one of the historians, as far as I know, has explained what actually happened, and even Corrsin, describing this event in detail, does not dot all the i's or cross all the t's. It was a strange irony of fate that Warsaw Jews could thank the antidemocratic system imposed on the country by St Petersburg for their electoral power. After the 1905 revolution the government had to agree to some semblance of general elections; it tried, none the less, to diminish the impact of worker and peasant votes, setting up a two-tier election through a curial system.

On the basis of the electoral system, made stricter by anti-Polish sentiment in 1907, Warsaw elected two deputies to the Duma. One of these was to represent the Russian population, though there were few Russians in the city—no more than 4 per cent. The other deputy was elected by the non-Russian population. The electoral college numbered 80 representatives for the bourgeois curia and only three for the workers' curia. Included in the electorate for the bourgeois curia were owners of real estate, owners of industrial and trading companies, renters of individual apartments, and employees of public institutions. It was probably not foreseen by the antisemitic government of St Petersburg that in Warsaw these regulations worked in favour of the Jewish middle class. In the elections to the first Duma the National Democrats won 54 per cent of the votes cast by electors in the bourgeois curia. In the elections to the second Duma 53 per cent, and in the third the results were similar (Corrsin, p. 30, does not cite numerical data). So, the National Democratic party elected their candidate three times, albeit without a large majority. But by the elections of 1912 Jewish pre-electors constituted 55 per cent of the voters for the bourgeois curia. Even the leader of the National Democratic Party, Dmowski, lost in the vote in the bourgeois curia, losing the chance to obtain a seat in the Duma. Theoretically, the deputy from Warsaw could now be a Jew. Neither the Jewish assimilationists nor the Orthodox Jews wanted that: they had no wish to provoke the Poles. Not being able to come to any agreement with the Nationalists, they offered their support to the Polish Progressives, with whom they had collaborated during the last elections in 1907. Corrsin is rather critical in his assessment of this group for its lack of consistency in committing itself to the principle of the equality of citizens and its yielding to the antisemitic agitation of the Polish press. It is perhaps worth while to note the connection of the Progressive Party with Freemasonry. Its candidate to the Duma, a lawyer, Jan Kucharzewski, who later became a historian, had been until recently a member of the National League, a precursor of the Endecja; he left when the National Democrats stated their opposition to the slogan of Polish independence.

The Jewish electorate set the following conditions: they would vote for a Pole who would speak out for the equality of Jews in the proposed electoral ordinance for local government. Kucharzewski wavered; with the existing electoral system, this would mean, in the future, a municipal council with a Jewish majority. Only the three socialists of the workers' curia were willing to support the principle of equal rights for Jews. The votes of the Jewish bourgeoisie were thus given to one of them, Eugeniusz Jagiełło, who became the deputy to the Duma. No one had ever heard of him. Corrsin exaggerates, however, in his assessment of him as a 'political nonentity' (p. 87); he turned out to be quite active in the St Petersburg Duma.

Several hours after the announcement of the results of the elections, the breaking of the windows of Jewish stores began, as a diarist relates. The election of Jagiełło was seen by the Polish press as a national disaster; even on the Jewish side consternation was widespread. Events had turned out catastrophically. This was not primarily because Dmowski, in retaliation for the defeat he had suffered, announced a boycott of Jewish businesses. The author is probably correct in suggesting (p. 103) that the boycott was not effective: a Jewish shop, run by members of the family, sold goods at lower prices than an elegant Christian shop. And the Jews did not allow themselves to be ousted from the wholesale trade. However, the Warsaw conflict of 1912 influenced Polish–Jewish relations between the wars; it hurt equally the Polish Jews and the Polish state.

The author does not pay attention to the crux of this sad story. The Christian electorate of Warsaw in 1912 was not prepared to accept the principle of equal rights for Jews in the forthcoming local-government elections. But these elections never took place. The Tsarist government, right up to the end, denied autonomy to the cities of the Polish Kingdom. Elections to the Warsaw city council took place only in 1916, after the Russians had departed. The influence of the Endecja under German occupation counted for much less. Polish and Jewish bourgeois groups came to terms as to the division of seats and there was not even any voting in the bourgeois curia. In the free Poland of post-1918 universal suffrage was established. The boundary of the city of Warsaw was expanded to include the suburbs, which were mainly Christian. Jewish parties, obviously, could not obtain a majority. It is evident that Kucharzewski could have accepted a compromise with the Jews in 1912 without hurting the Polish cause.

I shall end these comments about Corrsin's scrupulous and worthwhile monograph with two quotations which give conflicting interpretations of the phenomenon of Polish antisemitism. One of them is from the memoirs of Ludwik Krzywicki, a witness to those events, a fine sociologist and a socialist. He writes, in relation to 1912: 'The Endecja understood that antisemitic catch-phrases were useful to control crowds and arouse passion.'[1] The modern historian Roman Wapiński, far from being a nationalist sympathizer, holds rather that Endek antisemitism, 'understood instrumentally, was intended to create stronger ties between the Endecja and the Polish middle class, which was struggling against Jewish competition, especially in the Russian partition, and also to help in its struggle against the socialist movement.'[2]

STEFAN KIENIEWICZ

[1] L. Krzywicki, *Wspomnienia* (3 vols.; Warsaw, 1959), 282.
[2] R. Wapiński, *Narodowa Demokracja 1893–1939* (Wrocław, 1980), 129.

JÓZEF WRÓBEL
Tematy żydowskie w prozie polskiej 1939–1987
(Towarzystwo Autorów i Wydawców Prac Naukowych 'Universitas'; Kraków, 1991) pp. xi + 189.

This book by Józef Wróbel, which originated as a doctoral dissertation at Kraków University, is the first attempt at a comprehensive synthesis of a subject (Jewish themes in Polish literature) which is still a thorny one today; certain uncertainties and a structure which could have been more clearly organized are thus understandable faults: in the introduction, the author himself anticipates some criticism on these lines. Following the suggested guidelines in Błoński's famous article,[1] which encouraged the recognition of a 'Jewish school' in Polish literature, in which Jewish themes play as important a role as some other important motifs in contemporary Polish literature—the peasant motif, that of the eastern borderlands (*kresy*), and that of Galicia,—the Jewish motif is one aspect of the present-day 'search for roots' in Poland. The book's material, the author says, is drawn from

> literary works in which the Jewish issue is a central one ... Without losing sight of their literary value *sensu stricto*, the texts that have been analysed are considered as a testimony to the life of the Jewish world and its destruction. The intent to convey the specificity of each text (the author readily acknowledges) has not had a very positive influence on the coherence of some chapters. (p. 7)

The book is divided into six chapters, the first of which is devoted to the many attempts at commemorating the pre-war Jewish *shtetl*; the second is devoted to the relationship between the Jews and Communism (this is based almost entirely on the essay *Żydzi a komunizm* by Abel Kainer (pen-name of

[1] Jan Błoński, 'Autoportret żydowski', *Tygodnik Powszechny*, 5 (1982).

Stanisław Krajewski)); the third chapter, 'Job's Books', is divided into five sections and is concerned with the period of Nazi occupation and the extermination of Polish Jews. The last three chapters discuss the works of Henryk Grynberg, the exodus of 1968, and the current condition of the remaining Jewish writers.

The first chapter, 'The Lights of Shabbat are Turned off', a title borrowed by Aleksander Hertz, is dedicated 'to the attempts of writers who were outside Poland at the time of the war to resurrect the world of the dead' (p. 10), and discusses, above all, the works of Julian Stryjkowski and Kalman Segal. In this section the author underlines, in Stryjkowski's Galician trilogy, the importance of the breakup of the family and the consequent loss of traditional values (not only Jewish values, but human values in general); this breakup seems to prepare the ground for the impending catastrophe.

Polish writers such as Andrzej Kuśniewicz in *Nawrócenie*

regard the Jewish people as a critical element of the multinational mosaic, completing the picture of a dominant Polish presence ... The Arcadian vision of the coexistence of these peoples creates a barrier against the memories of the Second World War ... The extermination is only alluded to, and silence is kept each time that a description of reality would be required. (p. 28)

The author then laments the impossibility in Poland of objectively reconstructing the past, citing, incongruously, the novels of Isaac Bashevis Singer as an example of realistic historical prose, and forgetting that the consciousness of the recent catastrophe weighs on these works, as do a whole series of national stereotypes, which are not always complimentary to the Poles.[2]

The longest chapter is dedicated to the Second World War. The first part centres on the works of Adolf Rudnicki and Bogdan Wojdowski and on the novel *Przybysz z Narbony* [The newcomer from Narbonne] by Julian Stryjkowski. Rudnicki's writing, summed up in Kazimierz Wyka's expression as 'the function of solid memory', is different from that of his contemporaries, and from the writing of Zofia Nałkowska and Tadeusz Borowski (who are thematically closer to Rudnicki). His writing does not involve any stylistic revolution or formal research, since he is an example 'of the writer who does not give up in the face of the mechanisms which are destroying tradition, that biblical culture which is, for Rudnicki, not only word but a vision of the world' (p. 58). Discussion of *Przybysz z Narbony* is appropriate in the chapter devoted to the ghetto in Warsaw (let us not forget that the novel is dedicated to the insurgents of that ghetto). As

---

[2] Monika Adamczyk-Garbowska, 'Poles and Poland in I. B. Singer's Fiction', *Polin*, v (1990), 288–302.

Wróbel remarks, Stryjkowski makes an apology for the martyr figure while Wojdowski, in *Chleb rzucony umarłym* [Bread thrown to the dying], 'describes in a realistic way the atmosphere of the ghettos and the complexity of the choice between passivity and revolt'; the author then tries to read certain theses of Wojdowski's novel from a Christian perspective and translates some Jewish ethical concepts as evangelical prefiguration, which seems too contrived an interpretation (pp. 74–5). The section entitled 'Illusions of Liberals' concerns itself with the Artur Sandauer stories and with the image of the bourgeois Jew who is unable to understand at any level the reality of the extermination, because his own liberal-positivistic upbringing makes it impossible for him to do so; a good example being the paradoxical character of Chaim Rumkowski, re-created by Sandauer in *Kupiec Łódzki* [The merchant of Łódź]. This is a character that in world literature is epitomized by Serenus Zeitblom.[3]

Polish reaction to the Jewish extermination was indifference, as exemplified in a sentence in *Okupacja* [Occupation] by Stanisław Lukasiewicz (quoted at the beginning of 'On the Other Side of the Wall', p. 117); 'next to indifference, heroism is the basest vice'. The bad conscience of Polish literature finds its most famous expression right after the war in the story *Wielki Tydzień* [Holy Week] by Jerzy Andrzejewski. Wróbel also summarizes the essay by Madeline Levine on this novella, which he defines as 'sometimes incisive, sometimes controversial, sometimes even relentless in an outrageous way' (p. 120). Levine's purpose is to demonstrate, on deeper analysis, that some of the most negative anti-Jewish stereotypes emerge from Andrzejewski's text.[4]

The most interesting chapter of the book is dedicated to Henryk Grynberg, who was the subject of a long article published by Wróbel.[5] Grynberg 'is probably the last writer for whom being Jewish and Polish constitutes an artistic and existential drama'. He is also the last Jewish writer who speaks about the Shoah and who lived through it personally. In *Kadysz* Wróbel notices a sentence which seems to end a torment which has lasted for so many years. For the first time the autobiographic character of Grynberg, obsessed by the murder of his father during the war, asserts that, while

---

[3] Cf. Andrzej Werner, *Zwyczajna apokalipsa: Tadeusz Borowski i jego wizja świata obozów* (Warsaw, 1981), 22.

[4] Madeleine G. Levine, 'The Ambiguity of Moral Outrage in Jerzy Andrzejewski's *Wielki Tydzień*, *Polish Review*, revised as 'Catholicism, Anti-Semitism, and the Extermination of the Jews in Jerzy Andrzejewski's *Wielki Tydzień*, in John Micgiel, Robert Scott, and Harold B. Segal (eds.), *Proceedings of the Conference on Poles and Jews: Myth and Reality in the Historical Context, Held at Columbia University, March 6–10, 1983* (Institute of East Central Europe; Columbia University, NY, 1986), 355–74. Even though some of Levine's claims can be disputed, the essay is noteworthy for its unconventional approach to a work devoted to tradition.

[5] Józef Wróbel, 'Henryk Grynberg Calls Poland to Account', *Polin*, vii (1992), 176–91.

Poles saved his mother, a bandit killed his father. With this affirmation Wróbel maintains that it is time to consider closed the long period of the bitter 'reconciliation' between Poland and the writer. At this point we can mention that recently (February 1992) Grynberg went back to Poland for the first time since 1968. He was able to find the exact place where his father was murdered (a milk-container that the man was carrying with him when he died proved decisive evidence for the son) and, in the course of an encounter with the public, he admitted that until now he had considered himself 'on the Aryan side', and that he could 'reveal himself only now'.

In 'Exodus: March 1968' the stories *Dawid syn Henryka* [David, son of Henry] by Roman Bratny, 'a writer to whom one cannot deny a good sense for politics' (p. 145), and *Głupia Sprawa* [A foolish matter] by Stanisław Ryszard Dobrowolski, 'whose aggressive and coarse antisemitism can be read as a parody', are given as examples of writing in sympathy with the antisemitic campaign. 'The Uprooted' is concerned with works that have the problems of self-identification as the central theme, and therefore not only with Grynberg, but also *Sublokatorka* [The sub-tenant] by Hanna Krall, *Krzywe drogi* [Crooked roads] by Bogdan Wojdowski, *Siostry* [Sisters] by Barbara Toporska, and the stories by Stanisław Benski and Julian Stryjkowski.

Strangely absent from the bibliography is a full list of prose works on Jewish themes from 1939 to 1990. Only some diaries are mentioned, while essential titles such as *Umschlagplatz* by Jarosław Marek Rymkiewicz (Paris, 1988) —the first novel by a non-Jewish author to treat the *Shoah* effectively—or *Hipnoza* [Hypnosis] by Hanna Krall (Warsaw, 1989) are absent. Neither is it clear why one of the most famous poets, Stanisław Vincenz, has been excluded from the most interesting chapter on poetry dealing with the *Kresy*. As mentioned above, a better-organized structure would have facilitated a smoother and more useful reading: it would have been preferable to order the different works by theme, regardless of whether they were written by Jewish or non-Jewish writers, thus avoiding the prejudice of 'race' and classifying the confrontation between the way the minority perceives itself and its external appearance. Wróbel realizes how much the regime's position affects the way in which Jewish themes are received in Poland. For this reviewer, a sharper distinction between officially released works and those that were published unofficially would have been helpful, as would a comparison between the works of writers remaining in Poland and those who have emigrated (a separate study of Israeli literature written in Polish would have also been worthwhile). Despite these omissions, Wróbel's book remains a useful tool, one which at the moment is unique in the field of study that Krystyna Kersten describes as a 'minefield', where any word can be explosive, through which the student can only negotiate his way successfully with great discretion and tact.

LAURA QUERCIOLI

JAN T. GROSS
Revolution from Abroad: The Soviet Conquest of Poland's Western Ukraine and Western Belorussia
(Princeton: Princeton University Press, 1988)
pp. xxii + 334; illustrations

Jan Gross's fine piece of scholarly craftsmanship can be appreciated on several levels. Obviously it is in the first instance an exposition of the initial stages by which the basis was laid for the incorporation of Poland's pre-1939 eastern territories within the Soviet Union, a process that began, according to the author, with the Soviet military conquest of the present western Ukraine and western Belarus in September 1939. In six chapters, Gross explores the manner in which the Soviets remade the system of social organization in these territories. During the first weeks following the invasion, he contends, the occupying Red Army and NKVD transformed the state administration from a 'routine, dull and predictable bureaucratic instrument' into one that was 'arbitrary and capricious', which 'no longer attempted to shield its subjects from violence [but] now meted out violence against them' (p. 70). Subsequently, the elections held on 22 October 1939 to provide an ostensible popular mandate for the incorporation of the occupied territories into the USSR extended this transformation, according to Gross, by bringing virtually every individual citizen into direct contact with the state apparatus and subjecting his behaviour to public scrutiny. The exposure of all citizens before the authorities brought about as a result of the election campaign then made it possible, as Gross demonstrates, for the state effectively to induce obedience, whether by persuasion—through the restructuring of the educational system—or by coercion—through mass arrests, deportations, torture, and executions. Although, he notes, 'after World War II the Western Ukraine and Western Belorussia still had to go through important stages (like the collectivization of agriculture) before the Soviet regime stabilized', what happened in these territories between September 1939 and June 1941 offers in his opinion 'a comprehensive insight into the process of installing a Communist regime' (p. 225).

Gross's study, however, as he himself is aware, offers more than a mere description of this process. In attempting to explain how the Soviet conquerors managed so quickly and so thoroughly to establish a direct unmediated relationship between each individual and the state in which 'nothing, not even the most private family life, can be legitimately shielded from state interference and regulation' (p. 116), he develops a thesis that in a sense stands earlier theories of totalitarianism on their heads. The Soviets accomplished their goal, according to Gross, not, as most theories of totalitarianism would lead one to expect, 'by establishing new, state-controlled organizations and forcing people to join them' but by allowing citizens immediate access to the state's coercive apparatus for the settlement of their private disputes. This 'privatization of the public realm', to use Gross's term, served to entice the citizenry of the occupied areas into accepting the legitimacy of the occupiers, for it gave each individual the potential power 'to mobilize the state, in a highly personal fashion, to settle his problems'. Hence, he concludes, 'the real power of a totalitarian state results from its being at the disposal of every inhabitant, available for hire at a moment's notice' (pp. 119–21).

Such observations make Gross's study a contribution to normative sociology no less than to descriptive history. Perhaps even more noteworthy than these contributions, however, is the methodological lesson that the book provides—a lesson stemming from the evidence upon which Gross bases his conclusions and the manner in which he employs it for this purpose. This evidence is derived almost exclusively from personal testimonies, mostly recorded by Poles following the re-establishment of Polish–Soviet diplomatic relations in July 1941 and subsequently deposited among the collections of Polish materials housed in the archives of the Hoover Institution on War, Revolution, and Peace in Stanford, California. The use of testimonies in the type of reconstruction that Gross attempts is problematic, not least because the deponents cannot testify directly to the thinking of the Soviet occupiers but merely to the manner in which they perceived such thinking. And although Gross is careful to state that he has 'presented ... the phenomenon of the Soviets' seizure of power and imposition of their regime as it was experienced by ordinary people' (p. 225), it is clear that he is more interested in the nature of the phenomenon itself than in the manner in which it was perceived by its primary victims. In order to compensate for this distortion (as well as for other biases in the material, of which he takes note in his introduction), Gross has adopted certain principles of interpretation that those who employ similar source material in their work would do well to heed. In the first place, he has given greatest credence to eyewitness reports of specific incidents, favouring them over hearsay or general impressionistic statements. He has also recognized that a witness gains in credibility to the extent that he testifies about things that he did rather than about things that he thought or felt. And most important, he has drawn firm conclusions only when a large number of witnesses have mentioned more or less the same phenomenon: indeed, the most compelling feature of his work is the size of his sample, beginning with over 20,000 questionnaires gathered at the initiative of the Polish civilian and military authorities in the USSR and supplemented by materials in archival collections in London, Paris, Koblenz, Jerusalem, and New York. By following these principles Gross has avoided the temptation to use testimonies in what R. G. Collingwood called 'scissors-and-paste' fashion; rather, he has employed them as a basis for judicious self-generated statements.

In short, *Revolution from Abroad* is a major contribution to the study of Soviet and east European history and sociology on both the substantive and methodological planes.

DAVID ENGEL

WOLFGANG WIPPERMANN
Der konsequente Wahn: Ideologie und Politik Adolf Hitlers, with an essay by Saul Friedländer
(Gütersloh and Munich: Bertelsmann Lexikon Verlag, 1989)
pp. vii + 275; illustrations

A new book on Hitler has to compete with many predecessors. It also raises expectations, particularly if the author has recently published a long critical essay on the theme of biographies of Hitler (*Kontroversen um Hitler* (Frankfurt am Main, 1986)). In his new book, Wippermann consigns biographical details to an introductory chronological table, and then progresses to the serious business of demonstrating how Hitler's ideas related to Nazi policy in action. The fifteen selected themes range from women, Fascism, power and Prussia, to foreign policy, race, terror, and resistance. These are treated in alphabetical order, an arrangement that is not entirely successful. Sometimes, for example, one is left with the impression that Hitler's efforts to instrumentalize parts of Prussian/German history were as significant as his obsession with the verities of race. The prophylactic function of bad history, as a means of rendering the regime's ahistorical, racial vision normative, could have been stated much more explicitly. A few of the chapters, particularly those on the seizure of power and on the economy, are also rather slight, but the book as a whole is an impressive demonstration of how to relate ideologies to political consequences by one of the leading scholars in the field.

Wippermann gives a convincing account of how Nazi propaganda came to be all-pervasive, beginning modestly with the purchase of an Adler typewriter for the NSDAP's early propaganda office, and ending with control of the mass media and a *Volksempfänger* in every factory, bar, and home. He then discusses in greater detail three examples of Nazi propaganda in action: the alternative Nazi festive calendar; photographs of the Führer; and the poster cartoon figure of Kohlenklau ('Coal-snatcher') making off with a sack of coal. Many photographs of Hitler, who carefully censored his own image, show him putting his pet Alsatian Blondi through her paces. Despite the ever-present dog-whip, Hitler enjoyed the reputation of being an animal-lover. Inevitably, in his case, this laudable sentiment had its sinister side. Alsatians were bred in Germany from the late nineteenth century as a deliberate throwback to an aggressive and absolutely obedient dog-cum-wolf. For the Nazis, the Alsatian became an example of the triumph of breeding over nature, the canine analogue of what they envisaged for the human race. It comes as no surprise to learn that the SS empire included a firm with a monopoly on supplying dog food to the concentration camps, or that Jews and gypsies were forbidden to own dogs as pets. There is something highly inappropriate about attempts to humanize Hitler by depicting the broken-down old Führer deserted by all save Blondi: a 'friend', of course, who was poisoned in a lavatory closet. If Blondi represented the positive side of the Nazi racial vision, the figure of Kohlenklau can be aligned alongside the less subtle representations of Jewish-Bolshevik *Untermenschen*. Wippermann takes as his starting-point a chapter by the philologist Victor Klemperer (in his *Lingua Tertii Imperii*), who noticed Kohlenklau's passage into popular imagination while working as a forced labourer in a factory in 1943. Every petty pilferer was nicknamed Kohlenklau. But the figure itself was not as harmless as the alliterative name suggests. 'It' was composed of various elements from the Nazi visual repertory—webbed paws, a shifty, one-eyed glance, and a cloth cap at a rakish angle—and embodied the 'asocial', criminal, 'community-alien' type, the polar opposite of the 'honest' granite-jawed youths the Nazis used to reflect their self-image.

The strongest chapters in the book are those concerned with the Jews, race, terror, and the Left's fateful misanalysis of the specific properties of German National Socialism. Synthesizing much recent research on often quite obscure groups, Wippermann reminds us of the comprehensive nature of the persecution which stemmed from the Nazis' racial obsession. Skilfully, he draws out the thought-patterns linking the intended victims and correspondences in the evolution of persecution. Thus, in Hitler's mind, the so-called *Rheinlandbastarde*, of whom 500–800 were tracked down and sterilized by his regime, had been planted in Germany by the Jews in order to damage the nation's racial stock. Thus, Jews were often coupled together with gypsies in the regime's legislation; a conference was held on 21 September 1941 to 'co-ordinate' 'Final Solution of the Gypsy Question'; and in October Eichmann suggested appending 'a few wagonloads of gypsies' to the trains taking Jews eastwards. Of course, while stressing the comprehensiveness of the categories of the persecuted, Wippermann does not seek to deny the singularity of what befell the Jews. In a separate chapter he shows how the achievements of emancipation were reversed and then supplanted by a terror whose tempo was largely determined by the Nazis' economic and foreign-policy priorities. His detailed account of the flurry of discriminatory measures aimed at the Jews is a depressing monument to the denial of human dignity by the 'state and the desire of sectional interests to remove Jews from their sphere of activity'. Unfortunately, the author does not discuss the origins of the Final Solution in similar detail, or venture an opinion on the intentionalist/functionalist debate.

The chapter on terror and violence is also very effective. Using his own earlier work on conditions in Berlin, Wippermann traces the ways in which anarchic violence—typified by the 'wild' concentration camps—evolved into the legalized and systematic forms associated with the burgeoning SS empire. The author then shows how other forms of coercion, including youth custody centres, prisons, camps for gypsies, and labour-training centres, gradually assumed the character of the Dachau regime. His discussion of these less well known aspects of Nazi terror also stresses the role of, *inter alia*, academic, self-styled experts in criminal biology, the local authorities, and, in the case of disciplinary centres for slacking foreign workers, factory owners and managers who availed themselves of the terror apparatus to coerce their workforce. Wippermann's discussion of resistance is also a useful reminder of what is omitted from the conventional, and highly politicized, accounts promoted by the two postwar German regimes. In addition to the well-trodden ground of the KPD/SPD underground, minorities within the Churches, and a tiny section of the military-aristocratic élite, Wippermann discusses in detail left-wing splinter groups, the Jews, and Jehovah's Witnesses. His section on the Berlin-based Gruppe Baum, who in 1942 tried to burn down the exhibition 'Soviet Paradise', contains a thoughtful discussion of why resistance by Jews was so limited. The Jewish population was an elderly one, and as a trip to the largest cemetery in East Berlin makes plain, a population proud of its service to the Prussian-German state in peace and war. There was also the fact of massive and indiscriminate reprisals for acts of 'sabotage'. Following the fire in the Lustgarten exhibition in 1943, 500 Jews were arrested; half were shot and the rest were sent to Auschwitz. Jewish community leaders in Germany, Vienna, and Prague were warned of similar consequences in the event of further resistance. It was a massive price to pay.

In sum, Wippermann's book is an outstanding, original, and accessible survey of the translation of obsession into reality and human catastrophe. The book synthesizes much detailed research, including work done by the author, and the publishers have served him well with a thoughtful choice of illustrations. Wippermann's concern with the concrete is a refreshing change from the metahistorical confusions of the *Historikerstreit*, reflecting as it does work in the archives over a fifteen-year period rather than mere self-publicity.

MICHAEL BURLEIGH

YURY BOSHYK (ED.)

Ukraine during World War II: History and Its Aftermath. A Symposium

(Canadian Institute of Ukrainian Studies; University of Alberta; Edmonton, 1986) pp. xxii + 291.

The Canadian Institute of Ukrainian Studies at the University of Alberta is a major centre of research and scholarship in Ukrainian studies, particularly those concerning the modern period. The book under review, published under its auspices, deals with a most significant and sensitive subject of our century, the Second World War. A symposium on the Ukraine and Ukrainians during the Second World War was held in Toronto in 1985; scholarly papers on a number of issues concerning Ukrainians and related to the war situation read at this conference are published in this volume. The combination of historical research (Part I) with the issue of war criminals in postwar Canada and the United States (Part II) seems artificial and geared primarily to politics and publicity. The inclusion of some original documents (Part III) is both useful and illuminating. This review is concerned with the first part only, and will deal primarily with the issue of Ukrainian–Jewish relations.

Yury Boshyk, the editor, raises in his introductory remarks some crucial points concerning both information and attitudes. One might hope that the gradual opening of Soviet and Ukrainian archives to professional and unbiased research will be helpful. It is already the case that for some time Yad Vashem, the Israeli Remembrance Authority, has been permitted access to documentation in Soviet archives relating to the Second World War. These documents may shed new light on such a highly controversial issue as Ukrainian collaboration with the Nazis in the persecution and extermination of Jews. A continuing study by Dr Aharon Weiss of Yad Vashem on the Ukrainian underground in western Ukraine may also add considerably to our understanding of that period. As is well known, Jews and Ukrainians tend to present opposing views and interpretations of the war years. Historians on both sides are also divided in their views. A striking example is the first conference on Ukrainian–Jewish relations held in 1983.[1]

Orest Subtelny, in his discussion of the 1939–41 Soviet annexation of western territories, attempts to draw a comparison between the Soviet and Nazi occupations. Although until recently such an analogy would have seemed far-fetched, the latest exposures of Stalinist crimes make such an argument more plausible. It is also true that the meaning of Soviet and Nazi rule for Ukrainians, Poles, and Jews in eastern Poland (western Ukraine) was entirely different. Whereas for a Ukrainian nationalist Hitler could spell hope for independence, for a Pole he signified suffering and for a Jew death. Subtelny argues that the issue of collaboration should be examined in a more complex manner. He also points out the cumulative effect of Soviet behaviour towards Ukrainians during the 1930s and 1940s, and concludes that 'Ukrainians had good reason to view the Soviets as their primary enemy' and the Germans as a possible ally. The disturbing question in the moral sense is, however, whether Ukrainian national interests *vis-à-vis* the Germans justify a hostile and cruel behaviour towards their Jewish neighbours.

Bohdan Krawchenko's paper on Soviet Ukraine under Nazi occupation is perhaps the most thorough and balanced study in this volume. He is both honest and modest in stating that there are still issues and subjects which have not been studied sufficiently. He points out that we should be careful to differentiate between 'western' and 'eastern' Ukraine and to study the specificities of each area and situation. It seems that the Nazis used 'westerners' in order to influence the 'eastern', i.e. Soviet, Ukrainian population. Krawchenko states that the *Einsatzgruppen* struck at the Ukrainian nationalists as early as late summer 1941, when mass executions of Jews started. A most hated aspect of German rule in the Ukraine was the forced-labour programme, which changed the lives of millions of Ukrainians. Here again we face a major difficulty faced by Jews, i.e. to concede that the Ukrainians too were victims of the Nazi system. Ukrainians for their part usually resent the Jewish tendency to see the enormous and unprecedented tragedy of the Jewish Holocaust as exclusively directed against their nation. Krawchenko admits that Nazi racial doctrines and policies concerning Jews were different, but he also argues that the Ukrainians were *Untermenschen* as far as Hitler was concerned.

The most controversial statements, from a Jewish point of view, are undoubtedly those by Professor Hunczak. He is right to point out the

---

[1] Peter J. Potichnyj and Howard Aster (eds.), *Ukrainian–Jewish Relations in Historical Perspective* (Canadian Institute of Ukrainian Studies; University of Alberta; Edmonton, 1988).

importance of stereotypical judgements, prejudices, and ethno-centric beliefs among Jews and Ukrainians with regard to each other. He himself quotes a resolution of the Organization of Ukrainian Nationalists in April 1941 to the effect that 'the Jews are the most faithful supporters of the ruling Bolshevik regime'. This image of the Jews is still prevalent today among Ukrainians. It is true that Jews as individuals participated in Soviet rule during certain periods. However, this fact is simplified and exaggerated in Ukrainian opinion and writing, including Hunczak's. Jews are presented as a nationality group bent upon the destruction of Ukrainians.

Another gross error on Hunczak's part is his exaggeration of Ukrainian aid to the Jews. It is of course true that some Jews were indeed saved by their Ukrainian neighbours; this was, however, by no means a ubiquitous phenomenon. Hunczak claims that thousands of Jews entered the ranks of the Ukrainian Insurgent Army and that special Jewish partisan camps existed within the Ukrainian underground. Such an assumption is diametrically opposed to the current state of our knowledge as reflected in Jewish historiography.

Hunczak rightly points to the hesitation of some Jewish survivors to identify their Ukrainian saviours. Whereas it became quite fashionable to reveal Poles and others as 'righteous Gentiles', prevailing Jewish opinion, which casts Ukrainians in the worst possible light, hinders identification of those few who did help.[2] The question of Ukrainian attitudes towards Jews is yet to be fully researched. Both stances such as Hunczak's—that Ukrainians as a community displayed a positive attitude towards the persecuted Jewish population—and Jewish perceptions of every Ukrainian as a Nazi collaborator hamper our understanding of the problem.

Regretfully, it cannot be said that at least on the scholarly and intellectual level there is a growing Jewish–Ukrainian consensus about our common past, as is the case in the Polish–Jewish dialogue. The prolonged trial of John Demjanjuk in the Israeli courts added stress to traditional Ukrainian–Jewish tensions. On the other hand, some in the Ukraine seem to be willing to confront the past. In a free and liberal Ukraine the chance for an honest evaluation of history will be greater than within a nationally frustrated diaspora.

SHIMON REDLICH

[2] For a study of the most famous case see Shimon Redlich, 'Sheptyts'kyi and the Jews During World War II', in Paul R. Magocsi (ed.), *Morality and Reality: The Life and Times of Andrei Sheptyts'kyi* (Canadian Institute of Ukrainian Studies, University of Alberta; Edmonton, 1989), 145–62.

HALINA NELKEN
Images of a Lost World: Jewish Motifs in Polish Painting 1770–1945
(Oxford: Institute for Polish-Jewish Studies, 1991); pp. 144; 255 illustrations (32 pp. in colour).

Popular imagination of how Jews were visually portrayed by non-Jews in different periods of their interrelationship often evokes negative associations. As antisemitic caricatures have been so commonly reproduced they have successfully engraved in the minds and imaginations of many a revolting, stereotypical image, overshadowing depictions of a different nature. Rembrandt is usually cited as one outstanding example of a major artist who portrayed Jewish life and biblical themes in an unbiased manner, thus attracting the attention of scholars and laymen alike. But such themes were taken up by other artists too, and the issue of how Jews were portrayed is much more intricate than a mere division between positive and negative images. Indeed, in Rembrandt's day and during the following decades, Dutch, German, and Italian artists of varying stature showed a keen interest in Jewish religious life and practice, and perceptively documented it in a variety of works and styles, leaving behind a rich treasure-house of visual representations with many observations of contemporary Jewish life, seldom fettered by negative intent. Depictions of synagogues, Jewish ceremonies in the public and private sphere, and Jewish encounters with non-Jews hang beside portraits of individuals, rabbis and lay people, offering an opportunity to better comprehend the social and cultural ambience of the respective communities. Certainly these representations, to be reproduced in various media in the following generations, were not created in a vacuum but as a product of several forces, not least of which were the growing anthropological interest in foreign cultures and religions, the spreading of Christian Hebraism, and the flourishing of scientific exploration, which granted priority of place to direct observation. Moreover, such representations did not completely replace recurrent symbolic depictions of Jews, common in the Middle Ages, which were bent on portraying Jews and Judaism in a most unfavourable guise. All told, western and central Europe witnessed in the seventeenth and eighteenth centuries an unprecedented visual concern with Jewish manners and customs, challenging any simplistic categorization of a non-Jewish depiction of Jewish life in these countries.

But what of eastern Europe? A well-known sixteenth-century anonymous woodcut entitled *Lament over the Death of Credit* (reprinted as a colour plate in the volume under review, pl. I) places an elegantly dressed Jew beside a group of individuals, each one representing a different profession (e.g. a pharmacist, musician, goldsmith), and an Armenian, as they mourn Credit, who lies on a bier in front of them. The Jew seems to be wearing a prayer-shawl above a red robe, similar to that worn by another figure in the print. His presence, amid these other figures, appears commonplace, as if he were fully at ease in their company and considered to be one of them. No similar image exists in western and central Europe at that time or in the following generations. Was this characteristic of Polish representation of Jews? Reading and viewing *Images of a Lost World*, one is struck by a significant collection of paintings and drawings assembled to manifest the incorporation of Jews into diverse areas of Polish society, their active participation in the political and economic concerns of Polish society in the eighteenth and nineteenth centuries, and their interaction with Polish society. Providing a wealth of visual representations relating to Jewish life in Poland, many previously unpublished, from the days of partition to the Second World War, Ms Nelken is concerned to show 'how attractive the Jewish community was for the artists ... [who] reached beyond external representation and physical characteristics, in an attempt to grasp the intrinsic nature of Jewish traditions and way of life' (p. 140). Truly enamoured with these artistic works, Ms Nelken is convinced of their authentic portrayal of Jewish life and society within the Polish sphere, regarding them as a corrective to wrong-headed interpretations of Polish–Jewish relations. Her argument asserts emphatically that the sixteenth-century woodcut was by no means a rare phenomenon. Though this agenda is constantly present in the discussion, it does not cloud the value of the visual material under study, worthy of note for students of Polish and Jewish history.

However, Ms Nelken's study lacks a clear direction as it fails to offer an overarching principle by which to organize this valuable collection. It appears that the author has resorted to several. At times she opts for a historical presentation, using the major historical developments in the history of modern Poland as an important determining principle of the book; at times the rest is organized on geographical lines, focusing on several artists from a particular area; and at times the structure is thematic, so as to cover material that did not easily fall into any of the above divisions. However, seldom does the division contribute to the understanding of the work at hand. Take, for example, the section devoted to 'The Last Years of Poland's Independence, 1770–95', which deals exclusively with the celebrated Polish–French artist Jean-Pierre Norblin. Nothing in this section relates to the particular problems of the partition years, and though the author emphasizes that Norblin's work is 'exact in every detail' and offers a re-creation of the 'character and atmosphere of life in Polish towns at the end of the eighteenth century', she brings no evidence to corroborate such an important generalization. Herein lies an essential weakness of the book. To buttress her argument that this collection exhibits the integration of Jews into Polish society and portrays it authentically, Nelken ought to have resorted to other bodies of literary material. This is wanting throughout, so that significant doubts remain as to whether the visual material can be allowed to stand so independently. But that is only part of the problem. Nelken offers the reader very little in the form of interpretation, either historical or iconographical. While she brings to our attention some wonderful works of Norblin, such as his aquatints of Jewish personalities (executed in 1818), remarkably similar to works done in Germany at the beginning of the eighteenth century, and his *Horsefair in Warsaw*, she leaves us in the dark as to how she understands Norblin's choice of characters and how to unravel the interactions taking place in the latter work. The reader/viewer is left with these fine illustrations and some hints for further research.

In the following chapters one encounters many engaging portrayals of individual Jews, groups of Jews, and Jews together with Gentiles, alongside paintings of historical events (e.g. *The Funeral of Five Victims of the February Massacre, 1861*). Ms Nelken provides informative biographical details of individual artists but is less successful when it comes to more perceptive comments on the works illustrated. Furthermore, as the course of her argument is disjointed it is not at all clear why she chooses to discuss a particular painting and not another. In the section on Jan Feliks Piwarski (1795–1859), Nelken engages the reader's interest by showing some intricate works in zincograph, in which Jews are seen trading in various products, but then concentrates her entire discussion on the mathematician Abraham Stern portrayed in another work by the artist, providing information which is basically extraneous to the work *qua* artistic creation. Stern seems to have become more important than the artist, and thus one is again left with a query, wondering how to evaluate the artist's *œuvre*.

In perusing this volume one cannot help noticing the total reversal of the thematic focus of visual depictions of Jews and Judaism from that prevalent in central and western Europe in the period prior to the one covered here. The Polish material provides an overriding emphasis on Jewish occupations, habits, manners, and social involvement, while showing minimal concern with Jewish traditions, customs, and rituals. This discrepancy is remarkable and worthy of attention, for it offers a more complete visual rendering of Jewish life. One might have expected the author to relate to this phenomenon, as it may indeed support her thesis that the Jews were seen as an integral element of society. As their secular behaviour commanded more attention than their religious comportment, it could be argued that the separatist nature of Jewish life concerned Polish society less than their public presence—which is certainly not the case in western and central

Europe in the earlier period. But when it comes to those paintings dealing with religious themes, such as the striking series *Holiday of the Trumpets* executed by Aleksander Gierymski, Ms Nelken's treatment is wanting. What lies behind Gierymski's tremendous involvement with the *tashlikh* ceremony? Could this be seen within the context of portraying Jews in their public surroundings as opposed to their private abodes? How are we to interpret the presence of the non-Jews in the painting? Gierymski, like the majority of the artists who treated religious themes, refrained from penetrating into the interior of the Jewish home or the synagogue. Was this a coincidence, a problem of communication between artists and Jews, or a lack of interest in the inner workings of Jewish religious practice? On these and other issues the author is unfortunately silent, granting a future scholar of these works sufficient room for interpretation and for giving greater attention to the historical and social context in which the works were produced and further insight into the art-historical presentation.

Thus the representations in *Images of a Lost World* should be seen as a basic text opening the public's eyes to a world previously unacknowledged. For that service alone, performed with concern and competence, Ms Nelken deserves our recognition. She has done the spade-work without which future research would be much more complicated, and she has provided lay people and scholars with a book of much interest. The attractive volume, with fine reproductions in colour and black and white, is there for all to see and marvel. I would have preferred, however, a different title, better reflecting the images enclosed, and less playing up to nostalgic ruminations: perhaps *Images of a Vibrant World*.

RICHARD L. COHEN

VIVIAN B. MANN (ED.)
Gardens and Ghettos: The Art of Jewish Life in Italy

(Berkeley, Los Angeles, and Oxford: University of California Press, 1989)
pp. xx + 354; 192 illustrations

In the last three or four decades in the history of art the importance of catalogues from exhibitions has been steadily growing. From very modest origins as an inventory or rather a list of displayed works with some badly reproduced photographs, the catalogue has evolved into something which can enable us to preserve the memory of every great exhibition through a large album with fine pictures, with texts which provide a synthetic outline of a period, region, or specific phenomenon. Some of those publications are and will for a long time remain both a source of information and the first attempt at synthetic analysis.

These observations fit the catalogue published in connection with a large exhibition which took place at the New York Jewish Museum in 1989. The history of the Jews in Italy shown through the art produced in or for their communities during more than fifteen centuries unfolds before our eyes the specific history of this diaspora, so similar to and at the same time so different from all other diasporas in Europe. Let me cite a fragment of Primo Levi's novel *If Not Now, When?* (after the text of Emily Braun in the catalogue of this exhibition): the hero of this novel, a man coming from the eastern part of Europe, 'wondered if there were any Jews in Italy. If so, they must be strange Jews: how can you imagine a Jew in a gondola or at the top of Vesuvius?' And in another place: 'Italian Jews are as odd as the Catholics. They don't speak Yiddish. In fact, they don't even know what Yiddish is. They only speak Italian; or rather, the Jews of Rome speak Roman, the Jews from Venice speak Venetian, and so on. They dress like everybody else, they have the same faces as everybody else.'

The essays introducing the catalogue are: David Ruderman, 'At the Intersection of Cultures: The Historical Legacy of Italian Jewry'; Mario Toscano, 'The Jews in Italy from the Risorgimento to the Republic'; Vivian B. Mann, 'The Arts of Jewish Italy'; Richard Brilliant, 'Jewish Art and Culture in Ancient Rome'; Evelyn Cohen, 'Jewish Ceremonial Art in the Era of the City States and Ghettos'; Emily Braun, 'From Risorgimento to the Resistance: A Century of Jewish Artists in Italy'; Allen Mandelbaum, 'A Millennium of Hebrew Poetry in Italy'.

This enumeration alone gives an idea of how broad the presentation is and how many problems it tackles. Nearly all the authors stress the fact that Italy was the most liberal country for Jews, that the process of identification of the incomer with the city, with the state, and even with the whole country took place earlier than in any other European country. The ghettos were first established in the fifteenth century; the establishment of the Roman ghetto was ordered by Pope Paul IV in 1555. They were never strictly enclosed, and the Risorgimento established a freedom and equality of rights with Christians earlier than in other countries of Europe (excluding Holland, France, and England). Even the Fascist period was unexpectedly more liberal, and only Nazi pressure introduced racial laws in 1938. In consequence, Italy was the only country in the Berlin-Rome Axis where a large section of the Jewish population survived the Holocaust. Mario Toscano writes of this situation (p. 35): 'Unlike similar movements in Europe between the two wars, Italian Fascism was not characterized by the myth of race or by political, economic, or religious anti-Semitism.' And on the ideology of Italian Jews (p. 34): 'Within this context Jews took positions analogous to those of the rest of the population, and as a rule their choices stemmed not from their Jewishness, but from their social positions and political ideals. Although they moved in socialist and liberal circles, their numbers also included representative and militant Fascist (e.g., Margherita Sarfatti was a codirector of the political journal *Gerarchia*, while Umberto Terracini was one of the founders of the Communist Party).'

The phenomenon of the swift and total penetration of the Jewish population into the surrounding society, simultaneous with the conservation of proper tradition and its catalyst, namely religion, finds reflection in the works of art. It was this phenomenon which was the most specific, while the uniqueness of the religion and customs was not based on a separate language, a fact that I stressed above in the quotation from Primo Levi. One can say that the cement of this specific identity abides in Jewish solidarity, but—paradoxically—it is difficult to find such different and militant points of view in any other population.

When I looked into the book for the first time I was surprised by the similarity of many objects to those produced in different countries 'north of the Alps', and at the same time struck by the evident 'Italianism' of this art. The first illustration in *Gardens and Ghettos* shows the Tempio Israelitico in Turin (1880–4), which looks like many other synagogues, especially those in Germany, where at the end of the previous century the 'oriental' style had been adopted as the most suitable for Jewish houses of worship, just as neo-Gothic became the preferred style for churches and for the residences of English, German, and Polish gentry, neo-Renaissance was adopted by the French, Italian, and Russian bourgeoisie, and neo-Classical was the preference of totalitarian rulers.

Although the silver vessels in particular reflect very clearly the patterns of Renaissance, Baroque, or Classical styles, at the same time they have a very specific character. This is not only seen in such ceremonial forms as Torah crowns and finials, in particular religious symbols, but comes from a specific love for richness and density of ornament. The same is true of textiles, embroideries, and manuscripts. The study by Evelyn M. Cohen, one of the most interesting, shows very fine works of art where the Quattrocento blends this specific passion for ornamental richness with ancient traditions emerging from the Renaissance *maniera*. In the miniatures painted by Joel ben Simon in the middle of the fifteenth century one can find heads very similar to those of the *Wiener Musterbuch*, but even more striking is the fact that the zoomorphic and anthropomorphic letters can be compared to those in early Irish manuscripts. This does not mean that there is a direct connection, but rather a surviving memory of traditional form merged with an artistic capacity for easy adaptation. (I think that the same can be said about the specific Jewishness of modern literature even when the authors do not emphasize their Jewish origins, as in the works of Kafka, which are set in a world outside nations, states, and races.)

This matter comes to the fore when we observe the modern art created in Italy by Jewish painters and—in a much more limited way—sculptors. It seems that the organizers of the exhibition chose works related to the particular environment of Italian Jews, in a manner rather similar to the large exhibition of Marek Rostworowski in Kraków ('Jews–Poles'), but with the difference that in the Polish case the choice of exhibits was not based solely on the issue of how Jews saw themselves, but also on how non-Jews saw the Jews. The principle of selection adopted here has led to a preponderance of portraits. Personally, I should be more interested in a larger representation of 'pure art', from the following perspective: how Italian Jewish artists saw the surrounding world (or the world of their fantasy), not only how they saw other Italian Jews.

None the less, the New York exhibition and its attendant catalogue are artistic events of great importance. Once more the selection and presentation of normally dispersed pieces of art has opened a view into a world outside the common purview of most people.

TADEUSZ CHRZANOWSKI

Polska Sztuka Ludowa 43/1–2 (1989)

(special issue concerned with Jewish culture and folk art)

The periodical *Polska Sztuka Ludowa* has been of great service both to Polish ethnography and to Polish ethnology. For many years under the direction of Aleksander Jackowski it has published special issues devoted to selected problems (for example, in recent years, death, kitsch, or the art produced by mentally disturbed persons). The changes in our country have increased interest in the problems of the culture of national minorities. The special issue concerned with the culture of the Lemki (a Ukrainian ethnic group in the western part of the Carpathian Mountains) was a real success and sold out immediately after it appeared. In this volume the director and his staff have offered readers an issue concerned with some specific aspects of the Jewish religion, culture, and customs, especially in small, provincial communities.

By way of an overture, we are offered some fragments of Abraham Joshua Heschel's famous book *The Earth is the Lord's*. Hasidic mysticism, religious thought, and customs have always been particularly interesting for ethnologists, and there are thus a number of articles dealing with this religious movement, which arose two and a half centuries ago in the eastern part of the Polish–Lithuanian Commonwealth in the Ukraine. The article of Zbigniew Targielski deals with dance and music as the expression of Hasidic belief. Jacek Olędzki's essay about the *kvitlech* from Leżajsk (southern Poland) reveals some interesting new discoveries. *Kvitlech* are short prayers (requests or thanksgivings, similar to Christian volume votive and *ex voto* offerings) written on scraps of paper and placed on or beside the tomb of a revered person. In Leżajsk there exists one of the most popular Catholic sanctuaries devoted to the Virgin Mary, and in a small town not far from this place there lived quite a large Jewish population before the Holocaust, mostly Hasidim who revered a highly blessed man, the '*tsadik* miracle-worker' Noam Elimelekh (1717–87). It is a matter of some surprise that the petitions addressed to him were not only Jewish; many Catholic peasants also brought their requests to his tomb. Certainly in many of the articles in this issue of *Polska Sztuka Ludowa* we find reflections of the coexistence of Polish Jews and Polish peasants. The attempt to find a synthetic approach to this problem is developed in two studies by Ludwik Stomma and Władysław T. Bartoszewski. Stomma, in 'The Image of the Jew in the Structure of Polish Peasant Myths', uses pre-war statistics as a base for his study. But this material is sometimes treacherous. It is true that only a small part of the Jewish population lived in villages. But—and this fact is properly emphasized by Bartoszewski ('Relations between the Peasants and the Jews')—a very large number of Jews lived in small towns, closely linked with the surrounding agricultural population and even partly involved in agriculture. Tłoczek has named such towns from the region of Poznań 'agricultural towns'. For me, the arguments of Bartoszewski are more convincing than the structuralistic views of Stomma. But it can be said of both authors, born long after the Holocaust, that they know the facts but really do not know and understand the atmosphere and realities of the specific provincial structure of the Second Polish Republic. It should also be noted that even peasant society was at this time undergoing a major transformation.

In both essays, very interesting and stimulating as they are, there is a lacuna, a kind of embarrassment, in regard to the problem of Polish antisemitism. I think this is a crucial problem that we must concentrate on in the near future: there are too many myths and indeed complexes on both sides. It is our duty to break this taboo. But this is not really the task of *Polska Sztuka Ludowa*: it is cultivating its own ethnological 'path', which has proved quite fruitful.

Olga Goldberg-Mulkiewicz in 'The Mutual Penetration of Folk Elements between Polish and Jewish Communities' gives a short but convincing account of the interaction of formal influences in the popular arts and crafts.

Bogdana Pilichowska in 'Kraków Church Fair Toys Representing the Jews' discusses the phenomenon of small sculptured figures of 'praying Hasidim'. Those toys, mounted on springs, imitate the swaying character of Jewish prayer. Ewa Fryś-Pietraszkowa gives an outline of the participation of Jewish craftsmen in rural culture. This article discusses the relations between peasants and Jews more effectively than many theoretical speculations. There is a lot to be done in this field, going back to the first artists who depicted the life of the Polish countryside (Norblin, Orlowski, Płoński, Kielisiński, and a large crowd of painters from the second part of the nineteenth century). Alicja Maleta describes the memories of the present inhabitants of Gudec (a small town in southern Poland) concerning their former Jewish neighbours. This interesting subject finds a reflection in some very interesting documents: an account of a peasant from the region of Kielce (Tomasz Gajda) and an interview with Adam Zegadło, one of the most outstanding Polish folk sculptors, who often represents Jews in his works. Maria Fiderkiewicz describes opinions of the Jews from the region of Żywiec and Maciej Krupa summarizes an investigation undertaken in one of the local primary schools. The bulk of the children answered simply that they had not really heard about the Jews, and only 20 per cent had heard something from their parents or grandparents. The title of this report, in which film and television seem to be the most important sources of information, is 'The Fiddler on the Roof, or the Universal Jew'.

A very important part of the issue is made up of studies of Jewish art. Monika Krajewska and Andrzej Trzciński (complemented by a short anthology of translated Hebrew funeral inscriptions, compiled by Stanisław Krajewski) write about stone tombstones in the Jewish cemeteries in Poland. In this field quite a lot of research has recently been undertaken in Poland, but there is still an urgent need for further work as well as for conservation. Trzciński also contributes a short note about wall-paintings in a room in Tyczyn, which served formerly as a *sukkah*.

Perhaps the most interesting article in the field of the history of art is by Maria and Kazimierz Piechotka, the authors of a magnificent work on wooden synagogues in Poland (Warsaw, 1957). They discuss the wall-paintings in those buildings. Here we can see only the scraps of former riches: there are only two examples—from Germany, but so-called 'Polish synagogues'—which still exist. All the others were destroyed by the Nazis, leaving only some documentation and photographs. But even those scraps give us an idea of the characteristic richness and originality of those decorations. Once more we can observe the difficult but in some way blessed situation of Poland at the divide between East and West.

This special issue of *Polska Sztuka Ludowa* is without doubt a fine and valuable achievement. But not for the technical level of its production! Alas—like most scientific publications in Poland—the level is far below normal standards of printing. It is a pity, because the illustrations so badly reproduced in this volume are, from an artistic and documentary point of view, really excellent. Perhaps one could find sponsors who would make it possible to publish these materials as a separate book with high-quality reproductions. I am sure that such an edition would be a success.

TADEUSZ CHRZANOWSKI

JERZY MALINOWSKI
Grupa 'Jung Idysz' i żydowskie środowisko 'Nowej Sztuki' w Polsce

(Warsaw: Polska Akademia Nauk, Instytut Sztuki, 1987)
pp. 246; 68 black-and-white illustrations

The Jung Idysz [Young Yiddish] group—founded in 1918 in Łódź was the first and only important Jewish artistic group in the domain of painting and graphic art in Poland before the Second World War and the Holocaust. In his thoughtful and well-researched book, the Polish art historian Jerzy Malinowski succeeds in presenting a novel and on the whole convincing picture of both the internal and the external dynamics of Jewish artistic life in Poland at the beginning of the 1920s. He treats the history of the Jung Idysz group in close conjunction with the history and activities of the Jewish avant-garde between two focal points, Paris and Moscow. There can be no doubt that the flowering of Jewish artistic life in post-Tsarist and early Bolshevik Russia must have exerted in the crucial years 1917–19 a profound influence on the young Jewish artists in Warsaw and Łódź. After all, the Polish capital was an important stepping-stone for many Jewish artists from Russia and the Ukraine on their way to Berlin or Paris. So, for example, in the fall of 1921 the famous El Lissitzky stayed in Warsaw for a couple of weeks, contacted some Jung Idysz artists (most notably Henryk Berlewi), and published there an important theoretical article in Yiddish on 'Overcoming Art' ('Des goyner zayn di kunst', *Ringen*, 10 (1921 or 1922)). This article, which has remained unknown *goyner zayn* to the great array of Lissitzky scholars, has been rediscovered by Malinowski, translated into Polish, and published in the annex to his book (pp. 213–18): perhaps the most important of the many fortunate discoveries in this work.

To the Jung Idysz group belonged the now famous painter Jankel Adler, but also Wincenty (Icchak) Brauner, Marek Szwarc, Henryk (Henoch) Barciński, the poet Moshe Broderson, and the less well-known female artists Dina Matus, Ida Brauner, Pola Lindenfeld, and Zofia Gutentag. In 1921 Henryk Berlewi, the latter-day abstract painter, loosely adhered to the group. However, in late 1921 the group dissolved itself after most of its members left Poland to pursue their artistic education or careers in Germany.

The Jung Idysz artists espoused in their paintings (of which few have survived) and graphic works an artistic style which could be described as a Jewish variant of 'Late Expressionism'. Of course, the original impetus came from Chagall's vision of the *shtetl*; they were, however, mainly influenced by German Expressionist graphic art. Judged by German standards, much of their expressionist pathos appears pretty conventional and somewhat second-rate, as if its iconographical inception had already been permeated by the intellectual and stylistic demise of Expressionism proper in Germany in the years around 1920. Leaving Adler aside, only the linocuts of Szwarc and Wincenty Brauner display a febrile, intense graphic idiom which—this seems an interesting phenomenon—was to reappear in Polish art after 1945.

The Jung Idysz artists preferred linocuts to woodcuts. Linocuts allow softer, as it were fleeting, pictorial effects which on the whole do not appear in German Expressionism, which adhered to the woodcut as its favourite medium (Malinowski's generally precise stylistic analysis is a bit vague on this point). An interesting detail provides Barciński's *Half-nude* (illustration 36, linocut, 1919) with an astoundingly—for 1919—characteristically 'Picasso profile': probably a coincidence *avant la lettre*.

Malinowski displays in his book, as has already been said, a sure grasp as regards formal and comparative analysis and a good knowledge of German Expressionist art. He justly concentrates his attention—so few of the Jung Idysz works having survived—on the general cultural background, examining in detail the group's literary and art-theoretical pronouncements and its attitude towards Jewish tradition. An interesting point is the Expressionistically tinged predilection of some Jung Idysz artists for scenes and themes from the New Testament. Despite their fascination for the world of the *shtetl*, most of the Jung Idysz artists show a manifest desire to transcend the bounds of mere 'Jewish folkloricism'.

The edition itself is rather disappointing. The extremely shoddy printing technique shows the printing industry of the late People's Poland at its very, very worst (much of the underground literature published in Poland prior to 1988 was much more legible); the quality of the reproductions is characteristically poor. Despite these necessarily negative remarks, one has to acknowledge a certain thoroughness of both the author and the publisher: there are relatively few misprints. The notes are copious, but no bibliography has been provided and no summary in a foreign language. (The author, however, has recently published a short English-language article summarizing the main theses of the book: 'The *Jung Idysz* (*Young Yiddish*) Group and Jewish Modern Art in Poland 1918–1923', in *The Art of the 1920's in Poland, Bohemia, Slovakia and Hungary* (Niedzica Seminars, 6; Kraków, 1991), 67–72. Unfortunately, this summary is riddled with misprints, e.g. 'Bremen' for 'Barmen'. A revised version of it can be found in *Polin*, vi (1991), 223–30.)

SERGIUSZ MICHALSKI

JANET HADDA
Passionate Women, Passive Men: Suicide in Yiddish Literature
(New York: State University of New York Press, 1988)
pp. viii + 223.

No one will ever lack a good reason for killing himself.
CESARE PAVESE

Leave him in silence. Neither honour nor curse him.
RABBI AKIVA

Janet Hadda, an American psychologist and literary critic, deals—for the first time—with a peculiar subject, and does it in a peculiar way. She describes the role of suicide in Yiddish literature, its social implications and psychoanalytic reflections. The author first analyses thirteen short novels, most of them dating back to the period between the two World Wars, the Golden Age of Yiddish literature. Her study then focuses on three more recent works: *Di agune* [The deserted wife], by Chaim Grade, and *Der kunstmakher fun Lublin* [The magician of Lublin] and *Sonim, di geshikhte fun a libe* [Enemies: A love story], by Isaac Bashevis Singer. This last novel provides a clue to the entire essay, justifying, as it does, suicide as an answer to an unbearable existential condition.

Hadda's book rests on two theses, both stated in the introduction. The first, implicit in the title, begins with a sociological assumption:

a different and curious factor unites most of the literary suicides created by Yiddish authors: it is their failure to marry . . . The men who commit suicide are chronically withdrawn or inert, a condition that renders them incapable of sustaining the demands of marriage . . . The women, for their part, are too wilful to be tolerated by conventional standards. (p. 3)

This type of suicide, which occurs in the 'fictional works studied' (but which appears from the statistics not to be a phenomenon of real life), results from the existential inability of the characters to respond to the basic call of Jewish ethics, which is to create a family, to procreate, and to live in a comfortable and warm environment.

Hadda's major aim is to prove, against current interpretations, how the authors she analyses 'accept and forgive' suicide, which is 'ostensibly considered taboo and unpardonable' (p. 12). At the same time these authors see in it a negative response to marriage and family, which are always perceived as positive and constructive aspects of life. The other thesis applies psychoanalytical methodology to literary criticism in an attempt to provide a new interpretation. The author in fact devotes some very interesting paragraphs to this approach.

A very detailed index leads the reader through the complex web of themes with which the author deals. On the other hand, the book lacks a good bibliography of the novels and the reader is forced to trace them back in the footnotes.

It is quite surprising to find that the book gives the opposite of the expected ratio of male and female suicides. In the novels it is in fact mostly women who take their lives, while statistics from the real world show that 70 per cent of successful suicides are committed by men. Hadda's book shows that out of thirteen suicides in the corpus studied only five are committed by men. Two cases, Yasha in *Der kunstmakher fun Lublin* and Herman in *Sonim*, are actually suicides enacted in fantasy and reveal an attempt to escape from reality rather than an actual attempt to kill oneself. It would thus be interesting to understand why it was easier for a Yiddish writer to describe a woman's suicide, even though reality would suggest that it is mostly men who take their own lives.

As mentioned above, the last chapter, 'After the Holocaust', is of special interest. As a matter of fact, it seems to summarize and support the statement made by the author in the introduction concerning the surprising tolerance by Yiddish writers of suicide. According to Hadda, Singer comes to the point of proposing 'a somber and new suggestion . . . Singer seems to be suggesting that, for some survivors at any rate, the only importance in life is to keep in mind the destroyed Eastern European Jewish community. When this is no longer possible, perhaps suicide is an honorable, rather than a punishable act' (pp. 195–6). Singer's idea, although 'somber', is not truly original.

Throughout the book the author seems to be in agreement with the prevalent opinion that Judaism rejects and condemns suicide in a stronger way than other ethical and religious systems. (This opinion is not totally unsupported. It would suffice to recall the traditional sentence codified by Maimonides, according to which the suicide's relatives were not even allowed to mourn in public.) It is necessary, however, to ascertain whether this conception is due to an overlapping of Christian and Jewish ethics. There are several instances in which Jewish ethics do not wholly condemn suicide, and others where the position is loose enough to allow for a reading of suicide as a worthy action. The best example is the case of Masada's martyrs, who, according to the *Encyclopedia Judaica* (s.v. 'Suicide'), 'acted in accordance with their interpretation of *halakhah* which included slavery and subjection to a foreign power as one of those principles concerning which one was enjoined "to be killed rather than transgress"'. The issue becomes particularly delicate in the case of survivors of the Shoah whose bodies carry for ever the marks of 'slavery and subjection to a foreign power'. Bruno Bettelheim, Jean Amery, Paul Celan, and Primo Levi are only a few of the many names of survivors who were later actually victims of the *lager*s, those *lager*s that, as Hannah Arendt writes:

by making martyrdom, for the first time in history, impossible ... [and] by making death itself anonymous (making it impossible to find out whether a prisoner is dead or alive) robbed death of its meaning as the end of a fulfilled life. In a sense they took away the individual's own death, proving that henceforth nothing belonged to him and he belonged to no one. His death merely set a seal on the fact that he had never really existed.[1]

These tragic deaths met with a response from Establishment Judaism which for some was unexpectedly tolerant. Neither Bettelheim nor Primo Levi was buried in the corner of the cemetery allotted to those who had taken their lives, as Orthodox tradition would require. Survivors' suicides are not to be punished, being acts committed unconsciously: *shelo lada'at*. In this category are included, among others, suicides caused by 'pathological depression' and by 'a (subjectively) reasonable despair of life' (*Encyclopedia Judaica*). They could also be, paradoxically, the only possible way of martyrdom.

From this perspective, then, the peculiarity of the writers of the first half of the century becomes relative. Their cryptic tolerance was no more than a reflection of an attitude that, although pervaded by esoteric traits, was actually deeply rooted in tradition. Even Singer's position is no longer unique, and its provoking intention has faded so that it has become an integral part of contemporary Jewish thought.

LAURA QUERCIOLI

[1] Hannah Arendt, *The Origins of Totalitarianism* (New York and London, 1973), 450–1.

Obituaries

Stefan Kieniewicz
(1907–1992)

HE was tall, slim, and grey-haired and always wore glasses. He was a legend in the Department of History at Warsaw University. His name was spoken with awe and admiration, next to the names of Tadeusz Manteuffel, Marian Małowist, and Aleksander Gieysztor. I was then eighteen years old and my soul was revolting against the sickening world of Communist dictatorship that many accepted without protest.

I was eighteen years old and did not understand what was the basis of the strength and stature of these elderly men teaching history and writing about remote times. Stefan Kieniewicz seemed to me to be excessively careful. I knew neither him nor his make-up, neither his generational experience nor his intellectual achievements. And later, throughout the subsequent years, his books and essays were with me constantly. I still cannot get used to the fact that I shall never read a new essay of his again. He was a historian from an excellent pre-war school, and during the years of the Second Republic he won prizes and distinctions for his work on the nineteenth century.

Polish destiny, in a nineteenth century terrible and rich in events and individuality, invariably fascinated him. He wrote prolifically, staying under the influence of the tradition of the Warsaw school, and later under the influence of Marxism, which he was able to transform into an incomparable instrument for the analysis of our history. During the occupation he was connected with the Armia Krajowa (Home Army), then, as a professor at Warsaw University, he undertook in his research such complex subjects as the Galician massacre of 1846 and the peasant question. Always a faithful son of the Catholic Church, always stubbornly ferreting out the secrets of the Polish compromisers and Polish insurrectionists.

He was a magnificent historian, wise, enquiring, versatile, and fearless. From among the many works written by him, for me Stefan Kieniewicz will remain, first and foremost, the great chronicler of the January Insurrection. His monumental work constitutes the turning-point, not only in Polish knowledge of that time but also in Polish thought about the nineteenth century. Kieniewicz proposed this maxim for dealing with the nineteenth century: 'Be free of fanaticism, but not free of judgement.' He proposed critical thought, even though it be the contradiction not only of hagiography, but also of that strange methodology of the Stalin period when, according to a description by Tadeusz Manteuffel, Polish textbooks sounded as though they had been written by a foreigner, and an unfriendly foreigner at that. From the pages of Professor Kieniewicz's book a new and completely different picture of the Reds of 1863 revealed itself, a new portrait of Traugutt, a new image of the place of the Church and the presence of Jews in the Polish struggles for freedom. *Powstanie Styczniowe* [January Insurrection] by Stefan Kieniewicz is a marvellous testament to the writer's talent and intellectual shrewdness. It is also a testament to how much could be written in those times—of course, on condition that one had something of import to say.

I remember a meeting of the PEN Club on the anniversary of the regaining of independence by Poland. It was 1978. Kieniewicz spoke calmly but very soberly and critically. I remember the outrage in the hall from people expecting a heart-rending speech, and I remember my feelings of solidarity with the professor who suddenly, without ostentation, could demonstrate what integrity in research was, coupled with civil courage.

One of the last texts of Professor Stefan Kieniewicz that I read was a short essay in *Tygodnik powszechny* about the attitudes of German historians during the period of the Hitler dictatorship. Professor Kieniewicz was also reflecting on his own and on society's attitudes during the epoch of Communism's victory. That short reflection, calm and penetrating, had nothing whatever to do with the loud settling of accounts with German 'fellow-travellers with Nazism'. It was rather a voice in the discussion about how it really was—without beating a *tua culpa* on a foreign breast. For it was truth that fascinated Professor Kieniewicz. That devotion to truth dictated that he should remain in Poland through all those years, agree to countless compromises, often give way to pressure, and yet be, teach, continue his research, and educate succeeding generations of historians: in other words, maintain continuity. Today, when I read and hear about Polish continuity being ripped to shreds, I cannot help but feel that Professor Kieniewicz's life and work provide an important message for us. His is a voice of truth and seriousness in a world of prevarication and confusion. We shall return to his books more than once.

ADAM MICHNIK

Artur Eisenbach
(1906–1992)

ARTUR (AHARON) EISENBACH, who died in November 1992, was one of the last surviving representatives of that distinguished group of Polish Jewish historians who, in the years before the First World War and in independent Poland between 1918 and 1939, laid the foundation for the scholarly investigation of the Polish Jewish past. He was very conscious that he was a survivor from a lost world. On the occasion of his eightieth birthday in 1986, he reflected: 'my life's path has followed a course completely different from that of my colleagues ... except for a few members of the older generation.'

Eisenbach was born in Nowy Sącz in Galicia (Austrian Poland) in 1906 into what he described as 'a petty bourgeois family without any Haskalah traditions'. An unsuccessful attempt to make himself 'productive' by apprenticing himself to a locksmith led him to the conclusion that the only way to escape from 'provincial backwardness' was 'study'. Lack of funds forced him to drop out of the teachers' course at the Jewish Educational Seminary in Vilna, but he was eventually able to take his *matura* (secondary-school examination) in 1930 and enrol as a student at the Jagiellonian University in Kraków in October 1931. The following year he moved to Warsaw, where he managed to be accepted into the seminar of Professor Marceli Handelsman, himself of Jewish origin and the doyen of Polish nineteenth-century historians. The seminar had an enormous impact on the young Eisenbach: 'The meetings, discussions, and especially the methodological observations of Professor Handelsman were for me a revelation.'

He completed his MA (in Poland as in Scotland, a first degree) in 1935, with the highest grade. For his qualifying thesis he submitted an essay on 'The Legal and Political Position of Jews in the Duchy of Warsaw'. Unable to find a job in a university, he took employment in the offices of the Jewish Society for the Protection of Health (TOZ), where he soon became head of the statistical office, a position he held until the outbreak of the war. He continued to undertake historical research, influenced primarily by the Marxist school of Jewish historians, above all Raphael Mahler and Emanuel Ringelblum, whose sister he married. Stimulated by his work at TOZ, he published a number of articles on demographic and health issues, but his principal interest remained the problem of Jewish emancipation in the first half of the nineteenth century. He wrote several pieces on the position of Jews in the Napoleonic Duchy of Warsaw and began work on a doctoral thesis on this topic, an expansion of his master's thesis on the same subject under Professor Handelsman. The abundant material on the question that he found in the Polish archives was lost during the Nazi occupation, as were his other notes and library.

After the conquest of Poland in 1939, Eisenbach succeeded in fleeing to Buczacz, his wife's birthplace in Galicia, then under Soviet occupation. From here he moved to Saratov and Alma-Ata, spending the war in the USSR. His wife and child were unable to leave Buczacz and were murdered there by the Nazis in 1942. Many of Eisenbach's historical colleagues were trapped in Warsaw, among them his brother-in-law Emanuel Ringelblum, Ignacy Schipper, and Majer Bałaban, where they perished in the Shoah.

After his return to Poland in May 1946, Eisenbach worked in the Central Historical Commission of the Central Committee of Polish Jews which was set up after the war in an attempt to rebuild Jewish life in Poland. When the Jewish Historical Institute was established later in the year, he was appointed head of its archive, subsequently becoming a research worker. He became very close to the Institute's director, Bernard (Ber) Mark, a pre-war communist historian and publicist with a subtle and penetrating mind, who was able, until his death in 1966, to shield the Institute from the political pressures which were a feature of life in People's Poland, particularly in its earlier years. In the immediate postwar period Eisenbach devoted himself entirely to research on the Holocaust. This was, as he himself put it, a choice 'dictated by life itself', by his own tragic experiences during the war, and by the need to document the tragic fate of Polish Jewry and provide expert evidence for the trials of Nazi war criminals. He presented for his doctoral dissertation in 1953 a thesis entitled *Hitlerowska polityka eksterminacji Żydów w latach 1939–1945 jako jeden z przejawów imperializmu niemieckiego* [The Nazi policy of exterminating the Jews between 1939 and 1945 as one of the manifestations of German imperialism], which was published in the same year. His habilitation, which was published in 1955, was entitled *Pertraktakcje anglo-amerykańskie z Niemcami a los ludności żydowskich podczas drugiej wojny światowej* [Anglo-American negotiations with Germany and the fate of the Jewish people during the Second World War]. His writings in this period, dealing with very sensitive subjects, reflected the prevailing political orthodoxy. It was with some feeling that he observed in 1986, in a characteristically cautious manner: 'With a perspective of the more than fifty years during which I have undertaken historical research, I can now see clearly the great difficulties which stand before the scholar ... especially in times when the social sciences are politicized, with all the negative consequences this entails.'

After a decade of work in this area, Eisenbach began gradually to return to the theme to which he had devoted himself before the war, publishing extensively on a number of related problems, including the legal situation of the Jews in the late eighteenth and early nineteenth centuries, their position as an estate recognized by law, and the attitude of the different sections of the Polish 'Great Emigration' to Jewish emancipation. In 1966 he was made a member of the Committee for the Historical Sciences at the Polish Academy of Sciences and awarded the title of Professor.

The anti-Jewish campaign of 1968 was a very painful experience for Eisenbach. He had been appointed director of the Jewish Historical Institute in 1966 and came under very strong pressure to hand over its important archival holdings on the Second World War to the ascendant 'anti-Zionist' faction. These pressures he successfully and courageously resisted, at the cost of some smaller sacrifices and great personal suffering. He was subjected to vicious attacks in the press, and his articles in the *Polish Encyclopedia* were criticized for over-stressing Jewish issues. He was ultimately forced to resign as director of the Jewish Historical Institute, retaining only his position at the Polish Academy of Sciences, where, as he put it, 'there was a good atmosphere and I had magnificent friends'. He decided against emigration and 'was rescued from depression by my wife and family [he had remarried in 1948] and by intensive scholarly work'. Certainly, in the following years he produced a series of monographs on Polish Jewish problems in the first half of the nineteenth century which form the essential basis for any future work on this subject. They include *Kwestia równouprawnienia Żydów w Królestwie Polskim* [The question of the granting of equal rights to the Jews in the Kingdom of Poland] (1972); *Wielka Emigracja wobec kwestii żydowskiej* [The Great Emigration and the Jewish question] (1976); *Z dziejów ludności żydowskiej w Polsce w XVII i XIX w.* [Essays on the history of the Jews in Poland in the eighteenth and nineteenth centuries] (1983); and *Emancypacja Żydów na ziemiach polskich* (1987), which was published in English in 1991 as *The Emancipation of the Jews in Poland, 1780–1870*. He also continued to work on Holocaust themes, editing Ringelblum's diary and his essay on Polish–Jewish relations. In his last years he moved to Israel, where he had a nephew and where, active as ever, he was working on an account of Polish–Jewish relations in the nineteenth century.

Eisenbach's approach to his subject became more pragmatic in the 1980s. He stressed the need for scholarly detachment and for the historian to analyse the facts coldly and to examine historical developments objectively. He continued to stress that 'the key problems of Jewish history in Poland can only be explained in close connection with the central issues of Polish history and the evolution of other estates, groups, and classes of Polish society'. He had an encyclopaedic knowledge of the sources, both published and archival, and his work sometimes suffers from his obsession with detail. Yet he always retained a sense of what were the underlying issues and could expound them with great clarity. He would also go to extraordinary pains to ensure the accuracy of his work, as I learnt to my great benefit when I had the privilege of working with him to bring out the English version of *The Emancipation of the Jews in Poland*. Moreover, in spite of his determination to preserve academic detachment, like every great historian, he felt passionately about his subject-matter. The preface to *The Emancipation of the Jews in Poland*, in which he summed up his life's work, came straight from the heart:

In writing this book, I had a sense of participating in the dramatic decades-long striving of the Jewish community to abolish entrenched barriers, which were not only political, but also psycho-social. I must confess that it required a major effort of will to prevent my emotional involvement from affecting an objective presentation of the events. I leave it to my readers to determine whether I have succeeded in attaining such an objectivity.

ANTONY POLONSKY

'A Small Memorial Candle' for Adolf Rudnicki (1912–1990)

ADOLF RUDNICKI died in Warsaw on 15 November 1990. He was an author who, throughout the sixty years of his creativity, continually sought his own tone: from psychological prose and reporting to essays and concise parabolic stories. First and foremost, however, he was a poet of the murdered Jewish people. He was united with this theme to such an extent that what followed in his creative writing was barely noticed by the critics and generally misinterpreted. In order to understand him, it was necessary to transform the perspective from the realistic to the metaphysical, and to look for the source of his secret, multi-dimensional, symbolic prose in the Bible, Talmud, and Hasidic folklore, which this graduate of the Galaician *heder* blended with the Polish language.

Rudnicki made his début (together with such writers as Gombrowicz, Schulz, and Choromanski) with the novel *Szczury* [Rats] (1932), which was inspired by Freudian psychoanalysis, and revealed the interesting dreams in the subconsciousness and psyche of a weak man, lost, isolated, and encircled by evil. The novel lends itself to interpretation as an expression of the world-view of a tragic generation, the generation of 1910, over which hung the threat of apocalypse.

At the centre of Rudnicki's pre-war works stands man. The author attempted to present a universal vision of human nature; therefore he did not portray the specific Jewish environment from which he originated and which he knew best. There are similar developments in *Niekochana* [The unloved one] (1937), a subtle analysis of unreciprocated love, a feeling shown in a pure state, deprived of any supra-emotional conditions. The psyche of a sensitive, affectionate woman is the subject of astounding intuitive interpretations in all his later writings.

At the same time, Rudnicki moved from psychological to sociological analysis in the articles *Żołnierzy* [Soldiers] (1933) and *Doświadczenie* [Experiences] (1939), which painted a picture of war and its mechanized destruction of human individuality. Closest to this great theme is *Lato* [Summer] (1938), seemingly a story of a vacation in Kazimierz Dolny and a pilgrimage to a *tsadik* in Góra Kalwaria. In reality, however, it is a prophetic portrait of Judaism enclosed in its own separate society in the face of the danger which it perceives from outside. These works were severely assessed by the author himself in his postwar book *Kartka znalezionej pod murem straceń* [A card found at the wall of execution]:

> The war aged what I had written by a thousand years. I read full of amazement. I read with anger and disapproval. I read and don't understand... My works exude the stuffy atmosphere of papers abandoned in attics. War has already destroyed them, although it did not touch their physical form. The reflection of the great conflagration takes away from the readability of their pages, garbles their shapes like the ripples from a rock thrown off a bridge.

The extermination of the Jewish people, from whom Rudnicki was separated on the last journey, imposed upon him the obligation to be a witness to their inhuman death. The story from the series *Epoka pieców* [The epoch of the ovens] assured Rudnicki of an everlasting place in Polish literature. While others searched for a new way to describe the grimness of the past, Rudnicki reached back to the sources, to the biblical lament of Job, the treasury of the prophets, full of lyricism and pathos. He focused not on showing the massive extermination, but rather on the deep tragedy of the ethical dilemmas of individuals in specific situations in which history had placed them. An apocalypse passed over the world and, according to Rudnicki, there still existed love, heroism, loyalty, and the desire for ethical purity, as well as a tragic awareness of loss. *Epoka pieców* was never closed; Rudnicki's first recapitulation was *Żywe i martwe morze* [Dead and living seas] (1952), and he later completed *Kupiec Łódzki* [The merchant of Łódź] (1963), a penetrating analysis of the mechanism of subordination to a totalitarian government.

The epoch of the Holocaust has moved into the past; however, in the works of Rudnicki it has left an indelible trace. From that time on his works present 'the world after the end of the world', even when he is describing insignificant events such as holiday flirtations. Love in this world is like that in *Niekochana*, a sentence of isolation. Reality is invaded by evil, falsehood, insincerity, hypocrisy, a lack of authenticity; a man thus searches for a foothold outside of reality, because he has a presentiment of another actuality. On the surface this is realistic prose, but here is no imitated reality; the writing of Rudnicki is guided by dreams rather than consciousness. The dialogue of the characters is full of commonplace, familiar expressions which are far from natural. Their underlying rhythm is completely different: very likely imbued with the melody of the reading of holy writings on *heder* benches, or the chant of the cantor.

Rogaty Warszawiak [The cuckold of Warsaw] (1982), *Sto lat temu umarł Dostojewski* [Dostoevsky died a hundred years ago] (1984), and *Teatr zawsze grany* [The theatre which always plays] (1987) represent a different trend in Rudnicki's essays; at its beginning is *Niebieskie Kartki* [Blue cards], published in 1954. These books have retained their character; fragmentation of ideas, description, the ease of change in the direction of thought, moving from frequently trivial observations to philosophical reflections. Kazimierz Brandys writes about this style: 'The confusion of several styles is unlike anything else: essays and belles-lettres, intellectual reflections with reporting, journalism with morality.' Tomasz Burek wrote about the role and fate of these essays, especially those from around 1956, contained in the volumes *Ślepe lustro tych lat* [The blind mirror of those years] (1956) and *Prześwita* [Pre--dawn] (1957): 'The boldest, most honest, vibrant with passion from the administration of Stalinist justice... precisely these are condemned to oblivion, together with the book *Prześwita*, relegated to behind a curtain of silence.'

Rudnicki has always understood writing rather according to the manner of the late nineteenth century—as a calling, the choosing of a specific role: creation in words, but a perception different from that of his contemporary avant-gardists. His words are derived from the Bible and attempt to approach this absolute standard. His failure to adopt the canons of other contemporary writers is a symptom of his concern with the perfect form of a literary work: printing does not attain this standard of perfection, but has merely the status of a draft, which may be forgotten and ignored as a corrupt version of the true work.

About reality Rudnicki expressed himself only through literature; after several insignificant salutes to social realism he reached artistic independence, perhaps a little egotistical in his attitude. While history gathered speed and writing supported politics and vice versa, Rudnicki remained alone, unattractive, increasingly bitter. This radical individualistic attitude led to the volume *Sto lat temu umarł Dostojewski*, written to spite the nationwide solidarity and euphoria of the years 1980 and 1981. At that time he could not be officially published, and was unexpectedly circulated in Poland by an underground publishing house. The critics received him coolly, if not reluctantly. The eventual reconciliation between writer and critics came as a result of the widening circle of his readers following the publication of *Krakowskie Przedmieście pełnego deserów* [Krakowskie Przedmieście full of desserts] (1986) a book whose heroes are the already dead Arzejenski, Jastrun, Gombrowicz—all of his generation.

I saw Adolf Rudnicki for the last time in his apartment on Kanonia on 25 October 1990. We spoke of his literary plans, and there was nothing to presage the news which surprised me three weeks later. I thought of him as he had of death:

The first day after somebody's death, it seems impossible; you live in hope that you will see and meet him on the street. It is not possible to comprehend the death of someone dear; this means that it takes many stages.

You live, and together with you in your head, your rhythm, live phenomena to which you have become accustomed. Among these phenomena is he who had departed. Do not leave. Not yet.

JÓZEF WRÓBEL

Editors' Notes

THE JAN KARSKI AND POLA NIRENSKA AWARD

Professor Jan Karski has established at YIVO Institute for Jewish Research, New York, an endowment of $100,000 for a perpetual annual award of $5,000 to be made to authors of published works dealing with or otherwise describing the contribution to Polish culture and Polish scholarship of Poles of Jewish origin and Polish Jews. The award will be known as *The Jan Karski and Pola Nirenska Award*.

It is Professor Karski's wish that the jury awarding the prize should consist of the following six individuals:

1. *Dr Lucjan Dobroszycki*, Senior Research Associate at YIVO and Professor of History at Yeshiva University, as Chairman.
2. *Research Director* of YIVO Institute for Jewish Research.
3. *Research Director* of the Jewish Historical Institute, Warsaw.
4. *Dr Józef A. Gierowski*, Professor of History at the Jagiellonian University, Kraków, Director of the Research Centre of Jewish History and Culture in Poland.
5. *Czesław Miłosz*, poet and writer, 1980 Nobel Prize Laureate.
6. *Jerzy Turowicz*, editor-in-chief of *Tygodnik Powszechny*, member of the Polish Bishops' Conference Committee for Dialogue with Judaism, and Vice-President of the Society for Polish–Israeli Friendship.

The Jan Karski and Pola Nirenska Award will be of great importance in furthering Polish Jewish studies and creating a better understanding of the destroyed civilization of Polish Jewry.

BIBLIOGRAPHY OF POLISH JEWISH STUDIES

With volume 9 of *Polin* the editors hope to inaugurate an annual list of publications related to Polish Jewish studies. Since the task of collecting references is onerous, readers are asked to make us aware of all books and articles published and theses and dissertations completed on the subject, in any language, since 1 January 1993. Bibliographic references should be as full as possible, including the full name of the author, the title, the place of publication, the publisher and date, and the ISBN and price. References for works that might not otherwise have come to our attention would be particularly welcome.

Please address suggestions to: Professor Gershon Hundert, Department of History, McGill University, 855 Sherbrooke Street West, Montreal, Quebec, Canada H3A 2T7. Fax: 0101 514 398 8365. E-Mail: Hundert @ Heps.Lan.McGill.Ca.

Thank you.

Notes on Contributors

FRANCISZEK ADAMSKI is Professor of Sociology at the Jagiellonian University in Kraków and Chair of the Department of Social Pedagogy. He has written widely on religion, culture, and the family and is particularly interested in the influence of non-Catholic cultures on Polish culture. Among his books are *Modele małżeńskie i rodzinne i kultura masowa* [Marriage and family models and mass culture] (Warsaw, 1971); *Rodzina między sacrem i profanem* [The family between sacred and profane] (Poznań, 1986); and *Ateizm w kulturze polskiej* [Atheism in Polish culture] (Kraków, 1993).

STANISLAUS A. BLEJWAS is Professor of History at Central Connecticut State University, where he also co-ordinates the University's Polish Studies Program. He works in both Polish and Polish American history. He is the author of *Realism in Polish Politics: Warsaw Positivism and National Survival in Nineteenth Century Poland* (Boulder, Colo., 1982), and co-editor of *Pastor of the Poles: Polish American Essays* (New Britain, Conn., 1982).

SZYJA BRONSZTEJN is Professor of Statistics in the Department of Law and Administration at the University of Wrocław. His main interests are in the regional demography of Poland and the modern history of Polish Jews. Among his books are *Ludność żydowska w Polsce w okresie międzywojennym: Studium statystyczna* [The Jewish community in Poland in the interwar period: A statistical study] (Wrocław, 1963); *Procesy ludnościowe na terenach uprzemysłowianych: Doświadczenia polskie* [Population movements in industrialized areas: Some Polish examples] (Wrocław, 1980); and *Z dziejów ludności żydowskiej na Dolnym Śląsku po drugiej wojnie światowej* [The history of the Jews in Lower Silesia after the Second World War] (Wrocław, 1993).

ALINA CAŁA is Director of Research at the Jewish Historical Institute in Warsaw. She is the author of *Wizerunek Żyda w polskiej kulturze ludowej* [The image of the Jew in Polish peasant culture] (Warsaw, 1987) and *Asymilacja Żydów w Królestwie Polskim [1864–1897]: Postawy, konflikty, stereotypy* [The assimilation of the Jews in the Kingdom of Poland (1864–1897): Attitudes, conflicts, stereotypes] (Warsaw, 1989). At present she is one of the organizers of a project to assess the strength and nature of antisemitism in Poland today.

DAVID ENGEL is Professor of Modern Jewish History at New York University and co-editor of the journal *Gal-Ed: On the History of Polish Jewry*. He is the author of *In the Shadow of Auschwitz: The Polish Government-in-Exile and the Jews, 1939–1942* (Chapel Hill, 1987) and *Facing a Holocaust: The Polish Government-in-Exile and the Jews, 1943–1945* (Chapel Hill, 1993). At present, he is working on a study of the Jewish community in Poland after the Second World War.

BINA GARNCARSKA-KADARY was born and educated in Poland, where she worked in the Social Humanities Division of the Polish Academy of Sciences, while at the same time undertaking research for her doctorate. In 1968 she emigrated to Israel with her family. In 1971 she completed her doctorate at the Hebrew University. It was published (in Hebrew) in 1985 under the title *The Role of Jews in the Development of Industry in Warsaw 1816/20–1914*. She has worked since completing her doctorate in the Diaspora Research Institute of Tel Aviv University and published many articles on the social and material conditions of the Jewish working classes in *Gal-Ed*, *Shvut*, and *Tsion*. Her books, *The Jewish Proletariat in Interwar Poland* and *Po'alei Tsion Left in Prewar Poland*, will appear shortly.

JERZY HOLZER is Professor in the Institute of Political Studies at the Polish Academy of Sciences. His books include *Polska Partia Socjalistyczna w latach 1917–19* [The Polish Socialist Party, 1917–1919] (Warsaw, 1962); *Mozaika polityczna drugiej Rzeczypospolitej* [The political mosaic of the Second Republic] (Warsaw, 1974); and *'Solidarność' 1980–1: Geneza i historia* ['Solidarity', 1980–1: Origins and history] (Paris, 1984).

KAROL JONCA is Chair of the Department of Political and Legal Thought in the Faculty of Law at Wrocław University. He is a specialist in the history of modern political ideas and in Fascism and is the editor of *Studia nad faszyzmem i zbrodniami hitlerowskimi* (Wrocław, 1977). He has published many articles and ten books, most recently *Noc kryształowa z 9–10 XI 1938r. i casus Herschela Grynszpana* [The Kristallnacht of 9–10 November 1938 and the case of Herschel Grynszpan] (Wrocław, 1992).

ZBIGNIEW LANDAU is Head of the Department of Economic and Social History at the Warsaw School of Economics and principal editor of *Encyclopedia Drugiej Rzeczypospolitej* [Encyclopaedia of the Second Republic]. His main interests are Polish and general economic history in the twentieth century. He has written or co-authored many books, including *Plan Stabilizacyjny 1926–1930: Geneza, założenia, wyniki* [The Stabilization Plan 1926–30: Origins, principles, results] (Warsaw, 1965) and, with Jerzy Tomaszewski, *Zarys historii gospodarczej Polski 1918–1939* [Outline of the economic history of Poland 1918–1939]. (Warsaw, 1962); *Druga Rzeczpospolita:*

Gospodarka-społeczeństwo-miejsce w świecie [The Second Republic: Its economy, society, place in the world] and *Sprawa Zyrardowska: Przyczynek do dziejów kapitałów obcych w Polsce międzywojennej* [The Zyrardow affair: A contribution to the history of foreign capital in interwar Poland] (Warsaw, 1983).

ANNA LANDAU-CZAJKA works in the section dealing with interwar Poland at the Historical Institute of the Polish Academy of Sciences. She wrote her doctorate on the ideology of the extreme right in interwar Poland. At present she is preparing her Habilitation on antisemitic propaganda in Poland between the two world wars.

MARK LEVENE lectures in the Department of Modern History at the University of Warwick. He is the author of *War, Jews, and the New Europe: The Diplomacy of Lucien Wolf 1914–1919* (Oxford, 1992) and is currently working on a history of modern genocide.

EZRA MENDELSOHN is Professor at the Institute for the study of Contemporary Jewry and in the Department of Russian Studies at the Hebrew University of Jerusalem. He has written *Class Struggle in the Pale* (Cambridge, 1970); *Zionism in Poland: The Formative Years 1905–26* (London and New Haven, 1981); *Jews in East Central Europe between the Two World Wars*, (Bloomington, Ind. 1983), and *On Modern Jewish Politics* (New York, 1983).

ANNAMARIA ORLA-BUKOWSKA is completing her doctorate in anthropology at the Jagiellonian University in Kraków and has been studying Catholic–Jewish relations in Poland since 1985.

ANDRZEJ PACZKOWSKI is Professor at the Institute of Political Studies of the Polish Academy of Sciences in Warsaw and head of the research unit dealing with modern political history. His main publications are *Prasa polska 1918–1939* [The Polish press 1918–1939] (Warsaw, 1980); *Prasa i społeczność polska we Francji 1920–1940* [The press and the Polish community in France, 1920–1940] (Warsaw, 1986); and *Stanisław Mikołajczyk* (Warsaw, 1991).

RAFAEL F. SCHARF was born in Kraków in 1914. He graduated from the Hebrew High School and obtained a degree in law from the Jagiellonian University, where he was active in the students' academic organizations of the Zionist movement. He moved to London in 1938, where he was a foreign correspondent of *Nowy dziennik*, a Polish-language Jewish daily in Kraków. In the last war he served in the Intelligence Corps of the British

Army and for some time after the war was a member of a War Crimes Investigation Unit, preparing war-crimes trials. He is a co-founder of *The Jewish Quarterly*, a political and literary magazine now in its fortieth year of publication. He is a founder member of the Institute of Polish Jewish Studies in Oxford and a member of its Governing Council, and a member of the Editorial Board of the yearbook *Polin*. Active in the Korczak movement, he is a former vice-president of the International Janusz Korczak Society. He is an occasional lecturer at the University of Giessen in Germany, and author of numerous articles on Polish Jewish matters in journals in England, Poland, and Germany.

ROBERT MOSES SHAPIRO was educated at Johns Hopkins, Columbia University, YIVO, and the Hebrew University in Jerusalem. He teaches courses on East European Jewry, the Holocaust, and modern Jewish History at Yeshiva University. His research and writing concentrate on the Jewish community of Łódź during the twentieth century. He is a member of the Editorial Board of *Polin*.

DARIUSZ STOLA works in the Institute of History of the Polish Academy of Sciences in Warsaw. His research has concentrated on Polish–Jewish relations during the Second World War and mass migrations in Central Europe. He is preparing a doctoral thesis on Ignacy Schwartzbart, the Zionist leader from Kraków who sat on the Polish National Council in Angers and London during the Second World War. He has published articles in *Więź*, *Mówią wieki*, *Polityka*, and the *International Migration Review*.

JERZY TOMASZEWSKI is Professor at the Institute of Political Science and Head of the Mordecai Anieliewicz Center for the Study of the History and Culture of Polish Jews at the University of Warsaw. He is a member of the Council and Board of the Jewish Historical Institute in Poland. Among his publications are *Z dziejów Polesia 1921–1939: Zarys stosunków społeczno-ekonomicznych* [On the history of Polesie 1921–1939: An outline of social and economic conditions] (Warsaw, 1963); *Rzeczpospolita wielu narodów* [A republic of many nations] (Warsaw, 1985); and *Ojczyzna nie tylko Polaków: Mniejszości narodowe w Polsce w latach 1918–1939* [A fatherland not only for Poles: National minorities in Poland in the years 1918–1939] (Warsaw, 1985).

ALFRED WIŚLICKI is the son of Wacław and Natalia Wiślicki. He was born in Warsaw in 1913 and spent the war in the USSR. He is a specialist in building technology and in the history of technological change. He has lectured at the Polytechnics of Warsaw and Kraków.

Notes on Translators

ANNA CLARKE, academic and scholar, Ottawa, Canada, translated Yehiel Yeshaia Trunk, 'Poyln: Land of Sages and *Tsadikim*'.

ERICA NADELHAFT, doctoral student, Brandeis University, translated Alfred Wiślicki, 'The Jewish Boycott Campaign against Nazi Germany and its Culmination in the Halberstadt Trial', and the obituaries of Stefan Kieniewicz and Adolf Rudnicki.

THERESA PROUT, freelance translator, Somerset, UK, translated Alina Cała, 'The Social Consciousness of Young Jews in Interwar Poland', and Bina Garncarska-Kadary, 'Some Aspects of the Life of the Jewish Proletariat in Poland during the Interwar Period'.

SLAVONIC TRANSLATION SERVICES, Somerville, Mass., translated Dariusz Stola, 'In The Shadow of the Facts', and Stefan Kieniewicz's review of Stephen Corrsin, *Warsaw before the First World War: Poles and Jews in the Third City of the Russian Empire, 1880–1914*.

ANNA ZARANKO, editor, Oxford, translated Szyja Bronsztejn, 'Polish–Jewish Relations as Reflected in Memoirs of the Interwar Period', Anna Landau-Czajka, 'The Image of the Jew in the Catholic Press during the Second Republic', and Karol Jonca, 'The Expulsion of Polish Jews from the Third Reich in 1938'.

Glossary

Agudas Yisroel (Ashkenazi pronunciation; **Agudat Israel** in modern Hebrew pronunciation)   The principal political party of religiously Orthodox Jews in Poland. Founded in 1916, under the influence of German Orthodoxy, it had the backing of the Gerer Rebbe, leader of the largest Hasidic group in the **Congress Kingdom**. It was very hostile to Jewish radicalism and fought the Jewish socialist parties, especially the **Bund**. It supported a daily Yiddish paper, *Der tog,* and a network of private religious schools.

Akiba   The youth movement of the religious Zionists.

Al Hamishmar (Hebrew: lit. 'on guard'   A radical faction within the Polish Zionist Movement.

aliyah (Hebrew: lit. 'ascent')   Emigration to Erets Israel (Palestine).

Anders's Army   The army established in the Soviet Union in 1941 by General Władysław Anders under the auspices of the Polish **government-in-exile** in London. This army left the Soviet Union for Persia and the Middle East in mid-1942.

apikores, pl. *apikorsim* (Hebrew)   An unbeliever, a term used in the Talmud and derived from a corruption of 'Epicurean'.

Armia Krajowa (Polish: lit. 'Home Army')   The largest resistance movement in Poland during the Second World War, controlled by the Polish **government-in-exile**.

Betar   The youth movement of the Revisionist Zionist Movement.

Bund   General Jewish Workers' Alliance (Bund). A Jewish Socialist Party, founded in 1897. It joined the Russian Social Democratic Labour Party, but seceded from it when its programme of national autonomy was not accepted. In independent Poland it adopted a leftist anti-Communist posture and from the 1930s co-operated increasingly closely with the Polish Socialist Party (PPS).

Chadecja   The Christian Democratic Party (Partia Chrześcijańsko-Demokratyczna). In interwar Poland its main area of support was Upper Silesia. Its adherents were referred to as 'Chadecy', sing. 'Chadek'.

Chjena   The derogatory name (the word puns with the Polish for 'hyena') for the right-wing coalition of the Christian Democrats, the Peasant Party, and the National Democrats which ruled in Poland between May and November 1923.

Ciołkosz Archives   The archive established by the leader of the Polish Socialist Party in exile in London, Adam Ciołkosz, after 1945. Today in the possession of his widow.

Commonwealth (Polish: *Rzeczpospolita*) The term *Rzeczpospolita* is derived from the Latin *res publica*. It is sometimes translated as 'commonwealth' and sometimes as 'republic', often in the form 'Nobleman's Republic' (*Rzeczpospolita szlachecka*). After the union of Lublin in 1569 it was used officially in the form *Rzeczpospolita Obojga Narodów* (Commonwealth of the Two Nations) to designate the new form of state which had arisen. In historical literature, this term is often rendered as 'The Polish–Lithuanian Commonwealth'.

Congress Kingdom (otherwise Kingdom of Poland) A constitutional kingdom created at the Congress of Vienna (1814–15), with the Tsar of Russia as hereditary monarch. After 1831 it declined to an administrative unit of the Russian Empire in all but name. After 1864 it lost the remaining vestiges of the autonomy it had been granted at Vienna and was now officially referred to as *Privislansky kray* (Vistula territory).

Council of Four Lands The principal body through which the Jews governed themselves autonomously in the Polish–Lithuanian Commonwealth (*see* **Commonwealth**). The actual number of lands represented in the council increased in the course of the life of this body (from the late sixteenth century to 1764). Made up of delegates from the local **Kahal**s and regions, the Council generally met twice a year and was responsible for negotiating with the Royal Treasury the level of Jewish taxation and for levying taxes on the Jewish communities. In addition, it passed laws and statutes on internal educational and economic matters and other general concerns of Jewish life. A separate but similar body existed in the Grand Duchy of Lithuania.

curia Elections to the third and fourth **Dumas** were indirect, and different sections of the electorate elected representatives to a curia, which was responsible for selecting the representative to the parliament.

Duma The parliament with restricted but still significant powers established in the Tsarist Empire after the revolution of 1905.

Endecja Popular name for the Polish National Democratic Party, a right-wing party which had its origins in the 1890s. Its principal ideologue was Roman Dmowski, who advocated a Polish version of the integral nationalism which became popular in Europe at the turn of the nineteenth century. The Endecja advanced the slogan 'Poland for the Poles' and called for the exclusion of the Jews from Polish political and economic life. Its adherents were called 'Endeks'. *See* **Obóz Wielkiej Polskiej**.

Folkism A Jewish political party which favoured a non-territorial form of Jewish autonomy in the diaspora, in terms of which the Jews would control their own educational and social institutions, which would be financed through special taxes levied on the Jewish community. Though not hostile to Hebrew, the party argued that Yiddish was the national language of Polish Jews. The Folkists' main ideologue was the Nestor of East European Jewish historians, Shimon Dubnow. Their main spokesman in Poland was Noah Prilucki.

galut (Hebrew: *goles* in Ashkenazi pronunciation) The diaspora. The word literally means 'exile' and embodies a sense of the pain of the Jewish condition, which in traditional Jewish thinking will only be brought to an end by the coming of the Messiah.

gaon, pl. *gaonim* (Hebrew: lit. 'genius')   A term used to describe a man who had acquired a phenomenal command of the Torah. One *gaon* was Rabbi Elijah, the 'Vilna Gaon'.

gehenna (Hebrew; also *gehinom*)   Hell.

gemara (Hebrew)   Another name for the Talmud.

General Gouvernement   An administrative-territorial unit created in Poland during the Nazi occupation from some of the territory seized by Germany after the Polish defeat. The GG was established on 26 October 1939 and first comprised four districts: Kraków, Lublin, Warsaw, and Radom. Its capital was the town of Kraków and its administration was headed by Hans Frank. After the Nazi invasion of the Soviet Union, an additional province, Galicia, made up of parts of the pre-war Polish provinces of Lwów, Stanisławów, and Tarnopol, was added to the GG. On the territory of the GG the Germans pursued a policy of mass murder of the Jewish population and reduced the Christian Poles to slaves with no rights, who were to provide a reservoir of labour for the Third Reich.

Gordonia   A Zionist youth movement. Named after A. D. Gordon, a Zionist-socialist ideologue, who stressed the redeeming power of physical labour.

government-in-exile   After the German defeat of Poland in 1939, a government was established made up of the less compromised elements of the **Sanacja** regime and representatives of the democratic opposition and headed by General Sikorski. This government made its headquarters in Angers and after the fall of France it moved to London. It attempted to represent the Polish cause, but was abandoned by the Western powers at the Yalta Conference in February 1945, when it was decided that the pro-Communist government established in Poland by Stalin should be recognized on condition that it broaden its ranks by the addition of democratic politicians from Poland and the West and hold free elections. In practice, neither condition was fulfilled in any meaningful way.

goy, pl. *goyim* (Hebrew: lit. 'person', 'people')   A term used by Jews for non-Jews, sometimes with pejorative overtones.

HaBaD   An acronym derived from the Hebrew words *hokhmah*, *binah*, *da'at* (wisdom, understanding, knowledge). It was applied to a sect of **Hasidism** which developed in the Grand Duchy of Lithuania and whose leading advocate was Rabbi Shneur Zalman of Liozna (or Liady). He preached a more rationalistic and ordered faith than the Hasidism of central and southern Poland. The Lubavich dynasty of rabbis, also called HaBaD Hasidim, is descended from Rabbi Shneur Zalman.

hakhsharah   Agricultural labour organized by pioneering Zionist youth groups as preparation for settlement on the land in collective settlements (kibbutzim) in Erets Israel (Palestine).

halakhah (Hebrew: lit. 'the way') A word used to describe the legal part of Jewish tradition, especially in the sense of 'way of acting', 'habit', 'usage', 'custom', and especially 'guidance' and the norms of religious observance.

Ḥaluts (Hebrew: lit. 'a pioneer') A member of a youth movement which aimed to prepare emigrants for settlement on the land in Erets Israel. *See* **hakhsharah**

Hashomer Hatsa'ir (Hebrew: lit. 'The Young Guard') A pioneering Zionist youth movement.

Hasidism A Jewish mystical movement which grew up in the eighteenth-century Polish–Lithuanian Commonwealth. The Hasidim (from *hasid* (Hebrew) 'a righteous man') sought direct communion with God by various means including singing, dancing, and communion with nature. Originally opposed by the bulk of the Orthodox establishment in Poland, who described themselves as *misnagdim* (lit. 'opposers', i.e. of Hasidism), the movement soon became particularly strong in central Poland (the **Congress Kingdom**), southern Poland (**Malopolska** or Galicia), and the Ukraine.

Haskalah (Hebrew: lit. 'wisdom' or 'understanding', but used in the sense of 'Enlightenment') A rationalistic movement which emerged in the Jewish world under the impact of the European Enlightenment in the second half of the eighteenth century. It first became important in Germany under the influence of Moses Mendelssohn and soon spread to the rest of European Jewry, first in the west and then, more slowly, in the east. The *maskilim* (followers of the Haskalah), while retaining the Jewish religion, sought to reduce Jewish separateness from the nations among whom they lived and to increase their knowledge of the secular world. The movement also fostered the study of biblical rather than talmudic Hebrew and emphasized the poetic, critical, and scientific elements in Hebrew literature, aiming to substitute the study of modern subjects for traditional ones. In eastern Europe it opposed **Hasidism** and what it regarded as the relics of Jewish fanaticism and superstition. It also sought Jewish emancipation and the adoption by Jews of agriculture and handicrafts.

heder, pl. *hadarim* (Hebrew: lit. 'room') Colloquial name for a traditional Jewish elementary school.

Ḥemdat Shelomo Solomon Zalman Lipschits (1765–1839), first chief rabbi of Warsaw, known as 'Ḥemdat Shelomo' (Hebrew: 'the delight of Solomon') after his works of that name. He was chief rabbi of Warsaw from 1821 until his death and also founded a *yeshivah* in that city. A strong critic of the **Haskalah**, he led the opposition to the Assimilationists and to the rabbinical seminary they established in Warsaw, which was headed by Antoni Eisenbaum.

Hitachdut (Hebrew: lit. 'brotherhood') A non-Marxist labour Zionist party.

January Insurrection The ill-fated insurrection against the Tsarist monarchy which began in January 1863. After its defeat, the Russian government embarked on a determined effort to Russify not only the **Kresy** but also the **Congress Kingdom**.

Jewish Agency The international, non-government body, with its headquarters in Jerusalem, which was set up in accordance with the League of Nations Mandate for Palestine, to assist and encourage Jews to help in the development and settlement of Erets Israel. After 1948 it relinquished many of its functions to the government of Israel, but continued to be responsible for immigration, land settlement, youth work, and other activities financed by voluntary Jewish contributions from the diaspora.

kahal, kehillah (Yiddish: *kehile*) (Hebrew: lit. 'congregation') The lowest level of the Jewish autonomous institutions in the Polish–Lithuanian Commonwealth. Above the local *kehillot* were regional bodies, and above these a central body, the Va'ad Arba Aratsot (**Council of Four Lands**) for the Crown and the Va'ad lita (Council of Lithuania). The Va'ad Arba Aratsot was abolished by the Polish authorities in 1764, but local autonomous institutions continued to operate legally until 1844 and in practice for many years after this date in those parts of the Polish–Lithuanian Commonwealth directly annexed by the Tsarist empire, and longer in the **Congress Kingdom** and the remaining parts of Poland.

Karaites Followers of a heretical sect of Judaism, who recognized the validity of the written (*kara* in Hebrew means 'read') but not the oral law (the Talmud). In Poland many of the Karaites were descended from Tartars who had converted to this form of Judaism.

kiddush ha shem (Hebrew: lit. 'sanctification of God's Name') Martyrdom, the sacrifice of one's life rather than being forced into idolatry, immorality, or unjustified homicide.

Kresy The eastern provinces of Poland between the two world wars. Today parts of Lithuania, Belarus, and Ukraine.

kwitlech (Yiddish: 'notes') Notes left at the tombs of well-known *tsadikim*, asking them to intercede for the petitioner or the person on whose behalf aid was sought.

Litvak A Jew from the territories of the Grand Duchy of Lithuania (Litwa). In terms of Jewish stereotypes, the Litvak was a rationalist, an opponent of **Hasidism**, often a social radical, and also a miser. To themselves, the Litvaks were the incarnation of all the finest Jewish values.

luftmensh (Yiddish: lit. 'man of the air', 'man with his head in the clouds') A Jew with no obvious means of livelihood, but convinced that he will secure one by means of various far-fetched schemes. The archetypal *luftmensh* was Sholem Aleykhem's Menachem Mendel.

Malopolska (Polish: lit. 'lesser Poland') Southern Poland, the area around Kraków. Also referred to under the Habsburgs as Galicia.

maskilim   *See* **Haskalah**.

mitnaged (*misnagid*), pl. *mitnagdim* (Hebrew: lit. 'opposer')   The rabbinic opponents of **Hasidism**.

Mizrachi   The party of religious Zionists.

Obóz Wielkiej Polskiej (Polish: 'the Camp for a Greater Poland')   Extreme right-wing and pro-Fascist organization founded in December 1926 by Roman Dmowski because of his dissatisfaction at the weak reaction of the National Democratic Party (*see* **Endecja**) to the *coup* of May 1926 which brought Józef Piłsudski back to power.

pan   Polish: 'lord', 'master', or 'noble'. Also used today as the polite form of the second person singular.

pilpul (Hebrew)   Academic discussion of the Torah. Often regarded as a form of hair-splitting.

Po'alei Tsion (Hebrew: lit. 'Workers of Zion')   A Labour Zionist organization. It split into a right and left wing. The right wing was much more interested in settlement in Erets Israel (Palestine), the left wing in establishing links with left-wing non-Zionist parties.

porets (Yiddish)   nobleman.

Progressive Party   A moderate anti-chauvinist political grouping in the **Congress Kingdom** in the years before the First World War.

poyerim (Yiddish)   peasants.

Rebbe of Belz   Belz is a small town in East Galicia. The Rebbe of Belz was the *tsadik* with the largest Hasidic following in Galicia (Austrian Poland).

Revisionist Zionists   Followers of Vladimir Jabotinsky, who split off from the main international Zionist grouping in the 1930s and wished to pursue a more aggressive strategy to establish a Jewish state in Palestine.

Sanacja (from Latin *sanatio*, 'healing, restoration')   The popular name taken by the regime established by Józef Piłsudski after the coup of May 1926. It referred to Piłsudki's aim of restoring health to the political, social, and moral life of Poland.

Sejm   The central parliamentary institution of the **Commonwealth**, composed of a **Senate** and a Chamber of Deputies; after 1501 both of these had a voice in the introduction of new legislation. It met regularly for six weeks every two years, but could be called for sessions of two weeks in an emergency. When it was not in session, an appointed commission of sixteen senators, in rotation four at a time, resided with the king both to advise and to keep watch over his activities. Until the middle of the seventeenth century the Sejm functioned reasonably well; after that, the use of the *liberum veto* began to paralyse its effectiveness.

Sejm of the Four Lands   *See* **Council of Four Lands**.

Senate   The upper house of the **Sejm**. Its origin was the medieval Royal Council. It was composed of all the great officials of the government, the **voivodes**, hetmans, marshals, and treasurers, headed by the archbishop of Gniezno, who also served as *interrex* on the death of the king. The members of the Senate were overwhelmingly drawn from the class of magnates which came to dominate Polish society in the seventeenth and eighteenth centuries.

Stojalowczyk A follower of the radical peasant leader in Galicia, Fr. Stojalowski.

sukka Temporary shelter for the Sukkot (Ashkenazi 'Sukkes') festival.

Tarbut (Hebrew: lit. 'culture') The name of the Zionist Hebrew-language private-school system in Poland (and elsewhere in eastern Europe).

tashlikh (Hebrew: lit. 'cast') Religious ceremony in which Jews gather by a river, shore, or reservoir on the first day of the New Year (Rosh Hashanah) and say prayers for forgiveness that implore God to 'cast sin into the deep sea'.

tefillin (Hebrew) Phylacteries—a pair of small black leather boxes containing biblical verses on parchment, tied by leather straps around the left arm and the head and traditionally worn by men at weekday morning prayers.

tekhinot (Hebrew: *tekhines* in Ashkenazi pronunciation) Prayers in Yiddish published specially for women who could not read Hebrew.

tsadik (Hebrew: lit. 'the just one' or 'a pious man') A leader of a Hasidic sect (or community). Hasidim often credited their *tsadikim* or *rebbes* with miraculous powers and saw them as mediators between God and man.

Tse'irei Agudas Yisroel The youth movement of **Agudas Yisroel**.

tsitsit (*tsitsis* in Ashkenazi pronunciation) (Hebrew: lit. 'fringes') Jewish men and boys traditionally wear a four-cornered garment (the *tallit katan*) under their shirt—with tassels consisting of eight wool strings on each corner. These tassels are the *tsitsit*. A larger four-cornered shawl (the *tallit*) also adorned with *tsitsit* is worn at morning prayer.

Va'ad Arba Aratsot Hebrew: **Council of Four Lands**.

voivode (Polish: *wojewoda*) Initially this official acted in place of the ruler, especially in judicial and military matters. From the thirteenth century the office gradually evolved into a provincial dignity; between the sixteenth and eighteenth centuries the voivode conducted the local dietine, led the *pospolite ruszenie*, the *levée-en-masse* of the *szlachta* in times of danger to the **Commonwealth**, and occasionally governed cities and collected certain dues. By virtue of his office, he sat in the **Senate**.

voivodship (Polish: *województwo*) A province, governed by a **voivode**.

Wielkopolska (Polish: lit. 'Greater Poland') Western Poland, the area around Poznań.

Wojewoda *See* **voivode**.

World Jewish Congress An international Jewish organization established by Nahum Goldmann.

Index

A

acculturation 12, 44, 51, 389
 and Jewish press 189, 193
Adamski, Franciszek xix, 129–45
agriculture, Jews in 95–6, 102–3, 108, 177, 239
Agudas Yisroel xvi, 6 n. 3
 and *kehillah* elections 209, 210, 214–23, 225
 and Polish state 21
 studies of 11
Ajnenkiel, Andrzej 261
Akiba (Zionist movement) 294
Al-hamishmar faction 223
Aleykhem, Sholem 251–2, 290, 291, 300
Alliance Israélite Universelle 26–7, 139
Almog, Shmuel 8
Alter, Victor 213
American Jewish Committee (AJC) 28
American Jewish Congress 27
Anders, Gen. Władysław 335–8, 358, 372–7
Andrzejewski, Jerzy 88, 394
antichrist, and Talmudic religion 162
anti-Judaism, and Christian Church xix
antisemitism xv–xvi, xvii, 44, 77–9, 335–6, 372
 anti-Jewish boycott 31, 77, 196, 198, 199, 204, 210–11, 237, 391
 anti-Jewish jokes 81–3
 British 33
 conspiracy, international Jewish, accusations of 31
 deicide, accusations of xix, 85, 148, 152, 155–7, 204
 enemies, Jews seen as 80, 155–64, 200, 331, 335
 global domination, accusations of 139–40, 157, 159, 162–3, 173–5
 increase 70, 87–8, 184, 195, 210, 284, 327–9
 and Jewish artisans 232
 in Jewish historiography 4–11
 and Jewish press 191
 and nationalism 195–6
 Nazi xx, 347–8
 in Polish press 129–30, 133–5, 140–1, 149, 159–60, 165, 172, 198, 390
 and political parties xix, 22, 80, 194–205
 power, Jewish, accusations of 30–2
 in pre-independence Poland 3, 388–92
 ritual murder, accusations of 139–40, 157, 159, 162–3, 173–5
 and Roman Catholic Church xix–xx, 47–8, 78, 130, 149
 rural 78
 stereotypes of Jews 146–75
 and young Jews 47–50, 52–3, 80–1
 see also distinctiveness of Jewish community; expulsion of Jews; money: power of; pogroms; racism
apprenticeships 101, 228, 231, 233, 235–6, 246
Arabs, Palestinian 143–4
Arendt, Hannah 417
art:
 folk 410–13
 Jewish motifs in 404–7
 Jewish themes in Italy 407–10
 and Jung Idysz group 413–15
artisans, Jewish:
 earnings 235–6
 number 227–34, 237
 pauperization 229, 231–2, 234–5, 237, 244–5
 in *shtetl* communities 103, 213, 412
 see also proletariat, Jewish
Aryanism, and race 164–5, 167, 262
Askenazy, Szymon, memoirs 74
assimilation:
 and conversion 153–4, 201–2, 204
 decrease in 189, 325–9
 failure of in Kingdom of Poland 325–9
 increase in 90, 194–5
 of Poles 137
 and Polish intelligentsia 79–80, 387, 389
 rejection 199
 and Lucien Wolf 19–20, 22, 40
 and young Jews 42, 43, 44, 51–3, 63
assimilationism, in historiography 6, 7, 12
attitudes to Jews 76–86, 242
 in Catholic press 129–45, 146–75
 liberal middle class 194
 rural 78

attitudes to Jews (*cont.*):
  under German occupation 337–8
Auschwitz concentration camp 342, 400
Austria:
  peace treaty with 116
  and Polish Jews 19, 71, 255–8, 262, 275–6
autobiographies of young Jews xix, 42–65
  attitudes to Polishness 50–3, 74
  and crisis generation 63–7
  as history 64–5
  languages 43–4
  and self-awareness 44–50
  sources 42–3
  and value systems 54–5, 57–63, 64, 247
  see also memoirs
autonomy, Jewish 16–19, 20, 23, 39, 181, 184
  and Britain xix, 23–6, 29–36
  and United States 26–30, 31–2, 36
  see also *kehillah* system
Avremele, Reb 301–2, 304–6

B

Bader, Blima 50
Bąkiewicz, Colonel 338, 376–7
Balfour, Arthur 26, 31
Balfour Declaration 25, 144, 184
Banaczyk, Władysław 379
baptism of Jews 110, 123, 149–55, 157
Bartoszewski, Władysław T. 411
Beck, Józef 120, 127, 269, 284
Bezpartyjny Blok Współpracy z Rządem 6 n. 3
Beller, Ilex, memoirs 96, 105, 111
Belmont, L. 140
Benski, Stanisław 395
Berenbaum, Abraham 271–2
Berlewi, Henryk 413–14
Best, Werner 258, 260, 264
Betar (Zionist youth movement) 57, 294
Białystok, Jews in 252–3
Blatman, Daniel 365
Blejwas, Stanislaus A. 325–9
Bobrowski, Czesław, memoirs 77, 79–81, 87
Böhler, Friedrich 286, 289
Bolshevism, and Jews 31–2, 81, 138–9, 168–70
Bornstein, I. 228, 233
Borochov, Ber 251
Borowski, Stanisław, memoirs 77
Borowski, Tadeusz 393
Borski, Jan Maurycy 202
Bosak, Lipman, autobiography 45, 58–9
Boshyk, Yury 401–3
boycott:
  of German goods 282–9
  of Jews 31, 77, 196, 198, 199, 204, 210–11, 237, 391
Bracken, Brendan 360, 368
Brandys, Kazimierz 428–9
Bratny, Roman 395
Brauner, Wincenty 414
Brest–Litovsk treaty 18
Britain:
  and evacuation of Jews from Soviet Union 373
  and Jewish minority rights xix, 23–6, 29–36, 39–40, 333, 356–7
Bronsztejn, Szyja xix, 66–88, 232
Buffom, David H. 266
Bundism xvii, xxi, 294, 300, 312, 322
  and Communism 138–9
  in historiography 11–12
  and Jewish separation 72, 76
  and Jews under Nazism 340, 342, 360–3, 366 n. 21, 367–8, 370
  and *kehillah* system 181, 207, 209, 210–21, 225–6
  and municipal government 223–5
  and Polish government 20, 39–40
  trade unions 182, 248–9
  and young Jews 64
  see also Socialism
Burda, Andrzej 78
Burek, Tomasz 429
Burleigh, Michael 398–401

C

Cała, Alina xv, xix, 42–65, 325–9
Camp of National Unification (OZON) 203–4, 236–7, 256
Catholic People's Movement 203
Cecil, Lord Robert 37
censorship:
  and press controls 190, 191, 284
  and religious press 130, 131
Chadecja, *see* Christian Democratic Party
Chamberlain, Houston Stewart 134
Charszewski, I. 159, 162, 165
chauvinism, Jewish 10, 52–3
children:
  accusations of ritual murder of by Jews 148, 161
  friendships between Poles and Jews 47–9, 99–101, 112, 169–70
  Gentile 102
Chjena, *see* Christian Union of National Unity

Chmielnicki (Khmelnytsky) uprising 9
Chomyszyn, Grzegorz 88
Christ, as Jew 85, 166–7
Christian Democratic Party (Chadecja) 124
    and antisemitism 197–8, 200–1, 203, 207
Christian Social Union, and antisemitism 203
Christian Union of National Unity (Chjena),
    and antisemitism 197
Christianity, and anti-Judaism xix, 133–6,
    147–9, 197
Christianization 199
Christians, Palestinian 143–4
Chrzanowski, Tadeusz 407–13
Chudek, J. M. 152
Chwila 189, 218
Ciechanowski, Jan 351
citizenship:
    and 1918 peace treaties 116–18
    bill of 1920 116–17
    deprivation of 120, 127, 199–200, 256–62,
        275–6, 331, 334
    disputes over 118–20
    minority 14, 17–18, 21–2, 24, 115–16, 201
    see also loyalty; rights: civil
civic society, participation in 181–2
Clarke, Anna 301
Clemenceau, Georges 27, 35, 37
clubs, Jewish 73
co-operatives, Jewish 181
Cohen, Evelyn M. 409
Cohen, Richard L. 404–7
Comité des Délégations Juives (CDJ) 27, 34,
    35, 39
Commonwealth, Polish–Lithuanian 362–4,
    382–4, 411
Communism:
    in historiography 12
    and Jewish separation 72
    and *kehillah* elections 213, 219, 221
    and press control 190, 192
    and religious press 137–40, 163, 168–9, 172
    and trade unions 248–9
    and young Jews 42, 50, 54, 55, 64, 294
Communist Party of Poland (KPP) 64, 79
Communist Workers Party of Poland
    (KPRP) 72, 181
comparison, cross-national, of policies towards
    Jews in eastern Europe 13
concentration camps:
    and expulsion of Jews from Germany 255,
        265, 270
    Jews sent to 340–2, 363–4, 367, 400

consciousness, national:
    of Jews 202
    of young Jews 44–50, 51–3, 64
Conservative Movement 205
conversion of Jews 110, 123, 149–55, 156–7
Corrsin, Stephen D. 388–92
cottage workers:
    and artisans, 227, 230
    as potential supporters of Bund 213
    type of work 240
coup, May 1926 83, 123, 125, 127, 190, 198,
    208
craftsmen, *see* artisans
Crowe, Sir Eyre 24, 33
culture, German 70–1, 75
culture, Jewish:
    in historiography xvii, 6–7, 10, 12
    and proletariat 250–1, 297
    and race 166–8
    and separation 71–6, 329
culture, Polish xvii, 70–1, 75
    and Jewish settlement 136–7
    and Jews 44, 50–3, 63, 153, 168, 170,
        195–6, 327
culture, Russian 70, 75, 195
Czapliński, Władysław, memoirs 79, 80, 85
Czarkowski, Józef 75
Czerniaków, Adam 364, 366 n. 20

D

Dąbrowska, Maria 88
Dąbrowski, Eugeniusz 133
Daszyński, Ignacy Ewaryst 80, 384–7
Davies, Norman xvi–xvii, 9–10, 13, 347
Dawidowicz, Lucy 4, 7, 10, 299, 301
Delitsch, F. 134 n. 7
demography:
    and interwar poverty xvi, xvii
    Jewish 66, 90, 135–6, 177–8, 190, 201
    see also towns
Depression, Great, effects:
    on Jewish artisans 230–1, 234–6
    on Jewish press 183, 185
    on Polish Jews xx
    on Polish towns 92
dialect, use by young Jews 43
Dickstein, Professor 20
Diewerge, W. 272
distinctiveness of Jewish community in
    Poland 46, 74, 331
    and Jews' political status 201
    Russian Jewish immigrants 389

distinctiveness of Jewish community
 in Poland (*cont.*):
  used to justify antisemitism 194–6, 198, 205
  whether racial or cultural xix, 149,
   153–4, 164–75
Dmowski, Roman 14, 22–3, 31, 33, 34–5, 196,
  328, 390–1
Dobraczyński, J. 158, 160
  memoirs 78
Dobroszycki, Lucjan 206–7, 430
Dobrowolski, J. 166
Dobrowolski, Stanisław Ryszard 395
Drobner, Bolesław, memoirs 67 n. 4, 78–81,
  84
Drymmer, Wiktor Tomir 120, 126, 258
Dudziński, Janusz 125

E
economy, Jewish role in 9, 13, 77, 94, 125,
  141–3, 170
  pedlars 94, 98–9
  and Polish–Jewish conflict 195, 196
  see also agriculture, Jews in; apprenticeships;
   artisans, Jewish; boycott: of Jews;
   Depression; First World War; Łódź;
   poverty; professions; proletariat, Jewish;
   trade; trade unions, Jewish
Eden, Sir Anthony 334
education:
  levels of 178
  limitations on access for Jews 122, 198, 199,
   204
  and proletariat 243–6
  religious 93
  struggle for 54, 57, 247, 295, 297
  and trade unions 251
Ehrlich, Henryk 212
Eichmann, Adolf 256, 399
Eiger, Marek 77
Eisenbach, Artur 423–6
emancipation, Jewish 163, 389, 424, 425
emigration:
  forced, *see* expulsion
  increased 70, 201–2, 204–5, 212, 256
  in Jewish press 182
  to Palestine 60–1, 143–5, 184, 219
Endecja (National Democrats) 10
  and antisemitism 5, 8, 197–200, 202–3, 206,
   391–2
  and attitudes to Jews 79, 80, 87, 236, 261,
   328, 333–4
  and press 192

Engel, David 11, 330–44, 345–81, 396–8
Ertel, Rachel 186
Ettinger, Shmuel 6–7, 8, 10
Expres ilustrowany 188
expulsion of Jews from Germany in
  1938 255–81
expulsion of Jews from Poland:
  and the Catholic Church 160
  in 1918 22
  in late 1930s 126–7, 142–3
  in 1934: ONR proposals 200; ZMN
   proposals 204–5

F
Falanga, and antisemitism 200
'Feraynigte' Party 72
festivals, religious, in *shtetl* communities 82,
  107–8
Ficowski, Jerzy 298
Fiderkiewicz, A. 67 n. 6
Fiderkiewicz, Maria 412
Filipowicz, Tytus 205, 379
Fink, Hilda, autobiography 48, 51
First World War:
  effects on artisans 229
  effects on Jewish–Polish relations xix, 14–41
  Jews and Germany 196
Folkism xvii, 20, 39, 312
  and *kehillah* elections 221
  and young Jews 64
France, and Jewish autonomy 26–7, 35
Freemasonry:
  as enemy of Poland 200
  linked with Jewish international conspiracy
   theory 149, 162–3, 168, 172, 173
  and Progressive Party 390
friendship between Poles and Jews 47–9, 76–7,
  87
  in *shtetl* communities 96–7, 99–101, 112
Frydman, Sara, autobiography 54, 60–1
Fryś-Pietraszkowa, Ewa 412
Fuchs, Munio, autobiography 62
Fuks, Marian 176, 188, 190
funerals, in *shtetl* communities 106

G
Galicia:
  and antisemitism 8
  and Jewish press 188–9
  Jewish Social Democratic Party in 194 n. 2
  Jews in 71, 256–7, 275, 384–7
  peasant movement in 195

and *shtetl* communities 90, 91, 95, 103
  see also Kraków
Garncarska-Kadary, Bina xx, 238–54
Gaweł, Bolesław 83
Gawron, Walenty, memoirs 78
Geiger, Abraham 133 n. 6
Gelfer, Jakób, autobiography 49
Gentiles, see *goyim*
German, knowledge of 111, 178
Germany:
  expulsion of Polish Jews 64, 255–81
  peace treaty with 116
  and Polish Jews 25, 172, 196
  relations with Poland 19, 282–9
  see also Nazism
ghettos:
  in Catholic press 151, 172
  deportation from 339–41, 358, 362–8, 370–1
  and industrial workers 241, 250
  institution of 133, 199
  and isolationism 195
  Italian 408
  and Nazism 262
Gieguziński, Lejzar, autobiography 58
Giertych, Jędrzej 200
Gierymski, Aleksander 407
Glaser, Regina, autobiography 47–8, 51
Glikson, Paul 177
Globke, Hans 258
Głos Polski 188
Główny Urząd Statystyczny (GUS) 183, 189
Gobineau, Joseph Arthur 134
Golczewski, Frank 10
Goldberg-Mulkiewski, Olga 411–12
Gomulicki, Witold 290, 296
Gordonia (Zionist youth movement) 43–4, 294
Göring, Hermann 262, 269
government:
  in exile 11, 330–44, 345–81
  municipal 103, 181–2, 222–5, 391; see also *kehillah* system
goyim:
  Jewish attitudes to 44–9, 53, 100, 159–60
  neglect of in recent writing 90–1
Grabski, Władysław 122–3
Grade, Chaim 415
Graetz, Heinrich 133 n. 6
Granat, W. 166–8
Great Poland Camp (Obóz Wielkiej Polskiej) 198, 199, 204
Grimm, Friedrich 273–4
Gross, Jan T. 396–8

Grosser, Bronisław 251–2, 253
Grostern, Stefan 188
Grot-Rowecki, Stefan 85
Grünbaum, Yitzhak 4, 118, 119, 144, 219
Grydzewski, Mieczysław 77
Grynberg, Henryk 393, 394–5
Grynszpan family 266, 270–5, 276–8
Grynszpan, Herschel 262, 268, 270–5
Grzywacz, Józef, autobiography 43, 54
Gutman, Yisrael 4, 8, 374
Guttenplan, Aleksander, autobiography 54

H
Haberko, Piotr, memoirs 76 n. 44, 82
Hadda, Janet 415–17
Haecker, Emil 84
hakhsharah 7
Halberstadt trial 285–8
Halecki, Oscar 9
Haller, General 23
Halpern, Leopold 224–5
Haluts (Pioneer movement) 7, 8
Handelsman, Marceli 423, 424
Hartglas, Apolinary 283
Hartglas, Maksymilian 122, 123 n. 24, 124
Hashomer Hatsa'ir (Zionist scout organization) 58–9, 294
Hasidim:
  Alexandrov 310–17
  see also Orthodoxy
Haskalah 299, 326
Hatsefirah 326
Haynt 218, 224
Headlam-Morley, Sir James 16, 25–6, 29–30, 33–4, 37, 38 n. 90, 39
Hebrew:
  ban on 115, 121, 123
  and Jewish press 179, 183–6, 189, 219, 251, 297
  as language of worship 327
  in *shtetl* communities 111
  use by young Jews 43–4
ḥederim, in *shtetl* communities 93, 96
Heller, Celia xvi, xvii, 331
Hertz, Aleksander 393
Hertz, Y. Sh. 4, 8
Herzl, Theodor 139, 144
Heschel, Abraham Joshua 410–11
Hetnal, Adam A. 384–7
Hetnal, J. 162, 173
Heydrich, Reinhard 255, 263–4, 269–70
Himmler, Heinrich 264, 269

Hirszfeld, Ludwik, memoirs 71, 74, 75, 83
historiography:
   neglect of interwar years 89
   neglect of *shtetl* communities 90–1
   'optimistic' school xvi–xviii, 9–12
   'pessimistic' school xv, xvi, xvii, xviii, 9–12
   survey xviii, 3–13
   see also Holocaust
history, family 290–8
Hitachdut, labour Zionist party 223, 251
Hitler, Adolf, and Nazi policies 269, 287, 398–401
Hlond, August 170
holidays 72–3
   national 108
   religious 74, 82, 107–8, 109, 161
Holocaust xvii, 4, 339, 342–4, 353, 357–70, 393, 394, 428
   in historiography 7
   see also pogroms
Holzer, Jerzy xix, 194–205
Hoppe, Jan 256
Horowitz, Markus, autobiography 61
Horwitz, Zygmunt, autobiography 52
House, Colonel 28
Howard, Sir Esmé 24, 25, 32
Hübner, Zygmunt 118
Hudson, Manley 28
Hunczak, Professor 403
Hundert, Gershon David 382–4
Hunter Miller, David 28, 29–30, 36

I
identity, Jewish:
   and acculturation 189, 329
   and minority rights 39
   and young Jews 44, 50–3
Ilustrowany Kurier Codzienny 182 n. 15
industry, Jewish proletariat in 178, 239–42
inflation, effects 229–30
intelligentsia, Jewish:
   and emigration 70
   numbers 178
   and relations with Poles 73, 86
   and Socialism 72
   and unemployment 246
intelligentsia, Polish:
   and assimilation 137
   and attitudes to Jews 79, 86–7
International Court of Justice, and minority rights 15, 34, 37

isolationism, *see* distinctiveness of Jewish community
Italy, Jews in 407–10
Iwaszkiewicz, Jaroslaw 77, 85
Izraelita 326–7

J
Jablonowski, Roman 72 n. 26
Jabotinsky, Vladimir (Zev) 5, 10, 219 n. 52
Jackan, Samuel 188
Jackowski, Aleksander 410
Jagiełło, Eugeniusz 390, 391
Jakubowska, Hanna, autobiography 64
Jarzmonowski, Jerzy, memoirs 73
Jastrzębiec, K. 140
Jeleński, Jan 328
Jerzmanowski, Jerzy 83–5
Jesus, as Jew 166–7
Jewish Historical Institute 424, 425
Jewish Social Democratic Party, Galicia 194 n. 2
Jews:
   as chosen people 157–9, 163, 167, 173
   creativity of 6, 7
   images of in Catholic press 146–75
   and modernization xviii–xix, 63, 185
   'progressive' 194
   see also acculturation; Bundism; clubs; Communism; consciousness, national; demography; economy, Jewish role; education; emancipation; emigration; friendship; Galicia; ghettos; Haskalah; Holocaust; identity, Jewish; intelligentsia, Jewish; language; literature; loyalty, of Jews; marriages, mixed; memoirs; military service; nationalism; politics; Orthodoxy; parties, political; peasants; press, Jewish; Sabbath observance; schools; self-awareness; self-government; sexuality; *shtetl* communities; slaughter, ritual; Socialism; students; synagogues; towns; weddings; Zionism *and under individual towns*
Joint Foreign Committee of British Jews (JFC) 16–17, 35
Jonca, Karol xx, 255–81
Jóźwiak, Stanisław 379
'Judaeo-Communism' 137–40
Judaism, and Christianity xix, 133–6, 147–9, 197
Jung Idysz group 413–15
Jutro pracy 204

K

Kaczyński 342
Kakowski, Cardinal 130–1
Kalendarz apostolstwa modlitwy 147, 173–4
Kalendarz królowej apostołów 147, 156, 159–60, 162–3
Kalendarz królowej korony polskiej 147, 150
Kaliciński, Zdzisław, memoirs 69 n. 12, 76
Kaliciński, Zygmunt, memoirs 81–2
Kalisz:
   and *kehillah* elections 215
   and Jewish press 177, 186
'Kallos', autobiography 47
Kamińska, Maria, memoirs 69 n. 11, 70, 72 n. 27, 81
Kanowicz, Grigori 113–14
Karski, Jan 360, 368, 370, 430
Kartuska, Bereza 76 n. 45
Katzenelson, Itzhak 294–5
kehillah system 39, 181–2, 296, 313
   elections of 1936: background xx, 207–14; results 214–25
Kempner, Cecylia 386–7
Kersten, Krystyna 376 n. 28, 395
Keybote, Heinrich 272
Kieniewicz, Stefan 388–92, 421–2
Kingdom of Poland 70, 122
   and Jews in Warsaw 388–92
   see also assimilation
Kittenplan, Wilhelm, autobiography 64
Klausner, Joseph 133 n. 6
Kleinbaum, Moshe 296
Klemperer, Victor 399
Klopotowski, J. 130
Knobel Fluek, Toby, memoirs 96, 98–9, 101
Komorowski, General 340
Kopyto, Sara, autobiography 53–4, 60, 62–3
Korboński, Stefan 339–40, 362, 364–6, 371
Korczak, Janusz 78, 173, 297
Korfanty, Wojciech 261
Korn-Żuławski, Halina 68 n. 8
Korzec, Paweł xvi, 7, 331
Kossak, Zofia 154, 165–6
Kot, Stanisław 336, 338, 344, 350, 351, 373 n. 24, 374, 376
Kotarbiński, Tadeusz 88
Koło Patriotów Polsko-Żydowskich (Circle of Polish Jewish Patriots) 20
Kotula, Franciszek, memoirs 69 n. 12, 73, 77, 87
Kowalczyk, Józef 72 n. 27
Kowalski, A. F. 161, 166

Koźniewski, Kazimierz, memoirs 87 n. 101
Kraczkiewicz, Karol 350–1
Krajewska, Monika 412
Krajewski, Stanisław 392–3, 412
Kraków:
   Jewish population 66, 90
   kehillah system 222
   in memoirs 47, 290–1, 294
   press in: Catholic 327; Jewish 185, 187, 189
Krall, Hannah 395
Krasnowski, Z. 175
Krawchenko, Bohdan 402
Kreitman, Esther 295
Królowa apostołów 147, 152
Kruczkowski, Leon 88
Krupa, Maciej 412
Krzywicki, Ludwik, memoirs 70–1, 83, 87–8, 391–2
Kucharzewski, Jan 22, 390–1
Kuczka, P. 154, 163
Kudliński, Tadeusz, memoirs 86
Kulczyński, Stanisław 88
Kultur-Liga (Cultural Alliance) 251
Kultura 147, 149, 154, 160, 163, 165–7
Kuśniewicz, Andrzej 393
Kutner, Yehiel 299, 301–2, 305–6
Kwiatkowski, Edward, memoirs 83
Kwiatkowski, Eugeniusz 237
Kwiatkowski, Michał 379

L

Landau, Moshe xvi
Landau, Zbigniew xx, 227–37
Landau-Czajka, Anna xix, 146–75
Lange, Antoni 124
language:
   and ethnicity 111
   see also Hebrew; Polish; rights: linguistic; Yiddish
Laqueuer, Walter 339, 340, 363 n. 13
Lauche, Rudolf 286, 288–9
League of Nations, and minorities 15, 29, 33–4, 37–40
Leeper brothers 33
Left National Workers' Party 203
legislation:
   consolidation of in post-1918 Poland 115
   discriminating against Jews and other minority groups 8, 115, 120–7, 136, 199
   exceptional, limiting assimilation 201, 204, 205
Leshchinsky, Yakov 4

Leśmian, Bolesław 84, 297
Lestchinsky, Jacob xvi
Levene, Mark xix, 14–41
Levine, Hillel 383
Levine, Madeline 394
Levy, Oscar 139
libraries, popular 251–3
Lieber, Markus, autobiography 48, 54, 59–60
Lieberman, Herman 124, 352
Life is with People 89, 92, 96, 101, 106, 112–13
Lipiński, Edward 88
Lipski, Józef 263, 266
literature:
  Jewish themes in 392–5
  suicide in Yiddish literature 15–17
'Litvaks' (Lithuanian Jews) 70, 81, 326, 388–9
Lloyd George, David 26, 27, 30, 37, 144
Łódź:
  artisans 234
  Jewish industrial workers 240–1, 250
  Jewish population 66, 90, 136, 177
  Jewish provincial press 185, 187, 188, 192, 211
  kehillah elections 1936 219–22
  municipal government 182, 222–4
loyalty, of Jews xix, 168, 170–2, 175, 202, 387
Lublin:
  Jews in 66, 79, 136, 366
  and *kehillah* elections 215, 224
Lubomirski, Stefan 266
Lukas, Richard 9, 10 n. 19, 339, 365 n. 19
Łukasiewicz, Stanisław 394
Lwów:
  Jewish deaths 361, 367
  Jewish population 66, 90, 177, 245–6
  Jewish provincial press 185, 189
  kehillah elections 222
  pogroms 9, 80, 196

M

Macior, T. 140
Mack, Judge Julian 27–9
Maczyński, General Czesław 80
Madagascar, Jewish colonies proposed 145
Mahler, Raphael xvi, 4, 423
Maimonides, Moses 133, 417
Makabi sports association 73
Maleta, Alicja 412
Malinowski, Jerzy 413–15
Mały dziennik 147, 149, 164, 166, 171–2, 174
Manger, Itzik 71
Mann, Vivian B. 407–10

Manteuffel, Tadeusz 421, 422
Marcus, Joseph xvi, 11, 181
Mark, Bernard 424
marriages, mixed 49–50, 83–4, 110
Marrus, Michael 345
Marschak, Leopold 69 n. 13
Marshall, Louis 27–9, 30–1, 35–6, 37 n. 83, 38
Mayer, Arno 36
mayor, Jew as 103
Mazurowa, Maria Ludwika 84
Mead, Margaret 89, 90
Mein Kampf, compared with Talmud 160
Meltzer, Emanuel xvi, 10–11, 331
memoirs:
  family history 290–8, 301–22
  and Polish–Jewish relations xix, 66–88
  of *shtetl* life 90–1, 93–112
  and social stratification 68–71
  of young Jews 42–65
Mendelsohn, Ezra xv, xvii, xviii–xix, 3–13
Mendelson, Meir 306–10
Messianism, Judaic 134
methodology:
  comparative xix, 13
  use of memoirs 68
Michalski, Sergiusz 413–15
Michnik, Adam 421–2
middle classes:
  attitude to Jews 71, 194, 202, 232, 392
  Jewish 178, 296, 328, 390
Miedziński, Bogusław 203
Mikołajczyk, Stanisław 339, 342–3, 357, 361–2, 364, 369 n. 24, 370
military service by Jews 111, 172
  in Anders's army 335–8, 358, 372–6
  and citizenship status 117, 119
Milsztejn, N., autobiography 51, 53
Milton, Sybil 265
Mincberg, Lejb 210, 223
minorities, non-Jewish 69, 75–6, 168, 208
  Belarussian 5, 15, 39, 46, 81, 119, 123
  citizenship 115–20, 127–8
  German 5, 15, 32, 39, 332
  in Jewish historiography 8
  Lithuanian 15, 39, 81, 119, 123
  threat from 184
  Ukrainian 5, 15, 39, 46, 119, 123, 178, 387, 410
Minorities Treaty 1919 14–16, 22–34, 38–41
  and Britain 23–6, 29–35, 36–7, 39, 40
  and civil rights 116–17, 121
  and lack of Jewish unity 39–40

and United States 26–30, 31–2, 36–8, 40
  weaknesses 35–8
minority, Jews as 16–19
Mizrachi, and *kehillah* elections 216, 218
Młodzianowski, Kazimierz 119
Młodzież Wszechpolska (All-Polish
  Youth) 198
modernization, and Jews xviii–xix, 63, 185
Moltke, Adolf von 259–64, 274–5
Mond, General Bernard 84–5
money:
  lending 98
  power of 174–5
Montefiore, Claude 133 n. 6
Morgenthau, Henry 30
Morges Front 261
Mortkowicz-Olczakowa, Hanna 69 n. 13
Moskała, R. 168–9
Mowschowitch, David 16–17, 21, 40
murder, ritual, Jews accused of 148, 161
Muszyn, Chaja, autobiography 43–4

N
Nahlik, S. E., memoirs 67 n. 5, 68 n. 7,
  75 n. 40, 87
Najdus, Walentyna 384–7
Nałkowska, Zofia 393
Namier, Lewis 33
Narodowa Partia Robotnicza (NPR) 197
Nasz przegląd 182, 189, 285
Nasza obrona 283–4
Natanson family 20
nation-state:
  and Jewish rights 23–9, 35, 39–41
  Poland as 14, 19–20, 27, 38–9
National Council (Rada Narodowa) 248,
  332–4, 340, 352–4, 357, 362, 367, 379
National Democratic Movement 196
National Democratic Party:
  and attitudes to Jews 47, 78, 79–80, 117 n. 5
  and discriminatory regulations 124
  press 192
  in Warsaw 390
National League, and antisemitism 195–6, 390
National State Movement 204
National Unity Camp 126
National Workers' Party (NPR) 197, 201
nationalism, Jewish 6, 10–11, 19, 20, 329
  and Messianism 134
  and young Jews 60, 64
nationalism, Polish:
  and antisemitism 8, 52, 195–7, 329

and Jewish press 184
and restrictions on Jews 125–7
nationalization, calls for 201, 204–5
Nazism:
  and continuation of Polish policies xvi, xvii, 4
  and economic boycott on Jews 282–9
  effects on eastern Europe xx, 398–401
  and Jewish press 184
  repression of Jews 255, 257, 262, 338–44,
    345–81
  see also Hitler, Adolf
Nelken, Halina 404–7
Netzer, Shlomo xvi, 4
New States Committee (NSC) 28, 33, 36–8
Nisman, Beniamin 118
Noam Elimelekh 411
Noel-Baker, Philip 37–8
Non-Party Bloc for Co-operation with the
  Government (BBWR) 124–5, 206, 208,
  284
Norblin, Jean-Pierre 405–6, 412
Nowacyński, Adolf 198 n. 15
Nowodworski, Michał 130
Nowy dziennik 189
Nussbaum, Kalman 373 and n. 24

O
Obóz Narodowo-Radykalny (ONR; National
  Radical Camp) 200
Obóz Zjednoczenia Narodowego (OZON;
  Camp of National Unification) 203–4,
  236–7, 256
Odrodzenie (Renaissance) 198
Old Testament, and contemporary
  Judaism 157–9, 162
Olędzki, Jacek 411
Olszański, Tadeusz 93–4
Opalski, Magdalena M. 382–4
Opatów, eighteenth-century Jews in 382–4
Oppenheim, Yisrael 4, 7
Orla-Bukowska, Annamaria xix, 89–114
Orthodox League 20
Orthodoxy, Jewish xx
  and confessional schools 32
  in historiography 6, 7
  and Jewish separation 74–5, 326, 329
  and Polish state 20–1, 32, 39–40
  in *shtetl* communities 93–4
  and Yiddish 43
  and young Jews 42, 44–5, 48–50, 52, 55–7,
    63, 64
  see also Agudas Yisroel; Hasidism

Orzeszkowa, Eliza 51, 290, 328
Ostatnie wiadomości 188
Otiker, Yisrael 7
Otwinowski, Stefan, memoirs 69 n. 12, 85–6

P

Paczkowski, Andrzej xx, 176–93, 296
Paderewski, Ignacy 14, 20, 23, 31 n. 61, 34–5, 39
Pajewski, Janusz, memoirs 74
Pakentreger, Aleksander 177, 186
Palestine:
 as Jewish state 25, 26, 143–5, 184
 and young Jews 51, 60–1
Palten, Dr 265–6
parties, political:
 and antisemitism 194–205
 Jewish 40, 182, 208, 297
 and Jewish nationalism 19
 and Jewish separation 72
 reaction to Jews xix
 restriction on 208–9
 and young Jews 58–60
 see also under names of individual parties
partition, Austro-Hungarian 111, 115, 117, 121, 189, 229
 see also Galicia
partition, Prussian 111, 115, 195
partition, Russian 115, 117, 121–2, 189, 195–6, 229, 388–92
Party of Independent Socialists 72
passports, control of 255, 260–2, 263–4
patriotism, of Jews 51, 172
Patryk, Father 163
Peasant Movement, and antisemitism 195, 197
peasants:
 attitudes to Jews 45–6, 78, 232, 411–12
 conflict with Jews in Galicia 195
 Jewish attitudes to 46
 in *shtetl* communities 92–3, 95–6, 98–9, 295
pedlars, Jewish 94, 98–9
Peltyn, Samuel Hirsz 327
Peretz, Yitshak Leibush 251, 290, 299–301, 317–18, 322
Piasecki, Bolesław 200
Piechotka, Maria and Kazimierz 412
Pietrzak, Michal 190–1
Pilichowska, Bogdana 412
Piłsudski, Józef 22, 23, 80, 204, 385
 and *coup* of 1926 83, 123, 190, 208, 387
 see also Sanacja
Pinkas hakehilot 8
Piwarski, Jan Feliks 406

PLC, *see* Commonwealth, Polish–Lithuanian
Po'alei Tsion 60
Po'alei Tsion Left:
 cultural activity 73, 251
 and *kehillah* elections 1936 214–15, 220–1
 and trade unions 248
Po'alei Tsion Right 73
 and *kehillah* elections 1936 215–16
 trade unions 182, 248
pogroms 23, 77–8, 171, 328
 1918–20 9, 30–1, 39, 184, 189, 196
 1936 210, 211
 in historiography xvii, 5, 7, 9
 Reichskristallnacht 255, 272
Polish language:
 and Jewish separation 71
 use by Jewish press 183–4, 185–6, 187–9, 191, 192, 297
 use by Jews 34, 43–4, 50–2, 64, 111, 153, 178
Polish Democratic Union 205
Polish Emancipation Act 1862 21
Polish National Committee (PNC), and minority rights 22–3, 25
Polish Peasant Party Piast 124, 195
Polish Peasant Party (PSL) 195, 379
Polish Radical Party 205
Polish Social Democratic Party (PPSD) 194 n. 2
Polish Socialist Party (PPS) 72, 124, 181, 202, 206, 220
Polish–Soviet war 80–1, 171, 229, 385
Polishness, evidence of in memoirs 44, 50–3, 74
politics:
 involvement in 103–4, 181–2, 189, 206–7, 223, 297
 and Jewish press 193
 and young Jews 57–60, 64
 see also *kehillah* system
Polityka 204
Pollak, Jakub 138–9
Polonization 194, 195–7, 199–200, 204, 236–7, 327–8
Polonsky, Antony xv–xxi, 346, 423–6
Polska Sztuka Ludowa 410–13
Polski Związek Wydawców Dzienników i Czasopism 192
Popiel, Karol 261, 336, 374
Popławski, Jan Ludwik 328
Popular National Union (ZLN) 127
 and antisemitism 196–8

Posłaniec serca Jezusowego, and image of the Jew 147, 150, 152, 161, 168
poverty xvi–xvii, xviii, xx, 13, 69, 76, 86, 178, 295, 310–11
  increasing 231–2, 234–5, 237, 244–5, 248, 251, 253
  in *shtetl* communities 95
  and young Jews 54
Poznań:
  Jewish provincial press 187
  peasant movement 195
Poznański, Maurycy 69 n. 11
press, Catholic 75, 136
  audience for 178–81
  and image of the Jew 146–75
  and the Jewish question 129–45, 327
  and persecution of the Jews 359, 362, 364–7
  and press control 190–1
  size 183–4, 190
  see also antisemitism
press, German 178, 189, 192
  size 184 n. 19, 187, 190 n. 312
press, Jewish xx, 176–93
  areas of concern 182, 193
  journalists 192
  neglect of 176–7
  overseas 333, 355
  Polish-language 183–4, 185–6, 187–9, 191, 192, 297
  and press control 190–2
  provincial 185–8, 192
  readership 177–81, 188–90, 193
  size 183–5, 187, 297
  and trade unions 249–50
  see also Hebrew; Yiddish
press, Russian 178, 189
press, Ukrainian 192
  and press control 190–1
  size 184 n. 19, 187, 190 n. 31
Pro Christo:
  and antisemitism xix–xx
  and image of the Jew 147, 151–2, 153, 155–6, 160–1, 163, 164, 166, 168, 171–2, 174
Próchnik, Adam (Henryk Swoboda) 88, 386
professions:
  Jews in 136, 296–7
  restrictions on Jews in 127, 142–3, 204
  service, Jews in 87
proletariat, Jewish 69, 76, 238–54, 294
  cultural activity 251–4
  employment structure 239–42, 296
  and labour market changes 243–8
  organization 248–50
  see also artisans, Jewish
proletariat, Polish 5, 69, 76, 250
property, confiscation xx, 200, 204
'Protocols of the Elders of Zion' 138
Prus, Bolesław 389
Prystor, Aleksander 125
Prystorowa, Janina 125, 210
Prywes, Isaiah 306–10
Przegląd katolicki:
  and image of the Jew 146–7, 159, 162, 165, 169–74
  and the Jewish question 130–5
  and Jewish settlement in Poland 135–7
  and 'Judaeo-Communism' 137–40
  and roots of Christian–Jewish conflict 133–5
  solutions to Jewish question 140–5
Przegląd powszechny 131
  and image of the Jew 147, 153, 162–3, 166–9, 171–5
Przewodnik katolicki 147, 159, 162, 166
Przytyk pogrom 211
Putrament, Jerzy, memoirs 73, 78, 84–5

Q
Quercioli, Laura 392–5, 415–17

R
race, and difference xix, 149, 153–4, 164–75, 331
racism:
  and antisemitism 165, 167, 199, 201, 204
  Nazi 255
Raczkiewicz, Władysław 119, 353 n. 6
Raczyński, Edward 341, 342–3, 351, 355, 357, 359, 370
Rada Narodowa (National Council) 248, 332–4, 340, 352–4, 357, 362, 367, 379
Radziwiłł, Janusz 205
Rataj, Maciej, memoirs 80
Ratajczyk, Stanisław 120
Ratajski, Cyryl 118–19
Rath, Ernst vom, assassination 262, 271, 273–4
Redlich, Shimon 401–3
Reichskristallnacht 255
relationships between Poles and Jews 9–11, 66–88, 297, 326–9
  attitude of Church towards 156
  in eighteenth century 382–7

relationships between Poles and Jews (*cont.*):
  and Polish government-in-exile 4, 11, 330–44, 345–81
  roots of conflict 133–5
  in *shtetl* communities 96–112
religion:
  and Catholic Church 147–8
  freedom of 15, 21, 36, 74, 125–6
Renan, Ernest 321
Renner, Karl 17–18
Representacja Żydów Polskich (RŻP) 341, 368 n. 23
Republika 188
residence:
  habitual 116–17
  restrictions on Polish Jewish 199, 264
Revisionism, Jewish 10, 64, 216
revolution, Russian, Jewish involvement suspected 138–9, 168–9
Ribbentrop, Joachim von 263, 266, 269
Riga Treaty 116–18, 120
rights:
  civil xviii, 115–28, 199–202, 326, 390–1
  educational 36
  individual xix, 6, 17
  linguistic 21–2, 34, 37, 39, 121, 123–5
  in Minorities Treaty 14–15, 16, 19, 21, 23–34, 38–9
  political 35, 195, 199, 332–4, 355–6
  restriction 199
Ringelblum, Emanuel 423, 424, 425
Ritkes, Itche 311–13
Rogalski, A. 167
Roman, Antoni 237
Roman Catholicism:
  and antisemitism xix–xx, 47–8, 78, 130, 149
  and attitudes to Jews 78–9, 85, 91
  and conversion of Jews 149–55
  Jews seen as enemies of 155–64, 200
  and other faiths 147–9
  in *shtetl* communities 107–8
  and young Jews 45, 46–8
  see also press, Polish: religious
Romania, and Jewish autonomy 24, 29
Romer, A. 138, 142–3
Rosenberg, A. 134 n. 7
Rosnan, Ignacy 188
Rostworowski, J. 162, 174
Rotfarb, Abraham xv, 45, 52, 55, 62
Rowecki, General Stefan 340, 363–4
Rozen, Ajzyk, autobiography 57
Rozmaryn, Henryk 285, 287

Ruch katolicki 131
  and image of the Jew 147, 150, 158, 166
Rudnicki, Adolf 393, 427–9
Rudnicki, Kazimierz, memoirs 69 n. 12, 79, 86
Rudnicki, Sz. 198
rural communities, see *shtetl* communities
Russia:
  Jews in 17, 70
  and Warsaw 388–92
Russian, use of 70, 178, 189
Rycerz niepokalanej 147, 149, 152, 155, 157–8, 161, 164, 170
Rymkiewicz, Jarosław Marek 395

S
Sabbath observance 36, 161, 229, 319–20
  in *shtetl* communities 96, 102, 108–9
Salvador, Joseph 133 n. 6
Samuel, Sir Herbert 30
Samuel, Sir Stuart 30
Sanacja:
  and antisemitism 120, 199, 202–3, 204–5
  and artisans 236
  and *kehillah* system 208, 209
Sandauer, Artur 394
Sarid, Levi Aryeh 7
Schacht, Hjalmar 284, 286
Scharf, Rafael xx, 290–8
Schleifer, Dawid Moses ('Damaszek'), autobiography 44, 57, 59
Schoenfeld, Joachim, memoirs 94, 97, 103–5, 107, 110–12
schools:
  confessional 21, 25–6, 32–4, 52, 148, 198 n. 17, 296
  and patriotism 51
  relationships with non-Jews 46–8
  Sabbath 93
  secular 168, 212, 251, 328
  shtetl 93
Schulke, Commissar 272–3
Schulz, Bruno 100, 114, 298, 427
Schwartzbart, Ignacy 332, 333, 339, 341–2, 352–3, 355–7, 361, 364–5, 368, 379
secularization 54–5, 63 212–13
Sée, Eugène 26–7
Segal, Kalman 393
Segory, J., memoirs 77
'Sejmocracy' 190, 208
Sękowski, Marian 69 n. 9
self-awareness, of young Jews 44–50
self-determination, and Wilson 27, 28

self-government, see *kehillah* system
separation, Jewish 71–6, 113, 194–5, 198, 202, 326
  and Catholic press 147, 151
servants, Gentile 101–2, 107, 113, 170, 172, 174–5
sexuality, and young Jews 61–2
Shapiro, Robert Moses xx, 206–26
Shmeruk, Chone 12
Sholem Aleykhem (Aleichem) libraries 251–2
shtetl communities 12, 89–114, 178, 294, 317–20, 392, 411
  artisans 103, 213, 412
  funerals 106
  inns 99, 107, 172
  interaction and coexistence 96–112
  markets 92, 94–5, 97, 101, 112
  neglect in recent writing 90–1
  neighbours 104–6
  and provincial press 185–8
  rabbis 110, 301–6
  religious observance in 82, 93–4, 107–8
  structure and organization 91–6
  weddings 106
Shpeizman, Leib 7
Sikorski, Władysław 376
  and government attitudes to Jews 332, 334, 340, 342–3, 352–5, 360–2, 363 n. 13, 367
  and Polish Jews in Soviet Union 337
Singer, Isaac Bashevis 9, 299, 393, 415, 416–17
Siudak, Paweł 368 n. 22, 368 n. 22
Skryzński, Count 31
Skwarczyński, General Stanisław 203
slaughter, ritual (*sheḥitah*), ban proposed 74, 110, 125–6, 210, 211–12, 219, 331
Sławek, Walery 284–5
Sławoj-Składkowski, Felicjan 117 n. 5, 120, 203, 237, 260–1, 264
Słonimski, Antoni, memoirs 71, 86, 297
Słonimski, Chaim Zelig 326
Smigły-Rydz, Edward 141
Sobanski, Count 25
Sobieski, Wacław 79
Social Democracy of the Congress Kingdom and Lithuania (SDKPiL) 194
'Social Economic Bloc' 221
Socialism xx, xxi, 384–7
  and Pioneer movement 7
  rejection of Judaism 194
  in *shtetl* communities 93
  and young Jews 42, 57, 59, 327

see also Bundism; Po'alei Tsion Left; Po'alei Tsion Right; Polish Socialist Party (PPS)
Sodalis Marianus, and image of the Jew 147, 151, 156
Sommerstein, Deputy 256–7
Soviet Union:
  Jews in 4, 64, 135, 177, 350–4
  peace treaty with 116–18, 120
  and Polish army 335–8, 358, 372–6
  and Polish western territories 396–8
  Relief Apparatus 335, 350–2
  and Ukraine 401–3
sport, and Jewish separation 73
Springorum, Walther 258
Stańczyk, Jan 333, 353, 355–6
state, and Jewish problem xviii–xix, 5, 13, 129–45
stereotypes:
  in Catholic press 146–75
  of Jews 12, 90, 113
Stöckel, Ludwik, autobiography 46–7, 49, 61
Stojałowski, Father 78, 195
Stola, Dariusz 330–44, 345–81
Stomma, Ludwik 411
stratification, social 45–6, 68–71, 95
strikes 211–12, 249–50
Stronnictwo Ludowe (SL; Peasant Party) 195, 201–2, 332
Stronnictwo Narodowe (SN; National Movement) 198, 200
Stronnictwo Pracy (Party of Labour) 201
Stroński, Stanisław 342–3, 360–1
Stryjkowski, Julian 114, 290, 393–4, 395
Stuckart, Wilhelm 259
students, Jewish organizations 72
Subtelny, Orest 402
suicide, in Yiddish literature 415–17
Sutherland, Adam 20–1
Svobodnaya mysl 189
Świdrowski, Józef, memoirs 76
Świętochowski, Aleksander 328
synagogues:
  'progressive' 194
  in *shtetl* communities 93, 96, 108, 109
Szac, A., autobiography 49
Szajn, Izrael 183, 186 n. 24, 188
Szeintuch, Yechiel 177
Szelawski, J. 130
Szembek, Jan 259
Szereszewski, Rafał 282–3
Sztolcman, Hersz Wolf, autobiography 48–9, 61
Szwarc, Marek 414

T

Talmud, in Catholic press 157, 159–60, 162, 167–8
Tanenzapf, Ewa, autobiography 54
Tank, Maksym, memoirs 72 n. 27, 73, 86–7
Targielski, Zbigniew 411
Tartakover, Aryeh 4, 233, 242–3, 350
Tendlarz, Mojżesz, autobiography 54
Tesnière, Jean 271–2, 275
textile industry, Jews in 233, 240, 249–50
Thon, Ozjasz 61
toleration, religious 21, 164, 194
Tomaszewski, Jerzy xix, 9, 89, 90, 95–6, 115–28, 256 n. 3, 261
Toporska, Barbara 395
Toscano, Mario 408–9
totalitarianism, increase in 44, 53
towns:
    Jewish population 66, 71, 79 n. 63, 87, 90, 103, 119, 177–8, 291, 411
    Jewish proletariat 239
    and minority citizenship 119
    and provincial Jewish press 185–7
    small, see shtetl communities
Toynbee, Arnold 33
trade:
    in devotional articles 126
    Jews in 136, 167, 196, 239, 391
    shtetl Jews in 94–5, 97–9
trade unions, Jewish 71, 76, 182
    cultural activities 251
    growth 248–50
    and kehillah elections 1936 214, 219–21
Treblinka, Jews sent to 340, 363, 367
Trunk, Isaiah xvi, 4, 7, 300–1
Trunk, Yehiel Yeshaia xx, 299–322
Trzciński, Andrzej 412
Trzeciak, Stanisław 138
Tse'irei Agudas Yisroel 44, 59
Turków, Marek 285, 287
Tuszyńska, Agata 89, 100
Tuwim, Julian 77, 137, 173, 296, 297

U

Ukraine, in Second World War 401–3
Ukrainian Social Democratic Party 194 n. 2
unemployment 76
    and artisans 228–9, 231, 234–6
    and proletariat 239, 246, 248, 251, 295
    and young Jews 54, 57
Union of the Patriotic Left 205
Union of Social Activists 205

United States:
    and Jewish minority rights 26–30, 31–2, 36–8, 40, 333, 356
    Jews in 4, 34, 37, 135, 177
    Poles in 182
universities, limitation on Jewish students 122, 198, 199, 204
Unszlicht, J. 152, 157
Untermayer, Dr 282, 286
Urban, J. 153, 162

V

value systems:
    in Jewish press 193
    of young Jews 54–5, 57–63, 64
Vatican:
    and antiracism 165
    concordat of 1925 123
    and Palestine 143–4
Versailles, Little Treaty, see Minorities Treaty 1919
villages, see shtetl communities
Vilna:
    and Jewish culture 70, 73, 86–7
    Jewish deaths 361, 366, 367
    Jewish population 66, 70, 90
    and kehillah elections 215, 224
    provincial press 185, 215
Vincenz, Stanisław 395
violence, anti-Jewish xvii, 48, 211, 196, 205, 210, 255; see also pogroms
VJOD (Vereinigung Jüdischer Organisationen Deutschlands), and Jewish autonomy 19
Vogler, Henryk 69 n. 12, 73

W

Wald, Jula, autobiography 43, 44–5, 49, 50, 56–7, 62
Wallasch, Criminal Secretary 273–4, 278–9
Wapiński, Roman 392
Warsaw:
    artisans 231–2, 234–5
    deportation from 339–41, 358, 362–8, 370–1
    Jewish population 66, 90, 136, 161, 177, 388–9
    and Jewish press 184, 185, 186–9, 192, 218
    and Jewish separation 71
    Jews in industry 240–1
    Jews in local politics 182, 224, 313
    and kehillah elections 215, 219–20, 222
    libraries 252–3
    and Russian Empire 21–2, 388–92

Warsaw Positivists 194, 325, 327–9
Wassercug, Jozef 188
weddings, in *shtetl* communities 106
Weiss, Aharon 401–2
Weizmann, Chaim 23, 25, 31–2
Weizsäcker, Ernst von 268
Wesołowski, S. 141
Wiktorski, Paweł, memoirs 83, 84
Wilson, Woodrow 27–9, 32, 37–8
Winiarski, Bohdan 124
Wippermann, Wolfgang 398–401
Wiślicki, Alfred xx, 282–9
Wiślicki, Wacław 282–3, 285–8
Wiśniewski, M. 151, 160, 166, 168
Witos, Wincenty 122, 257, 261, 275
Wittlin, Józef, memoirs 67 n. 5, 78, 297
Wojciechowski, Stanisław 115
Wojdowski, Bogdan 393–4, 395
Wolf, Lucien xix, 16–18
  and minority rights 19–23, 26–7, 29–31, 33–40
women, in pre-First World War Poland 295
World Jewish Congress 282–3, 334, 339, 341, 350–1, 357, 361, 365, 368 n. 23
Wróbel, Józef 392–5, 427–9
Wühlich, Johannes 257–8
Wyka, Kazimierz 393

Y
Yad Vashem, and historiography 8, 338, 401
Yevstigniev, Colonel 373–4
Yiddish:
  ban on 21, 115, 121, 123
  and Jewish press 178, 179, 183–9, 251, 297, 389
  literature 295, 299–300, 317, 327, 415–17
  right to use 22, 39
  in schools 25–6, 32, 34, 37, 212
  in *shtetl* communities 103, 111
  use by Jews 43, 46, 64, 137, 327
  use by Poles 72
  used by political parties 194
Yidisher Vissenshaftlikher Institut (YIVO)
  archives xvii, 42–3, 53, 63, 247
  and Polish antisemitism 7, 54
youth:
  intellectual activity of 253
  memoirs 42–65
  proletarianization 243–7
  and separation 72–3
youth, Jewish, *see* autobiographies; education; schools *and under* antisemitism; assimilation; Bundism; children; Communism; consciousness, national; Folkism; Hebrew; identity, Jewish; nationalism, Jewish; Orthodoxy; Palestine; parties, political; politics; poverty; Roman Catholicism; sexuality; students; unemployment; Zionism
youth movements, Jewish, *see* Betar; Gordonia; Haluts; Hashomer Hatsa'ir; Tse'irei Agudas Yisroel

Z
Zajęty, W. 161
Zakon, Liebka 312–17
Zaleska, Zofia 379
Zaleski, August 22
Zaremba, Zygmunt 202
Zarwanizer, 'Leib', autobiography 48
Zegadło, Adam 412
Zeitlin, Hillel 218
Żelechowski, S. 174
Żelewski, Jan 144
Zelwiański, Hirsz 78
Zespól Stu (Group of a Hundred) 203
Zionism xvii, xx, 294
  and Britain 25
  in Catholic press 139–40, 143–4, 153
  and history of Poland xvi, 4–5
  Jewish attitudes to 11, 328
  and *kehillah* elections 209, 214–16, 218–22, 225
  and municipal government 222–4
  Pioneer movement 7, 8
  and Polish state 20–1, 31–2, 34, 39
  publications 186, 189, 218
  in *shtetl* communities 93–4
  and socialism 202
  and young Jews 42, 43, 50–3, 58–61, 64
Żongołłowicz, Revd 125
'Zosia', autobiography 55–6
Zwara, Brunon, memoirs 82–3
Związek Ludowo-Narodowy (ZLN) 196–8
Związek Młodych Narodowców (ZMN; Union of Young Nationalists) 204
Zygielbojm, Szmul 342, 353 n. 6, 357, 361, 364–5, 368

www.ingramcontent.com/pod-product-compliance
Ingram Content Group UK Ltd.
Pitfield, Milton Keynes, MK11 3LW, UK
UKHW021316180426
11947UKWH00015B/1254